Aleksandra Kollontai

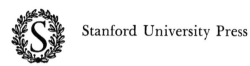 Stanford University Press

Stanford, California 1980

Aleksandra Kollontai

Socialism, Feminism, and the Bolshevik Revolution

Beatrice Farnsworth

Published with the assistance of the
National Endowment of the Humanities

Stanford University Press
Stanford, California

© *1980 by the Board of Trustees of the*
Leland Stanford Junior University

Printed in the United States of America

ISBN 0–8047–1073–2
LC 79–67775

To John, Dan, David, and Peter

Acknowledgments

M A N Y people have assisted me during the eight years that I worked on this study. Whatever remains that is questionable is here despite their advice and help. The manuscript has been read in whole or in part by Renate Bridenthal, Robert V. Daniels, Barbara Alpern Engel, Gregory Massell, and Richard Stites. I thank them, as well as the many other colleagues, friends, and students with whom I have discussed the book over the years. I am especially grateful for the innumerable hours my husband John spent patiently reading the manuscript in all its early drafts and final versions. He provided historical breadth as well as stylistic advice and encouragement. My son David willingly sacrificed days of college vacations and lent his editorial expertise to early and late drafts. My father, Max Brodsky, provided insights that improved an early section.

I am grateful to the staff of the University of Gothenburg Library for making available to me the correspondence between Kollontai and Dr. Ada Nilsson and Fredrik Ström. In 1973 the staffs of the Lenin Library in Moscow and the Academy of Sciences Library in Leningrad provided me with access to Soviet newspapers and journals. I wish to thank Slavic librarians Gail Persky at Columbia University and Marcella Stark at Syracuse University, and the Slavic reference service at the University of Illinois, for help in locating material. I owe a special debt to Wells College librarian Louise Rossman, who for several years has provided invaluable aid in tracking down Russian sources. To have proceeded without such help would have been impossible.

Preparation of this book has been aided by the financial support of the National Endowment for the Humanities, the American Philosophical Society, and Wells College.

Birgitta Bergman, Kerstin Larson, Dr. Theodore Lowe, and Gregory Zelenyuk helped with translations. Bernice Haber conscientiously typed the manuscript. Walter Ralls gave of his time in Washington to locate material.

I was privileged to be included in a productive conference called "Women in Russia: Changing Realities, Changing Perceptions," held on the Stanford University campus in 1975 and organized by Dorothy Atkinson, Alexander Dallin, and Gail W. Lapidus. Chapter 11, which grew out of the paper I presented at that conference, has appeared in slightly different form in D. Atkinson et al., eds., *Women in Russia* (Stanford, Calif., 1977). I owe special appreciation to my editor-critic, Peter J. Kahn, who for the past two years has read my manuscript in progress. His good sense and high scholarly standards have guided me in ways too numerous to list. Also my thanks to copy-editor Ruth Franklin.

And finally, Peter Farnsworth, who has lived with this manuscript for nearly all the ten years of his life, deserves to see in print that he has been a patient boy.

Contents

Twelve pages of photographs follow p. 240.

Preface

THIS is a book about a remarkable Bolshevik, Aleksandra M. Kollontai, the most prominent woman in Russia's Communist Party. Kollontai was a member of Lenin's Central Committee that carried out the Revolution in 1917, a Commissar (the only woman) in Russia's first Communist government, and the key figure in Russia's socialist women's movement. She functioned, to borrow the expression of one historian, as "the conscience of the Revolution." Still, the full scope of Kollontai's contribution as revolutionary and as feminist has never been analyzed. She died in political obscurity in Moscow in 1952 after retirement from the diplomatic service, into which the Communist leadership had shunted her. When she was remembered in the Soviet Union, it was not as a controversial feminist and a revolutionary leader but simply as the world's first woman ambassador. The Communist Party, just as it stifled her criticism, preferred that her radical contributions to revolutionary history and theory be excluded from the official record.

There is no women's movement in the Soviet Union today, although one did exist in the decade following the Revolution. Because Kollontai was at its center, the book is also about the Women's Section of the Communist Party (the Zhenotdel) which in 1930 fell before Stalinist centralization. One theme of this book is the tension between Kollontai and the Communist Party over the "woman question." Kollontai was convinced that little would have been done after the Revolution to bring women into public life without the efforts of a small group of Communist women who, although they rejected the label "feminist" as bourgeois and divisive of the proletariat, functioned within their own section of the Communist Party as socialist feminists.

The revival of the women's movement in the West has resulted in considerable interest in Kollontai and her leadership of the women's section of the Communist Party. This is as it should be. Kollontai went beyond Bebel, Marx, and Engels to provide Marxism with an important psychology of female liberation, but her contribution is sometimes misunderstood. Discussing Kollontai has its conventions. Because she, alone among the Bolsheviks, saw sexuality as a valid revolutionary theme, there has been a tendency to emphasize her writings on sexual relationships and romantic love. To do so is to risk missing the point. Kollontai believed in free sexuality, to be sure. But as early as 1913, in her essay on the "New Woman," Kollontai made clear her fundamental theme: to demand that women subordinate the emotional side of their lives and develop the kind of inner autonomy that would enable a young woman, like a young man, to decide to be an artist, or to join a revolutionary party. Mostly, she stressed the liberating potential of productive work. Particularly now, when the role of women in society is being debated, this needs to be understood, as does Kollontai's belief in female bonds as a dominant source of female strength. Indeed, the enduring friendships with women to which her life was testimony were ultimately more satisfying, she came to conclude, than her several episodes of romantic love.

Kollontai's faith in the potential of female bonding convinced her that if social change was to result from the Revolution, Russia's proletarian and peasant women would have to function as an interest group. Here, in her insistence that Russian women reorganize society and the family, lay an essential novelty. For its corollary was historically unique—that the social revolution in Russia would be a female undertaking led by the few Communist women in the Party. We need to know what resulted when Kollontai sought to put her concept into effect. Then we can begin to comprehend not only the unfolding relationship of the Soviet regime to the "woman question," but also the complexities of women's lives in the Soviet Union today. How the Communist leaders interpreted their pledge to social change and to women's equality, how they treated women in the Party, how Kollontai resolved the tension between her "feminism" and her commitment to working-class solidarity—these are central questions. They are of interest not only to students of Soviet history but to feminists, for they seek to assess the role of a separate women's organization within a larger political movement.

Since the tendency among historians interested in Kollontai is to explore her relevance to the contemporary women's movement, Kollontai as Bolshevik has been slighted. But because she was preeminently a political person, a book about Kollontai must go beyond the women's movement to analysis of revolutionary politics. I have tried

to interpret Kollontai's activities within the larger context of Bolshevik polemics and Soviet history. A main theme, then, is Kollontai's
stormy political career and her astonishing survival. Of the prominent members of the Bolshevik Central Committee that met in the
autumn of 1917 and voted to move toward a seizure of power, only
Stalin and Kollontai were still alive after the purges of the 1930's.
Stalin survived because he masterminded the assault on the Party.
But why Kollontai did remains an open question. That she endured
to die a natural death at 80, a year before Stalin's death, is the more
remarkable because she was a left-wing Oppositionist who grappled,
like all thoughtful revolutionaries, with the central problem of political thought: the relation between ends and means. A bold and
doctrinaire Communist, drawn to Bolshevism by Lenin's socialist internationalism rather than by his concept of Party organization, she
openly challenged authority. One of the organizers from within the
Party of the Workers' Opposition, the first (and unsuccessful) protest
against Communism's increasing repression, Kollontai tried in the
early years of the Revolution, when the climate was still relatively
open, to create a more democratic Party responsive to internal criticism. Kollontai's emphasis on the creation of "new people," and on
a more humane Communism encompassing artistic creativity and
workers' spontaneity, underscores the diversity of early Bolshevism,
which scholars have called attention to in recent years. A political
study of Kollontai becomes, then, an interpretation of the Bolshevik
Revolution through the prism of a socialist activist pursuing libertarian goals in an increasingly authoritarian system. That Kollontai
was one of those Communists who failed to hinder the development
of repression should not obscure the efforts of Bolsheviks like her.
Indeed, if this book adds meaningfully to that body of historical literature which seeks to persuade the informed reader that early Bolshevism differed qualitatively from later Stalinism, I shall be gratified.
I also trust that I have contributed to the growing literature that deals
with survivors, that I have partially illumined the fate of the old
Communist who managed to live through that other holocaust known
as the Great Purge. How Kollontai handled survival I have tried to
explain largely by means of her correspondence with her close friend
Dr. Ada Nilsson.

Stephen Cohen has pointed out in his introduction to *Bukharin
and the Bolshevik Revolution* that we know very little about the private lives and thoughts of the Bolsheviks, partly because of their

"common reticence" about such matters and partly because of their usual fate under Stalin. Only Trotsky has provided a full autobiography and uncensored private papers. But because Kollontai was not reticent about her intimate thoughts, and because she was a survivor, the biographer does have personal material. The Nilsson correspondence is, of course, invaluable. My bibliography will guide the reader to Kollontai's works that are autobiographical. Kollontai also wrote fiction, and it is likely that much of it depicts episodes from her own life. Although the ten volumes of Kollontai's memoirs—about 300 pages each—are essentially closed in the Central Party Archive in the Institute of Marxism-Leninism, since Stalin's death there has been a flurry of interest in Kollontai among Soviet scholars. Though Russians who have had access to the archive invariably take the dubious line that Kollontai regretted her Opposition and recognized her "mistakes," they have published valuable archival material. (Whether their interest in Kollontai reflects renewed female concern with the woman question is not clear but is suggested by the prominence of women historians within the group.) We now have a volume of memoir excerpts and several articles based on the archives, plus two Soviet biographies.

No book in the absence of documents in the Institute of Marxism-Leninism can claim to be definitive. But that Kollontai's memoirs, deposited in the Institute and written largely in the Stalinist era and under the eyes of the police, are totally candid seems unlikely. We know from her correspondence with Ada Nilsson that Kollontai revised her original diaries and destroyed old letters. Thus some questions may forever lack definitive answers.

B.F.

Aleksandra Kollontai

CHAPTER ONE

Socialism or Feminism?

FAILURE has its fascination. Aleksandra Mikhailovna Kollontai failed trying to create a social revolution in Russia. Her failure illustrates the limits to one leader's effective action, yet it also suggests, in the range of her aspirations, some alternative outcomes to the Communist experiment. For Kollontai's career bears witness to the fact that the social structure produced by Soviet Communism was hardly preordained.

Bolshevism was never monolithic. It has been pointed out that among the Bolsheviks, particularly those who came to the Party from an earlier and more general adherence to European radicalism, there existed competing intellectual schools having roots in populism, anarchism, and other non-Marxist ideologies.[1] To these should be added feminism. Feminism basically is the assertion of the equal rights of women. It implies the need to liberate women so that they may determine their own destiny free from traditional restrictions. At another level, nineteenth-century feminism was a political movement based on the belief that women needed to transcend divisions based on social, economic, or political class and unite to fight for equality within the existing capitalist system.

Early socialists advocated feminism, and one of the most enduring nineteenth-century bonds was the one that developed between socialism and feminism. But if socialism in the nineteenth century came to appear to encompass feminism, not all feminists were prepared to embrace socialism. For the socialist view of the aims of feminism was not the striving for legal and political equality within the existing system that many organized feminists meant, but a far deeper liberation of women from the oppression of a patriarchal family and a capitalist society. Socialists spoke not of feminism but more broadly of the "woman question."

The earliest prophets of socialism, the Saint-Simonians, preferred to wait for the voice of woman to decide her relationship to the fami-

1. Cohen, *Bukharin*, p. 5.

ly. But Aleksandr Herzen, one of the first Russian socialists, envisaged as early as the 1840's the potentially liberating impact of the socialist commune on the lives of women. "In communal life . . . woman will be more involved in general interests . . . [and] will not be so one-sidedly attached to the family." He also predicted that "In the future there will be no marriage, the wife will be freed from slavery."[2] Karl Marx, in the *Communist Manifesto* of 1848, pronounced the doom of the bourgeois family: under socialism, it would vanish.[3] The leader of German socialism in the late nineteenth century, August Bebel, warning that socialism could not succeed if the exploitation of women continued, urged women to join the ranks of the working class in order to destroy the established structure of male power that imprisoned both men and women. In 1903, the founding convention of the Russian Social Democratic Workers' Party, demonstrating its commitment to women, put a series of demands in its platform to protect women's interests as mothers and as workers.[4]

Socialists were generally convinced that organized feminism as it existed in Russia and elsewhere in Europe represented the special needs of educated and wealthy women, and that it expressed their desire to participate in the exploitative system, to partake of the privileges of the ruling class. Their struggle for sexual liberation was dismissed as frivolous. Marx, Engels, and Bebel distrusted the feminist demand for equality as essentially bourgeois.[5] The place of the working-class woman, the Marxists insisted, was beside the man of her class, not beside the women of other classes.[6]

Toward the end of the nineteenth century, young Aleksandra Kollontai became a socialist. She explained her entry into revolutionary ranks quite simply: "Women, their fate, occupied me all my life;

2. See Malia, pp. 268–75, for bonds between early socialism and feminism.
3. See Karl Marx and Friedrich Engels, *The Communist Manifesto* (New York, 1955), pp. 27–28; see also Engels, pp. 83, 89.
4. Bebel, pp. 4–5, 9, 378–79. For the 1903 platform, see USSR, [6], vol. 1, pp. 40–42. It demanded an end to women's employment in occupations harmful to their health; ten weeks of paid maternity leave; day-care centers for infants and young children in all shops, factories, and enterprises employing women; a half-hour free every three hours for women to nurse their infants; and the replacement of male government inspectors of labor conditions by female ones in industries employing women. It said nothing, however, about the withering away of the traditional family.
5. Meyer, p. 105.
6. Clara Zetkin said this in 1896 at the German Socialist Party's annual congress. See Honeycutt, p. 3.

women's lot pushed me to socialism."[7] This intriguing statement raises the question, Why socialism, why not simply feminism? Why did this Russian aristocrat committed to the liberation of her sex ignore Russia's feminist movement and turn her back on her own class?[8] I propose to show that Kollontai embraced socialism not so much from political or economic belief as from personal need. To know why Kollontai responded to socialism, and rejected bourgeois feminism, we need to understand her temperament, her family relationships, and her background. For it was these influences that determined her perception of socialism and feminism both.

Aleksandra Kollontai's birth in St. Petersburg in April 1872 was itself a social statement: her mother had left her husband, an engineer named Mravinskii, to live with an army colonel, Mikhail Alekseevich Domontovich, and gave birth to her daughter by Domontovich before her divorce was legal.[9] Such an unusual action—especially for a woman with two daughters and a son from her first marriage—marked her as one of the educated and independent-minded "new women" of the 1860's.[10] She was the daughter of a Finnish merchant, Aleksandr Masalin, who sold lumber in St. Petersburg. Domontovich, the man she first lived with and then married, was an aristocrat from an old Ukrainian landowning family who would eventually become a general. He traced his name to a thirteenth-century Prince of Pskov. Their daughter Shura, as the young Aleksandra was called, loved to hear the family legends; her favorite was a story that if a Domontovich arrived at the monastery in Pskov, bells would ring. As a child, the future revolutionary leader dreamed of going to Pskov, where bells would ring in her honor.[11] Kollontai later claimed, perhaps only partly in jest, that she did not follow the custom of socialist women and retain her maiden name after marrying because she knew her father would be distressed to see a Domontovich a hunted revolutionary.[12]

7. Itkina, p. 44. Elsewhere, Kollontai would offer a less convincing but more orthodox Bolshevik explanation. See below, pp. 9–10.

8. On Russia's feminist movement, see Stites, *Women's Liberation Movement*.

9. Kollontai (whose birthdate was April 1 [March 19, O.S.]) was adopted by Domontovich; see Kollontai, *Autobiography*, p. 9. Divorces were difficult to obtain without connections in the Holy Synod; on this topic see Stites, *Women's Liberation Movement*, p. 182.

10. The children of the first marriage were Adel', Evgeniia, and Aleksandr. Later, in her story "Liubov' trekh pokolenii," collected in *Liubov' pchel trudovykh*, Kollontai described a woman of her mother's generation who left her husband for another man.

11. Kollontai, *Iz moei zhizni i raboty*, p. 19.

12. Fortunato, p. 182.

The woman who became known in Russia for her attack on the bourgeois family would paradoxically recall her childhood as warm and happy. She felt very much loved, she tells us, not finding it embarrassing to recall (any more than did other Bolsheviks of similar background)[13] that she lived in a protective family where hunger and poverty were unknown. The famous advocate of free love and short-term marriage wrote approvingly of her parents, who loved each other into old age.

Her mother she endowed with a social conscience, which this remarkable woman may in fact have possessed, although the evidence for it is slight. Supposedly Aleksandra Domontovich reminded her children never to forget that their grandfather was a simple peasant. (Actually, Aleksandr Masalin, after some success selling tree stumps for the pavements of St. Petersburg, married a Russian noblewoman.) She encouraged a disciplined life, in which for example the girls of the family learned to make their own clothing, and she set much store by education. Shura had an English nanny and sufficient language instruction so that before the age of seven she spoke English, French, and German. Shura learned early to respect well-educated women.[14]

A young girl about Shura's age provided a model of the intellectually serious child, bright beyond her years, whom adults admired. She was Zoia Shadurskaia, whom Shura met when the Domontovich family lived in Bulgaria during the Russo-Turkish War of 1877. This friendship lasted into their old age (Zoia died before the beginning of the Second World War) and did more than provide Kollontai with a model to emulate. Zoia would live with Kollontai at a number of important points in her life: during her marriage, during some of the years she spent as a political émigré before 1917, and during the revolutionary era in Russia. Kollontai would love several men in her lifetime, but after her son Misha she considered Zoia the dearest person in the world.[15] A pale copy of Kollontai, Zoia would join her in political activities, even sign her oppositionist statements. She herself stayed in the shadow of her dynamic friend, neither seeking nor receiving personal recognition. We know little about this talented and

---

13. For Lenin's warm recollections of the pleasant aspects of gentry life, see Valentinov, pp. 158–59.

14. Kollontai, *Iz moei zhizni i raboty*, pp. 17–21, 31.

15. The family moved to Sofia in 1878 to join Mikhail Domontovich, who had been assigned to Bulgaria in 1877 during the Russo-Turkish War. For Kollontai's friendship with Zoia, see *ibid.*, pp. 34–36. For Zoia's admiration and loyalty, see Fortunato, pp. 183–85.

lovable woman who endeared herself to Kollontai by her sympathetic spirit and critical mind. Mutual admiration bound them. At some point it must have been tacitly conceded by both that Shura would be the leader and Zoia the follower.

In childhood their relationship was different. Then it seemed that Zoia would accomplish the great deeds. Zoia seemed to Shura to know everything: what a constitution was, how the planets moved, why Abraham Lincoln freed the slaves, what Garibaldi had tried to achieve. Even Mikhail Domontovich listened to Zoia, answering her questions as though she were an adult. Shura was not always so favored; for her there were usually banal questions from a busy man. "Do you like to live in Sofia, Shura?" "Papa always thought about other things when he spoke with me or with my sisters. It was as though we didn't exist for him."[16] From Kollontai this was a rare criticism of the first man she loved, and an insight into the kind of woman her father respected. One historian has suggested that the girl in the nineteenth century who became the aggressive, achieving, nonconformist woman was the intellectually precocious child who modeled herself primarily on her father and whose father, in return, treated her seriously and educated her as though she were a boy.[17] If so, perhaps Zoia's example showed the way for Shura Domontovich.

After the family returned to St. Petersburg, Mariia Strakhova, a model of the independent woman of radical political views and already tutor to Kollontai's older sister Zhenia, became Shura's mentor, too. Mikhail Domontovich rarely spoke seriously with ladies, but he enjoyed Strakhova's conversation, and Kollontai consequently looked up to Strakhova as someone her father respected. During family dinners, Shura's father and her tutor discussed the Balkans, criticized Bismarck, and even argued over Russian politics. General Domontovich warned Strakhova that she might get into trouble with her "dangerous ideas," that one day the police would come and pick her up.[18] Kollontai admired Strakhova because she could "argue with Papa."

Although she was not an active socialist, Strakhova brought the world of revolutionary women closer. Shura was nine years old in

16. Kollontai, *Iz moei zhizni i raboty*, p. 33.

17. Page Smith, *Daughters of the Promised Land* (Boston, 1970), p. 120. This pattern fits such American women as Harriet Beecher Stowe, Margaret Fuller, and Elizabeth Cady Stanton.

18. Kollontai, *Iz moei zhizni i raboty*, pp. 40–42 (on Domontovich's political troubles owing to his liberal views and his encouragement of Bulgarian constitutionalism), p. 43.

1881 when Sof'ia Perovskaia, an ascetic, 28-year-old noblewoman and member of the revolutionary "People's Will," was sentenced to hang for assassinating Tsar Alexander II.[19] Kollontai never forgot the day of the hanging. One cannot doubt that it was a political awakening. She was sitting at the piano with her sister Zhenia when they heard the gallop of police horses. Zhenia said, "They are hurrying to the execution," and she began to cry quietly. Soon Strakhova rushed in, pale and without her glasses. She could only gasp "It's done" before falling to the floor in a faint as Shura watched in fright.[20] The poet Pushkin had praised the historically creative role played by those leaders of the Decembrist movement who were hanged in 1826; Sof'ia Perovskaia had a similar impact on the female intelligentsia of late-nineteenth-century Russia.

By the age of fifteen Shura was diligently studying with Strakhova to earn the certificate that would enable her to become a schoolteacher or enter one of the higher educational institutes open to women. Although the family expected her to enter society, Shura objected. She had too many models of purposeful women: Zoia, Strakhova, and now even her older sister Zhenia, who was allowed to go to Italy to pursue a singing career. Once again Mme. Domontovich was defying convention: young women from "good families" did not become "actresses." But Zhenia became, as Evgeniia Mravina, a very famous singer. Shura's delight at being noticed in a theater as "Mravina's sister" gave way to another feeling. "I don't want to be only Mravina's sister, I also want to do something great with my life."[21] Shura dreamed. Like the women of the People's Will she might go to a faraway village and enlighten the peasants. First she would enter the Bestuzhev courses—one of the first Russian institutions of higher learning for women, and popular with the Petersburg intelligentsia. Her family objected. A friend persuaded her instead to attend private courses offered by a Frenchwoman.

Shura wanted not only to "go to the people" but to be a writer, and a writer not simply of stories but of ideas. The social critics

19. On Perovskaia, see N. Asheshov, *Sof'ia Perovskaia, Materialy dlia biografii i kharakteristiki* (Petrograd, 1921), and Figner, vol. 1, pp. 273–80.

20. For Kollontai's recollection of this scene, see her "Iz vospominanii," p. 79, and *Iz moei zhizni i raboty*, pp. 48–49.

21. Kollontai, *Iz moei zhizni i raboty*, p. 54. Kollontai's other sister, Adel', married a man 40 years her senior and lived a conventional life.

Pisarev and Dobroliubov became her models. Mariia Strakhova convinced Mme. Domontovich to invite a well-known teacher of Russian literature, Viktor P. Ostrogorskii, to come to the house each week to give her daughter supplementary lessons. At first Ostrogorskii did not take seriously a young woman who would probably soon be getting married; when he recognized her dedication, however, he set high standards for her writing. Stressing clarity, he trained the future revolutionary pamphleteer. (Kollontai later decided that Lenin, with his clear and forceful prose, exemplified Ostrogorskii's ideal.) It was Ostrogorskii who taught her really to know and to love Russian writers.[22]

As a young girl, Shura had read widely and voraciously, like many other sensitive and intellectually advanced children without any particular guidance. On the second floor of her grandfather's country estate, Kuuza, in Finland was a large library, its windows overlooking the garden, the big room a cool refuge on hot summer days. The collection was broad, encompassing in various languages the classics of several cultures: Corneille, Racine, and Molière; Tennyson and Byron; Schiller and Goethe; Pushkin and Gogol. One shelf held more contemporary literature—especially the novels of Turgenev—and another held the Russian monthly journals, among them *Fatherland Notes*, which Shura read as she grew older.

This young woman who aspired to be a writer fell in love in about 1890 with her lively and handsome cousin, Vladimir Kollontai, an engineering student. Her mother, despite her own unconventional pattern, cautioned Shura against marrying a poor man like Kollontai. Her father pointed out that she was immersed in the world of books and philosophical discourse, but that Vladimir enjoyed neither reading nor serious conversation; between her and this engineer there could be no spiritual closeness. Though she must have been pleased at this recognition that she was a woman of serious intellect, Shura nonetheless seemed to take the question of marriage as a contest of wills. For two years she insisted that she was in love. If she did not receive her parents' consent, she told her mother, she would leave—like her beloved heroine Elena in Turgenev's *On the Eve*.

The consent was finally given, and Shura married Vladimir Kollontai in 1893. Her father had been right: the marriage was not a success, and not only because Vladimir Kollontai lacked intellectual

---

22. *Ibid.*, pp. 58–61. Also see Kollontai, "Avtobiograficheskii ocherk," p. 261, for recollections of her education.

depth. Shura herself was emotionally immature, as an incident on her wedding day pointed up. That morning her pet dog killed her canary, and the discovery caused Shura to burst into tears. Describing the incident, Kollontai recalled her mother's rebuke: Was she not ashamed on her wedding day to cry like a child over a dead canary?[23] Not only was she emotionally too young; intellectually, she was still searching. The combination made it unlikely that she would be content with marriage.

A curious recollection seems significant. Prior to Shura's marriage there was some confusion because her birth certificate declared that she had been christened "Aleksandr," a boy. A trifling error, easily rectified, and surely not worth including in a memoir unless Kollontai wanted her reader to know by it that she was intended from birth for a man's life. For, as we shall see, that was how this nineteenth-century woman regarded the alternative to traditional marriage.[24]

One motive for marrying was her wish to be free, in this instance from her parental home and her mother's tender tyranny. Yet neither marriage early in 1893 nor motherhood later that year was for her a liberating experience. The myth of the haven of love plunged her into boredom as soon as it became reality. "I still loved my husband, but the happy life of a housewife and spouse became for me a 'cage.' "[25]

Aleksandra's dull and confining existence contrasted with the independence of Zoia Shadurskaia, who came to Petersburg in 1893 to study voice and lived with the newly married couple. Shura envied Zoia's freedom, her round of concerts, lectures, and student meetings. Soon Shura was spending her evenings not alone with her husband but reading and talking with Zoia, as in the best times of her youth. Together they discussed articles in Russia's "thick journals" and whatever they could find on the new science of Marxism, which in the 1890's was widely discussed among the Russian intelligentsia. When Vladimir Kollontai brought engineers home to work with him on mathematical problems, Zoia and Shura would try to draw them into discussions of current social and economic issues; but the men were soon bored. "Enough philosophy," Vladimir would laugh. Or

23. See Kollontai, *Iz moei zhizni i raboty*, pp. 64–68, for the circumstances surrounding her marriage.

24. *Ibid.*, pp. 67–68. For an example of the desire to live "a man's life," see Vera Zasulich's memoirs in Engel and Rosenthal, p. 69. On Zasulich in general, see her *Vospominaniia*.

25. Kollontai, *Autobiography*, p. 11.

if the discussion became heated, "Quiet, quiet . . . you'll wake the baby."[26]

Shura wanted to be loved, but she also felt a need to achieve. She reminded Zoia of her youthful dream of "great deeds." Now she had no time to be creative. She loved her little son Misha (Mikhail Vladimirovich) and her husband, but how could she be a writer if she lacked the opportunity to work? Attempts to share her concerns with her husband were disappointing. Vladimir Kollontai could not understand: How was he interfering? Was it that she no longer loved him?[27]

Zoia advised Kollontai to turn her domestic responsibilities over to the nursemaid her mother provided, lock herself in her room, and write. Kollontai explained the difficulties of working at home: you close the door and start to work but your child falls and begins to cry; he wants his mother, not his nurse, so you rush to see what is the matter. With such interruptions little could be accomplished.

Under these difficult circumstances, she wrote a short story. It concerned an older woman living in a loveless marriage who fell in love with a younger man, left her husband, and joined her lover. It was one of Kollontai's earliest attempts to attack the double standard that tried to prevent women from living freely as men did. She sent the story to one of Russia's "thick journals," which rejected it with the explanation that she had written propaganda, not literature. Zoia agreed that Kollontai's story was really an article; certainly the heroine lacked depth. Vladimir Kollontai teased his wife—perhaps the editor would have preferred a young and pretty heroine rather than a middle-aged one? Bruised by rejection, and angry at her husband's "light-minded" jokes, Kollontai announced she would never write fiction again.[28]

At this time, when Kollontai was seeking an adult identity beyond that of wife and mother, she came into contact with the desperate economic conditions of the working class. In later years, Kollontai would look back and artificially, but in orthodox Bolshevik style, identify the single incident that made her a revolutionary. It occurred, she said, during a trip in 1896 with her husband, one of his

26. Kollontai, *Iz moei zhizni i raboty*, pp. 70–72.
27. *Ibid.*, pp. 67–72.
28. *Ibid.*, pp. 71–75.

colleagues, and Zoia to Narva, where she visited the huge Kronholm textile works, which employed 12,000 men and women. The two engineers had been commissioned to draw up plans for the improvement of ventilation at the works, and Shura and Zoia joined them in a tour. Then Shura decided to inspect the workers' housing. In dingy barracks, the air unbearably stale and heavy, cots were lined up for the workers, married and single. Amid the cots children milled about, some playing, some crying. An old woman sat, supposedly in charge. Kollontai's attention was drawn to one little boy, about the age of her own son, who lay very still. He was dead. No one had noticed. When told about it, the old woman replied that such deaths were not unusual and that someone would come later and take him away.[29]

The horror of the barracks, the sights and smells of that day, decided her fate, Kollontai would later claim. In fact, she was drawn to socialism for other reasons as well, which as we shall see were probably more significant. But she was determined that the entire economic system had to change. What could be more inadequate than engineers making plans for improving ventilation? Down with capitalism; down with tsarism; political rights for the workers so they could defend their own interests! "I could not lead a happy, peaceful life when the working population was so terribly enslaved. I simply had to join this movement."[30] Of course, we know Kollontai saw her life as neither happy nor peaceful; but the traumatic events of the day at Kronholm focused her thoughts. She ceased to write feminist short stories and began instead seriously to study Marx.

Perhaps already the seeds of her later conflict with bourgeois feminism were sown. The feminists proposed that the unity of women transcended class lines, that the sexual division was more important than the economic. But how could sex divide the men and women who were struggling to get out of the barracks, or unite the women there with the wives of factory owners? Mariia Strakhova again became influential. Kollontai sought out her former teacher, who was engaged now in museum work—a model of the independent, socially

29. *Ibid.*, p. 79.
30. *Ibid.*, pp. 79–80; see also Kollontai's *Autobiography*, p. 11. On the other hand, a friend quotes Kollontai as saying that no single incident caused her to become a Marxist, that her socialist consciousness developed gradually. When pressed for recollections of events that influenced her, she mentioned not the visit to Kronholm but the sensational Petersburg strike of textile workers in 1896. See Fortunato, p. 183.

useful woman—and told her of her unhappiness. She loved her husband, Kollontai said, but married life was not what she had expected. Strakhova suggested that Kollontai needed purposeful activity and urged her to join in working on a "mobile museum" designed to supply educational materials to workers' evening schools. It was not what she wanted to do, but Kollontai hoped by this route somehow to find the way to the revolutionary underground.

At the Mobile Museum of Pedagogical Aids Kollontai met some of the new Marxists—Elena Stasova, also a student of Strakhova, and Vera and Liudmila Menzhinskaia. These three young women had been friends from childhood and would share Kollontai's future as a Bolshevik. Their mothers, Poliksena Stasova and Mariia Shakeeva-Menzhinskaia, had also been friends. Women of the 1860's, the elder Stasova and Shakeeva-Menzhinskaia were not only committed to the emancipation of women but also dedicated to the enlightenment of the Russian masses. Shakeeva-Menzhinskaia was one of the organizers of the Bestuzhev women's courses, and her husband, professor of history Rudol'f I. Menzhinskii, shared his wife's advanced views; all three of their children, Vera, Liudmila, and Viacheslav, in turn became Marxist revolutionaries.[31]

Elena Stasova's family was also prominent among the intelligentsia: her father was a well-known progressive lawyer; her mother and her aunt, Nadezhda, were committed to the liberation of women.[32] Elena had joined the underground Marxist organization in Petersburg, and by the turn of the century was to be its secretary. She used the museum as a place to receive illegal political literature smuggled in from abroad, where the editors of the organization's newspaper, *Iskra*, lived in exile. Elena was one of a small network of *Iskra* agents in Russia who received shipments, distributed them, and collected funds.[33]

Kollontai's recollections of this time of new associations reveal some of the motivations impelling her along the path to socialism and revolution. Although she and Stasova were to become lifelong friends, Kollontai sensed that the younger woman looked at her critically (Stasova was one year her junior). Stasova knew what she wanted

---

31. N. Iurova, "Sestry Menzhinskie," in Zhak and Itkina, eds., pp. 249–51. Viacheslav Menzhinskii eventually succeeded Dzerzhinskii as chief of the Soviet secret police.

32. For Stasova's recollection of these years, see her *Vospominaniia*, pp. 21–28.

33. Krupskaia, *Vospominaniia o Lenine*, p. 62.

in life and Kollontai feared that she must seem insufficiently serious to this young revolutionary. Occasionally Stasova asked Kollontai to deliver a letter or a package to an unfamiliar apartment; then the day came when she asked her to a meeting to help with some problems. Kollontai was overjoyed at the prospect of her first illegal meeting. But it turned out that the cell members simply needed Kollontai to raise money, for they knew that she was acquainted with many wealthy people in St. Petersburg. She was humiliated. Was she useful only for delivering packages and raising money?[34]

Kollontai was determined to prove to herself, to Stasova, and to the movement that she could be genuinely valuable as a Marxist. For despite Stasova's assurances that one did not need to have a deep knowledge of Marx to be useful—indeed, that it was far more useful to divest oneself of bourgeois notions of personal advancement and instead be totally dedicated to underground discipline—Kollontai was not content to engage in useful small tasks, even illegal ones. Stasova's words helped only to tide her over her immediate feeling of inferiority.

These two young women, who both devoted the greater part of their long lives to Bolshevism, provide an interesting contrast. Stasova, although one of the original members of the Petersburg Committee of the Russian Social Democratic Workers' Party, imposed limitations on herself and willingly filled a secondary, nontheoretical role all her life. Kollontai could not permit herself such narrow self-definition.[35] She craved distinction. She decided, contrary to Stasova's advice, to devise a course of study that would make her what she was not yet—a theoretical person, a writer of seminal ideas. Leadership in revolutionary movements seemed always to go to the theorists, and Kollontai was convinced that she, too, could be a leader.

When in 1898 the legal Marxist journal *Obrazovanie* published an article Kollontai wrote concerning Dobroliubov's views on environmental influences on the development of children, she and Zoia were jubilant. It seemed a sign that Kollontai was on her way to fulfilling her dream of becoming a Marxist writer. Only her father spoke frankly—at least paying her the compliment of taking her seriously. He told Kollontai that her writing was "not bad," but that her article

34. See Kollontai's *Iz moei zhizni i raboty*, pp. 85–87, for these early experiences with Stasova.
35. *Ibid.*, p. 88.

contained too many quotations and not a single original idea.[36] His honesty had the effect not of discouraging her but of strengthening her resolve to deepen her knowledge so that she could make a genuine contribution.

Despite her disapproval of Kollontai's desire to be a significant Marxist, Stasova gave her books on Marxism and on economics, and Kollontai began to read the other legal Marxist journals, *Nachalo* and *Novoe Slovo*. But this was not enough: for at least a year, she decided, she needed to go abroad to the University of Zurich to study Marxism with Heinrich Herkner, an economist whose book on workers she had just read. There, free from conflicts with her husband, she might live as a student, read all the works that were banned in Russia, and become a learned Marxist. Her little son Misha could stay with his grandparents. Her husband would have to understand; if not, that meant their marriage was over.[37]

Kollontai appealed to her father for emotional and monetary support. Unhappy with her plans to leave Russia, he agreed to finance her on the condition that she not tell her mother her reasons for going to Zurich. They would say that Shura needed to go to the Swiss mountains for her health. Perhaps General Domontovich was pleased that he had been right all along in warning his daughter against marrying a man who did not share her intellectual interests. What is curious is that he should have underestimated his wife's ability to empathize with Aleksandra's decision, since she had defied Russian convention in the 1870's more sharply than her daughter was about to do in the 1890's, when she took the by then well-worn path to Zurich to study at the University.[38]

One historian has pointed out the remarkable cohesion among women in late-nineteenth-century Russian gentry families. For example, a striking number of sisters were to be found in the revolutionary movement of the 1870's, and they received considerable support from their mothers.[39] Mme. Domontovich surely provided a model that inspired Kollontai, just as the mothers of Vera Figner, Sof'ia Perovskaia, Liudmila Volkenshtein, and the Subbotina sisters

36. *Ibid.*, p. 90.
37. *Ibid.*, pp. 89–90, and Kollontai, "Avtobiograficheskii ocherk," p. 262.
38. At the end of the 1860's, young Russian women, denied access to universities at home, began flocking to Zurich. By 1873 over 100 were studying there.
39. Barbara A. Engel, "Mothers and Daughters: Family Patterns and the Female Intelligentsia," in Ransel, ed., pp. 44–59.

profoundly influenced their revolutionary daughters. Vera Figner, imprisoned in the Schlüsselburg fortress for revolutionary activity in the "People's Will," dreamed of her mother as representing to her all that was meaningful in her own life.[40] Sof'ia Perovskaia, on the eve of her execution, wrote her mother a letter begging her to understand her action; her mother returned this devotion by sitting in her daughter's jail cell in her final hours, cradling her head in her lap.[41]

One explanation for this strong bond between mothers and daughters invokes the existence of tyrannical fathers against whom both generations of women tacitly rebelled. Another suggests that absent or ineffectual fathers proved no match for the impressively strong and sensitive mother. But the picture is more complex, for one can find nineteenth-century Russian intelligentsia families where support was offered to radical daughters by both parents, neither of whom was either ineffectual or tyrannical; by the same token, one can find examples (Angelica Balabanoff comes to mind) of the radical young woman whose last memory of home was her mother's curse as she left.[42]

For the woman like Kollontai fortunate to receive support from her family, the break with traditional life was more bearable. Kollontai's parents provided not only the models of strong-minded independence but also the emotional and financial backing essential for her venture. Without the assurance that little Misha would be happy with his grandmother, Kollontai would never have reached Zurich. In her memoirs, she recalled the anguish of that first night on the train from St. Petersburg. She wanted to be free, but what was this freedom? Weeping, she tortured herself with memories of the sweet little hands of her five-year-old son. She blamed herself for the pain her dear, loving husband felt at her departure. Of course he would not wait years for her—he would fall in love with someone else. What did she really expect from her freedom? Why did she want to go to Zurich? Did it really matter that she felt cramped, that she had ideals to achieve? Each station on the way to Zurich brought the renewed temptation to get off the train and go home. But to do so would be to deny her plans to become a truly useful Marxist. Forcing

40. See Figner, vol. 2, for ties to her mother, esp. Chap. 2 ("Pervye gody"), pp. 12–19, Chap. 28 ("Narushennoe slovo"), pp. 205–8, Chap. 30 ("Mat' "), pp. 214–16, and the poem "K materi" on p. 239.
41. *Ibid.*, vol. 1, p. 274.
42. On Balabanoff, see Bertram D. Wolfe's Foreword to her *Impressions of Lenin*, p. vii.

herself to remain, she began to write two letters, one to her husband telling how much she loved him, another to Zoia setting forth her reasons for abandoning family life and for choosing instead to fight for the working class and for the rights of women.[43]

Few people show more than Kollontai the truth of the notion that most young revolutionaries embrace a cause more for personal reasons than for abstract political ones. She would later recall that being "possessed" by revolutionary enthusiasm was a "sweet" spiritual state that closely resembled being in love.[44] Vladimir Kollontai watched in bewilderment as his wife abandoned one area of emotional involvement, their marriage, and entered another, the revolutionary movement. As an old woman near eighty, looking back over half a century, Kollontai would write that it still hurt her to recall the suffering she had caused so good a man as Vladimir Kollontai, who could not understand her need to enter "the man's world," as he called it, of politics. In his view, if she loved him and no one else she should have been content with a traditional wifely role.[45]

Partly a longing to see Misha, partly an eagerness to participate in the revolutionary underground brought Kollontai back to St. Petersburg in 1899, only a year after her departure for Zurich. With the death of her parents and the end of her marriage—for she never returned to Vladimir—Kollontai's household shrank to Zoia and Misha. She wrote of her pain at her father's death in 1902, a year and a half after her mother's, and the intensity of her reaction suggests that her sense of self derived primarily from him. There were many tragic times in her long life, Kollontai claimed, but at the death of her father she knew the anguish of irrevocable loss. The most dreadful moment came when Kollontai returned after the funeral to the quiet, empty house. She went into her father's study; in the corner was his familiar deep armchair, on the table lay closed a copy of *Macedonia and Eastern Rumelia*. At that moment, as she realized with full force that her father would never return to his desk, she was overcome with despair.[46] If there is truth to the assumption that exceptional women draw power from their relationship with fathers who treat them as persons of consequence, then Kollontai's grief at her father's death

43. Kollontai, *Iz moei zhizni i raboty*, pp. 91–92.
44. "Amerikanskie dnevniki A. M. Kollontai (1915–1916 gg.)," *Istoricheskii Arkhiv*, 1 (Jan. 1962), p. 131.
45. Itkina, p. 26.
46. *Ibid.*, pp. 35–36. For recollections that suggest Kollontai's identification with her father, see Palencia, pp. 20–24.

contained an added element. Alone, could she maintain her confidence?

In fact, her independence grew. The death of both parents cut Kollontai free. She was *from* the possessing class but no longer *of* it. With the passing of those who indulged her, and to whom she could turn, her dependency faded.

※※※

If her fate as a woman and her search for an identity drew Kollontai to political activity, why did she not join the feminists? The Western feminists had their counterparts in the Russian intelligentsia, educated upper-class women like Anna Filosofova, Anna Shabanova (one of Russia's first women doctors), and Nadezhda Stasova. Why did the feminists hold so little appeal for Kollontai?

Organized feminism's response to the "woman question" was, until 1905, basically conservative and apolitical, stressing education and useful employment. Through education women could open the doors to professional opportunity. Through philanthropy they could care for urban victims of poverty and ignorance—the peasant girls who came to the city, the abandoned women, the prostitutes. But this philanthropic work was by nature limited, and organizations financed and staffed by "charity ladies" from 1860 to 1917 managed to care for only a minute fraction of destitute women. In women's education, though, the results of the feminists' efforts were more impressive. In the 1860's and 1870's they managed to pressure the Russian government to open not only advanced high schools to girls of every social class but also universities and medical schools to women. Their ally in this struggle was the government's fear that young women who were leaving Russia to attend foreign universities (particularly the University of Zurich) were becoming radicalized.[47]

Yet the interests and temperaments of the nineteenth-century Russian feminists, who sought no alliances with the working class, undermined any definition of feminism in its broadest sense as representing the interests of all women. Philanthropists and patronesses, the feminists favored legal means to achieve their goals and were content with small deeds.[48] But this seemed too narrow to be considered fully liberating to many young women of the Russian intelligentsia.

47. As a result of its fear, the government issued a decree in the summer of 1873 ordering Russian women out of Zurich. See Figner, vol. 1, p. 120.
48. Goldberg, pp. 50–51.

Probably Kollontai's most direct knowledge of feminism came from observing the activities on behalf of women undertaken by the feminist mothers and aunts of her colleagues at the museum. These middle-aged feminists, with their moderate political style and their Russian Women's Mutual Philanthropic Society, must have appeared pallid in the 1890's to a young romantic like Aleksandra Kollontai, whose first heroine, Turgenev's Elena, left family and country to join her lover, Insarov, in the Bulgarian revolution. It was the women of the Russian revolutionary movement, who rejected the feminists, that presented exciting models.[49] There had been the women of the 1860's (erroneously called nihilists), who frequently contracted fictitious marriages with radicals to escape family oppression and strode with reckless boldness through university halls, disorderly student meetings, and radical circles of St. Petersburg. With their cropped hair and worn-out boots, often smoking cigarettes, they scorned the niceties of upper-class life. Like Chernyshevskii's heroine Vera Pavlovna, they wanted to do something useful and they demanded the immediate equality of the sexes. Going abroad to Zurich to study, or living in Russia in communal apartments, they invited rumors of sexual license, though in fact most maintained a strict personal code. The demand they made for "free love" meant simply freedom to love without social, religious, or economic restriction—not promiscuity.[50]

However intriguing an image of personal freedom the "nihilists" of the 1860's presented, it was the revolutionary women of the 1870's, the *narodniki*, who represented the sharpest alternative to bourgeois womanhood. Kollontai recalled her fascination with them.[51] For these revolutionaries, who wanted to change society itself (some by terrorism), the cause of women's emancipation no longer even existed. Vera Figner wrote: "We arrived abroad not to be pioneers of a movement to solve the woman question; to us it did not require any solving. It was a thing of the past."[52] Equality of men and women as a principle was established in the 1860's. Vera Figner, who was imprisoned for twenty years in the Shlüsselburg fortress, Sof'ia Perovskaia, who was

49. On radical women's rejection of the feminists, see Goldberg, pp. 84–85.

50. On the "nihilists," see Richard Stites, "Women's Liberation Movements in Russia, 1900–1930," *Canadian-American Slavic Studies*, 4 (Winter 1973), p. 462, and Stites, *Women's Liberation Movement*, pp. 99–114.

51. Kollontai, "Avtobiograficheskii ocherk," p. 262.

52. As quoted by Knight, p. 5, from Vera Figner, *Polnoe sobranie sochinenii* (Moscow, 1932), vol. 5, pp. 77–78.

hanged in 1881, and Gesia Gel'fman, who died in prison after giving birth to a child, became heroine martyrs. Kollontai's beloved Turgenev immortalized Sof'ia Perovskaia in a poem.[53] Revolutionary women worked side by side with men in an atmosphere of equality that seemed to mock the feminist premise of male oppression.

Kollontai could not have been satisfied with Russian feminism as it was defined in the late nineteenth century. As she grew in political awareness, probing political and economic theory, she came to recognize that the bourgeois feminists could do little for women of the working class. They could not affect the lives of the factory women whose children were perishing in the workers' barracks. Nor—and more to the point—could they really do anything for her.

Kollontai was trying to balance two conflicting needs, one to fulfill her maternal feelings, the other to accomplish "great deeds" in "the man's world." The Russian feminists might advance the status of some women, but their goals were tame; they did not aim to change the conventional family structure. Let there be no doubt: Kollontai was a feminist if by feminism we mean a woman's freedom to decide her own destiny, to express her thoughts fully, and to convert those thoughts into actions. She wanted to be free of sex-determined, stereotyped roles, free of society's oppressive restrictions. Kollontai's feminism postulated that woman's essential worth stemmed from her common humanity and was not dependent on the other relationships of her life.[54] And she decided that her quest could best be fulfilled through socialism.

Kollontai joined the socialists when she was already a mother—with all the anxieties that entailed. To be sure, she did not define herself as a mother. She was a person first. On occasion, she would even deny the depth of her maternal commitment. "Love, marriage, family, all were secondary, transient matters." But such a statement, made in middle age, did not accurately reflect her devotion to her son or the pain of separation from him.[55] A longing to be with her child contributed to her decision in 1899 to return to St. Petersburg, and throughout her career she hurried back from distant places to be with

53. "Porog: Stikhotvorenie v proze I. S. Turgeneva," in N. Asheshov, *Sof'ia Perovskaia* (cited in n. 19 above), p. 141.

54. On the development of feminist groups, see Goldberg, pp. 96–97. For a broad definition of feminism, see Barbara J. Berg, *The Remembered Gate: Origins of American Feminism. The Woman and the City, 1800–1860* (New York, 1978), p. 5.

55. For Kollontai's denial that love, marriage, and family were the core of her existence, see her *Autobiography*, p. 12. For the pain she felt at separation from her son, see her *Iz moei zhizni i raboty*, p. 91.

Misha during his school vacations, concerned that he know why his mother did not live like the mothers of his friends, often depressed, wondering whether he would ever understand her.[56] She could never have embraced an ideological movement that did not take into account women's role as mothers and include among its goals a radical restructuring of the family and women's relationship to it. Most of all, her ideology needed to hold open the promise of achievement in the larger world.

Kollontai was uniquely situated to understand the limitations of Russian feminism. The educational and professional opportunities that feminists were seeking in the late nineteenth century were already available to her as a woman of the upper classes. Nor did she lack nursemaids to help care for her child. As a mother she needed more—a supportive social structure to remove the inner conflict between the intellectual and the emotional sides of her personality.

Marxism, already flourishing among the intelligentsia in the late 1890's, provided that structure of meaning into which she could hope to fit her own idiosyncratic experience and by means of which she could remove the guilt from her discontent with the domestic role. Here was a positive perspective through which her disappointing marital experiences could be understood: one had to free oneself from the selfish bondage of private concerns and work in a socially useful way for the collective. By directing her away from the private and the familial, socialism promised Kollontai release from conflicts over the role of wife and mother. Socialism attracted her because almost from its inception it encompassed the woman question and offered solutions more comprehensive than those contemplated by Russian feminism. The early socialists advocated a public life for women, the disappearance of the bourgeois family, and the collective upbringing of children.[57] It is no accident that these ideas, which would eventually recede into a mythical haze in Soviet Russia, were the ones Kollontai would seize on and elaborate into communist theory.

Kollontai was one of the last of a type, the nineteenth-century radical Russian woman who joined the revolutionary movement from a

56. Mindlin, *Ne dom, no mir,* p. 136. Kollontai wrote of Misha, "What a joy it was to see his small, rosy face appear under the shadow of his cap and watch the seriousness with which he would deposit his small valise on the platform of some great European depot." Palencia, p. 52.

57. In the first draft of the *Communist Manifesto,* Engels included among the immediate measures to be taken by a communist regime the establishment of public child-rearing institutions. See Meyer, p. 95. Inessa Armand responded to socialism for reasons similar to Kollontai's. See I. F. Armand, *Stat'i, rechi, pis'ma,* pp. 81–86.

background of privilege and for motives only peripherally related to mainstream Marxism. Neither the fate of the proletariat nor the existence of economic deprivation equaled the situation of women in propelling her toward socialism. Kollontai's conversion was influenced primarily by the interests of one woman—Kollontai herself—who paradoxically wished to be free but also sought a cause to which she could give herself completely and that would in turn give structure and meaning to her life.

Kollontai was representative of many upper-class Russian women who broke with their conventional past and went to Zurich; but in certain ways she would always be unique. Unlike the "nihilists" of the 1860's, she would not change her outward style and remained all her life an elegant lady in the drab revolutionary ranks. Unlike so many of the revolutionaries of the 1870's (Vera Figner being an obvious example), she never sought martyrdom. The woman who as a little girl wanted to hear bells played in her honor lacked that fanatical moral rigor and urge to self-sacrifice that distinguished such revolutionaries as Perovskaia and that over the years drove many young Russian revolutionary women to suicide.[58] Asceticism was alien to her nature.

꙾꙾꙾

Perhaps because Russian Social Democracy was so small a movement at the turn of the century, Kollontai tended to perceive the political sphere that she entered as highly personalized. Two figures dominated: Vladimir Il'ich Lenin and Georgii Plekhanov. Lenin was an energetic young man in his thirties, Plekhanov the erudite and witty patriarch of Russian Marxism. In a sense, all Russian Marxists were Plekhanov's pupils. So for a time was Lenin. Then mentor and student became rivals. Ultimately, Plekhanov disagreed with Lenin on the question of party organization, the issue that in 1903 split the Russian Social Democratic movement at its London Party Congress into Bolshevik and Menshevik factions.[59] Although initially Plekhanov supported Lenin, their alliance as Bolsheviks (the faction claim-

58. For discussion of asceticism, suffering, and martyrdom on the part of revolutionary women, see Engel and Rosenthal, eds., pp. 9, 19–20. Also see Figner, *Zapechatlennyi trud*, vol. 1, p. 278. On suicide, see Knight, p. 17.

59. For Russian factionalism and the split between Bolsheviks and Mensheviks, see Valentinov; Theodore Dan, *The Origins of Bolshevism* (trans. Joel Carmichael; New York, 1970); and Leopold H. Haimson, *The Russian Marxists and the Origins of Bolshevism* (Boston, 1968).

ing majority support at the Congress) was only temporary. Soon Plekhanov repudiated the Bolshevik doctrine of tight party organization—Lenin's "cult of the professional revolutionary"—and accused the younger man of espousing ultracentrism and dictatorship *over* the proletariat.[60] In all the factional shifts and splits that marked Russian Social Democracy in the ensuing decade, one feature persisted: the two giants of Russian Marxism, Lenin and Plekhanov, Bolshevik and Menshevik, could not work together.

It was Plekhanov's personal charm, Kollontai thought, that inclined her toward the Mensheviks. She was "in love" with Plekhanov, she declared. Lenin also expressed love for Plekhanov, his teacher, about whom Anatolii Lunacharskii wrote, "It is a joy to recall those glittering eyes, that astounding intellectual agility, that greatness of spirit, or, as Lenin put it, that physical force of his brain, that aristocratic forehead crowning a great democrat."[61] Only slowly did Kollontai establish a political identity of her own that transcended hero worship.

Her friendship with Elena Stasova, who was secretary of the Bolshevik-dominated Petersburg Committee (as the Social Democrats in that city described themselves) naturally involved Kollontai with the Bolsheviks. With Stasova she led a circle of 25 to 30 workers, supposedly in geography lessons.[62] Underground party activity, mainly on the periphery of the movement, absorbed her: agitation, the distribution of illegal literature, protest meetings, student strikes and demonstrations. Through her work with Stasova, Kollontai might have come to join Lenin's Bolsheviks, despite her love for Plekhanov, but Lenin alienated her by his failure to attach sufficient importance to the development of spontaneity within the working class. Unlike other socialist groups, the Bolsheviks initially boycotted the Duma established in Russia after the Revolution of 1905. Kollontai believed, with the Mensheviks, that participation in the Duma encouraged worker spontaneity, whereas nonparticipation encouraged passivity and hindered working-class development. This ideological difference kept Kollontai's name from appearing on the masthead of

60. On Plekhanov see Lunacharskii, *Revoliutsionnye siluety*, pp. 38–49.
61. For Kollontai's view of Plekhanov, see her *Iz moei zhizni i raboty*, pp. 94–96. For the Lenin quote see Lunacharskii, *Revoliutsionnye siluety*, p. 48, and Ulam, p. 304.
62. The Petersburg Committee of the RSDRP ostensibly included members of both factions, but it was Bolshevik-dominated. On Stasova's connection with it, see her *Vospominaniia*, p. 89. For Kollontai's work with Stasova, see the former's *Iz moei zhizni i raboty*, p. 97.

the first legal Bolshevik newspaper in Russia, *Novaia Zhizn'*. Because she cooperated with the Mensheviks in the Duma by writing reports for their committees, they considered her one of them.[63]

෴෴

The woman question drew Kollontai to socialism; ultimately, it would preoccupy her. Feminism is first a personal impulse, directed inward. After freeing herself from established social standards, Kollontai reached out. According to a childhood friend, Evgeniia Fortunato, the liberation of women was Kollontai's favorite theme after her return from Zurich; Fortunato recalled her amazement when she first heard "Shurin'ka," her once light-hearted companion now transformed into an underground party member, exhort women to unite to fight for their equality in revolutionary struggle.[64]

Until 1905 Kollontai moved from one area of concern among socialists to another, seeking experience and exposure.[65] After 1905, however, the woman question became the focus of her activity because of the sudden prominence of bourgeois feminist organizations, which took advantage of the possibilities for reform inherent in the new constitution and the existence of the Duma.[66] Although we cannot document the onset of her political maturity, Kollontai's emotional embrace of socialism had given way by about 1905 to a mature, political analysis of the relationship of socialism to the woman question. The result was opposition to bourgeois feminism as a movement irrelevant to the lives of the working class. Thus in 1905, in reaction to the feminists, Kollontai began to organize a Russian socialist women's movement, a commitment that would last a lifetime. Regarding it as the core of her intellectual and emotional existence, she would return to the women's movement whenever she was thwarted elsewhere.

Among the feminist organizations, Kollontai's most formidable opponent was the Union for Women's Equality. Founded at the be-

63. Kollontai, *Iz moei zhizni i raboty*, pp. 102–10, 377, and "Avtobiograficheskii ocherk," p. 270. Women, of course, could not be elected to the Duma.

64. See Fortunato, pp. 182–83.

65. Her chief work prior to 1905 concerned Finland. *Zhizn' Finliandskikh rabochikh* (St. Petersburg, 1903) was considered in Finland a pathbreaking work and remained the only study of its kind until after the First World War. See Hauge, p. 16. For Lenin's appreciation of Kollontai's writings on Finland, see his letter to Bogdanov of Jan. 10, 1905, asking that Kollontai be mobilized to write articles on Finland for his new weekly *Vpered* (Lenin, *Sochineniia* [4th ed.; M, 1954], vol. 8, p. 27).

66. Kollontai, *Iz moei zhizni i raboty*, p. 100.

gining of the 1905 Revolution by a group of Moscow professional women and *intelligentki* who united to demand the vote, the Union became more threatening when, like the socialists, it demanded a full set of radical social and labor reforms and began to attract women from socialist ranks. Extending its efforts to peasant women, the Union could even produce massive petitions to the State Duma to end the oppression of women in the countryside by enfranchisement.[67] Some socialist women responded to the feminists and supported a "United Women's Platform." Kollontai, however, turned up at feminist meetings and spoke against the "idyllic" concept of collaboration between revolutionary socialists and bourgeois Equal Righters. Denying feminist assumptions that there existed a single "woman question," Kollontai publicly demanded that the socialist and proletarian women disassociate themselves from the feminists and rely for their liberation on the socialist party. She refused even to attend newly formed socialist women's clubs—although they were attractive to working women—because they lacked a clearcut class line. Until socialist women stated clearly that liberation had to be carried out by the working class alone and by means of revolution, Kollontai would not by her presence indicate approval of their activities.[68]

If Kollontai now seems naive in having assumed that the majority of Russian socialists shared her concern with the woman question, it never occurred to her to doubt at this time that her view of socialism, colored by its nineteenth-century feminist connection, was the prevailing one. Confident of the socialists' commitment, Kollontai thought she need only warn them of the feminist threat and remind them that they must give more attention in their program to the problems of Russian working women. When she did so she found for the first time how little the Social Democratic Party in Russia was concerned with the fate of the women of the working class and "how meager was its interest in women's liberation."[69]

How are we to explain the reluctance of the Bolshevik-dominated Petersburg Committee to support Kollontai? Ironically (for she was less controversial than Bebel), the Party applauded Bebel's theoretical interest in the woman question expressed in his call to women of all

67. Stites, *Women's Liberation Movement*, pp. 210–14.
68. Kollontai, *Iz moei zhizni i raboty*, pp. 101–6, and "Avtobiograficheskii ocherk," p. 268.
69. Kollontai, *Autobiography*, p. 13.

classes and disapproved of Kollontai's practical suggestions aimed solely at the working class.[70] To what degree was frank disdain for women involved? Many Party members scorned the notion that the passive Russian women, the "babas," could be a source of revolutionaries. The working class was too new in Russia, the Party too little rooted among the masses, and procedural questions too much disputed for the weak Petersburg Committee, torn by its own uncertainties, to take seriously Kollontai's warnings about the need to work among the mass of proletarian women. For some socialists, no area of Party work had lower priority.[71]

Despite the theoretical tradition that included resolution of the woman question among its goals, the Russian socialists regarded Kollontai's proposals uneasily, seeing women's liberation as a side issue that would be solved by the revolution. To deal with it explicitly, to make it a goal rather than a by-product, meant to be engaged not only in fruitless work but in dangerously divisive feminism. To a Marxist all that seemed needed was to adjust the economic base of society. To provide for separate work among women meant taking energy away from revolutionary activity of a direct sort.

※※※

The community of interest in the woman question that was missing in Russia Kollontai found abroad, in a budding international socialist women's movement in which Clara Zetkin, the leader of the semiautonomous socialist women's organization within the German Social Democratic Party, played the dominant role. At the Social Democratic Women's Conference at Mannheim in 1905, Zetkin's group impressed Kollontai with its agenda, which included women's suffrage, agitation among women in the countryside, and the recruitment of female domestic servants to the socialist movement. Zetkin strengthened Kollontai's view that the Russian Party must create an apparatus for drawing women to socialism.[72]

70. Similarly, the German Socialist Party hailed Bebel but shied away from Clara Zetkin. For Lenin's approval of Bebel on the woman question, see Klara Tsetkin [Clara Zetkin], "Lenin o morali i voprosakh pola," in Razin, ed., pp. 14–15.

71. Kollontai, "Pamiati bortsov revoliutsii," p. 8.

72. Kollontai, *Iz moei zhizni i raboty*, pp. 105, 377. The German socialist women's organization was semiautonomous (with its own leadership, finances, newspaper, and bureaucratic personnel) because women were not legally permitted to join political parties until 1908. After 1908, Zetkin found it difficult to exercise independence. By 1912, the socialist women's movement was effectively incorporated into the SPD bureaucracy and lost its separate identity. See Honeycutt, pp. 337–56.

Efforts of women like Zetkin to combat a lack of interest in work among women resulted in 1907 in a milestone—the first International Socialist Women's Conference, held at Stuttgart in connection with the Seventh Congress of the Socialist International. But Stuttgart, although Kollontai could not know it at the time, was a disappointing paradigm of the ambivalent relationship of the European socialist movement to the woman question.[73] If ever there was an issue on which Kollontai thought no question should arise, it was equal voting rights without distinction of sex. She was mistaken; "women and the vote" dominated the meeting. Socialist women vacillated, their willingness to compromise indicating that the principle of equality for women had still not entered into the "flesh and blood" of Social Democracy.[74] The decision of the Belgian, Austrian, and Swedish delegations to forgo suffrage for working-class women and to fight instead for universal male suffrage focused the debate. In Austria, for example, men were still fighting for a direct and secret vote, and the Austrian socialist women hesitated to prejudice that issue by a struggle for universal suffrage. The German socialist Lily Braun spoke for this "go-slow" view, using a rather inappropriate comparison. She hoped the socialist women would be as reasonable in accepting limitations on women's suffrage as they had been in accepting the ten-hour day, for which they fought without betraying their final goal of an eight-hour day.[75] However optimistically one may interpret the final vote in favor of Zetkin's universal suffrage motion, the tenor of the debates at Stuttgart suggested the weakness of international socialism's commitment to women's full political equality.[76]

In the fledgling international movement only Zetkin had gone be-

73. Kollontai represented Russia at Stuttgart. Her mandate came from the tiny group of socialist working women she had organized that spring. The previous year she had attended the German socialist conference at Mannheim as one of five foreign socialist participants. See Kollontai, *Izbrannye stat'i i rechi*, p. 399. For her views on Mannheim, see "Itogi Manngeimskago s'ezda."

74. Kollontai, *Izbrannye stat'i i rechi*, p. 85.

75. For vacillation among the women at Stuttgart, see Kollontai, "Dva techeniia," pp. 51–59, and *Izbrannye stat'i i rechi*, p. 88. For Lily Braun's position, see "Dva techeniia," p. 56.

76. Zetkin's motion read in part: "The socialist parties of all countries are duty-bound to fight energetically for the implementation of universal women's suffrage . . . which . . . is to be vigorously advocated both by agitation and by parliamentary means. When a battle for suffrage is conducted, it should only be conducted according to socialist principles, and therefore with the demand of universal suffrage for women and men." The women's conference accepted Zetkin's position by a vote of 47 to 11. The International Socialist Congress upheld it, but appended V. Adler's position giving each nation responsibility for determining the ways it struggled for electoral equality. On Zetkin's resolution, see Honeycutt, p. 307.

yond the earliest stages of politicizing women. In the years before the First World War she would succeed in organizing 175,000 socialist women. It was appropriate that Zetkin, who proposed at Stuttgart the establishment of an International Women's Secretariat, should become its first director when it was founded later in 1907, and that *Gleichheit (Equality)*, the German Social Democratic newspaper for socialist women, which Zetkin had been editing since 1892, should become its central organ.[77]

For Kollontai, Stuttgart had added significance. The meeting made Zetkin her mentor. The widow of a Russian revolutionary and the mother of two sons, Zetkin believed with Kollontai that for women motherhood was both a personal and a social function, and that it was socialism's responsibility to enable women to combine motherhood with a public role. But unlike other socialists—Lily Braun, for example, whose socialist purity had become suspect as a result of her concentration on the woman question—no one ever doubted Zetkin's Marxist respectability.

Zetkin's closest friend was Rosa Luxemburg. The brilliant leader of German Social Democracy on first meeting Zetkin dismissed her as a "sincere and worthy woman. . . ." But Luxemburg's biographer considered this friendship the most secure of her life. Luxemburg's indifference to the socialist women's movement was probably what enabled her relationship with Zetkin to be noncompetitive. Political affinities were taken for granted as both women automatically moved to the left on every issue, with Zetkin never hesitating to defer to Luxemburg on questions of Marxist analysis.[78] The course of Kollontai's friendship with Zetkin would not be as unclouded. These two combative personalities would clash as Kollontai, inspired initially by Zetkin's example, began to share the older woman's place as the dominant figure in the international socialist women's movement.[79]

꙰꙰꙰

After the dispersal of the Second Duma in 1907 and the arrest of the Social Democrats, the mood of reaction in Russia strengthened.

77. *Ibid.*, p. 7. Also see Quataert.

78. Nettl, vol. 1, p. 194.

79. In September 1915, Lenin apparently wrote to Kollontai asking if she would take Zetkin's place as head of the International Women's Secretariat—thus Kollontai in *Iz moei zhizni i raboty*, p. 193. The editor of that collection points out on p. 392 that no such letter has been found, but notes Lenin's criticism of Zetkin. For Lenin's disdain

Organizing the working class became more difficult as workers drifted away from both the Bolshevik and the Menshevik factions. Kollontai considered it essential that an appartus in the Party be designed especially for work among women, and stated so frankly in the spring of 1907 in an article she published in the Menshevik press.[80] A Women's Bureau would make possible concerted efforts to reach women and to keep track of those "broad-backed and kerchiefed" ones who occasionally attended Party meetings; one saw them once, then they vanished. But by the autumn of 1907, when Kollontai raised the question of organizing women in Petersburg, the few working women she had recruited were her sole allies.[81]

In her memoirs Kollontai recorded an unhappy episode showing that lack of support plagued Mensheviks and Bolsheviks alike, both women and men. Kollontai approached Vera Zasulich for advice on ways to organize Party activity among proletarian women. Zasulich's attitude toward young comrades was known to be exceptionally straightforward and friendly. Famous in Russia since 1878, when she shot a tsarist official who had ordered the beating of a political prisoner, Zasulich had become Plekhanov's close comrade and an intimate of Lenin and Krupskaia. The bohemian, untidy Vera Ivanovna was, like Kollontai, among the most humane of the socialists: "With Vera Ivanovna," Lenin commented, "too much is based on morality, on feelings." It was not only her heroic past that made Zasulich prominent, Trotsky recalled, "it was her astute mind, her erudition . . . and her exceptional psychological intuition."[82] Yet Zasulich proved hostile to the idea of a Bureau to work separately among women, claiming it would be divisive.[83]

Undaunted by her failure with Zasulich, Kollontai tried another tack. With the aid of the Union of Textile Workers and her few working-class supporters (including notably the sixteen-year-old book-

for Zetkin's pacifism, see Lenin to Kollontai, July 1915, in Lenin, *Sochineniia* (4th ed.), vol. 35, p. 148.

80. Although Kollontai does not identify the journal, it was probably *Russkaia Zhizn'*, a Menshevik daily published in St. Petersburg. On the Menshevik press in 1907, see M. S. Cherepakhov, *Russkaia periodicheskaia pechat' (1895–Oktiabr' 1917) spravochnik* (M, 1957). For Kollontai's participation in *Russkaia Zhizn'*, see her *Iz moei zhizni i raboty*, p. 379.

81. Kollontai, *Iz moei zhizni i raboty*, p. 109, and "Avtobiograficheskii ocherk," pp. 268–72. Kollontai's group of "conscious working women" included the weaver Antonova, the textile worker Anna Semenovna (Osipova), the dressmakers Solov'eva and Mariia Burko, and the nurse Efremova. *Iz moei zhizni i raboty*, p. 107.

82. Trotsky, *O Lenine*, pp. 16, 30, 40. For lively portraits of Zasulich, see Krupskaia, *Vospominaniia o Lenine*, pp. 44–45, and Trotsky, *O Lenine*, pp. 14–48.

83. Kollontai, "Avtobiograficheskii ocherk," pp. 271, 275.

binder Klavdiia Nikolaeva, who was to be a long-time associate of Kollontai), she established a legal club affiliated with neither socialist faction but open to both. It bore the innocent name "The Society for the Mutual Help of Working Women."[84] For most of Kollontai's young supporters, the forming of this club was their first serious political act; not so for Nikolaeva, who was no stranger to revolutionary activity and indeed had been arrested the year before.[85]

Kollontai's Working Women's Club, with its library and lectures, was open every evening and attracted as many as 200 to 300 women at a time from varied occupations. Kollontai was deeply involved with the life of the club in that winter of 1907–8, so when Zasulich appeared at the door one night, Kollontai was overjoyed: the doubter would see how receptive working women were to their own institution. But Zasulich condemned the club as a "superfluous enterprise" that divided the strength of the Party.[86]

Were the socialists justified in sensing a feminist danger in Kollontai's activities? Here we find a paradox. To draw working women to Marxism, Kollontai advocated the separatist methods of feminism. Encouraging women to form groups and inviting them to lectures "for women only" did, in fact, run the risk of leading women to develop a separatist, feminist consciousness. And yet this was also practical politics, a recognition of the uniquely backward state of Russian women, who were illiterate, superstitious, and accustomed to and accepting of exploitation. These women needed to be approached through discussions of health, child care, and sewing; to ignore the world in which they lived meant to lose them, whereas to draw them into a woman's group might be the first step toward leading them to political activity. The power of association, with its inner dynamic, might make of the timid working-class woman a recruit to socialism. Kollontai repeatedly made clear that the goal of female political consciousness was not separatism but working-class solidarity.

Kollontai's warning to the Petersburg Committee that the socialists were losing women students and *intelligentki* to the feminists and not gaining any women proletarians met with indifference or suspicion.[87] Such attitudes were reflected among Social Democrats else-

84. *Ibid.*, pp. 274–75.
85. For details of Nikolaeva's life, see G. Grigor'ev, "Skvoz' gody," in Zhak and Itkina, eds., pp. 292–95.
86. Kollontai, "Avtobiograficheskii ocherk," p. 275. This episode with Zasulich is not included in Kollontai's later memoirs of the period; cf. *Iz moei zhizni i raboty.*
87. "Avtobiograficheskii ocherk," pp. 272–73, and *Iz moei zhizni i raboty*, pp. 105–6.

where in Europe, where (with the exception of Germany) few special efforts were being made to raise the class consciousness of working women or to liberate them from their roles as housewives. Special groups and journals within the Party devised to reach women implied feminism, and socialists everywhere, as Kollontai learned, were as anxious as the Russians to avoid the charge that within their ranks they were harboring a left wing of the bourgeois feminist movement.[88]

Russian Social Democrats identified Kollontai with the woman question. As a result, the Petersburg Committee—despite her insistence to the contrary—suspected Kollontai of separatism, although they seemed indifferent to the very real attempts of the bourgeois feminists to split the working class. In the spring of 1908 Kollontai alone protested plans by the feminists to convene in the autumn an All-Russian Women's Congress that they hoped would result in a national Russian women's party. Kollontai unsuccessfully sought approval from the Petersburg Committee to organize a labor delegation to attend and explain why a united party was impossible.[89] Vera Slutskaia, a Bolshevik and a personal friend, tried to prevent Kollontai from participating. Ordinarily Kollontai respected Slutskaia's opinion; this time she ignored it.[90]

Why did Kollontai want to take a workers' delegation to the feminist Congress? Clearly the idea of a confrontation appealed to her. Personal antipathy to the feminist leaders and a desire for a forum to prove their inability to analyze the woman question also played their part. And this would be her first opportunity in Russia to act on a truly major stage—representatives of the foreign press and over a thousand women would be attending.[91] Kollontai could not resist this opportunity to be recognized as a public figure. The role of controversial leader was one she sought actively.

There were other motives. Though Kollontai insisted that socialists focus on the working class, was there no desire on her part to speak to bourgeois women? It would be a mistake to overemphasize an

88. Kollontai, *Izbrannye stat'i i rechi*, p. 102.

89. "Avtobiograficheskii ocherk," p. 276. Some Soviet historians have incorrectly presented the Petersburg Committee as encouraging working-class participation in the Congress. See Itkina, p. 51, and Bochkarëva and Lyubimova, *Women of a New World*, pp. 36–37.

90. For details of Slutskaia's life, see Svetlana Zimonina, "Sekretar' Raikoma: Vera Slutskaia," in Zhak and Itkina, eds., pp. 414–24.

91. A. Ivanova, "Dve tochki zreniia," in Artiukhina et al., eds., pp. 88–89.

ambivalent feeling, but Kollontai understood from her own experience the appeal of socialism. Lily Braun put it this way:

Socialism, angrily resisted by bourgeois society, nonetheless penetrated like the air we breathe through locked and barricaded doors and windows. In many of its traits it was virtually predestined to win the women over; just as, long ago, Christianity attracted countless female disciples because it appealed to sentiment, because it promised to help those "who are weak and heavily laden," so it is the sentimental side of socialism which today has such a strong effect on women, often without their knowledge, and most of the time without their wishing to admit it.[92]

The adjective "sentimental" is one Kollontai would not have chosen: socialism was her lifeline to the outside, nonsentimental world. Yet she was aware that socialism spoke to an audience broader than the proletariat. Kollontai knew that at the Women's Congress there would be bourgeois women aware of their cramped roles in society and as susceptible as she had been to the message of socialism.

Kollontai decided to lead a delegation to the Women's Congress without the permission of the Petersburg Committee. Using the Union of Textile Workers, of which she was a member, as her sponsoring organization, and her small apartment as a meeting place, Kollontai made her preparations. The Petersburg Central Bureau of Trade Unions undertook on her behalf to organize elections of delegates to the Congress, and some sympathetic members of the Working Women's Club, both Bolsheviks and Mensheviks, rallied to her support. As news of the forthcoming Congress spread through the factories, some working women who were hostile to the bourgeois feminists did gravitate toward the socialists.

During the two months before the Congress, Kollontai held about 50 meetings to coach the politically inexperienced working women. (She had suddenly become an "illegal" and had to dodge the police, a result both of the appearance of a pamphlet she had written calling on Finland to rise against the tsar and of her agitation among the textile workers.) Her core group included the workers Klavdiia Nikolaeva, Klavdiia Antonova, Mariia Burko, Anna Ivanova, and Varvara Volkova. Their efforts were amateurish, but Kollontai viewed their preparation of reports as essential political education.[93]

92. As quoted in Meyer, p. 109.
93. Kollontai, "Avtobiograficheskii ocherk," pp. 276–79. Their topics included women and politics, the budget of the woman worker, working conditions in industry, the need for protective factory legislation, child labor, the working woman in contemporary so-

Shortly before the Congress convened, the Petersburg Committee, aware that Kollontai was ignoring them and perhaps reassured that she did not intend to collaborate with the feminists, sanctioned working-class participation and delegated Vera Slutskaia and the Bolshevik Praskov'ia Kudelli to attend.[94] Kollontai was not delegated to be leader, but she dominated. Her group of some 45 working women, each carrying the red carnation symbolizing revolution, joined the 1,000 women who assembled in St. Petersburg on December 10, 1908, from all over Russia.[95] As Klavdiia Nikolaeva stepped into the huge Aleksandrovskii Hall of the City Duma, with its glittering crystal chandeliers, she faltered in the face of such unfamiliar splendor. Kollontai nudged her, "be bolder Klava, be bolder."[96] On that December day Nikolaeva could hardly have imagined that ten years later she would be chairing the First All-Russian Congress of Worker and Peasant Women in Moscow, and that a few years afterward she would head the Women's Section of the ruling Bolshevik Party.

In retrospect, the Petersburg Committee's suspicion that Kollontai intended collaboration with the feminists appears ludicrous. She attended the Congress not to cooperate but to oppose. Since the police were looking for her, Kollontai reluctantly designated Varvara Volkova to explain in her place why the bourgeois feminists and the proletarian working women had no basis for cooperation. Her speech, as read by Volkova, was simple and dramatic: the woman question, the feminists say, is a question of rights and justice; no, respond the proletarian women, it is a question of "a piece of bread." Even assumptions about the origins of women's concern with their lot were open to conflict: according to the bourgeois feminists, the woman question arose when the avant-garde of fighters for women's emancipation stepped out openly in defense of their trampled rights and interests; according to the proletarian women, it arose when millions of women, as a result of almighty capital, were thrown onto the market, driven

ciety, the position of servants, and the role of trade unions and clubs vis-à-vis working women. In short, a picture of the lives of working-class women would be presented to a bourgeois audience. For Kollontai's description of the Congress, see "Zhenshchina—rabotnitsa na pervom" feministskom" Kongresse v" Rossii," p. 6.

94. Kollontai, "Avtobiograficheskii ocherk," p. 279; Bochkarëva and Lyubimova, *Women of a New World*, p. 37. Some members of the Petersburg Committee opposed this decision to the end, and printed an appeal to working women not to participate.

95. The number of working women varies from 35 to 45. Kollontai recorded that the press noted their dramatic entry; *Iz moei zhizni i raboty*, p. 114.

96. Grigor'ev, "Skvoz' gody," in Zhak and Itkina, eds., pp. 295–96.

from their homes by the cries of hungry children and by the misery of their lives. Kollontai's speech asked what the feminists were doing to help working-class women. Could they produce one law for their protection achieved as a result of feminist influence?[97]

Kollontai was not being entirely fair. Some feminists' programs since 1905, as she knew, had included proposals for the amelioration of working conditions.[98] But Kollontai was concerned less with details than with caricaturing and discrediting the feminists. She argued that women would be fully liberated only through radical change. This meant abolishing all laws subordinating women to men; providing women with the right to be elected to all institutions of self-government on the basis of a direct, equal, and secret vote; providing legal protection of all areas of women's work; forbidding night work, overtime, and all work under conditions damaging to women or their future offspring; and guaranteeing enforcement of these rules by means of female factory inspectors to be chosen by the workers from among themselves. To this Kollontai added demands for maternity leave for eight weeks before and eight weeks after birth, and for free medical care during pregnancy. These were basically the provisions on the woman question incorporated into the Social Democratic Party Program of 1903.[99]

Kollontai denied that the feminists fought for similar demands, despite their talk about the unity of women's interests and the necessity for a general women's movement. She insisted that the world of women, like the world of men, was divided into two camps: the bourgeoisie and the proletariat. The feminists sought to make life better for women of a particular social category within the exploitative capitalist system. The proletariat struggled to eliminate the old, antagonistic class society. Do not try, she warned the feminists, to divide the working class by advocating a united women's organization.[100]

Soviet writers imply that Kollontai's demands on behalf of working-class women infuriated the feminists.[101] But in fact neither her call for universal suffrage nor her demand for the amelioration of working conditions and the establishment of maternity leaves could

---

97. See *Trudy* . . . , pp. 794–95.
98. Kollontai, *Sotsial'nye osnovy zhenskago voprosa*, pp. 2–3, acknowledges feminist interest in working conditions. See Edmondson for the several feminist programs.
99. *Trudy* . . . , pp. 798–99. For the 1903 party program, see above, p. 2.
100. *Trudy* . . . , pp. 799–801.
101. See, for example, A. Ivanova, "Dve tochki zreniia," in Artiukhina et al., eds., p. 90.

have outraged them, since some feminist groups had already incorporated into their programs a list of social and economic reforms. What the feminists did object to was Kollontai's premise that there could be no unity among women of different classes and the insulting implication that even if the feminists incorporated demands on behalf of working women, they were not prepared to fight for them seriously. Moreover, feminist leaders were mainly angry that Kollontai should send a workers' delegation into a unity conference with clear instructions to disrupt it.[102]

Although the workers' delegation was never as unified or as responsive to her direction as Kollontai would later claim,[103] feminist anger was justified. Nor had the feminists seen the whole of Kollontai's attempt to undermine their quest for unity: in preparation for the Congress she had written a book attacking Russian feminism that grew to 400 pages by the time it was completed (too late in the autumn to be printed in time for distribution at the Congress).[104] *The Social Bases of the Woman Question* developed themes Kollontai touched on in her speech prepared for the Women's Congress, and it did so in a strongly polemical way. We will see that this first full-scale study of the woman question by a Russian underscored not simply Kollontai's distance from the feminists but—and this was both less obvious at the time and ultimately of greater significance—her divergence from the Social Democrats as well.

However much Kollontai liked to repeat that the bourgeois feminists were limiting themselves to winning rights for women of their own class, she had somehow to contend with the fact that, since 1905 at least, one feminist group, the Union for Women's Equality, had been cutting across class lines. The Union appealed for universal suffrage and urged radical social and labor reforms: equal rights for peasant women in land reform, and welfare protection and insurance measures for working women.[105] In so doing, the Union was follow-

102. See Edmondson.
103. For Kollontai's assumption that she controlled the labor delegation, see "Avtobiograficheskii ocherk," pp. 279–80, and *Iz moei zhizni i raboty*, pp. 111–15. At the time of the Congress she recognized tactical divisions within the delegation, however, as her article "Zhenshchina—rabotnitsa na pervom" feministkom" Kongresse v" Rossii" shows (p. 7).
104. Publication was delayed because the manuscript was sent to Capri to be read by Maxim Gorky, friend and benefactor of the revolutionaries and publisher of many of their works.
105. Stites, "Women's Liberation Movements" (cited in n. 50 above), p. 465.

ing the lead of the new generation of liberals in Western Europe. To insist simply that the feminists cease beguiling proletarian women with misleading promises was accordingly insufficient by 1908, and Kollontai had to go further than she had in her speech to the Congress (which did little more than echo the Social Democratic Party Program) to explain how the feminists with their various lists of reforms failed to understand the actual needs of working women, and why proletarians needed not reform but revolution.

She proceeded by identifying the key feature in the struggle for the liberation of women: it was to fight "not against the outward forms of female inequality but *against the causes giving rise to them*."[106] The book argued, as the speech did not, the radical premise that for working-class women to be liberated, not only must the capitalist system be overthrown but the family itself must be restructured. Yet the problem of the family—so painful and sharp to Russian proletarian women—was of so little significance to the feminists that they failed to incorporate changes in the family into their platforms.[107] For this reason, their claim to be innocent of class bias was specious.

Men understood what the feminists did not: that the woman question was a matter not of liberation in the political arena, but rather of liberation at home. How frequently did the words "You could not live without me to support you!" spring to the lips of an angry man? How could true economic independence for women be possible unless the pattern of domestic life were altered so that the family ceased to be a closed individual unit?[108]

What Kollontai did not admit to the feminists was that the Social Democrats had equally failed to confront the issue of the family. Kollontai knew that no question concerning mutual relations between the sexes called forth so much disagreement, even among socialists, as that of whether to preserve the present form of the family in the future society. In the nineteenth century, Marx and Engels had written that the bourgeois family was doomed; but the question of the family was not central to Marxism, and no proposals for change in the structure of the family appeared in the 1903 program of the Russian Social Democratic Party. Indeed, at European socialist conferences as late as 1906 resolutions were still being offered that called for women to

106. Kollontai, *Sotsial'nye osnovy*, p. 224 (italics in the original).
107. *Ibid.*, pp. 187–89.
108. *Ibid.*, pp. 34, 128.

return from the factories to their role in the home when their husbands' wages improved.[109]

Not even socialist women were in full agreement concerning the family. Consider Rosa Luxemburg: in words that echoed Kollontai's own, she said that work, "that is to say hard, intensive work, which makes complete demands on one's brain and nerves, is, after all, the greatest pleasure in life"; but her views of women's relationship to love, marriage, and family were incompatible with her commitment to work. In a letter written in about 1898 to her lover, Leo Jögiches, she wrote:

My soul is bruised and it is difficult to explain exactly how I feel. Last night in bed in a strange flat in the middle of a strange city, I completely lost heart and asked myself the frankest question: would I not be happier instead of looking for adventure to live with you somewhere in Switzerland quietly and closely, to take advantage of our youth and to enjoy ourselves. . . . In fact I have a cursed longing for happiness.[110]

Elsewhere she wrote to Jögiches of her longing for a child. "Will this never be permitted? Never? . . . Oh darling, will I never have my own baby?"

Luxemburg's torment is the more poignant because it remained private and unresolved, her vision of love and maternal joy unrelated to Kollontai's counterimage of a society of collectives that would replace the individual family. Her letter to Jögiches was a dream of a very private life, a little nest with their own furniture, a few friends in for dinner, a summer in the country, a baby to care for.[111] Luxemburg so thoroughly repressed her womanly desires that not until after her death, when her letters were read, did friends know the pain she had endured.[112]

Kollontai's approach to the woman question was economic and social, that of the feminists legal and political. Kollontai charged the

<hr>

109. *Ibid.*, pp. 212–13. The idea of restructuring the home was not generally popular, despite a large theoretical literature on the subject. Nowhere in the 1903 program is there an echo of Marx's and Engels's assumption that the bourgeois family was doomed. See Marx and Engels, *The Communist Manifesto* (cited in n. 3 above), pp. 27–28, and Engels, pp. 83, 89.

110. Nettl, vol. 1, p. 163.

111. *Ibid.*, pp. 132, 144.

112. See Kollontai's tribute to Luxemburg and Liebknecht after their murder, in which she described Karl Liebknecht as the warm heart of German socialism and Rosa Luxemburg as its rational mind (*Izbrannye stat'i i rechi*, pp. 262–63). After Luxemburg's death and the publication of her letters, Kollontai understood her better. See Kollontai, "Pis'ma Rozy Liuksemburg," pp. 36–38.

feminists with thinking about the male-female relationship only insofar as it related to their own marital needs. For this reason, bourgeois feminists included among the issues they raised the future of church-sanctified marriage, and the questions of whether a husband might control a wife's earnings, whether he had the legal right to compel her to live with him, and whether he could take her children away by force. Although admitting that these problems were meaningful for working-class women and agreeing that they had caused misery to women of all classes, Kollontai denied that questions of legality could solve the future of the working woman's position in marriage and the family. The family was at base not a legal but an economic unit, its structure growing out of the economic system. Changes in the family were questions of economic relationships, questions that by their very nature were outside the ken of bourgeois feminism.

The feminists chose to consider marriage primarily in its legal aspects, but Kollontai brought the question of marital relationships and sexuality into the political forum, thus anticipating the widespread discussions of sexual mores in the Soviet Union in the 1920's. Having called attention to the curious failure of Russian feminists fully to discuss the marriage relationship, she observed that the few who occasionally considered the issue only reached the socially irrelevant conclusions already offered by European feminists, that marriage was a personal question to be resolved apart from the political and economic structure of society and by individual effort. If women "dared to" enter into a free marital union, ignoring self-protective economic factors, the problem of independence in marriage would solve itself.

Kollontai pointed out that the feminists were not considering the place in society of the woman of medium talents. For the woman of brilliance, beauty, or creativity, who could attract to her people eager to help, "daring" might be possible; but society must provide a means of survival and self-expression for women of average abilities with few economic advantages. Kollontai put the issue politically. Did the feminists believe that the contemporary class state, however democratically structured, could make free love possible? Would it take on itself the obligations relating to maternity and to the upbringing of children that were fulfilled now by the individual family? Only socialism could create the conditions that would enable women to be economically independent and that would at the same time protect them from the negative consequences of love free of economic considerations.[113] Only socialism could replace the family.

Kollontai's appearance at the Women's Congress brought swift retribution. She had intended to be silent, but a series of sharp interchanges with the feminists indicated her whereabouts to the police.[114] Rather than face years in prison, Kollontai prepared to flee Russia.[115] Her son, a fifteen-year-old in St. Petersburg, would remain in the care of close friends. Each night Kollontai sought a new refuge in order not to fall into the hands of the police. Old friends closed the door to her, and even her sister Adel' did not welcome her for fear of the harm that might befall her husband. On her last evening in Russia her friend the writer and poet Tat'iana Shchepkina-Kupernik gave a party for her at her home. Then Kollontai went to the freezing platform of the station to begin the trip to Germany and the life of a political exile, which was to continue until the Revolution of 1917.[116]

How shall we evaluate Kollontai's performance at the Congress, which forced her departure from Russia? Was it the foolhardy display of a woman who would risk even exile for the enjoyment of an exciting confrontation? Or was it the realistic behavior of a revolutionary who knew that her days in Russia were numbered? It would be only a matter of time before the police caught up with her if she continued to engage in revolutionary activity, and the alternative to action was extreme caution and silence. Was there much point for a revolutionary to remain in Russia forever dodging the police?

Many revolutionaries who had faced the same question, Lenin among them, were already abroad. In Europe she would find a community of socialists. She could write her revolutionary polemics with the resources of great libraries at her disposal. Misha, who was occupied in school, could visit during his vacations. The prospect was not a happy one, but neither was it altogether dismal. But to go into exile meant to abandon her beloved work. What a difficult time to leave Russia, she wrote to Plekhanov from Berlin in January 1909; now when she sensed some success in her efforts to awaken the Russian

113. Kollontai, Sotsial'nye osnovy, pp. 187–89, 194.
114. The feminists charged that socialist men were not truly committed to suffrage for women, citing the Stuttgart Congress. See Trudy . . . , pp. 494, 744, 784–87, for their charges and Kollontai's attempt to refute them as distortions of a complex situation.
115. Kollontai, "Avtobiograficheskii ocherk," pp. 279–80.
116. Itkina, pp. 54–56.

working women, when, for the first time, she saw women in Russia formulating their needs and raising their voices in defense of their interests as workers.[117]

She tried to keep in contact with the group she had brought together for the Congress. A warm letter from Varvara Volkova attested to her influence: hearing from Kollontai had inspired Volkova and the others not to abandon their cause and to try more vigorously to organize working women. What a pity that Kollontai was not with them; how much they missed and needed her! But it became difficult in the era of repression prior to the outbreak of the First World War for Kollontai's little group to continue its political activity. The police hounded them, closing down even their women's club. One of the victims wrote to Kollontai from Archangel with the news of their exile.[118]

Living abroad, Kollontai could do little to help her beloved women workers' movement beyond trying to keep the issues alive. This meant providing the much-needed literature that would polarize the women's movement and prevent working-class women from being lost to bourgeois feminism.[119] The woman question would remain in the political background. Not until 1914, shortly before the outbreak of the war, would the Russian socialists begin to take up the cause of women's liberation in a practical way—and then their interest was partly the result of factional competition between the Bolsheviks and the Mensheviks. As for the feminists, they never succeeded in creating a successful national women's party in Russia. Although Kollontai's lengthy attack on them, her *Social Bases of the Woman Question,* enjoyed success in Russia, it could take little credit for the defeat of the bourgeois women's movement, which was battered by political reaction and torn apart by internal dissension and bitter disappointment at the failure of the first two progressive Dumas to grant women the vote.[120]

A question remains. If the bourgeois feminists were committed to

117. *Ibid.,* p. 56. Itkina cites Kollontai's letter to Plekhanov.
118. *Ibid.,* pp. 56–57.
119. In 1900 Krupskaia had written a brochure, *Rabotnitsa,* describing the exploitation of women in field and factory and explaining the relationship of Marxism to their lives. There was little else. Kollontai wrote a pamphlet, *Rabotnitsa mat',* that was published in St. Petersburg in 1914. It contrasted the miserable life of the pregnant factory worker with the pampered luxury of the pregnant bourgeois lady.
120. See Stites, *Women's Liberation Movement,* pp. 219–22, on the decline of the feminist movement. For an example of the feminists' inability to agree, see *Trudy . . . ,* pp. 766–67.

the equality of women, as they surely were, why was it impossible for Kollontai ever to cooperate with them, to acknowledge that her doubts about her own socialist party established a common bond between herself and the feminists?[121] The answer must be that ideological differences were simply too fundamental. Collaboration with feminists, however sensible for practical goals such as factory protection and maternity benefits, risked harming the socialist concept of working-class solidarity. Kollontai was the revolutionary; the feminists were the reformers. The bourgeois feminists had no interest in fighting for a socialist solution to the woman question, which included the abolition of private property, the end of traditional marriage, and the withering away of the family. So long as their goals diverged, Kollontai militantly refused to recognize common ground.

At the same time, Kollontai needed continually to dissemble. The feminists never suspected that Kollontai intended *The Social Bases of the Woman Question* also as a challenge to the Russian Marxists "to build a viable women-workers movement in Russia."[122] In her zeal to remove the woman question from the marginal status to which Russian Marxists were inclined to assign it, in her effort to restore the nineteenth-century primacy of the idea that between socialism and the liberation of women there was a natural bond, Kollontai never revealed to the bourgeois feminists her difficulty in convincing either Bolsheviks or Mensheviks, as she moved between the two factions, to place among their goals a genuinely socialist solution to the woman question.

121. A double-edged memorial article in tribute to August Bebel, written in 1913, suggests Kollontai's doubts about the commitment of socialist men to the cause of women. See Kollontai, *Izbrannye stat'i i rechi*, pp. 113–24.
122. So Kollontai claimed in her *Autobiography*, p. 18.

CHAPTER TWO

Becoming a Bolshevik

NEVER was Kollontai further from Lenin and the Bolsheviks than in the years before 1914 when she lived in Berlin as a member of the German Social Democratic Party. Yet within a year after the outbreak of the World War and the resultant destruction of international socialism, Kollontai overcame her reservations and joined Lenin and the Bolsheviks. Her doubts, and the reasoning by which she resolved them, provide the theme for this chapter. The relationship between Lenin and Kollontai, partners in revolution, was grounded in ambivalence.

Socialists admired the German party as the "jewel of the International." Considered the party most determined in its opposition to war, it also encompassed the largest women's movement in Europe, led by Kollontai's mentor, Clara Zetkin, a member of the Party Control Commission.[1] In the years before the war Kollontai saw herself not as a socialist in exile but as an internationalist. She conducted her activities on a European scale, in Paris organizing a housewives' strike against high living costs, in Belgium helping to set the groundwork for a miners' strike, and in Sweden urging socialist youth to oppose militarism.

Not only did Kollontai ignore Lenin, she associated with Russians with whom Lenin disagreed. Among her comrades were the "soft" and humane Lunacharskii (whom Krupskaia would claim Lenin always really favored) and his great friend Aleksandr Bogdanov (a brilliant physician and party philosopher who had recently been Lenin's second-in-command).[2] Bogdanov invited Kollontai in 1911—along with Petr Maslov, a Menshevik agrarian expert—to give a series of lectures in Bologna at the party school that he and Lunacharskii had

1. Nettl, vol. 2, p. 607. By 1910 over 82,000 women belonged to the German party. Zetkin's journal, *Die Gleichheit*, the central organ of the movement, distributed 80,000 copies. See Kollontai, *Izbrannye stat'i i rechi*, p. 95.

2. For Lenin on Lunacharskii, see Krupskaia, *Vospominaniia o Lenine*, p. 169. For Bogdanov and Lenin, see Daniels, p. 14.

established. At Bologna leading intellectuals of Russian socialism spoke on the history of the workers' movement, on international politics, and on socialism in Russia. Each had a chance to develop a favorite theme: Lunacharskii, art; Trotsky, Tolstoy; and Kollontai, the woman question. There were practical lessons as well: how to organize conspiracies and use codes.[3]

That same year Lenin organized a rival school near Paris. Kollontai's negativism toward Lenin was especially noteworthy because her political views resembled his rather more than those of the extreme leftists Lunacharskii and Bogdanov. Lenin urged his party to work in the underground, but he had abandoned his earlier opposition to the Duma, coming to regard it as a useful revolutionary platform. Kollontai agreed with his arguments, both against those Mensheviks who wanted an open party with no underground activities and against extremists like Bogdanov and Lunacharskii who were opposed to legal participation in the Duma. But Kollontai was a romantic revolutionary who believed less in Lenin's theory of party discipline and hard organization than in Bogdanov's assumption that the party's task was to call forth and lead the broad revolutionary masses. She avoided Lenin out of loyalty not only to Lunacharskii and Bogdanov, whom he treated badly,[4] but to Plekhanov as well.

In their earliest talks together, before 1905, Plekhanov expressed to Kollontai his suspicion of Lenin, who reminded him of Bakunin with his narrow cult of the professional revolutionary; Kollontai understood that Plekhanov saw Lenin neither as comrade nor as disciple but as rival.[5] Ties to old friends, together with the rumors and frictions of émigré life, turned her ambivalence occasionally into antagonism. In a letter to Karl Kautsky, Kollontai reported from Paris that "this small band of people headed by Lenin is more and more isolated."[6]

Another area of tension, the woman question, heightened Kollontai's suspicion of the Bolsheviks. Most of the unhappy encounters between Kollontai and the Russian Social Democrats took place in St.

3. Hauge, p. 28, claims that Petr Maslov was Kollontai's lover and that her novel *Bol'shaia liubov'* was based on their relationship. Gorky and the historian Pokrovskii also came to Bologna. Lenin organized a rival school in 1911 at Longjumeau, near Paris; for his disputes with Bogdanov and Lunacharskii, see Daniels, pp. 9–34. On the Bologna school, see Livshits, pp. 124, 132–33.

4. See Lunacharskii, *Revoliutsionnye siluety*, pp. 19–20.

5. Itkina, p. 32.

6. See Pertsoff, pp. 33–34, for this undated letter (written in 1911 or 1912 from Paris) in the Kautsky Archive. On the tensions of émigré life, see Valentinov.

Petersburg during Lenin's exile. Yet there are indications that before the war, when Kollontai was regarded as a Menshevik (although she preferred to think of herself as an internationalist with ties to neither faction), she doubted Lenin's commitment to the woman question. In the spring of 1914, while she was preparing a report to the Third International Women's Conference, to be held in conjunction with the August meeting of the Socialist International in Vienna, Kollontai learned in confidence that the mandates of Menshevik delegates to the Women's Conference would be contested by the Bolsheviks. She was indignant at the maneuvering; they who had never been interested in the women's movement were now trying to dominate it.[7]

Kollontai tended to assume that she represented the embodiment of the woman question. Her attitude, understandable in relation to the bourgeois feminists, became less plausible when other socialists were involved—as Liudmila Stal' was to point out. Among the Bolsheviks in exile Stal', along with Krupskaia, Zlata Lilina, and Inessa Armand, shared Kollontai's commitment, if not her single-minded intensity. Krupskaia and Lilina are familiar to students of Russian history, if only because they were married to the Communist leaders Lenin and Zinoviev. Inessa Armand has also received attention because of her alleged relationship with Lenin.[8] Liudmila Stal' is less well known. The same age as Kollontai, she became her friend and a leader in the Russian women's movement. Born in 1872 in Ekaterinoslav, she was the daughter of the owner of a small factory and had been a party member since 1897. During her periods of exile from the capital, she worked alternately as a journalist and as a *fel'dsher*, or paramedic. By the time she left Russia in 1907 and joined Lenin's little group in Paris, she had been a strike organizer in Odessa and an underground party worker in Petersburg and Moscow. Arrested several times (once to find her three sisters in prison with her), she had already served a term in the Peter and Paul Fortress.[9]

These Bolsheviks, without prompting from Kollontai, planned to

7. The Women's Conference, according to precedent, was scheduled to precede the general Socialist Congress. The first two women's conferences were held at Stuttgart in 1907 and at Copenhagen in 1910. Pertsoff (p. 42) quotes Kollontai as twice expressing indignation to the Menshevik S. Iu. Semkovskii. See her letters in the Nicolaevsky Archive, Hoover Library, Stanford University.

8. On this relationship see Wolfe, pp. 96–114.

9. Flora Florich, "Vdali ot Rodiny (L. N. Stal')," in Zhak and Itkina, eds., pp. 447–48. See also "Liudmila Nikolaevna Stal' " in *Bol'shaia Sovetskaia Entsiklopediia* (2d ed.; M, 1957), p. 449.

organize Russian working women. In Paris, in 1911 or 1912, Stal' suggested to Louise Saumoneau, a leader of French socialist women, that they bring together Krupskaia, Inessa (as she was invariably called), and Kollontai to publish a journal for working women, perhaps abroad, perhaps in Russia.[10] Because Kollontai was considered a Menshevik, Stal's proposal that she participate was rejected. When the journal, *Rabotnitsa*, came into being in 1914, without Kollontai and under Bolshevik auspices, it was intended to attract proletarian women to the Bolshevik ranks.[11] The originators and first editorial staff worked separately: Krupskaia and Lilina contributed from Krakow, Inessa and Liudmila Stal' from Paris. A. I. Elizarova, K. Nikolaeva, E. F. Rozmirovich, and K. N. Samoilova worked in Russia. The journal was ostensibly legal. This is your journal, Krupskaia told the working women of Petersburg; send us your letters and articles. Articles discussed the need to fight for better working conditions and for sick funds, but some called on working women to join the revolutionary movement.[12] The editors therefore labored under fear of arrest; this eventually befell the Petersburg participants, who managed to use their arrest to protest unhealthy prison conditions.[13] Despite the inability of the editorial board to make common decisions, seven modest issues were published in 1914 before the journal was finally suppressed. Two issues were confiscated by the police because they called on working women to revolt.[14]

Lenin received the April issue of *Rabotnitsa*, which he praised in a letter to Inessa Armand: "Good work. . . . Mes félicitations à Ludm. et toi!"[15] The editors responded appreciatively. One of them, K. N. Samoilova, suggested from Russia that Lenin also submit an article.

10. Florich, in Zhak and Itkina, eds., p. 451.

11. Elena Rozmirovich wrote to Krupskaia from Russia of her distress that certain Bolsheviks contemplated including Kollontai. Rozmirovich saw only trouble in the idea of cooperating with Mensheviks. For the origins of *Rabotnitsa*, see Krupskaia, *Vospominaniia o Lenine*, pp. 217–19, and Bessonova, ed. The insurance campaign of 1912 in Russia played an indirect role in the origins of *Rabotnitsa*. In April 1912, the Duma passed a State Insurance Law that covered men and women workers employed in large-scale industry. Because women workers received equal rights with men in electing representatives to sick-benefit societies, the elections had a significance for the women's movement, as Krupskaia noted; *Rabotnitsa* could draw women into voting. See Bochkarëva and Lyubimova, *Women of a New World*, pp. 42–43.

12. Bochkarëva and Lyubimova, *Women of a New World*, p. 48. On the nature of articles, see Bessonova, ed., p. 27.

13. Pavel Podliashchuk, "Prekrasnaia Zhizn' (I. F. Armand)," in Zhak and Itkina, eds., p. 33; Samoilova, *V ob"edinenii-zalog pobedy*, p. 14.

14. Zhak and Itkina, eds., pp. 37, 299; Bochkarëva and Liubimova, *Svetlyi put'*, p. 39.

15. Bessonova, ed., p. 26.

They were not feminists, she pointed out, and they therefore welcomed the cooperation and opinions of men.[16]

The cause of women, instead of uniting the émigrés, became one more contest between Bolsheviks and Mensheviks. Liudmila Stal' advised Krupskaia in March 1914 to delegate a Bolshevik to report on the Russian working woman at the forthcoming International Socialist Women's Conference. Otherwise, Kollontai would surely step forth in the name of the Russian working woman. Instead, Inessa proposed that Krupskaia take to Vienna a delegation of as many Russian working women as possible. Lenin agreed: Kollontai must be prevented from speaking as the Russian delegate. So Krupskaia prepared a report on behalf of the Bolsheviks in the summer of 1914, as Kollontai did for the Mensheviks, for an International Women's Conference that never took place.[17] The war that came instead brought Kollontai into the ranks of Bolshevism, after German socialists shocked her by supporting the war and betraying the International.

When war broke out, Kollontai and her son Misha (who was with her on summer vacation) were arrested in Berlin as Russian spies. After a search turned up a mandate from the Russian Social Democratic Party delegating Kollontai to the International Women's Conference, she was released on the assumption that a Russian socialist could not be a Russian spy.[18] Misha remained in prison. Kollontai immediately sought out her socialist comrades, hoping that her friend Karl Liebknecht might intercede on behalf of her son. She learned that Liebknecht and the other socialist deputies were at the Reichstag, went there to see them, and thus happened to be in the German parliament at that disastrous moment for international socialism when the Social Democrats voted in favor of war credits. An acquaintance questioned Kollontai's presence: a Russian had no right to be in the Reichstag. The idea had not occurred to her. She had gone to the German parliament "as to her own." Here was the new reality: internationalism was destroyed. That evening, together with Liebknecht (who knew nothing about Misha), Kollontai wandered the streets of Berlin. Liebknecht, who shared her shock at the vote in the

---

16. *Ibid.*, p. 36.
17. For this correspondence, see Bessonova, ed., pp. 40–46, and Lenin, *Polnoe sobranie sochinenii*, vol. 48, pp. 303–4.
18. Kollontai, *Otryvki iz dnevnika*, pp. 14–17.

Reichstag and refused to abide by any notion of party solidarity, predicted that the international working class would never forgive the German Social Democrats for their action that day.[19]

Kollontai appeared curiously unaware of the antiwar activities of Rosa Luxemburg and Clara Zetkin. The small antiwar group in Germany would be known among local socialists as the "Rosa group." Luxemburg sent 300 telegrams to German officials who were considered to be oppositionist, inviting them to Berlin for an urgent conference. Only Clara Zetkin in Stuttgart immediately cabled support. Both women suffered depression that reportedly brought them close to suicide. Although Luxemburg termed Clara's reaction to the war "hysteria and the blackest despair," Zetkin acted boldly: through *Gleichheit*, the newspaper of the socialist women's movement, she tried to unite women against the war under the slogan "If men are killing, it is women's duty to come forward for life."[20]

Considering the meager support she received, Luxemburg might have welcomed Kollontai to her tiny antiwar group. If she did not, it was because Kollontai seemed of little consequence, one of Zetkin's women's-movement people.[21] Rosa Luxemburg could be cutting to those whom she considered her intellectual inferiors, and in Berlin in 1914, misled partly by condescension toward the women's movement and partly by Kollontai's elegance, she vastly underestimated the Russian. But Kollontai's analysis of the failure of German Social Democracy was as incisive as Luxemburg's own. Kollontai's initial unwillingness to accept the possibility that the German Social Democrats might destroy the International by voting support for the war was followed by a realization that came to historians much later: German socialism had become morally bankrupt. Kollontai recognized (as she was to do again in her own country) the decay of revolutionary ideals. Creativity was gone from German Social Democracy.[22] What

19. *Ibid.*, pp. 21–22. Kollontai's recollections of that day were also published in "Gigant dukha i voli: golos Lenina," p. 5.

20. Nettl, vol. 2, pp. 609–11; Itkina, p. 87. Kollontai quoted Zetkin in "Zhenskii sotsialisticheskii internatsional' i voina," pp. 3–4. Because Zetkin gave *Gleichheit* an antiwar cast, the journal was confiscated. Kollontai, *Iz moei zhizni i raboty*, pp. 156, 163, 386.

21. Luxemburg disparaged the socialist women's movement as "old ladies' nonsense" (letter of Luxemburg to Leo Jögiches, Sept. 18, 1900, quoted in Honeycutt, p. 251).

22. Kollontai had already criticized the German Social Democratic Party in her 1912 book *Po rabochei Evrope*, suggesting that a bureaucracy was growing up within it. As a result, she was for a time ostracized, as she recounts in *Iz moei zhizni i raboty*, pp. 121–25. On the "decay of ideals" within the German party, see her *Otryvki iz dnevnika*, pp. 53–54, and "Pochemu molchal" proletariat" Germanii v" iiul'skie dni?"

the Central Committee decided was sacred. The leadership avoided Liebknecht and feared Luxemburg, people whom Kollontai once regarded as the hope of the International.

꒫꒰꒫꒰꒫꒰

Eventually Misha was released from prison and Kollontai prepared to leave Berlin. In the city where she once had sought refuge she had become an outsider. Even among members of the socialist women's movement the mood had changed. When Kollontai suggested to a friend that working women demonstrate as pacifists against the war, the friend was amazed. A demonstration *now* against the war? The masses would never accept it. All that working women could do was to ease the suffering—establish infirmaries, for example. Exactly what the bourgeois women were doing, Kollontai thought.[23]

Kollontai described a farewell visit to Rosa Luxemburg as "brief" but "refreshing." Not even in her journal did she acknowledge the limited nature of their "friendship." Luxemburg referred cryptically to private political meetings, but she was disinclined to discuss with Kollontai her political activities. After a phone call to Liebknecht, Kollontai's one real comrade in Berlin, and a few nostalgic diary entries lamenting the once beloved German Social Democratic Party, Kollontai traveled in September 1914, an exile again, from Berlin to Copenhagen, and thence to Stockholm.[24] Until 1917 Scandinavia would be her home.

꒫꒰꒫꒰꒫꒰

What was needed was not simply the defeat of tsarist Russia or the Kaiser's Germany. Somehow the war must be ended and internationalism reestablished. But how? Kollontai's Menshevik guide Plekhanov proved no more helpful than the leaders of German Social Democracy: revealing a very Russian Germanophobia, Plekhanov expressed his hope for an Allied victory. Reversing the defensist argument of the German Social Democrats, Plekhanov argued that victory for imperialist Germany would mean the extinction of socialism in all European countries, Russia included. Kollontai sounded the pacifist call for "peace now," but Plekhanov said to Angelica Balabanoff: "So far as I am concerned, if I were not old and sick I would join the army. To bayonet your German comrades would give me great pleasure."

23. *Otryvki iz dnevnika*, p. 56; *Iz moei zhizni i raboty*, pp. 163–64.
24. *Otryvki iz dnevnika*, p. 74; *Iz moei zhizni i raboty*, pp. 168–71.

Balabanoff, his old Menshevik comrade, the Russian-born Italian socialist and pacifist, replied: *"My* German comrades! Are they not
yours as well? Who, if not you, taught us to understand and appreciate German philosophy, German Socialism—Hegel, Marx, Engels?"
Balabanoff left Plekhanov in Geneva. "Never, in all my life, have I
traveled with such a heavy heart," she recalled.[25]

Plekhanov became an "extreme patriot," and Kollontai rejected
him.[26] Her entry into the ranks of Bolshevism might have seemed a
logical next step, for Lenin, too, had concluded that the era of the
Second International was ended. After his initial disbelief that the
German socialists had really voted for war credits and that his beloved teacher Plekhanov had converted to chauvinism and betrayed
the working class, Lenin began elaborating his position on the imperialist war: it must be turned into a civil war. Since the Second International was destroyed, a Third must be created. But obstacles
stood in the way of what might have seemed a natural alliance between Kollontai and Lenin.

Lenin had moved from Krakow to Bern after the war broke out,
and his chief source of news about events in Russia was Aleksandr
Shliapnikov, a Bolshevik agitator who became Commissar of Labor
in the first Soviet government. After settling in neutral Sweden,
Shliapnikov sent Lenin news of Kollontai, with whom he had begun
a liaison, on October 24. "Comrade Kollontai is entirely for our
'Leninist position.'" Lenin wrote a qualified reply: "I rejoice with
all my heart if Comrade Kollontai is taking up our stand."[27] Bolsheviks were so few that Lenin's pleasure at the idea of a new recruit
must have been genuine; but his doubt about Kollontai's commitment showed more astuteness than did Shliapnikov's enthusiasm.
Kollontai welcomed Lenin's opposition to the war, but as a pacifist
she could not share his view that the war, rather than simply ending,
must be turned into a civil war.[28]

Kollontai tended to gravitate instead toward other socialists who

25. Balabanoff, *My Life as a Rebel*, pp. 120–21.
26. Kollontai, "The Attitude of the Russian Socialists," p. 60.
27. G. D. Petrov, "A. M. Kollontai v gody pervoi mirovoi voiny," pp. 85–86. Lenin's
reply is dated Oct. 27, 1914, and appears in Lenin, *Sochineniia* (4th ed.), vol. 35, p. 25.
28. For Kollontai's political views in late 1914 and early 1915, see her letter to F.
Ström criticizing Lenin's call for civil war: civil war was not a program and solved
nothing; that is what Lenin seemed to forget. (Kollontai to Ström, undated letter written in German, Univ. of Gothenburg Archive.)

were opposed to national patriotism. Lenin's Bolshevik organization was one of the two main rallying points for the internationalists among the émigré Russian Social Democrats. The other was the Paris daily paper *Nashe Slovo*, whose editors included Trotsky and Julius Martov. Kollontai was one of several non-Leninist internationalists who contributed from abroad. Others were G. Chicherin, Christian Rakovskii (a Bulgarian by birth), Ivan Maiskii, Karl Radek (a Pole), and M. S. Uritskii.[29] Eventually the logic of their internationalist position would impel them all toward Lenin's organization, despite their reluctance to support his narrow factionalism and commanding methods.

One might think that Kollontai became more receptive to Bolshevism because of her intimate relationship with Shliapnikov, Lenin's lieutenant.[30] Shliapnikov's appeal in 1914 emanated in part from his blunt Bolshevik militancy. In September 1914 Shliapnikov arrived in Stockholm from St. Petersburg to establish a northern link between Russia and Lenin in Switzerland; Lenin needed it for transporting personal letters, people, and literature through Stockholm.[31] Rare among Bolshevik leaders, Shliapnikov was a genuine proletarian. The son of Old Believers in Russia, he went to work when very young after only a little schooling. He was a socialist in his teens, then became a Bolshevik. Arrested several times, he left Russia in 1908. By trade a metalworker, he found employment in the factories of France, Germany, and England, learning French and a little German and English as he went. Early in 1914 he returned to work in St. Petersburg.[32] After the outbreak of the war he left for Stockholm, where in October he began receiving instructions from Lenin in Switzerland. Like Kollontai, Shliapnikov became involved with the Swedish socialists Karl Branting (a founder of the socialist party) and Fredrik Ström and Carl Höglund (Branting's youthful "opposition"). At the beginning of November Lenin's paper, *Sotsial-Demokrat*, arrived from Geneva. Shliapnikov, one writer recalled, "favored footwear for smuggling," and with the help of a cobbler he shipped

29. For contributors to *Nashe Slovo*, see Daniels, pp. 29–30.

30. According to Kollontai's *Otryvki iz dnevnika* (p. 4), she and Shliapnikov had been in contact earlier in Berlin. On Dec. 23, 1914, they jointly sent holiday greetings in a letter to Ström (Univ. of Gothenburg Archive). For Lenin's assumption in 1916 that Kollontai and Shliapnikov were a couple, see his *Sochineniia* (4th ed.), vol. 35, pp. 185, 497.

31. Lenin to Shliapnikov, letter of Oct. 27, 1914. *Sochineniia* (4th ed.), vol. 35, p. 125.

32. For his background, see the article "Aleksandr Gavrilovich Shliapnikov" in *Deiateli SSSR i Oktiabr'skoi Revoliutsii*, vol. 41, cols. 244–51.

Lenin's paper into Russia in boots. Friends described Shliapnikov in those early days as "a wonderful man . . . quiet and good-natured, never boisterous, . . . always dependable . . . not like a Russian at all. Above all, he had the ability, rare among Russians, to organize."[33] The man who became one of Lenin's closest comrades during the war years, the key figure in the northern underground, preserved the outlook and attitudes of the working man.

Although Shliapnikov surely brought Kollontai closer to Lenin, the facile assumption that he influenced her politically irritated her. In later years she wrote that "not a single one of the men who were close to me has ever had a direction-giving influence on my inclinations, strivings, or world view."[34] Kollontai was at least ten years Shliapnikov's senior, the mother of a grown son, and a woman with a sense of herself as an integrated, mature personality; all this suggests that Shliapnikov was an unlikely father figure or adviser. Yet it remains appropriate to question the extent of Shliapnikov's influence upon her. What was frequently true in other areas—that a woman who became prominent was usually introduced to the larger professional, political, or artistic world by an established man with whom she had a close relationship—was generally true in the ranks of Russian socialism as well. Even during the prerevolutionary years, when women participated in the Russian party on more politically significant levels than they did after the Revolution, men were usually dominant and women their loyal apprentices. The following vignette involving two Bolshevik couples—Elena Rozmirovich and her husband N. Krylenko, and Nadezhda Krupskaia and her husband V. I. Lenin—is suggestive. A Bolshevik comrade described a party conference in January 1915 that the two couples attended. Competing attitudes toward the war were hotly argued. "Comrade Rozmirovich did not speak; her point of view was developed by Comrade Krylenko. . . . Nadezhda Konstantinova did not speak. . . ."[35] But Kollontai was never the silent partner. Unlike other women who achieved eminence in socialism's male world, she did so without a masculine mentor, whether father, brother, husband, or lover. Shliapnikov may have heightened Kollontai's receptivity to Bolshevism, but the decision to join Lenin's ranks was her own.

33. Quoted in Futrell, pp. 87, 106.
34. Kollontai, *Autobiography*, p. 13.
35. Bosh, "Bernskaia konferentsiia 1915 g.," p. 181. For Rozmirovich and Krylenko, see Vavilina et al., eds., p. 65.

While the *Nashe Slovo* group remained diffuse and geographically scattered, the Bolsheviks were gathering an antiwar circle of their own in Scandinavia. Kollontai's antiwar activity with Shliapnikov led to her arrest.[36] But neither her arrest in Sweden, nor the lack of interest in internationalism among socialists in Denmark (where Swedish police brusquely escorted her), adversely affected her. She felt exhilarated in 1915 by the growth of the community of antiwar comrades.[37] In the summer the young Bolshevik Nikolai Bukharin arrived. Liudmila Stal' also came to Stockholm, delegated by Lenin to seek connections with Russia and channels for smuggling literature.[38] Kollontai had not yet become a Bolshevik, but she wrote to Lenin and Krupskaia of her happiness that they were working together against the war at a time when international socialism was devastated and one's friends often seemed to be speaking an alien language.[39]

But were they in accord? However gratifying her antiwar activity, however smooth the functioning of the northern link she and Shliapnikov were providing between Russia and the Central Committee in Switzerland (which in 1915 meant little more than Lenin, Zinoviev, and their wives), Kollontai still needed to clarify her political ideology. Years later she wrote that since the Bolsheviks were those who most consistently fought national patriotism, she officially joined their faction in June 1915 and entered into a lively correspondence with Lenin.[40] Her casual recollection obscured the intense self-questioning that occupied her during the last months of 1914 and the spring of 1915.

36. Kollontai's misgivings about advancing Lenin's slogan on transforming the World War into a civil war did not preclude her carrying out Lenin's request that she acquaint Scandinavian socialists with his manifesto "The War and the Russian Social Democrats." Her room in the Pension Karleson became a "headquarters" for Swedish socialists, where stormy discussions took place between party members and the leaders of the Swedish left wing, Carl Höglund and F. Ström. See G. D. Petrov, "A. M. Kollontai v gody pervoi mirovoi voiny," p. 86. Lenin scorned the antiwar activities of the Swedish leftists, describing Kollontai's friend Höglund as "a naive, sentimental antimilitarist." To Shliapnikov he wrote that they should be told to "either accept the slogan of civil war or stay with the opportunists and the chauvinists." Lenin to Shliapnikov, Oct. 27, 1914, in *Sochineniia* (4th ed.), vol. 35, p. 127.

37. Earlier, Kollontai called it a day of "ineffable joy" when she learned that both Lenin and Trotsky, although belonging to different factions, had militantly risen up against the war: "I was no longer isolated." Kollontai, *Autobiography*, p. 24.

38. On Stal', see Florich in Zhak and Itkina, eds., p. 455.

39. Petrov, "A. M. Kollontai v gody pervoi mirovoi voiny," p. 86. Petrov cites a letter in the Institute of Marxism-Leninism, but he does not provide a date. Presumably the letter was written late in 1914 or early in 1915.

40. Kollontai, *Autobiography*, p. 25.

She had begun to correspond with Lenin at the end of 1914, but he was displeased by her early letters. Kollontai wrote: "We hope that the struggle for peace will entail lifting the spirit of the Social Democrats in each country, bringing their demands into conflict with the purposes of the powers, resulting in that struggle, that 'civil war,' about which you speak, as the only correct slogan now." Sensing that Kollontai disagreed with his belligerency, that she was trying instead to advance the slogans of peace and disarmament, Lenin countered: "Apparently you do not entirely agree with the civil war slogan, which you relegate, so to speak, to a subordinate (I should say conditional) place behind the slogan of peace. And you underline that 'what we must put forward is a slogan that would *unite* us all.' Frankly, what I fear most of all at the present time is just this kind of indiscriminate unity, which, in my opinion, is most dangerous and harmful to the proletariat."[41] He added in his next letter the admonition that it was "useless to advance a goody-goody program of devout wishes for peace if at the same time and in the first place illegal organizations and civil war of the proletariat against the bourgeoisie are not advocated."[42]

"Antimilitary" was an expression that came naturally to Kollontai in 1915, only to be condemned by Lenin. How was it possible, Lenin asked Kollontai, for anyone to admit that on the eve of a socialist revolution the revolutionary class should be *against* arming the people? Such an antimilitarist attitude was not radical at all, nor revolutionary. Although Lenin attempted to soften his argument by seeming to direct it against her left-socialist friends in Scandinavia who had renounced arming the people, he had Kollontai in mind. "Only gradually," Kollontai later acknowledged, "did I arrive at the conclusion that there existed a logical connection between civil war and general armament."[43]

There ensued during the winter of 1915 a war of nerves, in which first Lenin and then Krupskaia tried to convince Kollontai that a

41. For Kollontai's letter, undated but probably written in Dec. 1914, see Petrov, "A. M. Kollontai v gody pervoi mirovoi voiny," p. 86. Also see her "Avtobiograficheskii ocherk," pp. 291–92, for her political position at this time. For Lenin's reply, see Krupskaia, *Vospominaniia o Lenine*, p. 243, and *Leninskii Sbornik*, vol. 2, p. 221, letter of Jan. 1915.

42. *Leninskii Sbornik*, vol. 2, p. 222, letter of Jan. 1915.

43. For Lenin's view, see Petrov, "A. M. Kollontai v gody pervoi mirovoi voiny," p. 90, and Lenin to Kollontai, spring 1915, in *Sochineniia* (4th ed.), vol. 35, p. 144. For Kollontai's recollection, see her "Avtobiograficheskii ocherk," p. 293.

pacifist demand for peace was a mistake and that only a call for civil war was appropriate. Their correspondence grew tense as each sought stubbornly to convince the other. Kollontai tried to persuade Krupskaia to disseminate socialist antiwar literature. Krupskaia, belittling Kollontai's slogan for peace as "sand in the eyes of the proletariat,"[44] urged Kollontai to forgo her pacifism and attend a Third International Socialist Women's Conference at Bern, which the Bolsheviks hoped would endorse civil war. Although Kollontai was invariably a force at such conferences, she did not participate in this one. The origins of the Bern Conference suggest why.

In November 1914 the Bolshevik Central Committee, through the editorial board of *Rabotnitsa*, suggested to Clara Zetkin, Secretary of the Socialist Women's International, that she call an unofficial conference to unite the antiwar left in favor of civil war. The Bolsheviks, reflecting Lenin's determination to thwart a socialist drift toward pacifism, wanted the meeting to be the start of a new left-wing revolutionary body, the core of a Third International. But other socialist women, including the pacifists Zetkin and Balabanoff, urged that the gathering be simply an international socialist women's call for peace. Zetkin was going to attend illegally, against the will of her government. She knew that many socialist women in Switzerland, England, Holland, and Austria were dependent materially on their party or their trade union and could not support the Bolshevik demand for defeat of their respective governments.[45] The lines of conflict were drawn.

When the sessions convened on March 26, 1915, the Bolshevik delegation sought to avoid overtones of pacifism and to insure that the meeting took a definite revolutionary stand.[46] But Zetkin opened the meeting by urging a women's movement against the war. Finally the Conference overrode the objections of the Bolsheviks and adopted a British resolution welcoming all efforts of nonsocialists toward peace; it also sent fraternal greetings to the International Congress of Pacifists due to take place at the Hague. Afterwards one of the Bolshevik women wrote: "It was clear that the delegates who met spoke different languages. The prevailing conception was that the

44. For Kollontai to Krupskaia, see letter of Feb. 10, 1915, in Petrov, "A. M. Kollontai v gody pervoi mirovoi voiny," p. 88. For Krupskaia's letters to Kollontai, see Nevolina and Orlova, eds., pp. 106–25.
45. For the Bern socialist women's conference, see Gankin and Fisher, pp. 286–302.
46. Krupskaia, *Vospominaniia o Lenine*, p. 242.

fundamental task was the struggle for peace. No one had the slightest idea about passing over to civil war."[47]

Lenin found the situation intolerable. He had accompanied the Bolshevik women to Bern, and from a nearby restaurant in the People's House he instructed their delegation to introduce his proposal to urge that the war be turned into universal civil war and that a Third International be created. But the Conference refused to endorse the Bolshevik position. The majority of the delegates who rejected Lenin's demand did not do so because it was too "radical," or because they approved of the Second International. Most of them simply did not want to break with the patriotic socialists at home because they wished to remain members of their respective parties in order to influence the rank and file.

An unofficial gathering seemed an unlikely forum for making decisions that committed their parties to specific actions. Some feared losing all influence in their parties at home if they acted independently abroad.[48] Krupskaia dismissed such an attitude as the familiar "self-abasement" of a women's conference.[49] Her observation was perceptive. But it minimized the very real conflict between the majority's desire to impress upon the masses the need to demand peace, and Lenin's determination to assure the future of the Bolshevik movement and to confirm a split with the leaders of the Second International.[50]

The Bolshevik delegation to the Women's Conference included Inessa Armand, Zlata Lilina, Anna Kaminskaia, and Elena Rozmirovich. If any of them thought it inappropriate for Lenin, rather than one of them, to be drafting their resolution, she remained silent. Each may have agreed with Krupskaia's sympathetic observation that it was "very difficult" for Lenin to act as a shadow leader when he longed to take a directing role.[51] Of a women's conference! The notion is bizarre. Had Kollontai been present, she would have resented again as she had in the past Lenin's attempt to manipulate a women's conference for Bolshevik purposes. Like Zetkin, Kollontai would have

47. Ravich, "Mezhdunarodnaia zhenskaia sotsialisticheskaia konferentsiia 1915 g.," p. 170.

48. Balabanoff, *My Life as a Rebel*, pp. 132–34.

49. Krupskaia to Kollontai, Apr. 17–19; see Nevolina and Orlova, eds., p. 122.

50. Balabanoff, *Impressions of Lenin*, p. 43, and *My Life as a Rebel*, p. 132.

51. For Lenin's effort to control the Bolshevik women's delegation, see Krupskaia, *Vospominaniia o Lenine*, pp. 244–45. Stal' was absent from the conference owing to illness. See Florich in Zhak and Itkina, eds., p. 454.

been concerned that the conference not break down and that socialist women remain united. Lenin might scorn "indiscriminate unity,"
but Kollontai shared Zetkin's enthusiasm for a demonstration that
socialist women of all countries (especially the belligerents, despite
their other disagreements) were as one in adhering to the socialist view that in case of war their duty was to bring about a speedy
termination.[52]

Did Kollontai not join the Russian delegation at Bern because she
knew that a battle between Zetkin and the Bolsheviks was inevitable?
Probably. There were warning signs. Krupskaia's harshness toward
Zetkin prior to the conference and her use in a letter to Kollontai of
the word "hypocrisy" to describe Zetkin's attitude signaled the tension that in fact emerged. When Kollontai corresponded with Krupskaia, she was evasive about her attendance. Even her memoirs leave
her absence inadequately explained. Soviet historians, who suggest
that by March 1915 Kollontai was firmly in the Leninist camp and
hoped to be present, account for her absence easily, if not consistently.
One contended that the warring governments would not permit Kollontai to travel to Switzerland. Another wrote that she had no time
to obtain a visa, and no money for the trip. Writing to a friend, Kollontai did cite a lack of money.[53] But she was a resourceful woman
who would not permit the absence of train fare to keep her from an
international women's conference. More likely, she welcomed an excuse to avoid making a political commitment.[54]

Instead, Kollontai sent a message of greeting and support in which
she condemned the chauvinist idea of defending the fatherland and
called on socialists everywhere to use the war crisis to obtain political
power for the working class. Yet we cannot assume, on the basis of
this ambiguous message and her later recollections, that if she had
been at Bern she would have voted for the Bolshevik resolution for

52. For Zetkin's views, see Gankin and Fisher, pp. 297–300. In an article published
early in March 1915 ("Zhenskii sotsialisticheskii internatsional' i voina"), Kollontai had
spoken out in favor of international solidarity on the part of socialist women against the
war, citing Zetkin's repeated calls for peace in *Gleichheit*.

53. On Kollontai's evasiveness about attending the Bern conference, see Nevolina and
Orlova, eds., pp. 116–17. For explanations of her absence by Soviet historians, see Itkina,
p. 100, and G. D. Petrov, "A. M. Kollontai v gody pervoi mirovoi voiny," p. 89. On her
lack of funds, see the undated letter to F. Ström (Univ. of Gothenburg Archive), which
speaks sympathetically about Zetkin.

54. For Kollontai's political mood early in 1915, see her *Nashe Slovo* articles: "Kopengagenskaia konferentsiia" (Jan. 29, Feb. 2), "Chto delat'? Otvet' sotsialistkam'" (Feb.
19), and "Zhenskii sotsialisticheskii internatsional i voina" (Mar. 7).

civil war.[55] We may conclude that had she attended she would have been torn. In her memoirs she observed that she was still a strong pacifist in the spring of 1915. Kollontai was not prepared to vote with the Bolsheviks for civil war, but neither did she share the respect that many delegates had for their socialist leaders at home. Had she been at the Conference, Kollontai would have been unable to suppress her disgust with the discredited heads of the Second International, whom so many of the women still supported. The great figures of the International seemed to her not even progressives, but rather "children of their age," mistakenly believing that "defense of the fatherland" was the duty of the proletariat.[56] A message of support to the Conference enabled her to avoid a conflict among her socialist friends and postpone a little longer a decisive confrontation with her own ambivalence toward civil war.

If Kollontai anywhere described the painful soul-searching that preceded her final decision in the early summer of 1915 to commit herself to Lenin's idea of armed conflict, such accounts have yet to come to light. We may guess that her acceptance of civil war was made easier by the knowledge that Karl Liebknecht was making the same transition. Liebknecht sent a letter to the International Socialist Conference at Zimmerwald in September 1915 that the participants read aloud (in the usual fashion) to the delegates. "Civil War, not civil peace!" Liebknecht wrote. " 'Civil War'—that is excellent!" Lenin exulted.[57]

⁂

Before turning to the subject of Kollontai as Bolshevik, it is appropriate to look further at Inessa Armand and Angelica Balabanoff, the two Russian leaders of the opposing factions at Bern, whose lives after the Revolution became closely intertwined with Kollontai's. Inessa, like Kollontai, was a romantic heroine, a mother of five children who left her husband to live with his brother and believed in a

55. See Itkina, p. 101, for Kollontai's greeting to the conference. Kollontai later claimed that the statement she sent to Bern was in the spirit of revolutionary internationalism and basically agreed with the Bolsheviks. See "Avtobiograficheskii ocherk," p. 292.

56. Kollontai wrote in "The Third International" (p. 2) that "the anarchist Kropotkin and the Marxist Plekhanov, the orthodox Kautsky and the wavering Vandervelde, Adler, and Vaillant, all can join hands, all are agreed upon the fatal, false, and absolute principle: first 'fatherland,' then the party."

57. For Liebknecht's letter and Lenin's reaction, see Gankin and Fisher, pp. 326–28.

woman's right to seek self-fulfillment and a socially useful life. The woman question attracted Inessa to socialism.[58] She concentrated first on the problem of the prostitute, the metaphor of women's oppression. She and Kollontai became the core of the Russian socialist women's movement. One friend remembered her at women's conferences surrounded by a crowd in red kerchiefs. Like Kollontai, Inessa was cultured, fluent in languages, a vivacious spirit; unlike Kollontai, though (and more like other revolutionary women), her dress was shabby and her style was plain. Grigory Kotov, a revolutionary in exile who was married to Liudmila Stal', met Inessa in Paris during their émigré days. Marveling at her inexhaustible energy, he called her a veritable revolutionary flame.[59]

In contrast to more sober women like Krupskaia, Inessa could be gay and light-hearted, as her correspondence shows. She and Zetkin, agreeing in January 1915 on the need to keep secret the idea for a conference of the socialist left, decided to discuss it in terms of a family wedding. Inessa humorously expanded the pretense for her own amusement, ending one letter with the news that she needed to stop writing and return to her ironing. How lucky you are, she teased Zetkin, to be unacquainted with such drudgery. She suspected that Zetkin did not know how to iron and insisted that she admit her deficiency. You women who are occupied with politics, how fortunate you are not to be doing housework.[60] "The house grew brighter when Inessa entered it," Krupskaia wrote after Inessa died, in a tribute to the woman whom many believed Lenin loved.[61]

Completely loyal to Lenin, Inessa was unable to resist his direction. She may have had no wish to do so, observed Balabanoff, who found her too rigid a Bolshevik. "The perfect—almost passive—executrix of his orders," she wrote of Inessa. "This does not imply that she had no personality or will of her own," Balabanoff went on: "I merely want to say that she was so saturated with the master's authority and infallibility that the possibility of any divergence was inconceivable to

58. Bertram Wolfe, in "Lenin and Inessa Armand," p. 100, cites Krupskaia's *Pamiati Inessy Armand: Sbornik pod redaktsiei N. K. Krupskoi* (M, 1926) for the view that the woman question drew Inessa to socialism.

59. For Inessa at women's conferences, see Vinogradskaia, *Sobytiia*, p. 222. For his impressions, see Kotov, pp. 115–22. See also P. Podliashchuk, "Prekrasnaia zhizn'," in Zhak and Itkina, eds., p. 35. Krupskaia also remarked on Inessa's energy despite her poor health in *Vospominaniia o Lenine*, pp. 215–17.

60. Armand to Zetkin, late Jan. 1915, in Nevolina and Orlova, eds., p. 112.

61. Quoted by Wolfe, p. 102.

her."[62] Lenin was the mentor, she the disciple. At the Bern Conference Inessa served as Lenin's spokeswoman to advance the Bolshevik proposal. "You carried out the work better than I could have done myself," Lenin told her after another meeting at which she spoke at his behest.[63]

Balabanoff shared Kollontai's Menshevik affinity and the bitter experience of breaking with Plekhanov because of his Russian chauvinism. An internationalist, well known in European socialist parties, politically she was closest to Kollontai. Sharing a temperament that would make it impossible for them to act ruthlessly against "the masses," both Balabanoff and Kollontai became outspoken oppositionists as freedom disappeared from the Party. Balabanoff explained in a suggestive remark that "Women have to go through such a tremendous struggle before they are free in their own minds that freedom is more precious to them than to men."[64] After the Revolution Balabanoff and Kollontai each fell into disgrace for their criticism. Balabanoff, unable to acquiesce in Bolshevism's manipulation of power, broke with the regime and left Russia. It is indicative of the bond between the two women that Balabanoff—though harsh in her judgments, and a puritan who rejected Kollontai's free sexuality—nevertheless wrote sympathetically about her decision to remain with the Party.[65]

When Kollontai became a Bolshevik in the summer of 1915, she celebrated her new affiliation by composing a pamphlet, "Who Needs War?" Her first publication for the Central Committee, it expressed not only a socialist's hatred of war and nationalism but also a Bolshevik's commitment to continuing the armed struggle as civil war. The text reached Lenin in September. Although her sentiments were similar to Liebknecht's, which he praised, Lenin's reaction was quali-

62. Balabanoff, *Impressions of Lenin*, p. 14. In fact, Inessa would lend her name in the spring of 1918 to the Left Communists who opposed Lenin's policies. See *Kommunist'*, 1918, no. 2–4 (Apr.–June).

63. Vinogradskaia, *Sobytiia*, p. 218, citing Lenin.

64. Quoted in Bryant, *Six Red Months in Russia*, p. 169.

65. My source of information concerning Balabanoff's puritanical aversion to Kollontai's sexuality is Ella Wolfe, a friend of Balabanoff (personal communication, May 1975). For Balabanoff's sympathetic view of Kollontai, see *My Life as a Rebel*, pp. 251–52. Kollontai remained loyal to Balabanoff and was distressed when the Party condemned her after her departure from Russia. See Kollontai to F. Ström, Nov. 10, 1924 (Univ. of Gothenburg Archive).

fied and somewhat patronizing. "Kollontai's pamphlet is good as to its purpose," he acknowledged in a letter to Shliapnikov, but the topic, he pointed out, was extremely difficult. To write about the war and its causes in a popular vein was hard. Krupskaia described Lenin's tact in dealing with the writing of others, his ability to suggest changes so skillfully that a person was hardly aware of being corrected.[66] Yet in Kollontai's case, he appears not to have exercised this skill. In a hurry to publish the pamphlet, and unable to contact Kollontai, he simply informed Shliapnikov that he had written her pointing out the need for corrections that he had in fact made. He hoped she would give her assent to them so that the pamphlet might be published quickly.[67]

Perhaps it was Lenin's inveterate need to rework what others had done to make it his own that lay behind some of his inconsequential changes. To Kollontai's description of the crippled victims of war—the blind, the deaf, the maimed—Lenin added the "legless," the "armless." Other revisions did clarify her meaning, demonstrating Lenin's skill at addressing the masses: where Kollontai wrote "as long as capitalism exists," Lenin substituted the more concrete "as long as private ownership in land, factories, etc. exists"; where Kollontai contended that the warring governments served the will of the capitalists, Lenin added that it was not possible for them to do otherwise, since they were made up of the capitalists and the landowners. Lenin thought that Kollontai's images of class conflict needed sharpening, and that her distinction between kinds of war—wars of self-defense versus imperialist wars—needed expansion, as did her discussion of imperialism.[68]

In her pamphlet Kollontai spoke in Lenin's terms to the workers in all countries, calling on them to turn the war into a civil war, to seize the land, the factories, the banks. And she turned Lenin's now familiar slogan into a vivid appeal, beseeching the soldiers at the front to cease firing on their "brothers" in the enemy armies, to say instead: "Comrade Workers, I know now that you are not my enemy. Give me your hand, comrade. We are both victims of our government's lies. Our enemy is behind us at home."

The Central Committee published Kollontai's pamphlet in 1916

66. Krupskaia, *Vospominaniia o Lenine*, p. 214.

67. Lenin to Shliapnikov, Aug.–Sept. 1915, *Leninskii Sbornik*, vol. 2, p. 241. The pamphlet was published without her consent to the changes, since she had already left on a lecture tour in the United States. See Itkina, p. 118, and below.

68. For Lenin's revisions, see *Leninskii Sbornik*, vol. 17, pp. 324–30.

and distributed it widely in Europe. Copies were sent to the United States. Despite the efforts of the tsarist police to confiscate it, "Who Needs War?" was even smuggled into Russia. "The warmest responses to your pamphlet are coming from the war prisoners," the Central Committee informed Kollontai.[69] Gratifying praise; but the corrected text of the polished and skillful brochure bearing her initials hinted that, despite her years of writing revolutionary tracts, the new Bolshevik recruit was in the eyes of Lenin a political novice.

An invitation to lecture from the German Socialist Federation in America took Kollontai to the United States in September 1915 to battle the prowar chauvinists. Lenin now had a representative in America, and he viewed Kollontai's activities there as an extension of his own.[70]

At first, it had seemed that the trip might not come off, since the socialists in New York did not reply to Kollontai's request for travel funds. Lenin wrote in dismay, "It will be very sad if your trip to America is completely disarranged. We have built not a few of our hopes on that trip." Lenin wanted Kollontai to establish contact with the socialist publisher Charles Kerr in Chicago to arrange for publication of the Bolshevik pamphlet "Socialism and War." She was also to try to bring together the left-wing internationalists, who might form a section of his projected Third International, and to manage somehow to secure financial help for the Bolsheviks. "No money, no money!! This is the chief trouble!"[71]

Lenin's frenetic letters made it clear that Kollontai was one of the chief partners in his fantasy of impending world revolution. The intensity of his instructions, his demand that Kollontai inform him of her prospective addresses in the United States so that his questions and instructions might reach her without delay, his insistence that she try to see the local Bolsheviks everywhere to "freshen" them up and *"connect them with us"*—all indicate his flawed image of the American political scene. Even his knowledge of the American socialist movement was erratic; he combined an occasional awareness

69. See G. D. Petrov, "O broshiure A. M. Kollontai, 'Komu nuzhna voina?'," pp. 110–11, and Itkina, p. 119.

70. Dazhina, ed., "Amerikanskie dnevniki A. M. Kollontai," pp. 135–36.

71. Lenin to Kollontai, Sept. 1915, *Leninskii Sbornik*, vol. 2, pp. 245–46; and Dazhina, ed., "Amerikanskie dnevniki," p. 133. Kollontai was unable to convince Kerr to print a full version of "Socialism and War" (a fact Lenin regarded as "incredible"). Nor was she able to alleviate Bolshevik financial problems: the conditions of her tour provided that the proceeds go to the German socialists. Dazhina, ed., "Amerikanskie dnevniki," p. 155.

with vast ignorance. *Appeal to Reason*, a little socialist newspaper in Kansas, he rated as "not bad." But of Eugene Debs, the most famous socialist in America, Lenin asked Kollontai, "and what is Eugene Debs?"[72]

The sheer number and detail of his questions attest to Lenin's respect for Kollontai's judgment. "Kollontaisha" is a "very capable woman!," Lenin enthused to Zinoviev.[73] Her ability to translate pamphlets into nearly any Western language delighted him: "Do you know Swedish?," he wondered in a letter after she had demonstrated her skills in French, German, and English.[74] Because he lacked confidence in his own knowledge of languages, Lenin was alert to such abilities in Bolshevik women like Kollontai, Armand, and Balabanoff. Lunacharskii recalled being touched at seeing Lenin's frank "None" in reply to the question "Have you a fluent spoken knowledge of any foreign language?" included in a questionnaire on display among the exhibits of the Red Moscow museum. Stasova, recalling Lenin's modesty about his poor language ability, has recorded that he spoke French and German well.[75]

Kollontai's American tour was grueling. Within four months she gave 123 lectures in four languages, frequently speaking in three languages during one evening.[76] A tendency to put what was personally painful behind her kept Kollontai from dwelling on the exhaustion and depressing isolation she experienced in the United States. The German Socialist Federation exploited her unmercifully.

10 December. On the train between Indianapolis and Louisville. I speak almost daily. I have been in America 62 days and I have spoken at meetings 53 times. Sometimes it seems to me that I will simply be unable to speak. I want to implore—let go of me.

11 December. Again on the train. Sometimes it seems that I don't have the strength to get up. . . . I want to bury myself in a pillow and weep, weep, weep. . . . What about Lenin? What is happening in our Party? Here one knows nothing. I want to be back in Europe. . . . Here I am in a vise, in bondage, I have no "freedom."[77]

72. Lenin to Kollontai, Nov. 1915, *Sochineniia* (4th ed.), vol. 35, p. 165.

73. Lenin to Zinoviev, July 23, 1915, *Polnoe sobranie sochinenii*, vol. 49, p. 101.

74. Lenin to Kollontai, Feb. 17, 1917, *Leninskii Sbornik*, vol. 2, p. 282. She did know Swedish.

75. Lunacharskii, *Revoliutsionnye siluety*, p. 19. Stasova, *Uchitel' i drug*, pp. 14–15.

76. Kollontai to Krupskaia and Lenin, Mar. 14, 1916, in Dazhina, ed., "Amerikanskie dnevniki," p. 156.

77. *Ibid.*, pp. 148–49.

She doubted the value of her effort. Did the audiences really absorb her message, or were they simply swayed by her emotion? "A splendid speech, it is just what we want: more revolutionary spirit in the movement." Warm praise was briefly exhilarating. But was she essentially just a political puppet, a Russian woman traveling at the invitation of German comrades for the struggle against the imperialist war, speaking for the reestablishment of the workers' International and revolutionary solidarity? She questioned her ability as a speaker and brooded over the correct internationalist responses that occurred to her not on the platform but only later in the night or the next day. Perhaps she was not a speaker at all—just a woman with a creative strain that she expressed by talk.[78]

In January 1916 Kollontai's thoughts centered on her return journey. But then came word from Misha in Russia that he might join her. "I did not sleep," she wrote, "due to my joyous emotions." She wanted to weep with happiness at the thought of seeing him. She noted frankly that she had been longing for the quiet familiarity of Norway, but the prospect of living with her son, of "seeing his dear face," overcame any reluctance to remain in America. Kollontai could combine the revolutionary's zeal with a mother's pride and somehow manage to sound convincing. Misha, a student at the Technological Institute in Petrograd, wanted to work in the automotive industry but to avoid activity connected with war. This was an empty hope, for Kollontai knew that automobiles were being used in the same bloody work as guns; but how indicative, she thought, of Misha's good and gentle nature! If her son came to America and thus avoided the war, life would still be kind to her. But what of the other suffering mothers?[79] She began to think of what work she might do in the United States. Then within a few days her plans fell apart. A telegram from Misha told her that he would stay in Petrograd. Although in her reply she explained that she would remain in America if he agreed to come, for unrecorded reasons she was unable to convince him to leave Russia.

Kollontai's diary entries suggest that her emotions were involved primarily with Misha and with close friends at home, particularly her childhood companion Zoia. Her relationship with Shliapnikov was evidently waning. When he wrote in February that he would be back

78. *Ibid.*, p. 149.
79. *Ibid.*, p. 151.

"in our old place," she wondered if it were Norway he referred to, adding laconically, "Of course, I am glad for him. . . ."[80] Later, when she prepared to leave America, she wondered what the future held and faced frankly the possibility that even in Europe there would be loneliness.

Kollontai's American journal conveys a strong sense of self, but one does not yet see the confident woman who was to impress observers during the Revolution. Certain episodes suggest a lack of self-esteem. When comrades from *Novyi Mir*, the Russian language daily published by socialist émigrés in New York, proposed that she remain in America as an editor, she refused, claiming insufficient experience. The work was attractive, and she knew there was a great need for someone to give the paper the correct internationalist direction, but she shrank from the undertaking. It would be different, she thought, if there already existed a group of like-minded internationalists with whom she could work. Instead of providing the leadership herself, she asked Lenin if he could suggest an editor who could expunge Plekhanov's influence and give *Novyi Mir* the proper tone.[81]

By 1916 Kollontai had consolidated her role as a Bolshevik on whom Lenin could rely to propagandize for the Zimmerwald Left. But to present her, as Leon Trotsky's biographer Isaac Deutscher does, as "one of Lenin's most fanatical adherents" is misleading, a reflection of Trotsky's bias.[82] Kollontai was not part of what Bukharin called the "obsequious coterie" around Lenin. Militarism and civil war were not the only issues on which Kollontai and Lenin differed.

Kollontai was an exponent during the war years of Luxemburg's thinking on the national question.[83] Luxemburg maintained, and Kollontai concurred, that national boundaries and appeals to nationalism were not only obsolete in an era of modern imperialism, when the world was being transformed into a single economic unit, but even contrary to socialist teaching. This view, supported by a group of younger Bolsheviks—Bukharin, and Piatakov and his wife Evgeniia Bosh—was directly contrary to Lenin's new thinking on self-determination. In the spring of 1915 Piatakov and Bosh, having acquired

80. *Ibid.*, p. 153.

81. *Ibid.*, pp. 155, 157. Itkina quotes Kollontai's observation that the work, although enticing, was not for her because she lacked experience. Itkina, p. 125.

82. Deutscher, *The Prophet Armed*, vol. 1, p. 242.

83. G. D. Petrov, "A. M. Kollontai v gody pervoi mirovoi voiny," p. 90. Petrov wrote that Lenin attempted to correct Kollontai's mistaken opposition to self-determination as well as to general armament.

some funds, proposed a new theoretical journal, *Kommunist'*; during its brief life it became the focus of Bolshevik disputes on nationalism.[84] Lenin, who stressed the tactical potential of nationalism for revolution in colonial and noncolonial areas, fiercely advocated the slogan of national self-determination; this the group around Bukharin and Piatakov just as vigorously resisted.

Krupskaia recalled 1916 as a tense time for Lenin.[85] He quarreled with everyone, Kollontai included. In the spirit of comradely equality, a hallmark among the Old Bolsheviks, Shliapnikov informed Lenin that the unpleasant situation could not be allowed to continue, that it was harming the Party.[86] In what may seem a paradox, Kollontai grew closer to the Bolsheviks as she joined "Bukharin and Co." and found herself again in disagreement with Lenin. The emotional impact of the altercation bound the Bolsheviks more tightly. Kollontai saw Lenin at his best as well as his worst. He ordered a halt to further publication of *Kommunist'*; yet as Kollontai read Lenin's lengthy reply to Shliapnikov, she sensed his need not only to advance his ideas but to have comrades understand him. In the same month that he received Shliapnikov's frank criticism he wrote to Kollontai expressing himself as "very grieved" that they disagreed concerning self-determination. Urging that they try to disagree without really quarreling, he added suggestions that increased her sense of being one of his closest comrades. Aleksandr should show her his reply to Bukharin, Lenin proposed. He knew he could rely on her discretion, for this discord in the Party must be known only to the very smallest circle.[87]

Kollontai undertook another trip to the United States in September 1916. This was prompted not primarily by political considerations, but, as a Soviet biographer wrote, by "a mother's heart."[88] Finally Kollontai succeeded in getting Misha out of Russia and safely to America. Living with Misha in Paterson, New Jersey, where he had found a job, Kollontai became a key person in the newly formed revolutionary enclave in New York, which was attempting to transmit its antiwar intensity to the disorganized American socialist move-

84. See Cohen, *Bukharin*, pp. 23, 36.
85. Krupskaia, *Vospominaniia o Lenine*, p. 271.
86. Gankin and Fisher, pp. 239–40.
87. Lenin to Kollontai, Mar. 1916, *Leninskii Sbornik*, vol. 2, p. 263. Despite a lapse in 1917 when she encouraged self-determination in Finland, Kollontai opposed the concept. In 1921 she called the slogan of self-determination misleading "bait." See Kollontai, *Rabotnitsa i krest'ianka*, p. 39. For defense of self-determination, see USSR, [10], vol. 2, pp. 185–87.
88. Itkina, p. 126.

ment, as Kollontai had tried before. Paterson depressed her, but the revolutionary tempo heightened, at least verbally, when Bukharin arrived in New York in November and Trotsky arrived in January. In the rear of a dingy basement at 77 St. Mark's Place, the exiles Bukharin, Trotsky, and Kollontai worked on the staff of *Novyi Mir*. Kollontai's presence, one Party member recalled, added a touch of foreign romance for visiting American Communists.[89]

In January Bukharin assumed the de facto editorship of *Novyi Mir*, a role that might have been Kollontai's. In an apprenticeship for his ten-year editorship of *Pravda* after the Revolution, Bukharin used *Novyi Mir* to publish regularly articles on neocapitalism, Marxism, and the state and the national question.[90] Had Kollontai become editor, readers of *Novyi Mir* might have been exposed instead to regular analyses of the woman question. We do not know how Kollontai felt about having a man many years her junior regard that position as natural for himself. Yet it is clear that even a remarkable woman like Kollontai, who could stand on a platform and exhort crowds, who could make her way alone in strange countries, sleeping in deserted train stations and dingy rooms as she waited for strangers to take her to her next meeting, still did not see herself in a dominant political role.

The Russians in New York were united in seeking to build support among the American socialists for Lenin's antiwar internationalism, but factions developed, as always, over how to achieve their common purpose. Trotsky, in particular, captivated the imagination of the American Left. One member recalled: "We intended to organize under the direction of Comrade Trotsky. Madame Kollontai, who was going to Europe, was to establish the link between the European and American left-wing movements."[91] (Kollontai left for Norway late in February 1917. The Revolution cut short these plans.)

The tension that in the future would exist between Kollontai and Trotsky was already apparent. In a letter Kollontai published in

89. Draper, p. 77. Lenin only learned that Kollontai was in America through her report on the Russians in New York. See letter of Feb. 17, 1917, *Leninskii Sbornik*, vol. 2, p. 282. For Kollontai's stay in 1916, see Dazhina and Tsivlina, "Iz arkhiva A. M. Kollontai," pp. 226–45. Shliapnikov was also in the United States in 1916 selling material on the Jews in Russia to Jewish socialists in order to raise money for his underground activity. See Futrell, pp. 110–11. For Kollontai's feelings toward Shliapnikov in 1916, see Dazhina and Tsivlina, "Iz arkhiva A. M. Kollontai," pp. 235–36.

90. Cohen, *Bukharin*, p. 43.

91. Draper, pp. 80–82; Sen Katayama, "Morris Hillquit and the Left Wing," *The Revolutionary Age*, July 26, 1919, p. 6.

January 1916 in the socialist journal *New Review*, she included Trotsky with the Mensheviks, a Russian group that, she told her American readers, was "unclear and unsteady" in its opposition to the war. Kollontai had heard from Lenin the previous summer that Trotsky was among those who were "most harmful" in their desire for unity with "the opportunists." At the Zimmerwald Conference in September Trotsky stood apart from the Mensheviks and Lenin both; but despite his independent position, Trotsky's interest in the creation of a Third International seemed obvious enough to those familiar with him or his writing.[92] In a later issue of the *New Review* Kollontai apologized, explaining that Trotsky's attitude was not identical to that of the Mensheviks, and attributing her "unfortunate mistake" in listing him as a Menshevik to the haste in which her letter was written.[93]

Nothing could convince Trotsky that haste alone could cause a Russian socialist to make an ideological mistake. For Trotsky, precise and judgmental, this was only the first of Kollontai's distressing misrepresentations of his views. Kollontai compounded the problem when she reported to Lenin what Trotsky later called "utterly worthless information" distorted by her "ultraradicalism." Kollontai informed Lenin that owing to Trotsky's arrival the right wing had been strengthened so that a Left Zimmerwald (antiwar) platform had not yet been adopted. On the basis of this news Lenin replied in unfortunate language: "I was sorry about the news of Trotsky's bloc with the 'Rights' for a struggle against Nikolai Ivanovich [Bukharin]. What a swine that Trotsky [is]. . . ."[94] To Trotsky those were "mistaken utterances," which he claimed Lenin later recanted by word and by deed. Trotsky insisted that he was in New York doing precisely what Kollontai says he was not doing: attempting to spread internationalist propaganda among American socialists. He had only scorn for his critics: "nothing was revolutionary enough" for Kollontai in those New York days.[95]

Kollontai's "ultraradicalism" harmonized with her temperament, but it was also the zeal of a convert. Once she had joined the Bolshe-

92. Lenin to Kollontai, summer 1915, *Leninskii Sbornik*, vol. 2, p. 235. On Zimmerwald, see Gankin and Fisher, pp. 321–24.

93. Kollontai, "The Attitude of the Russian Socialists," p. 61.

94. For Kollontai to Lenin, see Dazhina and Tsivlina, "Iz arkhiva A. M. Kollontai," p. 242. Kamenev, editing Lenin's letters in 1924, expunged the damaging phrase in Lenin's reply. See *Leninskii Sbornik*, vol. 2, p. 282. The words reappeared after Trotsky's defeat by Stalin. See Lenin, *Sochineniia* (2d ed.), vol. 29, pp. 290–93.

95. Trotsky, *My Life*, pp. 273–74.

viks she could only work for their principles with extreme measures: to form blocs, adopt programs, separate oneself from the waverers. Her readiness to report deficiencies on Trotsky's part may have been a projection of her own earlier misgivings about the ways in which international socialists should oppose the war.

꽃꽃꽃꽃

Kollontai had come to echo much of Lenin's militancy, yet some who knew her claim that she never lost her essential pacifism. "I doubt that she ever took seriously or literally," Bertram Wolfe has contended, "Lenin's desire to prolong the world war indefinitely by turning it into a civil war."[96] How then did Kollontai rationalize Lenin's emphasis on the need to arm the workers for civil war? She provided an insight when she wrote that she "shared Lenin's view . . . that the war could be defeated only by the revolution, by the uprising of the workers."[97] An "uprising" of armed workers was an amorphous concept that Kollontai pictured as something other than war and bloodshed. By chance the relatively bloodless Bolshevik Revolution in Petrograd in October 1917 approximated Kollontai's hope; the Civil War negated it.

Kollontai's diary suggests that her spirit never ceased to be pacifist. It was impossible, she wrote in 1916, to separate herself from the nightmare of war. She dwelt on battle images: snowy fields strewn with the dead and the wounded. Sometimes she felt she could not bear the war's torment.[98] A friend who was accustomed to Russians' lack of reserve still found Kollontai's intensity exceptional: Aleksandra Mikhailovna, Ivan Maiskii wrote, was "a very emotional person, perhaps even too emotional."[99]

Ironically, her pacifist hatred of war and internationalist yearning for socialist community brought Kollontai to accept Lenin's militarism. She became a Bolshevik in the summer of 1915 not because she had become an enthusiast for civil war or because she adhered to the Leninist organizational principles of 1903. Lenin's philosophy of organization was alien to an individualist like Kollontai. She was one of a group of international socialists who joined the Bolsheviks after

96. "I doubt that she ever ceased to be for a just peace, with neither victors nor vanquished, nor punitive treaties. . . ." Letter to the author from Bertram Wolfe, Jan. 16, 1974.
97. Kollontai, *Autobiography*, p. 27.
98. Dazhina, ed., "Amerikanskie dnevniki," p. 151.
99. Maiskii, *Vospominaniia sovetskogo posla*, vol. 1, p. 283.

the outbreak of war because, quite simply, there seemed no other course.[100] Kollontai would have agreed that probably Lenin's single most remarkable achievement was his confrontation of the socialist collapse in 1914.[101] Lenin's sense of the future, his concentration not on the dismal end of the Second International but on the constructive beginning of the Third, had restored her hopes for international socialism.

100. See Deutscher, *The Prophet Armed*, vol. 1, p. 233, citing a *Nashe Slovo* staff member. The workers' groups in Russia connected with Lenin seemed the only active internationalist force.
101. Nettl, vol. 1, p. 40.

CHAPTER THREE

"Magnificent Illusions": The Year of Revolution

BOLSHEVIKS shared the propensity of bourgeois memoirists to describe the precise circumstances in which they learned overwhelming news. She was riding in a trolley car in Oslo, Kollontai recalled, when she glimpsed a newspaper headline in large letters: REVOLUTION IN RUSSIA. "My heart began to tremble," she recalled, "literally tremble."[1]

Krupskaia remembered how one day in Zurich after lunch, "when Il'ich was about to go to the library and I had finished clearing away the dishes," a friend burst in: "There's been a revolution in Russia!"[2] Lenin's mind moved at once in new directions. The first person to whom he wrote was Kollontai. Why Lenin thought first of Kollontai explains much about their political relationship. There were, of course, practical reasons. Lenin needed an emissary to provide a route by which his messages could reach the Bolsheviks in Petrograd. If Kollontai were to remain in Norway she could be relied on to carry out orders. Who else could he trust so completely? Shliapnikov was already in Russia. Stalin and Kamenev were in Siberia. Zinoviev and Inessa Armand were with him in Switzerland. Lenin had other agents in Scandinavia, people close to him politically like Karl Radek, but they had not yet joined the Bolsheviks. Liudmila Stal' loyally smuggled literature to Russia, but she could not match Kollontai's revolutionary passion.

The decision to turn to Kollontai came from a still deeper need. Krupskaia observed that "Vladimir Il'ich was always having these periods of enthusiasm for people. He would seem to discern some valuable quality in a person and cling to it."[3] Kollontai's most "valuable quality" was her left-wing idealism. What Lenin would ulti-

1. Itkina, pp. 127–28.
2. Krupskaia, *Vospominaniia o Lenine*, p. 271.
3. *Ibid.*, p. 67.

mately see as a defect, her extremism, he judged in 1917 her most useful attribute.

It has been suggested that Lenin had not fully thought out his ideas while in Switzerland, that he did not yet propound the doctrine that the bourgeois phase of the revolution should be cut short, and that the proletariat should immediately attempt to seize power and thus bring about the next, socialist phase. Lenin had never openly rejected the orthodox Marxist law of revolution, which posited a sequence from autocracy to middle-class democracy, and only then to the proletarian, socialist revolution. But the possibility that a well-organized party might seize power at once was never far from his mind.[4] Although he had not set a schedule for immediate action, Lenin wrote to Kollontai on March 17 (4): "Our immediate task is to . . . prepare the seizure of power by the *Soviets of Workers' Deputies*. Only this power can give bread, peace, and freedom."[5]

Lenin held both ideas at once—the orthodox Marxist view, and the possibility of immediate seizure of power by the Bolshevik Party under the camouflage of the Soviet—but he sensed that Kollontai would be single-minded, her thoughts focused not on cautious cooperation and coalitions in Russia but on revolutionary internationalism and on the next, socialist phase. Thus he had written to her on March 16 (3): "*Never again* along the lines of the Second International! . . . By all means *a more revolutionary* program and more revolutionary tactics."[6] Their messages crossed. Kollontai had already wired that she was returning to Russia and requested instructions. Lenin responded, appreciative of her loyalty, but discouraged: "Much good it will do to send 'instructions' from here, when information is so pitifully scanty, while there are in Petrograd not only leading Party members but also officially designated representatives of the Central Committee!"[7]

Perhaps Lenin turned first to Kollontai, in whom he knew he would find unqualified enthusiasm for revolution, in an unconscious effort to rid himself of strategic uncertainty. In any event, Kollontai

4. Schapiro, pp. 30–31.
5. Lenin to Kollontai, Mar. 17 (4), 1917, *Leninskii Sbornik*, vol. 2, p. 292. In 1917 Russia was still using the Julian, or Old Style, calendar, which was 13 days behind the Gregorian, or New Style, calendar used in the West. To avoid confusion, I give in parentheses the Russian date of Lenin's letters from Switzerland and Kollontai's letters from Scandinavia.
6. Lenin to Kollontai, Mar. 16 (3), 1917, *ibid.*, pp. 289–90.
7. Lenin to Kollontai, Mar. 17 (4), 1917, *ibid.*, p. 291.

did not disappoint him: not only did she declare his slogan of civil war "magnificently vindicated," but she accorded him, in her refusal to take any steps without his authorization, greater stature as a leader than he actually possessed. Not sounding like the head of a tightly disciplined party, Lenin had asked Kollontai about her plans. But she, suggesting that the Party required total unity at such a moment, requested Lenin formally to authorize her return to Russia.[8]

The two entered into a rapport that would not survive 1917. When Lenin abandoned radicalism the following year, Kollontai was unable to follow him. A model of the Left Communist, Kollontai was doctrinaire and impatient. Attached to theory and program, somewhat utopian and emotionally democratic, she would heed her own compulsions.[9] She would pick up where she had left off in 1908, organizing a socialist women's movement and demonstrating by her radicalism that her enthusiasm for party discipline was limited to situations that involved immediate revolutionary action.

From Zurich, Lenin began thinking of the next step, the socialist revolution. But if he were to make a socialist revolution, Lenin knew that he would first have to radicalize his own Bolsheviks, for he sensed that the Party would be reluctant to move beyond a literal reading of Marx and the implication that conditions were not ripe in backward, peasant Russia for a proletarian socialist revolution. It has been suggested that Lenin realized he could change Party attitudes best by promoting and relying on people previously outside the Party's high command. Two groups thus became crucial: the Trotskyists, who would assume high positions on entering the Party in July 1917; and the left-wing Bolsheviks, who were mostly young and committed to action, and of whom Bukharin was the most prominent and able.[10]

The earliest signs that Lenin was embarking on a new radical policy and would rely on the leftists were his letters to Kollontai of March 16 (3) and 17 (4), in which the primary theme was noncooperation

8. Kollontai to Lenin, Mar. 17 (4), 1917, cited in I. M. Dazhina, "V vodovorote novoi Rossii i pis'ma A. M. Kollontai V. I. Leninu i N. K. Krupskoi v Shveitsariiu," *Novyi Mir*, 1967, no. 4 (Apr.), pp. 235–36. Kollontai returned to Russia on Apr. 1 (Mar. 19) with a Central Committee directive signed by Lenin. See Kollontai, "V tiur'me Kerenskogo," p. 27.

9. For one definition of a Left Communist, see Daniels, p. 7.

10. Cohen, *Bukharin*, pp. 48–49.

with the bourgeois government and preparation for the proletarian seizure of power. He wrote on March 17 of the need for preparations in Russia for arming the workers and having the Soviet seize power. Their immediate task, he told Kollontai, was to widen the scope of their work in order to arouse new social strata—backward elements such as the rural population and domestic servants—and to refuse *all* confidence or support to the new government.[11]

With an eye to Bolshevism's place in history, Lenin urged Kollontai to publish what he was writing to her if in Russia she found freedom of the press. It would provide material for a history of the recent past. And in a postscript, Lenin repeated: "Spread out! Arouse new strata! Awaken new initiative, form new organizations in every layer, and prove to them that peace can come only with the armed Soviet of Workers' Deputies in power."[12]

With the two letters to Kollontai, Lenin had embarked on what are called his "Letters from Afar." He hoped that Kollontai would forward the first two to *Pravda* for publication, but she was in fact so delighted with his apparent radicalism that she took them with her directly to *Pravda* headquarters, where Kamenev and Stalin, recently returned from Siberia, were among the new editors.[13]

On March 19 (O.S.), Kollontai arrived in Petrograd and *Pravda* announced the return of "the noted representative and writer of the International Social Democratic Movement."[14] From her first fiery speech against the war effort, Kollontai placed herself on the Party's extreme left, where, with Shliapnikov and Molotov, she acted in accordance with her interpretation of Lenin's instructions. For the leftists, who did not share Lenin's ambivalence, this meant a struggle against the war, against support of the moderate Provisional Government and its insistence that Russia stay in the war, and against the more cautious, conciliatory wing of the Party represented by Stalin and Kamenev. It would be a mistake to assume, however, that discord prevailed among the Bolsheviks in Petrograd. The reality of revolu-

11. Lenin to Kollontai, Mar. 17 (4), 1917, *Leninskii Sbornik*, vol. 2, p. 292.
12. *Ibid.*
13. Although Kollontai delivered the letters, the editors chose not to print them in full since they scorned cooperation with the Provisional Government. See the explanatory footnote in the English translation of Lenin's *Collected Works* (4th ed.; M, 1964), vol. 23, p. 407.
14. Kollontai, "Avtobiograficheskii ocherk," p. 295; *Pravda*, Mar. 19 (O. S.), 1917, p. 3. Kollontai's return was facilitated by a summons issued by Shliapnikov as a member of the Soviet. Kollontai, "V tiur'me Kerenskogo," p. 27.

tion was too exciting. Kollontai probably exaggerated only slightly when she rejoiced in the camaraderie she found. *Pravda*'s editors were working "without friction," she told Lenin, and dreaming that he might soon arrive.[15]

Of course, Bolshevism was never without its factions. Committed to the idea of an immediate proletarian revolution, Kollontai was one of a small group that in the spring of 1917 became radicalized (as they themselves realized) even beyond Lenin's hopes, a group so eager to move forward that they found "Lenin's circumspection" nearly conciliation.[16] As a spokeswoman for the extreme left, Kollontai spoke, wrote in *Pravda*, and organized demonstrations against the war and against the coalition of liberal democrats and moderate socialists in the Provisional Government headed by Aleksandr Kerensky, himself a socialist.

Exhausted and radicalized by war, and embittered by generations of repression, Russia's masses of workers, soldiers, and peasants were carrying out an immense social upheaval, seizing factories and estates without being under the control of any political party. A revolutionary leader might well conclude that the Bolsheviks must put themselves at the head of the spontaneous upheaval and provide direction, or risk having the revolution explode beyond their control.[17]

A believer in the concept of mass spontaneity, Kollontai saw the core of the Revolution not in her own Party but in the power of the Soviet, which in March 1917 ruled side by side with the Provisional Government.[18] She sought to become part of that unwieldy group of two to three thousand people with mandates, as one observer put it, "God knows from whom."[19] The Soviet of Workers' and Soldiers' Deputies was "the heart of the movement," she informed Lenin. But the Bolsheviks needed to increase their representation in the Soviet, where they were outnumbered by Mensheviks and SRs. Most members of its Executive Committee were not even duly elected but had simply seized their seats. Now they were complacent and lacked com-

15. For Kollontai's report to Lenin, see Dazhina, "V vodovorote . . . ," p. 238 (cited in n. 8 above).

16. Kollontai, "Avtobiograficheskii ocherk," p. 298. For example, Kollontai wrote that workers', soldiers', and sailors' delegates appeared before Lenin at the *Pravda* office in June 1917 pleading that it was time for revolution. But Lenin thought it was too early. Kollontai, "V tiur'me Kerenskogo," p. 45.

17. Cohen, *Bukharin*, p. 45.

18. For Kollontai on the Soviet, see Kollontai to Lenin, Mar. 26 (O.S.), 1917, in Dazhina," V vodovorote," p. 237.

19. The Menshevik Sukhanov's observation is cited in Ulam, p. 319.

mitment to revolutionary action. How she longed to be a member of the Executive Committee to strengthen Bolshevik influence!

Kollontai needed to obtain a mandate, and a resourceful comrade suggested she approach a union that had not sent delegates. The woodworkers' union was wavering; Kollontai need only persuade them to delegate her to the Soviet. She made her way to the damp basement headquarters of the woodworkers' union, where, at the direction of a soldier's wife who was the only person there, she sat and awaited the return of one Timofei Ivanych. The meeting went badly. The woodworkers insisted they were nonparty and suspected that Kollontai, a Bolshevik, was pro-German. They were "honest woodworkers," in favor of the war and opposed to the Bolsheviks, who stood for defeat. Mentally swearing at the comrade who had sent her into this "nest of militarists," Kollontai left empty-handed.[20]

It was the Bolshevik military organization, the "Voenki," that finally made her their delegate. Those for whom Kollontai was an unfamiliar sight in the Soviet asked how a woman delegate could come from a military committee, but the Soviet chose her nonetheless as director of the Bolshevik fraction and a member of its Executive Committee. There were several other women in the Soviet—including three or four Bolshevik working women—but for a long time Kollontai was the only woman on the Executive Committee.[21]

Her presence in the Soviet in a directing role, and as a delegate from the military committee, soon ceased to be startling. How she was regarded by her own Party is, however, a matter of some complexity. A collective image of Kollontai taken in 1917 would reveal ambivalent strains. A woman previously outside the high command, now a member of the Executive Committee of the Soviet, she spoke with authority on controversial issues, usually espousing what she understood to be Lenin's position. No Bolshevik in the spring of 1917 could be unaware that Kollontai was close to Lenin. And when Lenin returned to Russia in April, Kollontai was one of the Bolsheviks designated to greet him at the Beloostrov frontier station. The Petersburg Committee asked Kollontai to make a short speech and present Lenin with flowers. She extended her hand in greeting, but

20. Kollontai, *Iz moei zhizni i raboty*, pp. 244–47. Her account first appeared as an article in *Krasnyi Derevoobdelochnik*, 1927, no. 3, entitled "Mandat v sovet ot derevoobdelochnikov."

21. *Iz moei zhizni i raboty*, p. 248. The Voenki was created to direct the military work of the Revolution. See also "Avtobiograficheskii ocherk," p. 296, and *Autobiography*, p. 32.

another comrade chided "no speeches, just give Lenin a kiss." Krupskaia spoke anxiously of the many speeches Lenin had already endured—at every stop it seemed—as they traveled through Finland. He was so tired. Someone should give him a glass of tea. When the welcoming party boarded the train, Kollontai chatted with Lenin in one compartment. Krupskaia and Inessa Armand sat in another.[22]

The next day Lenin addressed the socialists—Bolsheviks, Mensheviks, and Independents—demanding an end to the partnership with the Provisional Government and all power to the Soviets. His advocacy of immediate socialist revolution seemed the delirium of a madman. Kollontai alone spoke in his behalf, and her support called forth "nothing but mockery, laughter, and hubbub." The meeting dispersed, and with it any chance of serious debate. The Menshevik Sukhanov used Kollontai's advocacy as an example of Lenin's "complete intellectual isolation."[23] A Russian folk saying comes to mind: "A chicken is not a bird; a woman is not a person." A jingle circulated in Petrograd:

> *Lenin chto tam ni boltai,*
> *Soglasna s nim lish' Kollontai.*
>
> No matter what Lenin babbles,
> Only Kollontai agrees with him.[24]

The Russian socialists may have laughed at Kollontai, but they also elected her to the Executive Committee of the Soviet. Still, her tokenism was clear to comrades and opponents alike. The bourgeois press branded her a mad *Bol'shevichka* and disparaged the "Kollontai party dresses."[25] Foreign visitors found her anomalous, especially after the Bolsheviks took power and Kollontai ascended to government office. For instance Jacques Sadoul, who came to Russia in 1917 as an attaché of the French military mission and decided to remain, noted her intelligence and eloquence but dwelled more on her sexual impact. The Minister of Public Welfare, he reported to Paris after a visit with Kollontai in her office, was dressed in clinging dark velvet that outlined her attractive supple body, which he could tell was free from any restraining garments. She was a very pretty woman with deep blue eyes and fine features, about forty years old. How strange, he wrote to a friend, to think of a pretty woman as a minister. And

22. "V tiur'me Kerenskogo," p. 41, and *Iz moei zhizni i raboty*, p. 251.
23. Sukhanov, vol. 3, pp. 41–42.
24. Kollontai, "Avtobiograficheskii ocherk," p. 296.
25. Kollontai, *Autobiography*, pp. 30–32.

on the basis of the effect their meeting had on him, Sadoul speculated on the political consequences if pretty women came to power.[26]

Bolsheviks who observed this animated woman—who the very day
after she returned to Russia had spoken out so boldly against the war
that she had to be warned against enraging the patriotic masses—
might have perceived Kollontai as supremely self-confident, a woman
who was at ease with her role in a man's revolution. To an extent,
such an image was valid. Yet an edge of insecurity revealed itself. She
wrote matter-of-factly in her memoirs about her mandate from the
military committee to the Soviet, but when N. Podvoiskii, leader of
the Military Organization of the Central Committee, first suggested
that she become a delegate of the military committee, Kollontai wondered if a group of soldiers would agree to being represented by a
woman.[27] Conscious of being in a world of men with traditional views,
she compensated for the sense that she was not fully welcome by a
boastful bravado: she wrote of her "followers" among the masses, the
factory workers and women soldiers who "numbered thousands"; of
her popularity as an orator; and of the workers, the sailors, and the
soldiers who were "utterly devoted" to her.[28]

In fact, she met with considerable hostility. Her support of Lenin's
April Theses established her as Lenin's friend but kindled resentment. She was jeered by small groups in the Soviet when she tried to
speak: "Leninka," they yelled, shouting her down. They told her
they knew what she was going to say.[29] Kollontai had to jump off
streetcars when people recognized her. Threatened, subjected to "incredible abuse and lies," she received countless hostile letters; yet it
was a point of pride never to request military protection, but to go
out alone, unarmed, without any kind of bodyguard. She was too en-
grossed in her work, she claimed, to think about danger. More likely
she felt that a woman could not afford the luxury of being afraid.[30]

Other factors were involved in the Party's collective image of Kollontai. Attitudes toward her were influenced not only by her status
as Lenin's comrade but also by her personal life. Trotsky recalled

26. Sadoul, p. 95.
27. Itkina, pp. 136–37.
28. Kollontai, *Autobiography*, pp. 30–32. These recollections, deleted before publication in 1926, appear in the original galley-proof included in the edition of the *Autobiography* published in 1971.
29. Kollontai, *Iz moei zhizni i raboty*, p. 257.
30. Kollontai, *Autobiography*, pp. 31, 39.

that Stalin's first attempt to establish a friendly camaraderie with him took the form of crude remarks made at Kollontai's expense. During the first revolutionary winter, Kollontai would begin a liaison with Pavel Dybenko, the young Commissar for Naval Affairs. Overhearing a telephone conversation in Smolny, the Bolshevik Party headquarters, Stalin recognized behind the partition the deep voice of Dybenko, who was speaking in an unfamiliar, tender tone. Stalin smirked: "That's him with Kollontai, with Kollontai!"[31]

Although Trotsky made it clear to Stalin by his demeanor that he found him "unendurably vulgar," his own manner of relating the episode suggests a certain titillation. In some circles in the Party, Trotsky recalled, people were gossiping over the fact that Dybenko, the "twenty-nine-year-old, black-bearded sailor, a jolly and self-confident giant," had recently become intimate with the aristocratic Kollontai, "who was approaching her forty-sixth year."[32]

Kollontai startled the Bolsheviks—most of whom, however free-spirited their theories, lived conventional lives—not only with her advocacy of freer sexuality, but, as Trotsky delicately implied, with her penchant for falling in love with younger men. First there was Shliapnikov, more than ten years her junior, with whom she had lived intermittently during the war years in Norway; then in the winter of 1917–18 she began her liaison and "unregistered" marriage with the "genial giant" Dybenko.[33]

Communists, even those lacking Stalin's crudity, were intrigued by what seemed a frankly sexual relationship between the cultured aristocrat and the huge peasant sailor. In the speculation aroused by Kollontai's liaison with Dybenko, more than one Bolshevik must have wondered why Kollontai was attracted to a man so different from the popular and good-natured Shliapnikov. In fact, Dybenko resembled Shliapnikov in one vital respect: he, too, represented the masses. As an intellectual contemptuous of her own class, Kollontai needed intimacy with the source of revolutionary strength. Guilty over her privileged past—when she went to Dybenko's village to visit his mother, Kollontai contrasted peasant life with her own mother's

31. Trotsky, *Stalin*, p. 244.
32. *Ibid.*, p. 243.
33. According to a friend, Kollontai and Dybenko began but did not complete registration for civil marriage. Palencia, p. 164. In any event, they regarded themselves as married, and Dybenko referred to Kollontai as his wife. See Goldman, p. 115. As mentioned earlier, Lenin and Krupskaia, in corresponding with Kollontai and Shliapnikov during the years of exile, indicated that they regarded them as married.

comforts[34]—Kollontai escaped from her intellectuality by incorporating into her life the "reality" experienced by "the people." Kollontai probably also believed in the concept of upper-class deprivation, in the image of the gentry-intellectual staring over a chasm of class at a more earthy existence. How genuine a proletarian Shliapnikov was when he informed Lenin that his theoretical disputes with Bukharin were boring! How spontaneous Dybenko would be when he defied party authority!

Had Kollontai lived unobtrusively, her sexual behavior would have been of little interest—a Bolshevik George Sand, but no threat. Instead, she made herself vulnerable by becoming involved in Bolshevik theory and policy, areas into which women rarely, if ever, intruded. More typical and acceptable to the Party was Kollontai's comrade, Elena Stasova, who headed the Party's secretariat. With three or four women assistants, Stasova quietly handled the correspondence, received callers, sent out directives, kept records of the Central Committee sessions, and managed the finances—tasks that in simpler days had belonged to Krupskaia, the Party's first secretary.[35]

In the face of the mixed views of Kollontai within Bolshevik ranks, it is noteworthy that she was the only woman chosen for full Central Committee membership in August 1917 (Stasova and Iakovleva were alternates), and that she received more votes than long-time Bolsheviks Stalin and Sverdlov.[36] It has been suggested that the assembled Party Congress in the summer of 1917 recognized as its leaders those Bolsheviks whose authority was associated with public presence and an orator's ability to hold an audience; by this reasoning Kollontai was especially fit for election, since she had become suddenly well-known for her brilliance as a revolutionary orator. Deutscher noted that after the decision to seize power, "Trotsky, assisted by the most effective agitators, Lunacharskii, Kollontai, and Volodarsky, was mustering the forces of the revolution." The Party would rely on Kollontai to speak at one gathering after another during the days prior to the seizure of power.[37]

34. Itkina, p. 192.
35. Stasova, *Vospominaniia*, pp. 133, 136.
36. Trotsky, *Stalin*, pp. 220–21. Kollontai's votes ran behind those of only Lenin, Zinoviev, Kamenev, Trotsky, and Nogin.
37. Deutscher, *The Prophet Armed*, vol. 1, p. 299; Robert V. Daniels, *Red October* (New York, 1967), p. 123.

But factors other than speaking ability were involved. The Sixth Party Congress met in August 1917 in abnormal and uncertain conditions: some Bolsheviks were in hiding as a result of the July uprising against the Kerensky government; others, among them Kollontai, had been arrested as German agents accused of spreading antiwar propaganda for German pay. Kollontai had been delegated by the Party at the end of June to attend an international meeting in Stockholm, and when she tried to return to Russia on July 13, after the uprising, she was arrested at the border by order of the Kerensky government and imprisoned in Petrograd for the remainder of the summer.

Kollontai could easily have avoided arrest had she taken the advice of friends and remained in Sweden. Within an hour after Karl Radek telephoned her with the news of the July uprising against the Provisional Government, he and another Bolshevik, Vorovskii (a Pole by birth), were sitting with Kollontai in a little cafe, assuring her that return to Russia meant certain arrest.[38] Looking back, she knew that of course she should have stayed in Sweden rather than chance prison, that she might have been more useful to the Bolsheviks in Sweden. But she did not want to appear cowardly before the Party.[39] Indeed, her prison memoirs reveal how essential to Kollontai's sense of self it had become by the summer of 1917 to be an active Bolshevik and how destructive she found political isolation. It is necessary therefore to digress for a few moments and consider her reaction to imprisonment.

Although she claimed that she was apprehended at the border by order of the Kerensky regime and subjected to boorish treatment as a spy,[40] she was in fact treated respectfully as an international social-

38. Kollontai, "V tiur'me Kerenskogo," pp. 25–26. During the "July Days," popular revolutionary uprisings got out of control and became riots. The Bolsheviks initially rejected any attempt to seize power as premature, but then led the riots. Kerensky denounced the Bolsheviks as German agents and threatened the leaders with arrest.

39. Kollontai, Autobiography, pp. 32–33. It was primarily for this reason (and her fear of being cut off from Russia) that Kollontai tried to return to Petrograd. For an attack on Kollontai in the Swedish press, see Rabinowitch, p. 31, and Kollontai, "V tiur'me Kerenskogo," p. 26. Kollontai lacked money for the trip and had to borrow from Vorovskii on account with the Central Committee. She thus scoffed at charges that she had German funds. "V tiur'me Kerenskogo," p. 26.

40. "V tiur'me Kerenskogo," pp. 28–29. Autobiography, pp. 33–34.

ist. Zoia Shadurskaia, reunited with Kollontai in Sweden and with her on the journey to Petrograd, was also arrested, as a result of her association with the "German spy" Kollontai. Zoia made sharp remarks about the resemblance of Republican Russia to old Mother Russia—different arresting officers, that was all. The officers, in turn, informed the two women that the Bolsheviks were traitors who had played into the hands of the enemy. But they were curious about the Party's intentions. What will happen if you overthrow the Provisional Government? Who will rule Russia then—the Bolsheviks? Kollontai gave assurances that the Soviet would rule—in accordance with Bolshevik control, to be sure—and that the government would be the Soviet.[41] The political argument suggests informality, not harshness, although a dining car waiter, more ridiculous than boorish, did chase Kollontai out when the prisoners attempted to enter to get something to eat. The spy Kollontai, the *Bol'shevichka* and enemy of the Russian Republic, could not eat on his train.

Her arrival in Petrograd at the Finland Station disoriented Kollontai, since it was from this same familiar platform that she had once left for happy summers at her grandfather's country house, Kuuza. Now she was passing along it on her way to Kerensky's prison. Kollontai displayed the customary Bolshevik incomprehension that the Provisional Government should be so undemocratic as to arrest members of a political party plotting its overthrow.

The anti-Bolshevik press in Petrograd delighted in the arrest of a female "spy." A malicious cartoon in the *Petrogradskaia gazeta* referred to her as that "Lenin woman" and scornfully depicted her as a now-humbled coquette, a fashionable lady in high-buttoned boots with French heels and a large, feathered hat. A clean-cut soldier followed with her baggage, like a servant, but one valise was marked "compromising documents" and the soldier held a bayonet.[42]

Zoia was freed in Petrograd, but Kollontai was taken to the Vyborg Women's Prison and questioned through the night. Where was her friend Lenin? If he were not a German agent, would he be hiding? The news that Lenin was still free delighted Kollontai. Her own imprisonment she expected would be brief. Her previous arrests, first in Germany, then in Sweden, had been token confinements. At the

41. "V tiur'me Kerenskogo," pp. 29–45, recounts the incidents from her arrest through her imprisonment that form the subject of this and the following paragraphs.
42. The cartoon appears in Rabinowitch, p. 31.

Beloostrov border station she had given the officer a telegram to send to the Executive Committee of the Soviet, assuming confidently that they could not countenance the arrest of one of their members.

In testimony to Kollontai's revolutionary appeal, the young officer who delivered her to the prison offered at the last minute to let her escape. Whether because she considered such an attempt doomed, or because she did not expect a long imprisonment, she rejected his offer, thinking how young he was. He then tried to ease her situation by asking at the prison if there were not a better cell for her, perhaps one with more light? As a guard replied, the Vyborg Women's Prison was not a hotel. Kollontai slept on a hard bunk in cell number 58. By order of the Kerensky government she was held under stricter conditions than the Bolsheviks who sat in The Crosses [Kresty] Prison. For Kollontai there were no walks, no visitors, no newspapers. But the prison guards regarded her kindly. The chief, a chatty man, was proud of his prison and wanted Kollontai to be comfortable. Did she not think the prison clean? And the bread, was it not better than elsewhere in the city? And the kasha for dinner, was it not tasty, cheap, and hearty? Kollontai was amused to see that the man was a real housekeeper.

Kollontai suffered in prison, not from brutal treatment but from anxiety, a result of being cut off from the Bolsheviks and revolutionary activity. She recalled Lenin's advice to revolutionaries that it was necessary to learn how to wait. How absurd for the prison authorities to assume that the Bolsheviks created the July uprising. She knew that in fact the Party had tried to hold it back, that Lenin had invariably dampened the enthusiasm of the delegates from the war and naval sections who came to him in the *Pravda* office, with his cautious "the time is not yet ripe, it is still too early. . . . Where are your forces? What are your preparations?"[43]

Now she was learning to wait. She wrote, she read, she mended her clothing, she tried to think.[44] But it was one thing to wait while busy, another to be alone. She envied the Bolsheviks in The Crosses Prison, who at least were together. Why was the Soviet silent? Where were the thousands whom she saw at meetings and who passed resolutions in favor of the Soviet? Perhaps the Party had been crushed. Lunacharskii, Kamenev, Trotsky, and Dybenko were among the imprisoned Bolsheviks, but Kollontai did not know how many had been arrested

43. "V tiur'me Kerenskogo," p. 37.
44. Kollontai to Zoia Shadurskaia, in Itkina, pp. 153–54.

and who was underground. Control of her life was out of her hands, and she could not adjust. Indeed, she became physically ill.[45]

Her sense of being cut off lessened somewhat after an old friend stopped to see her—Isaev, a prison inspector and left-wing Cadet whom she knew from the political banquets, literary clubs, and lectures of the days of 1904. Isaev was sympathetic, telling her that the Provisional Government was afraid to free her because of her inflammatory speeches.[46] After Isaev's visit the prison regime eased. Two wardens appeared in the door of her cell laden with bundles: white rolls, sausage, canned goods, butter, eggs, honey, and a note saying that "the sailors of the Baltic Fleet greet Comrade Kollontai."[47] She rejoiced. The Baltic Fleet had not been destroyed; it was still with the Bolsheviks and against the war, holding strong even without Dybenko, whom she learned from the prison chief was in The Crosses Prison. Kollontai and Dybenko had not yet become lovers, but she knew of the almost legendary leader of the Baltic sailors, a hero without whose presence she feared the fleet's revolutionary will could not hold.[48]

Thanks to Isaev's intervention, parcels were delivered to her from factories and shops, from workers' districts, and from the fleet. She learned that Shliapnikov was not arrested—good news that meant the metalworkers' union he led was still with the Bolsheviks.[49]

Kollontai's moods fluctuated. The packages and notes from workers and sailors cheered her, making her hopeful of release. When the packages mysteriously stopped coming, despair again took hold. It was only the end of August, but it seemed years that she had been in cell 58. She felt frightened and had episodes of hysterical weeping. The days seemed months. But some days she would awaken cheerfully, looking forward to her daily walk in the sunlight. Outdoors, she would close her eyes and breathe in the damp air, imagining that

45. Zoia heard that Kollontai had heart seizures and was anxious that she have medical attention. Kollontai hoped that a physician might ease her restrictions. She was appalled that the "humane" Provisional Government denied her visits from her son. "V tiur'me Kerenskogo," pp. 43, 48. Itkina, p. 154.

46. "V tiur'me Kerenskogo," p. 49. The Cadets were the Constitutional Democrats, one of the liberal parties formed in the 1905 era.

47. *Ibid.*

48. The prison chief also told her of an uprising among the Bolsheviks in The Crosses, which was located near the Finland Station, instigated by Dybenko and F. F. Raskol'nikov. Raskol'nikov was the leader of the Bolshevik sailors at Kronstadt in 1917, and the chairman of the Kronstadt Soviet. *Ibid.*, pp. 41–42.

49. *Ibid.*, pp. 50–51. Kollontai wrote her prison memoirs in 1927, after her relationships with Shliapnikov and Dybenko had ended.

she was in the woods. At such times, feeling stronger, she resolved that she could face imprisonment. Three years, five years, she could endure anything.

She did not have to. On August 21, a smiling prison chief appeared at her cell waving the order for her release. Her friends the writer Maxim Gorky and the engineer Leonid Krasin had paid a fine of 5,000 rubles and were waiting for her. Their reunion was joyful. Gorky and Krasin related the events of the summer. A Party Congress had been held. Kollontai was chosen as a member of the Central Committee.[50]

A few years later Kollontai would write, in a revealing sentence, that after her arrest she was elected to the Bolshevik Central Committee.[51] In this way, perhaps unwittingly, she connected cause and effect. No more than a small group of Bolsheviks shared Kollontai's revolutionary élan in the summer of 1917. A martyr in "Kerensky's prison," she had been an underground worker, one of Lenin's closest agents, an internationalist, a pamphleteer, an outstanding orator, and a committed revolutionary. Her election to full membership in the Central Committee without first having served as a candidate member was motivated by revolutionary enthusiasm in the Party; it was a gesture of friendship and solidarity to a Bolshevik who stood consistently on the left with Lenin, an indication that Lenin thought of her as part of his "general staff."

The Party regarded Kollontai not only as one of its most talented orators; she was accorded the further honor, rare for a woman, of at least temporary acceptance as a theorist. This is suggested by her inclusion early in October, along with Lenin, Trotsky, Bukharin, Kamenev, and Sokolnikov, in a committee appointed to prepare a Draft

50. *Ibid.,* pp. 50–53, for Kollontai's last weeks in prison. Krasin, an engineer and sometime Central Committee member, provided the Bolsheviks with funds from his millionaire friend Savva Morozov and from bank raids he organized. He was the first Commissar for Trade, Industry, and Transport. Lenin said of him: "Strange people these engineers. But in the future when we begin to build the new Russia . . . we will need not ten Krasins but thousands of Krasins." See Kollontai, *Iz moei zhizni i raboty,* p. 263. In 1925 Krasin was sent to London as Soviet ambassador. He died there in 1926.

The newspaper *Proletarii* wrote of Kollontai's release as a result of her heart condition. See Itkina, pp. 155–56. The Kerensky government put Kollontai under house arrest, from which she was later released by order of the Soviet. See Kollontai, *Iz moei zhizni i raboty,* p. 403. Kollontai lived under house arrest in the apartment of Vladimir Kollontai's second wife, who had cared for Misha during Kollontai's exile. Vladimir Liudvigovich Kollontai had recently died. See Itkina, p. 156.

51. "Avtobiograficheskii ocherk," p. 299.

Party Program, a theoretical document "of prime importance."[52] The tempo of events in October prevented the group from ever meeting, so that the Bolsheviks took power that month without a finished program.

꙰꙰꙰

A woman Communist to whom acceptance in the male world was important might have avoided concerns categorized as female. Thus Kollontai in the spring of 1917 might well have departed from the unpopular pattern she established in Petrograd during 1905, when she immersed herself in the woman question. It was a mark of Kollontai's commitment that she picked up where she left off when forced to flee Russia in 1908 and established the woman question as her primary sphere. A special joy in her return was reunion in Petrograd with the women who shared her concerns: Liudmila Stal', who like Kollontai arrived from Scandinavia; Inessa Armand, Krupskaia, and Lilina, who came from Zurich; and Nikolaeva, Samoilova, Praskov'ia Kudelli, Vera Slutskaia, and Stasova, who returned from exile in distant Russian provinces.[53]

Lenin's directive "Arouse new strata, awaken new initiative in backward areas" Kollontai interpreted as a call to work among women. One of her first articles for *Pravda* denounced the men of the Provisional Government for doing nothing for working-class women, whose demonstrations and demands for bread had ignited the Revolution in February. Were the women not the first on the streets? Were they not fighting and dying for freedom along with their brothers? She charged Rodzianko, the President of the Duma, with trying to keep working women out of the forthcoming Constituent Assembly and implied that only the bourgeois Equal Righters would benefit from the policies of the Provisional Government. In this fashion, Kollontai resumed her battle with her prewar enemies, the remnants of the feminist Equal Righters. The Provisional Government did give women the vote at the end of March 1917, but the Equal Righters would not disband, choosing instead to compete with the socialists for the support of the soldiers' wives, who were anxious for greater government benefits.[54]

52. Trotsky, *Stalin*, p 223. For her appointment as recorded in Central Committee Minutes, see USSR, [12], p. 76.
53. For Stasova's welcome, see Levidova and Salita, p. 236.
54. For her charge against Rodzianko, see Kollontai, "Rabotnitsa i uchreditel'noe sobranie," pp. 1–2. At the Sixth Party Congress in August 1917, Kollontai was named

Shortly after Lenin and Krupskaia returned to Russia in April, Kollontai spoke to them about the soldiers' wives; she feared that their desperate situation made them likely to succumb to the feminists' efforts to organize them into a union. Kollontai presented herself as the only Bolshevik interested in their problems. They could not live on their rations. They needed jobs. But how could the mothers work with no one to care for their small children? If the socialists did not show some concern, Kollontai warned, they might be lost to the Revolution.[55]

When Lenin agreed that of course the socialists should recruit soldiers' wives, Kollontai suggested that they create in the Party a commission or a bureau to reach these women. Krupskaia objected, recalling the failure of such attempts in Paris during the emigration. She did not have in mind a separate women's organization, Kollontai explained. She wanted simply to develop within the Party a responsible organ—call it a bureau—that would direct work among women. How many times since 1906 had she offered the same explanation! Lenin, not Krupskaia, appeared the more interested, and he suggested that Kollontai draw up a plan.[56]

Kollontai, Nikolaeva, and others sketched out a women's bureau, but Bolshevik women (including Inessa Armand) were not entirely enthusiastic. With Kollontai's encouragement, then, Inessa, Lilina, and Liudmila Stal' drew up an alternative sketch. But their changes (some of which Inessa disowned) were designed to avoid charges of feminist separatism. Kollontai hinted at friction within the women's movement as she defended the simplicity and good sense of her original plan that each Party organization create a bureau for work among women, with one member in the organization to bear responsibility for that bureau.[57]

Despite Lenin's interest, Kollontai's project faltered. Lenin's call

---

one of/the Bolshevik candidates to the Constituent Assembly. See "Avtobiograficheskii ocherk," p. 296, for discussion of soldiers' wives.

55. *Iz moei zhizni i raboty,* p. 268. Kollontai's interest in the soldiers' wives has been documented by participants in a demonstration in April 1917. Some 100,000 soldiers' wives marched on the government offices in Petrograd demanding higher rations from the charity women, the overseers of the poor. Kollontai was the only member of the Soviet to address the crowd. Mandel, p. 47.

56. *Iz moei zhizni i raboty,* p. 268.

57. *Ibid.,* p. 269. Kollontai's rough plan, worked out with Nikolaeva, is preserved in the archive of the history of the Party in the file "Movement of working women." This scheme of organization is almost the same as the one subsequently adopted and used through the 1920's. "Avtobiograficheskii ocherk," p. 297.

7

for new initiatives was oddly out of tune with old suspicions.[58] None-theless, organizational setbacks did not prevent Kollontai from re-cruiting either soldiers' wives or working women. The Party sent her that spring to direct a strike among the laundresses, 3,000 of whom were members of the Laundry Workers' Trade Union. Employed in private laundries, working in frightful conditions, they were fighting for living wages, an eight-hour day, and municipalization of the laun-dries.[59] The ugly strike, the first to face the Kerensky government, lasted for six weeks and broke the semblance of civil peace that ex-isted between the population and the Provisional Government. The number of striking laundresses grew steadily, eventually reaching more than 5,000. Laundry owners, in retaliation, occasionally resorted to criminal tactics such as throwing hot irons and pouring boiling water on the strikers. The Bolsheviks in the Petrograd Soviet passed a resolution to protect striking laundresses who toured laundries to gain support for the strike.

Kollontai found the strike meetings in May exhilarating, despite the frustrations of working, at times, with some of the most politically backward elements of the female proletariat. The demands of the laundresses were essentially economic; they wanted chiefly an end to starvation wages, but under Kollontai's guidance they also passed Bolshevik-inspired resolutions against the war and for the Soviets.[60]

The Bolshevik women's movement did not have the kind of cen-tralized bureau Kollontai wanted, but another institution proved useful—the revived journal *Rabotnitsa* (*The Woman Worker*). Sa-moilova, who considered a special party organization for work among women "superfluous," was among the Bolshevik women who favored instead a revival of this journal on the grounds that it would be an ideal means to rally women.[61] As she predicted, it became a natural center for developing the revolutionary energies of working women. Whenever possible, the *Rabotnitsa* staff used current issues like un-employment to turn women against the Provisional Government and toward the Party. E. Iaroslavskii warned women who lacked jobs now

58. On Party negativism and fear of feminism, see Stal', "Rabotnitsa v Oktiabre," p. 299.
59. Kollontai, *Iz moei zhizni i raboty*, p. 269; *Autobiography*, p. 32. For strike de-scriptions, see Bochkarëva and Liubimova, *Svetlyi put'*, pp. 63–64.
60. *Iz moei zhizni i raboty*, pp. 269–70. The strikers' demand for municipalization of the laundries went unmet.
61. Kollontai, "Pamiati bortsov revoliutsii," p. 9, and "Avtobiograficheskii ocherk," p. 297.

how much more grim their situation would be when returning soldiers needed work.[62] With high prices and growing scarcities the key issues of the day, the Bolsheviks aimed their appeal at the capital's poorest women. In May Kollontai wrote a special article linking the high cost of living to the war, and *Rabotnitsa* followed this with an appeal for a mass demonstration of working women, under the flag of internationalism, to protest the war. The idea seemed inopportune to more cautious Bolsheviks, since it coincided with a period of extreme official patriotism, but the meeting occurred and the crowd of thousands surpassed *Rabotnitsa's* expectations. Nikolaeva, Samoilova, Kudelli, and Kollontai were among the speakers, and a resolution of no confidence in the Provisional Government was passed after a speech by Kollontai. The newspaper *Rabochy Put'* (*Workers' Path*) caught the mood: the crowd sang the *Marseillaise* and cheered Comrade Kollontai.[63]

These were heady days for the *Rabotnitsa* women, as their influence grew among the working classes and they sensed the dismay of the bourgeois feminists. The latter, who supported the Provisional Government's war effort and believed in the victory of the Entente, ultimately had little appeal among the masses of working women and soldiers' wives, who hated the war.

Nikolaeva and Samoilova directed *Rabotnitsa* activities since Kollontai, as the revolutionary mood heightened, became overwhelmed with assignments. She had no time even to write articles. Lenin reproached her, urging that she produce more popular pamphlets like "Who Needs War?" But when could she write? She had four or five meetings a day, in barracks, in factories, on ships. Lenin insisted that one reached a broader circle through the press—then he sent Kollontai to speak to sailors in Helsingfors.[64]

It was not easy for Kollontai to accept the diversion of her energies. She regretted that her "beloved work" among women had to recede into the background, and that she could give only limited time to working women and to the soldiers' wives.[65] Yet she was heartened to

---

62. On the history and staff of *Rabotnitsa*, see G. Grigor'ev, "Skvoz' Gody," in Zhak and Itkina, eds., p. 299; Stites, *Women's Liberation Movement*, p. 302; and Vavilina et al., eds. For Iaroslavskii's warning, see Bochkarëva and Liubimova, *Svetlyi put'*, pp. 54–60.

63. The rally, held in the *Cirque Moderne*, is described in Bochkarëva and Lyubimova, *Women of a New World*, pp. 61–62. See also Kollontai, "Avtobiograficheskii ocherk," p. 297.

64. Kollontai, "Pamiati bortsov revoliutsii," p. 9, and *Iz moei zhizni i raboty*, pp. 9–10.

65. *Iz moei zhizni i raboty*, p. 267.

see that here and there colleagues were becoming more receptive to her ideas. Vera Slutskaia, once cool to a women's section, now proposed that a bureau for work among women be organized within the Petrograd Committee of the Party, with each district committee selecting a woman representative and sending her to work in the central bureau. The bureau would agitate only; the working women themselves would not be organized into a separate women's group.[66]

Varvara Iakovleva, whose Party activities centered in Moscow, urged in August that the Moscow Area Party Bureau, of which she was the secretary, begin propaganda and agitation among working-class women. Iakovleva argued that women, largely as a result of the war, had become a dominant element in the shops and factories but were still the most politically backward layer of the working class, the group most susceptible to bourgeois manipulation intended to destroy proletarian solidarity. A successful revolutionary struggle was impossible without a united working class—which meant including women. Accepting this argument, the Moscow Area Bureau proposed to create, in connection with its local committees, special commissions for propaganda and agitation among women, and to print, in addition to the Petrograd-based *Rabotnitsa*, special weekly pages in all Party newspapers designed to appeal to working-class women. The central Commission for Propaganda and Agitation would spread literature among the women, establish schools, and create other channels for communication. Such commissions were established in Moscow under Iakovleva's direction. But a larger indication of Iakovleva's success was the all-city meetings in Moscow attended by as many as 600 working women. The October Revolution, ironically, would cut into this organizing activity, but in its aftermath Iakovleva resumed her work among women, joined by Inessa Armand.[67] Most gratifying of all, at the beginning of October Kollontai, now a Central Committee member herself and acting with the support of Lenin's lieutenant Iakov Sverdlov (who after the Revolution would be Chairman of the Central Executive Committee of the Soviet), successfully proposed in the Bolshevik Central Committee that there be

66. Svetlana Zimonina, "Sekretar' Raikoma (V. K. Slutskaia)," in Zhak and Itkina, eds., p. 420. Although Slutskaia made the point repeatedly, there were protests against creating a Party organization for women. See Bobroff, p. 547. Slutskaia was killed in 1917, hit by a bullet while riding in a car.

67. Smidovich, "Rabota partii sredi zhenshchin v Moskve," p. 19. Smidovich worked under Iakovleva in the Moscow Commission for Propaganda and Agitation among working women. See also Kollontai, "Pamiati bortsov revoliutsii," p. 10.

created the nucleus of a Central Women's Bureau in the Party.[68]

Why did the Bolsheviks agree in the autumn of 1917 to what they had so long resisted: a section, however rudimentary, within the Party, devoted to work among women? Although the Bolsheviks invariably referred to women as the most backward, politically unconscious element of society, it has been suggested that the Party established a section devoted to organizing women for reasons opposite to the ones they proclaimed. That is, not the backwardness of women but rather the "tremendous growth" among working women, beginning in 1910, of "militancy, organization, and awareness of their own needs" compelled the Bolsheviks to relate to them in new ways.[69] It is true that the revolutionary potential of Russian working women was more apparent, but one cannot assume that their "militancy" impressed the Bolsheviks. We have Kollontai's testimony that her activity from 1917 to her ouster from Moscow in 1922 was a struggle to overcome resistance to devising means to recruit women. The Bolsheviks were more aware of the working woman in 1917 than they were in 1906, but with their negative estimate of the "baba," even when she was a worker in a factory or a participant in a strike, they needed always to be persuaded to pay her serious attention as a comrade.[70]

Still, after the February Revolution women received the vote, and Kollontai recalled that she and Sverdlov timed the proposal for establishing a women's bureau to coincide with the election campaign for delegates to the Constituent Assembly. A bureau trying to get out the women's vote might increase support for Bolshevik candidates.[71] What Bolsheviks did come to realize in the course of 1917 was the potential of the *Rabotnitsa* group, particularly of Kollontai, to organize working-class women. In October, having developed a network of ties with factories and shops throughout Petrograd, *Rabotnitsa*'s editors decided to hold a conference of women workers. Kollontai explained to the Central Committee that an organizing group had invited women representatives from the Putilov factory, the cable and pipe factories, the Treugol'nik works, and other enterprises to

---

68. Kollontai, "Avtobiograficheskii ocherk," p. 299; see also USSR, [12], pp. 75–76.
69. Bobroff, p. 541.
70. See Glickman.
71. "Avtobiograficheskii ocherk," p. 299. This reasoning recalls Bolshevik interest in 1912 in appealing to women in connection with the insurance campaign. See Chapter 3, n. 11.

help plan the conference, which the organizers hoped would be endorsed by the Petrograd Committee and attended by women delegates from all workers' organizations, whether factory committees,
trade unions, or district committees of the Party.[72]

Canvassing every factory and shop in Petrograd, the women assembled 600 delegates. Liudmila Stal' estimated that they represented
80,000 women workers.[73] Not all of the organizers were comfortable
with their success. Samoilova worried that a Women's Conference
might go too far toward allowing separatist feminist tendencies to
develop, and that it might antagonize Party members and lead to
further isolation of the woman worker.[74] Samoilova was realistic. The
gathering of women in Petrograd in November 1917 did increase
antagonism in certain quarters—certainly toward Kollontai—yet it
convinced others in the Central Committee that she could recruit
and influence the essentially apolitical working women of Petrograd.

Kollontai succeeded in demonstrating to the Central Committee
how non-Party working women could be rallied to the side of the
Bolsheviks by employing special means—in this case the non-Party
conference. The working women's conference of November 1917
came during a Party crisis. Zinoviev and Kamenev were leading the
opposition to Lenin's and Trotsky's insistence on one-party Bolshevik
rule. Kollontai used the conference to rally support for the majority
position, and her eloquence, Liudmila Stal' was certain, convinced
the women delegates to endorse Lenin's all-Bolshevik government
rather than a coalition of all Soviet parties. Kollontai's protégé, the
24-year-old Nikolaeva, led a delegation of nine working women to
Smolny Institute to announce the conference's support of a Bolshevik
government. She spoke, she said grandly, in the name of 80,000 working women of Petrograd.[75]

Lenin and Trotsky addressed the delegates. So too did Zinoviev,
who tried to convince them that the new government must be a coalition of all the socialist parties that had overthrown Kerensky. It was
no use. The working women preferred Kollontai's explanation that
the other socialist parties wanted not to share power but to take it

72. Stal', "Rabotnitsa v Oktiabre," p. 299. On Kollontai's explanation to the Central
Committee, see USSR, [12], pp. 76, 265.
73. Stal', "Rabotnitsa v Oktiabre," p. 299.
74. Kollontai reported Samoilova's views in "Pamiati bortsov revoliutsii," p. 9.
75. Stal', "Rabotnitsa v Oktiabre," pp. 300–301, and Grigor'ev in Zhak and Itkina,
eds., p. 301.

from the Bolsheviks by removing Lenin and Trotsky. Not without misgivings did Kollontai reduce to very simple terms the complex issue of the future of socialist democracy.[76]

For the first time since she joined the Social Democrats, Kollontai believed in the autumn of 1917 that she had gathered strong allies for the women's movement—Iakov Sverdlov, the Bolshevik Party's indispensable organizer and a key figure in Lenin's general staff, and Lenin himself.[77] Why Sverdlov became Kollontai's ally is difficult to say. Anatolii Lunacharskii's image of him is uninspiring. "It was as if he had no individuality," Lunacharskii wrote, "and no ideas of his own. He had orthodox ideas on everything: he was only a reflection of the general will and the general line. Personally he added nothing: he only transmitted what he got from the Central Committee or sometimes directly from Lenin. When he spoke in public, his speeches always carried an official character. . . . Everything was thought out, but only as far as was necessary. No sentimentality. No wit. . . . The man was like ice, somehow faceless."[78]

But let Sverdlov speak for himself, in a letter to Elena Stasova that she included in her memoirs. When Stasova's father died in May 1918, she wrote to Sverdlov from Petrograd, forlorn at her loss. He replied warmly, reassuring her that it was not true, as she feared, that she was tied to her comrades merely by a common ideology and mutual work. His feeling for her was entirely independent of Party connections. She was a dear, sympathetic friend who must not feel that with her father's death she had lost all meaningful ties. There were deep bonds, he reassured her, that existed even without blood relationships; such was his feeling for her, his dear comrade. He kissed her firmly, he ended effusively.[79]

Like Stalin, Sverdlov had spent his political life in the Russian underground, but the two men were far apart in their attitudes toward Communist women. As head of the Secretariat, the organ entrusted with the organizational aspects of Party work, Sverdlov was sensi-

76. See Deutscher, *The Prophet Armed*, vol. 1, pp. 333–35, for Lenin's and Trotsky's position; for Zinoviev's see M. Hedlin, "Zinoviev's Revolutionary Tactics in 1917," *The Slavic Review*, 1975, no. 1 (Mar.), pp. 19–43. Kollontai's misgivings are discussed below.
77. Sverdlov became chairman of the Central Executive Committee of the Soviet and titular head of state in Jan. 1918, succeeding Kamenev.
78. Lunacharskii, *Revoliutsionnye siluety*, p. 54.
79. Stasova; *Stranitsy zhizni i bor'by*, p. 102.

tive to women's subordinate status. He was also the father of two young children and the husband of a politically active Communist. Even after the Revolution it was necessary for the children to be with relatives in Nizhni Novgorod because there was no way to care for them in Petrograd. Something in Kollontai's portrayal of the situation of Russian women moved Sverdlov.[80]

Lunacharskii's view that Sverdlov merely followed Lenin does not contradict this picture, for Lenin too had come to support Kollontai's proposal for a Party group to organize women. Before the Revolution, Lenin seemed to Kollontai to lack commitment to the woman question. By 1920, Lenin would be explaining that there were not as many women in the Party as men because of the Party's past rejection of the need for separate bodies for work among the masses of women. Using the argument that Kollontai had been urging since 1906, and separating himself from the Party's previous view, Lenin came to insist that there must be commissions, bureaus in the Party, whose duty it would be to bring the masses of women workers, peasants, and petty bourgeois under Bolshevik influence. This would be not feminism, he argued, but revolutionary expediency.[81]

Although Lenin possessed that feel for reality, that marvelous sensitivity to the demands of the time that prompted him to adopt new tactics when old ones proved inadequate,[82] his concern, we know, was not so opportunistic as Kollontai had earlier suspected. His interest in the woman question had its source partly in his intuitive knowledge that for the Revolution to succeed women had to support it. In Paris, in 1911, Krupskaia and Liudmila Stal' had tried to organize the mass of emigrant working women. At every meeting, Krupskaia recalled, someone was bound to object, "What's the idea of a women's meeting, anyway?" Thus the effort petered out, though "Il'ich thought it a useful job."[83] By 1913, Lenin was writing articles for *Pravda* on the unique exploitation of female labor under capitalism and urging the founding of *Rabotnitsa*.

80. On Sverdlova, see Aleksandra Arenshtein, "Kamnia Tverzhe, (K. T. Novgorod-tseva-Sverdlova)," in Zhak and Itkina, eds., pp. 304–19. On Sverdlov, see Vinogradskaia, *Sobytiia i pamiatnye vstrechi*, pp. 164–87. Sverdlova has written of her life with her husband: K. T. Sverdlova, *Iakov Mikhailovich Sverdlov* (Moscow, 1957).

81. Zetkin, pp. 53–54.

82. This was Lunacharskii's assessment. See his *Revoliutsionnye siluety* (Moscow, 1923), p. 26.

83. Krupskaia, *Vospominaniia o Lenine*, p. 182. Maxim Gorky recalled how Lenin questioned workers about their lives. "What about your wives? Up to the neck in housework? But do they manage to learn anything, to read anything?" Gorky, p. 17.

Not even the support of Lenin and Sverdlov could entirely dispel the suspicion of feminism. There were still those who wanted no women's organizations. To say that the interests of women were separate seemed contrary to Marx's teaching that society was divided by class, not by sex. To those doubters Lenin replied with the scorn he directed toward people who presumed to invoke Marx in opposition to his own position. Principles were invoked by many revolutionary-minded but confused people whenever there was a lack of understanding. How did such guardians of "pure principle" cope with the historical necessities of revolutionary policy? All their talk collapsed in the face of necessity.[84] The Party had to find ways to draw women in. To meet this problem, special bureaus, commissions, and committees were essential.

In the autumn of 1917, the eve of the Bolshevik seizure of power, Kollontai's revolutionary optimism was at its peak. In those days she happily assumed that Bolshevik camaraderie was based on internal democracy, and that she was one of a circle absolutely loyal to one another. The meeting on the night of October 10 at which the Bolsheviks voted to seize power seemed to support her enthusiasm. The time and circumstances of the meeting were unusual: it was set to begin after ten in the evening at an address unfamiliar to Kollontai somewhere across the Neva, far out on the Petrograd side (near a river called the Karpovka). The apartment belonged to the Menshevik Sukhanov and his wife, Galina Flakserman; she, unlike her husband, was a Bolshevik. Galina Konstantinovna, who worked in the Petersburg Committee, had offered the use of her flat if a secret meeting place were ever needed, and it is a well-known story how she urged Sukhanov, who managed somehow to attend every other important revolutionary meeting, not to come home on the night of October 10.[85]

The meeting has not lacked chroniclers, although they have occasionally described the conspiratorial manner in which they arrived more precisely than the historic gathering itself.[86] As for Kollontai,

84. Zetkin, p. 54.
85. Sukhanov, *The Russian Revolution*, vol. 2, p. 556. Sukhanov remarked, "Oh, the novel jokes of the merry muse of History! . . . I don't actually know much about the exact course of this meeting, or even about its outcome."
86. Thus Varvara Iakovleva, a candidate member of the Central Committee, recalled that having been summoned from Moscow she joined Lomov and Sverdlov for the trip

she recalled that the tram car to the far end of Petrograd was over-crowded, but that a cab was too expensive. The meeting had already begun when she arrived. An unfamiliar figure sat on the divan with Kamenev. It was Zinoviev, whom she had not seen since before the "July Days," with a beard and his hair cut short. At the table sat Vladimir Il'ich, the other fugitive, who had arrived from hiding places in Finland. Ever since Kerensky had begun the search for him in July he had been absent from Party meetings. Clean-shaven, with a wig for disguise, he reminded Iakovleva of a Lutheran minister.[87]

As Lenin began his effort to convince the ten members of the Cen-tral Committee that the moment had come to prepare for the seizure of power, the meeting became tense. Iakovleva, who was asked to be secretary, began taking notes. Lenin stressed that support for the Bolsheviks was growing stronger among the masses. Kollontai, who was living with Pavel Dybenko when she published her recollections of the meeting in 1919, documented Lenin's view by emphasizing that Dybenko's Baltic Fleet was primed for an immediate rising in defense of the slogan "all power to the Soviet." The fleet demanded an answer from the Central Committee. To delay meant to lose the revolutionary moment.

Would the masses support an uprising? Were they reliable? Or were they actually opposed to action? Would there not be enormous damage if an uprising were unsuccessful? These questions focused the intense debate. "Two comrades, old tested revolutionaries, were doubtful." This low-key reference was Kollontai's tactful way of in-dicating the wavering of Zinoviev and Kamenev, whom she loyally never identified by name.[88] The group voted on Lenin's motion to prepare for the imminent seizure of power. Two voted no, but the rest of the members of the Central Committee present voted yes.

---

to Flakserman's. Early in the evening the trio met Dzerzhinskii and Trotsky; since they had time to spare, the group stopped for refreshment, then separated so as not to arouse suspicion as they traveled. Iakovleva, "Podgotovka Oktiabr'skogo vosstaniia v Moskovskoi oblasti," pp. 304–5.

87. *Ibid.*, p. 305. See Kollontai's account of this meeting in "Ruka istorii: Vospomi-naniia A. Kollontai," pp. 68–69. Present in addition to Iakovleva and Kollontai were Lenin, Zinoviev, Kamenev, Trotsky, Dzerzhinskii, Lomov, Bubnov, and Stalin. (Inter-estingly, neither Kollontai nor Iakovleva mentions Stalin.) Bukharin was not there. The two women's recollections make an interesting contrast. Kollontai wrote emotionally, at length, and in a vivid style. Iakovleva was laconic, occasionally insisting that she really could not remember what happened.

88. For the position of Zinoviev and Kamenev, see USSR, [12], pp. 86–92. In 1937, Kollontai offered a different interpretation of the role of Zinoviev and Kamenev at this meeting in an article in *Izvestiia*, slandering each.

The tension broke once the vote was taken, Kollontai recalled. And suddenly they all realized how hungry they were. They pounced on the cheese and sausage. Over glasses of hot tea they continued to argue. But the intensity and anger had dissipated. They bantered with the two oppositionists.[89] In the years to come Kollontai would watch this camaraderie among opponents vanish.

At daybreak, after a meeting that had lasted through the night, the long trip to the other end of Petrograd had to be made. But Kollontai's spirits soared. Could anyone doubt that she stood at the threshold of a great event in history? Could anyone deny that she was a key member of a revolutionary party responding to the mood of the masses? Was it possible to accuse the Bolsheviks of undemocratic procedures or vindictiveness toward a dissenting comrade? Was their spirit not one of good fellowship and solidarity?

Moreover, Kollontai sincerely believed that a Bolshevik government would express the will of the masses. For us to assume that the Bolsheviks came to power as a result merely of a conspiracy without mass support is to distort history, for the October Revolution had significant backing from workers and soldiers, particularly in Petrograd.[90] It is not within the scope of this chapter to determine whether Lenin and the Bolsheviks forced the issue in taking power or rather rode a groundswell of popular revolutionary feeling in doing so. Kollontai was convinced of the latter.[91] Yet she knew that she was part of a coup d'état. In fact, the Mensheviks and the SRs would walk out of the Soviet in protest against a Bolshevik seizure of power taken in the name of the Soviet but behind the backs of the other parties, thus leaving the Bolsheviks a monopoly of power. Kollontai would favor a Bolshevik government rather than a socialist coalition. And the roar of applause from the delegates for the fourteen Bolsheviks, Kollontai among them, who assumed their new places in the Presidium moments after the Second Congress of Soviets opened was for her the reassuring voice of the Soviet. That applause confirmed her belief that as a Bolshevik she was at the forefront not of a

89. Kollontai, "Ruka istorii," p. 69. She omitted all friendly references to "the two oppositionists" in later accounts of this evening. See "Na istoricheskom zasedanii" in her *Iz moei zhizni i raboty*, pp. 311–13. She also omitted her praise of Trotsky, whom she had called inspirational and steadfast in "Ruka istorii," p. 71.

90. For the role of the masses, see Rabinowitch.

91. For an interesting exchange of views on this question, see A. Rabinowitch and L. Schapiro, "An Exchange on the Russian Revolution," *New York Review of Books*, 10 (June 9, 1977), pp. 46–48.

conspiracy but of an insurrectionary rising of the Russian people: 1917 would be the glorious year when "we fought for the Soviet."[92]

The American journalist John Reed watched the Bolsheviks the night the Second Congress of Soviets, meeting in Smolny on October 26, confirmed their government in power. He saw "Lenin, gripping the edge of the reading stand . . . waiting, apparently oblivious to the long-rolling ovation, which lasted several minutes." The socialists sang the *Internationale*. "Alexandra Kollontai rapidly winked the tears back." It was the greatest moment of her life.[93]

Of Lenin's appointments to the Council of Commissars it has been said that "like a good conductor discerning the strength and weakness of each player in his orchestra, Lenin almost unfailingly distributed the instruments." With his long experience of dealing with extreme idealists in the socialist movement, Lenin knew it was wise to exclude them from influence on the really decisive issues and to harness their enthusiasm for the vital but secondary tasks. Kollontai's appointment as Commissar of Public Welfare was a typical example of such handling; Lunacharskii's as Commissar of Enlightenment was another.[94]

When Kamenev, on November 8, 1917, read to the Second Congress of Soviets the names of the members of the new government, Kollontai's was not included. Although this indicated that the post of Commissar of Public Welfare, to which she was appointed on November 13, was not among the first rank, it did not lessen her delight in being the sole woman in the Council and, so far as she knew, the only woman member of a modern government.[95] Lunacharskii and Trotsky each took over a former ministry in an almost light-hearted spirit, "as if the institution were about to dissolve in the paradox of their arrival."[96] Kollontai came to her ministry, still called "State

92. For examples of Kollontai's assumption that they fought for the Soviet, see *Iz moei zhizni i raboty*, pp. 248, 263.

93. The date was Oct. 26 (O.S.), or Nov. 8 (N.S.). See Reed, pp. 171–72, 177–78; and Kollontai, "Lenin v Smol'nom," in *Iz moei zhizni i raboty*, p. 317.

94. For these observations, see the Introduction and notes to Michael Glenny's translation of Lunacharskii's *Revoliutsionnye siluety*, pp. 18, 51.

95. Reed, pp. 185, 347; Kollontai, *Autobiography*, p. 35. Shliapnikov claimed that Kollontai was proposed as a member of a special "labor commission" (as a specialist on protective labor legislation) to advise the Commissariat of Labor, but that another comrade was chosen instead. See Shliapnikov, "K Oktiabriu," p. 26.

96. Sheila Fitzpatrick, "Cultural Commissars," paper presented to the American Historical Association, Dec. 1973.

Charity," thinking that she could establish a new pattern for people's government. Her dreams did not envisage the use of force, and she was consequently appalled at being confronted by former administrators who would neither surrender the keys nor allow her to take possession of her office. For Kollontai the pacifist it was another inner struggle: with tears streaming down her face she gave the order for arrests. Wielding power was uncongenial. " 'Is this you, Alexandra Kollontay, ordering arrests?' Afterwards I used to lie awake nights and wonder how I did it."[97]

Her initial problem stemmed not from any lack of innovative policies but from a severe shortage of funds to meet the overwhelming need for public assistance. The Commissariat was responsible for administering the welfare program for hundreds of thousands of war-disabled soldiers, the pension system, foundling homes, homes for the aged, orphanages, hospitals for the needy, workshops making artificial limbs, and a series of educational institutes for young women. The administration of playing-card factories (the manufacture of playing cards was a state monopoly) came under the direction of the Commissariat and provided revenue. To increase funds she lowered salaries of the professional social workers. Her own salary as Commissar was very low. Kollontai increased revenue by placing an exorbitant tax on playing cards. Through careful management she increased the meager pensions paid to crippled veterans, but the improvement was still far from lifting them out of misery.[98]

Kollontai tried, sometimes by decree, to help the war-disabled, to abolish religious instruction and introduce the right of self-administration by pupils in the schools for young girls (this was before the separation of church and state), to transfer priests to the civil service, to set up hostels for the needy and for street urchins, to reorganize orphanages into government-run children's homes, and to convene a committee of doctors to work out a free public health system for the whole country. The broad list suggested the range of her ideals more than her actual accomplishments. It is difficult to gauge how much Kollontai could do. The American journalist Louise Bryant, who liked to visit Kollontai in her office on Kazanskaia Street (now Plek-

97. Reed, p. 347, describes Kollontai giving the order for arrests. See Bryant, *Six Red Months in Russia*, p. 130, for Kollontai on the use of power.
98. Kollontai, *Autobiography*, pp. 35–36. Bryant reported that Kollontai's salary was equal to about 50 dollars a month. Bryant, *Six Red Months in Russia*, pp. 131–32.

hanov Street), thought that this "slim little person" worked untiringly and accomplished a tremendous amount.[99]

Everything she achieved came despite opposition. Former officials of the ministry continued their sabotage, shirking work and stealing vital supplies from milk to children's boots. Sometimes being Commissar seemed a burden beyond her strength. She remembered the old days before the Revolution when she traveled for the Party from country to country as a revolutionary agitator. How carefree they seemed! Well, the Revolution was here—but how often had she to tell herself "More courage, Kollontai!"[100]

The legal status of Russian women had improved immediately after the February Revolution, when the Provisional Government granted women full civil and political rights. Now the Soviet government went further, abrogating all legislation that subordinated women. No longer, for example, was a wife obliged to follow her husband if he relocated. Other laws gave women equal rights to hold land, to act as heads of household, and to participate as full members of rural communes. Restrictions were removed on divorce. Equal pay for equal work became law.

Kollontai introduced measures to protect women as mothers, an area the bourgeois feminists slighted. Her efforts to nationalize maternity and infant care set off a wave of "insane attack" in which Kollontai was accused of promulgating laws obligating girls of twelve to become mothers. A particularly vicious attack took the form of destruction by fire of a "Prenatal Care Palace" housed in a former school for young noblewomen still under the direction of a countess. In one wing of the old building Kollontai planned an exhibition room where courses for mothers could be held and model day nurseries established. One night, after a late and discouraging meeting of the Council of Commissars, Kollontai was awakened in the little apartment she shared with Zoia and Misha by a telephone call. The Prenatal Care Palace was on fire.[101]

Years later she wrote of the pain she felt as she stood on the street in the freezing cold looking at the destruction of her work. How

99. Bryant, *Six Red Months in Russia*, pp. 129–32.
100. Kollontai, *Iz moei zhizni i raboty*, p. 341, and "Iz vospominanii," p. 87.
101. Kollontai, *Autobiography*, p. 38, and *Iz moei zhizni i raboty*, pp. 340–41.

many sleepless nights had been spent planning the new institution, how many struggles with the old administration. An informal commission tried to establish its cause. Suspicion fell on the countess, who was wildly hostile to the Commissar of Social Welfare. The blaze had been confined to the wing that held Kollontai's new state facilities. Sailors who had come to fight the fire wanted to arrest the countess, but Kollontai restrained them. Zoia tried to comfort her. The building was old. Other Prenatal Care homes would be built.[102]

New work followed the setback. Kollontai's proudest accomplishment as Commissar was the founding in January 1918 of a Central Office for Maternity and Infant Welfare. The resolution signed by Kollontai began emotionally:

Two million babies, tiny lights just kindled on this earth, died in Russia every year because of the ignorance of the oppressed people, because of the bigotry and indifference of the class state. Two million mothers wet the Russian soil with their bitter tears every year as, with their calloused hands, they piled earth on the innocent victims of an ugly state system. Human thought . . . has at last come out into the open vistas of the radiant epoch where the working class can build, with its own hands, forms of child care that will not deprive a child of its mother or a mother of her child.[103]

Kollontai tried to implement the legislation she had advocated in her massive study *Obshchestvo i materinstvo*, undertaken when the Mensheviks in the Duma asked her to draft a bill on maternity welfare. The fundamental needs in this field, which Kollontai summed up at the end of her book, were promulgated by the Soviet regime in its first Social Insurance Laws. The decree providing for maternity leaves before and after childbirth was one of the regulations that most impressed the working woman.[104]

The original Soviet Family Code of 1918, although basically conservative, reflected some of Kollontai's hopes for the future: child care at government expense, clauses for insurance against illness and old age so that people need not depend on indifferent relatives, and

102. *Iz moei zhizni i raboty*, pp. 341–44.

103. *Autobiography*, p. 37. Kollontai's resolution is in Bochkarëva and Lyubimova, *Women of a New World*, p. 192. Kollontai's views on raising children under Communism are discussed in Chapter 5.

104. *Autobiography*, p. 20. See also Smith, p. 14. The first Conference of Petrograd Working Women, held in Nov. 1917, endorsed a report by Kollontai on the protection of female labor and on maternity welfare. The Conference resolution was used as the basis for decisions on mother and child care adopted by the Soviet government. Bochkarëva and Lyubimova, *Women of a New World*, p. 73. For Kollontai's participation in promulgating laws for maternity leave, see Itkina, pp. 174–75.

prohibition of adoption. This last clause reflected Bolshevik fear that adoption might serve as a cover for peasant exploitation of juvenile labor, and the belief that orphan children would be better cared for in children's homes away from petty bourgeois influence.[105]

Western historians of the early Soviet period tend to overlook the innovative image of participatory government held by Bolsheviks like Kollontai. She came to office in 1917 not only with a specific, if optimistic, program of social change, but also with fresh ideas of how Bolshevik Commissars should conduct themselves. She sought to organize her Commissariat along lines that reflected her larger image of humane relationships. She knew she was a novice in state administration, so she formed an auxiliary council in which experts, physicians, jurists, and pedagogues participated alongside the workers and minor officials of the Commissariat. Replacing the authoritarian idea of a single minister with the concept of collectivism, Kollontai sought to introduce self-rule, holding meetings at which all employees were present. Suggestions from scrubwomen would be as welcome as those from professional social workers. She replaced former bourgeois employees by cooks and workers, as if to demonstrate the validity of the famous image in Lenin's *State and Revolution* that any worker could run the state. A new life stirred in what had been a highly conservative entity.[106]

The cooperation and love Kollontai inspired among the lower-level employees astonished Louise Bryant. But Kollontai's predecessor, Countess Panina, the Minister of State Charity for the Provisional Government, was unimpressed. A well-educated, hard-working liberal who resembled Jane Addams, she was a lively and amusing woman who won praise even from the pro-Bolshevik Louise Bryant. "There are fine things about Panina," she wrote. As a liberal she did much for struggling Russia under the Old Regime in areas of education and culture. Even in the midst of revolutionary hardship—such as her own imprisonment by the Bolsheviks for refusing to hand over state funds—Panina liked to tell funny anecdotes. But she was invariably grim on one subject: Bolshevism and Aleksandra Kollontai. She flushed with anger when Bryant asked her reaction to the self-

105. This is discussed in Carr, *A History of Soviet Russia. Socialism in One Country*, vol. 1, pp. 45–46.

106. For Kollontai's innovations, see her "Iz vospominanii," p. 88, "Avtobiograficheskii ocherk," p. 300, and *Autobiography*, p. 36. For an observer's account, see Bryant, *Six Red Months in Russia*, p. 131. Shliapnikov, in "K Oktiabriu," p. 26, wrote of an attempt to establish the Commissariat of Labor on a collegial basis.

governing of charitable institutions. "Do you mean," she said, "the self-governing of children under six or people over one hundred?" She raged against the "absurd" Madame Kollontai who invited the servants to come and sit in armchairs at her meetings. What could they know of social reforms or technical training? She predicted that the Russian people would pay with their lives for Kollontai's experiments in participatory democracy.[107]

Kollontai's practice of nonauthoritarian relationships with her subordinates extended to her own behavior toward power. She seemed not to have internalized the commandment that Communists act in accordance with decisions of the Central Committee. Thus the Commissariat of Public Welfare evoked Party wrath by deciding on its own in mid-January 1918 to transform the famous Aleksandr Nevskii monastery into a home for war invalids. Pressed by ragged mobs of legless, armless, and blind veterans, who were organized into a union and threatened demonstrations, the Commissariat set out to find these war victims the shelter they demanded. A secretary (one Alesha Tsvetkov) located the "ideal" place: the Aleksandr Nevskii monastery, with its ample space and supplies of food and firewood. A decree was prepared requisitioning the building and supplies of the monastery; Kollontai, an enthusiastic opponent of the Russian church, immediately signed it.[108] The war-wounded were absolutely destitute, she told Louise Bryant. "They live in filth and beg for crusts."[109]

As Commissar of Public Welfare, she called on Dybenko, Commissar for Naval Affairs, for a detachment of sailors to take over the monastery. Sharing her opposition to the clergy, Dybenko happily complied, and the sailors arrived at the monastery. The monks, however, resisted. Ringing the bell, they summoned the faithful, who flocked to their aid. How the shooting began, Kollontai did not know. Emissaries from Smolny arrived to stop the fighting between the sailors and the defenders of the monastery. Some monks were among the casualties.[110]

The government subsequently reversed Kollontai's decree and ordered that the monastery not be taken, but too late to forestall street demonstrations and an Orthodox Anathema against the Bolsheviks. Lenin spoke to Kollontai, sternly explaining that arbitrary

107. Bryant, *Six Red Months in Russia*, pp. 122–34.
108. Kollontai, *Iz moei zhizni i raboty*, pp. 332–34.
109. Bryant, *Six Red Months in Russia*, p. 132.
110. Kollontai, *Iz moei zhizni i raboty*, pp. 334–35. Kollontai's clash with the church is discussed in Vvedenskii, pp. 122–25.

policymaking was impermissible. He regretted that Kollontai's clash with the monastery seemed likely to precipitate a decision concerning the question of separation of church and state.[111] And indeed, on January 20, 1918, the Council of Commissars decreed that henceforth church and state in Russia were to be separate.[112]

Except for her initial dismay at Lenin's criticism, Kollontai was unchastened. The clash with the church became a favorite story, and she referred to herself as a female Antichrist.[113] Sadoul's comment that "Kollontai triumphs" reflected her satisfaction that she had hastened a decision that denied government funds to the church.[114]

But it was a hollow victory. Lenin's joking remark that the Anathema of the church put Kollontai in the company of the Cossack rebel Stenka Razin and Leo Tolstoy did not mean that he took her action lightly. Bukharin recalled that Lenin laughed about even more serious matters.[115] Kollontai weakened her position in the Central Committee by displaying not only a defiance of party discipline but a lack of political skill. She failed to appreciate both the number of her opponents and the need to rally support to her side, for members of the government feared that the Soviet regime would be faced with religious as well as civil and foreign war.[116]

The excitement of the times created an atmosphere in which Kollontai could proceed, happily unaware that her comrades saw her as politically reckless. Much that occurred during the heady first months lent itself to subsequent romanticizing, especially the simplicity. A favorite story involved her first payment as People's Commissar: compensation to a peasant for his requisitioned horse (a function that did not even belong to her office). The man had traveled from his distant village to the capital and sought out Lenin in Smolny. As a result of his conversation with Lenin, the peasant waited for Kollontai at dawn with a note from Lenin on a small page torn from his notebook. Would Kollontai please settle the matter? Surely the Commissariat

111. Kollontai, *Iz moei zhizni i raboty*, p. 335.

112. Freedom of conscience was also guaranteed. For the text of the decree, see USSR, [1], vol. 1, p. 371. The Anathema against the Bolsheviks, dated Jan. 19, 1918, is printed in Vvedenskii, pp. 114–16.

113. Kollontai, "Iz vospominanii," p. 89, and *Iz moei zhizni i raboty*, p. 343.

114. Sadoul wrote that she succeeded both in having separation of church and state decreed and in having the budget for the religious sects ended. Sadoul, p. 222.

115. For Bukharin's recollection, see his letter in *Pravda*, Jan. 3, 1924, p. 5. Lunacharskii also observed that Lenin often expressed anger in what appeared a joking manner; see *Revoliutsionnye siluety*, p. 13.

116. Kollontai, *Iz moei zhizni i raboty*, pp. 332–33. On Bolshevik fear of religious war, see Sadoul, p. 222.

of Social Welfare had some cash?[117] She remembered the days of intense work, and the night sessions of the Council of People's Commissars, chaired by Lenin, in a small room with only one secretary who recorded the resolutions that were to shake Russia to its foundations. Sitting with her comrades around a table poorly lit by a hanging electric bulb, drinking glasses of hot tea if they were lucky, she felt an almost palpable spirit of unity. Afterward Kollontai would return to the small apartment she shared with Misha and Zoia, climb wearily up the dirty staircase to the fifth floor, hungry and cold, wondering if there was any bread at home, but convinced that she was living through her most glorious days.[118]

Years later Kollontai recalled the initial era of the Workers' Government as rich in "magnificent illusions."[119] She came to understand that despite the "real romanticism" of revolution she and her comrades were living in an unreal world. Decrees were the answer to all problems during this first period of Bolshevik rule. Usually they were propaganda rather than actual administrative measures. Trotsky candidly acknowledged that the Bolsheviks wanted to be certain that, if they were overthrown, the revolutionary guidelines would have been set.[120] In a moment of frankness during her first months as Commissar, Kollontai revealed her fear, shared by many Bolsheviks, that the Soviet Revolution would fail. Almost certainly thinking of the precedent of the Paris Commune of 1871, she took comfort, like Trotsky, in knowing that the Bolsheviks were the first to pronounce new revolutionary words, to issue new civic, economic, and family codes to guide the proletariat of the future.[121]

After her initial euphoria, Kollontai realized that she could not do much to help women. She criticized bourgeois feminists for ignoring the real needs of workers, but the Bolsheviks could not fulfill women's

117. Kollontai, *Autobiography*, p. 37, and "Pervoe posobie iz sotsobesa," in *Iz moei zhizni i raboty*, pp. 322–23.

118. *Autobiography*, p. 36, and "Lenin v Smol'nom," in *Iz moei zhizni i raboty*, p. 317. For a similar view of early Council sessions in Smolny, see Shliapnikov, "K Oktiabriu," pp. 41–42.

119. *Autobiography*, p. 35. This phrase was deleted before publication in 1926. It appears on the galley-proofs included in the 1971 edition.

120. Trotsky, *My Life*, p. 342.

121. For Kollontai's fears, see Sadoul, p. 96. For decrees relating to women, see Schlesinger, ed., and Lapidus, pp. 59–60. See also Chapter 5 below.

demands for shelter and milk for their children. The women insisted that the Bolsheviks keep their promises, and Kollontai tried to explain that they could not build a new life at once. But the women would not listen. Sailors and soldiers came to the Commissariat, too, begging Kollontai to take into the maternity homes their beloved girls while they were off at the front. But the homes existed only on paper.[122] What Kollontai could accomplish with inadequate funds was pathetic. A sympathetic visitor recalled the bleak succession of infant homes during the famine, rooms filled with starving babies with half-starved doctors and nurses trying to save them. The summer colonies were unsuccessful. Mothers feared leaving children in conditions of neglect. Lack of facilities turned children's homes into dreary places; those old enough to do so often ran away.[123]

Her frustration and helplessness, her fear that the Revolution would fail, were complicated by a more serious anxiety that she admitted to her French comrade, Jacques Sadoul: the suspicion that after her long exile abroad she did not really know the Russian proletariat. She saw them as an inert mass trailing far behind their Western European counterparts in political consciousness.[124]

Her realization had profound implications. What Kollontai admitted to Sadoul was nothing less than that she had deluded herself into thinking much could be accomplished, that she had failed to take into account Russia's backward, petty bourgeois, peasant mentality, which would make immediate and effective social reorganization nearly impossible. She was frank, but paradoxically she engaged in further fantasy, dreaming that she might bring Bolsheviks into accord with Mensheviks in a desperate effort to save the Revolution.[125] For Kollontai the idea was not wholly bizarre. Her commitment to an all-Bolshevik government was finally ambivalent. When Plekhanov, at a meeting of the First All-Russian Congress of Soviets in June 1917, pretended not to know her, she was hurt and regretted that her old idol was not with the Party.[126] Like Lunacharskii, whose sensibilities she frequently shared, she kept bright memories of Plek-

122. Kollontai, "Iz vospominanii," p. 87.
123. The sympathetic observer was Jessica Smith. See Smith, p. 172. For summer colonies, see Goldman, p. 173. For a vivid fictional account of the children's homes, see Gladkov's *Tsement*.
124. Sadoul, p. 96.
125. *Ibid.*
126. Kollontai, *Iz moei zhizni i raboty*, p. 262.

hanov, despite his betrayal of internationalism.[127] The illusion of socialist solidarity died hard; so, too, did other optimistic assumptions.

For Kollontai revolution was not an affair of battles and arrests, but rather an outpouring of spirits long oppressed. She had expected the Revolution to bring unity with other socialists in a great social movement to build a Soviet society.[128] She was beginning now to see her expectations as illusions. Soon she would see her most cherished illusions crumble.

127. For Lunacharskii on Plekhanov, see *Revoliutsionnye siluety*, p. 48.
128. Sukhanov remarked that Kollontai "rejected any alliance with those who could not and would not accomplish a social revolution!" See Sukhanov, *The Russian Revolution*, vol. 1, p. 288.

CHAPTER FOUR

The Brest-Litovsk Crisis and Three Bolshevik Women

WHEN Communists despaired of the future of Bolshevism, they would reassure themselves with thoughts of the international revolution that alone could salvage their daring experiment. Never did the Communists cling so tightly to internationalism as during that first winter in power, when they doubted their capacity to survive. For this reason, Lenin's decision in January 1918 to seek a separate peace with the Kaiser in order to take Russia out of the war came as an immeasurable blow.

From January through March Lenin pressed for the conclusion of peace with Germany, even though the German terms turned out to be unmistakably imperialistic—the kind of annexationist treaty he had earlier opposed in theory. If the Bolsheviks accepted such terms, they would be assisting imperialist aggression. For over two months a struggle raged within the Party over the question of peace or war. On the one hand, Lenin insisted that the terms, no matter how onerous, be accepted to win a breathing space for the new regime; on the other, a group that came to be called the Left Communists, headed by Bukharin and including Krestinskii, Uritskii, Bubnov, Dzerzhinskii, Lomov, Iakovleva, and Kollontai, urged revolutionary war against the advancing German army. "No one would have been more pleased than Il'ich if our army had been able to fight back, or if a revolution had broken out in Germany, which would have put an end to the war. He would have been glad to know that he had been wrong," the loyal Krupskaia wrote of the greatest Party crisis Lenin faced in his years of Bolshevik leadership.[1]

The anarchist Emma Goldman, recalling her months in revolutionary Russia, wrote that however widely they differed politically, nearly all the revolutionaries she spoke to in Moscow recalled the

---

1. Krupskaia, *Vospominaniia o Lenine*, p. 362.

Brest-Litovsk peace as the beginning of the decline of the Revolution, the ebb tide of the spirit that had carried each of them forward in 1917.[2] Lenin moved closer in the winter of 1917–18 to those on the right who had opposed or cautiously questioned his bold course in the fall. Bukharin headed those who were convinced, as he was, that Lenin's new policy would be fatal to the Revolution. The decision to sign a separate peace with imperialist Germany left Kollontai and the radicals who had supported Lenin in 1917 dispirited, bereft of the internationalism that had brought them together in 1914 and that they had counted on to sustain the Revolution.[3]

Historians have analyzed many times the bitter conflict among Party leaders during this crisis: Lenin's insistence on peace; Bukharin's advocacy of revolutionary war; Trotsky's ambiguous slogan "No war, no peace."[4] Hence we need not concern ourselves here with the intricacies of the struggle. But the crisis in the Bolshevik Party during the peace negotiations was a turning point in Kollontai's political career, so we will instead look at the controversy in another way and ask a different question. What was its effect not simply on Kollontai's future but on the political lives of the two other women who also served on the Central Committee, albeit in a somewhat lesser capacity, as candidate members? Varvara Iakovleva opposed the treaty, and Elena Stasova supported Lenin. The political fate of each was shaped, at least in part, by her reactions to the events of that winter and spring of 1918. Much has been written about the men during this crisis in the life of the Party, little about the women. Historians, focusing on the transmission and exercise of power, have been intrigued by the familiar conflict for primacy among men, and less interested in the women who seemed on the fringes of the struggle. Yet the experiences of Varvara Iakovleva, Elena Stasova, and Aleksandra Kollontai deserve attention, for they make clearer the political position of the *Bol'shevichka* in the months after the seizure of power.

The three women had much in common. Each came from a pros-

2. Goldman, p. 29.

3. For the internationalist argument, see the account of the Central Committee meeting of Jan. 11 (O.S.), 1918 in USSR, [12], pp. 170–71.

4. Lenin scorned Trotsky's position as an "adventurous gamble," which reflected his hatred of the treaty and his simultaneous recognition that it was impossible to continue the war. See Krupskaia, *Vospominaniia o Lenine*, p. 361. For analyses of this crisis, see Daniels; Schapiro; Cohen, *Bukharin*; and Wade.

perous background, each was an intellectual. Elena Stasova, as we have seen, was an early influence on Kollontai; and because she was also an old friend of Krupskaia's, with whom she taught in workers' Sunday schools, she became Kollontai's initial link to "the Il'iches," as Lenin and his wife were familiarly called. Kollontai described her friend as one of Lenin's earliest and most loyal comrades, efficiently executing Party decisions.[5] For Kollontai the concepts of loyalty and subordination conveyed the essence of Stasova's political contribution; they also described how Stasova perceived herself. Recalling her entry into the Petersburg Committee of the Social Democrats in 1898, Stasova noted that she asked to be in charge of technical matters, such as keeping track of addresses of revolutionaries. From 1903 on she was an *Iskra* agent closely associated with the Petersburg Committee. Even after the Revolution and some twenty years of political experience during constant disputes with other socialist factions, Stasova continued to see herself as a subordinate. Whenever Lenin asked her to undertake a political task, Stasova insisted on her inadequacy, claiming that she was "only an organizer," lacking theoretical ability.[6]

Stately and severe looking, Stasova knew she was seen as "stony," hard as steel. Kollontai described her differently, a warm friend always ready to help a comrade, "sensitive and responsive, as only a woman of great spirit could be."[7] Significantly, Kollontai praised Stasova's modesty, her unwillingness to push herself forward—qualities that Kollontai herself did not possess. Her warm tribute expressed appreciation of Stasova's loyalty. More than a decade after Kollontai's death, when the Party finally saw fit to rehabilitate her, the elderly Stasova wrote the introduction to a biography of Kollontai, praising her friend but even in 1964 cautiously acknowledging that Kollontai had made mistakes.[8]

Rash and impulsive action leading to "mistakes" of the sort Kollontai made was not congenial to Stasova. Uncomfortable with independent decision-making, Stasova preferred to follow orders. The crisis surrounding the ratification of the Treaty of Brest-Litovsk was a tormenting time for her because, called upon to vote as a Central

---

5. Kollontai, *Izbrannye stat'i i rechi*, p. 372.
6. Stasova, *Uchitel' i drug*, pp. 18, 22.
7. *Ibid.*, p. 21; Kollontai, *Izbrannye stat'i i rechi*, p. 372.
8. See Stasova's Introduction, "K Chitateliam," to Itkina. Kollontai's friend Marcel Body searched *Pravda* after Kollontai's death in 1952 looking in vain for an article about her. See Body, p. 12.

Committee member, she could not make a decision.[9] To conclude peace on the basis of the given conditions, or to break off the talks and begin the "revolutionary war" that the Left Communists proposed—how could she know? Stasova followed the course that came most naturally to her. She importuned both Sverdlov and Lenin for advice and guidance. The thought that the Bolsheviks, in concluding a separate peace with the imperialists, might be hurting socialists abroad disturbed her. Because she could not really grasp the essence of the matter—as she put it—she could not vote for Il'ich. But neither could she vote against him. Thus Stasova found herself at one Central Committee meeting simply abstaining, a position she considered impermissible at so difficult a time in the life of the Party. Ultimately Stasova chose what appeared the wisest policy: believing that Lenin had to be right, stifling her doubts, she voted with him for concluding the Treaty of Brest-Litovsk.[10]

Varvara Iakovleva was different, a woman of verve, given to independent action. Sources in Moscow remembered her in her later years as assertive and tactless, but honest. If Kollontai tended to romanticize her background, the opposite was true of Iakovleva. She diffidently recalled, looking back at her narrow, middle-class family, that it was hard to understand how she and her brother became revolutionaries. Kollontai recalled Iakovleva from 1917 as a fighter on the barricades in Moscow.[11] Others remembered her in more traditional ways, noting how pretty she was with her luxuriant brown hair braided around her head, her large brown eyes, and her lively, expressive mouth. Iakovleva shared Stasova's extraordinary talents for organizing, but she impressed people most by her high spirits. Did she ever get discouraged, her friend Polina Vinogradskaia wondered? A naive question, but one that suggested Iakovleva's impact on Communist contemporaries.

As a young woman from a well-to-do Moscow merchant family, Iakovleva graduated from the *gimnaziia* at sixteen in 1900 and began the study of astronomy at Moscow University under the well-known

9. Stasova, *Vospominaniia*, p. 157.

10. See USSR, [12], p. 204, for the Central Committee meeting, and Stasova, *Vospominaniia*, p. 157.

11. Moscow information provided in personal communication by Sheila Fitzpatrick. Kollontai's views are in her *Izbrannye stat'i i rechi*, p. 373. See Iakovleva's recollections in her biographical sketch of her brother, Nikolai Nikolaevich Iakovlev, and in her own autobiography in *Deiateli SSSR i Oktiabr'skoi Revoliutsii*, cols., 274, 278–80. Nikolai was killed in 1918 during the Civil War.

professor P. K. Shternberg, whom she later married and converted to Bolshevism. A member of the Party from 1904, and a participant in the events of 1905, she managed between arrests in 1906 and 1907 to complete her course of scientific study and take her state exams with a speciality in astronomy.[12] Iakovleva taught briefly in the Moscow city schools during these years. Arrested in 1910, she was exiled to Siberia (where she contracted tuberculosis) but escaped and joined Lenin abroad. Then in 1912 she reentered Russia illegally and, like Stasova, worked as a Bolshevik agent. Arrested again, she was exiled until the end of 1916.

Iakovleva and her younger brother Nikolai were among the young Muscovites who formed the close circle of friends among whom Bukharin, that circle's most famous member, began his Party career. Iakovleva's home was a lively, hospitable center where she and her Moscow comrades lived communally.[13] Secretary of the radical, pro-insurrection Moscow Bureau in 1917, Iakovleva was one of the Muscovites who, during the winter of 1918, worked with Bukharin and the young idealists of the left to defeat the peace of Brest-Litovsk. It would be better, she declared emotionally at a Party meeting in January, to die with honor under the revolutionary banner than to surrender to imperialism. Above all, the Russians had to ignite the international revolution in Europe.[14]

Kollontai, who joined the Moscow opposition along with Dybenko, was a notable exception to the youth of the group, closer in years to Lenin than to the leftists. If, as has been suggested, the opposition to the peace of Brest-Litovsk can be seen in terms of a generational conflict, then Kollontai's position emphasizes again her affinity with youth.[15] Kollontai was unique in that she was often more comfortable with the young than with people of her own age. Lenin, by contrast, frequently used the adjective "youthful" in a pejorative sense and denigrated the Left Communists as "infantile." Mistakes he attributed for the most part to "very youthful" Communists. He scorned "yellow-beaked fledglings" who thought themselves so "terribly

12. Vinogradskaia, *Sobytiia i pamiatnye vstrechi*, pp. 133–35.

13. *Ibid.*, p. 134. Iakovleva's husband, Shternberg, died in 1920 during the Civil War. Among the young Muscovites in their circle were I. N. Smirnov, Osinskii, and Sokolnikov, the first of whom became Iakovleva's second husband. On Iakovleva see also Krupskaia, *Vospominaniia o Lenine*, p. 190.

14. See Lenin's note about this Party meeting, held Jan. 8 (O.S.), 1918 in *Leninskii Sbornik*, vol. 11, p. 43.

15. Cohen, *Bukharin*, p. 64.

clever."[16] Whereas Lenin mistrusted spontaneity and was wary of youth, Kollontai glorified both.

An abortive mission in February 1918 to Sweden and the West to establish commercial and diplomatic contacts for the Bolshevik regime kept Kollontai from all but the first of the Central Committee meetings on the peace.[17] Thus it was not until the Seventh Party Congress in March 1918, when the treaty was being considered for ratification, that Kollontai assumed a prominent role among the oppositionists. She became at once a chief of the antitreaty faction, so vocal that a contemporary observer listed her ahead of Bukharin—a testimony not to the reality of Soviet politics but to Kollontai's charisma.[18]

Observers at the Seventh Party Congress, accustomed to the liveliness that made her one of the most popular of the Bolshevik leaders among European visitors, were startled by Kollontai's mood, which ranged from quiet despair to bitter outbursts of anger. Seeming sometimes to be moving in a trance, she reflected the atmosphere of crisis surrounding the signing of the treaty. A foreign correspondent witnessed an encounter that epitomized the tension: Kollontai bitterly accusing Lenin, whom she had buttonholed behind the tribune, of treason to the Revolution. "Enough of this opportunism!," she cried, "you are advising us to do the same thing you have been accusing the Mensheviks of doing, compromising with imperialism."[19]

Kollontai had absorbed Lenin's ideas too well. She remembered that he had written, in *Sotsial Demokrat* in 1915, that if the proletariat came to power in Russia, its government should immediately offer peace to all the belligerents on the condition that all colonial and dependent peoples be liberated. If, as was likely, neither the Central Powers nor the Entente accepted, Lenin predicted, "we should have to prepare and lead a revolutionary war" and "systematically arouse to insurrection" the socialist proletariat of Europe and the oppressed peoples of Asia, for whom revolution in Russia would provide "unusually favorable conditions."[20]

16. Klara Tsetkin [Clara Zetkin], "Lenin o morali i voprosakh pola," in Razin, ed., p. 17.

17. For Kollontai's assignment to this mission, see USSR, [12], pp. 64, 180, 284.

18. Sadoul, p. 266. Deutscher, *The Prophet Armed*, vol. 1, p. 389, lists the leaders of the antitreaty faction as Bukharin, Dzerzhinskii, Radek, Ioffe, Uritskii, Kollontai, Lomov-Oppokov, Bubnov, Piatakov, Smirnov, and Riazanov.

19. Williams, p. 246, quoting a reporter named Phillips from the *Manchester Guardian*.

20. Lenin, "Neskol'ko tezisov," in *Sochineniia* (4th ed.), vol. 21, pp. 367–68.

In a deeply felt speech on March 7, Kollontai, articulating Lenin's earlier concept, supported Bukharin and the revolutionary war faction. Life itself made the idea of a breathing space an impossibility. The old imperialist war had ended and a new period of civil war had begun, making peace impossible whether or not Russia signed the German terms. Lenin might deny now the need for a revolutionary war, claiming that preservation of the Soviet state was the best service that could be rendered to the European proletariat. Kollontai disagreed, and raised another question: Would signing the annexationist peace terms, conceived in the interests of capitalism, strengthen the solidarity of the international working class, or would the image of Soviet Russia succumbing to imperialism weaken the international revolutionary will?[21] The Bolsheviks probably would not survive in the short run, but as socialists they were ultimately dependent on the European working classes for the long-run struggle with the forces of imperialism, forces that Kollontai frankly acknowledged had grown stronger.

Kollontai announced what they all knew: revolutionary will does not grow stronger in time of peace. For revolution to occur in advanced capitalist countries, the strains of war were essential. Rosa Luxemburg said it earlier, at Stuttgart in 1907. The socialists must utilize times of imperialist war for revolutionary purposes. Kollontai spoke now of Finland, where the civil war she had hoped for a year earlier had finally occurred. If the socialists were successful, the civil war in Finland would spread; but if they were to sign the peace, they would betray the Finnish workers.[22]

Like Bukharin, Iakovleva, and the young Muscovites, Kollontai regarded the Russian Bolsheviks as only one detachment in the international revolution. The moment must be seized not to make a separate peace, of no real value militarily since Russia could not rebuild a conventional army during a so-called breathing space, but to create an international revolutionary army of which Russia would be but one division. She had little faith in the conventional Russian army's ability to fight on, for lack of discipline was too widespread. Nor did she seem to care. She was proud of having contributed to indiscipline. Unlike Lenin and Trotsky, she was opposed to central-

21. Under the Treaty of Brest-Litovsk, Russia lost 27 percent of her sown area, 26 percent of her population, a third of her average crops, three-quarters of her iron and coal, and 26 percent of her railway network. Schapiro, pp. 109–10.
22. For Kollontai's support of the Finnish workers, see USSR, [10], vol. 2, pp. 185–88. For her speech at the Seventh Congress, see USSR, [11], p. 92.

ized control of the military.[23] She pictured revolution in terms not of disciplined armies but of a spirit that would spread across Europe. "And if our Soviet republic is to fail," Kollontai concluded, "others will pick up our banner." The destruction of the Soviet republic would arouse revolution in the West. She had in mind the strikes and civil disorders not only in Finland but in Berlin, Vienna, and Budapest, and the efforts of her old comrades in Germany, Karl Liebknecht and Rosa Luxemburg, to build a new party.[24] The peace issue itself was intensifying the revolutionary movement in the West. The Soviet republic must not give the Berlin government the opportunity to say that peace had been concluded. We are not defending our fatherland, she declared bitterly (an angry rebuttal to Lenin's *Pravda* appeal "The Socialist Fatherland Is in Danger"), we are fighting for a workers' republic.[25] The first round of the decade-long battle in the Bolshevik Party between "Internationalism" and "Socialism in one Country" had begun.

Emotions ran deep on both sides. Lenin's appeal for support of the fatherland was calculated to touch Russian patriotism. His own feelings toward the Revolution were more complex than any sentiment that could be described as nationalism. The Revolution was his only child. Germany was only "just pregnant with revolution," he told the Central Committee, but we have "already given birth to a completely healthy child, a socialist republic that we may kill if we start a war."[26]

In appealing to the notion of world revolution, Kollontai and Iakovleva both seemed to be resorting to rhetoric. Certainly Krupskaia thought so when she wrote that the Left Communists talked themselves into "such ridiculous statements" as that it would be better to let the Soviet power perish than to conclude a shameful peace.[27] But far from being mere rhetoric, Kollontai's speech represented her concept of revolution, her reason for becoming a Bolshevik. The Frenchman Jacques Sadoul, who spent many hours during the winter of 1918 talking with Kollontai, called her the most passionately anti-

23. Sadoul, pp. 96–97.

24. The German Communist Party was founded in Dec. 1918 from the expelled left wing of the Social Democrats.

25. For Lenin's appeal, see *Pravda*, Feb. 22, 1918 (reprinted in Lenin, *Sochineniia* [4th ed.], vol. 27, pp. 13–14). For Kollontai's speech, see USSR, [11], pp. 91–93. For the arguments of the left, see the Central Committee minutes, USSR, [12], pp. 169–71.

26. USSR, [12], p. 168.

27. Krupskaia, *Vospominaniia o Lenine*, p. 361.

militarist of the Bolsheviks.[28] When it came to war and revolution, Kollontai and Lenin still spoke different languages. Revolution for her contained few military images; it was a burst of spontaneity, a banner to be picked up, a means to assure the end of all wars.

In isolating and highlighting the opinions of the women of the left, one runs the risk of making their behavior appear singular. We would do well to remember that in the multifaceted movement that came to be known as the Left Opposition in 1918 Kollontai and Iakovleva were only two members of a sizable radical group, and that their emotional speeches could be multiplied many times.

The intensity of feeling on the left could not keep Lenin from prevailing. The Seventh Party Congress finally yielded to Lenin's practical sense and on March 8 approved the Treaty of Brest-Litovsk. Both Kollontai and Iakovleva were dropped from the Central Committee. Immediately afterwards, in mid-March, the Fourth Congress of Soviets was held. Iakovleva and Kollontai, both of whom continued to oppose the treaty, attended. Kollontai was a member of the Presidium, and she again opposed the peace—again to no avail.[29]

In the face of defeat, both women resigned their positions in the Soviet government—Iakovleva withdrawing as Business Manager of the Supreme Economic Council, and Kollontai leaving the Commissariat of Public Welfare.[30] Kollontai explained to the Council of Commissars on March 18 that she could not continue to be part of the government's new turn toward what she called military politics.

With the ratification of the Treaty of Brest-Litovsk, the oppositionists turned their attention to domestic issues—notably to Lenin's decision, immediately following the Brest-Litovsk crisis, to reevaluate the regime's initial revolutionary economic policies. Workers' control of industry, in particular, threatened to become an illusion. This policy, which had given legal sanction to the factory seizures of 1917, seemed to Kollontai, Iakovleva, and others on the left the essence of revolution, the genuine expression of proletarian spontaneity. But by March 1918, workers' control had increased the economic chaos

28. Sadoul, p. 180.

29. Kollontai, *Izbrannye stat'i i rechi*, p. 423.

30. For Iakovleva's resignation, see *Leninskii Sbornik*, vol. 11, pp. 72–73. For Kollontai's resignation, see her "Avtobiograficheskii ocherk," p. 300. Kollontai gives March 18–19 as the time of her resignation.

caused by four years of war, further crippling Russia's industrial production. Lenin now decided that the government's survival depended on the reestablishment of managerial authority in industry: bourgeois managers and engineers must function as hired specialists; labor discipline must take the place of workers' control; and wage incentives must be restored.[31] Left Communists saw in this a major policy shift with the specter of bureaucratic centralization, supremacy of the Commissars, loss of independence on the part of local Soviets, and a general abandonment of government from below.[32] The pragmatic policies that Lenin labeled "state capitalism" and that strengthened his hopes for revolutionary survival suggested to Kollontai and Iakovleva that counterrevolution was imminent.

Whereas Kollontai and Iakovleva were dropped from the Central Committee during the Seventh Party Congress, Stasova was elevated to full membership, becoming the group's only woman. Bolsheviks in the months after the Revolution had a loose commitment to tokenism; one recalls Trotsky's idea that the Bolsheviks always include a "working girl" among their delegations.[33] A Communist woman, looking back a decade after the Revolution, remembered the early days when one often heard "We should have a woman, too."[34] Obviously, Communists were chiefly elected to the Central Committee because they could do something the Party needed done or because they were important to the *apparat* and too dangerous in opposition to leave out. Yet Party leaders still seemed to feel in 1918 that a token woman was necessary, and that was where Stasova came in. She was chosen mainly for her loyalty to Lenin, Stalin, and Sverdlov, not for her importance; she certainly could not match Kollontai's prominence in the Party (nor for that matter could Iakovleva). Kollontai was a full member of the Central Committee in 1917, when Stasova and Iakovleva were alternates. We saw in the previous chapter that Kollontai was chosen in October by the Central Committee, along with Lenin, Bukharin, Trotsky, Kamenev, and Sokolnikov, to serve

31. For this new course, see Cohen, *Bukharin*, p. 70, and Daniels, pp. 84–87.

32. See "Tezisy 'Levykh Kommunistov' O Tekushchem Momente," in Lenin, *Sochineniia* (3d ed.), vol. 22, pp. 561–71. Kollontai did not fully share the opposition of the Left Communists, led now by Osinskii and Smirnov, to all forms of labor discipline.

33. Sukhanov, *The Russian Revolution*, vol. 2, p. 553.

34. A former Zhenotdel worker, Niurina, cited in Winter, pp. 107–8.

on the commission to draft a new Party program.[35] And she was the only woman chosen for the Presidium of the Second Congress of Soviets, which ratified the new government. If one woman deserved the dubious honor of "token," it was Kollontai.

Their leftist extremism alone did not disqualify Iakovleva or Kollontai, for Bukharin, Krestinskii, Dzerzhinskii, Lomov, and Uritskii were all reelected (Uritskii, however, was demoted to candidate member). But the outspoken men on the left were formidable oppositionists whom it was necessary to placate, and Iakovleva's leftism was not counterbalanced by any such compelling reason to reelect her. If she were excluded, it would hardly be noticed. Situated in Moscow rather than Petrograd, she did not even attend most Central Committee meetings.[36]

Why Kollontai was dropped takes longer to explain. Oddly, just as Iakovleva was no force on the Central Committee, neither was Kollontai. She attended sessions more frequently, but like Stasova and Iakovleva she did not establish herself as a leader. The minutes for the autumn and winter of 1917–18 reveal a different Kollontai, a woman who sat on the sidelines and listened quietly to her male colleagues.[37] This was not the aggressive *Bol'shevichka* who ascended easily to the tribune and swayed crowds. Nor was it the orator who rose at the Seventh Party Congress to attack the treaty. Was there something about the atmosphere of the Central Committee that caused Kollontai to be subdued? Did the self-confident Bolshevik men, accustomed automatically to speaking to each other, signal to her that in the inner sanctum where men matched wits she was not fully a member?[38] Was it perhaps that the topics under discussion, the political situation on the war front and the technicalities of insurrection, were not as familiar to her as the topics that made up the woman question? When Kollontai did speak it was to report on a

35. USSR, [12], p. 76.
36. Two similarly undistinguished male members were reelected, Ia. A. Berzin and F. A. Sergeev, but they were loyal followers of Lenin.
37. Consider the meeting of Jan. 11 (24) on the question of peace. The full range of arguments was presented: Lenin, Trotsky, Bukharin, Uritskii, Lomov, Stalin, Zinoviev, Bubnov, Dzerzhinskii, and Krestinskii were all heard. Stasova and Kollontai were silent. USSR, [12], pp. 167–73.
38. That Kollontai was not quite an insider among Bolsheviks is suggested by Lenin's observation on July 26 (Aug. 8), 1917, that the Kerensky government "continues to arrest Bolsheviks (even Kollontai!)." *Sochineniia* (4th ed.), vol. 25, p. 186. That she joined the Bolsheviks only in 1915 may also have been a factor, though of course Trotsky and others joined even later.

forthcoming women's conference and to propose, with Sverdlov, linking the work among women workers with the Petrograd Committee.[39] Finally, as we shall discuss below, she spent much of her term on a mission abroad. But the fact remains that the Kollontai who sat in the Central Committee was a strangely passive figure.

One might suspect that Kollontai's demeanor reflected male chauvinism, but such an assumption would probably be exaggerated. Some men on the Central Committee may have been indifferent to Kollontai as a political presence, but it will not do as an explanation for her unaccustomed passivity and her subsequent ouster to place the responsibility on outside factors. None of the three women, on the basis of their undistinguished performance within the Central Committee, had made themselves essential to the Party leadership.

At least in Kollontai's case, there was an additional reason for excluding her. Kollontai was a troublemaker who tended to decide policy on her own. The most jarring example of her independence, we recall, occurred in mid-January when she high-handedly decided, as part of her effort to find a home for the war-wounded, to seize the Aleksandr Nevskii monastery. The outcry from the church forced Lenin to do what he had hoped for a while to avoid—decree separation of church and state.

The Central Committee decided at the time of her conflict with the church (January 19) to send Kollontai abroad as its representative in a delegation to establish close ties between Soviet Russia and left internationalists in Europe.[40] Thus it was that she missed the Central Committee discussions on the peace. It is possible that the timing of Kollontai's assignment abroad was fortuitous: she had, after all, been appointed in September as the Party's liaison with foreign countries.[41] More likely, the Central Committee wanted her out of the way for a

39. USSR, [12], pp. 75–76. At a Central Committee meeting on Sept. 20 (Oct. 3), 1917, Kollontai was asked to set up a group to organize channels of communication with foreign countries. She was to present a report about the group at the next session. See USSR, [12], p. 64. There is no record that this report was ever made; instead, at the next session at which Kollontai was present (Oct. 5 [18], 1917), she gave information about the proposed conference of women workers. USSR, [12], pp. 75–76. She spoke once more at the meeting on Oct. 20 (Nov. 2) on the state of affairs among Social Democrats in Finland. Again, this was an area of her own expertise. USSR, [12], p. 108.

40. The delegation was also to make preparations for convening an International Socialist Conference on the subject of the struggle for peace, a Conference that never took place. See USSR, [12], p. 284.

41. According to the Central Committee minutes, Kollontai and Larin were appointed on Sept. 20 (Oct. 3), 1917, to set up a group to organize channels of communication with other countries. See USSR, [12], p. 64, 180.

while. The suggestion incorporated in the original Central Committee notes that the trade union leader David Riazanov, and perhaps Kamenev, be sent along with her implies as much, since Riazanov, a cautious right-winger and a literal Marxist given to democratic scruples, was an inveterate troublemaker, and Kamenev was in disfavor.[42]

Kollontai further undermined her image of reliability in the Central Committee when at the beginning of 1918 she fell in love with Pavel Dybenko. Almost simultaneously the controversy over peace with Germany began, during which Dybenko was arrested on charges of treason. Though it cannot be proved, it seems likely that Kollontai's liaison with Dybenko further damaged her political credibility. Lenin told Clara Zetkin that he "wouldn't bet on the reliability . . . of those women who confuse their personal romances with politics."[43] If Lenin had in mind Kollontai's relationship with Dybenko, she became a victim of the stereotype that presented women as irrational and governed by their emotions.

Another factor, a scarcely conscious disapproval of Kollontai's personal conduct, may also have been involved. As late as the autumn of 1916, Lenin still thought of Kollontai as Shliapnikov's wife.[44] Lenin knew that it was in no way inappropriate to the moral standards of the revolutionary intelligentsia for Kollontai to break her relationship with Shliapnikov and begin living in an unregistered marriage with Dybenko. Still, he found the loosening of marital ties distasteful. Though he viewed the new morality philosophically, and would have denied having middle-class values, Lenin was personally a traditional bourgeois. He may have found awkward the presence of Kollontai and her lovers, past and present, on the Council of Commissars. Shliapnikov, moreover, had long been one of his most trusted lieutenants, whereas Dybenko was proving to be an irresponsible young man. In Lenin's eyes, Kollontai's stature may have diminished as a result of her intimacy with Dybenko.

42. The suggestion was not carried out. See USSR, [12], p. 180. The minutes of the Central Committee meetings in 1917 are peppered with rebukes to Riazanov for speaking without authority to do so and for behavior deemed unacceptable for a Party member, such as criticizing Party policies at trade union meetings. Riazanov was a former Menshevik, and he was charged at one point with offending the sensibilities of the revolutionary proletariat by publicly referring to a Menshevik as "comrade"! Kamenev was also a member of the right wing, and he and Riazanov had opposed the Bolshevik seizure of power in October as premature and led the opposition to the idea of an all-Bolshevik government.
43. Lenin to Zetkin, cited in "Lenin o morali i voprosakh pola," in Razin, ed., p. 20.
44. Lenin, *Sochineniia* (4th ed.), vol. 35, pp. 185, 497.

At this point, it is necessary to digress and consider the circumstances of Dybenko's arrest. The Frenchman Jacques Sadoul has given us a vivid account. He met Kollontai outside the Hotel National in Moscow on the morning of March 18, 1918, as she was buying fruit from a vendor. Her appearance shocked him. Exhausted and distressed, she seemed to have aged ten years. She explained that the fruit was for her husband, arrested on the most serious charge—treason.[45] Kollontai regarded the overt charge against him, treason for having surrendered Narva to the Germans, as meaningless. As they hurried across the street to the Kremlin, where Dybenko was being held, Kollontai explained that he had really been arrested as a reprisal by Lenin against a comrade who had dared to oppose the separate peace with Germany. The move was an effort to terrorize those Bolsheviks who might be inclined to engage in further opposition to the government's decision. Lenin, knowing Dybenko's energy and lack of discipline, feared that he might head south and lead his forces against the German army, breaking the peace terms. Worse, the Party suspected on the basis of rumors that Dybenko contemplated an overthrow of the government. Kollontai was especially alarmed because Dybenko's faithful sailors had sent an ultimatum to Lenin and Trotsky demanding their leader's release in 48 hours. She feared that the government might choose to execute Dybenko immediately without trial.[46] Even given such mitigating circumstances as Kollontai's anxiety over the possible execution of her husband, the tenor of her remarks was startling. Although she had just resigned from her position as Commissar in protest against government policy, Kollontai was still a member of the Party.[47] If Sadoul's account is accurate, then she presented to an outsider the bitter image of a Soviet leadership so panicky over prospects of internal revolt that it might summarily execute one of its own leaders.

Within the Party Kollontai's defense of Dybenko against charges of treason was assumed to be the result of her determination to save her lover rather than of her belief that he was innocent of the charges against him (however guilty he may have been otherwise of harboring hostile thoughts and half-formed plans to move against the government). By extension, her entire stance against the peace could be

45. Sadoul, p. 270. The government had by this time moved from Petrograd to Moscow, and the Fourth Congress of Soviets was under way.

46. *Ibid.*, pp. 270–71.

47. *Ibid.* Sadoul indicates that Kollontai had resigned as Commissar.

denigrated in retrospect as little more than support of Dybenko's own radical opposition to the treaty.

The view of Kollontai not as acting reasonably—reason being a male attribute—but as carried away by "female passion" is supported by the number of anecdotes that revolved around her love affair with Dybenko and her defense of him in 1918. One, which circulated around Moscow for several years, described Kollontai as irresponsibly deserting the government and fleeing with Dybenko to the Crimea after his temporary release into her custody in April 1918.[48] Another exploited Lenin's supposed "sentence" that the most appropriate punishment for the couple would be to have to remain faithful to each other for five years. In a letter to Paris, Sadoul described "poor Kollontai" as behaving foolishly, carried away by her love for Dybenko.[49] Dybenko, who was perceived as undisciplined and daring, was imprisoned as a threat to the government. No one regarded his sexual relationship with Kollontai as relevant to *his* conduct. Eventually he resumed his military command where he was needed. But Kollontai was considered lovesick. It is worth recalling Kollontai's own assessment that "not a single one of the men who were close to me has ever had a direction-giving influence on my inclinations. . . . On the contrary, most of the time I was the guiding spirit."[50]

Lenin's suspicion that Kollontai was no longer dependable may explain his failure to include her in his comments late in March concerning the Left Communists:

Since the conclusion of the Brest peace, some comrades who call themselves "Left Communists" have formed an "Opposition" in the Party, and in consequence of this their activity is slipping further and further toward a completely disloyal and impermissible violation of Party discipline.

Comrade Bukharin has refused to accept the post of member of the Central Committee to which he was appointed by the Party Congress.

Comrades Smirnov, Obolenskii, and Iakovleva have resigned from their posts as People's Commissars and as Business Manager of the Supreme Economic Council. These are absolutely disloyal, uncomradely actions that violate party discipline, and such behavior was and remains a *step toward a split* on the part of the above-mentioned comrades.[51]

48. Hauge, p. 42. Sadoul noted a press account that Kollontai had left Moscow for the Crimea with Dybenko. Sadoul had seen her three days earlier and expected to find her in Petrograd, where she told him she was going. Sadoul, p. 315.

49. Sadoul, p. 316.

50. Kollontai, *Autobiography*, p. 13.

51. *Leninskii Sbornik*, vol. 11, pp. 72–73.

Lenin wanted the Left Communists to resume their posts. Everyone, that is, but Kollontai.

A disheartened Kollontai nevertheless continued in the spring of 1918 to participate in Party activity, but whereas other Left Communists drifted back to the ranks before summer—Bukharin resumed his position on the Central Committee in May or June—she remained without a post.[52] Whether she was hoping to be asked to serve is not clear. Perhaps it no longer mattered. She opposed not only economic centralization but also the mood of the government in its militaristic harshness. She criticized the "militarism" visited upon the left—e.g. the brutal reprisals against the anarchists. When seen in the light of the "betrayal" of international socialism and the demise of workers' control, it reinforced Kollontai's fear that the end of the Revolution was near.[53]

We have seen several reasons why Kollontai was dropped from the Central Committee. In the summer of 1917 she had been a revolutionary idealist, an imprisoned agitator and brilliant orator. Less than a year later she was an oppositionist and clearly not a practical politician, easily dismissed as an unstable, emotional woman. Her idealism had embarrassed the government when she was Commissar, and her private life made some members of the leadership uncomfortable. Her performance on the Central Committee had been undistinguished. Not useful to the *apparat*, she was dropped. In 1918 the dutiful Stasova was a more congenial token than the maverick Kollontai.

❧❧❧❧

The Bolshevik government did not fall: instead the war came to an end. The peace of Brest-Litovsk ceased to be significant internationally with the defeat of Germany later in 1918. But for the women of the 1917 Central Committee, their behavior in the winter and spring of 1918 continued to affect their lives. Kollontai's career will be the subject of the remaining chapters. Here, I want briefly to consider the impact of the Brest-Litovsk crisis on the future careers of the other two women on the Central Committee. Elena Stasova, although in no way a formidable Communist, found her position solidified as a result of her loyalty to Lenin in March 1918. Stasova could

52. For evidence of her participation in Party work, see Lenin's notes on the Moscow All-City Party Conference, May 13, 1918, *Leninskii Sbornik*, vol. 11, p. 88.
53. See Kollontai to Sadoul, Apr. 17, 1918, cited in Sadoul, p. 316.

not be stereotyped as unstable and emotional. Nor did she irritate Party leaders by political extremism or overt opposition. It was easy to be patronizing toward Stasova, who was invariably appreciative. In short, she epitomized the token organization woman, a careful worker who loyally followed the wisdom of the male establishment. Paradoxically, because she made little contribution to the Central Committee, she was allowed to serve only briefly: elected once more at the Eighth Party Congress, she was dropped in 1920. Whatever her personal reservations, Elena Stasova continued to work faithfully in the Secretariat after Sverdlov's death in 1919 and Stalin's rise to control, no doubt attracted by the core of pragmatic power that Stalin represented. Her position in the Party remained as safe as it was undistinguished. Ultimately she would be edged into obscurity.

At least in the early years after Brest-Litovsk, Varvara Iakovleva did not suffer. After her exclusion from the Central Committee, Iakovleva's life followed a common pattern for Party members of the second rank. According to a friend, she ultimately came to regard her opposition to the Brest-Litovsk peace as an error, frankly admitting her mistaken judgment.[54] Throughout the 1920's Iakovleva worked as Deputy Commissar of Education, until she resigned in 1929 over disagreements on internal issues. Her resignation was accepted, and she was appointed Commissar of Finance of the RSFSR in the autumn of that year. Beginning in 1925 she made a brief return to opposition with her second husband, the Trotskyist I. N. Smirnov, but she separated both from Smirnov and from the Opposition in 1927. She remained as Commissar of Finance in the RSFSR from 1929 until 1937. That year she was arrested. Nearly twenty years afterwards, the issue of Brest-Litovsk returned to shatter her life. At Bukharin's trial in 1938, the most famous of the purge trials, the prosecution chose Iakovleva to bear witness against her old friend.

Earlier, in 1923, when the Party's perennial factionalism surfaced, the peace with Germany had been briefly revived as an issue. Bukharin found himself supporting Stalin, Zinoviev, and Kamenev in their struggle to keep Trotsky from the power they imagined he was plotting to seize. At that time, Bukharin candidly but unwisely reminded a workers' meeting in Moscow of the events of 1918. Pointing

54. Vinogradskaia, *Sobytiia i pamiatnye vstrechi*, p. 136. During the Civil War, Iakovleva organized working women in Moscow, earning Lenin's praise in a speech to the Fourth Moscow City Conference of nonparty working women on Sept. 23, 1919. Lenin, *Sochineniia* (4th ed.), vol. 30, p. 22.

out the dangers of Party factionalism that Lenin had been unable to end by his decree at the Tenth Party Congress in 1921, Bukharin recalled that factionalism was eagerly exploited by the enemies of Bolshevism. He disclosed that in 1918 at the time of Brest-Litovsk the Left SRs, trying to take advantage of the split in the Party, boldly approached the Left Communists with a plan to arrest Lenin and effect a change in government. Few political leaders have ever made a more unfortunate revelation. As someone commented of Bukharin, he was not a reserved man.

A group of former Left Communists, disturbed that Stalin and Zinoviev both seized on Bukharin's admission to attack in *Pravda* those Oppositionists in 1923 who had been members of the left in 1918, rushed to defend themselves. Iakovleva was among those (including Piatakov, Radek, and Preobrazhenskii) who protested in a letter to the editor that Bukharin was making too much of the episode with the SRs.[55] As they recalled, Piatakov and Bukharin had been approached in the lobby of the Party headquarters in Smolny by a Left SR leader who half-jokingly asked what the majority would do without Lenin. In March 1918 those who opposed Brest-Litovsk appeared to have a majority in the Central Committee, and Lenin had threatened to resign if the vote went against him. The treaty had been approved only because some of its opponents, including Trotsky, abstained from voting. It was at this point that the Left SRs had made their approach, suggesting a Bolshevik-SR coalition government under Piatakov. Piatakov and the others claimed in *Pravda* that Bukharin at the time had taken the episode as something of a joke. Bukharin replied in the same issue of *Pravda*. Why make light of the matter?, he asked, trying to demonstrate the dangers of factionalism. "This was a period when the Party was a hair's breadth from a split, and the whole country was on the verge of catastrophe."[56]

At Bukharin's trial, Prosecutor Vyshinskii insisted that the talks between the Left Communists and the Left SRs in 1918 had resulted not only in an agreement to overthrow the regime but also in a plot to arrest and kill those Bolshevik leaders who favored the peace—Lenin, Stalin, and Sverdlov. Varvara Iakovleva was among the former Left Communists called to testify against Bukharin.

55. Letter of Jan. 3, 1924, *Pravda*, p. 5.
56. Bukharin's reply, Jan. 3, 1924, *Pravda*, p. 5. The two letters appear under "Pis'ma v redaktsiiu."

Prosecutor Vyshinskii demanded of Iakovleva over and over in various contexts to repeat her charges.

V: What was the role of Bukharin in this affair?

Iakovleva: I have stated that Bukharin himself proposed that these negotiations (with the Left SRs) be conducted, and that he conducted them in conjunction with Piatakov.

V: That is, his role was a perfectly practical one, as a leader of this conspiracy?

Iakovleva: Yes.

V: You confirm to the Court that Bukharin also told you that the assassination of Lenin, as the head of the Soviet state, and Stalin and Sverdlov, as leaders of the Party and the government, was politically expedient and necessary.

Iakovleva: Bukharin spoke about that. Of course, he spoke of it cursorily, veiling it in a number of vague and unnecessary theoretical arguments, as Bukharin likes to do generally. He wrapped up this idea like a cocoon in a host of lengthy explanations, but he said it.

The President of the Court asked Bukharin if he had any questions to put to Iakovleva. Though he admitted guilt on certain political charges, Bukharin denied he had ever been involved in a supposed criminal plot to murder Lenin, Stalin, and Sverdlov. He tried to get Iakovleva to acknowledge that there had been no secret conspiracy in 1918, and that Party leaders with impeccable credentials—Kuibyshev, Iaroslavskii, and Menzhinskii—had also been Left Communists who opposed the peace, but Vyshinskii prevented him from pursuing that line of approach. Since Bukharin was the star of the Purge trials, Vyshinskii would not risk an error in the performance involving his most important victim. Iakovleva was thoroughly drilled and told a bizarre story in which the public opposition of the Left Communists in 1918 became a secret conspiracy and murder plot under Bukharin's leadership.[57]

Invariably the question occurs: How could Iakovleva falsely denounce her old friend? Do we not have assurances from Kollontai and others who knew her that Iakovleva was honest and indomitable, a brave fighter whose spirit seemed never to falter?[58] Iakovleva had a young child who had already been traumatized by the terrors of arrest. In 1936 the child's father, Iakovleva's former husband Smirnov, had been arrested and shot as a Trotskyist leader. In all likelihood

57. For Iakovleva's testimony, see Tucker and Cohen, eds., pp. 404–12.
58. Vinogradskaia, *Sobytiia i pamiatnye vstrechi*, p. 135.

Iakovleva falsely accused Bukharin to save her child's life and, perhaps, her own. Even if there had been no hostage she might have been unable to withstand the torture. She had been arrested and sent into exile in tsarist times, but in retrospect that was a relatively easy experience from which she was able to escape to the West. Although Solzhenitsyn withholds sympathy from the prominent Bolsheviks on trial after 1936, he is empathetic toward others who lied: "Do not condemn those who, finding themselves in such a situation, turned out to be weak."[59]

Iakovleva's testimony did not save her. She made a special request to her cellmates before she was shot: let them pass the word if they should ever escape that her depositions were lies that the investigators wrote and forced her to sign.[60]

Stasova was never arrested in the purges, even though she was a close friend of others condemned as enemies and her name appeared in their testimony. Like other Old Bolsheviks who escaped death, she was demoted, reflecting Stalin's dislike of the female *intelligentka* and his suspicion of Old Bolsheviks. She was isolated from the Party center but was allowed to live. In Medvedev's view, Stasova was one of those old friends of Lenin whom Stalin regarded as useful to him. Already in her sixties during the purge trials, she was one of Stalin's direct lines to the Leninist past. There had to be some Old Bolsheviks around to show continuity between the two eras, people who would be available to praise Stalin at command and call him the true Leninist.[61] Not until a few years before her death at age 96 did Stasova publicly defend Bukharin against the fantastic charges concerning Brest-Litovsk that Iakovleva had been forced to recite. After taking part in the denunciation of Stalin at the Twenty-second Party Congress, Stasova, almost on the eve of her death, was one of four Old Bolsheviks who wrote a letter requesting that the verdict of traitor against Bukharin be annulled, that his name be rehabilitated, and his honored place in the Party be restored.[62] Their appeal went unanswered.

As for Kollontai, her opposition to the Treaty of Brest-Litovsk affected her life not years later but at once. In Kollontai's case, her

59. Aleksandr I. Solzhenitsyn, *The Gulag Archipelago*, trans. Thomas P. Whitney (New York, 1973), vol. 1, p. 117.
60. Medvedev, p. 181. Robert Conquest reported that Iakovleva survived until 1944. See Conquest, *The Great Terror*, p. 400.
61. Medvedev, p. 308.
62. *Ibid.*, p. 185.

political future had already become clouded by March 1918. One historian has commented that 1917 was looked back upon as "the touchstone" in a Bolshevik's political career, the time when one's activity "forever enhanced or diminished" one's authority in the Party.[63] So Kollontai thought. She liked to recall that she had been closer to Lenin in 1917 than many of his older followers, and that she had been the only one of his comrades to take the floor in support of his April Theses.[64] It was another of her illusions to believe that this comradeship would continue and ensure her status in the Party. The objectionable aspects of her conduct during the first revolutionary year outweighed her earlier loyalty.

To Kollontai, her irreconcilable position on the left during the spring of 1918 seemed the reason for her political exclusion, for the onset of what she called "a dark time of my life." There were differences of opinion in the Party. "I resigned from my post as People's Commissar on the ground of total disagreement with the current policy. Little by little I was also relieved of all my other tasks. . . . The struggle was becoming increasingly irreconcilable and bloodier, much of what was happening did not fit in with my outlook."[65] She mistakenly assumed that the decision to exclude her was ideological. But as we have seen, Kollontai's role in the opposition was but one factor in her fall. Anecdotes and innuendos prompted by her "passion" cast doubt on her reliability. Kollontai's career would go through many changes in the years to come, but the events of 1918 influenced it, much as they influenced the careers of Stasova and Iakovleva.

The crisis of Brest-Litovsk, although it nearly tore the Party apart in 1918 and would be used to destroy lives twenty years later, did not at first create permanent enmities. Despite Kollontai's espousal of Left Communism, she maintained warm feelings for supporters of the treaty like Sverdlov and Stasova. Stasova did not join Kollontai during subsequent Party conflicts, but they remained close. Iakovleva, on the same side with Kollontai in 1918, did not join her in 1921 during the Workers' Opposition movement.[66] But her stance during

---

63. Cohen, *Bukharin*, p. 52.
64. Kollontai, *Autobiography*, p. 31.
65. *Ibid.*, p. 40. These remarks appear in the galleys of her *Autobiography* and were largely deleted in the published version.
66. Iakovleva sided with Trotsky and Bukharin, signing the Bukharin platform in Jan. 1921. See Lenin, *Sochineniia* (4th ed.), vol. 32, p. 28.

that conflict did not destroy Kollontai's warm respect for her.[67] Kollontai's friendships indicate that the web of loyalties that bound her to other Bolsheviks was determined more by personal feeling than by ideological affinity.

This is not to suggest that the small number of women prominent in the Party formed a warm and closely knit inner group of their own. Kollontai remained close to Iakovleva and to Stasova, but she feuded bitterly during the 1920's with others. Although Stasova and Iakovleva were involved in the socialist women's movement, it was for neither the core of her existence as a Communist. Perhaps their relative emotional distance from Kollontai's primary area of concern allowed their harmonious relationship, based in part on nostalgia for 1917, to continue.

The fight over Brest-Litovsk did not permanently alienate Bolsheviks from one another (although subsequent lines of cleavage followed closely those of 1917–18), largely because the experience of Civil War followed so quickly and served to reunite them. What other course of events could have created the series of compromises between Lenin and the Left Communists—in retrospect known as War Communism—that restored the revolutionary confidence of the Left and revived, if only temporarily, their illusion of progress toward socialism?

We have in this chapter concluded our examination of what Kollontai, in retrospect, would call the "magnificent illusions" of the first months of the Revolution. Some of those illusions had been badly shattered. Kollontai no longer believed that she would remain one of Lenin's close comrades. Moreover, the greatest illusion of all, that revolutionary internationalism, not national self-interest, was Bolshevism's highest goal, had not survived. We have accompanied Kollontai to the point where like many others she began to lose some of her faith in the rightness of Bolshevik decisions. But the Civil War renewed her spirit. How she responded to the crisis will be the subject of the next chapter.

67. Kollontai, "Zhenshchiny-bortsy v dni Velikogo Oktiabria," in *Izbrannye stat'i i rechi*, p. 373.

CHAPTER FIVE

Kollontai, Communism,
and the Family

AFTER the fight over ratification of the Treaty of Brest-Litovsk, Kollontai withdrew from overt opposition. The left, as we have seen, moved on to a new, ideological battlefront, protesting Lenin's modification of initial Bolshevik economic policies.[1] These early policies, which involved selective nationalization and sanctioned the workers' seizure of factories in 1917, had compounded the misery of four years of war and resulted in economic chaos. Lenin responded to this situation in April 1918 with a plan to use the skills of the capitalists. For just as Lenin had insisted that he must make peace with the German imperialists, now he concluded that internally he needed the cooperation and technical knowledge of bourgeois managers, centralized control over local soviets, and labor discipline to replace workers' control.[2] Lenin called his projected mixed economy in which limited state ownership would coexist with private management "state capitalism." Although the left opposed it, Lenin pictured it as a step forward because it would be centralized, calculated, controlled, and socialized.[3]

Kollontai protested privately against Lenin's "concessions" to the bourgeoisie.[4] If she did not become a leading member of the wave of opposition against state capitalism, it was because she was depressed and disheartened over the devastating loss of her positions on the Central Committee and the Council of Commissars and the downward turn of the Revolution. She was further drained by the effort of directing Dybenko's legal defense. In March, Kollontai feared that

---

1. For the left's position, see "Tezisy o tekushchem' momente" in *Kommunist'*, Apr. 1918, no. 1, pp. 4–9, which appeared as the joint statement of the editorial board. Kollontai was not a contributor to that first issue. Although she took no active role, she was listed on the masthead of subsequent issues.

2. Other initial Bolshevik policies included attempts to eliminate inequities in housing, establish an eight-hour work day, and end private landholding (although the peasant's right to work his new holding was affirmed). See Cohen, *Bukharin*, pp. 69–71.

3. Cohen, *Bukharin*, p. 70.

4. See Sadoul, p. 316.

Dybenko would be executed; in May, he was tried on charges of high treason and acquitted. But Kollontai could not prevent his expulsion from the Party.

The summer of 1918 brought the onset of the Civil War and foreign military intervention. The controversy over economic policies and the Left Opposition abruptly ended. With the outbreak of Civil War, which would last for three years, the Left Communists disbanded, the bases for their opposition having largely evaporated as new wartime policies took the place of state capitalism. Kollontai's own course in response to the Civil War, as well as that of others on the left, demonstrated the truth of her warning to the Seventh Party Congress that revolutionary will was strengthened in a time of struggle. One by one the leftists, Kollontai among them, closed ranks with the rest of the Party. The Civil War made her invaluable again as an orator. Kollontai returned not to a high government post in Moscow, but to the sphere of Party activity that in fact she had never wholly abandoned—revolutionary agitation.[5] Lenin knew the importance of accepting returning comrades without causing them to lose face. He warmly welcomed Kollontai back in October to "more active Party work," even agreeing that it was time to revoke Dybenko's expulsion. He promised to speak with Sverdlov about reinstatement.[6]

During the Civil War the Bolsheviks aspired to transform Russia, forcibly and hastily, into a War Communist society marked by requisition in the countryside and rationing in the towns.[7] The radicalism of this period may best be characterized not as a concession to the pressures of the left but as a response to peril. For example, the government resolved to nationalize every important category of industry in late June partly out of fear that large enterprises in occupied territories would be transferred to German ownership. The requisition

5. Her assignment in the spring and summer of 1918 was revolutionary agitation in Povolzh'e, an area that included Simbirsk, Kazan, Astrakhan, Tsaritsyn, Nizhni-Novgorod, and Saratov. For Kollontai in Povolzh'e, see Itkina, pp. 179–80, and Kollontai, *Izbrannye stat'i i rechi*, p. 423. She also managed to participate in Party activities in Moscow. See *Leninskii Sbornik*, vol. 11, p. 88. In the autumn of 1918, Kollontai was sent along with other women agitators into the textile areas north of Moscow. See *Izbrannye stat'i i rechi*, p. 423.

6. Lenin to Kollontai, Oct. 18, 1918, in *Polnoe sobranie sochinenii*, vol. 50, pp. 196–97. In October, Dybenko received a high army command in the Ukraine. He served there, in the Crimea, and on other southern fronts until the end of the Civil War. Dybenko had been arrested during the summer of 1918 in Sevastopol by the government of General Sulkevich and imprisoned until the end of September. See "P. E. Dybenko" in *Deiateli SSSR i Oktiabr'skoi Revoliutsii*, vol. 41, col. 132.

7. On the problems of this period, especially the black market, see Kritsman, pp. 116–19.

of grain and the promotion of class strife in the countryside originated in the hunger of the cities.[8]

Though it would be a distortion to imply that the Communists came to power with well-thought-out economic plans and programs, one risks another kind of error in presenting the regime's policies merely as *ad hoc* responses to emergency situations. For in doing so, we lose sight of Bolsheviks on the far left like Kollontai. For her, the policies of War Communism seemed appropriate to a society attempting to use the needs generated by war and revolution to change the lives of its people, especially women. Kollontai's concept of a radical bond between war and revolution was not new: history-conscious Marxists remembered that during the French Revolution the European war begun in 1792 against the opposition of Robespierre and sincere French democrats had by 1794 become essential to the fulfillment of the Revolution's radical program. Peace, with its relaxation of tensions, threatened to destroy "the narrow pathway to a democratic and moral world."[9] History, these Marxists knew, was full of ironic situations—and here surely was one repeating itself. Kollontai, the most antiwar and pacifist of the Bolsheviks, was finding, like the French revolutionaries before her, that war was a boon to her radical goals.

As Commissar of Public Welfare in 1917, Kollontai had regretted that she could accomplish little in the way of social reconstruction in poverty-stricken Russia. The Civil War enabled her to try out her ideas. There would be extreme centralization of industrial administration in the hands of the state, a state monopoly over labor, state-controlled administration of goods, and organized barter in place of commerce. As a result of state control, she anticipated that the children in the cities would be fed, and that the wounded, the elderly, and the foundlings would be cared for. In sum, the Soviet state would become socialist. Trotsky's unfriendly jibe of an earlier period, that nothing was too revolutionary for Kollontai, was equally apt in the era of War Communism.[10]

Because of her impatience for social change, Kollontai proved to be ambivalent rather than opposed (as were others on the left) to

8. For this view, see Cohen, *Bukharin*, p. 78. For War Communism, see Carr, *The Bolshevik Revolution*, vol. 2, pp. 151–268.

9. R. Palmer, *Twelve Who Ruled* (Princeton, N. J., 1941), pp. 277–78.

10. See Kollontai, *Polozhenie zhenshchiny*, pp. 151–52, 166, for her praise of War Communism and her long-range hopes for the disappearance of money and the introduction of labor conscription.

the greater authoritarianism that accompanied War Communism. Though within two years she would be leading the Workers' Opposition against the bureaucratic rigidity and militaristic spirit that by then had become part of government centralization, in the autumn of 1918 she rejoiced in the chance to use the crises of Revolution and Civil War to hasten a revolution within the family.

۞۞۞

It is important to understand Kollontai's concern that the Bolsheviks use power humanely. Although historians have implied that Kollontai's sympathies were limited to members of the Communist Party,[11] such an assumption, as we will see, is unwarranted. It was true that Kollontai had no wish to disturb the monopoly of Communist power, yet she constituted herself a spokeswoman for softer values and tried to impart to a less emotionally governed, tougher leadership her own compassion. Consider her article in *Pravda* at the beginning of October.[12] In an attempt to move those Bolsheviks who wanted to refuse aid to mothers of the former bourgeois classes, Kollontai described the women who had come to her Commissariat of Public Welfare begging for help for their children. They were from all groups—young soldiers' wives, women of the former landlord class, teachers, members of the intelligentsia—but they had in common their hungry children. Some of the women had been driven from their homes and had been forced to sell their last possessions to buy milk or to pay doctors' bills. These women may never in the past have been concerned with the unemployed mothers of the proletariat or their hungry children, but Kollontai rejected a vindictive policy toward them. Who would be punished but the children? However great the sins of the mothers, the Communists could not deny them aid. As a Communist, it was not appropriate for Kollontai to provide ethical reasons for her proposed network of public kitchens to feed the children and thereby aid the mothers. It was more politic to explain the disaster that might result if Communists were to permit women with children to cry for bread in the streets of Moscow. These mothers, ready to support any power that would feed their children, might become a force for counterrevolution. That she stressed Communist self-interest in smashing, by means of public feeding, what she

11. E.g. Schapiro, p. 294.
12. *Izbrannye stat'i i rechi*, p. 237, reprinted from *Pravda*, no. 210 (Oct. 1, 1918).

called the class foundations of the narrow, bourgeois family, did not negate her generosity.[13]

Kollontai's sentiments convinced some of the most bitter anti-Communists of her humanity. Thus one Russian feminist who opposed the Bolsheviks and condemned the women who became Bolshevik commissars, judges, and members of the *Cheka* for using power when they had it with the utmost cruelty exempted Kollontai: "Among those who are Communists by conviction there are others who must not be overlooked, educated and cultured women whose hands are clean from the blood shed in the time of Terror. The most prominent of these is Aleksandra M. Kollontai."[14]

Feminists in Russia, including those who were her enemies earlier, might welcome Kollontai's compassion, but they did not endorse socialism's vision of a revolution that included government responsibility for mothers and children. As for the Communists in 1918, in a country weighted down by hunger and war, the socialization of motherhood was largely an ideal to put off for the Communist future. Kollontai was not alone in regretting the still timid and small-scale government effort to aid mothers, but her interpretation of its cause was unique. Unlike other Bolsheviks, she blamed neither the war, nor the blockade, nor foreign intervention; instead she blamed the Communists themselves, particularly the women, whom she chastized as sluggish and inert.[15] The women in the Party were behaving not like Communist builders of a new world, but like traditional, passive women—delaying the practical, simple measures; failing to spark the spontaneity of proletarian mothers; and doing little about constructing maternity homes, nurseries, children's colonies and homes, and a broad network of children's kitchens. Communist women, accustomed to taking orders, were still waiting for someone to build for

13. *Ibid.*, pp. 239–40.
14. Selivanova, p. 20. When she wrote of the cruelty of Bolshevik women, Selivanova may have had in mind R. S. Zemliachka, a member of the 1904 Central Committee. Conquest (p. 80) describes her as a "brutal terrorist," Béla Kun's colleague in the slaughter in the Crimea in 1920, to which Lenin objected. For Kollontai's humanity, see Lenin, *Polnoe sobranie sochinenii*, vol. 51, pp. 85–86, for references to Kollontai's appeals on behalf of prisoners, and Itkina, p. 200, for Kollontai's interceding with Lenin on behalf of peasant women arrested during the suppression of the Antonov mutiny. A. S. Antonov, a former SR, led an anti-Bolshevik uprising during 1920–21 in the black earth region of Tambov. See Oliver H. Radkey, *The Unknown Civil War in Soviet Russia: A Study of the Green Movement in the Tambov Region 1920–1921* (Stanford, Calif., 1976).
15. Kollontai, *Izbrannye stat'i i rechi*, p. 240.

them. Trying to inspire her comrades by her own audacity, Kollontai used the pages of *Pravda* to exhort them to devise plans for aiding indigent mothers and children.[16]

Here was a brilliant and innovative idea, one of her brightest contributions to Bolshevism. Kollontai's program for social reorganization contained little that was original; rather, it was her call to Bolshevik women to respond to the challenge of revolution and war, to alter their sense of themselves as followers, and to lead in women's reorganization of the family that held the greater novelty. For its corollary was historically unique—that the social revolution in Russia would be a female undertaking carried out by Russian mothers, and led by the few Communist women in the Party.

Kollontai saw the question of nurturing as primarily a female concern, an idea that many modern proponents of women's equality tend to resist. Her explanation for her traditional perception of women's role was frank and very simple. Building the new socialist life was women's sphere by default, because daily life (*byt*) most affected them. They were the ones left at home to care for the children. They were the ones who had to keep them warm, often with no fuel; to feed them, sometimes with next to no food; to carry back-breaking loads of wood and water up long flights of stairs.[17] Yet more was involved. Kollontai's idealized view of the female character was also very Russian. Her woman was the resilient figure made familiar by nineteenth-century literature. Traditionally she was strong. Most of all she understood, from years of deprivation, how to create with her own hands "something from nothing."[18] The role of creating was always the woman's. Hope for the social revolution therefore rested with her. The men, workers and peasants both, occupied with the Red Front, the struggle with counterrevolution, and the need to change the system of economic production and build the apparatus of Soviet government, were not really interested in a new and revolutionary way of life. They could not be expected to set up dining rooms, communal houses, maternity homes, and institutions for the social upbringing of children.[19] Kollontai was not bitter or strident. She was matter-of-fact.

16. *Ibid.*

17. Smith, p. 147.

18. Kollontai, "Proizvodstvo i byt," p. 7. For this view of Russian women see also Dunham.

19. Kollontai, "Kak my sozvali pervyi vserossiiskii s"ezd rabotnits i krest'ianok," pp. 4–5.

She was also in a hurry. If Kollontai in October 1918 was no longer the brash commissar who without consulting others ordered the seizure of the Aleksandr Nevskii monastery, she was still among the most impatient of the Bolshevik leaders, especially with those Communists who did not share her sense of urgency. Though historians have marveled at the headlong rush toward socialism that marked the era of War Communism, Kollontai, in *Pravda*, condemned the pace as too slow. Female Communists were timid in launching social institutions, and male Communists were temporizing in appropriating to the state the private resources of the old order that would make social reconstruction possible. This latter theme dominated another article in October dealing with a different family question, the problem of the elderly.

Disposing of the myth that the family lovingly took care of its aged parents, deploring the reality of grudging support from sons and daughters, Kollontai called on the Communists to provide the elderly with homes and pensions. She described a plan to make old age a time of contentment rather than a "curse of poverty, loneliness, and idleness." Her enthusiasm for institutional care may sound naive today, in light of the growing disenchantment with the often dismal results of institutional solutions in modern industrial societies, but she could not anticipate in 1918 that institutions, whether children's homes, hospitals, or homes for the aged, might themselves grow prosperous and spawn their own professional bureaucracies while their pathetic inhabitants remained neglected. Kollontai saw simply that the aged were too often unwelcome among relatives. Thus she advocated communal homes whose inhabitants would live in dignity, making the daily decisions and running their homes by themselves. The need was urgent; the time for discussion had passed. Kollontai rejected the argument that revolutionary Russia lacked the facilities and personnel. She knew how to find them even during the Civil War. The well-built monasteries, the "black nests," should immediately be taken over by the state to become rest homes and sanitariums for the war-wounded and the elderly, and refuges for mothers and children.[20] Located outside the city, surrounded by meadows with kitchen gardens to provide vegetables and cows to supply milk for the sick and the young, they were ready-made sanitariums, fully equipped with beds, linens, utensils, and even separate "cells" for the very ill.

20. Kollontai, *Izbrannye stat'i i rechi*, pp. 243–45, reprinted from *Vechernie Izvestiia*, Oct. 30, 1918.

She sounded the Communist slogan: "He who does not work does not eat." And she asked if there was anyone who did not know that the monasteries were nests of parasites. Church property had already been nationalized. It was time to order the monks and the nuns to work.[21] She warned the Council of Commissars not to waste precious time mulling over the details. The forces of counterrevolution would benefit if the strength of the proletariat were not restored in rest homes.

Kollontai's provocative article in *Pravda* plunged her into the controversy she had initiated in January 1918 over the fate of the church in revolutionary Russia. Kollontai was consistently radical, demanding statewide implementation of revolutionary social goals. The occasional onslaught against the church, varying from place to place, and the sporadic local decisions to take over churches for secular use dismayed her as less than revolutionary.[22] We Communists, she charged in *Pravda*, however much we think we are campaigning against religious influence, are not doing enough.[23] She counted on the positive impact the Party could make among the masses to counteract the negative propaganda of the church. If people saw that churches and religious objects were respected, that priests were not being harmed, and that the immense church properties were being distributed to the peasants, they could be relied on to ignore the enraged priests' exhortations against Soviet power. Indeed, Kollontai's humanitarian call for social use of the monasteries does not seem in retrospect significantly more drastic than the selling of gold and silver religious objects undertaken in 1922 to raise money abroad for famine relief, a measure that was similarly resisted by the clergy.[24]

❧❧❧

Kollontai's blueprint for a social restructuring of the family, which appeared piecemeal in *Pravda* in the autumn of 1918, required not

---

21. *Ibid.*, pp. 248–49, reprinted from *Pravda*, Nov. 10, 1918.

22. See Carr, *Socialism in One Country*, vol. 1, pp. 49–50, on the sporadic nature of action against the church. Carr writes that in the chaos of the first weeks of revolution, the Bolsheviks had little time for consistent planning and action. Almost every step was either a reaction to an emergency or a reprisal for some threatened action against them. Even so obvious a measure as the separation of church and state was not announced until after Archbishop Tikhon issued an Anathema against the regime. Carr, *The Bolshevik Revolution*, vol. 1, p. 161.

23. *Izbrannye stat'i i rechi*, p. 252, reprinted from *Pravda*, Dec. 29, 1918.

24. See Carr, *Socialism in One Country*, vol. 1, p. 50.

only government plans but the active participation of the women of Russia. Lenin agreed that if women were to be liberated, they would have to accomplish the task themselves.[25] What for Lenin was an off-hand observation became for Kollontai a political imperative. Not only did she need to galvanize the hesitant but committed Communist women, she faced the greater problem of winning over non-Party working-class women. With hunger and deprivation intensifying their customary resistance to change, the masses of women were becoming dangerously alienated.[26] Quite simply, the women of Russia did not trust the Bolsheviks in the autumn of 1918, and there was no reason why they should have. The Revolution had not brought them the expected lightening of life. Their "breadwinners" were back at the front, now fighting for the Revolution but still away from the family. Their existence had become not easier but more difficult.[27]

How then to reach the women? A day-to-day, loose apparatus did exist for organization. A Women's Bureau, we recall, had been established in the autumn of 1917 at Kollontai's and Sverdlov's behest. *Rabotnitsa* was a focus for work among women, its staff organizing occasional rallies.[28] Weekly pages appeared in Party newspapers designed to appeal to working-class women. In Moscow the special Commissions for Propaganda and Agitation created by Inessa Armand and Varvara Iakovleva continued their work in connection with the Moscow Area Bureau. "All-City" and area meetings were held in Moscow and Petrograd for non-Party working women. Still, these efforts could not close the breach Kollontai feared was widening between the active leaders of the working women's movement and the broad masses of women who could see no real connection between their lives and the problems of the Soviet state.[29]

Kollontai saw the situation as Lenin did: the war was a catalyst for revolutionary change. It hastened the independence and revolutionary development of women, who in the towns and the countryside were

25. This was the recollection of Emelian Iaroslavskii, citing Lenin in *Kommunistka*, July 1923, no. 7, p. 4. Iaroslavskii explained that there was nothing feminist in the idea. It did not mean that women would work in isolation from men. Women would simply devote themselves in extra measure to developing those institutions by which their liberation from domesticity was to be accomplished.

26. Kollontai, *Rabotnitsa i krest'ianka v Sovetskoi Rossii*, p. 5.

27. Kollontai, "Kak my sozvali pervyi vserossiskii s"ezd rabotnits i krest'ianok," p. 4.

28. *Rabotnitsa* ceased publication in Jan. 1918 owing to a shortage of newsprint and was replaced by women's pages. Hayden, p. 154.

29. Kollontai, *Rabotnitsa za god' revoliutsii*, p. 21.

taking on the responsibilities of the absent men.[30] But Kollontai knew that special measures were needed to launch the educational process that would enable women to understand the larger, long-range impact of the Revolution on their lives. She proposed a dramatic first step, a conference that would bring women en masse to Moscow to meet with Party leaders and to learn how a new life could be built, based not on the traditional family but on the collective. A women's congress attended by top Communists, who would address the delegates as serious revolutionary fighters upon whom the regime was depending, might provide women with a new self-image. It might tap and reinforce what faith in their abilities the women had developed living alone and working during the war years. Returning to their homes, exhilarated by their positive contact with the Revolution, they could discuss in the factories and the villages how the Communists would assume the burdens of the family and ease their lives.[31] Thus Kollontai revived in the autumn of 1918 an earlier idea for an All-Russian Congress of Worker and Peasant Women.

A young Communist, a future member of the Women's Section of the Party, would remember that Kollontai called meetings to discuss an All-Russian Congress of Working Women in February 1918, while she was still Commissar of Public Welfare. In her office at 7 Kazanskaia Street, Kollontai and the staff of *Rabotnitsa* outlined plans.[32] But the tense winter and spring of 1918, when attention was riveted on the search for peace, was not the time to plan a meeting on the woman question.[33] Some Communists argued that the autumn of 1918 was no more appropriate. But in the worsening conditions of Civil War, Kollontai feared that the alienation of the masses of Russian women was becoming critical.[34] Goods were disappearing from the market; winter was coming, bringing cold and hunger. The eyes of proletarian women reflected an anxiety that Kollontai read as an accusation: "They promised us peace and bread, and they gave us

30. *Ibid.*, p. 4.
31. Kollontai, *Izbrannye stat'i i rechi*, p. 245.
32. Roza Kovnator, "Pervye shagi," *Kommunistka*, Nov. 1923, no. 11, p. 23. The Nov. 1923 issue of *Kommunistka* was a special fifth-anniversary retrospective on the First All-Russian Congress of Worker and Peasant Women. In addition to the article by Kovnator there were pieces by Kollontai ("Kak my sozvali pervyi vserossiiskii s"ezd rabotnits i krest'ianok"), Vera Golubeva ("S"ezd rabotnits i krest'ianok"), and Moirova ("Piat' let raboty sredi zhenshchin"). Rather than repeat the article titles in subsequent references, I will cite these in the form "Kollontai in *Kommunistka*, Nov. 1923, no. 11, p. —."
33. Kollontai, *Rabotnitsa za god' revoliutsii*, pp. 21–22.
34. Kollontai, *Rabotnitsa i krest'ianka v Sovetskoi Rossii*, pp. 4–5.

hunger, greater cares, and a new war."[35] The Communists, if they did not act dramatically to inspire the women, risked losing them.

꓿꓿꓿꓿

At the First All-Russian Congress of Worker and Peasant Women, which opened in Moscow on November 16, Kollontai gave a major speech presenting her blueprint for the future of the family. In its published form this became the famous pamphlet *The Family and the Communist State.*[36] For this reason alone the Congress would be of interest, but more was involved. By bringing together Communists of radical and conservative social views (and their bewildered constituents, Russia's working-class women) the Congress provided a microcosm of the tensions within Soviet society generated by the woman question.

The preparations for the Congress also deserve attention, for they mirror the socialist women's movement in Russia—its daring hopes crossed by internal doubts, its tentative and amateurish quality, and its uncertain support from the Party. Moreover, the development of the Congress shows the Communist women's need to rely on Kollontai even when they disagreed with her. She was not simply their political guide, but their liaison with the center of power; despite having been dropped from the Central Committee, Kollontai retained her eminence within the women's movement.

The Old Bolshevik Vera Golubeva, a long-time worker in the women's movement, gives us an insight into Kollontai's prestige in her recollection in a 1923 article of the uneasy and factious mood that dominated the first preliminary meeting in the autumn of 1918. Uncertain that the Party would permit them really to go forward, the women demanded to know what commitments Kollontai had received. Golubeva's experience in working among women had sensitized her to the likelihood that she would be called a feminist by other Bolsheviks, with the result that in the end the Party would provide neither workers nor money.[37] Kollontai explained that Sverdlov, the Soviet head of state, had been closely involved in the prepara-

35. Kollontai in *Kommunistka*, Nov. 1923, no. 11, p. 4.
36. Kollontai, *Sem'ia i kommunisticheskoe gosudarstvo.*
37. Golubeva in *Kommunistka*, Nov. 1923, no. 11, p. 16. Golubeva considered herself an expert on Bolshevism and the woman question. She participated in the early efforts to work among women organized in 1910–11 by the émigrés in Paris—Krupskaia, Stal', and Armand. In Minsk, after March 1917, she worked on orders of the local Bolsheviks agitating among soldiers' wives.

tory discussions and supported the idea of a congress.[38] A gathering of the sort Kollontai suggested seemed to him a good way to reveal the mood of the masses and enable the Party to find the correct approach.

Other members of the Central Committee, for instance Zinoviev and Rykov, did not endorse a non-Party women's congress.[39] Beyond the suspicion that a women's congress was potentially a troublesome, feminist enterprise was the feeling that organizing "babas" was "nonsense," a venture unworthy of Bolshevik attention during the Civil War.[40] Kollontai cited the favorable results from the less ambitious city and area meetings of working women that had been held during the first year of the Revolution: these had produced a greater number of active Communists among proletarian women and an increase in Party influence among the female half of the working population. But inevitably there were Communists who insisted stubbornly, now as in the past, that their ranks were open to each member of the proletariat, that women were fully equal, and that no one was preventing them from using their new political rights.[41] Kollontai parried such objections with the familiar argument that proletarian and peasant women were the most backward elements of Russia's population, lacking political consciousness. If they were to be reached, it would have to be by special means.

In an atmosphere marked by uncertainty, the women tentatively created a provisional bureau for organization.[42] Golubeva became secretary, but Kollontai was designated as liaison between the bureau and the Central Committee's Secretariat. She was responsible for passing the resolutions and decisions of the bureau on to Party leaders and then reporting back their replies.

The problem of location suggests the bureau's marginal status. Turned out of their first headquarters, a "corner" in the Second

38. Sverdlov was chairman of the Central Executive Committee of the Congress of Soviets and, as such, Soviet head of state.

39. Kollontai offered this recollection at a meeting of survivors of the 1918 meeting held in 1946. See "V. I. Lenin i pervyi s"ezd rabotnits," in Kollontai, *Iz moei zhizni i raboty*, p. 355. A year earlier, in November 1917, at a non-Party working women's conference, Zinoviev and Rykov had been "repudiated" in the name of 80,000 working women for their opposition to one-party Bolshevik rule. See Chapter 3 above.

40. Kollontai in *Kommunistka*, Nov. 1923, no. 11, p. 5.

41. Kollontai, *Izbrannye stat'i i rechi*, p. 255.

42. Workers in the localities would conduct the preelection campaign; the bureau would be responsible for planning the campaign and the program of the congress. Golubeva in *Kommunistka*, Nov. 1923, no. 11, p. 17. Eventually, all the working women who would be active in the Russian women's movement in the 1920's entered the bureau.

House of Soviets (where the Central Committee worked) because the "chatter" of the "babas" disturbed the men, the women located in a more remote area, a tiny room on the first floor. There Kollontai, Inessa Armand, and Varvara Moirova, one of Kollontai's protégées, wrote leaflets, articles for newspapers, and the resolutions they would put before the Congress.[43]

During the weeks of preparation some male comrades began to show interest, or at least curiosity, in the forthcoming Congress, even calling on the women to discuss their plans before Party and trade-union meetings.[44] But opposition still existed throughout the Party, and it was not limited to men. Communist women often preferred work that brought more excitement and prestige. Varvara Moirova, for example, found her own sister Zinaida unwilling to work among women. Zinaida rejected Kollontai's request that she travel to Tsaritsyn to conduct elections among women and accompany the chosen delegates back to Moscow. Protesting that she was needed for important work at the front, Zinaida objected to being sent to Tsaritsyn to "get delegates." Kollontai's reply, which illustrates her perception that Party activists often seemed to lack respect for the creative possibilities inherent in the people, suggests the difference in her own view not only of the woman question but also of the relationship of the masses to the Revolution as a whole. The question, she told Zinaida, was not of "getting" delegates, but rather of conducting elections among women who were still unclear about their own relationship to the Revolution. With local Party members involved in defending Tsaritsyn, some responsible Communist had to be sent to explain why women should come to a Congress. Simple women, many of them illiterate, they may never have been outside Tsaritsyn. They needed guidance not only in basic ideology—how to build the new socialist life—but in the most literal sense of being helped to reach Moscow without getting lost on the way.[45]

A few dedicated women, working with colossal energy, planned the campaign to bring delegates to the Congress. Kollontai, Inessa Armand, Golubeva, and Moirova worked in the Moscow area, and

---

43. Kollontai and Golubeva in *Kommunistka*, Nov. 1923, no. 11, pp. 5, 17. Golubeva mentions the tensions that plagued the women's organizing efforts. Sverdlov thought the women were pushing him beyond where he was prepared to go as they attempted to establish an apparatus for work among women within the Party. He cooperated after initial resistance.
44. Kollontai in *Kommunistka*, Nov. 1923, no. 11, p. 5.
45. Zinaida Chalaia, "V pervykh riadakh . . . ," in Zhak and Itkina, eds., pp. 266–67.

Samoilova and Nikolaeva directed propaganda in Petrograd.[46] Varvara Moirova recalled that Inessa and Kollontai provided the emotional energy that sustained the other women.[47] Moirova contributed on the practical level. The Communists who were being organized to go out into the provinces to conduct elections needed to be briefed on what to take along besides food. What kind of newspapers and brochures would be appealing? Moreover, female emissaries often had their own families to care for, so that Moirova had to consider each woman's situation and decide whether she would need help to replace her at home. It was also Moirova's task to make each emissary confident that the Party would carry through on its assurances of assistance.[48]

Congress organizers hoped for about 300–400 women. Privately, they feared that attendance would be poor, with no delegates coming from outside Moscow and Petrograd, and doubted that in less than two months' time they could have aroused sufficient political consciousness in working-class women to make them willing to journey to Moscow.[49] When the day arrived for the opening of the Congress, however, over a thousand delegates of various ages assembled in Moscow—a tribute to the efforts of the women workers who held innumerable meetings in factories and workshops in Petrograd and Moscow and who traveled, despite the dangerous conditions, to more distant areas—Simbirsk, Saratov, Tsaritsyn, and along the Volga.[50]

The huge number of delegates, a source of delight and astonishment, created chaos: neither food nor lodging was available in adequate amounts. The organizers needed immediately to provide for over a thousand women for about five days or a food riot would ensue. Kollontai "hung on the phone" through the night.[51] Sverdlov came to her aid, authorizing additional supplies and officially open-

46. Golubeva in *Kommunistka*, Nov. 1923, no. 11, p. 17.
47. Moirova in *Kommunistka*, Nov. 1923, no. 11, p. 9.
48. Chalaia in Zhak and Itkina, eds., pp. 267–68.
49. Golubeva in *Kommunistka*, Nov. 1923, no. 11, p. 17.
50. Kollontai, *Izbrannye stat'i i rechi*, p. 254, and in *Kommunistka*, Nov. 1923, no. 11, p. 6. The bureau followed the principle in conducting elections for delegates that an enterprise employing from 200 to 500 women workers could send one delegate; over 500, two delegates; and over 1,000, three delegates. Most delegates were from the proletariat; only about 10 percent were peasants. Itkina, p. 196. Inessa's and Iakovleva's earlier work in the Moscow area, carried out by their commissions for propaganda and agitation, resulted in aroused consciousness in the Moscow working women. Kollontai credited her two colleagues with the remarkable turnout in November 1918. Kollontai, *Rabotnitsa za god'*, p. 22.
51. Golubeva in *Kommunistka*, Nov. 1923, no. 11, p. 18.

ing the Congress. The support of the head of state elated the Bolshevik women and dispelled their fears that the Party might in the end fail to endorse the Congress.

How different this assembly looked from that first gathering of Russian women held ten years earlier, when the tone was properly bourgeois and the goals were merely reformist. Then the working-class delegates had numbered less than fifty; now they were over a thousand. For many of the kerchiefed women in wornout boots, quilted or sheepskin jackets, and men's army greatcoats who gathered in the great columned hall of the House of Unions, the Moscow Congress of 1918, at which Lenin himself appeared, was the first—and greatest—political event of their lives.[52] For the women organizers who knew that he had not yet entirely recovered from his gunshot wound, Lenin's presence was particularly welcome, the more so because it was unexpected.[53]

It was with deep satisfaction that the Bolshevik women, some of whom had been present in 1908 at the first Women's Congress, now convened a working women's congress in a socialist state. And yet it would be a mistake to regard their enthusiasm as a genuine triumph for the socialist women's movement. Would their problems not be as great as those that had faced the bourgeois feminists in 1908? The feminists had failed to establish unity among Russian women. Would it be easier for the Communists? With what ambivalence the audience, particularly the peasants, regarded the Bolshevik leaders! The Russian peasants had always distrusted and treated as "alien" the state and its officialdom. Many wondered why the October Revolution had brought them not peace but a continuation of war, hunger, and cold.[54] Could they rely on this new government, made up predominantly of urban Bolsheviks, which told them to abandon their familiar ways? What were they to make of Lenin's peculiar remark, in the spirit of his *State and Revolution*, that "each cook should be able to run the state"?[55] Could they trust these Bolshevik women—

52. For descriptions of the Congress, see Bochkarëva and Lyubimova, *Women of a New World*, p. 83. See the pictures of the Congress in Artiukhina et al., eds., p. 144 and in the Nov. 1923 anniversary issue of *Kommunistka*.
53. Zhak and Itkina, eds., p. 267. Lenin was shot as he left a Moscow factory after a speech on Aug. 30, 1918, by Fanny Kaplan, a former terrorist believed by some to have been an SR and by others, an anarchist. See Ulam, pp. 428–30 and Stites, *Women's Liberation Movement*, pp. 312–13.
54. Halle, pp. 94–95.
55. Moirova quotes Lenin to this effect in *Kommunistka*, Nov. 1923, no. 11, p. 9.

Kollontai, Armand, Nikolaeva, Samoilova, and Stal'—who did not act like women at all, but sat at the table of the Presidium?[56]

Among the speakers were Iaroslavskii and Bukharin, who shared a loose affinity with Kollontai in that they, too, had been Left Communists opposed to the peace of Brest-Litovsk.[57] Iaroslavskii, the most outspoken of the Bolsheviks on the need to root out religious superstition in the new Russia, spoke about the need for women to combat their old religious prejudices—a premature display of radicalism given the background of his listeners. Bukharin, who in a general way shared Kollontai's hope that women would grasp the opportunity afforded them by the Revolution to turn from their narrow, private interests toward the larger world, discussed events in Germany and what they signified for Russia and international revolution. Inessa Armand and Konkordiia Samoilova explained to the women the Party's projected plans.[58] Lenin exhorted the delegates by calling them the women's section of the workers' army and warning that there could be no socialist revolution unless they, the women, participated. The experience of all liberation movements taught him that a revolution's success depended on how much the women took part.[59] The women had to understand that Soviet power was the power of the working class without distinction of sex. They had to learn to take advantage of the Revolution to participate in the building of a new socialist life.

Lenin's sympathy for Russia's miserably exploited women should not be doubted. Yet on another, more private occasion, Lenin would be pragmatic, warning that unless the political backwardness of working-class women could be overcome, women, like little worms, would eat away at and undermine their husbands' will to fight.[60] Close attention to Lenin's speech suggests that he spoke as much to the Congress leaders as to the delegates, at least in his appeal for moderation. Aban-

---

56. Artiukhina et al., eds., p. 189.

57. The two men were part of the avant garde of the Party who in 1918 were seeking a break with tradition. Later, both would disagree with Kollontai on the issue of marriage and the family. For Bukharin's disagreement with Kollontai, see below, p. 171; for Iaroslavskii's, see "Moral' i byt proletariata v perekhodnyi period," pp. 138–53.

58. Samoilova reported on plans for commissions for agitation and propaganda and for delegates' meetings. See Kollontai, "Pamiati bortsov revoliutsii: tvorcheskoe v rabote tovarishcha K. N. Samoilovoi," *Kommunistka*, 1922, nos. 3–5, p. 10.

59. Lenin's speech was reported in *Izvestiia*, Nov. 20, 1918. See Lenin, *Sochineniia* (4th ed.), vol. 28, pp. 160–62.

60. Zetkin, p. 57. Kollontai also recalled Lenin's concern lest wives' complaints undermine their husbands' will to fight for the Revolution. Thus, he was anxious that she raise the political consciousness of working-class women. See *Izbrannye stat'i i rechi*, pp. 381–82.

doning for a moment his enthusiastic remarks to non-Party women in the audience, he gave cautious warning to Communist extremists. One assumes he had in mind Kollontai and her recent articles in *Pravda* when he urged that Communists be careful in fighting religious beliefs lest they cause harm by offending feelings. Here was an early hint of the Lenin who would warn in his last articles in 1923 against a revolutionary approach to building socialism and against change that would shake the old order to its foundations rather than slowly remolding it.[61] Lenin, cautioning the Communists to "shake" as little as possible, appeared conservative even in the era of War Communism when compared with Kollontai. He preferred propaganda and education, and he feared that by lending too sharp an edge to the struggle against religion the Communists would only arouse popular resentment. The strength of the Revolution lay in unity. The source of religious belief was poverty and ignorance; that, not the church, Lenin seemed to be saying, was the evil Kollontai and the radicals ought to combat.

Lenin received prolonged applause. The women sang the "Internationale." Few people in the huge hall realized that certain Party leaders, Kollontai perhaps most of all, were being urged to slow down. Beneath the surface rejoicing of the Congress of Worker and Peasant Women was a tension generated by disagreement over questions of social revolution. Kollontai's speech focused that unease.

Nikolaeva chaired the Congress, but Kollontai's role was pivotal.[62] The resolutions before the Congress had appeared as theory ten years earlier in her book *The Social Bases of the Woman Question*. Now in 1918 she addressed working-class women explaining how what had been theoretical would become a reality of daily life in revolutionary Russia. Kollontai and her comrades proposed the most radical resolutions, calling not simply for broad protection for mothers but for the destruction of the individual household and the establishment of the principle of state upbringing for children. The Congress also called for a fight against the double standard of morality and against prostitution. The real question, Kollontai knew, was how to draw worker and peasant women into construction, how to organize forms of work among them so that resolutions might be acted on. The slogan of the Congress, and of the socialist women's movement in Russia, became

61. For this interpretation, see R. C. Tucker, "Stalinism as Revolution from Above," in Tucker, ed., p. 82. For Lenin's thinking see his "O Kooperatsii" in *Sochineniia* (4th ed.), vol. 33, pp. 427–35.
62. *Bol'shaia Sovetskaia Entsiklopediia* (Moscow, 1954), vol. 30, p. 4.

"through practical participation in Soviet construction—to communism."[63]

How familiar was Kollontai with the mass of Russian working women she addressed in that huge hall? How relevant were her proposals to their lives? A few months earlier, we recall, Kollontai revealed her fear to Jacques Sadoul that she did not really know the Russian working woman. Away from Russia since 1908, she felt out of touch with the stolid and backward women who lacked the political consciousness of their Western counterparts. In fact, Kollontai knew the Russian working woman as well as, or better than, most Bolshevik leaders did. She had seen her daily during her months as Commissar of Public Welfare, pathetically impoverished, at times apathetic, but capable also of bitter complaint and therefore of counterrevolution. No one spoke more frankly to Russia's women than Kollontai about their potential either to hurt or to help the Revolution.

Earlier, rallying the working women of Petrograd to organize meetings and choose delegates, she warned them not to allow themselves any longer to be an unconscious stronghold for the enemies of the working class, "the priests, the kulaks, the petty bourgeoisie," who found working-class women passively receptive to their "lies" about Soviet Power.[64] As Kollontai warned women against the dangers inherent in their political backwardness, so she encouraged them to develop, reminding them of how they had sparked the Revolution in February 1917 by their demands for bread and peace.[65]

Whether Kollontai's remarks at the Congress were relevant to the immediate lives of either proletarian or peasant was another question. She knew enough about Russia to be aware that among the thousand delegates were many women—and not simply the peasants—who were alarmed over the prospect of a future in which their very manner of family existence was to be abandoned. To them she spoke in an apocalyptic mode, reminiscent of all utopians who see the entire past building up to a moment of crisis. She heralded a momentous event about to occur: the "red flag of the social revolution . . . already proclaims to us the approach of the heaven on earth to which humanity has been aspiring for centuries."[66] With this expectation, the question of relevance to daily life became momentarily inappropriate.

63. Kollontai in *Kommunistka*, Nov. 1923, no. 11, p. 5.
64. Kollontai, "Pis'mo k rabotnitsam krasnogo Petrograda," reprinted in *Izbrannye stat'i i rechi*, pp. 246–47.
65. *Ibid.*, p. 246.
66. Kollontai, *Sem'ia i kommunisticheskoe gosudarstvo*, p. 23.

Perhaps Kollontai's experience in the West, and her knowledge from years of work in international women's conferences of the socialist goals to which women aspired, provided her with the degree of distance she needed to be truly revolutionary. Kollontai asked the Russian women first to open their minds to the possibilities of a new life in which, thanks to revolution, they would no longer need to be dependent on men. Her speech was as much a reflection of her own past, and of her need to fight the emotional ties of the family, as it was a guide for Russia's women. In a fascinating way, her speech followed the outlines of her own liberation, which began with divorce. It was no accident that she started by discussing the right to divorce, which had been decreed shortly after the October Revolution, and by urging women not to fear their new freedom.

Having fought the bonds of traditional marriage, Kollontai announced dramatically that the old type of family had seen its day.[67] Bukharin had called the family a stronghold of conservatism, implying a kind of solidity; and in fact the Russian family in 1918, though damaged, was a still mighty fortress. If it were soon to disappear, it would have to be overthrown.[68] Kollontai's description, more impressionistic than objective, was based on her own assumption of the antagonism between the patriarchal family and this stage of revolutionary development. Family life, the key social institution of the capitalist state, the instrument most responsible for her personal frustration, was Kollontai's most compelling example of an institution holding women everywhere in subjection and hindering the development of a collective society.

For the Soviet state it was also an impediment, holding women back from more productive work outside the home. Kollontai reminded the women of the domestic situation of their mothers and grandmothers, whose housework, both in town and country, included spinning thread, weaving cloth, making leather, and generally creating new values whose surplus when sold on the market added to the prosperity of the country. The present-day urban housewife, on the other hand, only cleaned and repaired, doing unproductive and repetitive work that created no new value.[69]

Kollontai seemed, by extolling women's former domestic work, to be oddly nostalgic, even to be contradicting herself and undermining

---

67. *Ibid.*, p. 20.
68. For Bukharin's view, see Geiger, p. 52.
69. Kollontai, *Sem'ia i kommunisticheskoe gosudarstvo*, pp. 10–15.

her opposition to women's life within the confines of the patriarchal family. Or perhaps she felt that at least through their contact with the market economy such women of earlier generations had begun to win for themselves the means slowly to escape subordination.[70] But now the household was no longer useful either to society or to the individual woman; it needed to be replaced by collective housekeeping. When this change would occur she did not say. She implied that the time was near. She promised a Communist society in which someday there would be laundries, special mending shops, and housecleaning crews to replace wearying, individual efforts. She described public restaurants and central kitchens to which everybody might come and take meals.

A month earlier, Kollontai had outlined in *Pravda* her idea for a network of central kitchens all over Moscow, a model to be followed in other cities.[71] Districts should be broken into small parts and suitable locations for central kitchens found. These kitchens should be equipped with the help of area mothers, who would take turns being in charge, and supplied with fuel and provisions by the local Soviet. Public feeding would save food and fuel as a result of central planning. More significant politically would be the reaction on the part of women: they would see the state feeding their hungry children, and would realize that Soviet power was not mean, petty, or vengeful, but of a higher order than the former bourgeois government. That Kollontai understated the reluctance of most Russian women to give up their stoves did not mean that she assumed an enthusiasm for communal living. She hoped that the central kitchens would spark the beginning of a collective spirit in women, who might come to appreciate the time and energy saved in not having to market and cook.[72]

Here and there in 1918 central feeding was being discussed. It had even come into being on a small scale in some cities during the spring of 1918, but rather as an emergency measure to feed the hungry than as the social experiment Kollontai wanted.[73] To have serious social

70. *Ibid.*, p. 11.

71. *Izbrannye stat'i i rechi*, p. 241, reprinted from *Pravda*, Oct. 1, 1918.

72. For Russian women's reluctance to part with their stoves, see Smith, p. 192.

73. Its development was limited by Soviet poverty, the scarcity of food, and inexperience. Channels were created from the center, but nothing flowed through, as Kollontai explained in *Polozhenie zhenshchiny*, pp. 166–67. Nevertheless, in Petrograd in 1919 and 1920 almost 90 percent of the population ate in public dining halls, and in Moscow almost 60 percent. Kollontai admitted that the quality of the food was wretched, but she attributed the dismal results not to bad management (pointed to even by friendly observers) but to poverty and the Allied blockade.

significance, so that women could be free to give full energy to revolution, Kollontai knew that the idea would have to be implemented statewide.[74]

As for child care, Kollontai promised what women of her generation never had and what the worker and peasant women in her audience were not requesting: the collective would substitute for the family. The Communists were already planning institutions and programs to assume responsibilities that formerly devolved on mothers: day nurseries, kindergartens, children's colonies and homes, infirmaries and health resorts for sick children, free lunches at school, free distribution of textbooks, free clothing and shoes. Kollontai avoided the word, but her structure was authoritarian, the details of supervision meticulous. The child in the new society would be molded by socialist organization, passing the greater part of the day in playgrounds, gardens, and homes where intelligent educators would make him a Communist. He would grow up conscious of the greatness of the motto "Solidarity, comradeship, mutual aid, and devotion to the collective life." Kollontai used these examples to show that, as Marx and Engels had predicted, children would move out of family confines, with responsibility for their well-being passed on to the community.

From the point of view of socialist theory, Kollontai's imperatives were in proper order. Society's need to have women participate was primary, women's personal benefit secondary. But within the humanitarian asylum, all of women's problems would be met. As usual, when it came to the woman question, Kollontai pushed further than other Communists were prepared to go. It was in society's interest to aid the working mother, therefore the workers' state would assure a livelihood to every mother whether or not she was legally married. In this way the issue of motherhood without marriage, which socialists had earlier been reluctant to accept, Kollontai treated as settled.[75] Everywhere maternity homes and day nurseries would enable women to serve and be mothers at the same time. A woman need no longer fear that she would remain without support, little ones in her arms, if she was deserted by her husband. In the Communist world, a woman would no longer depend on a man; her own strong hands and those of the state would support her.

74. Kollontai, *Izbrannye stat'i i rechi*, p. 241.
75. The question was debated among socialists at the Second International Women's Conference in Copenhagen in 1910. See Kollontai, *Izbrannye stat'i i rechi*, pp. 99–100.

However much Kollontai tried to make the prospect seem alluring, she knew that her remarks were frightening, that her images were of an alien and even regimented life. Therefore, as we have seen, she pictured basically familiar roles. Women would be outside the home, working cooperatively, but still caring for children; they would be cleaning, but as members of housekeeping corps; they would be in charge of laundry, but instead of laboring individually would deliver their clothing to central places to be washed and ironed.[76]

And what of their children? Were the Communists going to destroy the family by separating children from their parents? On this point Kollontai was cautious. The nuclear family, she seemed to be saying, would remain untouched and children would return home at the end of the day. Here, too, Kollontai had to allay fears expressed by shouts of "We won't give up our children!"[77] Rumors frightened the women. Zlata Lilina, who bore the title of "People's Commissar for Social Planning in the Northern Commune"—a small, crop-haired, grey-eyed woman in a uniform jacket, sprightly and tough, Zinoviev's wife and the mother of young boys—was widely quoted as having said that the Party must rescue children from the nefarious influence of family life. "In other words we must nationalize them. They will be taught the ABCs of Communism and later become true Communists. Our task now is to oblige the mother to give her children to us—to the Soviet state."[78] It was consequently important for Kollontai to make clear that the small baby would remain at home with its mother, "while it is still learning to walk, clinging to its mother's skirts." Let the working mothers be reassured. The "Communist fatherland" was not intending to take children away from parents, "nor to tear the baby from its mother's breast." The "Communist fatherland" would take upon itself all the duties involved in the education of the child, but paternal love and maternal satisfaction would not be taken from those who showed themselves capable of appreciating these joys. Could this be called violent destruction of the family, a forcible separation of child and mother?[79] Only once did Kollontai reveal a trace of impatience. "Let the women of the working class cease to worry over the fact that the family as it is presently constituted is doomed

76. Elsewhere Kollontai explained that it made sense to bring women into the economy in areas where they were already adept and could make a contribution. See *Polozhenie zhenshchiny*, pp. 204–5.

77. As quoted in Stites, "Zhenotdel," p. 177.

78. For the alleged quotation, see Geiger, p. 72. For Lilina, see Serge, p. 71.

79. Kollontai, *Sem'ia i kommunisticheskoe gosudarstvo*, pp. 19–20.

to disappear. They will do much better to hail with joy the dawn of a new society that will lighten the burden of motherhood for women."[80]

By now it should be obvious that Kollontai's image of socialist womanhood assumed that the new woman would be a mother. It never occurred to Kollontai to consider those who might choose not to fulfill this role. An obvious reason lay in the collective's need for children to build the new society. I suspect, however, that Kollontai pictured socialist women as mothers for reasons that went beyond the society's need for children, that reached deep into the Russian symbolism of "Matushka-Rus," the enduring and capable mother. Kollontai's unexamined assumption that the Russian woman would of course bear children supports Vera Dunham's notion that the Russian ethos of the strong woman did not include the spinster.[81]

Kollontai tried to be circumspect at the First All-Russian Congress of Worker and Peasant Women, but she did not dissemble: insofar as *The Family and the Communist State* reflects what she actually said, she made a truly radical and authoritarian statement. Not only did it sound the death knell of the conventional family, it implied enormous changes in people's lives, especially men's. In place of the indissoluble marriage based on female servitude, the workers' state needed a free union of two equal workers. Thus the husband would cease to be not only the patriarchal figure but also the provider. Women were told in the name of the new regime that they need not depend on husbands for support: the state would assure them work.

Occasionally her revolutionary fervor burst through her moderation. There was nothing that women would not be able to do. She urged the delegates, in what were perhaps the most important words of the Congress, to return to their towns and villages with a new consciousness: no more would there be the word "baba." It was a brilliant symbolic gesture. Kollontai buried for a euphoric moment the pejorative epithet that traditionally signified the contempt in which working-class and peasant women in Russia were held.[82] Here was something her audience could respond to, and they did, shouting their approval as Kollontai offered them a new sense of identity and self-respect.

Emotions matter. The symbolism was profound and encouraging,

80. *Ibid.*, p. 22.
81. Dunham, pp. 459–83.
82. For this episode, see Itkina, p. 197.

and in a sense it was enough. Kollontai did not expect the Congress to accomplish matters of substance. Her political purpose was to begin the slow process of winning women to the Revolution. The Congress was to serve as a "beacon" (how often the Communists used that word in the early years, Trotsky remarked!) to show women how Soviet power, with their cooperation, could change their lives. If it succeeded, at least temporarily, in melding women together against the enemies of the Revolution, it might also accomplish a larger goal, that of giving the masses of women faith in themselves as well as in the Bolsheviks.[83]

Kollontai knew that husbands would resist the new concept of self she was providing their wives. Her reaction suggests ambivalence toward feminist creeds. Early on she had rejected feminism as a bourgeois movement that saw men as the oppressor, and the emancipation of women as an end in itself. But the empathy for women Kollontai manifested was surely a tendency she shared with the feminists. Sympathetic to the need for women to gain confidence and status, she showed an insensitivity to the feelings of deprivation of working-class and peasant husbands. Her recollection was remarkably casual: "Not all of them put up with it."[84]

A goal of the Congress was to give working-class women greater faith in themselves, and this the Communist organizers thought had been accomplished. It is impossible to document a growth in self-confidence on the part of the masses of women who returned home, no doubt bewildered and troubled by what they heard, but what can be documented is the greater self-confidence of the Communist women who organized the Congress.[85] Before the Congress, Communist women seemed to Kollontai insufficiently zealous. What she criticized as lack of zeal was really uncertainty—the fear of being labeled feminist, the reluctance to try only to fail. Their success in November 1918 in convening a huge Congress became a point of pride for the socialist women's movement in Russia. Five years later, on the anniversary of this first Congress, its organizers looked back, marveling at

83. Kollontai in *Kommunistka*, Nov. 1923, no. 11, p. 8; Itkina, p. 195.
84. Kollontai, *Polozhenie zhenshchiny*, p. 190.
85. There are hints that the women at the early non-Party congresses were in fact mostly passive or opposed to Soviet power. By 1920 a non-Party congress of 4,000 Moscow area women showed increased enthusiasm for the regime. Polina Vinogradskaia remarked on the contrast with earlier congresses in writing that instead of the few hostile participants and the crowd of passive listeners of the early days, one now saw women who wanted to build the new Soviet system. See Polina Vinogradskaia, "Odna iz ocherednykh zadach," *Kommunistka*, 1920, nos. 3–4, p. 31.

their accomplishment and recalling their triumph in bringing together over a thousand women of the proletariat. Not the masses of
backward Russian women but the women in the Communist Party
experienced a growth of confidence. Their subsequent disappointment would mock their early optimism.[86]

ᘒᘒᘒ

The Family and the Communist State is the more interesting in the
context of Kollontai's larger image of the impact revolution would
have on women's lives. She held in reserve, as it were, the idea of a
society of communes rather than of individual families—an idea she
could only allude to at the 1918 Congress.[87] I have suggested that the
"withering away of the family" was at one level a projection of Kollontai's own fight for independence against conventional marriage
and domesticity. By the same token, in projecting her conflicts outward, she tried to deal with her longing to be with her son. She presented overwhelming mother love, such as her own, as negative and
narrow. "The woman who is called upon to struggle in the great cause
of the liberation of the workers—such a woman should know that in
the new state there will be no more room for such petty divisions as
were formerly understood: 'These are my own children; to them I
owe all my maternal solicitude, all my affection; those are your children, . . . I am not concerned with them. . . .' Henceforth the worker-
mother, who is conscious of her social function, will rise to a point
where she no longer differentiates between *yours* and mine; she must
remember that there are now only our children, those of the Communist state, the common possession of all the workers."[88]

Kollontai never forgot her audience. In November 1918 she spoke
to women whose very existence revolved around motherhood. It
would have been an act of radical folly to question the value of a
mother's care. Lecturing to Party workers a few years later at Sverdlov
Communist University, Kollontai spoke more frankly. She agreed
that the bearing and nursing of children established a special relationship between mother and infant, but she differed from traditionalists
in her view of the duration of that need. Instead of the first year, Kollontai posited the first few weeks of a child's life as the critical time

86. See Golubeva's remarks on their naive expectation in 1918 that change would be
rapid in *Kommunistka*, Nov. 1923, no. 11, p. 18.

87. Kollontai's idealization of the commune is expressed in "Dorogu krylatomu
erosu!," *Molodaia Gvardiia*, 1923, no. 3, pp. 111–24, and in *Skoro (cherez 48 let)*.

88. Kollontai, *Sem'ia i kommunisticheskoe gosudarstvo*, p. 22.

when the exclusive attention of the mother was needed. During that period, there existed an important physiological tie between the nursing mother and the infant that made the mother's care essential; later, however, the mother's care was not as important.[89]

Kollontai repeated at the Sverdlov Communist University what she told the Women's Congress in 1918—that the workers' republic had no intention of taking children forcibly from their mothers, as the bourgeois world falsely charged. But mothers must understand that exclusive maternal love was not enough, that the child would need social education to become a group-oriented Communist. Mothers must learn to place their children in the healthiest environment—nurseries, kindergartens, children's homes—in order to help them to grow in the interests of society. Group play would emphasize "for us there is no mine and yours, for us everything is everyone's." Only then would the idea of private property atrophy.[90]

Could the mothers themselves provide the correct socialization? This was a subject Kollontai avoided, but it is clear she thought the possibility unlikely. For effective socialization to take place it was essential that children be placed in a situation where the responsible persons were themselves integrated in the desired cultural value system, where the patterns had previously been internalized into their own personalities. Few mothers in Russia could qualify. Without any formal knowledge of the new "sciences" of psychology and sociology, Kollontai grasped that the basic functions of the nuclear family were the primary socialization of children as members of society, and the stabilization of adult personalities.[91] It was these functions that socialists needed to remove from family control.

The language of spontaneity came naturally to Kollontai, but we have seen in the thinking of even this most libertarian of Communists the elements of authoritarianism. What of the mothers and fathers who resisted progress toward Communist life? History was assumed to be so overwhelmingly in favor of the commune that they would be swept along by the impetus of the workers' state looming behind the great universal family of workers. In those areas where Kollontai wanted the results to be immediately and socially correct, she relied in an automatic way on the power of "specialists": thus she wrote

89. Kollontai, *Polozhenie zhenshchiny*, p. 176.
90. *Ibid.*, pp. 174–76.
91. Parsons and Bales, p. 16.

that in children's institutions, "intelligent educators" would make of the child a Communist.[92]

Despite her assurances to the 1918 Congress that the Communists did not intend violently to destroy the family or forcibly to separate a child from its mother, Kollontai did anticipate an end to the family as a traditional living unit.[93] Elsewhere she chided her Bolshevik comrades who stopped short of this conclusion. She laughed at the bold revolutionary, reluctant to face the idea that the family was being destroyed, who comforted himself with the assumption that since there was nothing in the Communist program about the family that meant that somehow it could slip into Communist society. To those comrades who contemplated the destruction of the family with sadness, Kollontai directed pointed questions. What family were they nostalgic for? The enlarged peasant household? Or the nuclear family of the proletarian worker? Of course it was the latter, which meant they were longing for the small, isolated family that resulted from the capitalist system. How could these comrades defend such a family in connection with Communism? Did they propose, for example, that public feeding should exist only for single people, and that as soon as people were married women should go back to the pots and pans from which the Communists were trying to free them?[94]

In her polemic against the nuclear family Kollontai observed that there was no need to speak about children, since even the most fervent Communist defender of the family was convinced of the value of social upbringing. But then what was the family once deprived of cares about children and the household? It was nothing but a marriage union, without any economic or social responsibility, and ceasing therefore to be subject to the control and direction of the collective so long as it did not threaten the health of society.[95] Once the family was reduced to a simple marriage union, parents could separate freely, for they would no longer need to be concerned about their children's care. Here Kollontai made a jump that implied a smooth transition from freeing parents of *worry* about their children's material future to freeing them of *care* or *concern*. Neither in 1918 nor subsequently did Kollontai examine fully the larger ques-

92. Kollontai, *Sem'ia i kommunisticheskoe gosudarstvo*, pp. 18–23.
93. For Kollontai's assurances, see *ibid.*, p. 20.
94. Kollontai, "Sem'ia i kommunizm," *Kommunistka*, 1920, no. 7, pp. 17–18.
95. *Ibid.*, p. 18.

tion of the parent-child relationship. "Everyone" (meaning Communists) agreed that children should be brought up communally.[96] But she knew there was no single definition, let alone consensus, about what socialized upbringing (*vospitaniia*) implied for the family structure.

Turning to what other Communists said on the subject, we find a variety of views that tried to interpret what Marx and Engels meant when they wrote loosely in 1848 in the *Communist Manifesto* of the "abolition of the family."[97] Because of the wide scope their vagueness gave for individual interpretation, there was little agreement in the first decade of the Revolution. Did they mean only that the family would cease to exist as a bourgeois property-maintaining institution, Marx's hated center of small, household economy? Surely Marx and Engels intended at least that. But what of its structure? Would parents and children live together? On this point Marx and Engels were vague, not discussing parenthood in any detail and saying only that there would be "communal rearing of children." Even in the transitional era, "all children, once they were able to manage without maternal care, would be brought up and educated in state institutions."[98] If society was to rear and to educate, did this mean that the family under Communism would not live together? Were children to live with their parents part of the time? None of the time? All of the time? Were couples to maintain separate dwellings? Engels simply quoted the anthropologist Lewis Henry Morgan: "Should the monogamous family in the distant future fail to answer the requirements of society . . . it is impossible to predict the nature of its successor."[99]

Party policy held that it was incorrect to predict ways of life under Communism. But a small number of Communists intoxicated with the idea of the future speculated about the forms the family might take. That dreamer of bright dreams, Lunacharskii, pictured communal houses with well-organized quarters for children and adults connected by a heated gallery; parents would simply send their children to the appropriate quarters to be supervised by trained personnel. Lunacharskii also predicted an end to such categories as "my parents" and "our children,"[100] adding "whether there will be a free

96. *Ibid.*
97. Karl Marx and Friedrich Engels, *The Communist Manifesto* (New York, 1955), p. 27. (Originally published in 1848.)
98. Riazanov, p. 24.
99. Engels, p. 89, quoting Morgan.
100. Geiger, p. 48, quoting Lunacharskii.

family, without a head, or whether the family will break up entirely, we do not decide in advance. In a socialist society individual differences will not be eliminated, nor do we strive for that, and probably there will be different forms of the family."[101]

Individual schemes for children's homes and children's towns varied. L. N. Sabsovich, who advocated separation of children from parents from the earliest years, derided as petty bourgeois those who, speaking of biological ties, did not love all children as their own.[102] A radical pamphlet, probably written by Sabsovich, insisted that "one of the first results of the socialization of our education must be that children shall not live with their parents. From . . . birth they are to be in special children's homes in order to remove them . . . from the harmful influence of parents and family. We ought to have special children's towns."[103]

For the majority of Communists these were unwelcome fantasies. Krupskaia pronounced the dominant reaction to such "leftist" ideas about the family. "Men and women workers are right to refuse to give their children to children's towns. Socialist education must be organized so that parents and teachers both can take part in it."[104] There is reason to think that Lenin wished to see an end to individual housekeeping but not to the individual family. His famous conversation in 1920 with Clara Zetkin suggested as much.[105] One Communist has insisted that Lenin, like Krupskaia, continued after the Revolution to agree with the "renegade" Karl Kautsky at least on the question of the family. The German Communist, seizing upon Marx's reference to a "higher form of the family," inferred that the disappearance of the individual household meant not the end of marriage and the family but rather their transformation to a purified form free from materialist considerations and patriarchal inequalities.[106]

101. Smith, p. 92, quoting Lunacharskii. For Lunacharskii's further views, see "Kultura v sotsialisticheskikh gorodakh," *Revoliutsiia i Kul'tura*, 1930, no. 1, pp. 35–40, as cited in S. Frederick Starr, "Visionary Town Planning During the Cultural Revolution," in Fitzpatrick, ed., p. 289; and A. Lunacharskii, "Bol'nye storony komsomol'skogo byta," in Razin, ed., pp. 112–13. For proscriptions against predicting life under Communism, see Lenin to Kollontai as quoted in Itkina, p. 208.

102. Geiger, p. 48, citing L. N. Sabsovich, *Sotsialisticheskie goroda* (Moscow, 1930).

103. Such towns were considered for a time by the Town Planning Institute. For unidentified quote, see Winter, p. 150.

104. *Ibid.* The Krupskaia quote is from *O bytovykh voprosakh* (Moscow, 1930), p. 22, as cited in Geiger, p. 48.

105. See K. Tsetkin, "Lenin o morali i voprosakh pola," in Razin, ed., pp. 14–21, and the expanded version of this conversation in Zetkin, pp. 41–64.

106. Nor did Marx's reference mean the end of the individual dwelling, in the view of Riazanov. For his interpretation of Lenin's attitude on the family, see Riazanov,

Not even the women who organized the All-Russian Congress of Worker and Peasant Women in 1918 and shared Kollontai's belief that the family in its bourgeois form was an anachronism anticipated its demise in any uniform way. They agreed that the process of "withering" had already begun in 1918, that it was not moving quickly enough, and that it was the regime's responsibility to hasten the transition.[107] But transition to what was less clear.

An American who lived in Russia intermittently during the early 1920's was puzzled by the contradictions in Communist attitudes toward the family. On the one hand, certain Communists spoke glowingly to her of the beautiful homes they would build in the future, where babies would be taken away from their parents. Yet on the other hand, the Department for the Protection of Motherhood and Infancy, which was organized in January 1918, clearly looked toward enlightening mothers through posters, lectures, and consultations about the best methods of child care. Dr. Lebedeva, the head of the department, did not rule out the possibility of a future policy change, but she explained that Soviet Russia was not yet ready, materially or psychologically, for full-scale, collective upbringing.[108]

Some Communist women, accepting the premise that Marxists could not predict future forms,[109] looked forward simply to an end of housekeeping and daily child care—Kautsky's higher form of the family—and found that prospect sufficiently liberating. Others, though not discarding the concept of living with one's own husband and children, approved of the notion of separate children's homes located nearby, at least for older children. Sof'ia Smidovich, who worked among women in Moscow, told an American visitor, "I love my own children, but after all, how much do I see of them? I am at work all day, and usually in the evening too. . . . If they were in a

---

pp. 31–32. What many Bolsheviks rejected as "strange ideas" circulated in Russia during the Civil War (and again briefly during the ideologically intense First Five-Year Plan). N. Osinskii reported an example. "All individual life (not only family life) will disappear under socialism. There will be no more separate apartments; it will not be necessary to have separate rooms. . . . The whole life of a person, physical and mental, can be lived within the collective." Osinskii found such notions ridiculous: "To explain communism as a mechanical equalization and depersonalization is a petty-bourgeois interpretation. Home life under developed socialism will not be a barracks life." Winter, pp. 268–69, quoting Osinskii.

107. See for example Vinogradskaia's angry remarks to Trotsky, "Voprosy byta."

108. Smith, p. 179. For the organization of the Department for the Protection of Motherhood and Infancy under the Commissariat of Public Welfare, see Smith, p. 174.

109. As Krupskaia and other Communist women reminded Kollontai. See Vinogradskaia, "Serdtse, otdannoe narodu," pp. 186–204.

Children's Home they could come to me in my free time, and meanwhile they would be getting better training and better care than I can give them, and they would be living a more stimulating life."[110]

Eventually, and to another audience, Kollontai would stress the advantages of communal upbringing of children away from their parents.[111] In the autumn of 1918, however, aware that her position was too radical for the proletarian and peasant women assembled in Moscow, and that indeed it would receive uncertain support even from her sister Communists, she avoided references to physical separation.

The Bolsheviks may have seemed alike in their negativism toward the family, but in fact the prevailing Communist Party view diverged from Kollontai's in important ways. The Party agreed that the family's reactionary influence—its anti-Communism, its religiosity, its insularity, its patriarchal assumptions of inequality—had to be overcome. "We hate the bourgeois family," Lunacharskii wrote.[112] But from the outset, the regime moved not as Kollontai demanded toward destroying the family but, out of necessity and one suspects even preference, toward strengthening its very foundations. Consider a major social document of the autumn of 1918, the Communist Family Code. Although Kollontai helped frame it, the Code differed substantially from the spirit that inspired Kollontai's writing.[113]

Western critics who have assumed that the Soviet regime attempted in the early 1920's to destroy the family have confused government policies designed to undermine traditional features of patriarchy, the hallmark of the capitalist society, with an assault on the family as a unit. The two concepts were actually very different. The Family Code of 1918 did, in fact, weaken patriarchal concepts significantly, at least on paper. Kollontai's influence was reflected in clauses that made divorce easy to obtain even at the request of one partner, that eliminated a wife's obligation to follow her husband if he changed residence, and that allowed the couple the right to choose a family

---

110. Smith, p. 103.
111. Kollontai, *Polozhenie zhenshchiny*, p. 176.
112. Quoted in Smith, p. 92.
113. For Kollontai's involvement in promulgating the laws of Dec. 19, 1917, on freedom to divorce and Dec. 20, 1917, on civil marriage (as well as the law equalizing the rights of children born in and out of wedlock), see Itkina, pp. 174–75. On the 1917 marriage decree, see also Stites, *Women's Liberation Movement*, p. 363.

surname that might be the husband's name, the wife's, or a combination of both.

The observer unfamiliar with Soviet life might assume on the basis of the wording of the Family Code that husbands and wives thus became entirely equal. Where in the past the word "wife" might appear in a document, the Soviet regime substituted "spouse," thereby conveying the impression that rights and obligations of husbands and wives devolved equally on each. In fact, despite the use of the word "spouse," the understanding was general that because of economic realities "wife" was in fact intended. For example, under the heading "Rights and Duties of Husband and Wife," it was provided that the right of a spouse in need and unable to work to be maintained by the other spouse was preserved even in the case of divorce, until a change in the spouse's economic condition took place. "Spouse," it was generally understood, meant "wife."[114]

The purpose of the Family Code of 1918 was to preserve the family as a burden-sharing, mutually dependent group. Despite promises that looked to a future when personal obligations might be suspended and children and old people maintained by public care (and most likely included at Kollontai's prompting), the Family Code stipulated that for the present fathers, even unmarried ones, were responsible to share in a child's support, and that parents were bound to keep their minor children with them, to provide them with board, and to care for their education and development. Children were obliged to provide for their needy parents. People unable to obtain support from children, spouses, or parents because of their poverty were legally entitled to demand support from brothers and sisters. Religious beliefs were safeguarded. Parents were given the right to decide their children's religion.[115]

The Family Code of 1918 reflected the tension between the eagerness of radicals like Kollontai to provide for a future when the family would wither away and the determination of socially conservative Communists like Lenin to strengthen the family for the present. The continuing influence of conservative thinking was reflected in Soviet imagery. A little booklet published by the government in 1925 urging

114. Kollontai, of course, did not intend that it should. For this assumption see Commissar of Justice Dmitrii Kurskii, in *Brak i sem'ia*, p. 64.

115. For the Family Code of 1918, see USSR, [15], no. 76–77, art. 818, pp. 933–59. An English translation appears in Schlesinger, ed., pp. 33–41.

couples to register their marriages with the civil authorities bore on its cover the picture of a beaming peasant couple with three children scampering about. They looked, in the opinion of an American visitor, smug and happy enough to carry the caption "Own Your Own Home—Thirty-five Minutes from the Kremlin."[116]

Kollontai participated in framing the Family Code, but her influence was held in check and the Code did not reflect her radicalism. On balance, it was a conservative document that provided a more accurate key to the family's future than did *The Family and the Communist State*. Early Bolshevik legislation did not aim to undermine the nuclear family. The regime made divorce available so as to safeguard the new equality of women. Abortion was legalized in 1920— not for ideological reasons, but, we shall see, as an unhappy emergency measure to aid mothers who in conditions of hunger and civil war could not provide for children.[117] Thus the Bolshevik government's policy, as opposed to its rhetoric, was from the outset not to destroy (with Kollontai) but to maintain (with Lenin) the nuclear family.

For all her writing and speech-making, Kollontai's attack on the family as the obstacle to the transformation of women's condition raised problems that she failed adequately to consider, let alone resolve. The family hindered women's freedom and impeded the development of a more humane society, but Kollontai never questioned at what cost it might be replaced. What of the persistent idea that the family served as a bulwark of privacy? Nowhere did Kollontai deal adequately with the need for privacy in daily life. There is little evidence that she took it into account. Her plan in *Pravda* for communal kitchens to feed children contained a suggestive line, unfortunately all too brief. Mothers could pick up meals at the dining hall where their children were fed and bring them home where they might themselves eat more comfortably. In the Soviet communes established here and there in the 1920's the lack of privacy became an irritant.[118] But Kollontai mistakenly equated privacy with "narrow privatism." Pre-

116. Smith, p. 107.
117. Krupskaia, "Voina i detorozhdenie," p. 18.
118. For Kollontai's brief reference to privacy, see *Izbrannye stat'i i rechi*, p. 241. On the lack of privacy in Soviet communes, see Mehnert, pp. 170, 173, 178.

cisely to the degree that she ignored the need for privacy, she praised the communal spirit of the collective. To the nineteenth-century bourgeois notion—a result of the cleavage between the world of work and the world of leisure—that the individual private family was a refuge from a heartless world, Kollontai replied that in a humane socialist world that problem would be irrelevant. Socialist society would be total harmony. Despite her involvement in a political party whose history was one of perennial factionalism, Kollontai imagined a socialist future of personal accord and nonalienating labor from which no private retreat need exist. Far from viewing the family in benign Victorian terms as a refuge, she saw it as a narrow cell that fostered a selfish egotism.[119]

But it will not do as a theory simply to ignore the need for privacy and to condemn the family as narrow and selfish. Kollontai neglected to consider the family at its best, as an emotional bulwark for its children, as a source of parental warmth and affection—in brief, as what Shura Domontovich experienced as a child. Kollontai wrote glowingly of parental love for children, and she promised the women in November 1918 that the joys of parenthood would be preserved, that only its burdens would be removed.[120] But could the affectional functions remain vital and unimpaired in a vacuum, in a family no longer necessary as an economic unit or as a source of emotional sustenance?

Kollontai addressed this question elsewhere. To those who suggested that the family die away as an economic unit but maintain its vitality through its spiritual ties, Kollontai asked (anticipating current-day social scientists) whether those ties were sufficient to keep the family, reduced in its functions, from gradual decomposition.[121] She thought not. Consistently Marxist in her interpretation, she saw the emotional network of the family developing as a result of its daily material functions. If those functions were transferred out of the family onto society, the concomitant emotions would cease to exist within the family context and would grow instead within the collective. Kollontai anticipated that the affectional functions formerly part of the family would diffuse throughout the collective, so that the

---

119. For her negative view of the nuclear family, see *Sem'ia i kommunisticheskoe gosudarstvo*, pp. 22–23, and "Sem'ia i kommunizm," pp. 16–19. On the Victorian family, see Walter E. Houghton, *The Victorian Frame of Mind* (New Haven, Conn., 1971), pp. 341–93.
120. Kollontai, *Sem'ia i kommunisticheskoe gosudarstvo*, pp. 19–20.
121. Kollontai, "Sem'ia i kommunizm," p. 17. She anticipated the thinking of Bruno Bettelheim in *The Children of the Dream* and Christopher Lasch in *Haven in a Heartless World*.

collective would evolve more spiritual and loving tendencies within the Soviet people to replace the selfishly intense, emotional supports of the individual family.[122]

The Soviet Union, despite Kollontai, would never try to replace the family. As the lack of consensus in the early years suggested, there was insufficient commitment to communes, children's homes, and state-provided dining rooms.[123] Neither did the regime provide state care in place of the household; it did not go beyond establishing day-care centers for working mothers. We have to look elsewhere then, to other societies, if we wish to know what happened to the nuclear family when Kollontai's collective ideas were applied to it. Russians who rejected the family as totally as Kollontai did were not found in significant numbers in the Communist Party even in its early years. They were found, however, among the Jews who emigrated from the ghettos of Russia and Eastern Europe to Palestine and founded the Kibbutz movement. Because certain features of kibbutz life so closely approximated Kollontai's theories, it is useful to digress and consider briefly the Israeli experiment.

The Israeli kibbutz (the word means "group") is, by traditional standards, reminiscent of Kollontai's Communism in its absence of private property, its atheism, and its radical work-oriented social views. Its founders hoped that the group, or the collective, rather than the family would satisfy the emotional and economic needs of each member. When children were born, it was agreed that their security would come not from the family, which did not exist in the kibbutz in any structural or economic sense, but from the comradely peer group of equals. The idea that the "burdens" of parenthood should be carried by the collective, leaving only the "joys" to the parents, stemmed from the socialist desire to avoid relationships influ-

122. Kollontai, "Sem'ia i kommunizm," pp. 17–19.
123. Children's homes did not develop in accordance with Kollontai's dream of beautiful "palaces" where children, living apart from their families, would be socialized by trained specialists ideally from the working class. For the squalid children's homes during the Civil War, see Gladkov's novel *Tsement* and Goldman, p. 71. In 1922 the number of homes increased sharply owing to the famine. Their numbers dropped sharply when the central government withdrew support under the NEP. Closed institutions would cease to be of ideological interest in the Soviet Union. In 1924 the Department for the Protection of Motherhood and Infancy began farming children out to private homes, despite protests that this was a step backward ideologically. The mortality rate was cut in half. Smith, p. 178. Factory day-nurseries, after a sharp decline in the early years of the NEP, did subsequently grow.

enced by economic considerations and ties.[124] Kollontai expected a new kind of emotional ambience, less possessive and jealous, that would result from the extension throughout the collective of feelings previously reserved for a single relationship. So, too, did the Palestinian settlers, who wanted to escape from the overwhelming expression of feelings with which they were brought up.[125]

How the kibbutz handled parental relationships with their children did not vary widely from one wing of the kibbutz movement to the other. Kibbutz children lived from birth on (usually from the fourth day after delivery) not at home with their parents, but with their age-mates in separate children's houses within the small settlements where they were raised communally by members of the kibbutz assigned to the task.[126] The similarity between Kollontai's image of child-rearing and the reality of the kibbutz experience was the more remarkable since, according to the original settlers, their methods of child-rearing did not result from a plan but evolved from the needs of its members. No one knew what to do with the first children born in the original settlement. But since the women would not give up their share of the communal life and work, and the men were indifferent, they set aside a house where the children could live all day and put one woman in charge. Thus the system developed of children living in children's houses after the pattern of the first kibbutz.[127]

Observations of the kind of personality and sense of family the kibbutz experience produced lend support to Kollontai's assumptions. Collective upbringing resulted, as Kollontai thought it would, in a personality with different goals from those of the average traditional family, yet one that, to the surprise of the skeptics, was strong and healthy. Children raised in the kibbutz put less emphasis on personal identity and individual achievement and were less possessive. The child's peer group, which remained constant throughout his childhood, replaced the parents as a source of deep and lasting emo-

124. Bettelheim, p. 109. Bettelheim studied one kibbutz in depth in the late 1960's. His description bears a remarkable resemblance to Kollontai's sketch of the future in *Sem'ia i kommunisticheskoe gosudarstvo*.

125. On the other hand, members of the kibbutz also worried that the kibbutz-reared generation lacked feeling for one-to-one intimacy. Bettelheim points out (p. 139) that kibbutz children are rarely alone, and that intimacy is not held out as an ideal as it is in traditional societies. He found that an emotional flattening had resulted (pp. 307–8).

126. *Ibid.*, pp. 354–55, and p. 26 for variations.

127. *Ibid.*, pp. 32–40, quoting Joseph Baratz, *Degania, The Story of Palestine's First Collective Settlement* (Tel-Aviv, 1944?).

tional attachment.[128] All this is not to say that the concept of one's own parents and natural siblings disappeared. However attenuated the idea of the family seemed when judged by traditional standards, it proved more viable than Kollontai had anticipated.[129]

Much that has been written about kibbutz children validates Kollontai's theories of the possibility for personality change as a result of collective upbringing. The psychiatrist Bruno Bettelheim's observation that he has never seen children so different from their parents is particularly relevant. How one feels about personalities less emotional, less introspective, but remarkably well-adjusted to working with others will determine whether Bettelheim's conclusion will be regarded as positive or negative.[130] Kollontai, of course, would have rejoiced.

But could the kibbutz spirit have been created by means of forced collectives in a large and diverse nation? There was no way for the Bolsheviks, lacking consensus about the future of the family, to create in Moscow or in Petrograd, let alone on a national scale, Israel's tiny agrarian societies, its cultural cohesiveness and common values. Unfortunately, it is these tightly shared goals and group solidarity that probably provide the key to the success of institutional child-rearing.

If Kollontai pondered these problems, they did not inhibit her.[131] Nor did she face the unhappy fact that the interests of the state and the working mother in an industrialized workers' state were not necessarily identical with those of the young child. If in her zeal to be rid of the family she never studied what combination of institutionalized and individual care would produce the healthiest children, it was because she was not really thinking about the children. Her concern, as was true for the original socialist settlers of the kibbutz, was for the freedom of the adult.[132] Kollontai thought particularly of the mother.

128. According to Bettelheim (p. 123), the group came first, the kibbutz second, and the parents last in order of importance to the child.

129. The family does not exist in a structural-functional sense, but it does in a psychological sense. See Spiro, *Kibbutz*, p. 123. That the idea of the nuclear family persists as a place of privacy and affection suggests that it possesses a vitality that eluded Kollontai's analysis. Whether Kollontai was familiar with the kibbutz experiments is not known.

130. For a negative assessment of kibbutz-reared personalities, see Lasch, p. 220. For observations on reasons for the dissimilarities between generations, see Spiro, *Children*, pp. 336–41. Spiro rather more than Bettelheim discussed emotional disorders among kibbutz-reared children. See his section "The Adolescent Personality," pp. 316–42.

131. She did write of the lack of cooperation and ill-will in the community houses. See Kollontai, *Svobodnaia liubov'* (Riga, 1925), pp. 5–7.

132. Cf. Bettelheim, pp. 32–40.

The tenacity with which Kollontai clung to her illusion that the nuclear family was disappearing was motivated not only by her awareness that the family oppressed women in ways going deeper than daily domesticity but by an intuitive sense of congruence that convinced her that the authoritarian, patriarchal family could not comfortably coexist with the workers' state. That Kollontai would remember her pamphlet as *The Family and Communist Society* when in fact its title was *The Family and the Communist State* seems significant.[133] Kollontai delivered her famous speech under the influence of Lenin's *State and Revolution*, written a year earlier. The problem of the governing apparatus and of the overwhelming role it would assume in people's lives in the Soviet Union was scarcely anticipated in 1918. Rather than the state as directing and molding center, the powerful state would wither, as Lenin predicted, to be replaced by a looser society of collectives.

Again, Kollontai suggested ambiguities she did not try to solve. Though the patriarchal, authoritarian family would not be congruent with a decentralized workers' state, there was no reason to assume that a transformed, "new socialist family" made up of two Communist workers and their Komsomol children would be similarly incongruent. Kollontai's insistence that the family must disappear as a nuclear unit and be replaced by communes grew out of her fear that if any variant of the traditional family structure survived, women would be unlikely to maintain a sense of themselves as free and equal citizens who, in the interests of their work, might choose even to live apart from their lovers.[134] The reason why the "new woman" should not live within the family she explained in another, even more controversial, series of essays.

One historian has dismissed Kollontai's activities between her participation in the political crisis of Brest-Litovsk in 1918 and her leadership of the Workers' Opposition movement in 1921 as an excursion

133. For the incorrect title, see "Avtobiograficheskii ocherk," p. 300. For the problem of congruence in society, see Harry Eckstein, *Division and Cohesion in Democracy: Norway* (Princeton, N. J., 1966), for his "Theory of Stable Democracy," Appendix B. Perhaps intuiting *in*congruence, the Soviet Union abandoned its theoretical attack on the family—it had never advanced into practice—by the end of the 1920's as the regime hardened and moved toward greater authoritarianism. See Eckstein, pp. 17–19.

134. See Kollontai, *Polozhenie zhenshchiny*, p. 190 for the idea that Communist couples might live apart.

into "the harmless subjects of free love and communist family life."[135] They are harmless subjects if trivialized. In 1918 questions of family life were not regarded casually by those Communists who feared Kollontai's influence on Party youth.

Nothing in her inspirational speech to the First All-Russian Congress of Worker and Peasant Women could by itself have overly alarmed a Party loosely committed to the Marxian premise that the bourgeois forms of the family would wither. At the November Congress Kollontai referred briefly to a new kind of marriage, a "superior union of two loving and trusting souls."[136] In *The New Morality and the Working Class*, also published in 1918 but consisting of essays written earlier, Kollontai analyzed the features of a new relationship between the sexes, a marriage purified of its material elements. It was this publication that aroused controversy. *The New Morality* completed her assault on the family by attacking the traditional marital relationship and describing the "new woman" who could live without it.[137]

In studying family customs, anthropologists have confirmed the general proposition that marriages everywhere are primarily an exchange of goods and services and only secondarily an exchange of sentiments such as romantic love. Yet it is the former exchange that customarily makes husbands and wives mutually dependent. Marriages lacking material dependency have traditionally been regarded as more fragile and less likely to endure. Engels failed to discuss whether in his view human psychology allowed for the relative permanence of marriages based only on sexual love and compatibility without economic incentives. Russian Communists in the revolutionary era tended to see no problem. Trotsky was typical in predicting that when the bonds between husband and wife were freed from everything external, "genuine equality would at last be established. The bond will depend on mutual attachment. And on that account particularly, it will acquire inner stability."[138]

135. Schapiro, p. 291.
136. Kollontai, *Sem'ia i kommunisticheskoe gosudarstvo*, p. 21.
137. *Novaia moral' i rabochii klass* contained three parts: "Novaia zhenshchina," "Liubov' i novaia moral'," and "Otnoshenie mezhdu polami i klassovaia bor'ba." The first dated from 1913, the second and third from 1911. Together with *Sem'ia i kommunisticheskoe gosudarstvo*, it pointed Soviet Russia toward a society of collectives that would replace the individual family.
138. Trotsky, *Voprosy byta*, p. 45. The issue is with us today, as witness Lasch, pp. 137-41. The stability of marriages in the kibbutz is of interest here. According to Spiro,

Unlike other Bolsheviks, Kollontai recognized and faced frankly the likelihood that a marriage freed from economic concerns and family responsibility might falter after the initial romance and lose its stability as it ceased to be of material necessity to the partners. Kollontai was unique in that she not only welcomed this outcome but built a theory on it. In the future society a marriage might be extended, based on spiritual affinity, or it might be transient, based on passion and physical attraction. Both would be equally acceptable since each could give the collective healthy children.[139] She rejected the assumption that sex was not for the expression of transitory affection, but only a serious business between mature people who were prepared to accept the long-range consequences. Kollontai's espousal of a "new morality" provoked angry reaction within the Party, even among those Bolsheviks who may have conducted their own lives in accordance with the "new morality" but who balked at publicly advocating sexual freedom.

Once again the myth-maker, seeking always to be a "new woman" and to overcome her "atavistic" longing for an enduring and absorbing love, Kollontai proclaimed the merit of the comradely but short-lived relationship. She explained why the less stable marriage, with its greater flexibility in the relations of the sexes, corresponded to the needs of the proletarian class. Imagine a bourgeois financier who, in a moment of business crisis, withdraws his capital for his family's sake. Kollontai believed this would be seen as proper in terms of bourgeois morality, in which family needs come first. She compared him with the strikebreaker who, in the interests of his family, wanted to work during a strike. Would his comrades not urge him to put the interests of his class first?[140] Hence the stronger the ties of the individual couple or family, the poorer the outlook for workers' solidarity. The worse, too, for the liberation of women, who to be free had to learn to view love and the emotions within family relationships as men did—as only one part of their total existence.

The contention that "less stability" in the relations of the sexes

---

Children, p. 353, marriages within the kibbutz among the Sabra generation tend to be strong, stable, and intimate. His conclusion suggests the influence of group mores on the couple. The present-day kibbutz favors stable marriage, but earlier settlers were not so committed to the institution of marriage and their relationships were less enduring. Marital instability was subsequently judged detrimental to the welfare of the kibbutz. Spiro, *Kibbutz*, pp. 111–24. Conversations with Spiro indicate that it was the older women in particular who found the early, freer situation threatening.

139. Kollontai, "Sem'ia i kommunizm," p. 19.
140. *Novaia moral' i rabochii klass*, pp. 59–60.

coincided with the needs of the working class had a certain plausibility in the prerevolutionary era if one accepted the premise that people needed to be free for the uncertainties of battle. But after the Revolution was consolidated, if "comradeship" were to be the basis of the new morality among the proletariat, how did it benefit the working class that comradeship be short-lived? The answer was not clear. Kollontai's vagueness suggested that she had no obvious political explanation, only an intuitive conviction that new women, in the interests of their personal liberation, must not permit themselves to be entangled irrevocably in love for one man. They would be better served in the commune, which by dint of common and purposeful work would banish the "heavy weight of spiritual solitude" that impelled the bourgeois into romance.[141] In the commune, on the ruins of the former family, a new and looser union would arise, between two equal workers, "a union of affection and comradeship."[142]

Kollontai's *The New Morality and the Working Class* played a historically significant role. Occasionally by itself, more often together with other examples of her writing such as *Love of Three Generations* (in which she described Zhenia, the "new woman") it became a key document for Western commentators, who used it to illustrate the ideological basis for the sexual "anarchy" that flourished in Russia during the Civil War.[143] In the Soviet Union, Kollontai's theories, rather than providing the basis for a communal life, became a political embarrassment. The central image of *The New Morality and the Working Class*, that of a sexual crisis, a remnant of the bourgeois era marked by personal solitude, remained exclusively Kollontai's. Here and there Communists shared her views, but the Party never endorsed them. If there was a sexual problem in 1918 alarming enough to be

141. *Ibid.*, pp. 51–54.
142. *Sem'ia i kommunisticheskoe gosudarstvo*, p. 20.
143. For the use made of Kollontai's ideas in *Novaia moral' i rabochii klass*, see Schlesinger, pp. 69–71; Carr, *Socialism in One Country*, vol. 1, pp. 41–42; Smith, pp. 126–29; Geiger, pp. 44–48; and Halle, pp. 109–12. The "new morality" was a widely known doctrine of sexual revolution during the 1920's. Kollontai shared with Wilhelm Reich, Erich Fromm, Herbert Marcuse, and the "Frankfurt School" a commitment to social change and criticism of the authoritarian family, sexual repression, and puritan morality. There were differences, however. Marcuse, for example, saw Kollontai's commune as repressive because it emphasized the primacy of work. See Marcuse, *Soviet Marxism* (New York, 1961), pp. 233–34. The Frankfurt School combined Marx and Freud. Kollontai did not invoke Freud but was presumably familiar with his work. Greta Meisel-Hesse, whom she endorsed, was a student of Freud's. See Stites, *Women's Liberation Movement*, pp. 348–49. The Soviet professor A. Zalkind claimed that Kollontai was overly influenced by Freud in Em. Iaroslavskii, ed., *Kakim dolzhen byt'*, p. 151.

called a crisis, it was thought to be the result not of spiritual loneliness but of the very marital instability Kollontai found so promising for the socialist women's future. Bolsheviks in the early Soviet period attributed the problems they observed not to the phenomena Kollontai described—loneliness, possessiveness, and inequality, products of the *angst* of bourgeois life—but to the immediate upheaval of Revolution and Civil War.[144]

At the All-Russian Congress of Worker and Peasant Women in November 1918, Kollontai offered women a new self-image. Bury the word "baba," she urged. A few months later, at the Eighth Party Congress in March 1919, which she attended as a delegate from the Central Commission for Work Among Women,[145] she urged the Party to commit itself to the image of a new woman: a woman freed from family cares, not tied to marriage, part of the work force, a member of the Soviet. Many Party comrades, both male and female, were suspicious because of the sexual views expressed in *The New Morality and the Working Class*. But Kollontai was not an easy woman to discourage, and she sought, without any substantial backing, to incorporate her ideas on less stable marriages and the withering away of the family into the new Party program that was being drafted to replace the outdated program of 1903.[146]

Once more it was the cautious rather than the revolutionary Lenin who chided her. What did Kollontai mean, Lenin wanted to know, by the expression the "disappearance of the secluded family"? Where had the precise form the family would take under Communism been described? He reminded Kollontai that the Party program had to respond to practical needs. The Revolution needed to preserve the family from disintegration. There were children to be cared for.[147]

Lenin's rejection of Kollontai's efforts to force the Party to confront the question of marriage and the family indicated his awareness that while White armies were still undefeated, major social questions

---

144. Trotsky, *Voprosy byta*, p. 38, citing the conclusion reached by a meeting of Party propagandists in Moscow.

145. The Commission was connected to the Central Committee of the Party: it was created after the November 1918 Congress. See Kollontai, *Izbrannye stat'i i rechi*, p. 424.

146. For Kollontai's recollection of opposition to her ideas, see her *Autobiography*, p. 43.

147. For Lenin's remarks to Kollontai, see Itkina, p. 208.

could scarcely be approached. His good sense was accompanied, however, by a limited understanding of the woman question. He agreed with Kollontai that women had to be brought out of the home and into public life, and he shared her chagrin when Communist meetings seemed only vaguely concerned with the plight of women.[148] Yet although he had read *Anna Karenina* many times, Aleksandr Herzen's observation that marriage and the family loomed too large in women's psyche eluded him.[149] Lenin believed rather that "because she is engaged in housework a woman is still in a difficult position." For Lenin the woman question had a solution: once private property had been abolished, "to effect her complete emancipation and make her man's equal it is necessary for the national economy to be socialized and for women to participate in common productive labor. Then women will occupy the same position as men."[150] A large part of women's problems he attributed to insufficient attention to this point, which in theory every Communist considered "indisputable." "Do we take proper care of the *shoots* of communism that already exist in this sphere?," Lenin asked. He thought not. "Our press does not take the trouble, or hardly ever, to describe the best catering establishments or nurseries, in order, by daily insistence, to get some of them turned into models of their kind. It does not give them enough publicity."[151]

The Bolsheviks, following Lenin, placed excessive emphasis on domesticity as the source of women's subordinate status. A Party truism held that one of the "most degrading and soul-destroying forms of household slavery in which women find themselves . . . is . . . the kitchen," an aspect of "household slavery" that Lenin condemned as the "pettiest, dirtiest, heaviest, and dullest toil."[152] The kitchen received undue attention. Kollontai was ahead of her time in realizing that women's secondary position derived from the limitations imposed not by the kitchen but by emotional dependency. Thus she credited the early Utopian socialists—the Saint-Simonians, Fourier, and their successors—with appreciating the need to solve the woman question, but she pointed out that they, too, regarded women as com-

148. See Zetkin, p. 41.

149. For Lenin's rereading of *Anna Karenina*, see Krupskaia, *Vospominaniia o Lenine*, p. 217.

150. Lenin speaking to the Fourth Moscow City Conference of Non-Party Working Women, Sept. 23, 1919. *Sochineniia* (4th ed.), vol. 30, p. 25.

151. *Ibid.*, vol. 29, pp. 396–97.

152. As cited in Schlesinger, p. 282.

panions, helpmates, wives, or free lovers rather than as independent workers.[153]

To the extent that Kollontai's analysis of the woman question has relevance to the women's movement today, it lies in this insight. Neither her assumption that women should be mothers nor her prescriptions for communal living are likely to have widespread appeal to working women in modern industrial societies. It may be argued that in 1918 in Russia as well, proletarians and peasants, if they were to become new women, needed more than the communal dining halls that accompanied the Civil War. When Lenin, suspecting feminism, deplored the news that in Germany party workers were arranging discussion groups in which sex and marriage problems were given prime importance, he failed to understand that for women lacking class consciousness, discussion of marriage, the situation with which they most identified and in which they were most subordinate, was the obvious starting point.[154] He overlooked another factor, one that had become apparent to Kollontai in the 1890's as she prepared uneasily to leave husband and child to journey to the University of Zurich. If women were to enter the mainstream of Soviet life and build socialism equally with men, they would first have to overcome their guilt.

The Eighth Party Congress was disappointing on the woman question. A comparison of Kollontai's speech at the Eighth Congress with her recollection of what she had intended indicates that she abandoned her attempt to have the Party endorse her views on the new woman and the new morality. Instead, she switched from general principles to particular issues and in defeat tried to achieve at least a commitment to draw women fully into public life. As an opponent of bourgeois feminism, Kollontai would not express herself in terms that suggested antagonism between men and women. If she ever thought in such images, she applied an inner censorship, thus demanding not an end to male dominance in the Party and in government, but rather a commitment on the part of the Bolsheviks to bring women out of the family and into key roles in the work force.

After initial resistance, the program commission, having rejected Kollontai's points dealing with marriage relationships, did pledge to

153. Kollontai, *Polozhenie zhenshchiny*, p. 123.
154. Zetkin, pp. 44–46. In suggesting that German proletarian women should discuss not marriage but problems like the impact of the Versailles Treaty on their lives, Lenin overlooked the fact that such issues would not bring nonparty women to meetings.

work to draw women into the Party.[155] Recognizing the need to increase its strength by including proletarian and peasant women in the struggle for Communism and for Soviet construction, the Party promised to work to achieve this goal. It was a modest pledge.[156]

When Bukharin later in 1919 wrote *The ABC of Communism* to explain the newly adopted Party program, he avoided expressions that conveyed the idea of an attack by the revolutionary regime on the basic family structure. Religion, the state, banks, the monetary system—each would die out. But the family was left intact in all but its housekeeping and day-care aspects.[157] Bukharin's reference points were familiar: liberation of women from household slavery through the organization of community houses with central laundries and kitchens, communal nurseries, kindergartens, and summer colonies. Bukharin wrote that women must cease to be timid and diffident; they must enter public life. But he did not allude to Kollontai's precept that to be a new woman the "kommunistka" must change her priorities, that she must cease to live primarily for marriage, that her work must become a motivating force in her life.[158] Bukharin emphasized practical improvements, avoiding Kollontai's pejoratives about the narrow self-absorption of the isolated family. Nonetheless, he was one of the prominent Bolsheviks, along with Krylenko, Lunacharskii, and Trotsky, who at one time or another expressed the conviction that the family would disappear.[159]

The concept of "withering away" eluded Party consensus because to different people it meant different things. Most Bolsheviks, as we have already noted, neither expected nor hoped to see the demise of the nuclear family. Aleksandr Herzen had predicted years before that the bourgeois world, blown up by gunpowder, would arise again, once the smoke had settled and the ruins had been cleared, in a modi-

155. See Kollontai, "Avtobiograficheskii ocherk," p. 301.

156. See Kollontai, *Izbrannye stat'i i rechi*, p. 273. For this pledge, see USSR, [20], p. 435. At the first congress of the new Communist International in Mar. 1919, Kollontai proposed a similar resolution to commit the Comintern to drawing working women into the Communist movement. *Izbrannye stat'i i rechi*, p. 424.

157. Kollontai wrote that there was nothing about the family of the future in the Party program. See Kollontai, "Sem'ia i kommunizm," p. 18. Nothing was said about the family of the future in the 1903 Party program either. For the two Party programs, see USSR, [6], vol. 1, pp. 37–43 (1903), and pp. 408–55 (1919).

158. For Bukharin's views, see Bukharin and Preobrazhenskii, pp. 124–25. For Kollontai's view, *see Novaia moral' i rabochii klass*, pp. 8–9.

159. Bukharin's own family experiences were traditional. Krupskaia, for example, recalled a humorous incident involving Bukharin's maladroit cooking when his wife was ill. Krupskaia, *Vospominaniia o Lenine*, pp. 212–13.

fied form because it was not yet internally exhausted and the new world was not yet ready to replace it. Kollontai was not prepared to acknowledge in 1918, as the old order seemed to be crumbling, that Herzen had foreseen the tenacity with which both the revolutionary Party and the backward masses would cling to the familiar concept of marriage and family.

CHAPTER SIX

Director of the Zhenotdel

FOR two years, from the close of the First All-Russian Congress of Worker and Peasant Women in November of 1918 until she joined the Workers' Opposition in the winter of 1920–21, Kollontai immersed herself in Party work. First as an organizer during the Civil War and then as director of the newly founded Zhenotdel, the Women's Section of the Central Committee, she adapted her practice to the moderate possibilities that were all Russia's backwardness and Lenin's tactics permitted. But, as we shall see, Kollontai's ideological solutions to the woman question continued to be more radical than her practice implied, and frequently more radical than her comrades liked. Possibilities for friction increased when Kollontai extended her theories from the working woman in the factory to the peasant woman in the village and the prostitute on the street.

In the spring of 1919, the Central Committee sent Kollontai to the Ukraine to rally the population to the Soviet. Her father's stories of his youth in the area had prepared Kollontai for a land of country estates and peaceful backwaters. The reality was quite different. Moscow in 1919, despite the hunger, was a haven compared to the south of Russia, which was seething with civil war, Red and White terror, pogroms, typhus epidemics, and the disorganization of agricultural and industrial life. Along the road from the filthy station, hungry, exhausted people dragged emaciated children.[1]

Kollontai defended the Revolution in the south with comrades from *émigré* days and Brest-Litovsk controversies—especially Evgeniia Bosh and her husband Iurii Piatakov, who together headed the Soviet government in the Ukraine. Piatakov, bearded, tall, and dignified, barely escaped death at the hands of the Whites. His brother, less fortunate, was shot. Evgeniia Bosh, like Kollontai, was a militant

---

1. Itkina, p. 180.

Bol'shevichka. She had begun her political life in the Ukraine years earlier when, at the age of 21, she left her husband, the son of a factory owner to whom she had been married at sixteen, and immersed herself in socialist policies in Kiev.[2] During the Civil War Evgeniia slept with a revolver under her pillow and became a legendary heroine, famous for her handling of the Germans, the Whites, and the Ukrainian nationalists. A few years later, this brave oppositionist and follower of Trotsky, disillusioned and depressed, used the revolver to take her own life. But Kollontai would remember Bosh as she was during the Civil War, warm and exuberant, straining every nerve in struggle.[3]

No problem was more acute than military desertion. Frequently the most flamboyant Bolsheviks made the greatest contribution in combating it. On the Northwest front, Trotsky was "the soul of the resistance. . . . He was to be seen on horseback literally under machine-gun fire, bringing back stragglers to the front line."[4] Kollontai, too, was indefatigable. Making speeches, writing pamphlets, the former pacifist fought in the south to keep the Red Army soldiers at the front. If her propaganda was remarkably effective, it was because she spoke of feelings that others were reluctant or unable to express. She could not physically drag soldiers back to the front, but she could employ the manipulative weapons of guilt and fear. Her pamphlet "There Will Be no Deserters!," a vivid example of her ability simultaneously to empathize and to coerce, is worth pausing to consider. Here was a less familiar Kollontai, relentless and strident, occasionally even harsh, who appealed to the soldiers by raising and demolishing one by one the possible reasons for their desertion. Kollontai knew that the soldiers were worried about their families, who might be starving, knew that they feared they were needed in the villages to harvest the grain. Perhaps they were not sure why they were fighting. She assured them that the local Soviet was caring for their families, providing each mother, wife, or child of a Red Army man with a

2. For Piatakov, see Conquest, p. 9. For Bosh, see A. Solzhenitsyn, *Lenin in Zurich,* trans. H. T. Willetts (New York, 1976), p. 272, and "Evgeniia Bogdanovna Bosh" in *Deiateli SSSR,* vol. 41, part 2, cols. 42–43. Bosh and Piatakov escaped Siberian exile at one point by way of Japan and America. Lenin and Krupskaia referred to their new comrades as "the Japanese" when they joined forces with them in exile. Krupskaia, *Vospominaniia o Lenine,* p. 247.

3. Serge, pp. 194–95, describes Bosh in the Ukraine. For Kollontai on Bosh see *Izbrannye stat'i i rechi,* p. 373.

4. Souvarine, p. 243.

ration and seeing also that the grain was taken in.[5] But she warned that if the men deserted, their families would be deprived of rations. Worse, if the front fell, the enemy would overrun their fields, requisition their grain and horses, violate their women. In a personal tone, and using the familiar form, she warned men who might be thinking of deserting of their fate if the enemy entered their villages. "What would become of you, a former Red Army man? Do you think the enemy will pardon you? He will find you, wherever you are! He will mobilize you! He will force you to fight your brothers in the Red Army!" Kollontai reminded the would-be deserters of the tears of their wives and mothers. If the landlords, the generals, and the priests took power again, it would be their fault. The villagers would call them cowards. "There will be no deserters!"[6]

Other documents echo Kollontai's militancy and recreate the mood of Bolsheviks in the Ukraine. Early in 1920 three young women were executed by White Guards. The letters they wrote before they were shot were testimony to the effectiveness of Bolshevik agitation. "I am dying honorably," one young woman wrote to her comrades. "In eight days I shall be 22, but I am to be shot this evening. It's a pity to die like this, a pity because I have done so little for the Revolution. Only now I feel I am really a revolutionary and Party worker. . . . Soon, very soon, the whole of the Ukraine will breathe freely and constructive work will begin. It's a pity I shall not take part in it."[7]

Brave letters written by true believers told only part of the story. They did not convey the frightful uncertainty that presented the greatest danger for agitators like Kollontai. Traveling from one workers' settlement to another and from village to village, the Communists did not know when they would be greeted by sympathizers who, here and there, formed pockets of Soviet strength, and when by anarchist bandits or, as one Communist recalled bitterly, by "kulaks" ready to murder the Communists and welcome Denikin "with bread and salt."

Working frequently just behind the front lines, hastily departing in the midst of meetings when word was unexpectedly whispered

5. Kollontai, *Ne bud' dezertirom!*, pp. 4–5. Compulsory labor armies in the rural areas cultivated the fields and harvested the crops of families of Red Army soldiers. See USSR, [7], pp. 16–22. Families of Red Army men in the villages were generally exempt from labor obligation.

6. *Ne bud' dezertirom!*, pp. 5–15.

7. Cited in Bochkarëva and Lyubimova, *Women of a New World*, p. 80.

that the White army was approaching, Kollontai would sleep on
trains, exhaustion overcoming fear, despite bullets cracking through
the night. She proudly recalled that when she spoke on station platforms workmen in the crowd recognized her. "It's Kollontai," someone would say.[8] And the workers would listen to the unlikely agitator
who, we must keep reminding ourselves, was not a young Party
aktivistka but a middle-aged woman, formerly from the upper classes,
who spoke the special language of the Communist Party in the educated tones of the nobility. A comrade recalled the initial mistrust
with which working-class audiences regarded this beautiful "fine
lady." But after a few minutes suspicion dissipated in the face of Kollontai's eloquence, which was earthy and personal, and without condescension.[9]

Kollontai continued to carry out Party tasks in the south during the
summer—among Komsomol youth, trade unions, and working wom-
en. Dybenko, too, was in the area, having been reassigned to active
duty in the autumn of 1918. During the spring of 1919 he commanded
the Crimean Army and also held the post of Commissar for the Army
and Navy in the Crimean Republic. Kollontai saw him only occasionally, as a result of his military duties and her Party work. The Union
of Metalworkers sent her as their delegate in April to the All-
Ukrainian Congress of Trade Unions in Kharkov. For a month and a
half she lived in that city, working closely with Samoilova and laying
the basis for organizing working women.[10] After the evacuation of
Kharkov, Kollontai moved to the Crimea, serving as Chairwoman of
the Enlightenment Department in the Red Army. In that southern
region the scent of blooming magnolias and the splash of the sea occasionally made the Civil War seem unreal. But Denikin's forces advanced. On the eve of evacuation, the last call to the population from
the Soviet government came from Aleksandra Kollontai. From the
Crimea she went to Kiev, where she served as People's Commissar
of Enlightenment and Propaganda in the Ukrainian government
headed by her handsome, Rumanian-born friend Christian Rakovskii, who like Kollontai was one of the most broadly educated and

8. Itkina, pp. 180–83.
9. For the Communists' special language, see Selishchev. For workers' reaction to
Kollontai as a speaker, see Zaitsev, p. 171.
10. For Kollontai in the south of Russia during the Civil War, see Itkina, pp. 180–
83; Kollontai, *Izbrannye stat'i i rechi*, p. 424, and Kollontai, "Avtobiograficheskii
ocherk," p. 301. Kollontai and Samoilova established the working women's page in the
Kharkov Party newspaper. See Kollontai, "Tvorcheskoe v rabote tovarishcha K. N.
Samoilovoi," *Kommunistka*, 1922, nos. 3–5, pp. 8–11.

cultured of the Bolsheviks. She continued her activities organizing women, this time in partnership with Varvara Moirova, her comrade in the women's movement.[11] But as Denikin continued to advance, the Soviet government was forced in August to flee the city.

Returning to Moscow in September, settling into the big Hotel National that since the Revolution had housed Communist leaders, Kollontai immersed herself again in Party work. She had hoped first to be able to visit her son Misha in Petrograd, but there was no time. Her need invariably to subordinate her personal life disturbed her. She wrote lovingly to Misha, who was a student in the Technological Institute, about her longing to rush to Petrograd to see him, if only for 24 hours, but explained that she was unable to leave Moscow. There was urgent work to be done in connection with the First International Conference of Communist Women, which was scheduled to be held in July 1920. She wrote frankly of the conflict between her longing to be with him and the pressures of her work for the Party.[12] Elsewhere she described the torment of knowing that Misha must be hungry but having nothing to send him.[13] She feared for him in Petrograd, a city that had become "nothing but dust, darkness, and yawning emptiness."[14] Only the wonder of revolution sustained her. A few years earlier, socialism seemed an inaccessible dream; now she was part of a Communist government working to bring it about. The knowledge brightened her days and made bearable the ever-present deprivation.[15]

❧❧❧

Letters and diary excerpts leave no doubt about Kollontai's compulsive attachment to the Party and her identification with the Revolution. How the Party related to Kollontai in 1919 is less obvious. Clearly she was valued as an agitator. How much so was suggested by her appointment in the late summer of 1919 as the Central Committee's emissary to the Komsomol Central Committee. The middle-aged woman whose *New Morality and the Working Class* had been "bit-

11. For her propaganda work in the Ukraine, see Kollontai, "Avtobiograficheskii ocherk," p. 301. Before leaving Kiev, Kollontai sent 400 women Communists out of the threatened zone by special train. *Autobiography*, p. 42. For Kollontai and Moirova, see Zinaida Chalaia, "V Pervykh riadakh," in Zhak and Itkina, eds., p. 267.

12. For her letter to Misha, see Itkina, pp. 194–95. Kollontai missed the Conference in July 1920 owing to illness.

13. Kollontai, *Iz moei zhizni i raboty*, p. 357.

14. The poet Anna Akhmatova described Petrograd thus. See Haight, p. 57.

15. Kollontai, *Iz moei zhizni i raboty*, p. 358.

terly fought by many Party members of both sexes" less than a year before because they feared its effect on the morals of youth was now paradoxically delegated by the Central Committee to the Komsomol, the Young Communist organization.[16] Of course, this did not mean that the Party had decided to endorse her views; rather, it probably meant that Kollontai's controversial sexual theories were thought to appeal to youth. The Bolsheviks needed all the help they could get in the late summer of 1919, when they seemed on the verge of losing the Civil War. Their sending Kollontai to rally young people was a sign of their desperation.[17]

Kollontai's appointment to the Komsomol Central Committee was the more curious in that the Party, in making it, excluded her from the directorship of a new organ that should logically have fallen to her. In the autumn of 1919, when the Central Commission for Agitation and Propaganda Among Working Women was reorganized into the Section for Work Among Women (the Zhenotdel), Kollontai, the central figure in the Russian socialist women's movement since 1905, was passed over in the choice of director in favor of Inessa Armand.[18] Kollontai had little to say about the episode; and the fact that she never referred to being overlooked in favor of Inessa but instead assumed the credit for laying the basis for the Zhenotdel only empha-

16. See Kollontai's *Autobiography*, p. 43, for attacks on *Novaia moral' i rabochii klass*.

17. Another factor may have been involved. Lenin and Kollontai had a different sense of the relationship between women and youth. Lenin, who saw increased contact between women and youth as natural and mutually beneficial, urged Communist women to "cooperate methodically" with young people. For women it would be a continuation of motherhood, he thought, which would benefit them by extending their customary role to the social sphere. Tsetkin, "Lenin o morali i voprosakh pola," in Razin, ed., pp. 17–18. Kollontai, by contrast, saw such contact as a union of potential rebels, both dependent and sexually restricted by the traditional family.

18. After the Congress of Worker and Peasant Women in 1918, the Women's Bureau, with Sverdlov's help, had been reorganized into the Central Commission for Agitation and Propaganda Among Working Women. Its leaders were Kollontai, Moirova, Golubeva, and Inessa Armand. See Golubeva in *Kommunistka*, Nov. 1923, no. 11, p. 17; Bochkarëva and Liubimova, *Svetly put'*, p. 81; and Moirova in *Kommunistka*, Nov. 1923, no. 11, p. 10. The Commission was attached to the Central Committee and was in turn reorganized into the Zhenotdel. Beginning with the Central Commission in Moscow, a network of Women's Sections attached to the local Party committees fanned out into city and provincial districts. Kollontai, *Rabotnitsa i krest'ianka v sovetskoi rossii*, p. 6. The Zhenotdel also had representatives in each of the Commissariats to protect women's interests. Itkina, pp. 197–200. Kollontai became, with Bukharin, Krupskaia, Armand, Vinogradskaia, and Nikolaeva, one of the six editors of the Zhenotdel's monthly journal, *Kommunistka*. Bukharin may have been included to avoid charges of feminism and to safeguard ideological purity. Krupskaia was editor-in-chief. *Kommunistka* was the theoretical journal of the Zhenotdel, *Rabotnitsa* its weekly newspaper. There were several local women's magazines such as *Krest'ianka, Delegatka, Krasnaia Sibiriachka*. See Stites, "Zhenotdel," p. 183. Also see Hayden.

sizes that this must have been a painful memory.[19] Kollontai was rejected in favor of someone safer and more easily controlled. Inessa shared Kollontai's views on the "new morality," but like Krupskaia she was sensitive to Lenin's disapproval and unlikely to be recalcitrant. She was in any event as qualified by commitment and experience as Kollontai to be the first director of the Zhenotdel.

When Inessa died suddenly of cholera in September 1920, Kollontai was allowed to replace her as director despite the misgivings of Party leaders. Emma Goldman recalled an illustrative episode, Kollontai's eulogy at the funeral of the American Communist John Reed, whose death also occurred in 1920, in Moscow. "We call ourselves Communists," Kollontai said, "but are we really that? Do we not rather draw the life essence from those who come to us, and when they are no longer of use, do we not let them fall by the wayside, neglected and forgotten? Our Communism and our comradeship are dead letters if we do not give of ourselves to those who need us. Let us beware of such Communism. It slays the best in our ranks. Jack Reed was among the best." The Central Committee members, according to Goldman, exchanged looks of displeasure at such public frankness.[20] According to Angelica Balabanoff, Kollontai was a "frequent source of both personal and political annoyance" to the leaders. More than once the Central Committee asked Balabanoff to substitute for Kollontai in the leadership of the women's movement, "thus facilitating the campaign against her and isolating her from the women of the masses." Balabanoff understood what she called the "intrigue." She refused these offers, emphasizing that no one could do the work as well as Kollontai.[21]

Despite the uneasiness of the Party, Kollontai became officially in September 1920 what she had long been informally—the head of the Russian socialist women's movement, which now had an institutional home, the Zhenotdel. The Zhenotdel was unusual among Communist

19. For Kollontai's assumption that *her* work laid the basis for the Zhenotdel, see Kollontai, "V. I. Lenin i pervyi s"ezd rabotnits," in *Iz moei zhizni i raboty*, p. 355. Inessa's role in originating the journal *Rabotnitsa* in 1914 attests to her early commitment to the socialist women's movement. See A. F. Bessonova, pp. 25–26.

20. Goldman, p. 169.

21. Balabanoff, *My Life as a Rebel*, p. 251. When Clara Zetkin in the autumn of 1920 urged Balabanoff not to leave Russia but to stay and become Secretary of the International Women's Movement, Zetkin implicitly joined the group willing to shunt Kollontai aside. *Ibid.*, p. 290.

institutions in that it developed, from its beginnings in the autumn of 1917 as a Women's Bureau, not as a result of Party policy, but primarily as a result of an idea raised and shepherded by a few concerned Communist women. If not for this group, according to Kollontai, little would have happened in the area of special efforts to bring women into the Party.[22] Unfortunately for the Zhenotdel, its origins never ceased to plague it. Despite Kollontai's insistence that the Zhenotdel was not separate but subordinate to Party discipline and purpose, Communists tended to regard it as an institution cut off from general Party work rather than as an integral part of the Central Committee.[23] As a result, its members needed always to be alert to the charge of "feminism."[24] The Zhenotdel was particularly interesting because it absorbed much of the female talent within the Party and generated a vigorous institutional loyalty. Though it never operated separately, we will see that it did function as an interest group, a cause within a cause.

The women who joined the Social Democratic Party before the Revolution and became active later in the Zhenotdel tended to be from the educated upper class.[25] Of the eight-member staff of *Rabotnitsa*, one woman, Nikolaeva, was from the working class.[26] The others, if not all privileged, were educated and cultured. Two, Samoilova and Bonch-Bruevich, were daughters of priests. Of the six women who represented Russia in the International Women's Secretariat in 1920, none was from the working class.[27]

Zhenotdel women who joined the Party in 1917 or after were more

22. Kollontai, "Proizvodstvo i byt," p. 8.

23. For Kollontai's denial of separateness or even that Zhenotdel staff needed to be exclusively female, see "Doklad o rabote sredi zhenshchin na VIII S"ezde RKP (b), 22 Marta, 1919," USSR, [20], pp. 296–300.

24. Itkina, pp. 200–201. A women's section within the Communist Party was not unique to Soviet Russia. In 1921, Kollontai reported that Communist women's sections existed not only in Germany but in Bulgaria, Czechoslovakia, Sweden, Italy, and France. Kollontai, *Rabotnitsa i krest'ianka*, p. 26.

25. Only after the Revolution did the Party incorporate working-class women to any significant degree. The directors of the Zhenotdel illustrate the social pattern: the first two, Inessa and Kollontai, came from the upper classes; the third, Sof'ia Smidovich, was middle-class; and the last two, Nikolaeva and Artiukhina, were working-class.

26. The staff included, in 1917, K. Samoilova, A. I. Elizarova, P. Kudelli, V. Bonch-Bruevich, Z. Lilina, L. Stal', A. Kollontai, and K. Nikolaeva. Liudmila Menzhinskaia, an editor of *Rabotnitsa* in 1914 and a *Pravda* journalist who became a deputy director of the Zhenotdel in 1921, was also a well-educated woman from a cultured background. For Menzhinskaia, see N. Iurova, "Sestry menzhinskie," in Zhak and Itkina, eds., pp. 249–60, 564–65.

27. Kollontai, *Vsesoiuznaia kommunisticheskaia partiia (bol'shevikov). Tsentral'nyi komitet. Otdel po rabote sredi zhenshchin. Otchet.* (Hereafter *Otchet*), p. 15. The six were Krupskaia, Kollontai, Lilina, Stal', Samoilova, and Smidovich.

frequently from workers' families. Varvara Moirova, who worked with Kollontai on the First All-Russian Congress of Worker and Peasant Women in 1918, was an example. One of eight children, Moirova grew up in the Crimea, her mother a laundress, her father a shoemaker. Her younger sister Zinaida remembered that their mother cried when Varvara, then a *gimnaziia* student, and their older brother Nikolai joined in street demonstrations in 1905. Although in the orbit of her brother's revolutionary activity, Varvara graduated from the *gimnaziia* and even received a gold medal. She then enrolled in Higher Women's Courses in Odessa just before the war. She married a medical student, who on completing his studies went to the front, leaving Moirova with a small child. Her family responsibilities did not prevent her from being in the thick of student life, which meant involvement in the political struggle and friendship with Bolsheviks who worked in the Odessa underground. Either from the students or from the Bolsheviks, Moirova received a copy of Lenin's *What Is to Be Done?* Her sister Zinaida recalled how they read revolutionary literature together while Varvara's son slept nearby.

In the summer of 1917 Varvara Moirova became a Bolshevik, joining the Party in Odessa. She was chosen as a member of the Executive Committee of the local Soviet, and after October she became a local Commissar of Public Welfare. After the retreat of the Red Army during the Civil War, Moirova left Odessa and worked for the Party in Moscow, living with Zinaida (now a journalist and also a Party member) in a lively, very Russian atmosphere of conversation and comradeship.

Moirova's friendship with Kollontai probably began at this time, as they worked together organizing the November 1918 Women's Congress. Later, Moirova also worked with Kollontai in the Ukraine, remaining there as a member of the Commissariat of Public Welfare until Kiev was besieged by Denikin's forces.[28]

In the local branches Zhenotdel leaders were frequently from proletarian and peasant families. One, Vera Alekseevna, head of the Zhenotdel of Ivanovo-Voznesensk in 1926, was a peasant woman who at

28. After the liberation of Kiev and Kharkhov, Moirova worked with Samoilova organizing a Ukrainian Zhenotdel and became its first director. During the 1920's, Moirova served in Moscow first as Kollontai's deputy in the Zhenotdel and then as Zetkin's deputy in the International Women's Secretariat. The organization of collective feeding was her special interest. At the Sixth Comintern Congress she became a candidate member of the Executive Committee of the Comintern. In 1933 she received the Order of Lenin. She died in 1951. See Zhak and Itkina, eds., pp. 262–70, and Smith, pp. 194–95.

the age of ten had gone to work in a cigarette factory in the Ukraine for seven rubles a month. An American who visited her and the textile workers in her district described the Zhenotdel leader, who lived in tiny quarters in Ivanovo-Voznesensk with her three children and elderly mother. "Anywhere but in Russia, Vera's strange figure would have been followed by stares. . . . A rough boy's cap was pulled over her more than boyish bob, a nondescript rusty black jacket strained to make both ends meet across her expansive bosom, her short skirt exposed about six inches of white stocking above heavy black shoes encased in a pair of man's galoshes that grew to twice their size as we picked our way through the sticky mud to the Zhenotdel headquarters."[29] A dynamo of energy, Vera Alekseevna taught classes, presided over evening conferences, coordinated political and educational activities among factory women, and sent organizers out to the villages. Her assistant had only recently been a textile worker in the local factory.

Another working-class woman was Aleksandra Vasil'evna Artiukhina, a delegate to the All-Russian Congress of Worker and Peasant Women in 1918 and a member of the Central Committee in the mid-1920's. Born in 1889 into a weaver's family in Vyshnii Volochëk, Artiukhina joined the Social Democratic Party in 1910. From the age of twelve she worked in weaving factories. Her career sounded typical of the revolutionary woman: arrested and exiled several times, she became assistant director of the Zhenotdel in 1924, and director in 1927.[30]

How did backward Russian women respond to the initiatives of the Zhenotdel? Or to put it another way, how did the "fine ladies" who formed the original core of the institution crack the tough barrier of class? The women they sought to reach were people different from themselves, whose instinctive reaction was suspicion. One Zhenotdel leader recalled the hostile cries of "bread" and "down with the Bolsheviks" shouted by working women at a factory where she went during the Civil War. A working woman spoke to her sharply: she was not one of them. They were not fooled because she dressed in a working woman's shawl. She was really a fine lady. Had she ever

29. Smith, pp. 52–57.

30. On Artiukhina, see "Artiukhina, Aleksandra Vasil'evna," in the *Great Soviet Encyclopedia* (New York, 1973; trans. of 3d ed.), vol. 2, p. 383. On Armand, Nikolaeva, and Smidovich, see *Bol'shaia Sovetskaia Entsiklopediia* (2d ed., Moscow), vol. 3 (1950), p. 37; vol. 30 (1954), p. 4; and vol. 39 (1957), p. 404.

worked fourteen hours in a factory? Had her child been born on the shop floor, under the machines?[31]

If Communists like Kollontai, Samoilova, and Inessa Armand— "fine ladies" all—were able to bridge the gulf of class, it was because their appeal transcended class. Examples abound of instances in which the appeal by the Communist woman to the *rabotnitsa* was frankly woman-to-woman. Consider an episode in 1917, when the women in the Central Post and Telegraph Office refused to work. John Reed wrote of the opposition of women office workers to the Bolsheviks. The workers, "over-dressed, fashion-aping little girls, with pinched faces and leaky shoes," narrated their sufferings at the hands of the proletariat and proclaimed their loyalty to "all that was old, established, and powerful."[32] Lenin sent Kollontai to persuade this hostile group to cease their opposition. She had no success arguing the need to establish normal communications in the city; but when she began to speak to the telegraph workers as women and to describe Bolshevik intentions to lighten their lives, their mood changed and they applauded her.[33]

Because the Communist women identified so closely with their female constituency, the Zhenotdel was able eventually to overcome what might otherwise have been an impenetrable class barrier. The Zhenotdel was also spared another problem: the hostility workers' wives expressed when women agitators tried to stir up their husbands. Kollontai and her comrades in the Zhenotdel spoke to the women, not to their husbands, and they came not as outsiders seeking to organize the lower classes but as comrades in arms. They tried to live within the situation. Each of the former "fine ladies" was a propertyless revolutionary who, having cut all ties to the past, had no safe position to which she might retreat.[34]

Their problems in appealing to the proletarian and peasant women were hardly new: they had concerned revolutionaries in Russia for nearly a century. Few recorded their reflections as honestly or as warmly as Praskov'ia Ivanovskaia, a member of the populist People's Will. The daughter of a village priest, Ivanovskaia went to work in a rope factory in the 1870's among women who were driven "by the

31. The incident involved Smidovich. See F. Susloparova, "V stuzhu," in Zhak and Itkina, eds., pp. 432–33.
32. Reed, p. 266.
33. Itkina, p. 176.
34. For hostility to female agitators in Russia, see Mandel, p. 35.

most pressing need, by the cruelest misfortune." She believed that the illiterate women were eager to learn, but when could she teach them? How could she conduct propaganda among women who were totally exhausted at the end of the day? Ivanovskaia blamed herself for her failure. "A few girls were becoming interested in reading and had begun to drop in at my apartment, and in time I might have been able to propagandize and organize them." But conditions at the factory were too difficult and depressing, and Ivanovskaia left.[35]

Not all the women in the Zhenotdel entered with the same enthusiasm. Though the core who made up the first *Rabotnitsa* staff were dedicated to the socialist women's movement from the outset, some Zhenotdel workers were simply drafted by the Party into the Women's Section against their wishes. Kollontai recalled how older members of the women's movement like Konkordiia Samoilova scorned those who considered a Zhenotdel assignment demeaning.[36] These women did not embrace socialism because of a concern for the woman question; in the tradition of Rosa Luxemburg, they regarded women's emancipation as a by-product of a successful socialist revolution and saw no reason to devote time to "subsidiary" questions. For those who were disappointed or angered by an assignment to the Zhenotdel, who felt that to be limited to woman's work was to be less of a revolutionary, the first attitude to be changed was their own.

Vera Alekseevna recalled that after the Civil War, when she was requisitioned to work among women, everyone laughed. She who had taken part in strikes, who had been in jail more times than she could remember, who had been sent to the front to propagandize among the soldiers and had fought in the Civil War wearing men's clothing—she had become a member of the Women's Section! "They didn't think of me as a 'baba' at all. I didn't think much of the idea myself at first—I was so used to chasing around like a man, and wearing men's clothes. . . . But I had to obey Party discipline—and it turned out that I wasn't so badly suited for the work after all."[37] Zhenotdel work was hardly confining. Samples from Kollontai's organizational report at the end of 1920 under the heading "The Movement of Workers for the Month of November" show that comrades were commandeered

35. Engel and Rosenthal, eds., pp. 104–5.
36. Kollontai, "Tvorcheskoe v rabote tovarishcha K. N. Samoilovoi," p. 10.
37. Smith, p. 53. There were supposedly instances, on the other hand, of women who voluntarily became unpaid Zhenotdel organizers. See Bochkarëva and Liubimova, *Svetlyi put'*, pp. 83–84.

within that time to go from Perm to Smolensk, from Moscow to Kazan, from Odessa to Novgorod.[38]

Working among Bolsheviks like Kollontai, Inessa, Krupskaia, Nikolaeva, and Samoilova was sometimes enough to alter the views of unenthusiastic young recruits. Polina Vinogradskaia, one of the original members of the editorial board of *Kommunistka*, described her dismay when Elena Stasova assigned her to the Zhenotdel in 1920. She who dreamed of raising cities from ruin, of restoring the economy, had fallen into the Women's Section! Stasova was deaf to entreaties that she be assigned elsewhere.[39] But Stasova's turn was to come: that same year, having been removed from the Secretariat, Stasova was disheartened to be advised to go to work in the Zhenotdel. That kind of activity did not appeal to her, she replied stiffly to Krestinskii, the Party Secretary. Yet by 1921 she was doing impressive work in the Zhenotdel.[40]

As for Vinogradskaia, she appealed to Inessa Armand, claiming a lack of experience. But Inessa assured her that when she found how necessary the work was she would be satisfied. And indeed her frequent articles in *Kommunistka* were testimony to Vinogradskaia's ultimate dedication to the Zhenotdel. A scholarly woman who did not confine herself to the women's movement, Vinogradskaia published in the mid-1920's a learned article on the relationship between Marx and Lasalle, based on their correspondence.[41] Then she began a biography of Jenny Marx. Her husband, the economic theoretician Preobrazhenskii, was purged as a Trotskyite, but Vinogradskaia was spared. She lived to see *Zhenii Marks* appear in a fifth edition (1969) and to publish her own memoirs.[42] Looking back after forty years, she agreed that Inessa was right. A young romantic, she benefited from contact with the committed founders of the Zhenotdel.[43] Stasova,

38. Kollontai, *Otchet*, p. 6.

39. Vinogradskaia, *Sobytiia*, p. 199.

40. For Stasova to Krestinskii, see Stasova, *Stranitsy zhizny i bor'by*, p. 110. For Stasova in the Zhenotdel, see *ibid.*, p. 116. Kollontai credited Stasova with initiating Zhenotdel work among women in Central Asia. See *Rabotnista i krest'ianka*, p. 15. For the Zhenotdel in Central Asia, see Massell.

41. Vinogradskaia, "Vzaimootnosheniia Marksa i Lassalia po ikh perepiske," Kommunisticheskaia Akademiia Moscow *Vestnik* (1925), pp. 88–164.

42. Vinogradskaia, *Zhenii Marks* (Moscow, 1933). Vinogradskaia began her memoirs in *Novyi Mir*: "Oktiabr' v Moskve," *Novyi Mir*, 1966, no. 4, pp. 143–86, and "Serdtse, otdannoe narodu," *Novyi Mir*, 1969, no. 2, pp. 186–204. For her friendship with Trotsky, see correspondence as listed in G. Fischer, "Guide to the papers of Leon Trotsky and related collections in the Harvard College Library" (2d version, 1959).

43. Vinogradskaia, *Sobytiia*, pp. 199–200.

on the other hand, despite years of service in the Zhenotdel, never fully identified with her work among women, preferring at the end of a long life to be remembered in other capacities.[44]

Under neither Inessa Armand nor Kollontai would the Zhenotdel be monolithic. Commitment to a common cause—solution of the woman question—did not ensure either political or stylistic uniformity. Kollontai, Iakovleva, and Inessa were leftists at the time of Brest-Litovsk, whereas Stasova and Krupskaia supported Lenin. Vinogradskaia and Iakovleva became Trotskyists; Stasova and Smidovich followed Stalin; Nikolaeva became a Zinovievist.[45]

Although officially a section of the Central Committee, the Zhenotdel functioned, for reasons we will discuss elsewhere, as a relatively autonomous institution. Participatory democracy marked its style, and the pages of *Kommunistka* reflected the lively ferment of ideas to which each woman, no matter how young or how recent her Party membership, freely contributed.[46] This remarkable journal does more than provide insight into the workings of the Zhenotdel. *Kommunistka* tells us better than any other source about the Zhenotdel's concern for the quality of socialist life. A composite issue reflecting Kollontai's own thinking might include such titles as "The Protection of Motherhood," "The Family and Communism," "Drawing in of Worker and Peasant Women to the Social-Political Structure," "Labor Conscription and the Protection of Women's Work," "The Role of Public Feeding in the Lives of Working Women," and "On the Social Upbringing of Children."

As we might expect, an institution headed by Kollontai and based on collegiality was subject to intense disagreements. Kollontai's central concern—how to find the most effective means of "liberating" the Russian woman—itself became a subject of dispute when she focused on one of the most controversial issues in early Soviet society, labor conscription. The question became: did labor conscription, made

44. See Stasova, *Stranitsy zhizni i bor'by*, and *Vospominaniia*.

45. For Nikolaeva, see Daniels, p. 389. For Inessa as a Left Communist, see Chapter 2, n. 62 above, and Schapiro, p. 366. Vinogradskaia has suggested that Inessa and Kollontai worked poorly together, that Inessa found working with Kollontai uncongenial because their approaches to people and to organization differed. Vinogradskaia, *Pamiatnye vstrechi*, pp. 196–98. Vinogradskaia's bias against Kollontai is discussed in Chapter 10; still, Kollontai never suggested a close relationship between herself and Inessa.

46. For the Zhenotdel's relative autonomy, see the undated document "Ocherednye zadachi otdelov po rabote sredi zhenshchin," USSR, [16], vol. 1, p. 129. Negative aspects of its ambiguous status are discussed in Chapter 9. Kollontai avoided imposing her authority on younger members. See Itkina, p. 203.

universal in 1920, liberate or oppress Soviet women? Let us look first at the origins of the issue.[47]

The Soviet government in January 1920 proclaimed the Universal Compulsory Labor Law. Its architect was Trotsky, whose military tone was objectionable to many.

In a society which is in a transitional phase of its development and which is burdened with the inheritance of a distressing past, the passage to a planned organization of socialized labor is inconceivable without compulsory measures. . . . The weapon of state compulsion is military force. Therefore the militarization of labor, in one form or another, is inescapable in a transitional economy based on universal compulsory labor.[48]

The emotions generated by universal labor conscription are suggested by the title of a book on the subject that appeared years later in the United States: *The Origin of Forced Labor in the Soviet State*. Our question might begin with that bitter description. Was the promulgation of the decree on universal labor conscription an ominous day, the start of the ugly system of forced labor; or was it rather, as Kollontai called it, a great day—indeed, the greatest in the history of women?

Labor conscription was a response to the exigencies of the Civil War. Yet just as Kollontai earlier seized on the possibilities for socialism inherent in public feeding, so now she responded with enthusiasm to labor conscription. On her own, Kollontai elevated into an ideology, and attempted to convert into a revolutionary force for social change, an ad hoc emergency measure of the era of War Communism. That a libertarian like Kollontai should see potential for the transformation of the position of women in a measure opposed as oppressive by the Party's leftists seemed a subject for wonder.[49] Kollontai

47. At the Eighth Party Congress in March 1919, the obligation to work declared in the Labor Code of 1918 was elaborated and made general, and the initial assumption that compulsory work would affect only members of the former bourgeois and landowning classes was abandoned. What was left of voluntarism for other groups virtually ended with the mobilization decree of April 10, 1919. See Carr, *The Bolshevik Revolution*, vol. 2, pp. 202, 210.

48. For quotation, see Trotsky's "theses" on compulsory labor, *Sochineniia* (M-L, 1927), vol. 15, p. 111. For entire "theses", see pp. 107–14. For the text of the law, see "Decree of the Sovnarkom," Jan. 29, 1920, in USSR, [15a], no. 8, art. 49, p. 33. For an English translation of the Decree, see Bunyan, p. 110.

49. For Kollontai on labor conscription, see *Rabotnitsa i krest'ianka*, p. 41, and "Trudovaia povinnost'," pp. 25–27. The leftists were led by Osinskii, who in 1918 had taken Bukharin's place as the leading theorist of radicalism. They argued against centralized authority in any form, including labor discipline. See Cohen, *Bukharin*, pp. 72–74.

defended what to many was a bizarre stance. Women's greatest, most liberating day was not the one when they received legal rights equally with men; rather, it was the one when they were compelled by the state *to work* equally with men. That historic occasion revolutionized women's position. It is important here to understand that Kollontai welcomed the decree on labor conscription primarily because she anticipated the social and psychological reorganization that would surely result from it. Women would answer no longer to their husbands or families but to the collective. No longer would women be suffering creatures in need of protection for themselves and their young; they would become independent beings, sources of vital strength whose interests society respected.[50]

For Kollontai one of the most important features of the new labor law was the element of compulsion, the very aspect other leftists found most objectionable. What may at first seem aberrant becomes more comprehensible when we consider that Kollontai's preoccupation with women's need to be liberated was constantly being thwarted by women's distressing unawareness that the need existed. Kollontai depended on a degree of compulsion to alter women's perception of themselves and their role.

Did Kollontai believe so fully in the liberating potential of labor that she expected its effect to be immediate or total? After all, Russian women had been working in factories in large numbers since the second half of the nineteenth century, even participating in strikes— yet their self-image remained poor.[51] Their illiteracy, their poor incomes, and their exhausting double role as mothers and workers combined to reinforce feelings of inferiority. Men were in charge, patronizing the women workers at the machines and not accepting them either as equals or as comrades.[52] Kollontai understood that it was not enough for women to be employed. They had to see themselves differently.[53] Compulsory labor obligation would have this effect: no longer would timid women be able to stay at home and try to ignore the psychically debilitating consequences of masculine support; no longer would husbands be masters and providers. Women would have their own labor books based on their own labor. In a woman's book,

50. Kollontai, *Rabotnitsa i krest'ianka*, p. 41.
51. Glickman, p. 82. See also Bobroff for women in strike movements.
52. Glickman, pp. 80–83.
53. For the working woman's feelings of inadequacy, see Kollontai, "Proizvodstvo i byt," p. 8.

not her husband's, their children's names would be inscribed, thus establishing *her* role as provider.[54]

The German socialist Lily Braun, who shared Kollontai's concern with the liberation of women, wrote years earlier that "while the bourgeois woman seeks work as the great liberator, for the proletarian woman it has become a means of enslavement; and while the right to work is one of the noblest human rights, to be condemned to work is a source of demoralization."[55] Kollontai challenged assumptions that labor conscription "condemned" the Soviet woman to work. Rather, the Soviet woman was part of a collective that would —and this was the key—restructure its living pattern communally so that she might more easily participate in the economy. Under socialism women would be members of the work force without whose help the new order could not be built. With the restructuring of living patterns, episodes from the past would never be repeated. For instance, in a 1907 textile strike in Ivanovo-Voznesensk the demand had been made that women be released for a half day to do the family laundry.[56] Such a course would become unthinkable under the revolutionary regime. The Soviet state needed to preserve the working strength of women and to safeguard women's health in order to guarantee workers for the future. That meant an end to individual household drudgery and its replacement by communal forms, as well as a series of laws to protect mothers from working conditions harmful to their physical well-being.[57] In a society that regarded women not as low-paid labor but as vital members of the working collective, in a society that changed its living pattern to meet the needs of women, the working woman's self-image would respond positively. Labor conscription would at first make women's lives more difficult, but if women kept in mind the ultimate goal—building socialism—Kollontai thought they would be able to cope with the temporary burden.[58]

But Kollontai knew that if Soviet women were to accept labor conscription as more than an exhausting emergency device, they would

54. Kollontai, *Polozhenie zhenshchiny*, p. 145.

55. Meyer, p. 109, quoting Lily Braun, *Die Frauenfrage, ihre geschichtliche Entwicklung und ihre wirtschaftliche Seite* (Leipzig, 1901), p. 431.

56. Glickman, p. 81.

57. Kollontai, *Polozhenie zhenshchiny*, p. 171.

58. She explained how socialists' attitudes toward women and work differed from feminists': the socialists emphasized not a "meaningless" equality of work rights but the use of women's power to protect their own health as mothers as well as workers. *Polozhenie zhenshchiny*, p. 206.

have to be convinced that participation in a work brigade would really improve their lives. Thus she explained how the restructuring of life on a socialist basis could be integrated with the requirements of labor conscription. For example, the number of hours a person devoted to building communal facilities should be taken into account in reckoning his or her hours of obligatory labor. Only such stimulus would provoke broad reforms toward a liberating communal life.[59]

To understand Kollontai's faith in the revolutionary potential of labor conscription, we must keep in mind that the Communists would have to restructure society for the measure to succeed. In a prescient remark, Kollontai pointed out that unless life were reorganized communally, labor conscription would in fact be reactionary, leading not to liberation but to increased burdens.[60] A measure of her optimism was her assumption that the Communist Party would follow the rational, revolutionary course.

Labor conscription was highly ideological, touching attitudes not only about compulsion, authority, and social priorities, but even about women's innate potential to develop. Other women in the Zhenotdel endorsed labor conscription, but only Kollontai offered it as a panacea. Inessa Armand welcomed labor obligation as a means to develop forms for communal living.[61] Samoilova, although convinced that obligatory labor was essential, treated it as a wartime device and compared it to recruitment for the Red Army. Perceiving labor conscription primarily from the standpoint of the needs of the state, she asked what better way there was to acquaint the masses of backward women, especially the "parasitical" elements among them, with the value of collective labor. For those women who showed a lack of social awareness, obligatory labor would prove to be an educational step.[62]

There were also many skeptics. Vinogradskaia has written that even members of the Women's Section questioned the capacity of the average woman, wondering if mothers with children had the energy to

59. Ibid., p. 151, and "Proizvodstvo i byt," pp. 7–8.
60. Kollontai, Polozhenie zhenshchiny, p. 150.
61. Blonina (pseud. Inessa Armand), "Rabotnitsa i organizatsiia proizvodstva," p. 25.
62. Samoilova condemned critics who compared obligatory labor for women to the serfdom of tsarist times, charging that they were led by Mensheviks and SRs who were trying to undermine Soviet influence with the backward female labor force. She noted the protective laws for the pregnant, the new mothers, the elderly, and those with large families and asked if those laws resembled the conditions of serfdom. Samoilova, "Trudovoi front i rabotnitsa," p. 11.

respond to the call.[63] Could these exhausted women be convinced by Kollontai's promise that their obligatory labor would hasten social construction and their own liberation? Convincing in the pages of *Kommunistka*, Kollontai seemed less so in the context of the draining work women were actually doing. In the city, labor conscription extended to all women not having a work booklet, that is, not attached to some kind of shop, factory, or service, or involved in Party work. Women's auxiliary service took the form of sanitation jobs, snow removal, and the cleaning of courtyards and staircases. Women also unloaded firewood, sewed linen for the army, or tended the sick.[64] In the country, labor conscription might involve working in brigades clearing snow from railway tracks.[65] Only a woman with Kollontai's enormous spirit and, unfortunately, capacity for self-deception could overlook the widespread resistance to labor conscription and be convinced of its inspirational value in conditions of Civil War.[66]

Communists did not necessarily share Kollontai's extraordinary ability to recoup her energies. From time to time even Party members admitted they were tired. Zinoviev discussed the mood of Bolsheviks in 1920. "It is useless to deny that many militants are mortally weary. They have to attend 'Volunteer Saturdays' [*subbotniki*] twice or four times a month, out of working hours; excessive mental strength is demanded; their families live in difficult conditions; they are sent here today and there tomorrow by the Party or by chance; the result is inevitably physical exhaustion."[67] Zinoviev spoke realistically, but in terms Kollontai did not accept for herself. If momentarily she might be tired, she still clung to the feverish pace of the Communist militant in a seemingly inexhaustible way. The more this middle-aged woman immersed herself in work, the more she merged with the Revolution and felt strong.

Yet despite her support of labor conscription, Kollontai was mindful of the burdens daily life inflicted on Russian women. Until Soviet society was reorganized communally and social facilities were widely

63. Vinogradskaia, *Sobytiia*, p. 225.

64. For urban women's work, see Kollontai, *Polozhenie zhenshchiny*, p. 152.

65. For rural work, see USSR, [7], pp. 8–9.

66. References to work desertion suggest resistance. See USSR, [9], p. 14. On the role played by "politically conscious" women workers in the trade unions in combating work desertion, see Samoilova, "Trudovoi front i rabotnitsa," p. 11. The extent to which labor desertion laws were enforced against women deserters is not clear. A certain number of housewives without any legal excuse successfully shirked labor obligation.

67. See Zinoviev's speech of Sept. 1920 in USSR, [3], p. 148.

available, a sense of the possible prevailed. The Zhenotdel, which participated through its representatives in the *Glavkomtrud* (the Central Committee on Universal Compulsory Labor) in working out plans for extending work obligation to women and for determining measures for coping with work desertion, sponsored a list of exemptions reflecting the special needs of women conscripted to work.[68] Women from ages sixteen to 40 were obligated to work, but mothers were exempt for eight weeks before and after giving birth.[69] Mothers with children at home under the age of eight were to be excused from working if there was no one to care for the children. Women caring for a family of five were exempt, as were women tending a person too ill to be left alone. Work mobilization involving a change of location was not required of city women with children under fourteen or peasant women with children under twelve. There were exemptions for the sick and for women having lost 45 percent of their work capacity. The Zhenotdel also recommended that if women labored four hours at home, they should not have to work longer than four hours in a brigade. Nor should brigades that drew on the labor of housewives require them to travel any distance from their homes.[70]

One would be ill-advised to look to Kollontai for a balanced view of labor conscription as it functioned during the Civil War. She barely alluded to its negative and coercive aspects, praising it in Lenin's and Bukharin's terms as "comradely discipline" and the "self-organization" of labor rather than in Commissar of War Trotsky's terms as the "militarization of the working class." Reading her references to labor conscription, one would be unaware—except by inference—of the operational defects, the desertions, the need for labor discipline courts, and the black market.[71]

68. For Zhenotdel participation in elaborating measures to cope with work desertion, see Kollontai, *Otchet*, p. 11. Work desertion covered any failure to comply with the registration of call-up decrees, concealment of one's trade or profession, evasion of the call-up, leaving a job without permission, absenteeism, etc. A decree stipulated that expectant mothers and mothers of young children might not be imprisoned for work desertion or infringements of labor discipline. See Dewar, pp. 48–49.

69. *Polozhenie zhenshchiny*, p. 152. The upper age limit for women was lowered in 1920 from 50 to 40; for men it remained 50. See USSR, [7], p. 9.

70. For exemptions for women, see Kollontai, "Trudovaia povinnost'," p. 27, and *Polozhenie zhenshchiny*, pp. 152–53. Facilities to enable women with young children to work were insufficient. In the RSFSR in 1918 there were 78 factory and district day nurseries; in 1919, 126; in 1920, 565; in 1921, 668; and in 1922, 914. There were no permanent village day nurseries during the years of labor conscription. See Smith, p. 177.

71. For negative aspects of labor conscription and for references to labor discipline courts, see Carr, *The Bolshevik Revolution*, vol. 2, pp. 215–18. On how labor conscription worked, see the periodical *Izvestiia glavnogo komiteta po vseobshchei trudovoi povinnosti* (the official organ of the Glavkomtrud), 1920, nos. 1–7. USSR, [7], pp. 22–23,

꠵꠵꠵

The working class was the primary target of Kollontai's ambitious plan to develop "new women." So intensely did Kollontai concentrate on the proletariat that on at least one occasion she had to defend herself in an international arena against Clara Zetkin's criticism that she did not give sufficient attention to women of the intelligentsia. Although she denied any personal opposition to recruiting the *intelligentki*, Kollontai insisted that the socialist base must be among proletarian women.[72] But she knew there were other women to be reached: the students who could be persuaded to join the Women's Section, the prostitutes who needed to be brought into the legitimate work force, and the peasants who were far from the revolutionary fold. When the Zhenotdel moved its focus away from factory women, possibilities for disagreement and internal friction multiplied. Frequently it would be Kollontai's far-reaching and radical proposals that polarized opinion.

Kollontai delighted in Soviet youth. Students responded to her radical social ideas with the enthusiasm of the young, and this caused occasional misgivings among more conservative Zhenotdel leaders.[73] It was easy to talk about the Zhenotdel in the Central Committee school for Party officials, known as Sverdlov Communist University, where Kollontai gave a series of lectures in 1921. But other women remained psychologically and socially outside the revolutionary orbit and resisted the idea that the Revolution meant a new way of life. They required a more subtle approach. The remainder of this chapter deals with these other women, the peasants and the prostitutes, whom Kollontai, as director of the Zhenotdel, tried to incorporate into the revolutionary structure.

As a member of the Interdepartmental Commission for the Struggle with Prostitution, Kollontai drew up a plan to deal with the problems of the prostitutes. Earlier, before 1917, Kollontai had used working-class women's fear of slipping into a life of prostitution as a rallying point, explaining how their low wages, their miserable lot

discusses desertion. See also A. Anikst, *Organizatsiia rabochei sily v 1920 godu* (Moscow, 1920), for a review of labor militarization during 1920 written by a deputy chairman of the Central Committee on Compulsory Labor; Bunyan, especially his Bibliography, pp. 269–70; and Dewar, pp. 48–49.

72. Kollontai's speech at the Second International Conference of Communist Women. See *Rabotnitsa i krest'ianka*, pp. 44–45.

73. See, for example, Krupskaia's qualifying editorial remarks accompanying Kollontai's "Tezisy o kommunisticheskoi morali v oblasti brachnykh otnoshenii."

in the factories, and their lack of political influence made them vulnerable. It was the working woman's lack of political and economic rights under capitalism that made her helpless and a likely candidate for the yellow certificate of the prostitute.[74]

After the Communists came to power, they decreed an end to the tsarist system of police regulation of prostitution. The First All-Russian Congress of Worker and Peasant Women declared in 1918 that the Russian woman, a free and equal citizen, must no longer be subject to prostitution. Studies of Soviet society by Westerners concluded that in the aftermath of the Revolution prostitution disappeared, only to return under the New Economic Policy and the partial restoration of capitalism after 1921. In fact, though fewer in numbers, prostitutes continued all along to "poison" the atmosphere.[75] Moreover, Kollontai was disturbed at evidence that growing numbers of working women, servants, bourgeois office workers, and peasants were turning to prostitution as a secondary occupation. It could not be permitted in a workers' state, yet who in government during the days of the Civil War could spare attention for this painful social question?[76]

Other problems kept the regime from developing a uniform policy. Beyond the assumption that prostitution was incompatible with socialism, there was confusion. Kollontai described in *Kommunistka* how in one guberniia prostitution was ignored, how in another prostitutes were rounded up in the old way and put in camps, how in still another brothels flourished. She suggested an innovative first principle based on the assumptions of labor obligation, which had reached its peak in the first months of 1920: Let there be *no special measures for the struggle with prostitution*. Professional prostitutes must be treated like the rest of the work deserters who were apprehended for failing to contribute productively to the collective.[77]

74. Prostitutes were issued yellow certificates in Russia in the second half of the nineteenth century, a result of police regulation and supervision of prostitution. See Halle, p. 221. For Kollontai's early writing on prostitution, see "Zadachi rabotnits v bor'ba s prostitutsiei."

75. Women were still being reduced to instruments of pleasure, venereal disease was being spread, and the work force was being reduced. Kollontai, "Trudovaia respublika i prostitutsiia," p. 15. Halle (p. 224) was one of the writers who claimed that prostitution practically disappeared during the revolutionary era. Of interest is Souvarine's comment concerning prostitution among rural teachers whose average salary in the early 1920's was at times lower than 10 rubles per month. By 1925 their position had improved and "prostitution and mendicancy were tending to disappear." Souvarine, pp. 514–15.

76. Kollontai, "Trudovaia respublika i prostitutsiia," p. 15.

77. *Ibid.*, p. 17. Italics in original. According to Kollontai, the Orgburo accepted

Kollontai contributed the single unifying principle that the prostitute not be punished for prostitution *per se*. Before the law she should be held responsible only for deserting. She who was not occupied in socially useful work must be brought into the ranks of the workers. End the roundups, special institutions, camps, and colonies for prostitutes. Instead, labor books should be rapidly instituted throughout the Soviet republic. A prostitute should be treated as a work deserter —if ill, hospitalized; if healthy, placed in general work colonies, workshops, or training courses.[78]

Kollontai could be brisk in her prescriptions for the professional prostitute, but the women who resorted to prostitution for additional earnings represented a more complex problem that work books could not solve, for it was rooted in the deficiencies of Soviet life. To help these women the Zhenotdel had to struggle with the very character of society: work conditions had to be improved, food rations adjusted, living problems solved. Soviet Russia needed schools to prepare young girls for socially useful labor in order to eliminate one cause of prostitution—the absence of work habits and training. Communal houses, night lodging, and maternity homes were essential to reduce the feeling of loneliness and neglect that could force a woman to sell herself.[79] In the meantime, though, the woman with legitimate work who still resorted to prostitution should not be harassed. Her labor book, unless it could be proved fictitious, must protect her from any interference by the law in her private life. Kollontai argued, in an unpopular minority view, that as long as Soviet Russia was in the transitional era, with no generally accepted ethic about marital morality and no penalty for marriage relations entered into for reasons of economic calculation, it was not possible to punish working women who turned to prostitution for extra wages. Nor should her client be punished.[80]

Although Marxists (as well as feminists) traditionally pointed to

---

the Commission's theses regarding prostitution and the Moscow Soviet was putting the principles into operation. See *Otchet*, p. 11. (Report delivered in December 1920.) A survey of prostitutes in Petrograd in 1920 showed that the majority were 20 to 30. See S. Ravich, "Bor'ba s prostitutsiei v Petrograde," p. 21.

78. Kollontai, "Trudovaia respublika i prostitutsiia," p. 17. That Kollontai suggested printing labor books for all Russia implies they were still limited largely to Moscow and Petrograd. On labor books, see Carr, *The Bolshevik Revolution*, vol. 2, p. 202.

79. Kollontai, "Trudovaia respublika i prostitutsiia," p. 15. On the impoverished background of most prostitutes before the Revolution, see Halle, p. 220. See also Ravich, "Bor'ba s prostitutsiei v Petrograde," p. 21, whose survey showed the largest number of arrested prostitutes coming from the ranks of unskilled labor.

80. Kollontai, "Trudovaia respublika i prostitutsiia," p. 17.

the parallels between prostitution and bourgeois marriage, Kollontai found few supporters for her extension of this idea to Soviet society.[81] Was it not a form of prostitution, she asked, to live with a man because he had a room in the Soviet house? Was the wife who did not have to care for small children but who avoided labor conscription different from the prostitute?[82]

Sof'ia Smidovich, director of the Moscow regional Zhenotdel, disagreed. She was one of the Communists who accused Kollontai of mindlessly advocating prostitution.[83] Smidovich, who succeeded to the directorship of the central Zhenotdel in 1922 when Kollontai was removed, seldom agreed with Kollontai on questions involving female sexuality. Yet the two women shared experiences that gave them common ground as revolutionaries. They were both born in 1872; they both entered the Social Democratic Party in 1898; they both thought of themselves as Old Bolsheviks. The daughter of a prominent Tula lawyer, Nikolai Chernosvitov, Smidovich participated in two revolutions. As an underground worker in Tulu, Kiev, Kaluga, and Moscow, she too experienced prosecution and exile. Smidovich was married twice, first to P. V. Lunacharskii, and then after his death to Petr Smidovich, a highly placed Moscow Bolshevik. Arrested with her first husband in 1901, she was arrested again in 1910, this time leaving behind both her fifteen-year-old daughter and her eight-month-old son by Smidovich. Like Kollontai, she was frequently a worried mother, suffering in prison because of guilt over what she was inflicting upon her children. The image of her daughter weeping as her mother was taken away tormented her.[84]

Smidovich and Kollontai, each committed to the liberation of women, would argue often. The issue of the prostitute was one example. Kollontai's proposals for dealing with prostitution would cease to be viable with the demise of labor conscription in 1922, but the anger she generated among conservative Communists like Smidovich outlived that initial controversy.[85]

81. For the Marxist penchant to equate bourgeois marriage with prostitution, see Meyer, pp. 86, 92, 97. For a similar feminist view, see Charlotte Perkins Gilman, *Women and Economics* (New York, 1966), p. xxx.

82. Kollontai, *Polozhenie zhenshchiny*, pp. 192–93. For Kollontai's definition of prostitution to include married women who wished to avoid work, see Kollontai, *Prostitutsiia i mery bor'by s nei*, p. 4.

83. See Winter, p. 123, for Smidovich's attack on Kollontai.

84. F. Susloparova, "V Stuzhu," in Zhak and Itkina, eds., p. 428.

85. The Commissariat of Public Health in 1922 published a decree "On the Measures to Be Adopted in the Struggle Against Prostitution," which generally upheld Kollontai's principles. It called for special consideration of the problems of women and work so as

Working women in the cities and peasant women in the villages, whether or not they faced the slide into prostitution, all needed the enlightenment of the Zhenotdel. But it was the peasant woman, Kollontai came to believe, whose life was least changed by the Revolution, who most needed not only Zhenotdel support but a greater commitment from the regime. Kollontai, and by extension the Zhenotdel, reached the politically important conclusion that for social revolution to succeed, peasant women needed quickly to be drawn into its orbit. Though scarcely a fourth of the Communist Party was of peasant origin in 1920, and though debates in the Congresses during the Civil War at no point expressed the peasant view, the Zhenotdel dedicated itself early to a female version of the Leninist idea of a *smychka* (alliance) between proletariat and peasantry.

The Zhenotdel had no illusions about the difficulties it faced. Inessa Armand, when she was director, reminded the Zhenotdel organizers that the isolation of the village kept the peasant woman from seeing life beyond her own hut: she had not worked in a factory, like the city woman; she had not seen workers' demonstrations, let alone taken part in them.[86] Of course it was easier to agitate in the factories; women were more cohesive there and thus more quickly organized than the millions of peasant women dispersed throughout the villages of Russia would be. Samoilova, too, cautioned against a policy of simply continuing to organize women in the factories because work in the villages was so much more difficult.[87] Concentrating on the factories was tempting—particularly, as Inessa pointed out, when the Zhenotdel did not have enough workers to organize women in both city and village.[88]

Samoilova put in simple words the potential of a female *smychka.*

---

to avoid conditions thought to be conducive to the rise of prostitution. In italics it also warned: *Under no circumstances must the war against prostitution degenerate into a war against prostitutes.* There were to be measures taken against the agents of prostitution and medical treatment at dispensaries for prostitutes suffering from venereal disease. See the decree in Halle, pp. 225–26. In spite of efforts to combat it, prostitution flourished until the mid-1930's, when it was liquidated by a combination of forced labor, rehabilitation clinics, and police repression. See Stites, "Zhenotdel," p. 22. Serge describes roundups in the mid-1920's of prostitutes, who were sent to concentration camps in the far north. Serge, p. 207.

86. Blonina [Armand], "Volostnoe delegatskoe sobranie krest'ianok."
87. Samoilova, "O rabote sredi krest'ianok," p. 31.
88. Blonina [Armand], "Volostnoe delegatskoe sobranie krest'ianok," p. 35. Kollontai recalled the difficulty of organizing peasants as compared to the urban proletariat in *Iz moei zhizni i raboty,* p. 362.

Only recently peasant women had feared to go even the short distance to the village or *volost'* (rural district) Soviet, yet now all over Russia hundreds of peasant women were working in Soviets, even taking on responsible posts as representatives to the Soviets. Was this not a guarantee that the peasantry would eventually join the urban working class? It followed, Samoilova thought, that the Zhenotdel should work in the village.[89]

Ultimately the Zhenotdel supported Samoilova, but only after controversy. Indeed, even Kollontai hesitated initially. Believing with one group in the Zhenotdel[90] that politically and culturally there was a similarity of outlook between peasants, male and female, she first took the line that village work, so overwhelming in its scope, would be of little value. But she soon changed her mind, reaching the important conclusion that in those rural areas where the Party had already prepared the ground, the peasant woman was a more likely recruit to Communism than her husband.[91] The distinction leads to a further question. Should the peasant woman be considered in the same economic category as her husband? If he was a *kulak*, was she one as well?

Kollontai appeared to suggest that the peasant woman ought not to be categorized automatically with the peasant man. The peasant proprietor, not his wife, she explained, had a vested interest in maintaining his economic holdings and keeping subordinate to him the traditional peasant family, which included, of course, the woman. To him a new way of life meant little. How could it ease his situation? The peasant's wife, however, a silent slave in her family to brothers,

89. Samoilova discussed the peasant woman's need, even greater than the urban working woman's, for the kind of aid the Zhenotdel might provide. Samoilova, *V ob'edinenii zalog pobedy* (Moscow, 1921), p. 22. Samoilova believed that conferences of worker and peasant women were significant in bringing together urban and rural women, a means to destroy the antagonism between them which played into the hand of enemies of the working class. Samoilova, "O rabote sredi krest'ianok," p. 33. For examples of Zhenotdel concern for peasant women and regret over its limited success and weak beginning, see Kollontai, *Otchet*, p. 12.

90. For evidence of such a group, see Egorova, p. 33, and Blonina [Armand], "Volostnoe delegatskoe sobranie krest'ianok," p. 35. For Kollontai's initial reluctance to commit the Zhenotdel to the peasant, see Moirova, p. 11.

91. For Kollontai's views, see Moirova, p. 11, and Kollontai, *Polozhenie zhenshchiny*, p. 197. Inessa may have been ahead of Kollontai in stressing the need to work among peasant women. She explained that the isolation of the countryside worked against peasant women more than peasant men, since the latter at least went into the army and to political school, whereas the former remained at home, illiterate. See Blonina [Armand], "Volostnoe delegatskoe sobranie krest'ianok," p. 35. For literacy levels among peasant women, see I. M. Bogdanov, *Gramotnost' i obrazovanie v dorevoliutsionnoi Rossii i v SSSR* (Moscow, 1964).

husband, and father-in-law, did not live like a bourgeois lady. For her any of the changes in daily life about which the Zhenotdel spoke—collectives, dairy cooperatives, nurseries, central bakeries, laundries, and so on—were often appealing. For these reasons, Kollontai believed that the peasant woman, once reached, would grasp the essence of Communism more easily than the peasant man and become its supporter.[92]

By not defining the *krest'ianka* (the peasant woman) socially and economically in terms of her relationship to a particular man, Kollontai also emphasized her role as the representative of a family unit. There were many single women—usually war widows, wives of Red Army men, or wives of workers—who participated in obligatory labor in the countryside, in transport work, in seed campaigns, and in the apportionment and collecting of taxes in kind. All these activities required the aid of peasant women who, Kollontai came to believe, were losing their passivity as a result of their experiences in the Civil War.[93]

The idea that Kollontai appeared to convey—that the Party should concentrate on the *krest'ianka* in general, not simply on the poorest *batrachka* (rural day worker), using the peasant woman as a lever in the countryside—was a brilliant revolutionary tactic. But although in rural Russia there were more women than men, such an idea received little support during the era of War Communism.[94] Within the context of class war in the countryside it would have been counterproductive, conflicting with rural policies that were, of course, male-oriented. In the villages the Communist Party was conducting a class war aimed (during the years of War Communism) at winning over the *bedniak* (poor peasant), having the *seredniak* (middle peasant) as an ally, and combating the *kulak*.[95] Kollontai suggested a different emphasis, a rural war between the sexes. Peasant men, already

92. *Polozhenie zhenshchiny*, p. 198.

93. *Ibid.*, pp. 196–97.

94. Even Party members who agreed that creating genuine Communism required winning over the peasants were unenthusiastic about working among them, according to Golubeva ("Rabota zhenotdelov," p. 3). Massell claims that in Central Asia after 1923 it would be the Party's policy to use women as a lever for social change. See Massell, pp. 127, 132. Massell acknowledges that he is intuiting this "policy" from activity in the field and from articles by Zhenotdel workers in *Kommunistka*. He is dealing with "inferred programmatic doctrines and proposals," not necessarily with specific strategies. The themes he infers were never articulated rigorously enough to be considered formal propositions. Similarly, I infer from articles by Zhenotdel leaders that whether to recruit the more prosperous peasant women was a subject of disagreement.

95. Lewin, *Russian Peasants*, p. 69.

hostile to the regime, were additionally antagonized by the idea that their personal lives would be changed, that their wives would be taken out of the family and into public life. The Party had no desire further to alienate the important middle peasant by encouraging overly abrasive Zhenotdel activity. As for an appeal to the *kulachka* designed both to gain additional Communist adherents among women in the countryside and to undermine the *kulak* husband, although an interesting theoretical tactic, it was inappropriate ideologically.[96] The Zhenotdel was unlikely to encourage blatant rural feminism.

Kollontai, Inessa Armand, and Samoilova were bold innovators who saw early on the potential for alliance between proletarian and peasant women. But moving Zhenotdel activity into the village seemed to many women in the central organization politically risky. Although they wanted to win over peasant women, they did not care to act counter to overall Party policy. Thus, at first, a majority opposed even rural delegates' meetings, fearing that such gatherings in the village might further alienate the male peasant.[97] Nor was their concern unfounded. Though the delegates' meetings, according to Inessa Armand, did not necessarily elicit a negative response, the mere presence of a Zhenotdel organizer sometimes did. Peasant men, angry at the organizer for calling meetings, demanded to know what she was up to. Men beat their wives or daughters for attending meet-

96. When peasant women of all classes, including the *kulak*, were drawn into contact with the Zhenotdel, there was friction. Zhenotdel organizers, suspicious of the *kulak* wife, questioned her potential as a recruit. Policies toward the *kulachka* differed from area to area: some localities included her among the peasant delegates chosen for women's meetings; others excluded her. See Blonina [Armand], "Volostnoe delegatskoe sobranie krest'ianok," p. 35. For the problem of class stratification within the peasantry, see Lewin, *Russian Peasants*, pp. 41–80.

97. See Blonina [Armand], p. 34. The Zhenotdel considered the delegates' meetings, a notion devised by Inessa Armand, a highly successful recruiting device. Representatives of proletarian and peasant women were chosen in factories, shops, and villages, usually one from every 50 working women, here and there one from every 25. Kollontai, *Rabotnitsa i krest'ianka*, p. 29; *Izbrannye stat'i i rechi*, p. 373. Delegates served for three months, meeting weekly under the guidance of the local Zhenotdel. There were sessions on industrial and trade-union questions for proletarian women, on agricultural and village questions for peasants. See Smith, p. 48. Trained Party workers guided the delegates' meetings to matters the Party considered important. The women reported back to their constituencies, and new *delegatki* were chosen in due course. Delegates who remained in their own enterprises participated in *subbotniki* (Communist volunteer Saturdays) or Party campaigns connected with "Children's Week," "Red Army Week," etc. They joined commissions for the protection of labor, for the improvement of daily life, for the protection of motherhood. Frequently the *delegatka* helped in children's homes, assisted in dining halls, or organized a *subbotnik* to inspect infirmaries, to clean them, and to care for the sick and wounded. See *Rabotnitsa i krest'ianka*, pp. 7–8, 29–30; Itkina, p. 199; and the chapter "Krasnyi platochek" in *Svetlyi put'*.

ings or for showing an interest in Communism.[98] But the leaders who favored work in the countryside as well as in the towns made their point, and Samoilova provided guidelines for village work. Less imaginative than Kollontai, more narrowly ideological, she advised that the Zhenotdel concentrate on the poorest peasant woman, the batrachka.[99]

Members of the Women's Section might disagree on which category of peasant woman to recruit, but they agreed that peasant women had to be drawn out of their narrow concerns and turned toward the collective. Zhenotdel commitment to the villages prefigured later Bolshevik interest in wooing the peasants. Similarly, the Zhenotdel's innovative suggestions about method anticipated later Leninist thinking. In 1923, not long before his death, Lenin expressed regret that insufficient attention was being paid in the Party to the question of cooperatives. He found the ideas of nineteenth-century designers of cooperative communities relevant to the Party's problem of inculcating socialist concepts in Russia's peasant population.[100] The Zhenotdel applied a similar idea, earlier, to the peasant woman: Liudmila Stal', answering one delegate's questions about how to approach peasant women, recommended that the Zhenotdel concentrate on organizing cooperatively the thousands of women scattered throughout the countryside who were working at home in domestic industries. To avoid the opposition of economic planners who might charge her with harboring a non-Marxist fondness for small-scale, peasant industry, Stal' agreed that the desperate economic conditions of Russia in 1920 could only be solved by large-scale industry but urged that in the absence of the machinery and the skilled workers Russia use what was available.[101]

Here was an opportunity for the Zhenotdel to bring women into

98. The generation gap presented another problem. A mother might protest her daughter's becoming a Communist. See Blonina [Armand], "Volostnoe delegatskoe sobranie krest'ianok," pp. 34–35, for the generation gap and for male resistance to female political activity in villages.

99. Samoilova thought the batrachka the most likely recruit to Communism because she most resembled the urban factory woman. Samoilova, "O rabote sredi krest'ianok," p. 32. Samoilova also advised using Party workers familiar with the countryside and warned against relying on non-Party village school teachers, who could not be trusted to spread Bolshevik propaganda and should be limited to fighting illiteracy. Ibid., pp. 32–33. For Samoilova's guidelines on village work, see Egorova, "Kak organizovat' rabotu sredi krest'ianok," pp. 32–33.

100. See Lenin, "O kooperatsii," Sochineniia (4th ed.), vol. 33, pp. 432–35.

101. Stal', "Nasha rabota," pp. 14–15.

socialist cooperation, to organize them into artels, to combat the hunger and misery prevalent everywhere. At the same time, the Zhenotdel would be conducting propaganda, explaining to the women that, once organized into artels, they would become eligible for the help promised by Soviet protective labor decrees—especially the illness and maternity benefits. An idea with socialist potential, cooperatives unfortunately received too little government support.[102] "If the whole of the peasantry had been organized in cooperatives," Lenin fantasized in 1923, "we would by now have been standing with both feet on the soil of socialism."[103]

෴෴෴෴

The summer of 1921 brought the Second International Conference of Communist Women to Moscow, where they would learn from Kollontai about the Zhenotdel. Both the first and the second of these international gatherings took place prior to general Comintern congresses, the customary schedule for women's meetings during the days of the Second International. The Women's Conference would formulate plans to raise the political consciousness and increase the solidarity of working women of all countries, whereas Communist problems of a more general nature would be discussed later in regular Comintern sessions. That women from places as far apart as Mexico and India journeyed to Moscow for a conference did not mean, however, that a viable international Communist women's movement existed.[104] Lenin admitted as much when he told Clara Zetkin after the First International Women's Conference in 1920 that the Communists still did not have an international women's movement but would have to create one. He thought the Comintern was moving too slowly. The Second Comintern Congress in 1920 had posed the woman question,

102. Smith, p. 43, provides statistics for 1926–27 on peasant women and cooperatives showing that over 500,000 women were members of the Consumer Cooperatives and that 180,000 were members of handicraft cooperatives. A large number also joined agricultural cooperatives. But the proportion compared with male members was small, as was the numerical total. See Emel'ianova, pp. 215–17, for Zhenotdel efforts to develop cooperatives among peasants.

103. Lenin, "O kooperatsii," *Sochineniia* (4th ed.), vol. 33, p. 434.

104. The first women's conference in 1920 drew only about 17 delegates from Russia, Germany, France, England, Italy, Austria, Hungary, Denmark, Norway, Turkestan, Georgia, Sweden, Finland, Mexico, Latvia, and India. Kollontai, *Izbrannye stat'i i rechi*, p. 408. Indeed, the small group was composed hastily of women already delegated to the Comintern Congress. About 30 delegates came to the second conference in June 1921 from Germany, France, England, Sweden, Norway, Bulgaria, Switzerland, Azerbaijan, and Georgia. *Ibid.*, p. 341. Some countries denied the women visas to go to Moscow, so that they had to travel illegally. Vinogradskaia, *Sobytiia*, p. 235.

but a committee to draft resolutions, theses, and directives had made little progress.[105]

Kollontai devised a plan to unify the international women's movement.[106] She initiated efforts to develop an effective international network with a suggestion in 1920 that there be established a Women's Secretariat within the Comintern, rather than an independent body like the original Women's Secretariat.[107] With the Secretariat an integral part of the Comintern, the international solidarity of Communist women that had eluded the Second International might result. European Communist parties working in accordance with a unified plan would ideally follow the model of the Zhenotdel.[108] Kollontai was in earnest. A measure of her seriousness was the angry letter she sent in 1921 to the Swedish Communists from the International Secretariat criticizing them for their failure to follow Comintern directives to draw women into the movement.[109]

When Kollontai was chosen in 1921 by the Executive Committee of the Comintern to be deputy director of the International Women's Secretariat, she was already thinking in broad terms. Looking to the East, Kollontai praised the Third International for not limiting itself like the Second to work within the advanced capitalist countries of Europe. For a woman whose orientation was Western, Kollontai had a remarkable sense of the possibilities for Communist development. If the presence of Eastern women at the Conference seemed mainly a skillful use of theater, for Kollontai it was also a symbol promising the victory of Communism among Eastern women.[110]

Kollontai's report to the Second International Conference of Com-

105. Zetkin, pp. 41–42.

106. Illness kept Kollontai from the First International Women's Conference, which Inessa chaired. See Kollontai, *Otchet*, p. 15. But Kollontai helped prepare its agenda. See Kollontai, "Pervaia mezhdunarodnaia konferentsiia kommunistok, 1920g.," pp. 3–5. Along with Lenin, Krupskaia, and Zetkin, Kollontai was chosen as an honorary member of the Presidium.

107. See Kollontai, *Izbrannye stat'i i rechi*, p. 349, for the establishment of the Secretariat.

108. See Kollontai, "Tretii internatsional i rabotnitsa," in *Izbrannye stat'i i rechi*, p. 350.

109. This letter, dated Nov. 12, 1921, is in the papers of Fredrik Ström, Univ. of Gothenburg Library, Sweden.

110. See Itkina, p. 203, and Kollontai, *Izbrannye stat'i i rechi*, p. 350, for Kollontai's praise of the Third International. The International Women's Secretariat, which was connected with all Communist Parties, East and West, was to create under Kollontai's leadership centers for work among women in both the Near East and the Far East. Conferences would lay the bases for strengthening connections with the East and would sketch out Zhenotdel work on the basis of the special needs represented by different ways of life. See Kollontai, *Izbrannye stat'i i rechi*, pp. 316–18, 351. For Kollontai and women of the East, see Kollontai, "Posledniaia rabynia," pp. 24–26.

munist Women summed up her evaluation of the Zhenotdel's achievements as she neared the end of her first year as director.[111] If Kollontai believed that in its two and a half years of existence the Zhenotdel had achieved "colossal success" when measured against the overwhelming difficulties it had faced, her enthusiasm did not blind her to the grimness of Soviet life. It would be absurd, she knew, to suggest that in Soviet Russia working women were living well. Life may never have been as difficult as in this transitional period.[112] Millions of Russians were not "new women" but, as the Communist worker Somov in the Soviet drama *Inga* would say, still "suffocating in kitchen stench" and "carrying bruises from their beatings."[113]

Kollontai was proud of the new protections for mothers. But maternity legislation affected only women in shops and factories. And, even there, despite legislation, harmful working conditions often prevailed. Dampness, foul air, and poisonous gases still endangered workers' health. Kollontai reported truthfully that hygienic improvements were few and were carried out only in areas where there was pressure from Commissions for Protection of Work.[114] Emma Goldman, the Russian-born American anarchist, described a visit to a tobacco factory in 1920 where she saw pregnant women working in suffocating tobacco-laden air, "saturating themselves and their unborn with the poison." "The women are used to this atmosphere," the guide told her. "They don't mind."[115]

A strength of Kollontai's reporting was its honesty. However much working women were ultimately disarmed by a woman-to-woman approach, she knew that the majority did not believe that the Zhenotdel represented their interests. From labor conscription to nurseries, the Zhenotdel tried to force Russian women onto uncongenial, often frightening paths. Kollontai described practices of persuasion that were frankly manipulative but, she thought, successful. Women were made to feel guilty if they tried to shirk obligatory labor or failed to participate in the "voluntary" *subbotniki*. She pointed to the new uneasiness of women who rationalized their lack of social responsibility, blaming the household and lack of facilities for child care. If these deficiencies were corrected, surely they would be able to work

111. Kollontai made a preliminary evaluation in her lectures at Sverdlov Communist University, Feb.–July 1921. See *Polozhenie zhenshchiny.*
112. See Kollontai, *Rabotnitsa i krest-ianka*, pp. 7, 32.
113. Glebov, p. 263. See the discussion of this play in Chapter 9 below.
114. Kollontai, *Rabotnitsa i krest'ianka*, p. 14.
115. Goldman, p. 56.

for the Party, in the Women's Section and in the trade unions.[116]

Kollontai recalled that early in 1918 when they approached working women about building nurseries, women organizers sometimes met physical opposition from women who feared that their children would be put in public shelters. But the Zhenotdel was flexible, modifying its methods, deciding that it must demonstrate potential benefits by concrete means, working from practice to theory. First Zhenotdel workers built a nursery, then they slowly won over the women.[117] Dread existed on one side, enthusiasm on the other, but confidence grew on both sides with exposure. Reports from other Communists supported Kollontai's view that many women became disappointed by Party promises of child-care facilities that failed to materialize.[118] Calling on the government to increase facilities, Kollontai correctly predicted that working women would eventually find collective child-care institutions congenial.[119]

How much progress the Zhenotdel made in converting backward, apolitical women to the Revolution during the years of War Communism is difficult to determine. Reports were subjective. The number of actively involved and politically conscious working women was small. Kollontai reported that about 9 to 10 percent of Communist Party members in 1921 were women.[120] According to statistics for February–March 1921, in twelve gubernii there were 3,842 Communist women, of whom 2,406 were working women, 1,010 *intelligentki*, and 426 peasants. The number of delegates that the Zhenotdel recruited to their meetings in these gubernii came to 12,910. Kollontai estimated in 1921 that in all—by which presumably she meant the entire RSFSR—there were over 70,000 delegates (workers, peasants, and housewives), through whom over three million women had some connection with the Party.[121] As to the extent of that connection we can only speculate.

116. See Kollontai, *Polozhenie zhenshchiny*, pp. 183–84.
117. See *Rabotnitsa i krest'ianka*, p. 33, for Kollontai's view.
118. See "Protiv prosveshchennogo biurokratizma (a takzhe i neprosveshchennogo)" in Trotsky, *Sochineniia*, vol. 21, p. 73.
119. Praising Zhenotdel accomplishments, Kollontai described a network of nurseries established by the *delegatki*. *Rabotnitsa i krest'ianka*, pp. 32–33.
120. *Ibid.*, p. 7.
121. For these figures, see Kollontai, "Rabotnitsa i krest'ianka v Sovetskoi Rossii," in *Izbrannye stat'i i rechi*, pp. 326–27. Evidently the figures presented in *Rabotnitsa i krest'ianka*, p. 7 (6,422 Communist women in 12 gubernii), were in error and were scaled downward. The 12 gubernii surveyed were Moscow, Petrograd, Samara, Khar'kov,

Success was greater among proletarian women, less impressive among peasants, whose consciousness as a group, Kollontai admitted, the Zhenotdel still needed to penetrate. She was cautiously optimistic.[122] Women who only recently had been workers or peasants were seeing their lives change. Now they might be directing a political section in the army, organizing public feeding, struggling with starvation and epidemics. Some were even fighting illiteracy, constructing reading huts or taking part in political campaigns.[123]

In the first years of the Revolution, the peasant women lacked consciousness. They opposed the new regime, and work among them was slow to develop.[124] But Kollontai was convinced that whenever the Zhenotdel gave peasants special attention their orientation changed. When the Party called delegates' meetings and conferences of worker and peasant women, when the Zhenotdel began to teach peasant women ways to ease their lives, a broad circle of peasant women began to favor the regime.[125] Indeed, Soviet memoirs are filled with recollections of how a woman's self-image began to change when she heard her name called as a delegate. A member of the Central Executive Committee, a former peasant, would tell the story of her initiation into politics. "They elected me a delegate . . . and I cried all night. Where in the world did they want to send me?"[126] Another peasant remembered her pride upon being elected, how she felt suddenly different about herself. A factory worker recalled her fright, how she tried to refuse, alarmed by her own ignorance. But her coworkers assured her that she was sufficiently intelligent; and after all, she had someone at home to care for her children, so she must be a *delegatka*. Within perhaps three months of those initial meetings

---

Odessa, Kaluga, Briansk, Simbirsk, Tula, Ekaterinburg, Kostroma, and Lugansk. The total female population of the RSFSR according to the 1926 census was approximately 53,665,552. A sampling of female population by gubernii indicates the following approximate female populations: Briansk, 1,067,012; Leningrad, 1,485,175; Kaluga, 612,609; Kostroma, 431,710; Moscow, 2,431,318; Samara, 1,283,498; Tula, 800,672. See Lorimer, pp. 67–69.

122. See *Izbrannye stat'i i rechi*, pp. 326–27.

123. *Ibid.*, p. 339. Lewin, *Russian Peasants*, p. 121, provides statistics on the number of peasants in the late 1920's who were Party members. The number was small, as was the actual "proletarian element" in the rural Party. In the Ukraine, there were 200,000 *batrak* women and 100,000 women agricultural workers in the *Sovkhozy*, and of these only 84 were Party members. Kollontai recalled the greater difficulty in working among peasants and the need to know local customs so as not to alienate the peasants. Kollontai, *Iz moei zhizni i raboty*, p. 362.

124. See Kollontai's report on the Zhenotdel's slow progress among peasant women. *Otchet*, pp. 12–13.

125. *Polozhenie zhenshchiny*, p. 197.

126. Smith, p. 42, citing the story of F. O. Shupurova.

where at first it was difficult for the women even to be quiet, to understand the fundamentals of order, a *delegatka* became, in Kollontai's view, a sympathizer, if not a Communist.[127]

Kollontai trusted in the potential of delegates' meetings to destroy the political passivity of peasant women, who rarely took part in the deliberations of the *mir*, which instead of the village Soviet (*sel'sovet*) still dominated village life.[128] Democratic concepts such as voting for delegates to a larger unit might also work to break down the peasant way of thinking, which was centered in the patriarchal *dvor*, still the basic social unit, where the male heads of households continued to represent the other members of the family. Urging the peasant woman to vote for a delegate was one means of bringing her into the very different orbit represented by the Zhenotdel.

Kollontai identified signs suggesting to her that peasant women by 1921 were starting to think about their own lives. She pointed to the thirst for education on the part of young peasant women in the cities. In the Sverdlov Communist University, for example, 58 of 402 female students were peasants. In the *rabfaki* (workers' schools), 10 to 15 percent of the women were peasants. In various localities the percentage of peasant women in Party schools was still higher. She pointed to the increase in peasant women working in Soviet institutions, being chosen as members of uezd or guberniia Soviets or of executive committees, and occupying responsible posts in their local areas. During the first years of the Revolution the women members of the Soviets were exclusively proletarians, but now, by 1921, here and there peasant women actually outnumbered the proletarians. Only in the All-Russian Central Executive Committee was there not a single peasant woman.[129]

127. For recollections, see Bochkarëva and Liubimova, *Svetlyi put'*, pp. 86–89, and the chapter "Krasnyi platochek" on the *delegatka*. Kollontai's view is in *Rabotnitsa i krest'ianka*, p. 30. See USSR, [9], pp. 19–20, for the varying success of delegates' meetings in different gubernii.

128. See Lewin, *Russian Peasants*, p. 81. After the Civil War, the number of peasants taking part in elections to the *sel'sovet* was still small—22.3 percent in 1922, gradually increasing to 47.5 percent in 1925–26. There were still many villages in which no more than 10 to 15 percent of the peasants turned out to vote. From Soviet sources, Lewin concludes that the work of the *sel'sovety*, the basic element in the structure of government, was carried on without support from the mass of the peasantry. The Party imposed its own candidates. Lewin also discusses the revived vigor of the traditional *mir*. See *ibid.*, pp. 87–90.

129. *Polozhenie zhenshchiny*, p. 197. Another source supports Kollontai's optimism. Polina Vinogradskaia believed that the mood among non-Party women was changing. She recalled the earlier conferences with their few hostile participants and crowd of passive listeners. Now at non-Party conferences one saw women who wanted to help organize the nurseries and children's dining rooms. They were not for the most part

Even the patriarchal family seemed to her to be changing, particularly among young people. No longer, for example, was it unheard of for a woman to leave her husband. The more peasant women were chosen for the Soviet, and the sooner the countryside was mechanized and modernized and cooperative activity was strengthened, the quicker would be the liberation of peasant women.[130]

To the extent that Kollontai thought progress was being made, her conclusion was based on faith as well as evidence. A reading of Zhenotdel reports in *Kommunistka* suggests that one might easily have been pessimistic, concluding, for example, that work among the peasants lacked a mass character, that it was not following a single plan, and that insufficient numbers of peasant women were willingly entering into collective life or into Soviet construction. A great part of the work among the peasants was random, and dependent on the arrival of an energetic Zhenotdel worker from the center.[131] Still, *Kommunistka* carried reports of peasant women who, despite male ridicule, as early as 1920 organized work artels, sought to build children's nurseries, and requested further contact with advisers from the Women's Section.[132]

On balance, there seemed justification for Kollontai's optimism, particularly if the Zhenotdel could expand. Visitors familiar with rural Russia reported astonishment during the 1920's at the progress among peasant women in those few villages where the Zhenotdel was

---

young women who automatically anticipated new lives. Indeed, many were grey-haired, wrinkled peasants and proletarians wanting to rebuild. Some women did think they were too old to start anew, but those attending Zhenotdel conferences were receptive. Vinogradskaia, "Odna iz ocherednykh zadach," *Kommunistka*, 1920, nos. 3–4, p. 31.

130. *Polozhenie zhenshchiny*, pp. 196–98. If in the countryside the lives of women appeared still subordinate and little affected by the Revolution, Kollontai attributed the fact mainly to the unmechanized nature of agriculture, where muscular strength counted in determining a worker's status.

131. See USSR, [9], p. 25, for a breakdown by guberniia of effective work being done among the peasants. The regions around Moscow were in the lead. Despite the report's discouraging conclusion, the list of meetings and Zhenotdel activities in the countryside suggests an impressive effort. An article over the initials L. M., "Rabota sredi zhenskogo proletariata Povolzh'ia," in *Kommunistka*, 1920, no. 5, p. 41, indicated an interest among peasants in womens' meetings but a lack of organization. In rural areas, the Party's presence was still marginal at the end of the 1920's. Three-fourths of all villages experienced no organized Party activity. Rural Party membership had increased from 200,000 to 300,000 between 1922 and 1927, but there were still only 25 members for every 10,000 peasants. See Gail Lapidus, "Sexual Equality in Soviet Policy," in Atkinson et al., eds., p. 121, and Cohen, *Bukharin*, p. 443. For accounts of slow Party activity in rural areas and for references to recruitment of women in the countryside, see Lewin, *Russian Peasants*, p. 121.

132. See Tov. Lelia, "Kak organizovali krest'ianki trudovuiu artel'," *Kommunistka*, 1920, nos. 3–4, pp. 30–31.

active. Jessica Smith recalled a village meeting sponsored by the Zhenotdel in the late 1920's. "Some of the women spoke well, in clear, ringing voices." Others "spoke stumblingly, and had to be prompted, and one broke down before she finished, and rushed weeping from the platform. But it was a miracle to see this thing happening, to see the shining eyes of these hundreds of women in the dimly lighted hall, realizing for the first time that life held something for them beyond the dull routine of the past."[133]

At the Second International Conference of Communist Women, Kollontai praised the Zhenotdel. Toward the Soviet government that had not fulfilled its promises to draw women into political life on an equal basis with men, she was less generous.[134] "Look how many of us are here!," she exclaimed. "I am certain that the majority are businesslike comrades. But go into the Comintern, into the Central Executive Committee [of the All-Russian Congress of Soviets], and see how few women are there." At a meeting of the Central Executive Committee Kollontai counted four women. She protested that in Soviet Russia women were industriously carrying out tasks but were not being chosen for important posts. She demonstrated this failure at all levels, beginning with factory committees and ending with the central organs.[135]

Kollontai did not doubt that the Zhenotdel could change the situation. But she discouraged feminist separatism, invariably reminding Communist women that they must think in terms of the entire working class, male and female.[136] An excerpt from Kollontai's notebook

133. Smith, p. 37.
134. At the Eighth All-Russian Congress of Soviets in 1920, Kollontai and the Zhenotdel fought for a commitment to appoint proletarian and peasant women to positions of leadership in organs directing the Soviet economy, the factory committees, and the trade unions. See *Polozhenie zhenshchiny*, pp. 156–57. See Kollontai, *Autobiography*, p. 43, for resistance to a motion to this effect. It passed, but only after considerable effort by Zhenotdel leaders, particularly Samoilova. A year later, Kollontai protested that the resolution of the Eighth Congress to include women in the leadership existed only on paper. "Proizvodstvo i byt," p. 8.
135. *Rabotnitsa i krest'ianka*, p. 40. For figures to illustrate Kollontai's point, see p. 18. In the Plenum of the Petrograd Soviet there were 135 workers, 25 of whom were women. Among 194 members of boards directing textile workers in 38 gubernii, 10 were women.
136. For example, she suggested that the Zhenotdel eliminate women's pages since, except for their value in teaching women to read, they were not politically productive. They did not contribute toward educating men about Party work among women or toward bringing working-class men and women closer together. *Rabotnitsa i krest'ianka*, pp. 25, 34. For a description of women's pages and women's journals of

conveys the buoyant spirit of her first year as director. Kollontai knew that Party comrades jokingly referred to the Zhenotdel as "tsentro-baba," but what of it? There was too much work to be done! And she catalogued a frenetic round of activities recently undertaken with Vera Golubeva: first to the Orgburo; then to the Commission for the Struggle with Prostitution; next to a lecture by Vera Lebedeva, the director of the Section for the Protection of Mothers and Infants at the Commissariat of Health; then home to collapse on the couch and sleep for ten minutes; and then back to work.

Kollontai worked and lived in tiny quarters made crowded by Dybenko, with his huge presence; by her secretary, Mariia Dokshina; by a typist during the day; and by Misha, who in the midst of everything might arrive from Petrograd. People and noise were everywhere. But the confusion, the minutiae of daily living were hardly noticed. The success of the Zhenotdel, Kollontai wrote, overshadowed all else.[137] She did not anticipate in 1921 that the successes would be fewer and the problems greater in the years ahead.

※※※※

If the Zhenotdel seemed a bright hope to Kollontai, perhaps it was because other aspects of Soviet life, over which she had no control, appeared so grim. Few of the foreign women who attended the Second International Conference of Communist Women in the summer of 1921 could have suspected that the confident Zhenotdel leader who instructed them on ways to develop a women's movement was fighting a losing battle on several fronts. Kollontai seemed at the peak of her influence. Through the winter and spring of 1921 she was one of the prominent Communists chosen to lecture to students at the Sverdlov Communist University. She had not been a member of the Central Committee since 1918, but her role as head of the Russian socialist women's movement was recognized. Since the Zhenotdel was a section of the Central Committee, as its director she was attached to that prestigious organ. Periodically, when elections were held, she was chosen to be a member of the Central Executive Committee of the All-Russian Congress of Soviets.[138] When Kollontai's status began to

this period, see Bochkarëva and Liubimova, *Svetlyi put'*, pp. 84–85, and Emel'ianova, pp. 147, 197–98.

137. Itkina, p. 202.

138. See *Izbrannye stat'i i rechi*, pp. 424–25. In Dec. 1921, Kollontai was again chosen at the Ninth All-Russian Congress of Soviets.

decline in 1922 toward a low ebb like that of March 1918, it would be the result neither of her zeal on behalf of women nor of her controversial efforts to convert Communist youth to radical social and sexual theories, but rather of her leadership of yet another unpopular movement—the Workers' Opposition. It is to this subject that we now turn.

CHAPTER SEVEN

Lenin, Kollontai, and the Workers' Opposition

MAXIM GORKY liked to tell the story of Lenin's reaction to a remark by Julius Martov, who was once Lenin's "splendid comrade" and later became his Menshevik foe. There were only two Communists in Soviet Russia, Martov had written somewhere: Lenin and Kollontai. Lenin laughed, "long and heartily." Then he sighed, "What a clever woman she is!"[1]

Lenin's unhappy words recall his final clash with Kollontai, which began at the Tenth Party Congress in March 1921, continued through the Comintern meeting in June, and ended the following year at the Eleventh Party Congress. The issue revolved around Kollontai's leadership of the movement called the Workers' Opposition. Again, as in the Brest-Litovsk controversy, Kollontai believed that Lenin's policies were a departure from the revolutionary principles with which the Bolsheviks had come to power. This time no sweeping issues of internationalism were involved. Kollontai was trying quite simply to force the Bolshevik leaders to live by their own rules. Lenin's sadness when reminded of his old comrade reflected his awareness of how difficult it had become to implement her ideals. The last encounter between Lenin and Kollontai tells us much about Bolshevism, its internal contradictions and ambiguities, and the qualities that set it apart from the despotism of subsequent Soviet eras.

Signs of a clash between Lenin and Kollontai appeared early, for when Kollontai looked beyond the Zhenotdel she became disheartened: Soviet institutions seemed to be developing along lines alien to Communism and against the interests of the proletariat, and there were indications of a growing cleavage between the Party and the working class. Kollontai could not forget the joy of 1917. She was

1. Gorky, p. 54. Undated conversation.

nostalgic for the October days when everyone regarded the working class as the creator of Communism. Now she sensed vacillation and a deviation from the principle that Communist goals could be achieved only by the collective efforts of the workers. Kollontai isolated three fundamental causes of this: the breakdown of the economic structure; the ruthless pressure of hostile powers and White Guards as a result of the prolonged Civil War; and the Bolshevik attempt to create new economic forms in backward Russia, with its preponderantly peasant population.[2] To recover, the Party needed to face its problems. Instead, Bolshevism's crisis was made worse by a tendency to stifle free discussion in favor of "a blind subordination."[3] Kollontai was one of several Communists who, at a special Party conference held in September 1920, pressed for increased freedom of speech within Party organs. Zinoviev made an optimistic speech in response promising changes. Although the Communists applauded Zinoviev's promise of increased freedom to criticize within the Party, Kollontai remained skeptical. Typically, she requested permission to be heard, out of order, for just five minutes. She was not satisfied, she told Zinoviev, by his assurances. What kind of "free criticism" would be permitted? Party comrades at all levels must know that if they criticized Party policies they would not be sent off, in reprisal, to a warm climate to eat peaches.[4] The applause that followed her outburst demonstrated Party support. Many of the delegates understood that Kollontai's curious reference to eating peaches was a response to Zinoviev's ill-disguised maneuver to get rid of another critical Communist—Angelica Balabanoff, the first Secretary of the Comintern Executive. Zinoviev was trying to send her out of Moscow, ostensibly to take charge of a propaganda train to Turkestan.[5] Lenin as well as Zinoviev found Balabanoff irritating, and it was Lenin who replied to Kollontai, rejecting her "venomous" inquiry about whether Party freedom meant simply the right to be banished to eat peaches. He brushed aside Kollontai's concerns for free speech with his familiar argument that when the Soviet state was threatened by Kolchak and Denikin there could be no talk of freedom. "That is my answer to peaches."[6]

2. Kollontai, *Rabochaia oppozitsiia*, pp. 6, 10–11.
3. *Ibid.*, p. 41.
4. On Communist demands at the Ninth Party Conference for freedom of speech within the Party, see Schapiro, pp. 266–67. For Zinoviev's speech, see USSR, [3], pp. 139–56. For Kollontai's reference to "eating peaches," see *ibid.*, p. 188.
5. Balabanoff, *My Life as a Rebel*, pp. 238–39.
6. USSR, [3], p. 190.

It was more than his answer to peaches. The Soviet state was fighting to survive in 1920, but Lenin's attitude toward freedom of criticism had been no less ambivalent before Kolchak and Denikin became a threat. In 1902, in *What Is to Be Done?*, Lenin dismissed the cry for freedom of criticism by comparing freedom to a marsh:

We are marching in a compact group along a precipitous and difficult path, firmly holding each other by the hand. We are surrounded on all sides by enemies, and we have to advance almost constantly under their fire. We have combined . . . for the purpose of fighting the enemy, and not of retreating into the neighboring marsh. . . . And now some among us begin to cry out: Let us go into the marsh![7]

Freedom of criticism was still a marsh. Lenin would never cease to feel surrounded by enemies.

The September conference produced a new charter for Party democracy calling for more internal Party discussion and an end to the system whereby privileged bureaucrats ruled by edict. "Repressions of any sort whatsoever against comrades for the fact that they hold divergent views on certain questions resolved by the Party are impermissible."[8] But Lenin's blunt attack on Kollontai undermined in advance hope for greater freedom. Kollontai would write that the September conference and its promises changed nothing either in the Party or in the life of the masses.[9] On the other hand, the Party had affirmed internal democracy. And Lenin and Kollontai had drawn the lines of battle that foreshadowed their next two years of conflict. The months to come would find Kollontai seeking allies in her effort to force Lenin to put into practice the laudable promises and resolutions that expressed the will of the Party conference but seemed politically risky to the Party leaders.

꽃꽃꽃

Kollontai was angry over the harsh treatment of comrades who refused to be silent. Other Communists, in particular members of the trade unions, were developing their own grievances. The Workers' Opposition was a proletarian movement that arose among trade unionists during 1919. It originated in the discontent of workers, Party and non-Party alike, with the official policy of employing bourgeois specialists in responsible industrial positions. The Civil War

7. Lenin, *Chto delat'?*, *Sochineniia* (4th ed.), vol. 5, p. 328.
8. See Schapiro, p. 267, and USSR, [6], vol. 1, p. 509.
9. *Rabochaia oppozitsiia*, p. 8.

taught Party leaders that industry needed to be centralized, controlled, and planned. Technical specialists were required and, contrary to socialist principles of collegiality, so too was individual responsibility for management. Because the state had taken over industrial enterprises since the summer of 1918 and the onset of war, the issue was not whether to nationalize industry but how to administer the economy along socialized lines.[10] Were the factories to be turned into autonomous, democratic collectives based on the collegial principle, or were the industrial workers to be subjected again to managerial authority, labor discipline, traditional wage incentives, and the familiar scientific management of capitalistic industrial organization? Were the same bourgeois managers really to remain in control, the only difference being the state's title to the property?[11]

Bourgeois control, specialists, one-man management—these were measures the left refused to accept, regarding them as unnecessary for economic recovery and as deviations from a socialist economy. The Communist critics within the Party, primarily trade-union leaders like Aleksandr Shliapnikov and Sergei P. Medvedev, both of the Metalworkers' Union, attacked the use of specialists, protested against the diminishing role played by the workers in the control of industry, and denounced the growing rift between bureaucratic Party leaders and the working masses.[12] They demanded that industry be controlled by an All-Russian Congress of Producers, to be elected by trade unionists. During the winter of 1920–21, Kollontai decided that the Workers' Opposition was the appropriate vehicle for her own protest. Not only did she join the movement, she became a leader. We shall see why.

It is important to understand that Kollontai joined the Workers' Opposition despite her disagreement with some of its positions. If the leadership of the Workers' Opposition has been presented as monolithic, it is because the movement has been analyzed primarily from the perspective of the trade unions.[13] Here is an example of the kind of misconception that has resulted. E. H. Carr wrote concerning labor

10. The decree of June 28, 1918, nationalized all major branches of industry. A decree promulgated at the end of Nov. 1920 nationalized all concerns employing more than five workers with mechanical power, or ten workers without mechanical power. Both affected only legal title: owners remained temporarily in possession until such time as the *Vesenkha* (the Supreme Council of National Economy) took action. See Carr, *The Bolshevik Revolution*, vol. 2, pp. 176–78.

11. Daniels, pp. 107–10.

12. Schapiro, p. 222.

13. See Carr, *The Bolshevik Revolution*, vol. 2; Daniels; Schapiro; and Avrich.

conscription, a grievance of the trade unionists, that "it was natural that those who regarded labour conscription as a permanent part of a socialist economy also sought to incorporate the trade unions in the state machine."[14] Such a conclusion did not apply to Kollontai, who was one of Bolshevism's strongest advocates of conscripted labor but who also worked for the right of the trade unions to be the sole administrators of the economy. For her, labor obligation and labor discipline did not preclude a creative role for the trade unions.

From the outset, Kollontai and the trade unionists differed in their reaction to labor conscription. When the Soviet government issued Trotsky's decree in January 1920 on universal compulsory labor for men and women, Kollontai, we recall, hailed the day as the greatest in the history of women.[15] But earlier, when the proposal came up for informal consideration by the Communist fraction of the All-Russian Central Council of Trade Unions on January 12, 1920, Lenin and Trotsky were the only speakers who defended Trotsky's rigorous measures for handling labor.[16]

Although what opposition there was in Bolshevik ranks during the Civil War to conscription of labor tended to reside within the trade unions, and although Shliapnikov opposed Trotsky's "militarization of labor," a call to end the conscription of labor was not included in Shliapnikov's "Theses," which appeared in *Pravda* in January 1921.[17] Such a call might have been timely in the winter of 1921: the Civil War had ended, the Allied blockade had been lifted, and armed intervention in European Russia had terminated. Why Shliapnikov did not make it is not clear. Documentation of the Opposition and how it evolved remains sketchy. If, at some early point, Kollontai persuaded her good comrade Shliapnikov not to go beyond a general demand that Trotsky relax the methods of labor militarization, her initial influence on the movement was greater than has been presumed.[18]

14. Carr, *The Bolshevik Revolution*, vol. 2, pp. 220–21.

15. Kollontai, *Rabotnitsa i krest'ianka*, p. 41.

16. For the reception of Trotsky's proposals, see Bunyan, p. 92. For the text of Trotsky's "Theses" underlying the decree, see "Tezisy TsKRKP," in Trotsky, *Sochineniia* (M-L, 1927), vol. 15, pp. 107–14. Trotsky's "Theses" were adopted by the Bolshevik Central Committee on Jan. 22, 1920.

17. Shliapnikov's "Theses" are reprinted in Zorkii, pp. 235–42. For trade-union opposition to the conscription of labor, see Carr, *The Bolshevik Revolution*, vol. 2, pp. 216–21. For the notion that Shliapnikov opposed Trotsky's "militarization of labor," see Carr, *The Bolshevik Revolution*, vol. 2, p. 215.

18. See Bunyan, p. 190, for Shliapnikov's attack on Trotsky and for Shliapnikov's view that the time had come to relax the methods of labor militarization.

The Workers' Opposition in its early stages diverged sharply from Kollontai's views in other ways. Kollontai's late entry into the Opposition has been accepted without question.[19] But there are significant reasons why she did not join the movement until the winter of 1921, after the Party opened debate on the trade unions (late in 1920) and after the clash of views over the role of the unions had become public at the Eighth All-Russian Congress of Soviets in December. The Workers' Opposition, as it emerged at the Ninth Party Congress, made demands for which Kollontai could not have much sympathy. The trade unionists called not only for administration of the economy to be placed in the hands of the trade unions, but for the unions to be independent of the Party and the state.[20] Though Kollontai supported Shliapnikov in his call for a three-way separation of functions among the Party, the Soviet, and the trade unions, she could not accept the further notion that the trade unions be given autonomy within the Party. Shliapnikov's demand that the Communist fraction of the All-Russian Council of Trade Unions be an independent center of control of the Communist Party organizations in the trade unions was unacceptable to most of the Party leaders, Kollontai included.[21] Communists in the trade unions, as both the Ninth and Tenth Party Congresses decreed, would have to be subordinate, like all other Russian Communists, to the Central Committee of the Russian Communist Party.[22]

Particular reasons prevented Kollontai from endorsing exclusion from Communist discipline for any organization within the Soviet structure. As director of the Zhenotdel, she needed to combat suspicions that she and her comrades harbored separatist feminist ambitions tending to place them outside the Party orbit. Kollontai had early on committed herself publicly to the principle that all groups within the Communist Party must be subordinate to Party control. Beyond her commitment to principle, Kollontai, as director of the Zhenotdel, had a further motive to resist the trade-union demand. Conflicting, even antagonistic, pressures existed between the two interest groups, the trade unions and the Zhenotdel.[23] The Communist

19. See Daniels, pp. 127–29, and Schapiro, p. 290.

20. For the unions' call for autonomy, see Daniels, p. 126.

21. Kollontai did not include the demand in her *Rabochaia oppozitsiia*.

22. See the decrees passed by both the Ninth and the Tenth Party Congresses in USSR, [4], p. 559, and USSR, [2], p. 584.

23. On Soviet interest groups, see H. Gordon Skilling and F. Griffiths, *Interest Groups in Soviet Politics* (Princeton, N.J., 1971), p. 28.

fraction in the trade unions and the leaders of the Zhenotdel had been unable to work out an agreement to coordinate their work among the masses of non-Party women in the unions.[24] If the trade unions had the right of authority over Communists in the unions, women Party workers assigned by the Zhenotdel to propagandize in the factories might find themselves under the unwelcome direction of the trade unions rather than the Women's Section of the Central Committee. We will see elsewhere that conflicts between the Zhenotdel and the trade unions did develop over such questions of jurisdiction.

That Kollontai and Shliapnikov were close comrades did not mean that the trade unions and the Women's Section were also friends. And it was in the ruling Communist fraction of the trade unions, where opposition to official Party policy was fast gathering strength in 1920, that Kollontai found strong prejudice against women. Nor could she comfort herself with the idea that the minority of trade-union officials who formed the Workers' Opposition were an exceptional few who fought for women's equality in the unions. The evidence pointed in the other direction. The interests of women were not an Oppositionist cause. To be sure, the leaders of the Metalworkers were no more responsible than the heads of other unions for the fact that women in all fields occupied the lower paying jobs and earned less than men. But neither were they inclined, any more than men in other unions, to draw women into leadership roles.[25] Thus because of her leadership of the Zhenotdel, Kollontai had a special reason for protesting the trade-unionist call for independence from Party control.

It may be that Kollontai did not sign Shliapnikov's "Theses" on the Workers' Opposition when he published them in *Pravda* in January 1921 because they left unclear who was to control Party members in the unions. But at some point during this period the demand for full independence was abandoned, presumably because it was too controversial. If, as is possible, Shliapnikov, the most prominent of the trade-union leaders, responded to Kollontai's urging, we must conclude again that Kollontai played a more pivotal role in shaping the final program of the Opposition than has been assumed. The

---

24. Kollontai, *Izbrannye stat'i i rechi*, p. 320.

25. See Kollontai, *Polozhenie zhenshchiny*, appendix, unnumbered page, for a chart showing the large number of women in unions as compared to the small number of women in union leadership. Also see *Rabotnitsa i krest'ianka*, pp. 17–18.

draft resolution of the Workers' Opposition, when it was presented to the Tenth Party Congress in March, contained a new and surprising clause whose meaning was unequivocal and that Kollontai presumably took part in writing. It called for "Subordination of all Party and political work in the unions to the local Party organization and subordination of all members of the Party to the control of the local Party organization."[26] The way had been cleared for Kollontai to join the ranks of the Opposition, as she did sometime in January or February 1921. If she became an Oppositionist despite her disagreement with trade unionists over labor conscription and her skepticism about the quality of trade union commitment to working women, it was largely a result of concerns that made her reservations temporarily inappropriate. Kollontai feared not only that freedom of criticism was being crushed, but that the Communist Party was losing faith in the working class. If so, if the Bolsheviks separated themselves from their revolutionary base, they risked destroying the possibility of a workers' state. It followed that if Russia were not on a direct road to Communism, all that she had fought for in 1917—the activities of the Zhenotdel, the solution to the woman question—was also jeopardized. The emergence of a genuine proletarian movement, at a time when the Party seemed to be heedlessly turning away from the "direct class road" leading to Communism, heartened her by holding out the hope that disaster might be prevented. Therefore she welcomed as an ally the Workers' Opposition, with its trade-union composition and its premise that the rift between the proletariat and the Party must be healed, that the workers must be permitted to play a key role in the management of the economy.

We can now see why Kollontai joined the Workers' Opposition, but we still need to determine what caused her to become a leader. She could have lent support to the Workers' Opposition and left its actual direction to the trade unionists. She might then have continued to work in the Zhenotdel without risking her central role in the women's movement by another round of defiance. For battle lines were developing in the Communist Party in the winter of 1921 that recalled divisions and suspicions not seen in Moscow since the time of

26. Draft resolution presented to the Tenth Congress, as printed in Zorkii, p. 249.

Brest-Litovsk. If Kollontai remembered with pain the "dark time" of 1918 when her posts were taken from her, why did she jeopardize her position in the Zhenotdel by taking on a prominent role in a movement unpopular with Lenin? Part of the answer lies in Kollontai's attitude toward the Opposition's leaders. Let us look at Shliapnikov, head of the Metalworkers and the most prominent Oppositionist.

Students of the Workers' Opposition have assumed a more than casual link between Kollontai and Shliapnikov. Thus one historian has observed that "her close friendship with Shliapnikov gave extra zest to her advocacy of his views," others that she was Shliapnikov's mistress.[27] Shliapnikov, now "corpulent and unwieldy, with a large, round, moustachioed face," had of course lived with Kollontai for several years during their European exile.[28] They may have resumed— if briefly—their intimacy, although we know Kollontai considered herself married to Dybenko. (The conflicts of dual love, one relationship based on a long-time affinity of shared ideas and mutual warmth, the other on physical attraction, thread through her writing.[29]) More pertinent to the politics of the Workers' Opposition is another question. Was she inspired to lead the Opposition because of Shliapnikov's prompting, or was it rather Kollontai who influenced Shliapnikov? Kollontai would insist a few years later, as we have already had occasion to note, that none of the men she was close to ever influenced her thinking, but rather that she was the guiding force. It may have been so. We have seen that Kollontai was perhaps responsible for altering Oppositionist demands affecting the relationship of trade unionists to the Party. It also seems clear that Kollontai published her defense of the Workers' Opposition—a pamphlet that appeared in March, shortly before the Tenth Party Congress—because Shliapnikov's "Theses" published in *Pravda* in January seemed to her less than adequate. Thus she wrote that representatives of the Opposition were "not always able clearly to express and define" the roots of the controversy, that they were at times unaware that a question of principle was involved. In fact, two historically irreconcilable points of view were clashing: one-man management, a product of the individ-

27. For quotation, see Schapiro, p. 291; Daniels, p. 127, and Ulam, p. 469, both assume that Kollontai and Shliapnikov were still lovers.
28. Serge, p. 123, for the description of Shliapnikov.
29. See especially *Zhenshchina na perelome*, the essay "Dorogu krylatomu erosu!" (*Molodaia Gvardiia*, 1923, no. 3, pp. 111–24) and the short story "Liubov' trekh pokolenii" (in *Liubov' pchel trudovykh*).

ualist conception of the bourgeois class, and the Communist principle of the collective. Kollontai noted that the Opposition had no great theoreticians,[30] and she may have wished for a Bukharin or a Trotsky—at least the Trotsky of the old days, who had charged that only a bourgeois politician could distrust the working classes as intensely as Lenin did. Trotsky now, however, was opposed to proletarian *samodeiatel'nost'* (spontaneous, self-directed activity) and wanted the trade unions to be deprived of autonomy and absorbed into the machinery of government.[31] Perhaps she agreed with one observer that Shliapnikov, although fierce in his radical idealism, was "quite incapable" as a politician of "grasping and generalizing the essence of the conjecture [*sic*] that had been created."[32]

Kollontai, then, joined the Workers' Opposition and put herself at the forefront out of her conviction that lacking a Lenin, a Trotsky, or a Bukharin, the movement needed her. Not confident that the Workers' Opposition could effectively articulate its basic grievances, Kollontai assumed the mantle of the movement's theoretician, a role she enjoyed. She had decided in the 1890's, at the onset of her political life, that she wanted to make a significant contribution to socialist theory.[33] She did so many times, but never more impressively than with her March pamphlet *Rabochaia Oppozitsiia* (*The Workers' Opposition*). The most devastating attack upon the regime to come from within Party ranks, it transformed a dry discussion of the role of the trade unions vis-à-vis the Party into a broad-ranging theoretical questioning of the revolutionary integrity of the Party.[34] The controversy the pamphlet aroused raged for more than a year, and the movement that had given rise to it never resumed its original, limited form.

A Communist contemporary gave Kollontai credit for leading the Opposition. "Within the Russian Party," Angelica Balabanoff wrote, "the first organized opposition to the policies of both Lenin and Trotsky was led by a woman—Aleksandra Kollontai."[35] How are we to explain Kollontai's extraordinary impact when other Communists had earlier raised many of the same issues? Osinskii and Sapronov had already criticized the rapid degeneration of the Party and the

30. Kollontai, *Rabochaia oppozitsiia*, pp. 6–9.
31. Deutscher, *The Prophet Armed*, vol. 1, pp. 92, 507.
32. Sukhanov, *The Russian Revolution*, vol. 1, p. 43.
33. Kollontai, *Iz moei zhizni i raboty*, p. 88.
34. See Schapiro, p. 290, and Daniels, pp. 128–29.
35. Balabanoff, *My Life as a Rebel*, p. 251.

Soviets into a "parasitic bureaucratic system."[36] The answer is that no member of the left in 1921 reasoned with Kollontai's dynamic persistence or breadth of scale, and that no other Oppositionist produced a popular pamphlet like *The Workers' Opposition* that exposed the heart of the problem in easily understood language. Kollontai addressed herself not simply to the issue of the trade unions but to the fundamental ills of Soviet society, for she understood in 1921 what has only recently been pointed out—that the role of the trade unions in itself was "surrealistically irrelevant to the real situation in the country."[37] This recent judgment only ratifies Kollontai's position at the time that the root of the controversy was deeper than disagreements over the tasks and role of the trade unions, deeper than the crisis in agriculture and the fate of the economy.[38] The crisis was in the Party, where the Communists were floundering out of sight of their revolutionary goals. The Bolsheviks, priding themselves on their careful path, had fallen instead into a "marsh" of their own making.

Her analysis of the trade-union controversy was brilliant. She refused to take seriously the several positions that had been formulated in answer to the question posed by the Workers' Opposition: Who shall build the Communist economy? She was convinced that, contrary to Party opinion, there were really not many but only two points of view. One was that of the Workers' Opposition; the other was one that united all the rest of the groups, groups that differed in degree but not in substance.[39] Thus she dismissed the distinctions between Trotsky's idea that the trade unions be turned into organs of state—"production unions" that would operate on military lines under Party control—and Lenin's call for the unions to remain separate from the State, protecting the workers' interests and functioning also as schools of Communism. She mocked Bukharin, who wanted to see workers' democracy within the unions but who then shrank from the Opposition's demand that the working class create the Soviet economy! To all of them—Lenin, Trotsky, Zinoviev, and Bukharin—production seemed such a "delicate thing" that it was impossible to get along without directors. Their notion was that we must first nurture

36. Souvarine, p. 239. For Sapronov's and Osinskii's views, see USSR, [4], pp. 50–53, 115–27, 139–42. Sapronov protested Party bureaucracy and called for implementation of the decisions of the Ninth Congress. See Daniels, p. 138.

37. Cohen, *Bukharin*, p. 105. For Kollontai's view, see *Rabochaia oppozitsiia*, p. 6.

38. Bukharin wrote in *Pravda* on this latter point. See Cohen, *Bukharin*, p. 105.

39. Kollontai, *Rabochaia oppozitsiia*, pp. 21–22.

the workers, teach them, and only when they grow up liberate them from the teachers in the Supreme Council of National Economy and let the industrial unions take control over production.

The several points of view expressed by the Party leaders in their separate "Theses" coincided in one essential feature—for the present, we shall not give the trade unions control over production. Trotsky, Lenin, Zinoviev, and Bukharin may have differed in stating the precise reason why they believed the workers should not be entrusted with running the industries, but they all agreed that at the present time management over production must be saddled upon the workers by a bureaucratic system.[40]

What has been noted by one historian, that Lenin's handling of the Workers' Opposition was an example of his marvelous political skill, seemed obvious at the time to Kollontai.[41] Lenin, with his sure political instinct, played the role of broad-minded conciliator, playing off one group against another, denouncing Trotsky's theses as "completely incorrect." But Kollontai knew that whereas the Workers' Opposition looked to the unions to manage and create the Communist economy, Lenin, together with Bukharin and Trotsky, did not trust the masses.[42] Unconvinced by Lenin's show of bitterness, aimed alternately at Trotsky and Bukharin, she predicted agreement between the groups now furiously opposing each other. She would not be surprised if the sponsors of the different economic reforms, with the single exception of the Workers' Opposition, came to a common understanding at the approaching Tenth Party Congress, since there was no essential controversy among them.[43] Thus Kollontai swept aside the arguments that had been filling the columns of *Pravda* for weeks and anticipated the outcome of the Tenth Congress—at which unity was stressed, factionalism banned, and the Workers' Opposition crushed.

꙳꙳꙳

Kollontai's efforts to democratize early Soviet society have been recognized and appreciated, but underestimated. Thus we read that Kollontai's arguments in favor of increased democracy were "strictly limited in their appeal to the Communist Party," that they did not,

---

40. *Ibid.*, pp. 25–26.
41. See Ulam, p. 470, on Lenin's political skill.
42. *Rabochaia oppozitsiia*, p. 30.
43. *Ibid.*, p. 36.

"in any form, criticize the domination by the Communist minority over the majority of the proletariat." Moreover, the interests of the peasants, as opposed to the proletariat, concerned her still less.[44] This conclusion appears superficially plausible, particularly with regard to Kollontai's lack of concern for traditional peasant interests.[45] Her assumption that only the peasants benefited from the Revolution surely had an odd ring in the winter of 1921, when the peasants still groaned under the burden of forced requisition of grain. But I want to argue that Kollontai's commitment to the urban working class was no less powerful than her attachment to the Party. Indeed, a goal of her campaign in behalf of the Workers' Opposition was to provide for the diffusion of democratic forms throughout the industrial proletariat precisely to compensate for Communist political rule.

The conflict that ensued from Kollontai's dedication to Party and proletariat both, and her means of resolving it, may be understood by comparing her with Rosa Luxemburg, whose outlook she had shared ever since she first read Luxemburg's "Reform or Revolution" at the turn of the century. There Kollontai had encountered this statement: "Socialism by its very nature cannot be decreed. . . . [T]he negative, the tearing down, can be decreed; the building up, the positive, cannot. New territory. A thousand problems. Only experience is capable of correcting and opening new ways."[46] Similarly, Kollontai scorned the "absurdly naive belief" that it was "possible to bring about Communism by bureaucratic means." She criticized those who decreed, where it was necessary to create.[47] But Luxemburg added a conviction Kollontai could not endorse: "Without general elections, without unrestricted freedom of press and assembly, without a free struggle of opinion, life dies out in every public institution, becomes a mere semblance of life, in which only the bureaucracy remains as the active element."[48]

Rosa Luxemburg enjoys the reputation of being more broadly democratic than Kollontai. But Luxemburg was never a member of a party in power. Had the German Communists been victorious, as a minority group, no doubt Luxemburg would have modified, at

44. Schapiro, p. 294. Italics mine.
45. But see the discussion in Chapter 6 of Kollontai's views of the female peasant.
46. Rosa Luxemburg, "Sozialreform oder Revolution?," in her *Gesammalte Werke* (Berlin, 1972), vol. 1, part 1, pp. 369–70. See also *The Russian Revolution* (Ann Arbor, Mich., 1961), pp. 70–71. This pamphlet originally appeared in 1922 as *Zur russischen Revolution.*
47. Kollontai, *Rabochaia oppozitsiia,* p. 14.
48. Luxemburg, *The Russian Revolution,* p. 71.

least for a time, some of her democratic principles. She was no less revolutionary than Kollontai. At the end of December 1918, although she knew the masses in Germany would withhold their support, she participated, albeit reluctantly, in an ill-fated attempt to seize power. Luxemburg was too much the militant to reject a temporary dictatorship aimed at keeping her party in power. Kollontai was trying, as Luxemburg would have done had she been a member of a weak, revolutionary government, to find ways to mitigate the evils of the necessary period of dictatorship. Kollontai did not believe it was possible to allow free elections and a multiparty system in Russia after 1917 and still maintain the revolutionary structure. Yet nothing indicates that she believed only Communists could be elected to the proposed All-Russian Congress of Producers. The idea that non-Party unionists could be eligible was not excluded by Kollontai's proposed regulation that "All appointments to the administrative economic positions shall be made with consent of the union. All candidates nominated by the union are nonremovable. All responsible officials appointed by the union are responsible to and may be recalled by it."[49]

Communist leaders were not certain what the Workers' Opposition intended this ambiguous clause to mean. Trotsky, making his confusion known, affords us a glimpse of his distress that the Party no longer had the support of the working class. He angrily cited Zinoviev's prediction that if Shliapnikov's Congress of Producers were to assemble, 99 percent of it would be non-Party men, Socialist Revolutionaries, and Mensheviks. Calling Zinoviev's observation "a monstrous exaggeration" that "should be stricken immediately from the record," he asked, with shrill sarcasm, if Zinoviev wished to enlighten the Third International with the news that in Russia the workers' state consisted of 1 percent of the working class stifling the voice of the other 99 percent.[50] Although Trotsky found Zinoviev's indiscretion appalling, he admitted that even if the percentage were reduced significantly there would still remain a very large number of dissatisfied workers who would not vote for the Bolsheviks. Shliapnikov assured Party leaders that they had nothing to fear, that an All-Russian Congress of Producers would of course be composed of Communist delegates nominated and elected through the Party cells.[51] Though

49. Kollontai, *Rabochaia oppozitsiia*, p. 37.

50. Trotsky in a speech of Mar. 14, 1921, at the Tenth Party Congress. See USSR, [2], pp. 350–51. For Zinoviev's anxiety about the proposed Congress of Producers, see Zinoviev quoted by Carr, *The Bolshevik Revolution*, vol. 2, p. 227.

51. For Shliapnikov's disclaimer, see USSR, [2], p. 388.

there is no hard evidence to support the view, Trotsky's and Zinoviev's assumptions, coupled with Shliapnikov's hasty disclaimer, suggest that Kollontai had not excluded the possibility that the unions might elect non-Communist workers to an All-Russian Congress of Producers.[52] Although it was not Kollontai but Shliapnikov who in 1917 had advocated a coalition government, the situation was different now: the Bolsheviks no longer had the support of the workers that had so exhilarated Kollontai in 1917.[53] Kollontai may have hoped that through an All-Russian Congress of Producers elected freely by the unions the Party could preserve this single, absolute link with the working class.

The language of her pamphlet was consistent with such a hope. Kollontai's call to the Party to allow the proletariat full scope to develop economic and social forms was an effort to compensate for the political control of a Communist minority over the majority. Thus she charged that the Party did not trust the creative abilities of workers' collectives, that it wrongly sought salvation from the industrial chaos not through the hands of workers but through the scions of the capitalist past. Consider what she called the key question: Who shall develop the creative power in the sphere of economic reconstruction, the class organs or the "Soviet machine"?[54] Her conclusion that the unions must create the Communist economy, because in the unions the class identity was purer than in the heterogeneous Soviet economic apparatus, reflected concern for the vast majority of non-Party workers in the unions. Ironically, Kollontai argued from a traditionally liberal and democratic concern for the majority: we have half a million Party members in the unions, but the unions consist of seven million workers.[55] Creativity, the search for new forms of production, for new incentives to increase productivity, could arise only in the bosom of this natural class collective. *"Only those who are directly bound to industry can introduce into it animating innovations."*[56]

She pointed to the Party's unconscious emulation of the bourgeois

52. See Schapiro, p. 294, for the contrary opinion that only Communists would be eligible for election under Kollontai's plan.

53. For workers' support of Bolshevik goals in 1917, especially in Petrograd, see Rabinowitch, p. 312.

54. Kollontai, *Rabochaia oppozitsiia*, p. 9.

55. *Ibid.*, p. 28.

56. *Ibid.*, p. 7. Italics in original. A literal Marxist, Kollontai regarded the proletariat, not the Party, as the bearer and creator of Communism. The Party simply "reflected" the class point of view of the proletariat. *Ibid.*, p. 48. It followed, therefore, that no part of the working class should be excluded from the creative economic process, and that the proletariat should control it.

past: the Party was contradicting itself by claiming to be creating a system that expressed new moral values while at the same time giving to authority a traditional, hierarchical form and expecting from the masses passive acceptance. Kollontai thought as Rosa Luxemburg did. To build Communism, the mistakes of the proletariat were preferable to the wisdom of its leaders: "Errors committed by a truly revolutionary movement" were historically "more fruitful than the infallibility of the cleverest Central Committee."[57]

Lenin was not really wrong when he classified Kollontai's emphasis on proletarian economic creativity as anarcho-syndicalism.[58] Much in the Workers' Opposition was reminiscent of the theories of Bakunin, for whom the people in their revolutionary essence were a secularized form of "holy Russia." Lenin also knew that much was reminiscent as well of what he had advocated in 1917 in *State and Revolution*. We might question Kollontai's faith in the proletariat's potential for creativity in a shattered, predominantly peasant country. Yet she was not suggesting that the anarchy of the initial factory committees of 1917 be recreated; she looked to the trade unions to supervise and coordinate.[59] The Revolution had been carried out in the name of the working class, with workers' control of production as part of the revolutionary platform. Lenin's first promise to the Soviet regime after the Bolshevik seizure of power had been "we shall institute workers' control over production."[60] And, as Kollontai warned, the masses were not blind. Workers could see the leaders' distrust.[61]

Kollontai had in mind the unhappy model of German socialism on the eve of the First World War.[62] Although she did not cite her earlier

57. Rosa Luxemburg, "Leninism or Marxism?," in *The Russian Revolution*, p. 108. This article first appeared in *Iskra* in 1904 as "Organizatsionnye voprosy russkoi sotsial-demokratii."

58. See USSR, [2], p. 116.

59. See *Rabochaia oppozitsiia*, pp. 36–37. Within two weeks of the Revolution, Kollontai exulted that the workers, through the trade unions, would be in control of industrial production. See her letter of Nov. 24, 1917, to F. Ström. Ström Archive, Univ. of Gothenburg. For trade-union recognition that "workers' control" must be under the regulation of the unions, see the resolution of the Second All-Russian Congress of Trade Unions, Jan. 23, 1918, in USSR, [21], pp. 112–14.

60. See Sukhanov, *The Russian Revolution*, vol. 2, pp. 623, 629, and Lenin's speech in *Sochineniia* (4th ed.), vol. 26, p. 215. In Lenin's words, the Soviet government would "establish workers' control over production." See also the "Resolution" of the Petrograd Soviet that pledged to "institute workers' control over the production and distribution of goods," in *Sochineniia*, vol. 26, p. 210. The original decree on workers' control issued by the Council of Commissars in Nov. 1917 did not specify that workers' control would be regulated by the trade unions. See the decree "O rabochem' kontrol'" in USSR, [15], 1917, no. 3, art. 34–35, pp. 39–40.

61. Kollontai, *Rabochaia oppozitsiia*, pp. 16–17.

62. *Ibid.*, pp. 5–6.

statement of faith in proletarian spontaneity, which appeared in 1915 in *Kommunist, The Workers' Opposition* raised the same specter of a bureaucratic party cut off from the masses, of an uninspired, self-satisfied leadership and a passive rank and file. From class-conscious fighters, the German proletariat had been reduced by such a party to a dull herd that passively followed its leaders to war in 1914.[63] Would her own Russian comrades similarly abandon revolutionary principles?

Kollontai had a remarkable sense of how little the Bolsheviks, whatever their rhetoric to the contrary, identified in practice with the working class. As a measure of the degree of her alienation, she even went so far as to contrast the Russian workers as they went to war in 1914, believing that their leaders knew best, with the Russian workers who in 1921 were not suffering quietly, who were not accepting as superior the wisdom of Party leaders.[64] Russian workers were illegally striking in 1921. She unsettled the Bolsheviks by informing them that the workers were asking whether they were really the prop of the class dictatorship or just an obedient herd serving as support for those who, having severed all ties with the masses, carried out their own policies and built up industry without any regard to proletarian opinions and creative abilities.[65] After three years of revolution, the condition of the workers' lives not only had failed to improve but had become worse. Hygiene, sanitation, and working conditions in the shops seemed the lowest priorities. The Party had gone no further in trying to solve the housing problem than moving workers' families into inconvenient bourgeois mansions. In the heart of Moscow, workers still lived in filthy, overcrowded workingmen's quarters, one visit to which made Kollontai wonder if there had been a revolution at all.[66] And she saw an unhappy precedent being set in the ever-growing inequality between the privileged in Soviet Russia and the rank-and-file workers: because of Soviet poverty, of course, the housing problem could not be solved in a few months or even years, but the worker saw and resented the disparity between the Soviet official's life and his own. Kollontai was one of a number of Bolsheviks who were committed to the notion that it was the Party leaders, not the masses, who

63. Her 1915 article was entitled "Pochemu molchal" proletariat" Germanii v iiul'skie dni?"

64. *Rabochaia oppozitsiia*, pp. 5–6.

65. *Ibid.*, p. 20.

66. *Ibid.*, pp. 17–18.

should bear the hardships of daily life. They were best able. For it was the leaders who had the compensating satisfaction of seeing their long-held ideals being realized.

Zinoviev had promised at the Ninth Party Conference practical measures to eliminate the inequality in living conditions between the responsible socialists and staff workers on the one hand and the working masses on the other.[67] Nothing significant was occurring. Kollontai protested that whenever it was necessary to repair houses occupied by Soviet institutions the government could find both the materials and the labor. The Party would not dare try to shelter its specialists in huts like those in which the masses still lived and worked. There would be such a howl that the entire housing department would have to be mobilized to correct the chaotic conditions that interfered with the productivity of "the specialists."[68]

Soviet leaders were uneasily aware of how thin a proletarian layer was available as a social base for developing Communist ideals. The working class, it is said, had "nearly vanished."[69] Kollontai pointed out how few workers were actually involved in government. She quoted the People's Commissar of Supplies, A. D. Tsiurupa, who claimed that only 17 percent of the people who served in his Commissariat were workers. More than 50 percent were tradesmen and salesmen, most of them illiterate. Though Tsiurupa took comfort in the "democratic composition" of his office, Kollontai resented the presence of petty-bourgeois elements that brought decay into Soviet institutions. All the more reason to give free scope for economic creativity to the seven million workers in the trade unions who were still available to run the industries.[70]

67. See USSR, [6], vol. 1, p. 511.
68. *Rabochaia oppozitsiia*, p. 19.
69. See Lewin, "The Social Background of Stalinism," in Tucker, ed., p. 112. For statistics on the decline in number of industrial workers, see Kritsman, pp. 52–53. See Carr, *The Bolshevik Revolution*, vol. 2, pp. 197–98, for the decline in the urban population. By the autumn of 1920, the population of 40 provincial capitals had declined by a third from their 1917 levels—from 6,400,000 to 4,300,000. The population of 50 other large towns declined by 16 percent from 1,517,000 to 1,271,000. The larger the city, the greater the decline. Petrograd lost 57.5 percent of its population in three years, Moscow 44.5 percent.
70. See *Rabochaia oppozitsiia*, p. 11, for Kollontai's quote of Tsiurupa, and p. 28 for Kollontai's figure of seven million workers and 500,000 Party members. Not all the seven million listed in the unions as members were industrial workers.

If Kollontai seemed relatively sanguine about the continuing availability of a proletariat as a base for social experiments, it may have been because she saw a social base not necessarily apparent to leaders for whom the word "worker" usually held a male connotation. It is not without significance that Kollontai chose examples to illustrate working-class initiative in part from the socialist women's movement. She noted how many times workers' own attempts to organize dining rooms, day nurseries for children, transportation of wood, and so on had died from red tape. Wherever there was a move by the people themselves to equip a dining room, store a supply of wood, or organize a nursery, refusal always followed refusal from the central institutions: there was no equipment for the dining room, no means of transporting wood, and no adequate building for the nursery. And how much bitterness was generated among working men and women who knew that if they had been given the opportunity to act, they themselves could have put the project through. How painful to be refused materials when they had already been found and procured by the interested workers! Initiative slackened, the will to act died. "Let officials themselves take care of us." As a result, a harmful division was generated: we are the toiling people, and they are the Soviet officials on whom everything depends. Similarly in the Party, every independent attempt, every new thought was considered a "heresy," a violation of Party discipline, an attempt to infringe on the prerogatives of the center.[71]

Kollontai was simultaneously one of War Communism's greatest supporters and its sharpest critic. This reflected not so much a contradiction as an entirely accurate perception that War Communism was composed of at least two layers, the heroic and the military. And though Kollontai applauded the heroic assault that had torn down the old bourgeois society and substituted collectivism, labor obligation, work books, food rations, egalitarianism, and the (for her) joyful ethic that he or she who does not work does not eat, the military side of War Communism was grim. It brought rule by administrative decree, summary justice, and a Communist arrogance that underlay the assumption of the bureaucrat's superiority.[72] The bleak side of War Communism caused her protest that nothing was being done in the

71. *Rabochaia oppozitsiia*, p. 38.
72. See Tucker, ed., p. 92. For Kollontai on the military mentality in the Party, see *Rabochaia oppozitsiia*, p. 41. Lenin referred to the predilection for giving peremptory orders and commands as *komchvanstvo*, or "Communist arrogance." See Tucker, p. 402.

Party to encourage spontaneous action in the masses, *samodeiatel'nost'*. Rather, the contrary prevailed: at every meeting working men and women were called upon "to create a new life, build up and assist the Soviet authorities"; yet no sooner did they attempt to carry out these admonitions than some bureaucratic institution, feeling it was being ignored, hurried to cut short the efforts of the over-zealous initiators. Kollontai understood what the American writer Max Eastman wrote after living in "the workers' state." The Revolution was controlled by men who "were not celebrating the triumph of the proletariat, but the triumph of the idea of the proletariat."[73]

At the Tenth Congress Lenin accused Kollontai of railing against bureaucracy without offering ways to eliminate it. In fact, she did supply suggestions. But, as she pointed out, to be effective they needed first to be applied to the Party. If the Communists were overwhelmed by bureaucracy, it was because they were afraid of criticism and had ceased to rely on the masses. If the Party opened itself to internal criticism, the Soviet institutions would follow, becoming again alive and vital, rather than laboratories for stillborn decrees.[74] That was the first condition: in the name of the Workers' Opposition, democratic principles must be applied not only for the present, but also in times of internal and external tension.

The second condition for restoring the Party to health was the expulsion of all nonproletarian elements (an early and more or less benign version of the Party purge). The stronger the Soviet authority became, the greater the number of middle-class and sometimes even hostile elements that joined the Party merely for personal advantage. Reasoning that the most revolutionary nonworker elements had joined during the first period of Soviet rule, Kollontai proposed the reassessment of all nonworker members who had joined the Party since 1919, reserving for them the right to appeal within three months the decisions arrived at. Every applicant to membership or reinstatement must work a certain period of time at manual labor before becoming eligible for enrollment.[75] By the time of the Tenth Congress this proposal was expanded into a draft resolution demanding that manual labor be made compulsory for all Party members—no matter what their status. For three months each year they were to live and

73. Eastman, p. 329. For the stifling of workers' initiative, see *Rabochaia oppozitsiia*, p. 38.
74. *Rabochaia oppozitsiia*, pp. 40–41.
75. *Ibid.*, pp. 41–42.

work like genuine proletarians.[76] (The Russians never adopted this concept. The Chinese Communists did.)

Multiple office-holding too must end. Years later, Trotsky regretted the "extraordinary closeness and at times actual merging of the Party with the state apparatus," remembering the harm it did to the freedom and elasticity of the Party regime.[77] Kollontai saw the problem in 1921, criticizing members of the Central Committee who occupied high posts in the Soviet government and proposing limits on the number of Party members who could act simultaneously as Soviet officials. Finally, to eliminate bureaucracy and revive Party health, it was necessary to restore the practice of submitting important questions of Party activity and Soviet policy to the rank and file.[78]

Kollontai's relationship to the Opposition was not without ambivalence or tension. To be a leader of a trade-union movement meant also to modify temporarily her own inclinations. One searches in vain through *The Workers' Opposition* for the usual demand for increased Party attention to the woman question. For Kollontai, its absence was remarkable. The need for more women in positions of leadership in Soviet institutions, including the unions, was obvious to the director of the Zhenotdel; as we know, she seldom missed an opportunity to speak of the problem. Her failure to mention it supports the suspicion that the Workers' Opposition would have been unenthusiastic about it.

Kollontai began her pamphlet by posing the question, What is the Workers' Opposition? She answered that it was a movement aimed at transferring the direction of the economy into the hands of the trade unions, i.e. an All-Russian Congress of Producers. It was, beyond that, a set of proletarian grievances: hatred of the bureaucrat and the bourgeois specialist, resentment of the privileged Party member, fear that the workers were being put in last place. What the Workers' Opposition was not (though she did not say it) was a movement sensitive to or interested in the aims of the Women's Section. To suggest that Kollontai was merely compromising—her own accusation against the Party leadership—would be insufficient. Kollontai, as a leader of two interest groups, faced immensely difficult choices. If she omitted

76. Unless they were medically exempt. The text of the draft resolution appears in Zorkii, pp. 244–50.
77. Trotsky, *The Revolution Betrayed*, trans. Max Eastman (New York, 1970), p. 95.
78. *Rabochaia oppozitsiia*, pp. 43–45.

reference to the woman question in a broad-ranging critique of the Communist Party, she would be less than honest. If she appealed to the Party rank and file to join the Workers' Opposition and included demands on behalf of women, she risked alienating supporters and jeopardizing her usefulness to the Opposition. And if the Workers' Opposition did not prevail, if the Party were not reformed, could the woman question be solved? The key issue for her in March 1921 was the desperate need to transform the Party, to weaken its bureaucratic authoritarianism, and to provide scope for her beloved spontaneity. And so Kollontai, making the familiar trade-off, subordinated the woman question to what seemed the larger purpose.

The Workers' Opposition stands as one of Bolshevism's most impressive documents: critical and harsh to be sure, but neither despairing nor disillusioned. Shliapnikov had become bitter by 1921; Kollontai had not.[79] She ended her pamphlet with characteristic optimism. "Il'ich will listen to us, ponder and think over [what we say], and then will decide to turn the Party rudder toward the Opposition. Il'ich will be with us yet."[80] It may seem paradoxical to offer Kollontai's *Workers' Opposition* as an example of Bolshevism at its best when it was rejected by most of the Party's leaders. I see it, however, as a monument to the bright promises with which the Bolsheviks took power, a statement in which Kollontai, writing not as an outsider but as a loyal Communist, defended the heroic hopes of 1917. I would argue further that the degree of anger the pamphlet aroused reflected the degree to which it provoked the leadership's own doubts. *The Workers' Opposition* was a testament to Bolshevik anxiety.

Kollontai functioned as a Communist Cassandra, strident and slightly mocking, subjecting the "most popular" Bolshevik leaders to the sharpness of her pen, warning them that the masses, although they loved Lenin and were fascinated by Trotsky, were crying "Halt, we won't follow you any longer." This was not the Kollontai who sat quietly at Central Committee meetings in the autumn of 1917 and winter of 1918 and let Lenin, Trotsky, and Bukharin have the floor. It was, however, the Kollontai who in another arena in 1918 attacked Lenin personally for betraying the principles of international socialism and who subsequently lost her position on the Central Committee and in the Council of People's Commissars. Memories of her

79. For Shliapnikov, see Serge, p. 123.
80. *Rabochaia oppozitsiia*, p. 48.

downfall in 1918 contributed to the vigor of her defiance in 1921.

Though she assumed a leading role in the Opposition, Kollontai maintained a certain distance from her co-Oppositionists and even criticized them. At times, she said, there was much indefiniteness and absurdity in their expressions, demands, and motives; even their basic positions might differ.[81] If Kollontai felt superior to other members of the Opposition in her ability to articulate the demands of the movement, she also saw herself as more able than other Bolsheviks, even those on the Central Committee, to interpret the needs of the working class. One by one she disparaged her comrades—for example Zinoviev, whose speech at the September conference, despite its promises, changed nothing in the Party or in the life of the masses.[82] Those leaders—Lenin, Trotsky, Bukharin, and Zinoviev—who lacked her faith in the proletariat, who refused to turn over control of production or expropriated industries to the trade unions, and who reduced the unions to mere schools for the masses failed to understand that the unions were not only schools for Communism but its creators as well, because they had lost sight of the "creativeness of the class."[83]

A question of absorbing interest to students concerned with the role of women in the Communist Party inevitably arises. How did the male leadership, particularly Lenin, take criticism from a Communist woman? Did they relate differently to Kollontai because she was a female leader? Did they regard her arguments less seriously, and assume—in the manner of one Western historian, who called Kollontai a figurehead—that despite her ability Kollontai was not really a leader, but rather that she followed Shliapnikov? If it is true that in times of stress people act like themselves, only more so, then the confrontation between Lenin and Kollontai that followed the publication of her pamphlet is ideally suited to exploring these questions.

Angelica Balabanoff recalled that she had never seen Lenin so angry as when Kollontai's pamphlet was handed to him at the opening of the Tenth Party Congress. Kollontai suggested the same thing when she later described how Lenin quickly leafed through *The Workers' Opposition*, the pamphlet that was in the hands of most of

81. *Ibid.*, p. 9.   82. *Ibid.*, p. 8.
83. *Ibid.*, pp. 27–28.

the delegates, and shook his head in disapproval.[84] There had been a time in their revolutionary past when Lenin, the master pamphleteer, revised one of Kollontai's wartime brochures because of her difficulty in writing about a complicated subject in a popular yet meaningful way. Kollontai had learned her lesson. How well could be gauged by the bitterness of Lenin's invective at the Tenth Congress as he denounced the Workers' Opposition in general and Kollontai's pamphlet in particular.

Lenin's anger, his reiteration of the phrase "Kollontai's pamphlet," suggests that it may have been the existence of the pamphlet that infuriated him. Kollontai's audacity in using against him his own favorite propaganda device, the popular pamphlet, when he had schooled her in the art, left him gasping. If, as Balabanoff recalled, he had never seemed so angry, it may also have been the result of the timing of the publication. A week before the Congress opened a serious revolt had broken out at the naval fortress at Kronstadt in the Gulf of Finland, where the sailors were attacking the Bolshevik government that they themselves had helped to power.[85] "When you sent in the final proofs, you knew about the Kronstadt events," he charged, adding, "and it is at a time like this that you come here, calling yourselves a Workers' Opposition."[86]

Lenin's manner of addressing a Party assembly has been described many times. He was free of Trotsky's flashing oratorical devices, but the effect of his matter-of-fact rhetoric was extraordinary. Max Eastman wrote that it was as though "he was taking us inside his mind and showing us how the truth looks."[87] Maxim Gorky, musing that it was very difficult to convey the impression Lenin made, described the unity, comprehensiveness, and strength of his speech as a "veritable work of classic art: everything was there, and yet there was nothing superfluous, and if there were any embellishments, they were not noticed as such, but were as natural and inevitable as two eyes in a face or five fingers on a hand." Gorky recalled the enthusiastic whispers one would overhear as Lenin spoke, his arm extended, the hand

84. See Balabanoff, *My Life as a Rebel*, p. 252. For Kollontai's recollection, see both Mindlin, *Ne dom, no mir*, pp. 366–70, and Itkina, p. 213.

85. Under the slogan "free soviets," the sailors established a revolutionary commune in Mar. 1921 that survived for 16 days until an army was sent across the ice to crush it. Avrich, p. 3.

86. USSR, [2], p. 115.

87. Eastman, p. 335.

slightly raised. "Now, *he* has got something to say!" It really was so. Lenin's conclusions "were not reached artificially, but developed by themselves, inevitably."[88]

Lenin, mustering his self-control, began in a moderate tone by trivializing the Workers' Opposition. He made sharp observations about the "astonishing luxury of discussions and disputes within a Party shouldering unprecedented responsibilities and surrounded by powerful enemies."[89] In a later report, he spoke about the trade-union discussion as having "taken up so much of the Party's time," calling it a discussion that must have "bored most of you," an "impermissible luxury" in the face of "crop failure, a crisis, ruin, and demobilization."[90] He warned of the dangers of Kronstadt—the petty-bourgeois counterrevolution, Lenin called it. The Bolsheviks were awaiting news of the mutiny at Kronstadt. The country was in the midst of an economic breakdown and a peasant crisis. These were the Party's real problems. They could be solved, according to Lenin, only by granting concessions to advanced capitalist states so that the Soviet government could rehabilitate its economy with machinery and technical aid from abroad, and only by appealing for peasant support. Raising the specter of counterrevolution, Lenin warned that the bourgeoisie was trying to pit the peasants against the workers, that behind a façade of workers' slogans they were trying to incite the petty-bourgeois anarchist elements against the workers. If successful, their plots would lead directly to the overthrow of the dictatorship of the proletariat and the restoration of the old landowner and capitalist regime.[91]

Kollontai, when her turn came to speak, reacted as though she were indifferent to Lenin's magnetism and the power of his argument. Indeed, it was almost as if he had not spoken. She ignored the direction of Lenin's remarks and shifted the emphasis away from the crises in agriculture and industry back to what she called the fundamental problem: the Party's failure to carry through on its initial ideals. She tried to force Lenin to confront the issues *she* had raised in *her* pamphlet: was Soviet Russia not a workers' state? What of Bolshevik resolutions to increase proletarian initiative and spontaneity, to cleanse the Party of alien elements? What of Party democracy? Why were Party members evaluated behind the scenes, and decisions

88. Gorky, p. 15.
90. *Ibid.*, p. 27.

89. USSR, [2], p. 2.
91. *Ibid.*, pp. 33–36.

taken secretly over whom to keep and whom to send to distant places?[92]

Kollontai's remarkable ability to resist what one author has called Lenin's "gravitational pull" needs explaining. In part it was a result of her conviction that she was right, but in part it also had to do with the circumstances of her adherence to Bolshevism. She had never been a member of Lenin's sect, the little group of Russian political émigrés in Geneva who became known as the "Bolshevik colony." Indeed, during the prewar years Kollontai distrusted Lenin. Ultimately, she was drawn to Bolshevism not because of Lenin's irresistible appeal but because of his commitment to internationalism and to a Third International. No evidence suggests that she regarded Lenin, only two years her senior, as innately superior or, as some Bolsheviks called him, the *starik*, the wise old man.[93]

Kollontai's resolve not to be diverted from questions of revolutionary promises, and her implication that he had not discussed the real reasons behind Kronstadt and other proletarian discontents, goaded Lenin into dropping his moderate tone.[94] When Lenin spoke again it was not to respond to Kollontai's probings about Party democracy and proletarian spontaneity but to destroy the Workers' Opposition in general and Kollontai's pamphlet in particular. Its very name, the "Workers' Opposition," outraged him. "Indecent," he called it.[95] Whoever came to the Congress with such a pamphlet at this moment of crisis was "trifling" with the Party. "Comrades," he said, "I entreat you all to read this pamphlet. You could not find a better argument against the Workers' Opposition than Comrade Kollontai's pamphlet *The Workers' Opposition*." Lenin's bravado was made less convincing by his need to devote much of his speech to Kollontai's brochure, to quote from it repeatedly and to explain, as he put it, why the counterrevolution was assuming an anarchistic, petty-bourgeois form and why the speakers from the Workers' Opposition failed entirely to realize the danger.[96]

Attacking Kollontai and Shliapnikov, accusing them of anarchism, syndicalism, and petty-bourgeois demagoguery, Lenin tried to link

92. *Ibid.*, pp. 100–102.

93. On Lenin's attraction, see R. C. Tucker, "Introduction," in *The Lenin Anthology* (New York, 1975), p. xlv. For Lenin as *starik*, see Valentinov, pp. 72–73.

94. For Kollontai's provocative remarks, see USSR, [2], p. 101. For Lenin's anger, see *ibid.*, p. 112.

95. *Ibid.*, p. 115.

96. For Lenin's speech, see *ibid.*, pp. 115–24.

them to Kronstadt—although as Kollontai angrily objected, members of the Workers' Opposition were the first to respond to the call on March 10 to go to Kronstadt to put down the rebellion.[97] Her husband Dybenko was leading a division across the ice.[98] It was possible to link the Opposition to Kronstadt only in the vaguest sense. The two groups shared a negative affinity—opposition to stifling Party control. Kollontai attributed the uprising to the expansion of the dictatorial state and its economic machine. Lenin, though he knew better, implied that the mutiny was the work of Socialist Revolutionaries and White Guards.[99]

Kollontai was committed to the primacy of the Party in a way that the sailors were not. With Kronstadt's fundamental demand for Soviets without Bolshevik control she had no sympathy. Yet her need to recapture the revolutionary purity of 1917 resembled the sailors'. Opposing Kronstadt, Kollontai acted consistently. She understood in 1921 that the sailors intended to oust the Bolsheviks from power, and her reaction to the threat was similar to her response in 1917 to the call for a coalition government. Now, as then, she shared the leaders' unwillingness to tolerate a political challenge.

Lenin was determined to present his old friends from the underground as leaders of a treacherous deviation, and he stressed Kollontai's and Shliapnikov's potential for disruption. "When Party comrades talk as Shliapnikov has done here—and he always talks like that at other meetings—and Comrade Kollontai's pamphlet says the same thing . . . we say: we cannot go on like this, for it is the kind of demagoguery that the Makhno anarchists and the Kronstadt elements jump at."[100] Lenin once wrote, and he still maintained, that demagogues were the "worst enemies of the working class." They were dangerous because they aroused "base instincts in the masses" and were "the worst enemies because in the period of disunity and vacillation when our movement is just beginning to take shape, nothing is easier than to employ demagogic methods to mislead the masses."[101]

Lenin charged that the Workers' Opposition simply wanted to

97. *Ibid.*, p. 300. For a list of the delegates sent to Kronstadt from the Tenth Congress, see pp. 765–68.

98. For Dybenko at Kronstadt, see Avrich, pp. 194, 202–3, 213.

99. See Reichenbach, p. 19, for Kollontai's interpretation of Kronstadt. For Lenin's explanation, see USSR, [2], p. 33.

100. USSR, [2], pp. 123–24. Nestor Makhno, an anarchist partisan in south Russia, led a formidable army against the Soviets. He was defeated in Nov. 1920.

101. Lenin, *Chto delat'?*, *Sochineniia* (4th ed.), vol. 5, pp. 431–32.

argue, that it gave the Party nothing but generalities. Then he contradicted himself by isolating the elements in Kollontai's pamphlet that most distressed him. He derided Kollontai's praise of "class-conscious and class-welded people," an expression he turned into an epithet and used many times in the course of the Congress. He asserted that the Opposition held that the "organization of the management of the national economy is the function of an All-Russian Congress of Producers." He scoffed at the arguments about freedom of speech and freedom of criticism, which in his view had no particular meaning. "You cannot fool us with words like 'freedom to criticize.' " He ended ominously, "I think the Party Congress will have to draw the conclusion that the Opposition's time has run out and the lid is on it. We want no more oppositions!"[102]

What agitated Lenin more, one suspects, than Kollontai's call for Party democracy (which he treated vaguely, contrasting real democracy with "just talk" but not defining either) was her implication that he lacked confidence in the working class.[103] It was, after all, a horrendous charge and he angrily denied it. "It is absolutely untrue to say that we have no confidence in the working class and that we are keeping the workers out of the governing bodies." Rather, "we are on our last legs for want of people and we are prepared to take any assistance with both hands, from any efficient person, especially a worker. But we have no people of this type." He dared the Opposition to carry their charges to their awesome but logical conclusion: a revolutionary party that had no confidence in the working class and did not allow workers to occupy responsible posts ought to be ousted![104]

Lenin denied Shliapnikov's and Kollontai's accusation that he attempted to terrorize the Opposition with the word syndicalist.[105] Yet he mocked Kollontai's call for an All-Russian Congress of Producers to direct the economy: "As for the syndicalist deviation—it is ridiculous. That is all we have to say to Shliapnikov, who maintained that the All-Russian Congress of Producers, a demand . . . confirmed by Kollontai, can be upheld by a reference to Engels."[106] But Shliapnikov and Kollontai did not have to go back to Engels. Lenin knew—as Kollontai told him—that they need go no further than the Party Program of 1919, which declared that the trade unions "must actually

102. USSR, [2], p. 118.   103. *Ibid.*, pp. 114–15.
104. *Ibid.*, p. 122.   105. *Ibid.*, p. 116.
106. *Ibid.*, p. 380.

concentrate in their hands the entire administration of the whole public economy as a single economic unit."[107]

Lenin could have acknowledged that the Party Program was no longer valid; he might have candidly urged his critics to forget for a time what he had written in *State and Revolution*. Instead he insisted that an "All-Russian Congress of Producers" was neither Marxist nor Communist. He charged the Workers' Opposition with putting a false construction on the Party Program, which in his reading said "the trade unions *should eventually arrive* [*dolzhny priiti*] at a de facto concentration in their hands of the whole administration of the whole national economy, as a single economic entity."[108] It was Lenin who was misconstruing what had been an implicit and accepted revolutionary goal in 1917.

He was bitter. It was easy to write "there was something rotten in our Party." Of course there was excessive bureaucracy. He acknowledged the "bureaucratic ulcer": it had been diagnosed and had to be treated in earnest. But why did not Comrade Shliapnikov when he was Commissar or Comrade Kollontai while she was Commissar teach the Party how to combat bureaucracy? If you know how to make the bureaucracy smaller, "share with us please, dear comrades, your knowledge."[109]

Lenin persisted in misunderstanding Kollontai's use of the term bureaucracy. He defined it in a nontheoretical sense to mean red tape, inaction, negligence, heavy-handedness, a "paper swamp"; she replied more broadly that bureaucracy was the direct negation of mass spontaneity and self-directed activity.[110] The harm in bureaucracy lay not only in the red tape, as some comrades would have us believe, but also in the solution of all problems by means not of open exchange but of formal decisions handed down from the central institutions. "Some third person decides your fate; this is the whole essence of bureaucracy."[111] When Kollontai was Commissar of Public Welfare, she did, we recall, attempt to eliminate bureaucratic approaches by collective decision-making.[112]

107. For Kollontai's reminder, see *Rabochaia oppozitsiia*, p. 37. For trade unions and the Party Program of 1919, see Schapiro, pp. 285, 319. For the resolution itself, see *Vos'moi S''ezd (RKP) (b): Protokoly* (Moscow, 1933), pp. 392–93.

108. USSR, [2], p. 380.

109. *Ibid.*, pp. 121–22. For Lenin on the bureaucratic ulcer, see *ibid.*, p. 39.

110. For Lenin on bureaucracy, see *Sochineniia* (4th ed.), vol. 35, pp. 459–61.

111. For Kollontai on bureaucracy, see *Rabochaia oppozitsiia*, pp. 39–40.

112. For Lenin's earlier rejection of collegiality in favor of one-man management, see Carr, *The Bolshevik Revolution*, vol. 2, p. 192.

1. Kollontai at age six, 1878, from Dazhina, ed., *Iz moei zhizni i raboty.*

2. Kollontai with her husband, Vladimir, and their son, Misha, in 1897, from Dazhina, ed., *Iz moei zhizni i raboty.*

3. Misha with his maternal grandfather, General Mikhail Domontovich, from Halvorsen, *Revolutionens ambassadør.*

4. Kollontai with Misha in 1915, from Itkina, *Revoliutsioner, tribun, diplomat.*

5. "In Honor of the Second Revolution," a postcard showing (clockwise, from top left) Trotsky, Lenin, Lunacharskii, Spiridonova, Zinoviev, Kamenev, Raskol'nikov, and Kollontai. The inclusion of Spiridonova, a Left SR, is a reminder that in the early days of the October Revolution the Left SRs were in coalition with the Bolsheviks. Courtesy of the Hoover Institution Archives.

6. The Council of Commissars
in 1918, showing Kollontai seated
to Lenin's left and Dybenko
standing behind her and to her
left, from Dazhina, ed., *Iz moei
zhizni i raboty.*

7. Inessa Armand and her
children, from I. F. Armand,
Stat'i, rechi, pis'ma.

8. Sof'ia Smidovich as a young woman, from Bochkarëva and Liubimova, *Svetlyi put'*.

9. Varvara Iakovleva, from Vinogradskaia, *Sobytiia i pamiatnye vstrechi.*

10. Shliapnikov, from Futrell, *Northern Underground.*

11. Dybenko in 1916, from Mawdsley, *The Russian Revolution and the Baltic Fleet.*

12. The *Rabotnitsa* editorial board in 1917, showing (clockwise, from left), Nikolaeva, Kudelli, Samoilova, Bonch-Bruevich, Stal', Kollontai, and Elizarova. From Kudelli, comp., *Velikii oktiabr'*. . . . Reproduced courtesy of the Hoover Institution Archives.

Первая редакционная коллегия журнала „КОММУНИСТКА"

1920

1923

т. Н. К. Крупская.
Несменяемый редактор „Коммунистки".

т. Ольминский.
Старейший член партии (с 1898 г.).

т. Инесса Арманд.
Инициатор журн. „Коммунистка".

т. Н. Бухарин.
Ответ. редактор газеты „Правда".

т. К. Николаева.
Работница. Член Петроградского Губкома. Вождь петрогр. работниц.

т. П. Виноградская.

т. А. Коллонтай.
Один из первых инициаторов работы среди женщин, ныне замполпреда Норвегии.

13. The *Kommunistka* editorial board in 1920, showing (clockwise, from top) Krupskaia, Bukharin, Kollontai, Vinogradskaia, Nikolaeva, and Ol'minskii; in the center is a portrait of Inessa Armand, who was dead at the time this retrospective article in *Kommunistka*, 1923, no. 7, was written. Reproduced courtesy of the Hoover Institution Archives.

14. Kollontai (far right) and Zetkin (second from right) seated among the Presidium of the Second International Conference of Communist Women, 1921. From Itkina, *Revoliutsioner, tribun, diplomat.*

16. Evgeniia Bosh, from a memorial article written by Preobrazhenskii, in *Proletarskaia Revoliutsiia*, 1925, no. 37(5). Reproduced courtesy of the Hoover Institution Archives.

15. Iakov Sverdlov, from a memorial article in *Kommunistka*, 1923, no. 11. Reproduced courtesy of the Hoover Institution Archives.

17. Kollontai at the tribune, from *Kommunistka*, 1923, no. 11. Reproduced courtesy of the Hoover Institution Archives.

18. Kollontai in the mid-1920's, a signed photograph reproduced courtesy of Mrs. Bertram Wolfe.

19. Angelica Balabanoff in old age, from Ronald Florence, *Marx's Daughters: Eleanor Marx, Rosa Luxemburg, Angelica Balabanoff* (New York, 1975).

10. II. 1941

Alexandra Kollontay

Envoyé Extraordinaire et Ministre Plénipotentiaire
de l'Union des Republiques Sovietiqus Socialistes

Kära Ada, tack för de
underbart vackra gula
rosorna till den 7 nov.

och för all Ditt vänskap!

10/11. 41.

20. Kollontai's diplomatic calling card, here with a note of thanks to her friend Ada Nilsson "for the yellow roses on the 7th of November."

21. Kollontai in 1952, the year of her death, from Dazhina, ed., *Iz moei zhizni i raboty.*

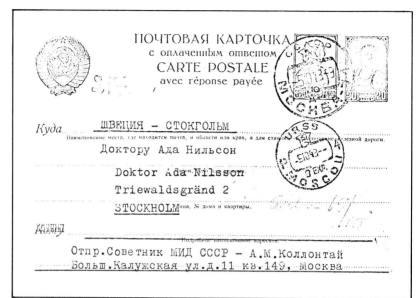

ПОЧТОВАЯ КАРТОЧКА
с оплаченным ответом
CARTE POSTALE
avec réponse payée

Куда ШВЕЦИЯ — СТОКГОЛЬМ

Наименование места, где находится почта, и области или края, а для станций наименование железной дороги.

Доктору Ада Нильсон

Doktor Ada Nilsson

Triewaldsgränd 2

STOCKHOLM

Улица, № дома и квартиры.

Отпр.Советник МИД СССР — А.М.Коллонтай
Больш.Калужская ул.д.11 кв.149, Москва

4/X 48.

My dearest friend Ada,
just a short but warm
greeting to you. How are you?
I have no news about the
womens conference, not yet. But
I hope, that our meeting most
Take place in this autonne,
I feel better, because Micha
is now pentiionerad and
his health is better,
My life is the same, as before,
very quiet, but I have books,
and every morning I write
or put in order my memoires.
Dear, dear Ada — you are all-
ways in my thoughts and in
my heart. I long to see you,
Love to friends and most
to yourself. Alexandra.

22. A postcard from Kollontai, in retirement in Moscow, to her "dearest friend Ada."

Lenin did not believe that it would be possible to cope adequately with bureaucracy. For all his talk about a bureaucratic ulcer (a minor ailment after all) another remark more accurately conveyed his view: we cannot struggle fully with bureaucracy and practice democracy consistently because we lack the strength.[113] If the regime lacked the strength, it was, according to Kollontai, for the reason Lenin had admitted elsewhere—that the Party was seriously ill.[114] For Kollontai (as for the Left Communists in 1918 and the Democratic Centralists)[115] it was precisely bureaucratism that sapped Party strength. But until the Party heeded the demands of the Workers' Opposition, the sickness would remain.

An awkward question arose. Could a sick Party function as the vanguard of the proletariat? Presumably not. The Bolsheviks, Lenin in particular, were incensed by Kollontai's implication that the Workers' Opposition had come to reflect the proletariat more closely than the Party as a whole did. Take, for example, Kollontai's contention that the Workers' Opposition was the foremost part of the proletariat, that its connection to the working masses was direct, through the unions rather than fragmented among Soviet institutions.[116] Or her assumption that the Workers' Opposition was the proletariat itself, its very flesh, connected with the machines and the mines, the class-welded, class-conscious, class-consistent Party of the industrial proletariat.[117] Iaroslavskii dismissed these remarks as amusing pretensions: the leaders of the Workers' Opposition spoke about themselves in such solemn tones, as the very flower of the working class![118] Bukharin ridiculed Kollontai's supposed claim to superior proletarian sensibilities by reading aloud embarrassing excerpts from an article on motherhood she had published in *Kommunistka*. The essay, entitled "The Cross of Maternity," concerned a play called *The Miracle*, which had appeared on the Berlin stage in 1914, shortly before the war. It was an unfortunate lapse in Kollontai's Communist sensibility. Kollontai appeared to be glorifying the madonna as a symbol of the compassionate, all-forgiving mother. Bukharin, who was one of the original editors of *Kommunistka*, called the passages

113. USSR. [2], p. 115.
114. See Avrich, p. 31, for Lenin's remark.
115. For the Democratic Centralists, see Daniels, p. 95.
116. *Rabochaia oppozitsiia*, p. 6.
117. *Ibid.*, p. 5. Lenin taunted Kollontai with these remarks at the Tenth Congress. See USSR, [2], p. 117.
118. See Iaroslavskii's Introduction to Zorkii, pp. 5–6.

in praise of the madonna "disgusting Catholic sentimentalism—
poshlost'." He was appalled that Kollontai considered it appropriate
for a Soviet audience.[119] Bukharin was condescending about Kollontai's further "nonsense" that would put all Communists to work at
manual labor for three months of the year. Did the Workers' Opposition really think anything worthwhile would be accomplished by
taking Foreign Commissar Chicherin, for example, away from his
diplomatic responsibilities, and placing him at a factory bench?[120]

Bukharin might joke, but Lenin repeated Kollontai's phrases as if
to exorcise them. Her notion of the Workers' Opposition as the "class-
conscious, class-consistent, class-welded" vanguard of the proletariat
he regarded as a travesty, and her pamphlet as heretical. The pamphlet called on the Party to rely on the spontaneity of the working class,
when Communists knew, as Lenin had long since explained, that
working-class spontaneity could not lead to socialism.[121] When Kollontai urged that the Party permit the working class to reconstruct
life on a new, Communist basis, since the workers know best "where
it hurts us the most," she was being profoundly subversive.[122] The
former Menshevik was denying a cardinal Bolshevik assumption that,
as Marxists, the ruling Party best knew the "real" interests of the
people. To Lenin, those like Kollontai who worshiped the spontaneity of the working class were, in fact, endangering the workers
by encouraging them to distrust all those who would bring them political knowledge and revolutionary experience from the outside.[123]

Since Kollontai dared pretend to a greater proletarian sensibility,
since she presumed to question Lenin's faith in the working class,
Lenin retaliated by maligning her loyalty. He declared that when
someone, under the guise of helping, wrote such a brochure as *The
Workers' Opposition*, that person must be unmasked.[124] He accused
his opponent of working toward a split. Kollontai's insistence that
"there will be no split" became a weapon to distort and turn against
her. Lenin quoted scornfully: "The Workers' Opposition will not,
and must not, compromise." And with a show of disbelief he added
ironically that this did not, however, mean that it sought a split. Not

119. USSR, [2], p. 325. See Kollontai, "Krest materinstva."
120. USSR, [2], p. 325.
121. It could lead only to trade unionism. See Lenin, *Chto delat'?*, *Sochineniia* (4th
ed.), vol. 5, p. 347.
122. *Rabochaia oppozitsiia*, p. 18.
123. See Lenin, *Chto delat'?*, *Sochineniia* (4th ed.), vol. 5, p. 431.
124. USSR, [2], p. 115.

at all. Its task was entirely different. Even in the event of defeat at the Congress it would—and he quoted—"remain in the Party and step by step, stubbornly defend its point of view, save the Party, and straighten out its line."[125]

A German Communist recalled the way Lenin argued. When he was up against hostile opinions, his voice used to take on a note of incomprehension as though he found it impossible to believe that anyone could fail to understand anything so obvious—even when the matter was far from obvious.[126] Now Lenin pondered in mock incredulity: what could Kollontai possibly mean, "not seek a split"? The delegates showed their appreciation of Lenin's rhetoric with the customary laughter and applause.[127] But Kollontai was no doubt correct in her suspicion that the applause indicated more the delegates' love for Lenin than their endorsement of what he said.[128] Kollontai's meaning was clear enough. The Workers' Opposition did not intend to set up a new party in opposition to the Bolsheviks. Lenin, attempting to undermine Kollontai's credibility as a comrade, used Trotsky as an example of a right-thinking Bolshevik—an inadvertent endorsement of Kollontai's view that when it came to the question of autonomy for workers Lenin, Trotsky, and Bukharin were really in agreement. He and Trotsky often disagreed, Lenin said, but Trotsky understood the need to compromise. Whereas Trotsky, his rift with Lenin healed, could say "of course we will unite, because we are Party people,"[129] Kollontai was saying "we will not compromise but we will remain in the Party." Such an attitude would not be permitted. There would be no more playing, no more factions. "We don't need opposition now, comrades."[130] Lenin's response was in the vein that Kollontai urged the Party to abandon: he invoked the psychology of crisis to justify repression.

Lenin's remarks contained hints of forcible exclusion. He welcomed every assistance in getting democracy working, he said, but when the people were exhausted it would take more than talk. Everyone who wanted to help was an asset. But when the Opposition said that they would "make no concessions" and would try to save the

125. For Kollontai's insistence that there would be no split, see *Rabochaia oppozitsiia*, p. 48. For Lenin's reaction, see USSR, [2], p. 119.

126. Reichenbach, p. 17.

127. USSR, [2], p. 119.

128. Mindlin, *Ne dom, no mir*, p. 368.

129. USSR, [2], p. 122.

130. *Ibid.*, p. 118.

Party from within, Lenin countered "Yes, if you are allowed to stay!"[131] That remark cast doubt on Lenin's charge that the Workers' Opposition planned to set up another party in opposition to the Bolsheviks. It showed that he did not believe Kollontai *intended* to provoke a split. Consider the angry question with which he greeted her. She was sitting with Jacques Sadoul when Lenin came up to them. "Do you realize what you have caused?," he asked, implying a lack of premeditation on her part. "It is a call to a split. It is the platform of a new party. . . . And at such a moment! It is syndicalism."[132]

One would like to know the words Kollontai and her friend Sadoul exchanged after Lenin strode away. Sadoul was selected early on, we recall, to share Kollontai's anxieties. Of the Frenchman, another Communist wrote, "I loved his lively, mocking intelligence, his epicurean nonchalance, his political adroitness."[133] Perhaps it was Sadoul's lack of self-righteousness and his moderation and good sense that caused Kollontai to trust him. Kollontai and Sadoul knew that the Workers' Opposition did not want to leave the Party. If Kollontai anticipated a split, it was of a different sort. Long before Djilas wrote his *New Class*, Kollontai predicted the development of a bureaucratic and privileged class in Soviet Russia that would live on a scale different from the worker. The real "split" would not be the Workers' Opposition breaking to form another party; it would be the loss to the Communist Party of the working class. Kollontai was also warning, when she protested against the new class, that Old Bolsheviks would increasingly be pushed aside. She spoke from her own pain. Long-time Communists like Kollontai and Shliapnikov were hurt when they saw less idealistic careerists who joined the Party after the Revolution being put in positions of trust.

✳✳✳

Looking back at the Tenth Party Congress more than 50 years later, one is struck by Bolshevism's boisterous egalitarianism and vitality. The minutes of the Congress illustrate remarkably that camaraderie that Kollontai warned the Communists they were about to lose. Maxim Gorky, who wrote of Lenin's exceptional attitude toward Party comrades, recalled how Lenin was sometimes sharp with

131. *Ibid.*, p. 119.
132. Recollection from Kollontai's diary, cited in Itkina, p. 213. Lenin did, however, fear the possibility of a split in the Party. See Avrich, p. 31.
133. Serge, p. 237.

people when arguing with them, how he pitilessly ridiculed them, even laughed at them in a venomous fashion. "But how many times, when judging the people whom yesterday he criticized and rebuked," Gorky added, "was there clearly evident the note of genuine wonder at their talents." Gorky believed that it was "impossible to consider as Lenin's equals even the greatest people in his Party," but Lenin himself "didn't seem to realize this."[134]

Kollontai and Lenin battled as equals. She conducted herself as though she were speaking not to a man who had become a legend in his own lifetime, a leader whom Max Eastman described as "the most powerful man I ever saw on the platform," but simply to a respected comrade.[135] She announced that Lenin's report on behalf of the Central Committee was not satisfactory, that it did not deal adequately with the Party's sharpest problems.[136] And Lenin repeated in a mocking sort of way that Kollontai claimed that his report did not satisfy her.[137] Lenin's remarks did not suggest that he underestimated Kollontai's leadership. His anger toward Shliapnikov may have been more intense, but he still condemned Kollontai harshly, never doubting that the brochure was her work *alone*. Lenin was too astute a judge of character not to recognize in the pamphlet signs of Kollontai's secure confidence, that quality by which she announced that she was a person of independent thought. Lenin's anger revealed that he understood all too well Kollontai's impact. Kollontai not only dared to question Lenin's commitment to the working class, she signaled a new danger—the potential appeal of the Opposition to Communist youth.

Earlier in the year that danger had been demonstrated. A. Barmine recalled Kollontai's dramatic appearance before the young men at the War College of the Red Star. Representatives from each of the competing groups came to the College to speak before the Tenth Congress. (The Central Committee had decided to allow the election of delegates to the Congress on the basis of platforms—the closest the Communists came to a multiparty system.) That Barmine described Kollontai's arrival in terms of her physical appearance and dress indicates his own difficulty in accepting as natural a "female orator of the first rank." Dressed in black, with sophisticated simplicity, ele-

134. Gorky, p. 53.
135. Eastman, p. 334.
136. USSR, [2], p. 100.
137. USSR, [17], p. 46. This sentence does not appear in later editions.

gant even in revolution, Kollontai at nearly 50 was still, he thought, a beautiful woman who showed no signs of age. The young men who listened attentively as she denounced the bureaucracy and demanded a return to working-class democracy were impressed by the fiery speech of this prominent leader who was married to their fellow student Pavel Dybenko. When the moment for voting came, of 300 Communist students, 250 sided with Kollontai and the Workers' Opposition.[138] Such a threat had to be crushed.

If there was any sense at the Tenth Congress that Kollontai had ventured in an inappropriate way beyond the parameters of her role as leader of the Zhenotdel, it was not apparent. In fact, Trotsky's follower Krestinskii (one of the three Party secretaries), a Bolshevik who shared many of Kollontai's fears and democratic inclinations and who himself would soon be sent out of Moscow, charged that Kollontai could have exercised more authority in dealing with Party problems had she been willing to. As a director of a section of the Central Committee, she had the right to participate in the meetings of the Orgburo (Organizational Bureau), a smaller body within the Central Committee responsible for the general direction of organizational work and Party appointments. But Kollontai attended its sessions only when matters touching on the Zhenotdel were being discussed. Krestinskii criticized Kollontai for being judgmental about others when she wasted time—as he put it—with the Workers' Opposition. The time could have been better used preparing memoranda for the Orgburo. She, less than anyone, had the right to protest Bolshevik deficiencies.[139]

We have seen that Party leaders did not question the independent nature of Kollontai's leadership. But Lenin's perception of Kollontai's significance did not exclude the possibility that he might take advantage of the fact that his antagonist was a woman. One ought not to overstate occasional episodes, for Lenin indulged in invective against all Bolsheviks who disagreed with him. But Lenin did attempt to embarrass Kollontai with a suggestion of sexual looseness on her part—a line of attack he would have been unlikely to direct at a man. A favorite device in tsarist days had been to imply that sexual promiscuity accompanied female radicalism.[140] Lenin ventured in the same

138. Barmine, pp. 91–92. See Daniels, pp. 140–41, on the election of delegates.
139. USSR, [2], pp. 110–11. Krestinskii charged that only one other Bolshevik—Nevskii—attended sessions only when his special interests were involved. *Ibid.*, p. 111.
140. See Figner, vol. 1, p. 120. Figner, discussing the government's decree in the summer of 1873 ordering female students home from Zurich, noted that the women

direction. Repeating Kollontai's presumptuous remark about the "class-welded, class-conscious" comrades of the Opposition, he declared his pleasure in knowing that Kollontai and Shliapnikov were in fact thus united. His observation greatly amused the audience, many of whom knew that Kollontai, living since 1918 in an unregistered marriage with Pavel Dybenko, in prerevolutionary days had been considered married to Shliapnikov.[141] Balabanoff recorded her own outrage over the episode. Remarking on the lengths to which Lenin would go in pursuit of his strategic aims, even against an old comrade, she praised the dignified calm with which Kollontai met Lenin's attack.[142]

※※※※

At the Tenth Party Congress the Leninists commanded a large majority. Thus it could have been predicted that the Workers' Opposition would be badly defeated when it came to voting on the platforms. Nor could it have come as a surprise, in the context of Kronstadt and the bitterness of the pre-Congress fights, when the Congress ordered the rapid dispersal of all groups that had formed on the basis of one platform or another. Failure to execute this decision would lead to immediate and unconditional expulsion from the Party.[143] Kollontai was astonished when she heard that Shliapnikov was chosen for the Central Committee. A leader of the Workers' Opposition elected! Then she understood that by including Shliapnikov in the inner core Lenin hoped to disarm him more easily. But after the meeting Shliapnikov supposedly whispered to Kollontai "We will continue to fight."[144]

Lenin exulted in his final speech over the results of the Congress: "We know that, united at this Congress, we will really get rid of our differences, be absolutely united."[145] Despite his success in controlling the Tenth Congress, Lenin could not have been less accurate in his prediction of the future of Bolshevism. The Tenth Party Congress

---

were said to be living in free love unions. See also Stites, "Women and the Russian Intelligentsia," pp. 41–43.

141. See USSR, [2], p. 117, for Lenin's remark. For the audience's boisterous reaction, see USSR, [17], p. 48. "Noisy applause" is omitted from the 1963 edition (USSR, [2]).

142. Balabanoff, *My Life as a Rebel*, p. 252.

143. See Daniels, p. 148, for the Party decision against factionalism and for the secret provision by which the Central Committee, on a two-thirds vote, could expel from the Party even Central Committee members found guilty of factionalism.

144. See Mindlin, *Ne dom, no mir*, pp. 371–72.

145. USSR, [2], p. 555.

would be the last one totally under his control; by the Eleventh he would be a sick man, unable to participate in the sessions. As for Kollontai, the Tenth Congress would be the last she would attend as the prestigious leader of the Women's Section of the Central Committee. Nor could either Lenin or Kollontai know that the Tenth Party Congress was also the scene of their last confrontation. Other Party leaders would soon take Lenin's place in "unmasking" Comrade Kollontai.

CHAPTER EIGHT

An Appeal to the Comintern

"We talked passionately of our sick Party: sick, but what else on earth is there?"
—*Victor Serge*, Memoirs of a Revolutionary

THE severe centralization characteristic of War Communism was replaced in 1921 by the less rigorous, but also less socialist, New Economic Policy (NEP). Kollontai continued to lead opposition to Party policies, but now with additional grievances. Her resentment of the political retreat represented by the partial return of free enterprise combined with her original protest on behalf of the neglected worker and against the privileged bureaucrat. Joined by Shliapnikov, Kollontai became bolder, antagonizing the Central Committee in this round of opposition by carrying her protest against Bolshevik policies to the Comintern. The Party retaliated in 1922 by appointing Clara Zetkin to a Comintern investigating commission and thereby pitting her against Kollontai, her longtime comrade in the international socialist women's movement. Later that year, at the Eleventh Party Congress, Kollontai fought an attempt to oust her from the Communist Party. The move to exclude Kollontai failed, but she was forced from leadership of the women's movement.

At first, in the aftermath of the Tenth Party Congress, it seemed as though Kollontai had turned away from opposition and back to the Zhenotdel. Rather than polemical tracts on behalf of the trade unionists, she prepared reports for the Second International Conference of Communist Women, which, as we saw in Chapter 6, met at the end of June 1921. The cause of the Workers' Opposition at no point became associated publicly with that of the Zhenotdel. No evidence suggests that any of the prominent leaders of the Workers' Opposition with whom she was closely associated—Shliapnikov, Medvedev, Lutovinov, or Kuznetsov—supported Kollontai's simultaneous effort to overcome male prejudice against women in their own area, the trade unions.

Thus Kollontai fought for the interests of women against the trade-union bureaucracy without the aid of her comrades from the Workers' Opposition. At the end of May, in an article in *Pravda*, she attacked the policies of the Fourth All-Russian Congress of Trade Unions, then meeting in Moscow. The meeting hall was crowded with some 2,000 delegates, but Kollontai had to search to find the few women among them. A token female delegate who sat in the Presidium was not even a trade unionist, but rather one of the Communist Party members with whom the Bolsheviks packed the unions. In the pages of *Pravda*, Kollontai wondered how there could be so few women present when in some unions women were in the majority. Could there really be no clever union women capable of leadership? Or did the reason for their absence lie elsewhere? Women were not in leadership because the Communist Party and the trade unions had failed to put into practice their several resolutions concerning the need to draw women into public life. The Eighth Congress of Soviets had resolved to include women in all economic organs. The Ninth Party Congress had resolved to draw working women into the construction of Communism through the unions as well as the Soviets. The Third Congress of Trade Unions had resolved in 1920 to work actively among the female proletariat. It was to no avail. Kollontai added a sharp observation: if the Party intended to heed its own decision taken at the Tenth Party Congress that the unions be regarded as schools for Communism, it must conduct educational activities among women as well as men. It should use the Women's Section to carry out educative efforts to eliminate the strong male prejudice against women that existed among the rank and file in the trade unions, as well as in its bureaucratic leadership.[1] She planned to take up the unhappy situation of women in the trade unions when she reported to the Second International Conference of Communist Women in June.

Indeed, Kollontai might have limited her activity during the summer of 1921 to the Second International Conference of Communist Women, had Party policies not taken an alarming turn. The New Economic Policy was legalizing some of the very defects of Soviet

1. According to Kollontai, the Party fraction in the unions had not put the resolution of 1920 into effect. For her indictment of unions and Party both, see Kollontai, "Profsoiuzy i rabotnitsa," *Izbrannye stat'i i rechi*, pp. 319–21.

society against which Kollontai protested at the Tenth Congress. Although she was a prominent Bolshevik, Kollontai seemed only to become aware gradually, after the Tenth Congress, of the major policy reversals that would be taking place—an indication of the piecemeal manner in which they evolved. Her apprehension at the time of the Tenth Congress, however, suggests that she half-consciously anticipated such changes. Consider her warning that the peasantry, with its petty-bourgeois proclivities and sympathies, demanded freedom of trade—and her grudging acknowledgment that acquiescence to peasant demands would be proof of the regime's political wisdom. But a sense of history caused Kollontai to warn that, however sensible for the Party to appease the peasant momentarily, the future historian would find it a dangerous digression from the class-oriented revolution, and a backward search among the debris of the bourgeois past.[2] If Kollontai sensed some of the difficulties that would ensue from the combination of industrial backwardness and agrarian revival, nowhere did she anticipate the ugly solution those difficulties would provoke by the end of the decade: violent collectivization and forced-draft, massive industrialization.

Kollontai's answer to the malaise of Soviet society was intensification of the Revolution. Lenin responded in the opposite way. After three and a half years of misery and hunger, Russia, he was convinced, could not have socialism forced upon her. Not for generations could the mentality of peasant Russia be altered to allow the entry into socialism.[3] Peasants and workers both were expressing discontent, occasionally violent, with the economic policies of War Communism.[4] The peasants demanded both an end to requisitioning and a legalization of the market. The strikes and industrial unrest that began in Petrograd at the end of February, aggravated by fuel and food shortages and demands by workers to be able to trade freely with the villages for food (which they had already begun illegally to do), impelled Lenin to announce at the Tenth Party Congress an end to the forcible collection of food from the peasants.[5] A tax in kind would be sub-

2. Kollontai, *Rabochaia oppozitsiia*, pp. 14–16.
3. See Schapiro, p. 311, and Lenin's report to the Tenth Party Congress on Mar. 15, 1921, USSR, [2], pp. 403–15.
4. One ugly recollection conveys the desperate mood. "Savage peasants would slit open a Commissar's belly, pack it with grain, and leave him by the roadside as a lesson for all. This was how one of my comrades died." Serge, p. 116.
5. On illegal markets during War Communism, see L. N. Kritsman, "Geroicheskii period velikoi Russkoi Revoliutsii," *Vestnik Kommunisticheskoi Akademii*, vol. 9 (Moscow, 1924), pp. 116–19.

stituted for the arbitrary food quotas, which Lenin hoped would increase peasant incentive to produce. The tax marked the first step. Two other aspects of the NEP that Lenin did not mention at the Tenth Congress were to unfold later: greater freedom of internal trade (meaning that the peasant could trade his surplus with whomever he chose rather than only with the state), and the granting of concessions to private capitalists so that they might run industrial enterprises.

Kollontai, who became one of the bitterest opponents of the NEP, recognized that, however grim the extenuating circumstances, to allow what was not taken from the peasants to be sold on the free market was in fact to return to capitalism. She might have accepted what may have been Lenin's more limited intention, to confine normal market relations to "localities," which would then exchange or barter goods directly with the state.[6] If this was Lenin's aim, it failed immediately. Buying and selling swept the country. Restrictions on free trade were therefore eliminated.

Kollontai stubbornly resisted the move toward free trade as a break with Bolshevism and a reversal of the basic socialist principles of the Soviet state. Outraged, she saw the NEP as treachery to the Revolution, and was thus receptive to suggestions that she protest to the Communist International against the policy of the Russian Communist Party. At the forthcoming Comintern Congress she would be a member of the Russian delegation and the representative of the International Women's Secretariat, a prestigious spokeswoman, sitting in on the Comintern Executive Committee (the IKKI).[7]

Although Kollontai's Soviet biographer Anna Itkina, a former worker from the Zhenotdel, tells us that Kollontai's oppositionist friends insisted that she speak in their behalf, obviously she was not coerced.[8] Yet after the Tenth Congress Kollontai's role as an oppositionist was ambivalent. How she must have longed for the simplicity of her earlier encounters with the bourgeois feminists, when issues were clear-cut, loyalties unconflicting, and battles invigorating. Resolutions on party unity and against factionalism taken at the Tenth

6. Cohen, *Bukharin*, p. 124.

7. On the IKKI (Ispolnitel'nyi komitet kommunisticheskii Internatsional), see Carr, *Socialism in One Country*, vol. 3, part 2, p. 977. The representative of the Women's Secretariat in the IKKI was entitled to have a consultative voice on general issues, to attend all meetings, and to vote on issues pertaining to the women's movement.

8. Itkina, pp. 213–14.

Congress had created a nearly impossible situation for Communists like Kollontai, who took party discipline seriously. Factionalism was banned, but in his statement on party unity Lenin warned that although every person who voiced criticism must be mindful of the Party's situation in the midst of enemy encirclement, so too must every person "strive in practice to correct the Party's mistakes."[9] Kollontai suffered over the ambiguity. Would it be within the spirit of Lenin's speech to criticize the Bolsheviks at the Comintern Congress? Or would it violate discipline? She suspected the latter. For Kollontai, party discipline was not an external set of regulations but an internalized pattern of behavior. Unfortunately, Lenin was simultaneously Bolshevism's primary figure of authority and the focus of Kollontai's antagonism. Thus she had begun her remarks at the Tenth Congress by reiterating her high regard and deep, special feeling for Lenin before launching into criticism of his policies.[10] Once she decided in the summer of 1921 to oppose Lenin at the Comintern Congress, she made up her mind to inform him of her intention beforehand. If she thought he might reassure her that to speak out was not to break discipline, she was disappointed: Lenin, startled and wondering if she expected his blessing, made a jocular observation that both of them knew was no indication of his real attitude.[11]

As the Comintern Congress got under way, Kollontai was still troubled and doubtful about her decision to oppose. She stood in the lobby beforehand worrying whether silence would be cowardice. Similar thoughts had plagued her in the summer of 1917, when she decided to return to Russia from Sweden, though she knew that the Provisional Government had a warrant out for her arrest. Uneasily— she was not a fearless fighter—Kollontai steeled herself and mounted the tribune. Her speech did not even touch on the relationship of the trade unions to the Party; the issue of workers' control had been rendered obsolete by the onset of the NEP. Neither did she refer to the factional fighting of the past year. She spoke, rather, from her fear that the NEP meant suppression of the Communist spirit that had prevailed during the tumultuous months since 1917.

It was not surprising that she began by justifying her action, informing the comrades that she spoke in the name not of the Russian delegation but of a small minority in the Russian Communist Party.

9. USSR, [6], vol. 1, p. 529. 10. USSR, [2], p. 100.
11. Itkina, p. 214.

She explained that she was breaking discipline because Communists had a higher obligation than simply to obey the Party. That obligation was to the Communist International, which, as she explained elsewhere, was not a chance gathering of comrades but the highest Communist body.[12] It was the Kollontai of 1915, speaking in the lofty internationalist spirit of her *Nashe Slovo* articles, wanting it known that within Russian ranks were Communists who were troubled by changes in internal policies.[13] The NEP, by giving capitalism the opportunity to flourish once again in Russia, threatened to destroy what advances the Revolution had made in the direction of socialism.[14] Kollontai knew that Russia was forced to this policy by the delay in the international revolution. But—and perhaps for the first time—Kollontai publicly faced the possibility that the international revolution might be a long way off. In the atmosphere of the NEP, the working class was losing faith in its abilities, and the peasantry was being encouraged to see itself as the basis of Soviet society. A petty bourgeois spirit would soon flourish.[15] Russian Communists had become accustomed since 1917 to looking hopefully to the coming revolution in Europe. Kollontai turned the situation around, pointing out that the European working class would be looking to Moscow for help when revolution occurred in Europe, but that if the NEP continued the workers would find instead of a strong and politically conscious working class in Russia only a dispirited proletariat. Thus she nimbly adopted another theme, the need to preserve a strong kernel of revolutionary will among Russia's proletariat that would support revolutions elsewhere.

Parts of Kollontai's speech left her vulnerable. She mistakenly argued that world capitalism had outlived itself. (In this view she was not alone. A year earlier, Bukharin had predicted the imminent collapse of capitalism.)[16] She exaggerated the political consciousness of Russian workers, insisting incorrectly that the proletariat had become psychologically attuned to the principles of Communism and accustomed to having its needs met by the state.[17] But much that she said was thoughtful and disturbing. Her remarks have been described as cautious, since she did not detail the bitterness of Bolshevism's fac-

12. USSR, [8], p. 198.   13. USSR, [18], pp. 367–68.
14. *Ibid.*, p. 369.   15. *Ibid.*, pp. 367–69.
16. See Carr, *The Bolshevik Revolution*, vol. 2, p. 199. Carr cites Bukharin's *Ekonomika perekhodnogo perioda* (1920).
17. USSR, [18], pp. 369–70.

tional struggle.[18] Still, she made serious allegations. Delegates who regarded Lenin with awe heard her question whether Lenin believed in the creativity of the working class—the charge that, as we have seen, distressed him most. In an egalitarian style that was familiar to Old Bolsheviks but that must have seemed to her audience to border on insolence, Kollontai remarked that it was characteristic of Lenin to attach great significance to mechanical strength as a factor in production, but little significance to the creative powers of the proletariat.[19] Adopting the NEP, the Party was forgetting its mission to create new people and a new social order. The Soviet state might raise its productivity with the NEP, but at the same time it ran the risk that the working class might lose faith in the Communist Party.[20]

Kollontai spoke in German, the official language of the international assembly, and then repeated her speech in both Russian and French. A friend thought that perhaps she did not trust the interpreter.[21] But it was Kollontai's custom at international gatherings to speak in several languages. It was a tribute to internationalism that in the past had endeared her to other socialists.[22] The Bolsheviks, as we shall see, were unmoved.

As she mounted the podium to speak, there were derisive smiles on the faces of Bukharin, Zinoviev, Kamenev, Rykov, and Radek, and whispers passed among them.[23] Although Lenin was Kollontai's primary target, he sat quietly while Trotsky and Bukharin sought to demolish her protest. Their anger was proportional not so much to Kollontai's remarks as to their own doubts and fears. Trotsky began by admonishing Kollontai for her aggressiveness in pushing her name forward as a speaker. Did she forget that it was contrary to Party custom to enter one's own name on the list of the Comintern Congress speakers? Ordinarily, questions for discussion were put forth not by an individual but by a delegation, and then only after having been scrutinized beforehand in the Party Central Committee. He bantered with Karl Radek to the amusement of the audience over whether Kollontai should be called an Amazon or a Valkyrie. Then he abruptly abandoned his half-hearted attempt to put Kollontai's remarks in the framework of unseemly female behavior. Kollontai's implication

18. See Daniels, p. 162, and Schapiro, p. 332.
19. USSR, [18], p. 369.
20. Ibid., p. 370.
21. Reichenbach, p. 21.
22. For an example, see Mindlin, Ne dom, no mir, pp. 159–60.
23. Reichenbach, p. 21.

that the Bolsheviks lacked faith in the working class was too serious for humor. His anger suggested that for him, as for Lenin, that allegation was the most infuriating. Trotsky reminded Kollontai that the Russians were still encircled by capitalism. If Kollontai's little group believed that the workers could not understand why the regime was willing to offer concessions to capitalists in return for much-needed machines, then it was Kollontai's side, not Trotsky's, that lacked faith in the working class![24]

Bukharin, a man of private doubts, spoke also from his own anxiety, and in so doing unwittingly revealed additional facets of Bolshevik infighting. He claimed to find particularly comical Kollontai's prediction that the Party was creating a "new class" of bureaucratic specialists that would become stronger, a new bourgeoisie against whom it would be necessary to carry out a "third revolution."[25] Bukharin was really projecting his own fears, which he would express more fully elsewhere.[26] For it was not Kollontai but Bukharin who used the expression "new class." Bukharin was responding not to Kollontai's speech so much as to disturbing memories—perhaps of their private conversations.[27]

Not surprisingly, Kollontai and Bukharin, two of the most humane and least authoritarian of the Bolsheviks, were also the most concerned about the Party's alienation from the masses.[28] In a brief outburst, Bukharin's frustration revealed itself: "What does Kollontai want us to do?" For all her anxiety, no one really knew what she was proposing. We make noises about initiative, but how are we to develop working-class initiative? Kollontai had provided some suggestions: workers' control of industry and the freedom to criticize. Bukharin credited neither. Propose something concrete to us. Until then, enough with pointless criticism![29]

Lenin was expected to add final remarks. Instead, he declared his agreement with Bukharin and declined the opportunity to say more.[30]

24. USSR, [18], pp. 372–74.

25. *Ibid.*, p. 379.

26. See Cohen, *Bukharin*, pp. 143–44.

27. *Ibid.*, p. 131. The notion of a "third revolution" had been raised against the Bolsheviks since 1917 by anarchists in the Ukraine, the Kronstadt rebels, and the oppositionist Workers' Truth group in 1921; Cohen calls it the fantasy of the Party's mad hatters. During the 1920's, the "third revolution" came to imply a sweeping away of the rural bourgeoisie and Nepmen.

28. See Cohen, *Bukharin*, p. 145. For Bukharin speaking about himself in humanistic terms, see Nicolaevsky, pp. 16–17.

29. USSR, [18], p. 381.

30. *Ibid.*, p. 382.

One would like to think that Lenin kept silent out of regard for a woman who had been his loyal follower in 1915 when he had only a handful of supporters. But such sentiment was out of character. More likely, Lenin chose not to dignify Kollontai's charges by disputing the indisputable—his faith in the proletariat—in an international congress.

At no point either at the Tenth Party Congress or at the Congress of the Comintern did the Bolsheviks deal effectively with Kollontai's demand that the Party permit internal criticism. It was entirely fitting, however, that this demand should be associated with Kollontai. Perhaps no one in the Lenin years regarded the Party's potential to turn against its own members as ominously as she did. We recall her foreboding in March 1918 in her conversations with Jacques Sadoul at the time of Dybenko's arrest. Again in 1921 she confided her fears to an outsider, the German Communist Bernhard Reichenbach, a member of a sympathetic left-wing splinter group of his party.[31] She told Reichenbach, who was in Moscow for the International Congress, that she was going to oppose Lenin at the Comintern Congress because the NEP was treacherous to the Revolution. Since she feared she might be arrested, she gave him her manuscript copy of *The Workers' Opposition* for safekeeping. He in turn gave the manuscript to a messenger going to Berlin a day or two later.[32]

It was not unusual for Kollontai to worry about her manuscripts. Before her trip to the United States in 1915 she had given the Swedish socialist Fredrik Ström her manuscripts with careful instructions to follow in the event of her death.[33] In the case of *The Workers' Opposition*, which was already published, Kollontai expected that the Party might confiscate existing copies. Only a limited number had been printed, and efforts had already been made to interfere with their distribution.[34] Her instinct to rely on foreign Communists—an indication of the sincerity of her internationalism—in this instance had serious consequences. When Kollontai later asked her German

31. Reichenbach, a cofounder of the German Communist Party, was a leader of the left wing that called itself the *Kommunistische Arbeiter Partei Deutschland* (KAPD). In the spring of 1920, the KAPD split off from the German Communist Party. In April 1922, the KAPD formed, together with Dutch and Bulgarian opposition groups, the so-called Communist Labor International, which was at times referred to as the Fourth International. See Schapiro, pp. 330–31.

32. Reichenbach, p. 21.

33. Kollontai to Ström, no date, Ström archive, Univ. of Gothenburg Library.

34. Only 1,500 copies of her pamphlet had been published—with difficulty. She corrected Riazanov, who put the figure at 1,500,000. See USSR, [2], p. 100.

friend to return her manuscript, he told her that it was safe in Berlin. Indeed, the German Communists were having it translated into German and published. Presumably their high-handed action was a gesture against Kollontai as well as the Russian leadership. According to Reichenbach, the German left wing heard that Trotsky had taken Kollontai in hand and that behind the scenes she had submitted to party discipline and recanted.[35]

Kollontai did not recant, but neither did she vote against the new resolution approving the policy of the Russian Communist Party.[36] Rather, she remained in the limbo of ambivalence. She was to write of her appearance at the Comintern Congress: "I finished speaking. I walked through the hall to the exit. No one paid any attention to me. I knew it would be this way. But it hurts. It hurts very much . . . nothing is more dreadful, more painful, than discord with the Party. Why did I speak?"[37]

If Kollontai were going to restore herself to the Party's good graces, the autumn of 1921 would have been an appropriate time. She had experienced a hint of the painful isolation she knew in 1918 when, as a member of the Left Opposition, she lost her Party positions. The publication of her pamphlet abroad was a signal that if Kollontai were to retreat it must be at once, before she became too deeply drawn into oppositionist activities. Legitimate causes pulled at her. As her articles in *Kommunistka* in the autumn indicated, the situation of the Zhenotdel remained precarious.[38] The women Communists who were fighting for their institution's right to exist needed her. Nevertheless, Kollontai decided in February 1922 to resume active opposition.

That month, 22 supporters of the Workers' Opposition decided to appeal to the Comintern against the Russian Central Committee and without its prior knowledge. Kollontai was not one of the original signatories. She added her name later, the twenty-third, an indication of her difficulty in reaching the decision to oppose.[39]

Kollontai lost the directorship of the Zhenotdel sometime in February. Although the directorship may have been taken from her coincidentally with the new wave of oppositionist activity, it was more likely that Party leaders moved against her after becoming aware of

35. Reichenbach, p. 22.
36. Schapiro, p. 332.
37. Itkina, p. 214.
38. See, for example, "Ne uprazdnenie, a ukreplenie."
39. USSR, [8], pp. 750–52.

her renewed contact with the Opposition.[40] If Kollontai signed the "Appeal of the 22" after being removed from office, her act was additionally brave. Already in disfavor, she was risking the fate she had protested against since the Ninth Party Congress: banishment. And as one Communist asked, "What militant from Moscow . . . would expose himself with a light heart to transfer to Archangel, Irkutsk, or Vladivostok, real exile in accordance with Tsarist tradition . . . ?"[41]

As the delegate of the International Women's Secretariat to the Executive Committee of the Communist International (the IKKI), it was logical that Kollontai be chosen by the Opposition to present the "Appeal" to the Executive Committee.[42] Unlike Kollontai's speech in July, which was largely an expression of hostility to the NEP, the "Appeal of the 22" echoed her earlier attack on the Party. Because the Appeal was directed over the head of the Central Committee rather than to it, and because it was signed by a group, it was more damaging than her earlier pamphlet. The Opposition wanted the world Communist movement, which trusted the International, to know how the Russian Party was moving away from the working class:

Our directing centers are carrying on an unrelenting, disruptive fight against all, especially proletarians, who allow themselves to have their own judgment, and in case of the expression of this within the Party they take all kinds of repressive measures. . . . The Party and trade-union bureaucracy . . . ignore the decisions of our congress on putting workers' democracy into practice.[43]

Bureaucrats in high places used threats of exclusion and other repressive measures to force Communists to elect not those they themselves wanted but those the bureaucrats wanted. The result was careerism, intrigue, and servility. Workers, in response, were leaving the Party. In March of the previous year Kollontai had written "there will be no split."[44] Now the Opposition implored the Comintern, because the situation was so grave, to help avert the danger of a split in the Party.[45]

A special Commission of the Comintern was appointed to hear both

40. See *ibid.*, p. 753, for Shliapnikov's account of illegal searches of his apartment. Kollontai and Shliapnikov both recounted approaches by agents provocateurs.
41. Souvarine, p. 326.
42. See USSR, [8], p. 752. A copy of the appeal was sent to the Central Committee.
43. *Ibid.*, pp. 749–50.
44. Kollontai, *Rabochaia oppozitsiia.* p. 48.
45. USSR, [8], pp. 749–50.

sides, but the Bolsheviks, who controlled the International Executive, handled the situation in a way that promised them the least embarrassment. The Commission was carefully selected. Each of its members was someone who, for one reason or another, was unlikely to oppose the Soviet leadership.[46] Shliapnikov objected privately that including a cipher like Marcel Cachin, a pathetic failure as a revolutionary, to sit in judgment was a special insult to the Opposition.[47] Kollontai must have been similarly disturbed, but for other reasons, by the appearance of her old friend Clara Zetkin on the Commission. The meeting between Zetkin and Kollontai was a drama within a drama. The Bolsheviks were exploiting the tensions between two women who were being driven apart in 1921 by conflicts both personal and political.

Once Zetkin and Kollontai had been close. In the years before the World War, Kollontai willingly and eagerly moved into Zetkin's orbit. Clara Zetkin, the founder and organizer of the International Socialist Women's Movement, provided a welcome role model for the Russian newcomer, strengthening Kollontai's resolve to create within the reluctant Russian Social Democratic Party institutions for work among women such as Zetkin described. At prewar international women's conferences Kollontai invariably voted with Zetkin, but Kollontai's analysis of problems was apt to be more sophisticated and thoughtful, a hint that the younger woman would not always follow her mentor's lead.[48]

Clara Zetkin, particularly in the prewar years, argued against bureaucratism in the German party and fought for intraparty democracy. She insisted on the need for a women's organization within the proletarian movement, and she was outspoken in her battle against

46. The Commission included C. Zetkin, M. Cachin, C. Kreibich, and A. MacManus. See Schapiro, p. 333.

47. *Ibid.* Deutscher labeled Cachin a pathetic failure in *The Prophet Unarmed*, vol. 2, p. 359. Victor Serge said Cachin "would strive always to follow the strongest current of opinion. . . . A rather intelligent man, who could see practically everything that was going on, he—for a long time I am sure—experienced considerable anguish; but he never rebelled." Serge, p. 167. Cachin had opposed the Bolsheviks in 1917 and had come to regret it. He was anxious to avoid further humiliation, and the Bolsheviks exploited his anxiety by appointing him to the Commission. See Albert S. Lindemann, *The "Red Years": European Socialism Versus Bolshevism, 1919–1921* (Berkeley, Calif., 1974), pp. 151, 179.

48. See Kollontai's account of the dispute at the International Socialist Women's Conference in Copenhagen in 1910 over the demand of Danish women that typesetters be allowed to work at night, "Vtoraia mezhdunarodnaia zhenskaia konferentsiia v kopengagene v 1910 godu," *Izbrannye stat'i i rechi*, pp. 95–105. Zetkin rejected the demand as feminism. Kollontai's analysis was more sophisticated.

male prejudice among German Social Democrats.[49] But it was not likely that a friendship between strong-minded and combative people like Zetkin and Kollontai could evolve without friction. Zetkin probably resented Kollontai's failure to support her fully in her long feud with Lily Braun, a flamboyant and beautiful woman from the Prussian upper classes who came to social democracy in 1895 from feminism, a background Braun found difficult to overcome. Kollontai voted with Zetkin against Braun at socialist conferences, but she did not share Zetkin's resentment of her. She may have suspected that part of the problem between Zetkin and Braun lay not only in Braun's reformist and feminist tendencies but in her individualism, her ambition, and her cavalier failure to respect Zetkin's leadership in the socialist women's movement. Braun was deliberately abrasive, particularly when she neglected to discuss Zetkin's contribution to the proletarian women's movement in her well-known book *The Woman Question*. This insult was the more egregious in light of Zetkin's obviously central role and her efforts earlier to provide a place for Braun in the German movement. In her reaction, Zetkin revealed uneasiness about the possibility of a potential rival. She wrote to Karl Kautsky condemning Braun as false, selfish, nasty, and malicious.[50] Kollontai, on the other hand, described Braun as bright and original.[51] She even quoted frequently in her own work from Braun's "offensive" book.[52]

Kollontai's personal relationship with Zetkin was further jeopardized in 1912 by the appearance of Kollontai's book *Po rabochei Evrope*, which criticized the stuffy and self-righteous leaders of the German and Austrian Social Democrats, suggesting that a bureaucracy was growing within their ranks.[53] Anonymous reports condemned her as an ingrate and a traitor to her adopted party. Her German friends who had not read the manuscript were incensed by what they heard about it. Among the Germans, only Karl Liebknecht rallied to Kollontai's support. Later, when the book became more widely available, the Germans decided that their condemnation of Kollontai had been excessive and restored her to the party's good graces. Zetkin wrote Kollontai a friendly letter.

49. See Honeycutt, p. 328.
50. *Ibid.*, pp. 317–18. Braun's book is *Die Frauenfrage—ihre geschichtliche Entwicklung und wirtschaftliche Seite* (Leipzig, 1901).
51. Kollontai, *Iz moei zhizni i raboty*, p. 118.
52. See especially *Sotsial'nye osnovy zhenskago voprosa*.
53. See *Iz moei zhizni i raboty*, p. 118.

The strains between Kollontai and Zetkin before the war seemed trivial after 1914. When the German Social Democrats in the Reichstag voted in August for war credits, Zetkin endeared herself to Kollontai by being one of the first to denounce openly the position of the socialist majority. Zetkin and Kollontai both were arrested for antiwar activity. The two women acted jointly in the international women's movement, each bravely championing the cause of internationalism, Kollontai in the pages of *Nashe Slovo* and Zetkin in her own journal, *Gleichheit*, the organ of the socialist women's movement since 1891. Then in 1917 the dynamics of the international women's movement and the relationship between Zetkin and Kollontai subtly changed. Kollontai returned home, exultant over the downfall of the tsarist government. Zetkin suffered an enormous blow: in May the German Social Democrats (the SPD Executive) deprived her of her major work, her directorship of *Gleichheit*, because of her criticism of the majority socialist support of the German war effort.[54]

The Russian women soon met with success in their attempts to develop a socialist women's movement within the Russian Party. After the Revolution they revived their newspaper, *Rabotnitsa*; they won their battle for a Women's Bureau; and in 1920 they launched their theoretical journal, *Kommunistka*. Zetkin still provided a model,[55] but the focus of the socialist women's movement was moving from Germany to Moscow. The First and Second International Communist Women's Conferences, we recall, convened in the Russian capital in 1920 and again in 1921. Inessa Armand dominated the first, Aleksandra Kollontai the second—advising the delegates on which strategies to pursue and which programs to develop in their own fledgling socialist women's movements.[56] Since 1907 and the first International Women's Conference at Stuttgart, Zetkin had viewed Kollontai as her protégé. But as director of the Zhenotdel in the country of the first successful Communist Revolution, Kollontai, not Zetkin, became the central figure in the international women's movement.

Zetkin had come to Moscow late in 1920, "ill and hysterical," overwrought by poor health and ugly memories of the recent murder of her dearest friend, Rosa Luxemburg. Zetkin was in no state to become an oppositionist. Nevertheless, her readiness to embrace the

54. Honeycutt, p. 458.
55. *Ibid.*, p. 7.
56. See Kollontai, *Rabotnitsa i krest'ianka*, pp. 21–48.

regime rather than to join with Kollontai and Balabanoff as its critics shocked her old friends. To their dismay, Zetkin succumbed to calculated flattery. Because of her prestige as a veteran leader of the working class and a founding member of the German Communist Party, Zetkin was accorded a place of honor. Balabanoff described what she called the unhappy effect of Soviet power and prestige upon even "the most intransigent of revolutionaries," as Zetkin, her former mentor, became fascinated by the tribune and applause. She was still so weak that she sometimes had to be carried on and off the platform. Zinoviev, the head of the Comintern, stage-managed Zetkin's appearances, according to Balabanoff. "Look at this white-haired veteran of the movement," he would say when he introduced her. "She is a living testament to the approval all great revolutionaries give to the tactics of our great, invincible Party." Then as Zetkin began to speak, Zinoviev would write in a note to the translator, "Abbreviate; cut her speech. We can't waste so much time on her eloquence." Balabanoff discovered that Zetkin loved the atmosphere with which the Bolsheviks surrounded her. Party leaders let her think she was influencing policy, but secretly laughed at her naiveté. Balabanoff regretted that she could not prevent Zetkin from becoming a willing tool of Zinoviev and the Bolshevik leadership.[57]

Thus in March 1922, as the Comintern Commission assembled to pass judgment, it was not the stalwart of 1915 who listened to Kollontai and Shliapnikov denounce the Russian Party, but an aging and weakened woman. Zetkin knew that Kollontai spoke to her as well as to Lenin, for Kollontai had earlier, at the Second International Conference of Communist Women, implied that Zetkin should concentrate more on the proletariat by rejecting Zetkin's advice that the socialist women's movement give more attention to international agitation among women of the working intelligentsia, such as teachers and office workers. Kollontai had insisted that the Communists first establish themselves firmly among the women in the factories.[58] Continuing in March 1922 to emphasize the necessarily dominant role of the proletariat in the workers' state, Kollontai and Shliapnikov developed the theme of a Party grown sick and repressive largely because it had lost touch with the workers. Three hundred and six workers left the Moscow organization between May and August. Kol-

57. Balabanoff, *My Life as a Rebel*, p. 289.
58. Kollontai, *Rabotnitsa i krest'ianka*, pp. 44–45. See Carr, *Socialism in One Country*, vol. 3, part 2, pp. 980–81, for the persistence of this issue.

lontai condemned a situation that particularly appalled her: when workers went on strike, Red Army men were sent into the factories as strikebreakers. In a workers' state!

The Party was repressive. It failed to implement the decisions of its own congresses. Free criticism was not permitted. The Party had even sent a provocateur to urge Kollontai and Shliapnikov to join a Fourth International—grounds for exclusion! Shliapnikov, a member of the Central Committee, told of his apartment in Moscow being searched and his mail opened. Both reported that members of the Workers' Opposition who had signed the "Appeal of the 22" were already being summoned before the Central Control Commission, the first sign of repression.[59]

Zinoviev and Trotsky, whom one observer noted "dominated without effort" the congresses of the Third International, defended the Party.[60] The Commission listened to both sides and, of course, decided in favor of the Party. It pointed out that the dangers cited by Kollontai and Shliapnikov were no surprise in these difficult times, that the leadership was aware of the problems and was taking steps to alleviate them. Shliapnikov and Kollontai were not helping the Party to resist the dangers, but rather were giving comfort to the Party's enemies, Mensheviks and White counterrevolutionaries. The Commission repeated the resolutions of the Tenth Congress against factionalism and warned that continuation of their activities might put the Workers' Opposition outside the ranks of the Third International. Any harm that might befall the Russian Communist Party, they added piously, would harm not only Soviet Russia but the Comintern as well.[61]

It has been suggested that the Commission may actually have been unaware of the seriousness of the charges against the Russian Party.[62] But however misinformed her colleagues, Zetkin knew better. She had already heard the same charges from her friend Balabanoff, whom she called "one of the few honest people left in the movement."[63] Angelica Balabanoff had informed Zetkin a year earlier that she was refusing to collaborate with the Bolsheviks any longer and was preparing to leave Russia. Zetkin, who since the death of Rosa Luxemburg regarded Balabanoff as her closest friend, pleaded tearfully with

59. USSR, [8], p. 754.
61. USSR, [8], pp. 755–56.
63. Balabanoff, *My Life as a Rebel*, p. 290.

60. The observer was Souvarine, p. 190.
62. Schapiro, p. 333.

her to remain, suggesting that she could be appointed secretary of the international women's movement. It was an indication not simply of Zetkin's attachment to her friend but of her attachment to status and her insensitivity to pushing aside Kollontai, who since the autumn of 1920 had been director of the Moscow section and the representative of the Secretariat in the IKKI.[64] But Balabanoff would not acquiesce in the deterioration of the Party or the eclipse of Aleksandra Kollontai. She was fond of Zetkin, but she regretfully concluded that Zetkin's willingness to work with the Bolsheviks was "one of the bitter personal disillusionments of my life." Like Kollontai she had been Zetkin's friend and disciple; now, however, she could no longer look to her in either role.[65]

Balabanoff could not forgive Zetkin for allowing herself to be used. But Zetkin's behavior was not difficult to understand. Ill and growing old, she had been disappointed before by a political party and had suffered. The moral failure of the German Social Democrats in 1914 had so depressed her that friends feared she would never recover from the shock.[66] For years Zetkin had fought the good fight. Now, although she belonged to the newly founded German Communist Party and was one of its representatives in the Reichstag, she enjoyed being in Soviet Russia, a witness to the Revolution. She wanted to believe in the Bolsheviks rather than in Aleksandra Kollontai, who with her relentless criticism was ready to correct even a veteran like Zetkin at an international women's conference.[67]

The tension of their political disagreements exacerbated their rivalry. The International Women's Secretariat that was established by the Comintern in October 1920 seemed to fall informally into two halves: a Moscow section directed by Kollontai and a Berlin section headed by Zetkin. Kollontai's implication that this division created difficulties for the Secretariat, and contributed to its inability to

64. Carr, *Socialism in One Country*, vol. 3, part 2, pp. 977–78.

65. Balabanoff, *My Life as a Rebel*, p. 290.

66. *Ibid.*, p. 130; Nettl, vol. 2, p. 609, discusses Zetkin's and Luxemburg's suicidal feelings upon the outbreak of the World War.

67. Kollontai may have reminded Zetkin of old enemies. It is not too far-fetched to believe that Kollontai's combativeness revived Zetkin's unhappy memories of her earlier rival Lily Braun, also an outspoken former noblewoman who refused to accept Party dictates. Superficial similarities may have caused Kollontai to seem more and more like "the beautiful, the glamorous Lily," whose independent actions Zetkin once denounced as being "as false as her complexion." Zetkin to Karl Kautsky, Nov. 1901, cited in Honeycutt, pp. 317–18. For Lily Braun and German socialism, see Meyer, pp. 107–12.

function, may have reflected her own displeasure with Zetkin.[68] Zet-kin, for her part, assumed the superior role. She edited a monthly journal, *Die kommunistische Fraueninternationale*, which started publication in Berlin in April 1921 and continued for four years. The international orientation of its title was a pretension that *Kommun-istka* in Moscow did not mirror.[69]

Kollontai's loyal friends protested Party attempts in 1922 to oust her from the women's movement. Balabanoff recorded her own dis-may.[70] Other Communists reproached the Party indirectly. Liudmila Stal', who worked with Kollontai in the International Secretariat and who had been her friend since prerevolutionary days in Stockholm, declared her loyalty in an article in *Proletarskaia revoliutsiia*. With-out referring to current problems, Stal' recalled a more serious split, when others were being condemned and it was Kollontai who whole-heartedly supported Lenin and the majority of the Central Commit-tee. Stal' wrote about November 1917 and Zinoviev's and Kamenev's resignations from the government at the crucial moment of its for-mation, and she reminded the Party how Kollontai, then Commissar of Public Welfare, had rallied the working women of Petrograd to the support of Lenin and Trotsky.[71]

Zetkin indicated no regret in 1922 that Kollontai was being pushed out of leadership of the international socialist women's movement as a result of her appearance before the Comintern Commission. Zetkin

68. See Kollontai, "O rabote mezhdunarodnogo zhenskogo sekretariata," and her re-port to the Second International Communist Women's Conference, June 1921, reported in *Pravda*, June 12, 1921, p. 1. Another account claims that Kollontai indicated that the Comintern disapproved of the division, that it subsequently rebuked the Berlin Secre-tariat, and that the Berlin Secretariat then became an auxiliary and purely executive section of the International Secretariat in Moscow. For this see Carr, *Socialism in One Country*, vol. 3, part 2, p. 978.

69. Carr, *Socialism in One Country*, vol. 3, part 2, pp. 978–79. Whatever rivalry ex-isted between the Moscow and Berlin sections was presumably diminished by the re-organization of the Secretariat after the Second International Communist Women's Con-ference. Instead of two directors, it had six, Kollontai and Zetkin among them. Kollon-tai's association with the Secretariat ended in 1922, after her participation in the appeal to the Comintern by the Workers' Opposition. Despite Zetkin's continued presence, it would seem that the Secretariat did not function very effectively without Kollontai. No International Women's Conference was held in connection with the Fourth Comintern Congress in November 1922. Zetkin, however, was at the height of her prestige in Mos-cow. The IKKI appointed her in the late autumn of 1922 as the single Women's Secretary. See *Pravda*, Dec. 7, 1922. Zetkin shifted the balance of the International Women's Sec-retariat back to Berlin. In 1926 the organ was downgraded to a women's department of the Executive Committee of the Comintern. See Stites, *Women's Liberation Movement*, p. 343.

70. Balabanoff, *My Life as a Rebel*, pp. 251–52.

71. Stal', "Rabotnitsa v Oktiabre," pp. 299–301.

was being used to take her old friend's place in the game of "discredit one's comrade" already under way in Moscow. On the one occasion when Zetkin could have paid tribute to Kollontai's pioneering work in the Russian socialist women's movement, she chose not to. In a curious replay of the past, Clara Zetkin followed the pattern of Lily Braun, who had hurt Zetkin by omitting from *The Woman Question* any meaningful discussion of her contribution. When Zetkin published her reminiscences of Lenin, which focused on talks with him concerning the woman question and the Zhenotdel, she in turn ignored Kollontai and her contribution.[72] Zetkin may never have admitted, even to herself, either her sorry role or the fact that Balabanoff and Kollontai had been right in 1921 in their dismal predictions for the Russian Party. She spent much of her time during the 1920's in the Soviet Union. As the Party grew increasingly repressive, Zetkin was unable to ignore its deterioration. Like many others, she criticized the regime, primarily in private conversation.[73]

Kollontai and Shliapnikov had pushed too far in 1922 with their appeal to the Comintern. The result was a bitter confrontation a few weeks later in March at the Eleventh Party Congress. The question occurs, Why did Kollontai participate in so hopeless a venture as an appeal to the Communist International against the Russian Communist Party, which was basking in its prestige as the directing organ of the first successful Communist state? As a delegate from the International Women's Secretariat to the IKKI, and as a prominent Bolshevik, she knew that the Bolsheviks dominated the Comintern. Its Executive was headed by Zinoviev, and its meetings were held in the Kremlin, attended by Bukharin, Radek, and Trotsky. She knew, as Angelica Balabanoff, the first director of the Comintern had known, that the Bolsheviks controlled the Executive.[74] She shared the knowledge of another friend, the German Communist Bernhard Reichen-

72. The one oblique reference to Kollontai is negative. Zetkin quoted Lenin to the effect that he would not bet on the reliability of those women who mixed personal romance with politics. See "Lenin o morali i voprosakh pola (iz vospominanii Klary Tsetkin)," in Razin, ed., p. 20.

73. Ella Wolfe attests that Zetkin congratulated Bertram D. Wolfe for his outspoken criticism of the Stalinists. (Personal communication, May 1975.) Zetkin did, however, occasionally exert pressure on the regime. For example, in 1922 she joined with Serge, Sadoul, and Souvarine in trying to mitigate the political persecution of the Russian Socialist Revolutionary Party by the Central Committee. See Serge, p. 164.

74. Balabanoff, *My Life as a Rebel*, p. 241.

bach, that within the Executive Lenin's authority was taken for granted by the Russian representatives, that "when Lenin had his say, the question was settled."[75] Was she so innocent, then, as to call on Lenin, the shadow leader of the Comintern, to act against Lenin, the Chairman of the Council of Commissars of the Russian government? In a sense she was doing just that, and it was not as naive as it seemed. She did not expect the Comintern to take action. She hoped rather, both in July 1921 and again in February 1922, to influence Lenin by the audacity of her disclosures. Her appeal to the Comintern was a symbolic plea to the institution that Lenin himself had established in 1919 as the highest Communist body.

Kollontai's action did not have the result she hoped for when she wrote "Il'ich will be with us yet." But she had correctly gauged the depths of Lenin's reaction: although the Party at no point denied the Opposition the right to go to the Comintern, the appeal was the single deed that most outraged Lenin and the Central Committee.

The Eleventh Party Congress set up its own commission to investigate the activities of the Opposition. In its report the commission regretted the ingratitude of Opposition leaders like Shliapnikov, who was chosen at the Tenth Congress in a gesture of conciliation to be a member of the Central Committee, and Kollontai, who was delegated for work in the Comintern. Both had refused to respond to these gestures of Party unity in the proper spirit. Rather, along with Medvedev, the two had preserved, inspired, and headed an illegal factional organization.[76] The commission, made up of Zinoviev, Stalin, and Dzerzhinskii, recommended that the three unrepentant leaders be expelled from the Party.[77] The Central Control Commission concurred.[78]

꒚꒚꒚꒚

The Workers' Opposition movement—its activities and its relationship to Bolshevism—has been investigated elsewhere.[79] Here I want to consider primarily Kollontai's response to the recommendation of the investigative commission to expel her from the Party. Lenin, al-

75. Reichenbach, p. 17.

76. See the commission report in USSR, [8], pp. 702–10.

77. *Ibid.*, p. 710. In addition to Kollontai, Shilapnikov, and Medvedev, the Commission recommended expelling two other leaders, Mitin and Kuznetsov. See Carr, *The Bolshevik Revolution*, vol. 1, p. 216, for the members of the commission.

78. For the report of the Central Control Commission, see USSR, [8], p. 177.

79. See Daniels and Schapiro.

ready ill, attended the Eleventh Party Congress only to present and discuss his opening report and to make a closing speech. Kollontai spoke primarily to the members of the Central Control Commission who had looked into her allegedly illegal activities.[80]

Lenin warned that the Bolsheviks were still in a difficult situation, surrounded by enemies of the Soviet state.[81] Yet Kollontai was curiously immune to anxieties about enemy encirclement and infiltration, to what has been described as "an acutely neurotic fear of dangers for the movement."[82] When her turn came to speak, she appealed once more to the Bolsheviks to abandon their beleaguered state of mind, a legacy of the underground and the Civil War, and begin to live in accordance with their own pledges. She disputed the charge that she was the leader of an illegal, anti-Party faction, denying that any faction existed. She denied that she had breached Party ethics by appealing to the Comintern with false information that defamed the Party. And she rejected charges that she had cooperated with Communists abroad who were seeking a Fourth International. Fighting for her right and the right of her comrades to remain in the Party, Kollontai insisted that they had not violated but had rather upheld Party rules.

What was she guilty of?, she demanded to know. It was a question that had been asked many times before in Russia, and that would be heard many times in the future. She turned their accusation back on her accusers: the problem was not that she was the guilty leader of an illegal faction but that the Party refused to abandon its "state of siege" mentality.[83] The Central Control Commission, still caught in the psychology of a military regime, thought in terms of leaders, ranks, and factions. She denied that "the 22" were a faction. And, unwittingly undermining her insistence that she was not a leader, she testified that the "Appeal" was not the result of conspiratorial and prolonged planning because *she* delivered it to the Comintern conference and *she* knew. There were not even enough copies to be distributed to each member of the conference Presidium; indeed, there had been so little advance preparation that the document was

80. The special commission's investigation ranged over her participation in the Workers' Opposition and her contribution to the life of the Women's Section. Members of the Zhenotdel—Smidovich, Golubeva, and Elizarova—testified. See USSR, [8], pp. 702–10.

81. For Lenin's speech, see *Sochineniia* (4th ed.), vol. 33, p. 287.

82. See Lewin, "The Social Background of Stalinism," p. 112.

83. For the military mentality of the Party, see Kollontai, *Rabochaia oppozitsiia*, p. 41.

translated only into French.[84] The Control Commission was flattering her by accusing her of leading an illegal faction despite the fact that her name appeared as number 23 on an "Appeal" signed by 22 Party members. The twenty-third signatory could not be the leader of the previous 22, some of whom had been her political teachers!

Nor was she guilty of conspiring with Communists abroad to publish her pamphlet. She reminded her comrades that frequently their own statements were misquoted by the bourgeois press; it was beyond the power of any of them in Moscow to control what foreign splinter groups published. She could do no more than she had already done: protest that her pamphlet was being published in an organ of the Fourth International with which she had no connection, and ask that such unauthorized publication cease.[85]

Aron Sol'ts, speaking earlier for the Central Control Commission, recalled that Kollontai was once a Menshevik, implying that old associations were being held against her. Such infuriating innuendos were intended to obscure the issues, she knew. Fighting to restore a set of comradely relationships that were ceasing to exist, she reminded the Eleventh Congress that she was a longtime Bolshevik. How many Communists had written a brochure for the Central Committee as far back as 1915? And who among the Bolsheviks could forget her participation in organizing the Zimmerwald Left?[86]

These were side issues. Kollontai brushed them away, focusing on the main point, trying by force of logic to destroy the case against her. She intuited correctly that the call to exclude the Opposition from the Party was a punishment for the appeal to the Comintern. Yet Party leaders admitted that the 22 were fully within their rights to appeal to the highest Communist body.[87] If, as she had shown, the 22 were not an illegal faction; if, as the special commission admitted, they did not violate Party discipline by turning to the highest Communist body with their protest—where then was their guilt? Kollontai denied that the substance of their appeal was the problem. She recalled the speeches of the previous day of Comrades Kosior and Osinskii and insisted (over an objection from the floor) that their protests

84. USSR, [8], pp. 197–98.
85. See n. 31 above on the Fourth International. It is worth recalling that Kollontai's pamphlet was marked "only for members of the Tenth Party Congress" and that only 1,500 copies were printed.
86. USSR, [8], p. 197. For Sol'ts's remarks, see ibid., p. 176.
87. This right was upheld in the Resolutions of the Eleventh Congress. See ibid., p. 579.

against Party policy were sharper than anything contained in the "Appeal of the 22."[88]

Kollontai was in deadly earnest about living by the letter of Party law. She knew that the Tenth Congress had confirmed a Communist's right to criticize. She was remarkably frank about her interrogation. She reported that the Control Commission had asked if she would acquiesce in the Comintern's directive that she not engage in factional activity. Kollontai agreed that she would. But she added that when the Control Commission had asked her if that meant that she would cease her protests, she replied no, she would not. She was defiant, reminding the Party Congress as she had reminded the Control Commission that it was the obligation of each member to criticize and correct Party errors.[89]

This indefatigable woman, having disproved, if only to her own satisfaction, the charges against her, subjected the Party again to the dismal facts of Communist life—as if by repetition she could refute the investigative commission's accusation that "the 22" had given a distorted picture to the Comintern.[90] She claimed that the Opposition was being honest when it informed the Comintern that the Russian Communist Party had become alienated from the working class. In 38 of the most industrialized gubernii, only 44 percent of the workers were Party members. In a factory with some 900 workers, when Party members called a meeting to vote on a resolution only twenty workers voted and four abstained. The working class was becoming inert. She rejected the argument that the situation was beyond Party control, that it was the result of "objective conditions."[91]

According to one dissident Communist, the Left Opposition was defeated because of its "mystical theory of the Party." Boris Souvarine contended that "the Opposition were lost by their idealization of the very evil they proposed to attack under another name."[92] Souvarine's thoughtful insight did not apply to Kollontai, at least not in 1922. Her focus of attack *was* the Party. She repeated the theme of her pamphlet: the sickness of the Russian Communist Party was not the result of the problems of economic reconstruction, famine, or the threat of foreign intervention—the arguments of the Bolshevik lead-

88. *Ibid.*, p. 199. For Kosior's views, see USSR, [8], pp. 125–28. For Osinskii's, see *ibid.*, pp. 86–89.

89. *Ibid.*, p. 199.

90. See the commission report in *ibid.*, p. 706.

91. See *ibid.*, pp. 199–200.

92. Souvarine, p. 345.

ers. The sickness was the result of the suffocation of thought.[93] And if the Opposition was driven from the Party, working-class passivity would increase. Once more, she implored the Party not to exclude comrades who signed the "Appeal" but rather to open up the Party. Kollontai identified the signs of that moral sickness which, as another Communist observed, in some fifteen years brought on the death of Bolshevism.[94]

Kollontai at the Eleventh Party Congress insisted on her own rather quixotic perception of recent Party history. The Tenth Party Congress has come to be known historically for its stress on the theme of Party unity and its ominous endorsement of a resolution ordering the end of all factions at the risk of expulsion. Kollontai had another view of what had been important at the Tenth Congress: she challenged Party leaders to heed the resolutions about workers' democracy and about freedom of internal Party criticism. Both were still paper resolutions.[95]

Party leaders ignored Kollontai. But within a year of the Eleventh Congress appeared the "Appeal of the 46," in which Trotsky led a group of Bolsheviks in calling for reaffirmation of the Tenth Party Congress resolution on internal Party democracy. Ironically, it would be only five years before Trotsky, fighting to remain in the Party, and protesting far more radically and defiantly than Kollontai, would defend even factions. He would cry out to the same body before which he had indicted Kollontai and the Workers' Opposition that "any serious group . . . when it is confronted by the dilemma whether it should, from a sense of discipline, silently efface itself, or, regardless of discipline, struggle for survival—will undoubtedly choose the latter course . . . and say: perish that 'discipline' which suppressed the vital interests of the movement." And he warned in words that recalled his own earlier action against Kollontai and Shliapnikov: "Beware, lest you should find yourself saying later: we parted company with those whom we should have preserved and we preserved those from whom we should have parted." [96] The Central Control Commission would spurn Trotsky, just as it had earlier rejected Kollontai. Sol'ts, for example, the tough chairman (who did not suspect that his

93. See USSR, [8], p. 200.

94. Serge, p. 185.

95. For Kollontai's challenge, see USSR, [8], p. 200. For the Resolution on Party Unity, see USSR, [6], vol. 1, p. 529. The resolution calling for freedom of internal Party criticism was drawn up and introduced by Bukharin. See Eastman, p. 412.

96. Deutscher, *The Prophet Unarmed*, vol. 2, pp. 346–47.

own turn was to come), scorned Kollontai's "pretense" that the appeal to the Comintern was not the work of an illegal and secret faction but that it all happened by chance in "half an hour."

Did any of the Bolsheviks shrink from expelling old comrades like Kollontai? Were there any outside the Opposition who perhaps asked in 1922 questions Trotsky would raise too late? Surely there were. For the Eleventh Party Congress did not in the end endorse the investigative commission's recommendation that the "leaders" of the Workers' Opposition—Kollontai, Shliapnikov, and Medvedev—be excluded from the Communist Party. Instead, the Congress approved a curious set of resolutions entitled "On Certain Members of the Former Workers' Opposition" that repeated the commission's case against the three but stopped short of its demand for expulsion. The resolutions adopted by the Congress condemned the Workers' Opposition but upheld its right to turn to the Comintern.[97] The Congress censured Kollontai on several counts: for her anti-Party speech at the Comintern Congress, which gave ammunition to elements of the press hostile to the Bolsheviks; for her failure to disown her pamphlet *The Workers' Opposition*, which was being used abroad by harmful groups striving to set up a Fourth International; and for her supposed statements in that pamphlet that a split was inevitable, that it only remained to select the proper moment. This last charge was patently false, but the resolution repeated that Comrade Kollontai expected a split if the Party failed to adopt the views of Kollontai, Medvedev, and Shliapnikov. The report also noted Kollontai's alleged regret that there were so few factional meetings, a distortion of her view that the Bolsheviks must be what they always were, a vigorous and argumentative body. If her perception of the Party was that of a romantic revolutionary, it was also an accurate description of Old Bolshevism.

Despite its damaging indictment, the Eleventh Congress concluded simply by repeating the threat made earlier by the Comintern. If Comrades Kollontai, Shliapnikov, and Medvedev continued to display a similar attitude toward the Party, they would be expelled. How it happened that the Congress agreed with its special commission's findings yet failed nevertheless to uphold its recommendations, we do not know. The meeting in which the Congress discussed the commis-

97. See n. 87 above. Lenin in his speech at the Eleventh Congress affirmed the right to appeal to the Comintern. See *Sochineniia* (4th ed.), vol. 33, p. 288. For Sol'ts's scornful remark, see USSR, [8], p. 205.

sion's report was secret, and its proceedings have not been published.[98] It has been assumed that the Central Committee suffered an embarrassing defeat at this meeting, that the Congress defied the Committee— and by implication Lenin—by refusing to expel the three Opposition leaders from the Party.[99] Although such an interpretation is plausible, a different scenario may have taken place.

Lenin, who was absent after discussion of his opening report and played no part in the special commission's investigation, returned to the Congress to deliver his closing speech. The meeting in which the Congress discussed the special commission's report took place immediately prior to his final remarks.[100] Lenin presumably was in attendance, then, at the secret meeting. And it may have been that Lenin permitted the Party to retain within its ranks the three censured leaders because he could see little point in creating additional divisiveness by expelling them. Kollontai and Shliapnikov had already been punished. Shliapnikov was being dropped from the Central Committee.[101] Kollontai, who had lost her directorship of the Zhenotdel, was also being removed as Secretary of the International Socialist Women's Secretariat. Lenin's closing speech, in which he stressed Party unity, suggests that he may have preferred to retain the Opposition leaders within the Party's ranks—perhaps to convince himself that Bolshevik solidarity did exist. He pointed out in his speech that Party solidarity was the feature that most distinguished the Eleventh Congress from the preceding Tenth, and he boasted—as if it were better somehow that Kollontai, Shliapnikov, and Medvedev *not* be expelled—that only a very small part of the Opposition had put itself outside the ranks.[102] Nor were Lenin's remarks at the close of the Eleventh Congress those of a leader who had just suffered a surprising and serious defeat. Rather, they were the conclusions of a man who sounded relieved that a situation had gone well.[103] If so,

98. This information is contained in a footnote to the proceedings of the Eleventh Congress. See USSR [8], p. 807.

99. Schapiro, p. 336.

100. USSR, [8], p. 807.

101. See Lenin's reference to an earlier attempt in the Central Committee to expel Shliapnikov from the Party—an attempt that failed of the necessary two-thirds vote. Lenin may have preferred by the end of the Eleventh Congress to retain Shliapnikov in the Party, but his anger toward his old comrade was unabated. Lenin, *Sochineniia* (4th ed.), vol. 33, p. 288.

102. Evidently Lenin referred to the expelled Communists Mitin, Kuznetsov, and Miasnikov. See USSR, [8], p. 807, n. 188.

103. For example, Lenin was pleased that the disagreements over the trade-union issue and the NEP were less sharp than he had anticipated. *Ibid.*, p. 521.

the final act of the Eleventh Congress, which overruled the investigating commission's recommendation, may have occurred not, as has been supposed, in opposition to Lenin's wishes, but rather in agreement with them.

Kollontai was not expelled from the Party. It would appear that Lenin wanted her still to remain; and indeed he expressed privately to Gorky his regret at the necessity of her political demise, a sentiment that accords well with his reluctance after the Tenth Congress to attack his old comrade publicly. At the Comintern Congress, we recall, he deferred to Bukharin. At the Eleventh Congress he withdrew after an angry barrage at Shliapnikov, remarking that Trotsky had already dealt with the significance of Kollontai's pamphlet.[104]

Lenin's respect for Kollontai, his awareness that her analysis of Party ills was in a sense correct, would not inhibit him from sending her away. Kollontai would soon be assigned to minor diplomatic work in Scandinavia, which meant isolation from any meaningful connection with the center of Communist power. Lenin was exhausted with opposition in general and with Kollontai in particular. He was tired of being reminded of what he already knew: that the workers' lives were not what they should be, that the Party was failing to fulfill its promises, and that he had abandoned what he had written in *State and Revolution*. One historian summed up Lenin's unease: "There was always a Shliapnikov, Kollontai, or Osinskii ready to challenge him on a matter of principle, recalling to him and others Lenin's previous and quite different views on this or that question."[105]

Lenin no longer needed Kollontai. If it was true that he distrusted the colorful gesture and word, he was probably never entirely comfortable with her style.[106] Kollontai's flamboyance was even less congenial to him now, when it had ceased to serve a purpose. Her remarkable ability to sway crowds mattered little with the Revolution accomplished and the Civil War ended. When Lenin referred to "that foolishness of the Smolny period," and the "time of enthusiasm and chaos,"[107] Kollontai, with her uncompromising idealism, was an integral element of what he was putting behind him.

There was more. Kollontai, we recall, had never adhered to Lenin's

104. Lenin, *Sochineniia* (4th ed.), vol. 33, p. 288. Note in this speech to the Eleventh Congress of Mar. 28, 1922, the contrast between Lenin's anger at Shliapnikov and his relative restraint toward Kollontai.
105. Ulam, p. 461.
106. Deutscher, *The Prophet Armed*, vol. 1, p. 341.
107. Ulam, p. 458.

organizational principles. She became a Bolshevik, as did many others, because she was an antiwar internationalist. If after the Tenth Congress Lenin intended that Bolshevism return to the more rigid structure of its early post-1903 years, if his ideals were now discipline, order, and organization, Kollontai had to go.[108] She had defied the Central Control Commission with the vow that as a Bolshevik she had a commitment to disagree, and she had pledged never to cease her criticism.

What separated Lenin and Kollontai as much as anything else was their attitude toward law. Lenin made his contempt for legalism known, whereas Kollontai believed in the letter of Party law. How ironic that the laws of intra-Party democracy, which Lenin evaded and Kollontai upheld, were his own.[109]

Lenin and Kollontai represented two opposing poles of Bolshevik political thought that emerged with full clarity in 1922. She clung to the "revolutionary-heroic" tradition of 1917, whereas he, with his New Economic Policy, moved further along the pragmatic route he had staked out at the time of Brest-Litovsk. Of course Kollontai would insist on a Communist's duty to protest; it was a right upheld by Party congresses. Of course Kollontai would despise the NEP; the very concept of economic retreat was the antithesis of revolutionary heroism.[110] The more Lenin became pragmatic and moderate and —odd as the notion sounds—responsive to public opinion (the primary explanation for the NEP), the more Kollontai could be counted on to protest the deradicalization of Bolshevism.[111]

The ills of Soviet society, which both Lenin and Kollontai recognized, contributed still further to their estrangement, since their analyses of the causes and their ideas for the cures were at odds. Recall the problem of bureaucracy. Kollontai blamed alien elements and the Party leaders for abandoning Party democracy. Lenin blamed Russian social conditions that were as yet unripe; historical circumstances had forced the Revolution too early.

108. See Daniels, pp. 29–30, on the antiwar internationalists who joined Lenin.

109. For an example of Lenin's attitude toward legalism, see A. Mikoyan's account of a meeting Lenin held during the Tenth Party Congress—the Congress at which he outlawed factions. At this meeting, Lenin engaged in the very factionalism he was simultaneously declaring outlawed by surreptitiously planning to call together the adherents of his "Platform of the Ten." See Tucker, *Stalin as Revolutionary*, p. 298.

110. Her attitude toward the NEP changed somewhat by the mid-1920's. See Chapter 11.

111. As she did earlier. When Lenin briefly adopted state capitalism, Kollontai quietly opposed. See Sadoul, p. 316.

We are already familiar with Kollontai's radical recommendations to counter bureaucracy. Her suggestions were very much in the heroic tradition of fierce assault: begin with the Party, opening it up to the workers; criticize the sickness at the center, restoring the system to life and vitality.[112]

Lenin recognized toward the end of his life the "vile bureaucratic bog," the "paper swamp," as he called it; but he recommended that to fight against bureaucratism and red tape there be a *"checkup on fulfillment."*[113] Lenin thought not of mass participation from below but of streamlined efficiency. And for that rather elitist purpose he urged that there be formed another committee![114]

To a young Communist (sounding much like Kollontai) who objected that spontaneous activity was possible only if bureaucratic administrative centers were swept away, Lenin responded not as an impatient revolutionary but as a realistic statesman. "The fight against bureaucratism in an utterly worn-out peasant country takes a long time and has to be carried on tenaciously without losing heart at the first setback."[115] The young Communist referred to a famous passage in Engels's *The Peasant War in Germany*: "The worst fate that can befall the leader of an extreme party is the forced necessity to take power at a time when the movement has not yet sufficiently matured to rule the class that it represents and to carry out measures for consolidating its rule." Lenin replied with the suspicious irritation of a revolutionary leader weary of being upbraided by doctrinaire Communists. "Your reference to Engels is to no purpose. Wasn't it some 'intellectual' who prompted you to make it?"[116] It was precisely intellectuals like Kollontai whom youth found appealing, and whom Lenin wanted removed from positions of influence.

I should like in the remainder of this chapter to return to an earlier question that we can now better assess: the relationship of the

---

112. See Kollontai, *Rabochaia oppozitsiia*, p. 44.

113. Italics in original. See Lenin's letter of Jan. 1922 to A. Tsiurupa, who in 1922 replaced Stalin as Commissar of the Workers' and Peasants' Inspection, an organ Lenin conceived as a force for popular control over the bureaucratic apparatus. *Sochineniia* (4th ed.), vol. 35, pp. 459–61.

114. He proposed "a very small (four to six people) apparatus consisting of highly experienced and tested assistants (an office manager, his assistants, a secretary, etc.)." *Ibid.*, p. 459.

115. This letter of May 1921 was to M. F. Sokolov. See *ibid.*, pp. 418–20.

116. *Ibid.*, p. 419.

Communist leadership to the women in the Party. In a previous chapter, I asked how the Party treated criticism when it came from a woman in the leadership. The circumstances and decisions surrounding Kollontai's appeal to the Comintern make the answer obvious. When she became a threat and a leader in her own right, the Bolsheviks treated a woman no differently from a man, meting out the same punishments—mainly the loss of Party positions, and if the provocation seemed irritating enough, diplomatic "exile." The ranks of Soviet diplomats swelled in the early 1920's with Communist troublemakers.[117] By charging Kollontai with leading a faction, the Party officially recognized her dominant position. For tactical reasons, Kollontai denied at the Eleventh Congress that she was a leader, but she saw herself as one, we know. A few years later this would be clear when Kollontai wrote to Fredrik Ström, recalling in a proconsular sort of way what she and Comrade Shliapnikov were fighting for in 1921.[118]

The situation of a woman who achieved power in Bolshevik ranks and then lost it had no real precedent. The closest parallel to Kollontai was Angelica Balabanoff, who in recognition of her popular status in internationalist ranks served briefly as the first Secretary of the Comintern. We recall Zinoviev's efforts to send her away from Moscow on specious missions, lest she embarrass the Party before foreign visitors by speaking about internal Communist repression. Kollontai and Balabanoff were removed not because they were women, but because they insisted on violating party discipline.

Ultimately, Kollontai's experiences as a leader of the Workers' Opposition and as its defender before the Comintern may not provide an entirely useful model to enlighten us about the role of women in the Communist Party. Like the queens and princesses of history, she was an exception. Most Bolshevik women found their roles becoming increasingly less significant as the Communist system grew stronger. Moreover, Kollontai was almost alone in pursuing leadership beyond the ranks of the women's movement.[119]

117. See Souvarine, pp. 328–29, and Chapter 12 below. Shliapnikov notes that after the Tenth Congress all those who supported the Workers' Opposition were removed from their posts—"kicked out" or transferred. Shliapnikov, "Nashi raznoglasiia," in Zorkii, p. 146.

118. Kollontai to Ström, undated letter, Univ. of Gothenburg Library.

119. Ironically, the existence of the Zhenotdel may have been partly responsible for the circumscribed roles and relatively low status of Bolshevik women. It served as a

The relatively low status of women in the Party has been explained in several ways. One theory, which may be approached cautiously, holds that an already authoritarian revolutionary movement grows even more rigid and exclusive after coming to power. The men, as a result of their military conquest, gain a heightened sense of their own masculine power and are not likely to share it with women—even with women comrades from the underground. Applied to Bolshevism after 1918, this theory is plausible. The era of War Communism, or the "heroic period of the Great Russian Revolution,"[120] impressed on Bolshevism a new spirit or culture. Kollontai (as well as Osinskii) spoke of a militarization of Party life. "The political culture of the movement," Robert Tucker has written, "underwent a certain militarization and grew more authoritarian."[121] In these changed circumstances, most Bolshevik women suffered a decline in status. Consider the women who were active Bolsheviks before 1917, distinguished heroines of the revolutionary era: Armand, Bosh, Kollontai, Krupskaia, Rozmirovich, Samoilova, Stasova, and Iakovleva.[122] Two, Inessa and Samoilova, died early. The others found their status as revolutionary activists diminished. Not one of them ever sat on the Politburo. Only Kollontai, Stasova, and Iakovleva ever served on the Central Committee during the initial Soviet period, and Iakovleva was only a candidate member. Elena Stasova was a prominent example of a woman who lost stature. Elected to the Central Committee in 1912, in 1917, and again in 1919, she was then dropped. Krupskaia was another woman who played a politically significant role prior to the Revolution. But her prerevolutionary position as Secretary of the Bolshevik Party did not become powerful until it was taken from her after the Revolution. Its increase in importance was due partly to the successful Revolution, but it was not her immediate successor, Elena Stasova, who made it a power base. Iakov Sverdlov began the

---

convenient, out-of-the-way place to assign them. Paradoxically, it also served as an irritant to Communist men. See Chapter 9.

120. This was Kritsman's title for his book on War Communism. For the theory of the heightened sense of power gained by men in a revolution and their reluctance to share the newly won power with women, see Gregory J. Massell, "The Limits of Sexual Equality in the Soviet System," paper prepared for the Conference on Women in Russia, Stanford University, May 1975. Prior to the Revolution, when the Party was smaller and weaker, women played a greater role.

121. See Tucker, *Stalin as Revolutionary*, p. 208.

122. Of 248 people singled out as eminent persons in the revolutionary era to be included in *Deiateli SSSR i Oktiabr'skoi Revoliutsii*, only eight were women. See R. McNeal, "Women in the Russian Radical Movement," p. 160.

process. Stalin completed it.[123] Once it became a position of power, the Party Secretaryship remained a man's role.

When it came to choosing Central Committee members Evgeniia Bosh was overlooked, although she was surely deserving. Bosh has been described as "one of Bolshevism's greatest personalities." A "forgotten woman," Solzhenitsyn has called her. Before the Revolution she had edited *Kommunist'*, with Bukharin and Piatakov. Later she was a heroine of the Civil War in the Ukraine, where with Piatakov she headed the first Soviet government. She directed Soviet organization and the resistance to the German invasion. In 1918, she was entrusted by the Central Committee and the Cheka as well with the fate of Penza province. A gifted woman, her book *A Year of Struggle: The Struggle for the Regime in the Ukraine* has been called by Victor Serge a remarkable contribution to the history of the Civil War.[124] Bosh joined the Trotskyist opposition in 1923. A year later, after its defeat, exhausted and ill, condemned to inactivity, depressed over the failure of workers' democracy and the divisions within the Party, she shot herself. The Bolsheviks held no national funeral for this militant Oppositionist. No urn was placed in the Kremlin wall, although some of her comrades believed she had earned the distinction. Preobrazhenskii objected to the Communists' failure to honor properly one of the Revolution's great figures, but he was overruled.[125]

Elena Rozmirovich and Evgeniia Bosh were sisters. Although not a heroine of her sister's stature, Elena Rozmirovich was an important Bolshevik who deserved greater political recognition than she later received. Rozmirovich was accustomed to making a political contribution, and before the Revolution her views had been respected. Secretary of the Bolshevik fraction in the Fourth State Duma, she was ultimately forced to emigrate to Western Europe, where she played a theoretical role in Bolshevik politics. In late 1914, Rozmirovich and two other young Bolsheviks living in the village of Baugy near Lausanne (Krylenko and Aleksandr Troianovskii, her husband) became

123. Krupskaia was elected only once to the Central Committee, in 1934, when she was already an old woman. See Appendix II, "Composition of the Chief Party Organs," in Daniels, pp. 422–33.

124. For Bosh, see Serge, pp. 194–95, and V. Serge, *Year One of the Russian Revolution*, trans. Peter Sedgwick (New York, 1972), p. 389. The Russian title of Bosh's book is *God bor'by: Bor'ba za vlast po Ukraine* (Moscow, 1925). Solzhenitsyn's comment on Bosh is in A. Solzhenitsyn, *The Gulag Archipelago, 1918–1956*, trans. T. P. Whitney (New York, 1975), vol. 2, p. 17.

125. See Serge, pp. 194–95. On Bosh's death, see Deutscher, *The Prophet Unarmed*, vol. 2, p. 383, and Souvarine, p. 334. For memorial article, see E. Preobrazhenskii, "Evgeniia Bogdanovna Bosh," *Proletarskaia Revoliutsiia*, vol. 5 (37), no. 2 (1925).

friendly with Bukharin. Rozmirovich, Krylenko, and Bukharin formed a loose political alliance, which became known informally as the Baugy group. The three decided to publish and edit their own newspaper, *Zvezda* (*The Star*), a decision Lenin resented since he regarded *Zvezda* as a potential rival. In 1917, Rozmirovich was a member of the Military Bureau in Petrograd, a subordinate organ of the Bolshevik Central Committee. She conducted propaganda among the soldiers of the Petrograd garrison, edited the newspaper *Soldatskaia Pravda*, and later served on the Central Control Commission.[126] Bukharin and Krylenko, the other members of the old Baugy group, continued in vital political roles—Bukharin as editor of *Pravda* and member of the Politburo, Krylenko as head of the Commissariat of Justice. Elena Rozmirovich became an administrator of the Lenin Library.

To the interesting theory that Bolshevik women lost status largely because men were reluctant to share their newly won power with them can be added another observation. A French socialist, criticizing her own party, noted that though in theory women were accepted as equals in socialist parties, in practice only the woman who came in company with her husband, father, or brother was received without objection.[127] Bolshevik women usually had a male mentor. Inessa Armand followed Lenin, as Stasova looked to Sverdlov. Lilina was the wife of Zinoviev. Bosh was married to Piatakov. Iakovleva was the wife of I. N. Smirnov and the sister of the revolutionary Nikolai Iakovlev. Rozmirovich was married to Troianovskii. Vera and Liudmila Menzhinskaia were the sisters of Viacheslav Menzhinskii, successor to Felix Dzerzhinskii as head of the secret police. Sof'ia Smidovich was married to Petr Smidovich, an Old Bolshevik who was president of the Moscow Soviet in 1918. Though it was true that a Bolshevik was unlikely to marry outside of his or her political circle, invariably the wives and sisters of prominent Bolshevik men occupied minor roles.

Communists themselves mentioned that the notable Bolshevik woman usually had a male mentor. Thus the heroine of Anatolii Glebov's play *Inga*, a Communist intellectual and factory manager

126. On Rozmirovich, see the autobiographical sketch in *Deiateli SSSR*, and Gankin and Fischer, p. 805. On Troianovskii, who was later Soviet ambassador to Japan and the United States, see Nicolaevsky, p. 12. On the Baugy group, see also Cohen, *Bukharin*, pp. 22–23, and Krupskaia, *Vospominaniia o Lenine*, pp. 239–40.

127. The Party was reluctant to accept a woman who came on her own account. M. J. Boxer, "Socialism Faces Feminism: The Failure of Synthesis in France, 1879–1914," in Boxer and Quataert, eds., p. 102.

described as the equal or superior of any man around her, was regarded by Communists as a curiosity. An explanation had to be found for her prominence. The Old Bolshevik Somov recognized that it was not customary for a woman to attain her managerial position. He understood how it happened. "I admire Inga. I like her decisiveness, her firmness. . . . But, after all, she is—how shall I put it?—a laboratory product. She had to have a father exiled abroad—a remarkable Bolshevik! . . . You won't find many like Inga."[128]

Kollontai and Balabanoff were unusual. Not only did they lack a male mentor, they were also among the few Communist women who achieved eminence in areas unrelated to the socialist women's movement.[129] We may find an explanation for their high status in another similarity that linked them, one that was hardly tangible, but that contributed nevertheless to their achievement in Communist ranks: Kollontai and Balabanoff did not simply feel equal, they believed themselves to be superior. We recall that in Kollontai's *Workers' Opposition* she disparaged Bolshevik leaders for an insufficient understanding of the working class and chided her oppositionist comrades for obtuseness on the theoretical level. Whereas Kollontai may have come to regard herself by 1921 as superior intellectually, Balabanoff saw her own superiority in moral terms. When she refused Zetkin's appeal that she remain in Moscow, Balabanoff congratulated herself. "Had I yielded to pressure . . . my life would be quite different from what it is, but I would have missed the greatest satisfaction of my life —the knowledge that I have been strong enough to swim against the stream." Again, when she said goodbye to Lenin: "If you think I have done good work, I have merely done my duty; if you think I have done better than others, again, I have done nothing more than my duty. You cannot give me what I desire. I would like to have the moral and political possibility to remain in the country of the Revolution."[130] A slim, small woman with dark braids framing her face, she was beginning to age, but she remained the eager militant insisting on living like a poor student. Reflecting later on her choice to leave Russia rather than compromise her socialist principles, Balabanoff concluded: "It gives me immense joy to be able to appear as I

128. Glebov, p. 263.
129. Nikolaeva and Artiukhina, one a Zinovievite, the other a Bukharinite, each served as director of the Zhenotdel. Each also served briefly on the Central Committee. See Daniels, pp. 422–33.
130. Balabanoff, *My Life as a Rebel*, p. 290, and *Impressions of Lenin*, pp. 151–52.

am, with a clear conscience; it is a piece of luck for which I envy myself."[131]

The self-righteousness and self-esteem of these two women were irritating, no doubt, but it would not have been possible for women of greater humility to challenge the Bolshevik leadership. A humble Kollontai could not have gone over the head of the Central Committee to deliver the appeal to the Comintern, any more than she could have fought for her right to remain in the Party. The conclusion is inescapable and remarkably commonplace. Even in Soviet Russia, among men schooled on Herzen, Chernyshevskii, Bebel, and Engels, to become fully equal a Communist woman needed to feel superior.

131. Balabanoff, *Impressions of Lenin*, p. 152. The description of Balabanoff is from Serge, pp. 105, 184–85.

CHAPTER NINE

The Zhenotdel During the NEP

WHEN she protested to the Comintern against the NEP in the summer of 1921, Kollontai did not include the cause of the Women's Section in her appeal. Perhaps she did not want to cloud her argument by introducing an unpopular issue. Elsewhere, Kollontai sharply criticized the ways in which the NEP adversely affected the Zhenotdel.[1] Indeed, during the months that remained between the loss of her Zhenotdel directorship in the winter of 1922 and her enforced departure from Moscow the following autumn, Kollontai became absorbed in a depressing sort of way with the negative relationship of the NEP to the woman question.

Kollontai and Sof'ia Smidovich, her successor as director of the Zhenotdel, watched in dismay as funds for social experiments were withdrawn by the central government. The social revolution begun under War Communism, which featured labor obligation, children's homes, and public dining rooms, instead of developing receded into the nostalgia associated with the great heroic era. The Zhenotdel would limp through the 1920's, the successive directors after Kollontai presiding over an institution that refused to die but that could not grow. Yet it is important to understand that although Kollontai did, with good cause, blame the NEP for undermining the mission of the Zhenotdel, the NEP was not ultimately responsible for the failure of that institution to thrive and to achieve the integration of women into Soviet political and economic life. As this chapter will show, during neither the War Communism years nor the relatively more relaxed era that followed the onset of the NEP did the several elements of Soviet society approve of the intrusion of the Women's Section into their lives. Within Soviet society, in the village and the factory, in the trade union and the local Party organization, the Zhenotdel met opposition. Even the central government was indifferent in practice,

---

1. See in Kollontai's final lecture at Sverdlov University her references to a joyless depression and to the suspension of the Zhenotdel's ability to construct new forms. *Polozhenie zhenshchiny*, p. 199. For the Central Committee's recognition of the problem and official pledges to support the Zhenotdel, see "O rabote zhenotdelov v sviazi s novoi ekonomicheskoi politikoi," decision of TsKRKP, Nov. 22, 1921, USSR, [16], vol. 2, p. 204.

if not in theory, to its future, although the Zhenotdel was a section of the Central Committee. It is to this last problem that we turn first.

Because Kollontai lost her post as director of the Zhenotdel in February 1922 and was fighting to remain in the Party, she did not figure prominently in the struggle over the Zhenotdel waged at the Eleventh Congress. When the Party assembled in March, Sof'ia Smidovich, the new director, and Viktor Nogin, another Old Bolshevik who had been a speaker at the historic Congress of Worker and Peasant Women in November 1918, brought the dismal situation of the Women's Section before the Party. Nogin, a moderate who in 1917 had warned of the political terror that would result if the Bolsheviks established a one-party government, now reported on behalf of the watchdog Central Revision Commission.[2] He criticized the Party's condescending attitude toward the Zhenotdel, calling it an "unhealthy" one designed to cause Zhenotdel members to feel unequal. Nogin provided vignettes that revealed the Women's Section's peculiar status: at one meeting of the Orgburo the representatives of all the sections of the Central Committee but the Zhenotdel were present; at another, the director of the Zhenotdel brought up a business matter, was allowed to ask one question, and then was told to wait outside before she could raise another. These were but a few of the indignities that seemed intended to demean the Women's Section. He could describe more; something had to be done.[3]

Sof'ia Smidovich agreed. Zhenotdel women were not treated as equals. But if they were regarded as of "second rank" at the Party center, things were worse at the local levels.[4] The few qualified workers the center assigned to the provincial sections were scorned by Party comrades because of the "unimportant" nature of their work. Smidovich believed that Zhenotdel methods for reaching non-Party women had proved effective and would be more so—particularly among peasant women—if given increased Party support. Instead, despite official resolutions to the contrary, the Party showed little in-

2. See USSR, [8], p. 67. The Central Revision Commission was an elected Party body with three members. It inspected the way business was handled in the central Party bodies. See USSR, [6], vol. 1, pp. 639–40.

3. See Nogin's report, USSR, [8], p. 67. A significant indication of the Zhenotdel's secondary status was the separation of its headquarters, located in a Moscow flat, from those of the Central Committee in the Kremlin. See Stites, "Zhenotdel," p. 182.

4. See USSR, [8], pp. 456–58, for Smidovich's report. For confirmation of Smidovich's view of conditions at the local levels, see Kollontai, Otchet, pp. 4–5.

terest in supporting even the invaluable delegate's conferences. Indeed, at the local levels the Women's Sections were regarded as so unimportant that one might occasionally be liquidated, its work amalgamated with general propaganda and agitation.[5]

As early as 1920, its leaders protested suggestions that the Zhenotdel be abolished and its tasks distributed among Party agitational sections (known in the Communist jargon of the day as "Agit-Prop"). Konkordiia Samoilova argued at the time that it was senseless, when the Zhenotdel's work was yielding tangible results, to speak of the organization ending. The outcome could only be negative. Zhenotdel reports for the year 1921 indicated that in provinces where a Women's Section did lose its fight for the right to an independent existence, and where its organization was turned into a subsection of the Agit-Prop, such subordination did not result in closer merging of the central Zhenotdel with general Party work. The Agit-Prop sections did not bring anything new into the work among women; in fact, they were little interested in it. The result was simply that the central Zhenotdel was even more isolated from Party activity.[6] Zhenotdel reports contained depressing examples of provincial committees ordering Zhenotdel workers out on other assignments, and even prohibiting agitational campaigns in connection with the reelection of delegatki.[7]

By the beginning of 1922, Kommunistka reported fears at the Fourth All-Russian Meeting of Guberniia directors that the Zhenotdel might be liquidated. Although a representative sent by the Central Committee, L. Sosnovskii, the head of the Central Committee's Agit-Prop department and the editor of Bednota, assured the directors that the Party relied on their work among proletarian and peasant women, the Zhenotdel remained unconvinced.[8] Its members knew that Kollontai had had to defend it against charges that it was divisive —seeking by means of "feminist" activities to split the working class.[9] How often had she explained that, on the contrary, the Zhenotdel brought worker and peasant women "into the general proletarian struggle." The institution had its staunch advocates, but they had

5. Smidovich to the Eleventh Congress, USSR, [8], pp. 456–58. Also see Kollontai, "Ne uprazdnenie, a ukreplenie," pp. 25–27.
6. See Samoilova, "Organizatsionnye zadachi," p. 27.
7. See USSR, [9], pp. 18–19.
8. For Sosnovskii, see "Itogi 4-go vserossiiskogo soveshchaniia zavgubzhenotdelami," Kommunistka, 1922, no. 1(18), p. 2.
9. Itkina, p. 201.

become fewer. In its first two and a half years the Zhenotdel lost some of its best friends: Iakov Sverdlov died in 1919, followed by Inessa Armand in 1920 and Konkordiia Samoilova in 1921.[10] A shaky institution could ill afford to lose supporters. So invaluable had Sverdlov's aid become that, upon his death in 1919, Kollontai wrote an emotional essay telling Russia's working women that with the death of Sverdlov they lost a comrade who really understood the need to work among women, to raise their class consciousness, and to organize them for political activity. Sverdlov's death, though a sad loss to the entire Party, meant special grief for the newly developing women's movement.[11]

With Sverdlov gone, the Zhenotdel could and did still turn to Lenin and to Trotsky. Anecdotes abound about how Lenin helped. Trotsky too was generous. We have Kollontai's testimony that Trotsky, "although he was overburdened with military tasks," unfailingly and gladly appeared at Zhenotdel-sponsored conferences.[12] Still, sacrifices of personal time on the part of a few leading men did not mean long-range government or Party commitment. What success the Zhenotdel was to have would ultimately depend not on the help of a few key individuals in the Central Committee, but on the Women's Section's relationship to the Party as a whole and to the Soviet organs of government.[13] Precisely in these areas the Zhenotdel was most severely rejected.

Out of this unhappy background, Sof'ia Smidovich, a brusque and practical woman, gave the Party a choice at the Eleventh Congress that Kollontai would not have offered: if the Zhenotdel was necessary, then the Party must provide it with more trained workers both for the provinces and for the central apparatus, who would try to counteract the lack of local support; if not, it would be better to liquidate

10. For Samoilova's biography, see V. Morozova, "Kompas u Kazhdogo Svoi," in Zhak and Itkina, eds., pp. 398–413. Samoilova's husband, a revolutionary lawyer named Samoilov with whom she had lived since 1905, died in 1918 in Astrakhan where he had been sent by the Party to stock bread for Petrograd. *Ibid.*, p. 413.

11. See *Izbrannye stat'i i rechi*, pp. 266–67, and Vinogradskaia, *Sobytiia i pamiatnye vstrechi*, pp. 164–87, for another appreciation of Sverdlov.

12. See Kollontai, *Autobiography*, p. 42, for Trotsky's help. The young Zhenotdel worker Roza Kovnator recalled a meeting of worker and peasant women in Moscow in the winter of 1921 when Lenin arrived very late and spoke despite his preoccupation with a deteriorating economy, a hostile peasantry, and the Workers' Opposition movement. Afterwards, Kovnator told Lenin's sister Mariia how much it meant both to the audience and to the Zhenotdel that Lenin came. Mariia glumly replied that she knew they valued Lenin's appearance but that her brother was exhausted. See Zhak and Itkina, eds., p. 492.

13. For this awareness within the Zhenotdel, see USSR, [9], p. 10.

the local sections than to allow them to drag out their miserable existence.[14] Some members of the Zhenotdel believed that a little progress was better than none. Smidovich evidently disagreed.

Kollontai and Smidovich shared a similar outrage at the Central Committee's lack of commitment to the Zhenotdel, which was one of its own sections. But Kollontai's attachment to the institution was too deep for her to contemplate failure, although she knew before she assumed the directorship in 1920 that the Party had considered abolishing the Zhenotdel.[15] We know that Kollontai's directorship was taken from her in 1922 as a political punishment. It is difficult to imagine her leaving by choice. Smidovich, on the other hand, presumably did leave by choice after two years, moving on to the more prestigious and formidable Central Control Commission.

It fell to Molotov at the Eleventh Party Congress to express in a few laconic words the Party's attitude toward the Zhenotdel. Commenting in his capacity as secretary of the Central Committee, Molotov did not speak to the substance of the problem, lack of Party support. Nor did he refer to the obstacles the Zhenotdel met on a daily basis. Instead, he remarked that the Women's Section had gone through a difficult time in which it lacked real leadership. The problem, he implied, lay not in the poor attitude of the Central Committee but within the organization. Perhaps a more competent director . . . ? Kollontai was a convenient scapegoat, since she was already under attack. The Eleventh Congress, we recall, was considering expelling her from the Party for her leadership in the Workers' Opposition.[16] Molotov revealed more than a lack of appreciation of Kollontai's work: in retrospect, his words were a gloomy portent, an indication that the Central Committee was not going to alter its negative attitude. Thus the Party's pledge at the Eleventh Congress to end the liquidationist attitude toward the Women's Section, and henceforth to strengthen the organization, meant little.[17] Party attitudes did not change; moreover, as Kollontai feared, the NEP caused the future of the Zhenotdel to appear more uncertain. One immediate effect, for example, was reduced government investment in childcare.

14. See Smidovich, USSR, [8], pp. 457–58. For Party reluctance to give the Zhenotdel the required people, see Vinogradskaia, "Itogi III-go vserossiiskogo soveshch. zavgubotdelov po rabote sredi zhenshchin," p. 4.
15. Samoilova indicated as much in an eloquent defense of the work of the Zhenotdel in "Organizatsionnye zadachi," p. 27.
16. See Molotov's remarks, USSR, [8], p. 58. For a sense of Kollontai's direction of the Zhenotdel, see her Otchet, pp. 1–16, and USSR, [9].
17. For this pledge, see USSR, [8], p. 558.

The number of factory day-nurseries and homes for mothers and infants fell sharply.[18] A resolution offered at a conference on women spoke of the NEP's "catastrophic effect" on the work being done among mothers, and articles in *Kommunistka* reflected the alarm among workers in social institutions like nurseries. Under the NEP these women did not know how much longer their institutions would exist.[19]

Need for these institutions would not abate. During the 1920's, homeless children were described as Russia's "greatest evil" and "a living reproach to our conscience." Official figures admitted to seven, eight, perhaps nine million abandoned children, living by begging and stealing, the older ones by prostitution and crime. Krupskaia blamed the problem not on misery and lack of concern, as in the old days, but on unemployment and the extreme poverty of the peasants.[20] The Communists were not entirely responsible for either situation, but only they could provide the social remedies.

Kollontai, on behalf of the Zhenotdel, spoke boldly to the International Communist Women's Conference against postponing the social revolution. Any postponement hurt the liberation of women.[21] She sounded optimistic, yet she could not ignore the direction of Soviet policy after the summer of 1921. She was particularly reluctant to recognize the fate under the NEP of obligatory labor, the cornerstone of her image of women's liberation. There was no reason for Kollontai to have assumed earlier, at the Tenth Party Congress, that Lenin's announcement of an end to requisitioning grain from the peasants spelled the doom of labor conscription. Trotsky, at that time, insisted that militarization of labor, as he called it, was not affected by a tax in kind and that his labor policies were independent of War Communism.[22] The Platform of the Ten, the program that Lenin's group presented at the Congress, reassured Kollontai and

18. In 1922 the number of homes had increased owing to the famine. Their numbers dropped when the central government withdrew support under the NEP. In 1924 the Department of Motherhood and Infancy began farming children out to private homes despite protests that it was a step backward ideologically. The mortality rate was cut in half. Smith, pp. 177–78.

19. See Smidovich, "O novom kodekse," p. 47, and Smidovich, "Nashi zadachi," pp. 18–20. Also see V. Moirova, "Obshchestvennoe pitanie i byt rabochei sem'i," *Kommunistka*, 1926, no. 10–11, p. 45, and a report of a local Zhenotdel directors' meeting in which the negative effect of the NEP on their work was discussed. "Itogi 4-go vserossiiskogo soveshchaniia zavgubzhenotdelami," *Kommunistka*, 1922, no. 1(18), pp. 2–3.

20. Souvarine, pp. 420–21.

21. Kollontai, *Rabotnitsa i krest'ianka*, p. 42. See *Izbrannye stat'i i rechi*, p. 352, for a reprint of Kollontai's article in *Pravda* of Nov. 13, 1921, and her resistance to any government attempt to back away from its commitment to solving the woman question.

22. See Deutscher, *The Prophet Armed*, vol. 1, p. 497.

Trotsky that labor conscription would continue. One role of the trade unions as stipulated in that platform was to carry out decrees on different compulsory labor obligations.[23]

For several months after the Tenth Party Congress, compulsory labor laws remained intact.[24] Yet events soon showed that labor conscription as a Communist institution was drawing to a close—if for no other reason than that compulsory labor laws were incompatible with a revival of free enterprise. Large-scale industry remained in the hands of the state but was being decentralized administratively and split into a number of trusts, which were ordered to operate on principles of cost accounting preparatory to entering the market on a competitive basis. The trusts thereby gained the right to hire and fire. The centralized state machinery that had mobilized and allocated labor on a national scale was becoming irrelevant in a market economy.[25]

In April 1921, a decree removed the main restrictions on the movement of workers from one job to another. The measure took effect slowly, its results only gradually becoming apparent through the summer and autumn of 1921.[26] In June and July, with orders being issued that still spoke in terms of labor service, there was no reason for Kollontai, preparing her report to the Second International Conference of Communist Women and praising labor conscription, to think that compulsory labor had ended.[27] But by November 1921, when further decrees were issued limiting the categories of persons liable to being called up for labor service and limiting service itself to natural emergencies, even the most committed believer should have recognized that labor conscription was being halted with the end of the Civil War. The director of the Zhenotdel was one of the last to capitulate. An article in *Kommunistka* in November 1921 suggests that Kollontai was still not accepting the demise of obligatory labor.[28] A further decree was required in February 1922 before labor conscription as practiced under War Communism ended.[29] A year after

23. Kollontai, *Rabochaia oppozitsiia*, p. 26.

24. Bunyan, pp. 261, 265.

25. *Ibid.*, p. 266.

26. Carr, *The Bolshevik Revolution*, vol. 2, p. 317.

27. For the continuation of orders speaking in terms of labor service, see *ibid.*, p. 318. For Kollontai's praise of labor conscription at the International Women's Conference, see *Rabotnitsa i krest'ianka*, p. 41.

28. Kollontai, "Proizvodstvo i byt," pp. 7–8.

29. See Carr, *The Bolshevik Revolution*, vol. 2, pp. 317–18, on the end of labor conscription.

the promulgation of the tax in kind that ushered in the NEP, compulsory labor legislation had essentially been revoked.

One Old Bolshevik, formerly a leading exponent of War Communism, offered an apologetic view of what seemed his own past folly. Bukharin saw the transition to the New Economic Policy in 1921 as the "collapse of our *illusions*."[30] Kollontai, on the other hand, continued to defend practices now being abandoned: labor conscription, public feeding, ration books, and wages in kind instead of money.[31] Long after the demise of War Communism, she persisted in believing in its basic notion: that through enthusiasm and compulsion the Bolsheviks could, in a short time, change the economic system of Russia and begin seriously to alter patterns of thinking. She resisted—because she knew it to be untrue—the notion Bolsheviks tried later to advance that only a few romantic dreamers had seen War Communism as a direct road to socialism.[32] The collectivist policies Bukharin called "illusions" seemed to her still in the early 1920's what Lenin once called "a final stable form," whereas the NEP appeared a bitter betrayal.[33]

Kollontai knew that the harshness of daily life eased a little after Lenin inaugurated the NEP. For the peasants, it meant an end to the hated requisitioning; for urban workers, it meant the legal right to go freely into the countryside to buy food. Trade between city and village revived. Although for most Russians the NEP was blunting the edge of discontent, in the Zhenotdel the NEP was causing despair. By the autumn of 1922, with the return of a free economy, women were losing their jobs. Seventy percent of the initial cutbacks involved women, and Kollontai feared that the Soviet Union had fallen into a grim depression.[34] She was convinced that for women disaster had occurred. If War Communism and its policies of labor conscription had been the great breakthrough, the NEP and its resultant unemployment was the "new threat."[35]

30. Bukharin as cited in Cohen, *Bukharin*, p. 139 (italics in original).

31. Kollontai, *Polozhenie zhenshchiny*, pp. 166–67.

32. Victor Serge recalled that War Communism during its lifetime was simply called Communism, "and anyone who, like myself, went so far as to consider it purely temporary was looked upon with disdain." Serge, p. 115.

33. Lenin's remark in 1919 is quoted in Cohen, *Bukharin*, p. 87.

34. See *Polozhenie zhenshchiny*, p. 199. Under NEP cutbacks, women were the first to be discharged. Women metalworkers decreased from 15 percent in 1920 to 12.1 percent in 1923 and to 9.2 percent in 1926. In the textile industry the cut was less sharp—from 63.9 percent in 1920 to 59 percent in 1926. See Serebrennikov, p. 52.

35. The expression was Kollontai's and she publicized it in *Kommunistka*. See "Novaia ugroza," p. 6.

Kollontai understood an important point, that unemployment, like work, was a force with effects. By removing women from the labor market, the NEP was throwing her back into the domestic slavery from which the Revolution had recently begun to liberate her. A year earlier the Revolution had been making progress toward affirming the principle of equality between the sexes. The "new woman"—working, becoming economically independent of a man—was developing an inner freedom that would make her the envy of even the most comfortable beneficiary of family life.[36] Soviet literature provided examples. In Glebov's play *Inga*, Veronica, a pampered wife, laments to the female Communist factory manager, "Oh, how I envy you! You are so talented, so energetic! And most important of all, how you burn with your work!"[37]

Women were learning, if slowly, to depend on themselves, understanding that they could not count on a man for support when at any moment he might be mobilized for the front or called on for Party work. Kollontai had no illusions, however, about the reality that faced most women even before the NEP. The vast majority in 1921 were dependent, their earnings a small portion of the family budget. The Zhenotdel seemed the only Communist group truly concerned that an equal right to work was not equality and that economic independence for women was a "paper slogan."[38] Despite the Communist conception of women's equality, despite the pledges made at Party congresses to draw them into the economy, the regime was failing to protect women from traditional discrimination during periods of unemployment. In the autumn of 1922, women who were being thrown out of jobs had two choices: prostitution, or the search for a husband as a means of support. Just as she refused to distinguish between the prostitute and the legal wife who shirked labor obligation, Kollontai sympathized with unemployed women who were turning to the streets.[39] The NEP meant that women were again doomed to relate to men from the viewpoint of material advantage, and men, sensing the revival of dependency on the part of women, would soon return to the ideal of the bourgeois family. If women were losing their

36. *Ibid.*, p. 6.
37. See *Inga* in Glebov, pp. 234–35.
38. See Smith, p. 26, for the continuation of this downward trend. The average pay of women in all industries at the end of 1926 was 41.7 rubles a month, that of men, 60 rubles. For "paper slogan," see Kollontai, "Proizvodstvo i byt," p. 8. Also see *Polozhenie zhenshchiny*, p. 159.
39. See Kollontai, "Sestry," pp. 23–26.

jobs, if their strength in the work force was ceasing to be considered by the economic organs of the state, how could they be "comrades"? How could there be speeches about the equality of women in marriage and the family?[40]

Here and there official concern was shown for unemployed women. The Commissariat of Labor issued an order in February 1922 prohibiting the dismissal of unmarried pregnant women without permission of the Labor Inspection.[41] Women and men were to be treated on an equal basis, but mothers with children below the age of one were to be given preference.[42] This kind of measure, undertaken by the trade unions or the Commissariat of Labor to safeguard women's jobs, proved insufficient. There were too many unemployed men, many of them demobilized soldiers, whom the conservative business managers of state enterprises usually preferred to hire.[43]

When it came to the woman question, Party decrees served more as apologies for what was not being done than as guides to action. Thus a Party resolution of 1924 insisted that "the preservation of female labor power in industry is of political significance" and directed Party organs to take appropriate measures.[44] In the milieu of the NEP, the decree meant little. The NEP hindered the Zhenotdel not only by increasing female unemployment but by making it unlikely that women would be able to improve their skills or upgrade their

40. Kollontai, "Novaia ugroza," p. 6.

41. See Sobranie zakonov 1922, no. 18, art. 203, quoted in Grunfeld, p. 28.

42. See Dodge, p. 60. This same decree provided that unmarried women and mothers of small children were not to be deprived of any housing that went with the terminated job or any kindergarten privileges until they had found new work. An unemployment problem had briefly arisen earlier when the end of Russia's participation in the war resulted in women being turned out of their jobs in favor of returning veterans. Kingsbury and Fairchild, p. 84. Many factory committees and trade unions in 1918 were allowing women to be dismissed. Thus in Apr. 1918, the Petrograd Council of Trade Unions and Factory Committees insisted that dismissal should be based on need rather than sex with special preference given to unsupported women with babies. See Smith, pp. 16–17, for trade-union decrees opposing the firing of women to provide jobs for men.

43. For preference given to men despite official policy, see Serebrennikov, p. 58. Another ominous trend, from the point of view of Kollontai's longtime efforts to safeguard the health of the working mother, was signaled by the attack on protective legislation as a cause for female unemployment. In Nov. 1924, Commissar of Labor V. Schmidt spoke at the All-Russian Trade Union Convention of the need to revise protective laws such as those dealing with night work so as to facilitate the employment of women. See Grunfeld, p. 28. We recall that Kollontai regarded feminist slogans of equality at work as meaningless: the socialist emphasized not "equality of rights," but the expedient use of woman power to protect women's health as mothers as well as workers. Polozhenie zhenshchiny, p. 206.

44. See USSR, [6], vol. 2, p. 89.

work qualifications. This key problem, which Kollontai identified even before the start of the NEP, was now intensifying.[45]

During the War Communism era, Kollontai illustrated lectures with charts showing the relative wages of men and women workers in various branches of industry. In all areas the men earned more.[46] In Soviet Russia women were customarily unqualified, untrained workers. Unless sufficient technical and professional training for women were provided, the principle of "equal wages for equal work" proudly announced by the workers' republic would remain an empty slogan.[47]

There were other reasons why the training and the wages of women lagged. Until there was collectivization of the household, women would have neither time nor energy to learn new skills.[48] The more energy women had to waste on nonproductive household chores, the less they would have for factories and shops.[49] Communist women alarmed by the dismal outlook for women's employment sought during the early NEP years to warn Party leaders. Varvara Iakovleva, writing in *Kommunistka* in 1923, pointed out that the training courses for women that did exist were being cut under the NEP almost to the point of elimination. As a result, the level of work for which women were qualified might actually fall. Iakovleva urged the

45. See *Polozhenie zhenshchiny*, p. 159. Kollontai also publicized the issue in *Pravda*. See *Izbrannye stat'i i rechi*, p. 321, for a reprint of "Profsoiuzy i rabotnitsa," *Pravda*, May 22, 1921.

46. According to tables she provided for the end of 1920, in the tobacco industry women's wages were about 58 percent those of men, in the textile industry 60 percent, in the paper industry about 46 percent, and in the sewing industry 86 percent. See *Polozhenie zhenshchiny*, p. 209.

47. See *ibid.*, p. 159. Observers reported that women, on one pretext or another, were put in a lower category even when they were doing the same work as men. Many men, particularly in the villages, refused to work for the same wages as women. See Smith, p. 26. For similar observations, see Souvarine, p. 419.

48. Kollontai, "Proizvodstvo i byt," p. 7.

49. *Ibid.*, p. 7. The Zhenotdel also got no government cooperation in its efforts to upgrade women's skills. The *praktikantstvo* (apprenticeship) system, devised as an administrative training program, was not popular. Government agencies, trade unions, Soviets, and other organs, whose personnel were already overworked, were reluctant to devote time to the political and technical training of inexperienced *delegatki* assigned to them. See Carol Hayden, "The Bolshevik Party and Work Among Women, 1917–1925" (paper presented to the Conference on Women in Russia, Stanford University, May 1975), p. 13. See P. Vinogradskaia, "Itogi III-go Vserossiiskogo soveshch. zavgubotdelov po rabote sredi zhenshchin," p. 4, on Party organizations hindering Zhenotdel work. Another problem arose over who was to pay the apprentice's wages. In some instances, the central government took over payment when local institutions refused. In other instances, the local cooperatives and Soviets were forced to assume payment. The *praktikantstvo* system was later abandoned because the government withdrew money to pay apprentices. See Hayden, "The Zhenotdel," p. 165.

Zhenotdel to alert the trade unions and the Komsomol, so that a long-range plan might be evolved to increase the numbers of young women enrolled in factory trade schools.[50]

The factory trade school to which Iakovleva referred, the *fabza-vuch*, as it was called, played a potentially important educational role. Each factory was supposed to have a certain percentage of apprentice worker-students taking courses for from two to four years. They worked a few hours in the factory and a corresponding number of hours in the school, where they were given the theoretical knowledge necessary for the more highly skilled branches of the trade. Visitors during the 1920's observed, however, that the proportion of women in the schools was always lower than that in the factory.[51]

Iakovleva set before the Zhenotdel a list of ways to increase the number of women in the schools. The Zhenotdel must begin by establishing a connection with factory schools in each guberniia, since each school determined the number of places for young women. Zhenotdel workers must then become familiar with each school (and not simply on paper): What kind of training did each school provide? What relationship did the training bear to the work in the factories? How many young women were working in a particular enterprise in relation to the number of men? What were the working conditions like? How many women were unemployed in the area, and how many young people lived in the area? Only with such knowledge could anything be done about getting more young women into the factory trade schools. It would require a vast amount of work for the Zhenotdel to be in constant and close contact with factory trade schools, but Iakovleva considered it essential.[52] Her list was admirable, illustrating not only her ability to find solutions but the somewhat tactless approach for which she was known. If Iakovleva had been director of the Zhenotdel rather than simply its friend, she would have understood that the Women's Section could carry out her proposals only if it had government and union cooperation and a staff beyond some twenty workers at the center.[53]

The central government needed to aid the Zhenotdel by increasing technical and professional training for women along the lines that Kollontai and Iakovleva suggested. It needed to expand collective in-

50. V. Iakovleva, "K voprosu," p. 16.

51. Smith, p. 28.

52. Iakovleva, "K voprosu," p. 16.

53. For Zhenotdel organization, see Stites, *The Women's Liberation Movement*, p. 335.

stitutions and to direct government agencies to cooperate in good faith with the Zhenotdel. For the Party to continue through the 1920's to issue resolutions about women's equality without knowing how, or indeed whether, they were to be implemented was pointless. There was always the risk that women—particularly peasant women, with their traditional mistrust of authority—would withdraw entirely from the Zhenotdel network, frustrated by the perceived discrepancy between the section's promises and the reality of their lives.

At the height of War Communism, Kollontai anticipated that labor conscription would lead to a healthier, more comradely relationship between the sexes.[54] The NEP undermined this concept by encouraging the revival of the kind of woman that Kollontai considered a throwback to the past—the "dolly," the "parasite," the *Nepmansha* (NEP girl). Usually from the former bourgeois classes, the "dollies" were those powdered ladies who, forced to work during labor conscription, used their jobs to strike up advantageous acquaintances. Now they were unemployed and spreading their influence in the less ideological atmosphere of the NEP.[55]

Kollontai scorned the "dolly," who understood neither the importance of obligatory labor nor the social significance of bearing children, and who merely clung to the bourgeois right to enjoy herself. She was concerned about the impact of these parasitic women on the psyches of working-class men. As a Marxist, Kollontai conceived of people as products of their social environment. With the demise of labor conscription, one no longer had any social means of shaming the "dolly"; free now to encourage a vulgarized, bourgeois ideology, she was in a position to keep men from growing internally in their views of women. Not simply the bourgeois "NEPman," but the working-class man was being reinforced in the age-old view of women as household servants and instruments of pleasure. Party workers who a couple of years earlier had lived only for the Revolution were falling under the influence of feminine wiles. Kollontai portrayed such situations in her novel *Vasilisa Malygina*, in which a young woman, Nina Konstantinovna, seduces the proletarian Vladimir and makes him her "protector" as well as her lover. Kollontai pictured Nina as "painted and powdered," interested only in clothes and men, a real *burzhuika*. After the Revolution, she is taken on as an office worker. Her aim is

54. See *Polozhenie zhenshchiny*, p. 152, for Kollontai on ways in which labor conscription would improve the image of the peasant woman in the eyes of the male peasant.
55. Kollontai, "Novaia ugroza," pp. 6–7.

to ensnare a man who will provide for her. A wily woman who winds herself around a man like a snake, she completes the corruption of Vladimir, who is already falling victim to NEP luxury.[56] Kollontai feared that in the atmosphere of the NEP the *"Nepmansha,"* the "dolly," would replace the "new woman" as a role model.[57]

Kollontai had abundant reason to resent the NEP. It damaged the Zhenotdel by curtailing its social welfare activities, by increasing female unemployment, and by jeopardizing the image of the economically independent "new woman." One might argue as well that under the NEP the government was more indifferent to Zhenotdel goals for socialist living than might have been the case had War Communism prevailed. The Soviet government in the 1920's seemed not much interested in encouraging experiments in collectivism, to which the Zhenotdel was committed. Lewin, for example, has described the complaints of peasant *kolkhozy*, which also felt neglected by the regime and objected not only to being ignored by the Party, but to government negativism that was hindering the collective movement.[58]

It was not that the Party disputed the theoretical value of the collective institutions to which it had pledged itself in its Party Program in 1919.[59] Rather, the Party was ordering its priorities, its time schedule differently. The regime opposed the Zhenotdel's proposals in part because they required a large initial investment that most Communists believed should be deferred.[60] But economic resources are always

56. See *Vasilisa Malygina*, pp. 242, 248, which appeared in a collection of Kollontai's novellas including *Sestry* and *Liubov' trekh pokolenii* under the general title *Liubov' pchel trudovykh*.

57. For Kollontai's fear that Communists would fall under the influence of the "dolly," see "Novaia ugroza," p. 8.

58. See Lewin, *Russian Peasants*, pp. 115–19, for the regime's neglect of the *kolkhozy*. At the Conference of kolkhoz members held in Moscow in Feb. 1925, a number of speakers called attention to the failure of the local Soviets and local party organizations to assist the *kolkhozy*. Lewin concludes that it is remarkable the movement survived at all without assistance and guidance, since it was made up of *bedniak* who were largely illiterate.

59. An exception should be made concerning children's homes, about which there was considerable disagreement. A. Rykov argued that in the homes the state was bringing up idlers who did not know how to work. See Carr, *Socialism in One Country*, vol. 1, p. 45.

60. The Women's Section's belief that such arguments were short-sighted was given expression later during the First Five-Year Plan by the economic planner Sabsovich, who stressed the increase in gross productivity that would result from the employment of women. He argued that collectivized services in the socialist city would ultimately cut the cost of provisioning, not only to the collective but to the individual. In the short run the cost could be passed on to the citizens, who would be able to afford the increase

limited. Where they are allocated is a question of relative values. No doubt collectivism did not rank high during the NEP. Yet the NEP was not responsible for the Zhenotdel's fundamental problems; they were manifest before the effects of the New Economic Policy could be felt.[61]

Why the Party continually downgraded the Zhenotdel cannot be explained fully by citing a lack of interest in collectivism during the years of the NEP, Russia's insufficient financial resources, or even Party fear that the Zhenotdel was divisive and threatened to split the working class.[62] It has been said that the more quickly one changes a situation the more one brings along from the past.[63] So it was with Bolshevism in relation to the woman question. When the Congress of Soviets in 1920 opposed a resolution to bring women into positions of leadership—a resolution that had been endorsed by the Party Congress a year earlier—it was because many men did not approve of the decision to draw women into public life. Fear of social disruption was an element. At the Eighth All-Russian Congress of Soviets, after Kollontai proposed that worker and peasant women be drawn into government, a young peasant jumped to the platform and banging his fist on the table shouted, "I will not let my wife be taken into the Soviet! I have eight children. How can she go into the Soviet?" A large section of the Congress, said an observer, seemed to be sympathetic.[64]

As for the government, concern not to offend the personally conservative masses of workers was accompanied, one suspects, by a touch of unease among the predominantly male Bolsheviks at the prospect of appearing to be taking the *baba* too seriously. Thus the women of the Zhenotdel had repeatedly to remind a reluctant Party that the work of the Women's Section must be given some priority. Polina Vinogradskaia's plea written in 1920 would remain relevant through the 1920's: Would the Central Committee assign the Zhenotdel a number of "responsible old Party workers" and all comrades not engaged in other activities to work among women? And would the Cen-

---

because there would be two wage-earners in the family. See S. Frederick Starr, "The Anti-Urban Utopias of Early Stalinist Russia" (paper prepared for the Conference on the Cultural Revolution in the USSR, 1928–1933, Russian Institute, Columbia Univ., Nov. 22–23, 1974), pp. 33–34.

61. Mandel, p. 53, refers to "the famous" Zhenotdel, belying the beleaguered status of the organization from the outset.

62. For this fear, see Itkina, p. 201.

63. See Lewin, "The Social Background of Stalinism," p. 126.

64. Winter, p. 111. The Eighth Congress took place in December 1920.

tral Committee circulate a letter, again to remind localities about the importance of working among women?[65] Kollontai wrote in *Kommunistka* in 1921, as she had written earlier, a directive that could have been repeated each year. The Zhenotdel needed continually to insist on the inclusion of working women in all local commissions concerned with the organization and improvement of the life of the working class.[66]

We have seen negativism toward the Zhenotdel within the central government, and we have suggested a general resistance to the idea of evolving sex roles. To demand that the Party fulfill its promises and encourage women to assume public authority meant to jeopardize not only familiar comforts but to undo the very barriers between male and female roles on which many men (and women too) relied for a sense of security. We are also told "it is an axiom that people cannot be taught who feel that they are at the same time being attacked."[67] In fact the Zhenotdel *was* perceived as a threat. We find examples of hostility toward the Zhenotdel in the lower levels of the Party, in the Komsomol, and among ordinary Russians in the factory, the village, and the trade unions. Resistance was strongest among men, particularly husbands. The Zhenotdel organizer harassed and made life miserable for men who drank or abused their wives, with the result that a large segment of Soviet society resented the Zhenotdel.[68]

Literature provides examples. In Glebov's *Inga*, the Zhenotdel worker Mera threatens Boltikov, an alcoholic factory worker who beats his wife, with a trial designed to make an example of him. Boltikov protests, speaking for every man, "What do you mean— trial? Who are *you* to try *me*? . . . I can't beat my wife, eh? . . . I have always beaten her!"[69] Husbands threw papers from the Women's Section into the fire. Wives were forbidden to go to meetings, and those who braved male disapproval often arrived with bruises inflicted by men angry that their wives were learning to read and to write.[70]

65. Vinogradskaia, "Itogi III-go vserossiiskogo soveshch. zavgubotdelov po rabote sredi zhenshchin," p. 5.

66. Kollontai, "Proizvodstvo i byt," p. 7.

67. Gordon Allport as quoted in Massell, p. 397.

68. See N. Astakhova, *Tovarishch Olga*, p. 130.

69. See Glebov, pp. 275–76. The same theme is expressed in N. Kochin, *Devki* (M, 1929), p. 186, when a disgruntled husband complains "a guy can't even beat his wife, nor make her work—not even argue with her. They've made up special laws for women in Moscow." Quoted in Gasiorowska, p. 79.

70. For examples of male opposition to wives' participation, see Vinogradskaia, *Sobytiia*, p. 205; and L. Stal', "Rabota sredi zhenshchin v Terskoi oblasti," *Kommunistka*, 1920, no. 5, p. 39. Trotsky reported references to the women's organizations as po-

The word *delegatka* was not respected in the popular idiom. She was just a *baba* chosen at a meeting by other "old women."[71]

The Communist writer F. Gladkov provided a remarkably perceptive portrayal of the conflict between the Zhenotdel and the lower levels of the Party in his novel *Tsement*, about the early 1920's. The Communist Red Army leader Gleb Chumalov, returning to his town after three years of Civil War and looking for his wife and little daughter, finds that his once cheerful cottage has become "an empty hole" with grimy windows and dirty floors. His wife Dasha, whom he used to take into his arms and carry like a child, who planted red geraniums in the window boxes, has become a stranger in a red kerchief, a "new woman," who calls him "comrade" and advises him to register with the factory committee for his food ration. She eats in the communal restaurant. Within minutes after his arrival she leaves. The Party has ordered her on a *komandirovka* (a mission) into the countryside for a few days.

Dasha, who is a director of the local Zhenotdel, takes Gleb to visit their child, Nurka, in a nearby children's home, a former mansion of the bourgeoisie, now named "Krupskaia." Gleb is appalled: children wander about "like goats," crying, fighting with each other, scratching their heads and armpits, their faces wan and their eyes sunken.[72] "The poor wretches will starve. The Zhenotdel ought to be shot." But Dasha replies that if there had been no Women's Section the children would have died. The Zhenotdel has work to do: "our children have lived like pigs. . . . Everything possible must be given to them, . . . they must eat, play. . . . For us nothing, but for them—everything . . . even if we have to die."[73]

The men in the local Communist Party scorn the Women's Section but sound foolish and somewhat frightened. Comrade Shuk warns Gleb that the women's front is a dangerous place.[74] "They'll bite us to death, claw us to pieces and deafen us with screeching." He calls the women "a committee of devils." And his fear of "new women" is expressed in anger: "Not one of them will bear any more children as long as she lives. The whole damned gang of them is going

tentially destructive of marriages. See L. Trotsky, *Voprosy byta* (M, 1923), p. 43. One of the earliest fictional portrayals of the theme of female awakening and marital breakdown is Neverov's "Mar'ia the Bolshevik" (1921). See "Mar'ia-Bol'shevichka" in Aleksandr Neverov, *Izbrannye proizvedeniia* (M, 1958), pp. 195–200. For a discussion of the story, see Gasiorowska, p. 35.

71. See Selishchev, p. 214.   72. Gladkov, pp. 46–47.
73. *Ibid.*, pp. 53–54.   74. *Ibid.*, p. 60.

to boycott us."[75] And when Dasha proposes to start crèches for babies in homes of the former bourgeoisie, her Party comrades hoot: "Hear, hear! Ah, these women—they peck like hens and crow like cocks! They're sure handing it to us brothers!"[76] A group of women propose Dasha to chair the local Party group, but Communist men loudly object. Let women have equal rights, but "let them wait a little longer. . . . We need a beard on the chairman."[77] The non-Party women the Zhenotdel is trying to organize are themselves ambivalent about change. She would be a fool, one woman tells another, if she let the Women's Section convince her to quit her children, her husband, and her home.[78]

Author Gladkov seemed to admire Dasha, whom he pictures as strong and determined. We see Dasha being congratulated at the *chistka*, the Party cleansing.[79] "Here is a real member of the Party . . . a real worker and militant. Our Party can only be proud of such Comrades."[80] But what did the Communist Gladkov really think of comrades from the Zhenotdel like Dasha, who spoke out at party meetings, rejected their husbands, and put their children into homes? Consider a scene at the children's home where Dasha went each morning and evening to kiss Nurka.

The little girl has become all bones, and is flickering out like a candle, dying from day to day; the doctors are puzzled about what is wrong. Gladkov and Dasha both know: It is not only a mother's milk a child needs; a child is nourished also by a mother's heart and tenderness. A child fades and withers if the mother does not breathe upon its little head, if she does not surround its sleep with her care.

In a moving scene, Dasha, saying goodnight to Nurka, asks her "What do you want? Tell me." And Nurka replies "I want to stay with you . . . so that you'd never go away and always be near." She is sitting on Dasha's lap, and Dasha can feel her warmth. Dasha puts Nurka to bed and leaves the children's home. She does not go as usual down the road to the Women's Section, but rather walks into a thicket, where she flings herself down on the grass. And there she lies crying for a long time, digging with her fingers into the mold.

75. *Ibid.* These insults are deleted from later (for example, 1947) editions.
76. *Ibid.*, p. 87 (deleted from 1947 edition).
77. *Ibid.*, p. 80.
78. *Ibid.*, p. 292 (again deleted from 1947 edition).
79. At a *chistka*, unsuitable members are questioned, accused, and ousted.
80. Gladkov, p. 332.

The fault lies in her, Dasha, and she will never be rid of her guilt. But it is not her own fault, Gladkov explains.[81] It has come from somewhere outside, from life, from Revolution. Gladkov understood Dasha's grief, but he punished her further with Nurka's death.

꛰꛰꛰

Negativism toward the Zhenotdel continued throughout the 1920's, permeating not only the lower levels of the Party but seemingly most of the workers and peasants as well. Visitors to Russia's villages reported anecdotes about the Zhenotdel that if true provided good reason for male resentment, and that if apocryphal indicated how a negative image of the Zhenotdel had already entered the realm of Russian myth and folklore. One was the story of a modern Lysistrata, Aksinia Karaseva, who lived in the village of Vertevka. Aksinia, the victim of an abusive husband who resented her political activity, conspired with the local Zhenotdel to organize a female boycott. Supposedly, the women of the village assembled in the schoolhouse and refused to rejoin their families until the men signed a statement promising no longer to abuse their wives. The men, so the story goes, protested but eventually signed.[82]

The Communist writer Anatolii Glebov, a First Secretary of the Theater Section of the Russian Association of Proletarian Writers (RAPP), described toward the end of the decade in his play *Inga* two "new women," supposedly products of Zhenotdel ideology, who reflected the Women's Section's lack of popularity after nearly ten years of existence. Instead of Dasha, the pioneering and semiliterate women's leader in *Tsement*, we meet the more sophisticated Inga and Mera. Inga, the Communist intellectual, dedicated to her work, is superior to the men around her but is portrayed as a failure as a woman. She cannot have children and torments her lover Dmitri by thinking of her work when she should be paying attention to him. Even in a society dedicated to work Inga sounds harsh. She will not permit anyone to bind her, and she resents Dmitri's expectation that she will sacrifice her work. Dmitri loves Inga, but she stifles and oppresses him in a way that his former wife never did. He doubts that a mate could be found for a woman like Inga.[83]

Mera, a Zhenotdel organizer and factory worker, is no more appeal-

81. *Ibid.*, pp. 294–95.   82. Smith, pp. 44–46.
83. Glebov, p. 292.

ing. Glebov uses her to caricature the Zhenotdel. A Jewish intellectual who has been married seven times and wants to demolish the family, Mera shrills "Pots? Diapers? Jealousy? To hell with it!" Somov, the man of good sense, the old Communist worker, chides her; in a few words, in which he explains that millions of working women need the family, he undermines the Communist Kollontais. "You, the intellectual women . . . dream about various kinds of free love. But *they* . . . my God! . . . There are so many other things of much greater importance!"[84]

When at the play's end Mera taunts the unhappy Dmitri, who must choose between his wife Glafeera and his lover Inga, with the advice that all three should live together, she strikes a discordant note from the rejected sexual anarchy that had marked the era of Revolution and Civil War. In his portrayal of Mera, Glebov implies that the Zhenotdel represents sexual looseness. Neither of the models—the hard-driving, self-conscious Inga, or the uppity Mera—both caricatures of the intellectual heroines of 1917, were suitable new women. Instead, we are invited to sympathize with Glafeera, a gentle and humble factory worker who is struggling to educate herself politically. But unlike Inga, her success will not threaten the ego of husband Dmitri, whose love she is trying to regain and whose transgressions she forgives. Nor will she violate Communist morality. "You may live like that if you want to," she advises the promiscuous Mera from the Zhenotdel, "but we will blaze our own trail!"[85]

The Zhenotdel is portrayed as still doing its job of shaming reactionary male chauvinists. The alcoholic foreman in the clothing factory is ridiculed by Communist workers. But when he protests that he fought in three wars against tsarism and the bourgeoisie, and that a machine gun riddled him, when he complains that for 40 years he has worked without trouble, but that now the whole factory is full of bossy "baba departments" who will not leave a fellow alone,[86] we can presume the sympathies of the audience.

We might surmise that a generational difference existed among Communists in their perception of women's roles. No Women's Section existed in the Komsomol, where no one thought it would be

84. *Ibid.*, pp. 262–63.   85. *Ibid.*, p. 293.
86. *Ibid.*, pp. 248, 277.

needed. Among youth growing up with equal educational opportunities and educated in accordance with socialist principles, a special
section to work among women seemed superfluous. As it turned out,
it was not. Youth might feel sexually free, but there was reason to
believe that young men in the Komsomol held fairly traditional ideas
about sex roles in society and resented being displaced by women.[87]
In the Moscow Komsomol, as elsewhere, women in the mid-1920's
held few positions, and young women did not hesitate to report that
young men initially opposed their work and tried to keep leadership
of the organization in male hands.[88]

An indicator of tension between the two institutions was the Zhenotdel demand that the Komsomol show more interest in attracting
young women to the Party and regularize their haphazard contact
with the Zhenotdel by organized cooperation. It was time for the
Komsomol to adopt methods already tried and proven by the women.[89]

Another institution in Soviet society that remained opposed to the
Zhenotdel was the trade unions. A Zhenotdel director in the Ivanovo-
Voznesensk textile district described the open obstructionism of her
male comrades. Although there were only two women on the guberniia
Trade Union Executive Committee, and it had been decided that two
more should go on the slate for the new committee, some of the men
objected that women were insufficiently educated for such posts. The
Zhenotdel director wore down their resistance, but only after hours
of insisting that women would never learn if men did not let them
take responsibility: a year of experience was more educational than
five of study.[90]

Kollontai took on the problem of trade-union antagonism in several speeches, presenting tables showing the large percentage of
women in the unions and the tiny proportion in leadership positions.
Even in those unions where women were in the majority they were
invariably missing at the top.[91] Women were overlooked for admin-

87. See Mehnert, p. 223, for the persistence of a sexual double standard among young
Communist men.
88. See Smith, p. 64.
89. See S. Vol'naia, "Soiuz molodezhi i otdely rabotnits," *Kommunistka*, 1920, no.
6, pp. 11–12.
90. Smith, p. 55.
91. In the sewing industry, where women made up 69.1 percent of the union membership, they held only 25.7 percent of the directing roles. In the tobacco industry
comparable figures were 67.8 percent and 36.6 percent, in textiles 60.2 and 9.3, and
in the paper industry 34.3 and 10.1. Figures are for Jan.–Mar. 1921, except for the paper
industry which are for 1920. See tables in *Polozhenie zhenshchiny*, pp. 157–58, and
Rabotnitsa i krest'ianka, p. 18.

istrative positions not simply because they lacked self-confidence (although that was a factor). In the case of the trade unions, their failure to be selected was also the result of the distrust of men who were trapped by attitudes from the past and unwilling to accept women in responsible positions.[92]

Kollontai reasoned that the unions lacked socialist consciousness toward women because they had no group working within them committed to women's equality. She drew a devastating parallel between the unions and the Party at large before the founding of the Women's Bureau and the Commission for Agitation and Propaganda Among Working Women, when the situation was similar. Then no one did anything on behalf of women. The task before the Women's Section, therefore, was not simply to strengthen the self-confidence of the working woman but to agitate among working men to effect a radical change in their relationship toward female union members.[93] A resolution taken at a conference of Zhenotdel leaders in 1920 in fact urged that special instructors be assigned within the trade unions to carry out Zhenotdel work. These Communists would bring the broadest possible strata of working women into participation, first by introducing women into governing positions in the trade unions.[94]

There was still the problem of male prejudice. How much it reflected trade unionists' resentment of female competition for jobs, and how much a simple opposition to women in authority, was not really clear. Whatever the cause of the prejudice, Kollontai understood that until the Zhenotdel combated it the inferior position of women in the unions would continue. Although she knew the extent of negative feeling toward the Zhenotdel in the unions, Kollontai suggested a series of maneuvers by means of which the Women's Section might force the trade unions to activate their own resolutions.[95] In addition to putting Zhenotdel workers in the unions, she urged that the Zhenotdel make use of union publications in order to popularize the Party commitment to include women in socialist construction. Special women's pages in trade-union publications would be counterproductive, since the purpose was to reach the men.[96]

92. Kollontai, "Proizvodstvo i byt," p. 8.

93. *Ibid.*, pp. 8–9.

94. See Vinogradskaia, "Itogi III-go," p. 3, and Samoilova, "Organizatsionnye zadachi," *Kommunistka*, 1920, no. 6, p. 26.

95. Kollontai, "Proizvodstvo i byt," p. 9. See USSR, [9], pp. 10–11, for tension between the Zhenotdel and the trade unions over proposed Zhenotdel work in the unions.

96. Kollontai, "Proizvodstvo i byt," p. 9.

The unions, believing that the Zhenotdel was divisive and threatened their own authority over the workers, opposed Kollontai, arguing that it was the union's role to represent both male and female
workers. Although the unions insisted that this was what they were
in fact doing, they lacked interest in the woman worker. In the factories where work among women rested on the Zhenotdel organizers
—whom the unions already resented—what one Zhenotdel director
called a "we and they" attitude developed. The factory committees
failed to take any initiative, refusing to put subjects of special interest
to women on their programs. When the women did come to meetings,
they were greeted with "Well, let's hear what the babas have to say!"[97]

The conflict between Kollontai, as director of the Zhenotdel, and
the trade unions first broke into the open in 1921—the same year in
which Kollontai led the Workers' Opposition. A former worker in the
Women's Section has written of the battle to abolish the Zhenotdel
waged by certain trade unions in 1921 under the flag of a fight against
feminism. The controversy grew so intense that Kollontai requested
the Politburo to consider the urgent matter of the relationship between the trade unions and the Zhenotdel, since the fierce dispute
raging around the issue was disrupting Zhenotdel work.[98] The Zhenotdel was not abolished—as the trade unions would have liked—but
neither did its activity in the midst of the trade unions increase significantly, as Kollontai had hoped. The Central Committee resolved
toward the end of 1921 that the strengthening of the Zhenotdel connection with the trade unions could be achieved only if the Party fraction
in the trade unions designated women workers to coordinate union
work among women with the work of the Zhenotdel.[99] Work among
women in the unions, it seemed, would be directed not by the Zhenotdel but by the unions. Within a few years, the Trade Union Congress voted to place the responsibility for work among women on the
factory committees as a whole, instructing the unions to include questions of special interest to women in their general program. Zhenotdel
organizers continued to be active in every factory. Tension between
the trade unions and the Zhenotdel did not abate.[100]

97. Smith, p. 56.

98. Itkina, p. 201.

99. For Kollontai's expectation, see *Rabotnitsa i krest'ianka*, p. 18. For the Central
Committee's resolve to encourage trade union support of Zhenotdel goals, see USSR,
[16], vol. 2 (M, 1922), p. 204.

100. Smith, p. 56, reporting a conversation with the head of the Zhenotdel in Ivanovo-
Voznesensk.

Kollontai's position appeared paradoxical. On the one hand, as a leader of the Workers' Opposition, she was jeopardizing her place in the Party by fighting for the right of the trade unions to control industry; on the other, she was denying to the trade unions another right they jealously guarded, to be the sole representative of the interests of all the workers. For Kollontai there was no contradiction. The trade unions should be in charge of the economy, regulating it and controlling production. The Zhenotdel, for its part, should be able to affect union policy. If the Zhenotdel were a force within the unions, and if the unions were to take their place at the head of the economy, Party indifference to the role of women might be circumvented. Kollontai's theoretical plan broke down when trade-union leaders proved no more comfortable than other Communists with bringing women into leadership.

༄༅༄

By the mid-1920's a negative image of the Zhenotdel had become fixed in Soviet society. Dasha abandoned her child to die in a children's home and made life miserable for her bewildered husband home from the Civil War. Mera urged promiscuity on good Communist workers. Both women were crude caricatures of Kollontai, but they endured in the popular mind, symbolizing the aggressive, abrasive (and somewhat self-righteous) *Zhenotdelovka* badgering people to alter their lives for the worse.[101]

We are left with a puzzling question. Why did the Party disregard Sof'ia Smidovich's challenge at the Eleventh Congress and let the Zhenotdel limp along for the rest of the decade? We have seen how throughout the 1920's critical elements of Soviet society—the factory workers, the peasants, the local Communist officials, even members of the Central Committee—feared and resented the Zhenotdel or were at best indifferent to its fate. But it was not lack of popularity at the grass roots that hobbled the Zhenotdel as much as lack of central government (meaning Communist Party) support.

Although we do not have an exact picture, we may surmise that the Party center was as fragmented on this issue as it was on others. Some members of the Party—Sverdlov, Lenin, Trotsky, and presum-

101. See the recent disparaging reference made by a woman intellectual concerning the superfeminist of the "women's department type" (*Zhenotdelskogo tipa*), whom she was pleased to report was a phenomenon of the past. Hough, p. 366. Occasionally Kollontai caricatured herself, as her provocative remarks to Louise Weiss suggest. See Weiss, vol. 2, p. 120.

ably Nogin, Sosnovskii, and S. V. Kosior—thought that the Zhenotdel was making an important contribution.[102] But by 1924 Lenin and Sverdlov, early supporters of a Women's Section, were gone. On balance, the Zhenotdel still had some friends who believed in the institution and its mission, but they were either too few or their convictions too lukewarm to build a consensus for full support.[103]

We will see in the following chapter that when the Zhenotdel was finally disbanded in 1930, a sense of relief was felt in some quarters of the Central Committee—an interesting example of congruence between the lower levels of society and the authoritarian Party above that governed it. Of the various causes that Kollontai defended based on promises made by the Party in its program of 1919, workers' control was the most likely to be accepted by Soviet citizens, equality of the sexes in public life and an end to traditional domesticity the least likely.[104] Workers' control of industry had popular support from the outset: workers, after all, spontaneously seized factories in 1917. If any part of the Party program could have been preserved, it should logically have been that revolutionary pledge. The opposite was true with the transformation of the relationship between the sexes. What was remarkable was not the hostility at the grass roots toward the Zhenotdel, but the faith on the part of a small group of women Communists that within a few years after the Revolution they could by external means alter people's most deeply held prejudices.

102. S. V. Kosior had been a Bolshevik since 1907 and was of worker origin. See Itkina, p. 181, for his aid to the Zhenotdel in the Ukraine in 1919. See also Conquest, p. 14. Nogin died in 1924.
103. The 1930 report in which Kaganovich discussed the demise of the Zhenotdel indicated a split in Party support for the Women's Section. See Chapter 10 below.
104. For the Party Program of 1919, see USSR, [6], vol. 1, pp. 409–30.

CHAPTER TEN

Socialist Feminism

KOLLONTAI remained in the Party despite efforts at the Eleventh Congress to expel her, but the structure of her life disintegrated. She had to endure not only public humiliation, the loss of her Party position as director of the Zhenotdel, and virtual banishment,[1] but also the private pain that came with the end of her marriage to the Bolshevik military hero Pavel Dybenko.

When she received an appointment as Soviet representative to the legation in Norway in the autumn of 1922, she knew that her fate could have been worse—an assignment on another continent, for example, rather than to a beloved Scandinavian country.[2] She was philosophical, expecting diplomatic work to be a formality, and anticipating time in which to write.[3] But separation from Soviet politics was difficult. Although Kollontai joined no faction, she did not easily end opposition, particularly against government neglect of the woman question. Kollontai conducted a singular struggle for the next few years before ceasing to fight the battles of the women's movement. Her effort was independent and also uninvited, an intervention from afar largely by means of articles in the Soviet press, that were unwelcome both to Sof'ia Smidovich, her successor as director of the Women's Section, and to Krupskaia, the editor of *Kommunistka*. The Moscow leaders of the Zhenotdel were reluctant to reject Kollontai, a founder of the socialist women's movement; but aware of their institution's vulnerability, they drew away from her after 1923, made uneasy by Kollontai's "feminism."

1. Others too were banished: before Trotsky's exile in 1928, Piatakov, Preobrazhenskii, and V. Kosior joined Rakovskii in Paris; Kamenev was appointed ambassador to Mussolini; Antonov-Ovseenko went to Prague; and Safarov, the Zinovievist leader of the Komsomol, was sent to Constantinople. Thus were the leading Oppositionists dispersed. Deutscher, *The Prophet Unarmed*, vol. 2, p. 338.

2. Supposedly, the intention was to send her to Canada, but Canada objected. Kollontai's initial appointment in Norway was as first secretary of the Soviet trade delegation. Thinking she might be assigned to Sweden, she wrote to Ström asking if "Branting would stand me in Sweden." See undated letter to Ström, Ström Archive, University of Gothenburg. At the end of October 1922 Kollontai was appointed counselor of the delegation in Christiania (Oslo). For details, see Hauge, pp. 53–55.

3. Kollontai, *Autobiography*, p. 44.

It will be recalled that Communists defined feminism in negative terms to mean not simply a defense of the interests of women and a fight for their equality, but a separation of women from the larger working class in rejection of men and in recognition of bonds among women that transcended those of class. Feminism meant separate organizations for women that threatened Party control and divided the working class. Feminists were interested not in the well-being of the collective but rather in bourgeois notions of female self-fulfillment.[4]

Kollontai did not simply share the Bolshevik perception of bourgeois feminism; she was its chief advocate. It is the more significant, then, that within a few years of the Revolution she would offer Communist women a new interpretation of feminism shaped to the working-class state. But her definition of working-class, or socialist, feminism that appeared in *Pravda* in 1923 failed to convince most Bolsheviks, as did her essays and short stories exploring the nature of male-female relationships. Her insistence that private as well as public life must change in response to the Revolution was rejected in a narrow sort of way as bourgeois feminism. It is to the controversy in *Pravda* that we turn first.

Bebel wrote in the 1870's that women must not wait for men to help them, just as workers could not wait for help from the bourgeoisie. But within the Soviet system separate female action involved inherent tension, although prominent Communists like Lenin, Trotsky, and Iaroslavskii, echoing Bebel, called on women to organize themselves for collective life.[5]

When some Communist women suggested innovations, they were censured—even by their female comrades—as "feminists." Consider the episode initiated during 1923 in *Pravda* by Vera Golubeva and defended from abroad by Kollontai. Golubeva was one of the imaginative Communists within the Zhenotdel who kept the institution

4. Feminists sometimes candidly acknowledged the truth of the charge. Thus the nineteenth-century feminist E. Shchepkina summed up the difference between feminists and socialists. "The two principal modes of human activity," she wrote, "are individual and collective. People like feminists, possessing greater scope, time, and means to express themselves in individual action, do so, hoping to place their personal stamp upon the activity they have engaged in. This, at bottom, was the underlying impulse of feminism." Stites, *Women's Liberation Movement*, p. 231.

5. Iaroslavskii cited Lenin in *Kommunistka*, 1923, no. 7, p. 4. For Lenin's view that "the emancipation of working women is a matter for the working women themselves," see his speech to the Fourth Moscow City Conference of non-Party working women, Sept. 23, 1919, in *Sochineniia* (4th ed.), vol. 30, p. 26. For Bebel, see Meyer, p. 98.

vital after the deaths of Samoilova and Inessa and the banishment of Kollontai. On the fifth anniversary of the First All-Russian Congress of Worker and Peasant Women, Golubeva wrote in *Kommunistka*: "Reading now the reports and resolutions of this Congress, one is simply astonished to see with what ease they projected the full transformation of the old world, the state raising of children, change of marriage relations, destruction of the domestic economy, etc. Now five years after the passing of these resolutions, when we have met such difficulty in the path of our advancement toward Communism, now we know that everything in these resolutions . . . has not been realized."[6]

A few months earlier Golubeva had demanded change. Writing in *Pravda*, the newspaper one Communist termed "the open tribune" and "an intermittent survival of democracy," she had bluntly stated what was common knowledge. The Party had no real interest in the Zhenotdel. As an institution it received insufficient support; therefore, it could accomplish little.[7] Unemployment among women, a result of the NEP, made the achievement of Zhenotdel goals more difficult, now that fewer women worked in factories where they could receive effective political education. Golubeva suggested that the Zhenotdel expand its methods by organizing "special societies" of non-Party, unemployed women dedicated to the Zhenotdel goal of full equality and liberation from domesticity.[8]

The response in *Pravda* was hostile. Why "special societies"? What could they do that the Zhenotdel was not attempting? One woman wrote that Golubeva obviously had a different concept of the Zhenotdel's purpose. Party work among housewives was never its task. Another denied that work among peasants was, as Golubeva charged, mostly "on paper." A Zhenotdel worker named Niurina questioned Golubeva's fears, arguing that the current situation of female unemployment was only temporary, that the worst was past since women now made up 28.8 percent of production workers. Clara Zetkin was harsh, charging rather unfairly that Golubeva proposed societies for the bored wives of Nepmen.[9]

6. See *Kommunistka*, 1923, no. 11, p. 18.
7. *Pravda*, Feb. 1, 1923, p. 3. For praise of *Pravda*, see Souvarine, p. 326.
8. *Pravda*, Feb. 1, 1923, p. 3. Golubeva's suggestion that societies might include men did not prevent charges of feminism. Kollontai reported such charges against Golubeva in *Pravda*, Mar. 20, 1923, p. 4.
9. For responses to Golubeva, see *Pravda* issues of Feb. 7, 1923 (p. 4), Feb. 9, 1923 (p. 4), and Feb. 10, 1923 (p. 4). Golubeva replied, reviewing the charges against her, in the *Pravda* issue of Apr. 13, 1923.

From Norway, Kollontai monitored the activities of the Zhenotdel, trying to influence the institution she had recently headed. Joining the *Pravda* debate, Kollontai argued (correcting Zetkin) that Golubeva's special societies made sense during the NEP since the Soviet state was not providing women with employment. Golubeva was suggesting not that the Zhenotdel be destroyed, but simply that it augment by more flexible means the delegates' meetings, its standard method of reaching factory and peasant women. These meetings alone could not cope with the masses of politically "unconscious," dependent women, the isolated housewives who were outside the network. Yet it was the unemployed housewives, whose numbers were increasing, that the Zhenotdel needed to reach and to influence. Dismissing as "pious nonsense" Comrade Niurina's argument that unemployment was a temporary phenomenon, Kollontai argued that even if the process of drawing women into production were to be resumed rather than halted, it would take years before significant numbers of Russian women were independent from men and from the family.

Kollontai reminded the Communists of the small percentage of women who belonged to the Party—9.2 percent in the cities and 4.2 percent in the country. The work of the Zhenotdel was barely begun. Delegates' meetings had yielded "brilliant results" in the first years of the Revolution, when masses of women had been conscripted into the work force. Now something more was needed. She cited the example of the backward Near East, where the Zhenotdel organized women's clubs, not delegates' meetings. The Party should extend those clubs throughout Russia, basing them on projects of interest to housewives, who, their attention engaged, would become susceptible to Communist influence. It was not a question of a new principle, Kollontai explained; it was simply a question of a new method.[10]

Kollontai understated the novelty of her position. For the first time she advocated separate women's groups, which earlier she had rejected.[11] What is more, for the first time she did not deny the possi-

10. Kollontai in *Pravda*, Mar. 20, 1923, p. 4. Also see Golubeva in *Pravda*, Apr. 13, 1923, for why delegates' meetings alone were ineffective. The Zhenotdel did attempt later in the 1920's—at least on paper—to bring housewives into the network of delegates' meetings. By the mid-1920's, delegates were chosen for one of every ten workers and one of every 100 housewives and peasants every year by as large a number of women as could be gotten to participate. The women thus elected met twice a month under the leadership of a trained Party worker. By 1926, there were half a million delegates elected throughout the country, 64 percent peasants, 20 percent workers, the rest housewives, office workers, and domestic servants. See Smith, p. 48.

11. Earlier, in 1921, Kollontai had seen separatism as permissible only in the East

bility of feminism existing within Communist ranks. Rather, she affirmed it: instead of condemning feminism or warning against it, she offered a definition of the term giving it working-class connotations. Acknowledging that Golubeva was being called a feminist, Kollontai asked what the charge meant. Feminism was a "terrible word" only in the conditions of bourgeois society, only if the working woman strove for liberation within a bourgeois framework. What, after all, was feminism but the aspiration of women to establish their own rights? And however much working men might object, Kollontai insisted that those rights did not oppose the interests of the proletariat but, in a workers' state, fused with them.[12]

One must marvel at the casual way in which Kollontai offered the Communists this brilliantly simple definition. Since the turn of the century she had used the term "feminist" as an epithet, usually against the organized bourgeois feminists, who aspired to split the workers' movement along male-female lines, but occasionally against tendencies in Bolshevism.[13] Now suddenly feminism became a goal. She explained her acceptance of the term she had previously spurned: in bourgeois countries, the working class must fight the feminists; but it was in no way harmful, when power was in the hands of the working class, for women to unite and to become, as it were, "socialist feminists." The setbacks to women's equality under the NEP increased the need for Soviet women to join together as feminists to struggle for socialism. Kollontai called on the Zhenotdel, therefore, to put itself at the head of Golubeva's proposed societies and give them the proper Communist direction.[14]

where, because of custom, women would not attend meetings with men. See Kollontai, *Rabotnitsa i krest'ianka*, p. 25, and n. 13 below.

12. *Pravda*, Mar. 20, 1923, p. 4. My thanks to Carol Hayden for calling my attention to this article.

13. For example, Kollontai opposed "Sections," an organizational device that had coexisted for a time with delegates' meetings, because of the risk of feminism (meaning separatism) inherent in permanent women's groups. How Golubeva's special societies differed from the "Sections" is difficult to see. Made up of female recruits who were lacking in consciousness and who needed enlightenment, they would entail the same risks. As permanent groups, they would embody the threat of separatist organizations with a life distinct from the Party.

14. *Pravda*, Mar. 20, 1923, p. 4. Possibly Kollontai was resorting to her tactic of justifying Zhenotdel activity by appealing to the Communist instinct for self-preservation. But she seemed genuinely fearful that Soviet Russia was not entirely free from the dangers of a revived bourgeois feminism. Hayden, p. 166, notes that *Rabotnitsa* resumed publication in Jan. 1923 in a Zhenotdel effort to counteract the influence of a developing non-Party feminist press that was receiving wide distribution among women workers. See Stites, *Women's Liberation Movement*, pp. 306–13, on the other hand, for the political demise of Russian feminism.

However convincing the logic by which Kollontai incorporated feminism into the framework of the Soviet state, her explanation rested on a shaky assumption—that power in Soviet Russia was in the hands of the working class. But was it? Only two years earlier Kollontai had condemned the Party for its distance from the proletariat and the privileged positions of its bureaucrats, suggesting that the Party was ceasing to be the vanguard of the working class, that indeed the workers were deserting the Communists. Her words in 1923 were a reflex, revealing how difficult it was even for oppositionists like Kollontai to divest themselves of the belief that the Party still embodied the politically conscious proletariat.

No doubt the assumption of a workers' state sounded plausible in 1923. Lenin was still alive; Stalinism was an unknown term. But to the end of her life, Kollontai, like Trotsky and other Bolsheviks, persisted in seeing the Soviet Union as a workers' state—no matter how much she opposed its policies—because it preserved the structure of the October Revolution: nationalized industry, a planned economy, and a social welfare program couched in a hopeful Marxist ideology.

Her advocacy of feminism within a socialist context tended to liberate Kollontai from a set of restrictions that had frequently hampered her arguments. Since before the Revolution, Kollontai had been trying to convince the Party that her work among women was not simply ethically or socially desirable, but economically and politically essential to the socialist state. This pressure caused inconsistency. Kollontai told the International Communist Women's Conference in 1921 that the broad mass of women had ceased to be the bulwark of counterrevolution, that after two and a half years of special work the Zhenotdel had managed to awaken political consciousness in working women and to teach them to be active participants in the construction of a new society. Women's passivity toward and distrust of the Revolution and Soviet power existed now only in the remote areas where there was still no Women's Section.[15]

Yet it was the Party's need to reach the backward masses of non-Party women, the potential counterrevolutionaries, that Kollontai had used as her justification to the Eighth Party Congress in 1919 for the existence of a special apparatus in the Party to work among women.[16] If by 1921 most women had ceased to be counterrevolutionary, the Zhenotdel might logically be cut back. Instead, Kollontai

15. *Rabotnitsa i krest'ianka*, p. 7.
16. See USSR, [20], pp. 296–97.

demanded a strengthening of its work to bring women more fully into socialist construction. If she had not needed to justify the Zhenotdel as politically expedient, if she could have presented it instead, frankly, as a source of benefit for women, her reasoning would have been less tortured.

Kollontai came close to such candor in 1923 when she advocated special societies. The fundamental question, whether the deeper ties were those of sex or class, seemed to her no longer relevant. In a workers' state committed to women's full equality, women could appropriately unite to press for fulfillment of that commitment. Yet Kollontai still pointed to old dangers—in this case a possible resurgence of the bourgeois "Equal Righters"—to bolster her position. Perhaps in the conditions of the NEP, and the seeming resurgence of the bourgeoisie, Kollontai questioned what earlier she had affirmed: that with the bourgeois class reduced to a few remnants, the Communists no longer had to struggle against bourgeois feminism.[17] Or her warning may have been tactical. More important, Kollontai provided in 1923 a theoretical framework within which to justify employment by Communists of frankly feminist (meaning separatist) devices: special women's clubs and societies, not simply to entice women to build socialism, but to overcome the psychological obstacles to equality—passivity and lack of faith in their own abilities.[18] In the concept of special societies, the potential of working-class or socialist feminism reached its most sophisticated expression: these were to be unions not simply of urban factory women and village peasants, but implicitly of all Soviet women. In retrospect, not least significant was Kollontai's assumption that such interest groups, pressing for equal employment and collective living arrangements, had a role to play in the Soviet state.

Had she been its director throughout the years of the NEP, Kollontai might have influenced the Zhenotdel to accept her definition of working-class feminism. Still, anxiety to avoid suspicions of feminist separatism was deeply ingrained. Not even Communists with the impeccable credentials of Krupskaia and Inessa Armand were immune. Krupskaia, for example, in a memorial article thought it important to vouch that there had never been a trace of feminism (mean-

17. For her warning of the bourgeois danger, see *Pravda*, Mar. 20, 1923, p. 4. By contrast, see *Rabotnitsa i krest'ianka*, p. 24, for Kollontai's view in 1921 that Russian Communists no longer had to fight the bourgeois danger.

18. For Kollontai's concern with the Russian working woman's weak sense of independence (*samodeiatel'nost'*), see "Proizvodstvo i byt," p. 9. For Kollontai on female passivity, see *Rabotnitsa i krest'ianka*, p. 23.

ing separatism) in Inessa's work among women.[19] The scorn young Communist women felt toward feminists (whom they believed traditionally affected men's clothing) was illustrated in a story told by a female visitor to the Soviet Union during the 1920's. When she appeared one day wearing a man's shirt, a shocked *komsomolka* observed: "Women don't wear those, they are men's blouses. It was only in the last century that women dressed like that, as a protest against their treatment. Now women are free. . . . *Please* don't wear it. . . . It's politically incorrect. It's historically inaccurate."[20]

If Kollontai's response to Golubeva's proposal to establish special societies was a surprising and useful redefinition of feminism, the reaction of other Bolsheviks was predictable. The Twelfth Party Congress in April 1923 took note of Golubeva's special societies, ignored Kollontai's explanation, and rejected them as a feminist deviation that threatened to separate women from the working class. Criticizing the "separatism" and "feminism" exhibited by certain members of the Zhenotdel, the Twelfth Congress resolved that to counteract Zhenotdel inadequacy the work of the delegates' meetings among non-Party women be strengthened.

Sof'ia Smidovich, the Zhenotdel director, welcomed the resolution.[21] Why she reacted positively to it but negatively to the idea of special societies is, at first, puzzling. Smidovich shared Kollontai's and Golubeva's distress over the Party's neglect of the women's movement. The presence of only four women as voting delegates among the 400 members of the Twelfth Congress, when the Party had a membership of some 22,000 women, appalled her. She blamed the remnants of bourgeois "chauvinism," the sluggish, inert attitude of certain Communists toward women, and hoped it would not happen again.[22]

19. Krupskaia, "Inessa Armand," *Kommunistka*, 1920, no. 5, p. 19.
20. Winter, pp. 51–52.
21. For the resolution see USSR, [5], p. 685. Smidovich thought it would help the Zhenotdel repair the deficiencies of the delegates' meetings, end lack of discipline, and be more systematic. It was time, she wrote, to stop underestimating the delegates' meetings, to cease questioning their right to exist. See Smidovich, "XII s"ezd partii o rabote," pp. 4–5.
22. Smidovich, "XII s"ezd partii o rabote," pp. 4–5. In 1923 the Communist Party had 381,400 full and 117,700 candidate members. See Rigby, pp. 52–54, for membership figures and discussion of discrepancies in the sources for the years up to 1932, and p. 361 for a table on the sex structure of CPSU membership, 1922–1967. There were fewer female delegates at the Twelfth Congress than at preceding congresses: at the Ninth and Tenth Congresses, for example, women were about 5 percent of the voting dele-

Smidovich deplored Communist neglect of women but opposed Golubeva's alternatives largely because she erroneously believed, after the Twelfth Congress, that the Party had changed its course. "Full Party direction" of the Zhenotdel, the Party's new slogan, heartened her.[23] Ironically, "Party direction," so ominous to other Soviet institutions, seemed to promise what the Zhenotdel wanted: attention from the Central Committee. Smidovich's hopes were understandable. They added poignancy to her role. She wanted to believe that the Party approved of her as director, that it was ready, therefore, to support the Zhenotdel adequately. Despite the disappointing history of previous promises, she grasped at the pledge of the Twelfth Congress to combat "feminist deviations" by a rededication to Zhenotdel goals, in the hope that Party leaders were belatedly replying to her earlier challenge.

Smidovich may have feared that with their talk of special societies, Kollontai and Golubeva were raising the specter not only of feminism but of factionalism.[24] Her fear of a female faction was rooted in Party recognition that under the NEP it was not dealing adequately with the woman question. Special societies of unemployed, non-Party women, Smidovich thought, might attempt to substitute themselves for Soviet institutions.[25] The cautious qualities that made Smidovich

gates; at the Eleventh, women were less than 2 percent—nine out of 513 delegates. See Hayden, p. 166.

23. The Eleventh Congress had resolved to end liquidationist sentiment. See USSR, [8], p. 558. And, indeed, one writer reported no liquidationist sentiment at the Twelfth Congress. See unsigned article, "Chto skazal XII partiinyi s"ezd po rabote sredi rabotnits i krest'ianok," Kommunistka, 1923, no. 5, p. 13. For Smidovich's optimism, see "XII s"ezd partii o rabote," p. 5.

24. Factionalism was defined as "the emergence of groups with special platforms and a certain striving to close ranks and create their own group discipline." See Tucker, Stalin, p. 296. The Tenth Congress, in a resolution not published with the rest of the documents emanating from it, empowered the Central Committee to enforce a ban against factions even involving Central Committee members. A two-thirds vote of the combined total membership of the Central Committee and the Central Control Commission was required for demotion or expulsion of a Central Committee member. For discussion, see USSR, [8], p. 577.

25. Smidovich, "Soveshchanie zavedyvaiushchikh," pp. 10–11. For Party recognition of tensions in the area of work among women, see Chapter 9 above and USSR [5], p. 685. Zhenotdel progress in providing social services for women in the early 1920's was extremely limited. In Oct. 1923, Kovnator reported that the Zhenotdel had created 545 children's institutions in all of Russia, and that 909 summer day nurseries had been organized for the children of peasant women. In Jan. 1925, in Leningrad, a city with about 50,000 women workers, the local Zhenotdel reported about 53 centers for child care in the factories, serving 2,270 children. In Nov. 1924, Nikolaeva protested that the government's housing policy was contrary to Zhenotdel aims: in workers' housing, for example, no central kitchens were being built. For decreasing emphasis on the emancipation aspects of Zhenotdel activities in late 1920's, see Hayden, pp. 169–70.

an ideal candidate for the Central Control Commission caused her to suspect the intentions of the more adventurous Kollontai and her protégé Golubeva.

꘎꘎꘎

Did the pledge of the Twelfth Party Congress significantly improve the status of the Women's Section? A glance ahead seems appropriate. Closer Party control of the Zhenotdel meant that subsequent directors would be members of the Central Committee. It did not mean that its directors would wield more power. Rather, the directors would be subject to political storms. Klavdiia Nikolaeva, Kollontai's old friend and Smidovich's successor, rose and fell in the mid-1920's with the left-wing Zinovievists who were opposing Stalin and Bukharin. Similarly, her successor, A. V. Artiukhina, enjoyed some eminence with the Bukharinites.[26] When the moderates, the so-called Right Opposition to Stalin headed by Bukharin, Rykov, and Mikhail Tomskii, came under attack in the late 1920's, Artiukhina was removed.

To interpret Nikolaeva's and Artiukhina's loss of the directorship as part of a larger move to crush opposition to Stalin, who by the late 1920's was the supreme leader of the Party and the state, still does not explain the decision taken in 1930 finally to end the Zhenotdel. A more accurate guide to Party motivation was the resolution at the Twelfth Congress warning against the danger of feminist tendencies that "could lead to the female contingent of labor breaking away from the common class struggle."[27] Subsequent resolutions identified the danger of viewing the woman question in isolation from the common struggle of the working class.[28]

At the end of the decade, as the relatively fluid and tolerant NEP was abandoned, the Zhenotdel fell victim neither to the lack of popularity we saw in an earlier chapter, nor to internal friction, but to the larger purposes of Stalinist centralization. Stalin's consolidation of power within the central Party apparatus and his crash program of industrialization and collectivization in the countryside was accompanied by a reorganization of the Central Committee Secretariat in

26. Following the Fourteenth Party Congress, Artiukhina explained that the Zhenotdel's task was to propagandize among women against Zinoviev's Leningrad Opposition. See A. V. Artiukhina, "XIV S"ezd VKP (b) i nashi zadachi," *Kommunistka*, 1926, no. 1, pp. 10–15.

27. See USSR, [5], p. 685.

28. See USSR, [6], vol. 2, pp. 88–89, for resolutions of the Thirteenth Party Congress.

1930. The Women's Section (and with it its journal, *Kommunistka*) was abolished, its activities assigned to sections in charge of agitation and mass campaigns.[29]

The assumption that centralization of the Party apparatus caused the demise of the Zhenotdel is supported by the similar fate that year of the only other similar organization, the *Evsektsiia*, or Jewish Section of the Communist Party. Both groups in their composition and goals "breached the sexual, ethnic, and organizational unity of the Party."[30] Another parallel supports the view that interest groups like the Zhenotdel that functioned with some degree of autonomy could not survive the end of the NEP and its social and economic pluralism. Just as the Women's Section and the Jewish Section spoke for particular constituencies, so too did the trade unions.[31] The Party intruded into the trade-union organization in 1928 with the election of five Stalinist leaders to the Central Trade Union Council.

In the case of the expendable Zhenotdel, the Party took more drastic steps. Instead of imposing a new Stalinist leadership, it liquidated the organization, the fate that Zhenotdel workers always feared. Politically, it was appropriate that L. Kaganovich, Stalin's lieutenant, delivered the report announcing the Party's decision to abolish the Zhenotdel, while the Zhenotdel's last director, A. V. Artiukhina, a defeated Bukharinite, concurred. Kaganovich tried heavy-handedly to be tactful. Some people, he said, had objected to the abolition of the Zhenotdel; others cheered that "it was about time." He agreed with neither side. The Zhenotdel had accomplished a big job during its ten years. He was not one to regret its existence. But now that its work was complete, now that women had been drawn into the Soviets, the unions, and the

29. See Lapidus, "Sexual Equality in Soviet Policy," p. 123. For Party justification of abolishing the Zhenotdel, see *Pravda*, Jan. 17, 1930. Women's Departments were preserved in the Central Asian Party organization until the mid-1950's. On the reorganization of the Party apparatus, see M. Fainsod, *How Russia Is Ruled* (Cambridge, Mass., 1965), pp. 191–93.

30. Lapidus, "Sexual Equality in Soviet Policy," p. 124. For the stormy history of the Jewish Section, see Gitelman. Both organizations functioned not only to transmit the influence of the Communists but to defend the interests within the Party of constituencies that the organizations' supporters argued could not be reached and mobilized without a special apparatus designed for that purpose. Neither institution was more than tolerated by the Party. Both the Zhenotdel and the Evsektsiia were relatively autonomous by default.

31. The unions between 1921 and the late 1920's were not simply supposed to ensure Party influence over non-Party industrial workers and maintain production; they were chiefly expected to represent the interests of the workers during a regime of "state capitalism." Under the crash industrialization program inaugurated in 1928, however, maximizing productivity became the unions' main responsibility. See Daniels, pp. 344–48.

Party, the Zhenotdel had fulfilled its purpose. As Kaganovich defined it, that purpose was remarkably limited. Even the 13.5 percent of women in the Party in 1930 was unimpressive, only a small improvement over the figures Kollontai offered in 1923 of 9.2 percent in the cities and 4.2 percent in the country.[32]

Kaganovich did not conceal his suspicion that the Women's Section was feminist, i.e. separatist. He implied that with the end of the NEP and with the needs of heightened industrialization, the Zhenotdel's social concerns were inappropriate. Women were to be mobilized not as women but as workers. A separate Women's Section acted not as a progressive center but as a brake on progress.[33] Kaganovich agreed that opposition to women's full equality was still strong in 1930 and needed to be overcome. The responsibility lay now not with the Zhenotdel but with the entire Party.[34] It was a pious conclusion. Artiukhina echoed Kaganovich, rationalizing that the Central Committee, in placing responsibility for work among women on the whole Party, had in fact elevated work among women *to a higher level*. Artiukhina, an Old Bolshevik, a factory worker from the age of twelve whose Party career had been spent among working-class women, knew better. Nearly every word belied her attempt to be optimistic and revealed what the Zhenotdel really thought about the reasons for its demise. She warned Communist women not to say that the Zhenotdel had been abolished because it was considered harmful, not to speculate whether somewhere, someone prevented the Zhenot-

32. See Kollontai, *Pravda*, Mar. 20, 1923, p. 4. Kaganovich illustrated his conclusion that the Zhenotdel had accomplished its purpose—drawing in women—by pointing to the 301,999 women members of the Soviets, the 3,078,000 women members of the trade unions, and the 56,608 women members of factory committees. As for Party committees, women in 1929 had increased to 20.1 percent, as compared with 7.1 percent in 1927. The numbers, he thought, were evidence that a separate section for work among women was no longer needed. See Kaganovich, "Reorganizatsiia partapparata i ocherednye zadachi partraboty," *Kommunistka*, 1930, no. 2–3, pp. 3–5, and Artiukhina, "Zhenrabotu vesti vsei partiei v tselom," *Kommunistka*, 1930, no. 2–3, pp. 6–7.

33. At the Sixteenth Party Congress, Kaganovich noted that peasant women were providing much of the resistance to collectivization and implied that their political backwardness might be blamed on the Zhenotdel's excessive concentration on problems of everyday life rather than on political education. See *XVI S"ezd Vsesoiuznoi Kommunisticheskoi Partii (b). Stenograficheskii Otchet* (Moscow-Leningrad, 1931), p. 70. If the Party hoped by abolishing the Zhenotdel to divert attention away from the concept of women as a group, it succeeded. An index of Party resolutions and decrees includes 301 entries on the subject "women" for the period 1917–30, but only three for the next three decades. Lapidus, "Sexual Equality in Soviet Policy," p. 124.

34. Kaganovich, *Kommunistka*, 1930, no. 2–3, p. 5. He explained that delegates' meetings would be retained. Special methods of mass agitation among women should still be conducted—especially in the East. They would be led by Women's Sections within the section for agitation and mass campaigns.

del from functioning. Such talk was incorrect, bore no relation at all to the Party line, and was forbidden.[35]

꙰꙰꙰꙰

Kollontai hardly anticipated in 1923 the gloomy fate of the Zhenotdel seven years later. But her article in *Pravda* justifying feminism within a workers' state was an example of the kind of "deviation" the Party hoped to eradicate. Her essays, short stories, and novellas exploring relations between the sexes, giving literary form to her concept of socialist feminism, only deepened suspicions within the Party that Kollontai was, after all, divisive.

Kollontai focused in these works on the lives of Soviet women. Her most direct message appeared in a simple short story that lashed out both at government indifference and at the regressive effect of the NEP on relations between the sexes. She sent the story, called "Sestry" ("Sisters"), to *Kommunistka*. It told of a young couple, both Party members, whose lives had been disrupted by the NEP. The wife had lost her job because of employment cutbacks and because she had a husband to support her. Her working-class husband began to move in a corrupting, bourgeois ambiance, drinking and staying out—in all, rather pleased that his wife was unemployed and thus better able to do housework. One night he brought home a prostitute. The embarrassed woman, unaware that her companion was married, apologized to his wife. The husband slept in a drunken stupor as the two women talked and found a common "women's language." At dawn, after the prostitute had left, the wife decided to go out and find her. For were they not "sisters," unemployed working-class women, each with only one means of earning her livelihood?[36] The bitter, didactic tale, which put in literary form Kollontai's earlier fears of the damaging effect of the NEP on male-female relationships, dismayed the Zhenotdel, although as a revolutionary statement it was above reproach. The leaders of the Women's Section seemed not to understand that Kollontai was doing more than merely protesting economic cutbacks, that she was protesting Communist failure to achieve with the Revolution a more honest and equal relationship between men and women.

The Zhenotdel leaders disassociated themselves from Kollontai, who still had a popular following, especially among students. We have

---

35. Artiukhina, *Kommunistka*, 1930, no. 2–3, pp. 6–7. Italics appear in the original.
36. Kollontai, "Sestry," *Kommunistka*, 1923, no. 3–4, pp. 23–26.

seen Smidovich's opposition to Kollontai's efforts from abroad to influence the Zhenotdel. Now it was the turn of Krupskaia and Vinogradskaia. The editorial staff of *Kommunistka* published "Sestry" but with a rebuke to its author. Acknowledging that cutbacks in employment among women were a tragic state necessity, the editors made a pathetic effort to counter Kollontai's conclusions. Why had neither of Kollontai's fictional victims appealed to the Party for help? If Kollontai's heroine had been a simple factory woman rather than an office employee, she could have turned to her trade union. Trade-union aid might not have been sufficient, but it would have provided moral support, they insisted lamely.[37]

Kollontai's unseemly gloom distressed *Kommunistka*'s editors. But remembering that Kollontai had only recently been one of them, they were restrained. Only Polina Vinogradskaia refused to be bound by loyalty to an exiled comrade. Later she would claim that Krupskaia encouraged her to write an article criticizing Kollontai, a vicious denunciation published in the literary journal *Krasnaia Nov'*.[38] Either Krupskaia was reluctant to sponsor an attack on Kollontai in her own journal and preferred to have a young, less well-known Communist take responsibility, or another member of *Kommunistka*'s editorial board—it might have been Kollontai's friend Bukharin—withheld approval.[39] In any event, Vinogradskaia's attack did not appear in the pages of *Kommunistka*.

Professing amazement that such a dismal story could come from the pen of a woman who was still regarded as a leader of the women's movement, Vinogradskaia wondered why Kollontai thought "Sestry" appropriate for publication in *Kommunistka*. If Kollontai felt herself a responsible leader, she should have constructed a story that did not depict the dark corners of life. Vinogradskaia insisted, in an early example of what would come to be called socialist realism, that Communists from whom the masses sought answers should not sow dejection, hopelessness, even panic.[40] Vinogradskaia accused Kollontai of deviating further by espousing "feminism," of forcing on the

37. *Ibid.*, p. 26. For Kollontai's earlier expression of the same fear about the effect of the NEP on male-female relationships, see "Novaia ugroza," pp. 5–9.

38. The claim appeared only in 1969, in Vinogradskaia, "Serdtse, otdannoe narodu," p. 193. Vinogradskaia's attack was made in the Oct.-Nov. 1923 issue of *Krasnaia Nov'*, and was entitled "Voprosy morali, pola, byta i tov. Kollontai."

39. Kollontai's references to Bukharin in *Vasilisa Malygina* suggest their continuing friendship. Bukharin was the only Communist leader other than Lenin whom Kollontai mentioned by name. See *Vasilisa Malygina* in *Liubov' pchel trudovykh*, p. 184.

40. Vinogradskaia, "Voprosy morali, pola, byta i Tov. Kollontai," p. 203.

reader her single, fully worked-out conclusion "down with men."[41] But Vinogradskaia distorted Kollontai's conclusion, which was not an attack on men but rather an implicit call for "new people."

Kollontai developed her concept of "new people" more explicitly in essays published in 1923 in the Komsomol journal, *Molodaia Gvardiia*, called "Letters to Working Youth."[42] One praised the marvelously sensitive poetry of Anna Akhmatova who, although she was unsympathetic to the Communists, wrote about women and love in ways Kollontai hoped would induce in Communist youth a greater awareness of the nuances of sexual relationships. Another developed Kollontai's theories of relationships between the sexes, expanding on what had appeared earlier in her *New Morality and the Working Class*. Although she had once written (in *The Social Bases of the Woman Question*) that between the "emancipated woman of the intelligentsia and the toiling woman with calloused hands there was . . . an unbridgeable gulf,"[43] Kollontai chose an emancipated, intellectual poet, Anna Akhmatova, to inspire working-class youth. Despite the great poet's lack of revolutionary consciousness, Kollontai understood that the spirit of contemporary women infused her poetry. Akhmatova, giving voice to a woman's point of view, wrote of women who were demanding change, who needed some independence from love and who wanted to work in a time of social transformation. Akhmatova examined attitudes toward her sex. Two themes repeated themselves in her poetry in an unconscious dialectic: one was man's inability to recognize the individuality of the woman he loved; the other was the striving of women to combine love with creative work. Kollontai put Akhmatova's themes in a socialist framework. Communists forging a new culture could not solve the woman question with the one-sided, masculine approach typical of the bourgeois past, in which a man loved a woman but did not really see her. For most men, woman was still Eve—woman in general. Men in whom the customs of bourgeois ideology were still strong seldom noticed that women, encouraged to live primarily for emotions, were being asked to sacrifice their own worth—the "white bird" within them of which Akhmatova sang. For Kollontai, one example from Akhmatova's poetry sufficed. When her lover called it absurd for a woman to be a poet, and Akhmatova asked what was it that he loved in her if he did

41. *Ibid.*
42. Kollontai, "Pis'ma k trudiashcheisia molodezhi o 'drakone' i 'beloi ptitse,'" pp. 162–74, and "Dorogu krylatomu erosu! (Pis'mo k trudiashcheisia molodezhi)," pp. 111–24.
43. *Sotsial'nye osnovy zhenskago voprosa*, p. 19.

not recognize that she was a poet, she spoke for all women striving to express themselves.[44]

As vigorously as Kollontai called for a new relationship between the sexes, other Communists, joining Vinogradskaia, pushed back. Paradoxically, it was two young Communists from the lower ranks of the Party who publicly opposed as feminism Kollontai's praise of Akhmatova. B. Arvatov and G. Lelevich, the "vigilante" critics as they have been called, denied that working women could respond to the non-Communist Akhmatova. They insisted that Kollontai, praising Akhmatova, was not operating within a Marxist framework: she concentrated on the "battle of the sexes," revealing a feminist subjectivism with which Communists had nothing in common. Arvatov objected to Kollontai's separation of the woman question from the larger social problem, her thinking not in Marxist but in feminist terms by grouping together women who struggled for their independence against love as though the struggle alone rather than its object determined their political affiliation. Would Kollontai include Cleopatra, Madame de Staël, and Sarah Bernhardt among the proletariat?

Arvatov anticipated by over twenty years the condemnation of Akhmatova by Stalin's lieutenant Andrei Zhdanov when he called Akhmatova's poetry the work of a martyr, an hysterical bourgeoise who relished pain and suffering. He counted in one book the word death 25 times, melancholy seven, sorrow seven, and so on. Believing that Akhmatova could influence youth only in individualistic, neurotic ways, Arvatov declared himself appalled that Kollontai would recommend advice so harmful to youth as a means to understand women.[45] Lelevich spoke for the Association of Proletarian Writers (which had declared class war on the literary front) and fatuously repeated Arvatov's word count, agreeing that any poet so immersed in concepts of death and suffering must simply be morbid. He seconded Arvatov's view that Kollontai's endorsement of Akhmatova's poetry should be rejected as feminism.[46]

Lelevich for the Association of Proletarian Writers, Vinogradskaia for the Zhenotdel—each in a narrow way tried to reduce the beauty of

44. For Kollontai's discussion of Akhmatova, see "Pis'ma k trudiashcheisia molodezhi," pp. 166–68.

45. Arvatov, pp. 148–51. Zhdanov issued a similar statement in 1946 to accompany Akhmatova's expulsion from the Union of Soviet Writers and to prohibit publication of her work in the Soviet press.

46. Lelevich, pp. 188–94. Kollontai's comrade N. Osinskii also recognized Akhmatova's greatness. Lelevich called Osinskii outrageous for saying Akhmatova was Russia's foremost poet. *Ibid.*, pp. 178, 188, 200.

Akhmatova's poetry to neurasthenia and to denigrate Kollontai's empathy with her. Denying that questions of sexuality could provide revolutionary themes, Vinogradskaia professed bafflement that *Molodaia Gvardiia* considered appropriate for publication a feminist article that concentrated on themes as irrelevant as women in love.[47] Vinogradskaia's anger lay partly in awareness that freer sexuality increased the misery of working-class life in a society that had not yet built the social institutions to provide for its consequences. But still her bitterness was exceptional. The editors of *Krasnaia Nov'* apologized to Kollontai in a subsequent issue for Vinogradskaia's attack. The editors might not agree with Kollontai, but they wanted it known that she was a fighting comrade and not the bourgeois lady Vinogradskaia rather cruelly portrayed as being out of touch with proletarian reality, enjoying diplomatic comfort in Norway, and indulging in her favorite hobby—questions of sexual morality.[48]

Vinogradskaia was not only harsh, she was also inconsistent. She accused Kollontai of being absorbed with men, sex, and love, but at the same time charged her with joining feminists in rejecting men. Although Vinogradskaia did not notice the contradiction, it was not difficult to explain. We see the political reasons underlying Kollontai's concerns, her important argument that the patterns of male-female relationships, since they influenced women's role, must be transformed and become a factor in revolutionary planning. But political considerations were only part of her motivation. If in 1923 Kollontai appeared preoccupied with questions of love, if she was drawn to the poetry of Akhmatova and attracted to the feminist idea of bonds between women, it was also out of response to her own pain. Kollontai needed to turn to Akhmatova's testimony to a woman's strength to endure the loss of love because her private life was in disarray.

꿈꿈꿈

Her five-year marriage to Pavel Dybenko—which began during the first year of Revolution when, as she liked to recall, they fought together for the Soviet—was ending. Dybenko had fallen in love with a young woman. The trauma of unhappiness caused Kollontai's thoughts to turn inward to questions of emotions, of communication

47. Vinogradskaia, "Voprosy morali, pola, byta," pp. 182, 209. *Molodaia Gvardiia's* editors did note that because of the numerous controversial points in Kollontai's article, they published it with a view to opening it to discussion. For editorial note, see *Molodaia Gvardiia*, 1923, no. 2, p. 162.

48. For the editors' apology, see *Krasnaia Nov'*, 1923, no. 7, p. 306.

and trust between men and women who were not only lovers but Communists. She pondered a complex issue. If they were Communists, why were they not really comrades?

Kollontai's "Letters to Working Youth" prophesied a new kind of relationship between men and women. Her novels, on the other hand, reflected ambivalence toward any emotional relationship with men. Revolutionary women tended to avoid elaboration of their personal lives. Kollontai was the exception. In *Vasilisa Malygina*, Kollontai wrote a fictional but thinly disguised account of the end of her marriage to Dybenko. *Vasilisa Malygina* is the story of Vasia, a young working-class woman and Communist Party member who falls in love with Volodia, a fellow Communist with anarchist leanings. Vasia and Volodia begin living together during the Civil War. Eventually he becomes a successful NEP entrepreneur who succumbs to bourgeois pleasures, one of which is a love affair with a member of the former bourgeoisie, a powdered and pampered *Nepmansha*, Nina, a young woman who is looking for a man to take care of her. Although the occupations of the protagonists are changed, the novel is a series of unhappy episodes that trace the disintegration of the Kollontai-Dybenko relationship.[49]

By putting this story on paper Kollontai sought not only to work out ideas suggested to her by Akhmatova's poetry but also to free herself from the need to relive mentally the episodes of her passionate love for Dybenko. She put in the novel all of what Kollontai's Soviet biographer alluded to primly as the "difficult ordeals" of life with Dybenko,[50] beginning with his other brief affairs during their enforced long separations and Kollontai's decision that she could not drop him simply because he had hurt her. "A poor thing, her love, if she would leave him the first time he had made her suffer." In her account of Volodia she retold the agony of the harsh knock at the door and Dybenko's arrest for treason in 1918. In 1923 it still seemed to her that she had never lived through anything more dreadful than the night they took Dybenko away. By herself, she defended this "big, helpless, childlike man," for who would understand him if not she? She trusted Dybenko "as much as it was possible to trust anyone."[51] To her he seemed a romantic revolutionary, whose harshness and obstinacy were only on the surface. If he was sometimes embit-

49. See *Vasilisa Malygina* in *Liubov' pchel trudovykh*.
50. Itkina, p. 194.
51. *Vasilisa Malygina*, pp. 107, 113–14. Kollontai's references are to Volodia, but it is Dybenko she describes.

tered by disappointment with the Revolution, if he was occasionally foulmouthed, abusive, and insubordinate, she was able always to reason with him.[52]

Her novel described the five years Kollontai lived as Dybenko's wife, alternately adoring and worrying about her husband, a military commander who did not maintain discipline,[53] a lover who was occasionally unfaithful, a man who drank too much and liked to show off. Then in 1922 when life was bleak, when for a second time she was deprived of her official positions and was fighting for the right to remain in the Party, she went on a trip to Odessa to be with her husband, who had received a military command there. In Odessa (which in the novel becomes "a southern city") she discovered that he had fallen in love. In the novel, his lover was a Nepgirl. In fact, Dybenko was living with an orphan of nineteen.[54] This painful triangle, only slightly disguised, forms the primary focus of the book.

Central to the fictionalized account of the demise of Kollontai's marriage was her portrayal of Volodia-Dybenko as less strong and decisive than she. Vasia-Kollontai in the end appears the resolute, controlling figure. It may not have been Kollontai's intention, but Volodia emerges as very human, an affectionate man who weeps with the torment of having to decide between his new young love and his beloved mentor. Although it was in the interest of her emotional well-being to portray herself as strong and Volodia-Dybenko as never having ceased to love her, if Kollontai's vignettes were drawn from reality, then Dybenko's love indeed seemed real. Volodia is convincing when he tells Vasia that he cannot picture life without her, and when he reaches for understanding with the plea that she not desert him: "not now, help me, advise me."[55] Between him and the young girl there is no common ground. She is not a comrade. She can never be a friend like Vasia-Kollontai. He takes care of the girl and feels responsible for her; yes, he loves her, but not as he loves Vasia, for whom his feelings are stronger and deeper. "I can't see any course without you. . . ." And he reminds Vasia how he always wondered what she would say, what she would advise. "You've been my guiding star, and I need you!"[56]

52. *Ibid.*, pp. 79, 107. Souvarine recalled (p. 258) that Dybenko tried to leave the Party in 1918 when the death penalty was reinstituted.

53. *Vasilisa Malygina*, p. 78.

54. See Hauge, p. 50, for the episode in Odessa.

55. *Vasilisa Malygina*, p. 179.

56. *Ibid.*, pp. 252–53, 270.

The suicide attempt that figures in the novel approximated what actually happened. In his anguish over having to make a choice, Dybenko attempted to take his own life with his revolver. The bullet missed his heart, but it penetrated his lung and caused a severe infection.[57] Kollontai remained in Odessa to nurse Dybenko through his recovery, but when he kept calling in his delirium for the young girl, she returned to Moscow.

She wrote a melancholy letter that cried out for refutation. Assuring Dybenko that she was not the wife he needed, she described herself as a "person" (*chelovek*) before she was a woman. Once she had helped, but now she could only hinder him. He needed another kind of wife, one who would not overshadow him but who would create a home, be with him, take care of him. He knew that she was not suited for that role, that she scorned domesticity. So why should he doom himself to continue so difficult a life? And in a few pain-filled words Kollontai urged him to take his share of "youthful happiness."[58] In the past Kollontai had seemed to surmount gracefully the taboos of sex across generations. Shliapnikov, we recall, had also been her junior. But unease over their difference in age—Dybenko was 34 and she was 51—may have convinced her that their marriage would sooner or later end. In her novel she recalled the protest of the husband that he was young and wanted to live.[59] It was a poignant memory.

Dybenko visited Norway in 1923 in an attempt at reconciliation. The effort failed, despite the love that bound them, the emotion that Kollontai called an "ember of passion, smoldering under the ashes of anger and estrangement." Of their last days together, she wrote "They were strange days, . . . sultry, gloomy."[60]

If Dybenko, as Volodia in the novel, was altogether understandable, Kollontai emerged as more complex. It would be interesting to know if she consciously meant to portray herself as rigid and uncompromising, a somewhat self-righteous Communist. If, as seems likely, Vasia was in large part Kollontai, then Kollontai, the advocate of the new woman, apparently also saw herself as possessive, the kind of woman whom elsewhere she pitied. Volodia-Dybenko offers Vasia-Kollontai what should appeal to her. He points out quite reasonably that they

57. Hauge, pp. 50–51, based on an account provided by E. Lorentsson. A close friend of Kollontai, Lorentsson claimed that the novel was autobiographical.

58. Excerpts from Kollontai's letter appear in Itkina, pp. 193–94.

59. *Vasilisa Malygina*, p. 208.

60. *Ibid.*, pp. 271, 277.

might go on as they had in the past. For "were we ever together before? We never had any family life. We were always working, saw each other only for a moment. . . . Shall we live that way again? . . . Would you like that? Each to live for himself. And when we miss each other, we'll meet. Will you? . . . We mustn't break off. . . . We don't have to part. . . . That's what hurts." But Kollontai could not easily be her "new woman." Indeed, sexual jealousy is the central theme of the novel. She was consumed by it; it grieved her but she could not control it.[61] "He asked her to pity him! Had he pity for her? Had he not tormented her? . . . All night long he had made love to another woman."[62] "Her heart was heavy with unspeakable pain . . . her beloved, her comrade, was betraying her, his friend."[63] He had talked about her with a strange woman "as if she were not his friend and comrade, but some enemy." And she "wanted to moan like a wounded animal, to sob loudly . . . for it was all over."[64] These lines constitute the emotional heart of the novel—not the somewhat artificial ending in which Kollontai has Vasia give up her husband, urging him to live with his lover while she lives with her unborn child, who will be brought up communally. What did she need a man for! That's all they could do— be fathers![65]

Vasilisa Malygina was no stilted Soviet novel with its stereotyped woman—the kind of novel that within a few years would become the norm in Soviet literature. It was a feminist novel in that it emphasized the twin concepts of female self-realization and sisterhood. It was also a departure from Kollontai's earlier writing, for at some point Vasia begins to feel compassion for Nina, the *Nepmansha*. This suggests that Kollontai now accepted a doctrine she had always fought against prior to the Revolution: that between women bonds existed transcending those of class. In a remarkable passage, Vasia explains her feelings toward Nina: "I sympathized with her as a sister, for she had known a woman's pain, and had suffered as much as I."[66] That the "*Nepka*" Nina and the Communist Vasia both lived in a working-class state did not make Kollontai's "feminism" less irritating to Bolsheviks.

We must keep in mind that Kollontai, contrary to what her detractors said, was not espousing feminism in the narrow, prerevolutionary

---

61. *Ibid.*, p. 271.
63. *Ibid.*, pp. 184–85.
65. *Ibid.*, p. 303.

62. *Ibid.*, p. 218.
64. *Ibid.*, pp. 251, 222.
66. *Ibid.*, p. 301.

sense of bourgeois individualism, or of separate organizations that threatened to divide the working class; rather, she was exploring the postrevolutionary possibilities of the socialist feminism she proclaimed in *Pravda*. And within Kollontai's pluralistic socialist feminism, women could band together under the guidance of Communist institutions in pursuit of their newly won rights, befriending each other despite their class origin. Golubeva's special societies; Vasia's "fine group [of] mostly women weavers," with whom she planned to live with her baby collectively at the weaving works; even Nina the Nepgirl —all could find a place.[67]

If Kollontai seemed to be accomplishing the difficult feat of synthesizing Communism and feminism, thus making it politically possible for women to be Communists and feminists both, she herself seemed burdened with other tensions. Consider for example Kollontai's "Letters to Working Youth." They called for a new, more sensitive man as partner to a liberated woman. But in her novels the Communist heroine rejected love for the warmth and camaraderie existing among Communist workers. Just as Vasia leaves Volodia in *Vasilisa Malygina*, in another novel, *Bol'shaia liubov'*, Natasha, the young Communist worker, leaves the Communist theoretician Senia. The best known of Kollontai's Communist heroines was Zhenia in "Liubov' trekh pokolenii" ("The Loves of Three Generations").[68] Indeed, Zhenia became notorious. The story of Zhenia has been much interpreted, usually to prove that Kollontai was irresponsibly and deliberately advocating promiscuity among the young. That was far from her purpose, but Zhenia did reflect Kollontai's fascination with the possibility of a life of camaraderie lived without romantic love. Artistically, "Liubov' trekh pokolenii" was no more ambitious than "Sestry." Each narrative took the form of a diary designed to convey a message. Where "Sestry" emphasized the bonds between women, "Liubov' trekh pokolenii" stressed the advantages of comradeship over romance, of work over emotional entanglement. The Austrian psychiatrist Helene Deutsch, who devoted a section of her *Psychology of Women* to Kollontai's Zhenia, called Kollontai's story an important cultural and historical document because it expressed faithfully the

67. *Ibid.*, p. 294.
68. "Liubov' trekh pokolenii" appeared with "Sestry" and *Vasilisa Malygina* in the collection *Liubov' pchel trudovykh*. The book was translated into several languages, and in Germany alone went through several editions.

ideas of women in the first period of the Russian Revolution.[69] The three generations were represented by Ol'ga, a "highly responsible" Party organizer; Ol'ga's mother, a typical propagandist of the 1860's, still active and in charge of a traveling library; and Ol'ga's daughter Zhenia, twenty years old, a Communist, and like her mother and grandmother devoted to her work. Here we find a neat Marxian dialectic in which the sexual patterns of the first two generations oppose each other and are then carried forward into a new resolution in the third. The grandmother, Mariia Stepanovna, is not unlike Kollontai's own mother—a "progressive" in her personal life, a woman who left one husband and married another, but a woman committed to monogamous marriage. Ol'ga, her daughter, resembles Kollontai. Her commitment is to "free love," which she posits against her mother's ideal of a freely contracted love marriage. Ol'ga, believing in freedom from conventional marriage ties, finds herself in love simultaneously with two men, one a comrade whom she loves spiritually, the other a man whose politics she does not respect but whom she loves sensually. Ol'ga's mother, whose morality is entirely oriented toward love for one man, can only disapprove of her daughter's conflict.

But the real focus of the story is Ol'ga's daughter Zhenia, the third generation. She begins a casual affair with her mother's lover, describing it in simple terms as an extension of the Marxist philosophy of the abolition of private property to love: Comrade R., who lives with mother and daughter in their one-room apartment, is not her mother's private possession. Ol'ga claims that it is not the affair she finds so distressing as the heartlessness and cynicism of the pair, for whom there is no love and no passion. Ol'ga, remembering how she suffered and struggled to rid herself of the entanglements of love, cannot fathom their coldness. Their involvement with each other is "vulgar debauchery." Zhenia becomes pregnant and plans an abortion, but she does not even know who the father is![70]

Although Helene Deutsch wrote with a psychiatrist's insight, she was unaware of how personal a document "Liubov' trekh pokolenii" was. Kollontai's story seemed to Deutsch "particularly valuable" because Kollontai raised problems dispassionately without any desire to solve them, neither praising nor condemning.[71] Deutsch was more per-

69. See Helene Deutsch, *The Psychology of Women* (New York, 1944), vol. 1, p. 358.
70. Kollontai, "Liubov' trekh pokolenii," pp. 36–37.
71. Deutsch, *The Psychology of Women*, vol. 1, p. 358.

ceptive than Soviet critics, who assumed with shrill disapproval that Zhenia spoke for Kollontai. But to conclude as Deutsch did that Kollontai was detached and objective would be inaccurate. Rather than a cool observer faithfully depicting sexual mores during the revolutionary era, Kollontai was closely involved in the situation of her protagonists. We hear her first as Ol'ga, protesting that in Zhenia's sexual relationship there is no love, no suffering, no joy, no regret—nothing but the cold conviction of her right to pluck pleasure, now here, now there.[72] But as Zhenia she objects to a love relationship, because "one must have time to fall in love" and she has no time. Party activity has taken complete hold of her and her comrades, so they simply take advantage of the few short hours of release available to them. There is nothing binding.[73]

Zhenia, the Communist *aktivistka* who had lovers but no time to fall in love, emerged as a rather depressing stick figure despite Kollontai's effort to portray her in a friendly way. If she was utterly unconvincing in her wide-eyed protest that of course she loved her mother but that her affair did not concern her, it was because Kollontai did not really know the figure she projected. She was not the first author who did not understand her own creation. If Zhenia felt no sympathy for her mother, if it did not occur to her that her mother was suffering, it was because she was unable to empathize with another human being. Totally free of guilt, she viewed her liaison with Comrade R. simply as the result of living in a one-room apartment. Deutsch charged that any love Zhenia professed for her mother was infantile; Zhenia gladly received it but was unable to consider her mother's feelings. Zhenia was heartless. The Communist professor Aron Zalkind was similarly harsh, dismissing Zhenia's philosophy as "a disease, not a class idea."[74]

Deutsch called Zhenia incapable of human feeling. She failed to perceive that Zhenia was, in fact, not human. Though it is true that during the Civil War one could find young men and women who lived like Zhenia, the fact is not entirely relevant to Kollontai's story. Zhenia was Kollontai's fantasy of a more autonomous, less painful life lived without entangling emotions. Kollontai portrayed Zhenia not because she was encouraging youth to be promiscuous, as Communists charged, but because she needed in 1923 to convince herself, as

72. "Liubov' trekh pokolenii," pp. 43–44.
73. *Ibid.*, pp. 44–45.
74. Deutsch, *The Psychology of Women*, vol. 1, p. 372. For Zalkind's comment, see Halle, p. 110.

she tried to build a new life without Dybenko, that there were viable alternatives to romantic love.

Kollontai's fantasy of a flight from love was a cry of pain rather than a thought-out position. Her more persistent theme, which we can trace back to 1913 and the publication of her essay "Novaia Zhenshchina" ("The New Woman"), held that love should play a subordinate role in a woman's life and that her primary commitment should be to work. Zhenia tempted Kollontai. But that Kollontai did not intend Zhenia as a serious model was suggested by her anticipation of what she called the "mournful question," certain to come from some young reader, of whether the only escape from love's bondage was to break with it. In reply, Kollontai described a better alternative—that men develop a sensitivity toward women as comrades and treasure that individuality in women about which Akhmatova wrote.

Ultimately, Kollontai's deepest commitment was to the socialist commune, in which there flourished neither escapees from love nor women alone, but "new people" bound by friendship and "many-sided love." Recalling in her "Letter to Working Youth" Aleksandr Herzen's novel *Who Is Guilty?*, Kollontai evoked the triangle in which one partner needs to make the painful choice between two individuals. If one loved one person with a physical passion and another with a spiritual devotion based on years of shared ideas, did one need to be torn apart in the choosing? Not in the collective of the future. Instead of the tyranny of individual love, a network of warmth would so support the individual that sexual passions could be made tractable. Hurt, jealousy, and possessiveness would disappear because there would be neither isolation nor loneliness. Neither the self-absorbed couple nor sexuality would dominate. Each would be relegated to a lesser place, and collective work would be the generating motor and the unifying force.[75] The friendship and mutual commitment of the collective would replace a couple's need for each other and provide emotional

75. Kollontai, "Dorogu krylatomu erosu!," p. 123. Ironically, H. Marcuse used Kollontai's collective, so alarmingly loose to most Bolsheviks, as another example of Soviet repression. See his *Soviet Marxism* (New York, 1961), pp. 233–34. See Kollontai, "Tezisy o kommunisticheskoi morali," pp. 28–34, for her attack on the concept of the couple as harmful to the collective. For example, Kollontai saw the right of a wife to be transferred to the area where her husband worked as damaging to the collective bonds of the group. See "Tezisy o kommunisticheskoi morali," p. 30. For Kollontai's description of the future commune, see *Skoro (cherez 48 let)*. A close parallel to Kollontai's commune was the early kibbutz, which also rejected the isolated couple. For sexual insecurity of aging women in the kibbutz when marriage was only a love union, see Spiro, *Kibbutz: Venture in Utopia*, pp. 113–17, 217–35.

solace to a greater extent than could the single spouse. The "Letter to Working Youth" might well have been entitled "Conversations with Myself." Kollontai was using social ideology also to mask her individual motives. Just as she tried in 1918 to shake free of excessive maternal love as a byproduct of writing *The Family and the Communist State*, so she sought in 1923 to exorcise her own jealousy and sexual possessiveness.

Kollontai acknowledged her limitations and conflicts in a frank autobiographical sketch, in which she admitted that she was still far from being one of the positively new women "who take their experience as females with a relative lightness and, one could say, with an enviable superficiality. . . . After all, I still belong to the generation of women who grew up at a turning point in history. Love, with its many disappointments, with its tragedies and eternal demands for perfect happiness, still played a very great role in my life. An all-too-great role!" Two years after her separation from Dybenko she was still emotionally in pain. Thus she added of her love, "It was an expenditure of precious time and energy, fruitless and, in the final analysis, utterly worthless. We, the women of the past generation, did not yet understand how to be free."[76] Ultimately, she would decide that deep bonds of female friendship—her love for Zoia Shadurskaia, for example—were more valuable and enduring than sexual love.[77]

Writing novels reinforced her commitment to creative work and emotional detachment. But much as Kollontai tried to divest herself of preoccupation with painful memories by transferring them to literary form, the process was slow. There were moments of despair when, despite the distractions of diplomacy, she felt herself a discarded, middle-aged woman cast out by the Central Committee and abandoned by her lover. She wondered why she was always far from those dear to her: her son Misha and her friend Zoia. She dared not think of Pavel Dybenko. There were times when she questioned the choices she had made that denied her the possibility of warm and simple happiness. But she banished self-doubt. She wrote to Zoia that, as always in moments of suffering, it was work that rescued her. "As you might guess," she told Zoia after Dybenko's departure from Norway, "no one here suspects what I am going through. I work to the utmost." She tried to absorb herself in the unfamiliar details of the purchase of

76. Kollontai, *Autobiography*, p. 7.
77. Nilsson, "Det Stora Uppdraget," *Vi*, 1961, no. 35, part 1, p. 9. Kollontai's commitment to the bonds of love among women is discussed in Chapter 12 below.

herring and sealskins and the sale of grain. For, as she concluded, "It is better this way. . . . It is essential."[78]

٭٭٭

For Kollontai, a strange new chapter began in Norway in October of 1922. Her intervention in the affairs of the Zhenotdel was, at best, intermittent and long-range. From the time she took up her duties as a member of the Soviet legation to her departure at the end of 1925, Kollontai knew that she must try to establish a life without the women's movement and the daily excitement of party politics. Her days turned out to be busier than she had anticipated; Norway had initially seemed mainly a place to write. She was appointed head of the legation and became the official Russian representative. She set herself the tasks of effecting the *de jure* recognition of Soviet Russia and of reestablishing normal trade relations, which had been broken by war and revolution.[79] Strenuous work and new experiences were only briefly diverting. For a time Kollontai enjoyed the publicity she received as the first woman ambassador. We do not know if she was aware that it was "the fashion, in diplomatic circles, to sneer at her, to tell stories of her bygone adventures and to suggest that even now she seeks fresh ones."[80] Kollontai simply wearied of the sterile life of the diplomat and the daily routine that absorbed her energy but in the end bored her. The "façade" of diplomacy, combined with personal considerations (to be discussed later), caused Kollontai to ask to be relieved of her diplomatic position. Although she knew that a Communist did not easily "resign," and that she would not be permitted to resume political life in Moscow, she left Oslo in December 1925 with no intention of returning. She did not anticipate that she would become embroiled in what would be her last campaign to influence the woman question.

78. Itkina, p. 194. See Mindlin, *Ne dom, no mir*, p. 389, for Kollontai's self-questioning.
79. Kollontai's upgrading to Minister to Norway was announced in Feb. 1923. A trade agreement was concluded at the end of 1925. Kollontai, *Autobiography*, p. 47. For details of the Norwegian years, see Body, pp. 12–24.
80. Quoted from a 1931 diplomatic report in Hauge, p. 276.

CHAPTER ELEVEN

The Last Battle: The 1926 Marriage Law Debate

WHEN Kollontai arrived in Moscow from Norway late in December 1925, the regime was revising the marriage law that she had helped to frame in 1918. Despite her tenuous status as a banished Communist who had just resigned her post, she plunged into a highly visible and, as it turned out, lonely fight against the government's new proposals. The day would come when Kollontai's strength would be that of a victim, a survivor; in 1926, it was still that of a bold combatant.

As in 1923, when Kollontai became involved from afar in the politics of the Zhenotdel, her concern was unwelcome. Sof'ia Smidovich, who headed the Party's renewed campaign against Kollontai, decided that the former director of the Zhenotdel advocated ideas too radical for the "transitional era." Kollontai's final battle to influence the course of the socialist women's movement was the occasion of her last collision with Smidovich. The two former directors of the Zhenotdel, each committed to the liberation of women but each convinced of the correctness of her own path to that goal, demonstrated their different perceptions of Soviet women. The stakes were lower and the battle less brutal than that going on in the Politburo, but the Bolsheviks in the socialist women's movement were struggling just as futilely with each other to arrive at an essentially similar Communist future. That success ultimately eluded both Kollontai and Smidovich —that their movement and its institutional home, the Zhenotdel, would at the close of the decade be brought to an end—suggests the tragedy of their situation.

To understand the final conflict between Kollontai and Smidovich over revision of the marriage law, it is necessary to explore first the legal and social status of marriage as it was legislated in the Soviet state. Among students of Soviet history, a view prevails that in the 1930's family policy "changed from a radical to a conservative one," from an attack on the traditional family to support of it.[1] Such a theory encourages the notion that in the 1920's the regime held an advanced attitude toward women and a casual view of marriage, which suddenly gave way to a conservatism imposed by Stalin. Superficially this may seem to have been so; but as an interpretation of Bolshevik social policy during the first two decades of Soviet power, such a view is misleading.[2] It overemphasizes the influence of Communists like Kollontai and ignores what should by now be apparent—that at nearly every turn Kollontai met strong Party and government opposition to her ideas on marriage and family.

Stalinist social legislation in the 1930's represented not a reversal of policy but rather the triumph of certain traditionalist strains within Bolshevism that had been strong throughout the 1920's. Early Bolshevism was not monolithic, for we have seen Communists opposing each other not only on political and economic issues but also on social ones. Thus those revolutionary principles that presumably underwent conservative change in the 1930's—women's genuine equality and independence from men, the noninterference of society in the relations between the sexes, collective responsibility for the upbringing of children, the absolute right of divorce, and the legalization of abortion—were in fact from the outset sources of tension and conflict within the Party. Furthermore, we know that the Soviet regime, however impeccable the socialism of its rhetoric, never disdained the family in practice. Soviet society was too backward, the problems of economic reconstruction too vast, and the commitment of its leaders ultimately too ambivalent for fundamental innovation to occur in this intimate area.

If not a zeal for social experimentation, what did motivate the rush during the first revolutionary year to enact new marriage laws? In the area of marriage and divorce, the Communists saw an opportunity for legislation to overcome the backwardness of tsarist Russia. Determined to combat the influence of the church, the new Bolshevik government

1. See, for example, Geiger, p. 321. For other suggestions that the Communists launched an attack on the family in the 1920's, see Alex Inkeles, *Social Change in Soviet Russia* (New York, 1961), p. 5; J. D. Clarkson, *A History of Russia* (New York, 1969), p. 573; and Nicholas Riasanovsky, *A History of Russia* (New York, 1963), p. 621.
2. Geiger, for example, refers to the "radical family legislation of the early years" (p. 321). Inkeles, Clarkson, and Riasanovsky present similar views.

declared in the fall of 1918 that henceforth it would recognize only marriages registered with the civil authorities.[3] As for the absolute right to divorce granted in 1917, it was regarded as one of the great achievements of the October Revolution, intended to indicate at once that the Communists wanted freedom for women, traditionally subordinate and bound to their husbands. But the institution of marriage, far from being undermined, was to remain stable, despite Kollontai's efforts to influence policy in contrary ways at the Eighth Party Congress. A new kind of marital union would simply take the place of the traditional one; by no means could the family, in accordance with the venerable socialist slogan, begin to wither away.[4] What we have come to know as Kollontai's vision remained for a distant Communist future. Meanwhile, the Soviet family had responsibilities to fulfill.

The original Bolshevik marriage laws, far from being socialist, were no more than modern and Western, as Bolsheviks themselves acknowledged. A member of the Supreme Court of the USSR explained this when a new marriage law was being debated in 1925.

Our existing legislation on family and marriage relations was created by the methods of bourgeois law. This legislation has not and cannot have anything communist in it as some comrades are trying to prove. The new law that is being submitted to the present session of the All-Russian Executive Committee for approval likewise has nothing communist in it. . . . Under the prevailing conditions we are compelled to construct our law according to the methods of bourgeois law. The project for the Code of Laws on Marriage, Family, and Guardianship as drafted by the Council of People's Commissars contains nothing that would go against bourgeois law. . . . The State puts the matter thus: if two people propose to get married, these two must, first, undertake to help each other, and second, if they intend to have children, undertake to keep these children, feed them, rear them, and educate them. In a communist society this care is undertaken by the society itself, without making its individual members bear these responsibilities. But during the period of transition we are forced to follow the methods of the bourgeois countries.[5]

3. See "Kodeks zakonov ob aktakh grazhdanskogo sostoianiia, brachnom, semeinom i opekunskom prave," Oct. 17, 1918, nos. 76–77, art. 818, in USSR, [15], pp. 933–59. Excerpts appear as "Code of Laws Concerning the Civil Registration of Deaths, Births, and Marriages of October 17, 1918" in Schlesinger, ed., 33–41. Church marriages that predated the introduction of obligatory civil registration on Dec. 20, 1917, had the validity of registered marriages.

4. For the Communist belief that the traditional family would wither and disappear, see Engels, pp. 83, 89, and Karl Marx and Friedrich Engels, *The Communist Manifesto* (New York, 1955), pp. 27–28.

5. Statement of P. A. Krasikov, cited in Schlesinger, ed., pp. 133–34.

Why then, if the marriage law was already conservative, was there a need in 1925 to change it? Though the 1918 marriage code had included such "un-Communist" provisions as male responsibility for women, parental responsibility for children's upbringing, and the legal obligation of relatives for each other's economic well-being,[6] the regime thought it necessary midway through the 1920's to back away from its Communist ideals still more. The reason for this was that the transition to the New Economic Policy in 1921 had resulted as we have seen in burgeoning female unemployment. We recall that the NEP meant not only a partial restoration of private enterprise but the end of labor conscription, a feature of War Communism that had provided work and rations for great numbers of people, especially women. Under the NEP, as we indicated earlier, 70 percent of the initial job cutbacks resulting from the partial restoration of free market conditions involved women, the least skilled members of the labor force.[7] Simultaneously, as the government reduced its investment in protective arrangements—primarily child care—after 1922, the number of homes for mothers and children fell sharply.[8] For hundreds of thousands of unemployed women who had not registered their marriages with the civil authorities, the situation was potentially perilous: should their husbands leave them, they would be without means of support.

By 1925, after four years of wide-scale female unemployment, the struggle against church weddings did not seem as urgent to the government as the need to protect women, the "weaker" party in marriage.[9] The Council of People's Commissars reacted by abandoning its policy of recognizing only marriages registered with the civil authorities. It proposed to the All-Russian Central Executive Committee in October 1925 a new family code that would make unregistered marriages legal.[10] The purpose, Commissar of Justice Dmitrii Kurskii explained, was to safeguard women by extending to nonregistered, *de facto* wives the right to receive alimony. Further, the government proposed to add to the 1918 law, under which a destitute spouse "unable to work" was entitled to her husband's support, the broader right to alimony simply

6. See USSR, [15], pp. 933–59; Schlesinger, ed., pp. 33–41.
7. Kollontai, "Novaia ugroza," p. 6.
8. Smidovich, "O novom kodekse," p. 47; Smidovich, "Nashi zadachi," pp. 18–20.
9. This was explained in a note to the 1926 draft of the "Code of Laws on Marriage, Family, and Guardianship of the RSFSR," quoted in A. Godes, "The Conception of Legal and of *De Facto* Marriage According to Soviet Law," *Sovetskaia Iustitsiia*, 1939, no. 19–20, translated in Schlesinger, ed., p. 360.
10. See the projected marriage code of 1925 in *Brak i sem'ia*, pp. 25–35.

"during unemployment." Though this right would apply to "either husband or wife," Kurskii explained, it was "primarily intended to safeguard the women. And it is right that this should be so."[11]

In the highest echelons in 1925 a battle was raging between Trotsky and Stalin, but on the popular level debates over the proposed changes in the marriage law were sweeping Russia. That support for or opposition to the proposed changes did not break down along Left Bolshevik–Right Bolshevik lines, but were above Party factionalism, is precisely why the controversy was important. It illustrated Kollontai's belief that there persisted within revolutionary Russia more fundamental schisms within Party and society: the traditional division between the sexes and, to a lesser extent, the friction between generations. These schisms, as we will see, transcended not only temporary political alignments but even, at times, the rural-urban cleavage. For the future of Kollontai's ideas about women and the family in Soviet Russia they were to be enormously significant. Before turning to examine the debates over the proposed new marriage law first in the Central Executive Committee and then, more broadly, among Party women as reflected in the press, let us first see why the issue of changes in the laws governing marriage should have generated such excitement.

The provisions of the 1918 marriage law concerning alimony and the distribution of property in the event of divorce were only applicable to couples who had registered their marriages with the proper authorities. Thus it was easy for men to protect themselves from the possibility of having to pay alimony or share property in a divorce by simply failing to register their marriages. As Kurskii's assistant in the Commissariat of Justice, Brandenburgskii, commented, it was impossible to deny that even after eight years, *"de facto* [i.e. unregistered] marriages preponderate in our life."[12] Rural and urban men alike feared a new alimony law whose provisions could not be evaded simply by failing to register a marriage. To each the proposed law was a threat—even though rural and urban households were established on very different bases.

Urban men were unhappy about the proposed new marriage code because it included an article suggested by a delegation of women workers that provided for the equal division of property acquired by the spouses during marriage in the event of a divorce. For urban

11. Excerpt from a meeting, 2d Session of the All-Russian Central Executive Committee, RSFSR, as published in *Brak i sem'ia,* p. 64.
12. Schlesinger, ed., p. 104.

women, this was appealing: property acquired by one spouse or by mutual effort would become common property to be divided in a divorce. In the past, a nonworking wife who ran the household and took care of the children had not received any share of what her husband made—as the "provider," he kept everything. Under the new law this injustice would be remedied.[13]

The village family, on the other hand, did not consist of the economically isolated married couple, as the city family did. The rural couple was involved rather in an extended peasant household. The *de facto* marriages that the new law would recognize meant to the peasants not the unregistered church marriages they were accustomed to in the countryside but rather a "loose" living together associated with city life. Though there was rural objection to the recognition of *de facto* marriage on the grounds that it would increase the intrusion of "city ways" into the countryside, the peasant's primary objection stemmed from the possible economic threat of alimony to the *dvor*, the peasant household. The Land Code of 1922 had stipulated that the possessions of the *dvor* were common property belonging to all members of the extended household, including women and children. Did this mean an equal division of all holdings of the *dvor* for the wife in case of divorce? This was not clear. At least one commentator wondered in 1925 whether peasant women were not better off under the Land Code of 1922 than they would be under the proposed marriage law: after all, he thought, the 1922 code did assure wives a share in the entire property of the *dvor*, whereas the proposed law would have her share only in her husband's property acquired after marriage. However, other clauses in the complex 1922 code had been designed to prevent the splitting up of farms and to permit the separation of movable goods only. Were these principles of the land code to be preserved in the new marriage code? The matter was confusing, and the peasants were not alone in wanting clarification.[14]

A common assumption held that alimony suits were numerous in the towns but uncommon in the countryside. But as Kollontai pointed out in her report to the International Conference of Communist Women in 1921, divorces were increasing among peasants. Particularly in villages where the Zhenotdel was active, women were no longer always willing to remain in unhappy marriages. Thus,

13. The 1918 marriage code had not established community of property in the hope of further undermining marriages of economic calculation.
14. F. Vol'fson, "K diskussii o proekte semeinogo kodeksa," *Brak i sem'ia*, pp. 8–9.

there were quite a number of alimony suits in the villages: in some regions one-third of all the cases heard in the People's Court concerned alimony claims.[15] It was apparent, at least to the peasants, that those provisions of the new marriage code that would extend alimony to wives in unregistered marriages were going to add to the burdens of the entire peasant household. Much of the controversy over the proposed new marriage code in the Central Executive Committee focused on this issue.

It is striking that during the daily debates over the proposed new marriage law in the Central Executive Committee at the end of 1925, the factional issues being fought over elsewhere in the Party's ruling circle never surfaced. If they were reflected at all, it was only in occasional elliptical remarks. So much were the participants absorbed in the unfolding conflict between the sexes that most of the delegates, whether rural or urban—including Mikhail Kalinin, the President of the Central Executive Committee, as well as jurists from the People's Commissariat of Justice—acted as though they were unaware of the Left Oppositionists' demand for rapid industrialization at the expense of the peasants. A delegate to whom the deeper nature of the dispute had become obvious expressed concern that alimony was leading to "nothing but a campaign of ill-feeling against women."[16] She spoke correctly.

As the debate continued, it became clear that members of the government did not always appreciate the nature or the scope of their own proposals. This failure of communication was illustrated by a series of exchanges between a peasant delegate and the Public Prosecutor, N. V. Krylenko. The peasant pointed out that since rural husbands and wives rarely lived by themselves but in most cases lived with the entire family, the relatives all suffered in the event of a separation: "I divorce my wife. We have three children. My wife immediately appeals to the court and I am ordered to pay for the children. As there is a common household, the court decides that the entire household must contribute. Why should my brother be punished?" Krylenko objected: "The brother will not be called upon!" The peasant tried again: "If we live together the whole family suffers. If I am ordered to pay 100 rubles and the family owns two

15. Schlesinger, ed., p. 151.
16. The delegate was a Comrade Gnilova, speaking at the 3d Session of the Central Executive Committee, Nov. 1926, as quoted in Schlesinger, ed., p. 140. See also "Zakony-zhizn'-byt, iz sudebnoi khroniki," *Brak i sem'ia*, pp. 43–44.

cows and one horse, we shall have to destroy the whole household."
He used another example: "Two brothers live together; one of them
has six children, the other is a bachelor but has fathered a baby. For
a year he has not paid for it; then the court orders him to pay 60 or
70 rubles and the whole household has to be ruined."[17]

Whereas to the peasant delegates nothing seemed more unfair than
permitting the payment of alimony to interfere with peasant agriculture, to the sponsors of the projected law, notably Kurskii and
Krylenko, a woman's right to support was basic. To the latter, the
peasant in his endeavor to preserve intact the economic strength of
the *dvor* would be forcing an unemployed woman onto the streets;
he would be penalizing an innocent woman who had been divorced
by her husband or forced to leave him because of intolerable conditions in the still patriarchal *dvor*.[18] Kurskii and Krylenko reassured the peasants that the courts would take into account the duration of the marriage, the work contribution of the wife, and her
actual need, and would seek to award alimony in a way least likely
to hurt the economy of the *dvor*. In particular, they stressed that they
would not force it to part with its chief asset, land; on this point the
1922 land code would not be superseded.[19]

Now we must ask exactly how well the Land Code of 1922 had been
protecting peasant women. After all, why should the peasant have
resisted new alimony laws and the legal recognition of *de facto* marriage if he were already abiding by a theoretically more comprehensive land code that entitled a wife to an equal share of the land, the
buildings, and the economic products of the *dvor*?[20] In fact, the 1922
land code made the woman an equal member of the *dvor* only in the
case of a legally recognized marriage and only as long as she remained
married, and it did not guarantee that she could take from the *dvor*
what she might consider her rightful share upon divorce. Because
the code allowed only movable goods to be taken from the *dvor*, and
because no demand for a division of goods could be made where less
than two years had elapsed since marriage, protection for women in
divorce was less than effective. There were reports of women who had
lived and worked in a family for over three years being ejected from

17. Excerpt from discussion of the marriage code in the 2d Session of the Central
Executive Committee, Oct. 1925, as quoted in Schlesinger, ed., pp. 107–8.

18. See Kurskii's summary in Schlesinger, ed., p. 117.

19. *Ibid.*, pp. 89–90.

20. For this assumption, see I. Rostovskii, "Brak i sem'ia po teorii tov. Kollontai,"
Brak i sem'ia, p. 140.

the *dvor* with a few sacks of potatoes and pounds of flour. There was also the phenomenon one journalist called a "wife for a season," in which a peasant proprietor married a girl in the spring only to abandon her in the autumn.[21]

Opposition to further expanding the number of women eligible for alimony by recognizing *de facto* unions emerged as a male-female issue. To peasant anxiety that alimony threatened the well-being of agriculture was added the general argument that giving alimony to women who had lived in unregistered marriages would increase sexual looseness and lead to debauchery. Nor was this feeling the result of purely peasant prejudice, as the historian E. H. Carr has suggested.[22] Aron Sol'ts of the Central Control Commission pleased many urban men when he insisted in a public debate with Krylenko in Moscow that only registered marriage should carry material consequences; but Sol'ts, alarmed that women might be encouraged by the proposed law to enter sexual relationships in order to get alimony, had in mind enforcing stricter morality, whereas the men sought protection against lawsuits.[23] In the Central Executive Committee, delegates spoke critically of the woman who lived with a man and tried to conceive a child so that she could receive one-third of his wages.[24] David Riazanov, founder and director of the Marx-Engels Institute, was prominent among those Bolsheviks who insisted with Sol'ts that in the interests of societal stability only registered marriage should be legal.[25] Riazanov also would have liked to see a decrease in divorce rates. Krylenko, on the other hand, was indignant at suggestions that a Soviet citizen's right to divorce be in any way infringed.[26]

There was suspicion that a desire to avoid work would create alimony-seekers. What if women, feigning illness, abused the institution? Admitting that the proposed law had a "danger spot" in the extension of alimony during unemployment, Kurskii thought that in practice there would have to be further clarification, such as registration at the labor exchange to establish the cause of unemploy-

21. Schlesinger, ed., pp. 106, 89, 117.

22. For the view that the moral objection to legalizing *de facto* marriage was limited to peasant prejudice, see Carr, *Socialism in One Country*, vol. 1, p. 47.

23. For the Sol'ts-Krylenko debate, see report in *Izvestiia*, Nov. 17, 1925. Smidovich notes male applause for Sol'ts in *Brak i sem'ia*, p. 93.

24. Schlesinger, ed., p. 96.

25. *Ibid.*, pp. 150–51. See also Riazanov, p. 21, for his views on sex and marriage.

26. Schlesinger, ed., pp. 150–51, 106.

ment.[27] Instead of exploring the fundamental issue, the lack of job opportunities for women under the NEP, additional questions suggested new areas for conflict. If a marriage were unregistered, how would the court know it existed when a woman, naming some man as her husband, sought alimony? What would distinguish a *de facto* marriage from a casual relationship? The lawyers began to argue. What is a wife? What are a "wife's rights"?[28] The definition of marriage elaborated by the Council of People's Commissars—the fact of living together, a joint household, and the announcement of such to a third party—produced its own confusion. What about the Communist couple whose Party work caused them to live for years in separate cities? Were they not married?[29]

There was another area of concern. Would recognition of *de facto* marriage lead to an increase in religious marriages and a general strengthening of the church? Millions, content with religious marriages, might not bother to register. Since the 1918 marriage law requiring registration had been promulgated, priests were obliged to ask couples if they had registered their marriage. If the new law were passed, the priest would no longer have to do this.[30] The peasant, in particular, would continue to be emotionally satisfied with a church ceremony.[31] Thus went the case against recognizing the *de facto* marriage.

꙰꙰꙰

If alimony was seen as a threat to the peasant economy, and if a significant number of Party members believed that extending alimony to *de facto* marriages would on the one hand encourage "immorality" and on the other reinforce the church, why did the new marriage law propose to legalize unregistered marriages? The answer, as we have seen, was that so many marriages continued to go unregistered.[32] Kurskii, citing Lenin, gave assurances that someday,

---

27. *Ibid.*, p. 117.   28. *Ibid.*, p. 111.
29. *Ibid.*, pp. 93, 112.   30. *Ibid.*, p. 95.
31. Dem'ian Bednyi, " 'Vser'ez i . . . ne nadolgo' ili sovetskaia zhenit'ba," *Brak i sem'ia*, p. 122, supported this point of view in a widely quoted verse. Bednyi wondered why the Russian, loving festive song and ceremony, would want to register a marriage in a crowded, smoke-filled clerk's office.
32. Why marriages went unregistered was explained in part by Max Eastman, who lived in Moscow in intellectual and artistic circles not necessarily representative of the proletariat. "Marriage . . . was not much in vogue in revolutionary Russia in those days. Together with bathing suits and epaulettes, lawyers, and other impediments to social freedom, it had been largely swept away by the revolution of October, and had not

under Communism, there would be communal rearing of children.[33] But for now, he maintained, in this transitional era between the old and the new, it was essential that the family (in other words, the husbands) be made responsible.

A woman delegate, referring to David Riazanov's moral scruples, added later: "If Comrade Riazanov intends to abolish de facto marriages, why has he not, in the sixty years of his life, arranged matters in such a fashion that we beget children only after registration, for now we beget them before registration, some before and some after. . . . We must recognize the de facto marriage. Who are the women bearing children? A widow, a young girl. . . . But we refuse to recognize the de facto marriage. We do wrong, comrades!"[34]

There was evidence that even in the countryside, where recognition of de facto marriage was generally opposed, younger people differed from their elders on this subject. At some of the meetings to discuss the proposed marriage law, young people, ambivalent toward the extended household, supported recognition of nonregistered marriages.[35] Party youth in particular favored recognition, although the Komsomol did not necessarily endorse the government plan. According to Kurskii, opinion in the towns, especially at discussions held in workers' quarters, was overwhelmingly in favor of the extension of legal protection to de facto marriage.[36] In fact, Izvestiia noted in reporting on the discussions throughout the provincial press that it was the women in the towns who favored the proposal to equate de facto with registered marriage, whereas the men were opposed for reasons of self-protection.[37] As the enthusiastic reaction of men to Sol'ts's argument indicated, a good number of urban workers along with the peasant patriarchs would have preferred to see the status quo maintained. Still, the dichotomy between town and country seemed significant enough to cause Preobrazhenskii, a leading supporter of Trotsky's Left Opposition, to insist along with the government that "once we have, in the towns, taken a firm

yet come back. The Moscow I lived in was, in its sexual code, a sort of generalized Greenwich Village. Getting married, when it did happen, was commonly called by the rather disrespectful name of 'registering.' It consisted of appearing together in a small dingy office about the size of a hall bedroom and signing your two names in a paper-bound ledger—also the names you intended to be called by after the feat was accomplished." Eastman, pp. 434–35.

33. Schlesinger, ed., p. 91.
34. Ibid., p. 141.
35. Ibid., pp. 125–26.
36. Ibid., p. 126.
37. Izvestiia, Jan. 9, 1926.

stand for the code . . . we cannot turn back from the code because some peasant *dvors* are behindhand with it." [38]

The government could simply have issued the new marriage law by decree in November 1925. But the Commissar of Justice, made uneasy by the widespread and quite unexpected opposition he met in the Central Executive Committee, wondered whether the project might not need further examination. [39] To an extent that seems astonishing today—in light of the rigidity that in less than a decade would overwhelm Soviet life—prominent Communists such as Kurskii, Riazanov, and Kalinin were scrupulously concerned that the new law be discussed widely since, as Kalinin said, it was one that would deeply affect life and morals. Kalinin reminded Krylenko, who was irritated by the delay, that the Party had long ago decided to invite the masses to participate in the process of making legislation; he wondered if the peasants' sensibilities had perhaps been neglected, and if the women's organizations had made known their final views. [40]

When the marriage law came up again in the Third Session of the Central Executive Committee, dissatisfaction was no less sharp despite a year of additional discussion. Although at least 6,000 village meetings had been held, according to calculations made by the Commissariat of Justice, attitudes remained the same. The peasants continued to oppose recognition of *de facto* marriage, the one feature of the law the government insisted on retaining. [41] To many delegates the law still seemed fair neither to peasants nor to workers but only to Nepmen, profiteers of the partial restoration of capitalism, who alone under the New Economic Policy had the money for alimony. As one delegate put it, "the law says the court will set alimony, but how do you collect it? You go to the peasant, he says he has nothing: 'This cannot be sold, that cannot be sold.' " A peasant woman, a delegate, objected, "We cannot wait until an extra lamb or an extra piglet is born on the defendant's farm. Even his cow should be sold and the proceeds devoted to the child's upkeep." [42] Among workers,

38. Schlesinger, ed., pp. 145–46.
39. *Ibid.*, pp. 118–19. Kurskii objected to Riazanov's contention that the marriage code had been insufficiently discussed locally. He had clippings to prove that the project had been widely argued in the press, if not in all *volost'* (rural district) and town meetings.
40. Schlesinger, ed., pp. 119–20.
41. *Ibid.*, p. 121.
42. *Ibid.*, pp. 147–48.

too, there was a lack of cash for paying alimony; but to enforce penalties for nonpayment in the countryside was even more difficult than it was in the towns.[43]

The concerns of the Russian peasant supported the socialist conviction that attitudes engendered by private property were a source of social backwardness. The experience with the proposed new marriage law seemed to validate Lenin's early view that, however pernicious, the factory system was "progressive" because by drawing women into production it led to their independence from the oppression of the rural, patriarchal family.[44] Still, there was pathos in the peasant situation. The anxiety over who would get the cow and the horse—or worse still, a part of the land—was sadly ludicrous. Within a few years, during forced collectivization, the peasants would lose everything.

※※※

A main theme of the NEP was that peasant agriculture should be encouraged and that the middle peasant not be alienated. How curious then that no attempt was made either in the Party or in the government to assuage peasant fears by producing an alternative to the hated institution of alimony. The debate in the Central Executive Committee served not only to document dissatisfaction with the government's new marriage law. It illuminated a more fundamental problem, the need to instill in Soviet society the basic socialist concepts of collectivism. It would have been remarkable if among Bolsheviks there had been no voices in the mid-1920's to insist that the new marriage law be based, not on the demeaning assumption of a man's economic responsibility toward a woman, but on the socialist assumption of equality between the sexes and on society's collective responsibility toward its members in need. In fact, only one prominent Bolshevik made these points—Kollontai—while she was temporarily in Moscow, presumably awaiting a new assignment.[45]

Kollontai's negativism toward the NEP had diminished somewhat during her three-year absence from Moscow. It would be an exaggeration to imply that she accepted the NEP with enthusiasm—"Nep-

43. Vol'fson in *Brak i sem'ia*, pp. 20–21.
44. Lenin, *Sochineniia* (4th ed.), vol. 3, *Razvitie kapitalizma v Rossii*, pp. 480–81.
45. Kollontai arrived in Moscow from Berlin in late Dec. 1925 and requested a health leave for the winter and spring. She returned to Berlin early in 1926 for medical treatment and remained there through July. See Body, p. 18.

man" and "Nepmansha" remained derogatory terms[46]—but like other Communists she assumed that the NEP would persist. She was will-ing, moreover, to admit that she may have been wrong. Reversing her earlier assumption that female employment would continue to de-cline, and pointing to Russia's steady economic recovery since 1923, Kollontai predicted that despite mass unemployment steady expan-sion of the private sector would mean an eventual increase in em-ployment for women. Growing government resources, she thought, would make possible further investment in public facilities to re-place the individual household.[47]

Before offering a counterproposal derived from this dual premise, Kollontai explained why she considered the government's projected new marriage law unacceptable in a society hoping to be socialist. Rather than being progressive, the proposal revealed the Party's fail-ure, after eight years in power, to evolve an appropriate family policy. The government was creating categories of women—registered wives, unregistered wives, and casual lovers—and since the first two were now made equal in their rights, the third was necessarily deprived. Who were these "casual" women the new law refused to defend? Often they were poor peasant girls going to the city to work in fac-tories and shops and living in conditions of frightful congestion. And what was the new law going to do for those registered and unregis-tered wives it was intended to defend? They were to be encouraged to abase themselves in court, to beg for their legal sop from unwilling men probably too poor to pay. Kollontai scoffed at the pointlessness of socialists defining marriage or seeking to strengthen it by legisla-tion—as though abandoned, unemployed women could be aided by such means. Unlike those who agreed that alimony had failed but argued in the press and the Central Executive Committee that the courts must find ways to enforce payment, she insisted on the funda-mental proposition that women who served society by providing it with future workers deserved society's support.[48]

How would Kollontai's theory be converted into practice? Writing in *Kommunistka* in 1921, Kollontai had anticipated the gradual but steady withering away of the isolated family and its replacement by

---

46. See Kollontai, "Brak i byt," p. 372.

47. On the economic recovery, see Carr, *Socialism in One Country*, vol. 1. For Kol-lontai's earlier pessimism concerning female employment during the NEP, see Chap. 10 above and Kollontai in *Pravda*, Mar. 20, 1923, p. 4.

48. Kollontai, "Brak i byt," p. 371.

communal living. In 1923, in her "Letters to Working Youth," she clung still to the communal dream. But now in 1926, adapting herself to the less ideological mood of the NEP, she modified her radical enthusiasm. Where she had consistently proposed government protection for mothers in the form of state subsidies before,[49] now she discarded the idea of direct state aid from existing government resources and proposed instead to abolish alimony and create a General Insurance Fund. To it the entire adult working population would contribute on a graduated scale, the lowest contribution being two rubles a year. With 60 million adult contributors, the fund could count on an initial minimum of 120 million rubles, which would make possible the establishment of day nurseries and homes for children, and homes for mothers in need. Moreover, it would provide support for single mothers unable to work and for their children up to the age of one year. Later, as the fund grew, this child support could be extended until the age of three or four. Yes, Soviet society was poor, but Kollontai pointed out that its rate of economic growth in the mid-1920's was impressive. Within two or three years of its founding, the General Insurance Fund would no longer be a burden.[50]

Another important aspect of Kollontai's proposal was her plan for the creation of marriage contracts that would safeguard the interests of housewives. By these contracts, a couple would voluntarily conclude an agreement upon marriage that would determine their economic responsibilities toward each other and their children. A rather weak idea that at first glance seemed to have deserved the criticism it received, it was predicated on the assumption that Zhenotdel activists could manage the herculean task of organizing a network in the countryside to teach backward peasant women how to safeguard their economic interests. For example, the Zhenotdel would explain to peasant women how they might keep their earnings from the sale of cloth and dairy products.[51] Kollontai's idea of a marriage contract was clearly market-oriented and appropriate in the context of the NEP, though it was probably impractical given the limited scope of the Zhenotdel in the countryside. Nonetheless, we should keep in

49. Kollontai, *Sotsial'nye osnovy zhenskago voprosa.*
50. See Kollontai, "Obshchii kotel ili individual'nye alimenty?"; "Brak i byt," pp. 363, 378, and "Brak, zhenshchiny, alimenty," p. 1, for the substance of Kollontai's argument in 1926.
51. Kollontai, "Obshchii kotel," p. 2.

mind that Kollontai was thinking about the matter in long-range socialist terms.[52]

A small group of followers and students responded warmly to Kollontai's optimistic proposals, which kept alive the hope that revolution still lived in NEP Russia, but the great majority of Party members rejected them. "For us young Communist women," a Party worker recalled, "Kollontai was a lofty example of a revolutionary fighter, and we aspired to imitate her."[53] Another student, underscoring generational differences within the Party, wrote to *Komsomol'skaia Pravda* claiming that most students supported Kollontai and suggesting as a temporary means of strengthening her proposed General Insurance Fund a five-kopek tax on wine, theater tickets, and various amusements.[54] From reports on the debates in the Central Executive Committee, one senses that there were women delegates here and there who would have accepted Kollontai's plan had the government endorsed it. One, a peasant, declared that "above all we lack children's homes."[55] Another, echoing the same sentiment, wondered why the proposed code ignored the casual marriage. A member of the Zhenotdel pointed out that according to the code many women would be left completely without aid, and she warned against cutting off the little channels of socialist public assistance that already existed to provide help to the destitute.[56] A woman member of the Presidium of the Central Council of Trade Unions wrote that if Kollontai's proposal for a general fund were to be discussed widely it would receive support.[57]

Some of Kollontai's critics were moderate, even mildly sympathetic. Iurii Larin, whose articles on anti-Semitism and alcoholism

52. Kollontai's marriage contract idea was called unrealistic by Smidovich in "Otmenit' li registratsiiu braka i sistemu alimentov," p. 2. But Article 13 of the final text of the marriage code affirmed that married parties might enter into all kinds of agreements with regard to their property. A complementary section added that such agreements became legally void as soon as one of the parties considered his or her interests to have been violated. The People's Commissariat of Justice wrote only the first part, but Kurskii explained that the Council of People's Commissars introduced the addendum in an effort to safeguard the interests of the weaker party. Thus, the Zhenotdel would have had legal backing to aid women in cases of injustice in connection with marriage contracts. See Schlesinger, ed., p. 116.

53. Itkina, p. 203.

54. *Komsomol'skaia Pravda*, no. 65 (248) (Mar. 1926), p. 4.

55. Schlesinger, ed., p. 99.

56. *Ibid.*, p. 136–39.

57. "Za i protiv predlozheniia tov. Kollontai," *Brak i sem'ia*, pp. 142–43. (A series of short statements by different people.)

had shown him to be, like Kollontai, a person concerned with social issues, observed that her idea for a General Insurance Fund accorded with the Party program for future state support for all children. In principle, of course, it was acceptable; but for now he considered it impracticable.[58] Others implied that replacing alimony with a general fund was unfair to the peasant majority, who would never willingly pay an extra tax to benefit mostly city women and children; and to compel payment would run counter to the NEP policy of lessening burdens on the peasantry.[59] Criticism of the fund on the grounds that the peasants would be opposed tended, however, to ignore the fact that the peasants vigorously objected to the government's own project. Kollontai's General Insurance Fund had the advantage of removing what to the peasants was the greatest threat, that the household might be forced to provide support for one member's abandoned wife.

Those who believed that the threat of alimony had the singular virtue of discouraging immorality and divorce in the countryside were particularly scornful of Kollontai's innovative marriage contract. Not only did it seem too ridiculous an idea to take seriously, but its spirit was said to be capitalist, not communist. Why, one critic asked somewhat irrelevantly, should economic calculation be a part of marriage?[60] Those who accused Kollontai of inconsistency in presenting the public with, on the one hand, a "fantasy" in which the individual was liberated from the responsibilities of providing for a family and, on the other, a *meshchanstvo* ("petty-bourgeois") proposal for marriage contracts missed her point.[61] Her critics completely failed to understand that Kollontai was attempting the difficult task of maintaining a sense of revolutionary purpose within the context of the NEP.

Urging increased taxation, Kollontai seemed to the Right to be thinking along the lines of Trotsky and Preobrazhenskii, who were arguing for systematic pressure on the peasants. But the Left Oppositionists sought increased taxation of the peasants to provide economic support for rapid industrialization, not social experiments. Indeed, Trotsky felt it was too soon for radical social experiments, by which the Party would run the risk of falling on its face and being

58. *Ibid.*, p. 141.
59. Smidovich, "Otmenit'," p. 2.
60. Rostovskii in *Brak i sem'ia*, pp. 138–39.
61. *Ibid.*, p. 140.

embarrassed before the peasantry.[62] Thus Kollontai's plan was supported by neither the Left nor the Right factions within the Party. The Right's contention that Kollontai's plan for a two-ruble-per-year tax ran counter to government economic policy, and that by putting pressure on the peasantry it resembled the measures proposed by the Left, was an exaggeration.

Among top-echelon Party leaders, only Trotsky, with his characteristic interest in social problems, took the time to discuss publicly the proposed new marriage code. The assumption on which Kollontai's proposals were based—collective responsibility for those in need—aimed at building an increased socialist awareness among the people. Trotsky argued the other way around—that socialist awareness had to be developed first, that the state could not build new social institutions without cooperation from the masses.[63] But how was a socialist consciousness to be created if the Party did not, slowly but steadily, introduce socialist measures? The need for developing socialist attitudes was underscored by some of the reactions to Kollontai's plan. Here, for example, is how one working woman reacted: "Comrade Kollontai's tax is altogether unsatisfactory. . . . How can anyone speak of a general taxation of all men, when only one man is concerned in the begetting of a child? What affair is it of the community? The matter is far simpler: if you are the father, you must pay!"[64] Even Trotsky, curiously insensitive to the Thermidorian aspects of the government's new marriage code, was indignant about the grounds on which Sol'ts and Riazanov opposed it. To think that in Soviet society anyone could be so "thickheaded" as to deny a mother the right to help simply because she was not a registered wife; women needed all the protection they could get. Describing Soviet marriage legislation as socialist in spirit, Trotsky regretted that society lagged so dismally behind it.[65]

Trotsky shared with most of Soviet society a view of women that

62. Trotsky, *Sochineniia*, vol. 21, p. 49. For Trotsky's view that the time was not yet ripe for social experiments, see Trotsky, *Voprosy byta*, p. 46.

63. Trotsky, *Sochineniia*, vol. 21, pp. 71–72.

64. "Za i protiv predlozheniia tov. Kollontai," *Brak i sem'ia*, pp. 143–44.

65. Trotsky, *Sochineniia*, vol. 21, p. 434. Iaroslavskii, "Moral' i byt proletariata v perekhodnyi period," pp. 150–51, expressed identical views. Supporters of the marriage law liked to picture its opponents (in Krylenko's words) as philistines. Krylenko argued that Soviet policy was moving toward economic and political equality of the sexes despite opposition from philistines and peasants. A footnote in Trotsky, *Sochineniia*, vol. 21, p. 514, quotes with approval Krylenko's arguments in favor of the new marriage law.

led him to praise as socialist legislation that Kollontai condemned as petty-bourgeois. Nor was Trotsky's perception necessarily "un-Marxist." Marx once filled out a "confession" for his daughter Laura revealing that the virtue he admired most in men was "strength"; in women, "weakness." Both Marx and Engels believed that the weak had to be protected from the strong, that men had to protect women. This notion ran through the debates over the new marriage code, countering the socialist assumption that the collective should provide social security for its members. Few Bolsheviks shared Kollontai's view that women were inherently strong and needed freedom from the debilitating protection of men that alimony represented. The new marriage code, in its assumption that women were weak, continued to project the image of woman as victim.

Much of the reaction in the Party against Kollontai's plan for a General Insurance Fund to eliminate alimony stemmed from opposition to Kollontai and to the "new woman" she projected. Pointing to her allegedly loose sexual views, critics accused her of seeking to corrupt Soviet youth by encouraging irresponsibility. Kollontai's critics reminded readers of her "Letters to Working Youth," which offered the image of a commune where one could love more than one partner, and her "Liubov' trekh pokolenii," which featured Zhenia, the "new woman" who had lovers but no time to fall in love. Like Polina Vinogradskaia earlier, these critics presented her as the promiscuous advocate of a "new morality," a woman preoccupied with questions of sex and love.[66]

The leaders of the Party's opposition to Kollontai in 1926 were Sof'ia Smidovich, now a member of the powerful Central Control Commission, and to a lesser extent Kollontai's old friend Emelian Iaroslavskii, also a member of the Central Control Commission and a Stalin supporter. The journals for which Kollontai had written in 1923, *Molodaia gvardiia* and *Kommunistka*, were now less open to her. Smidovich and Iaroslavskii, on the other hand, had free access to the Komsomol youth publications *Molodaia gvardiia* and *Komsomol'skaia pravda*. They intimated that whereas the regime sought stability in marital relations, Kollontai advocated the opposite:[67] Kollontai was saying "the collective will support the children, so why remain together once love is gone?" Without a doubt, she was unique among prominent Bolsheviks in seeking to incorporate the concept

66. For the most slashing attack, see Lavrov, pp. 136–48.
67. See, for example, Smidovich, "Otmenit'," and Iaroslavskii, "Moral' i byt," p. 150.

of free sexuality into the revolutionary framework. Other Party members spoke about "new people" but saw them inhabiting a distant, communist future. Iaroslavskii, although giving assurances that someday under communism there would be no need for moral laws, was in line with dominant Party attitudes when he warned that it was for bourgeois not proletarian youth to flit from flower to flower indulging in Kollontai's "love of the worker bees." In fact, Iaroslavskii recalled, for eight or nine years he sat in prison and sexual abstinence had done him no harm.[68]

Iaroslavskii, reluctant to attack Kollontai personally, was actually rather mild.[69] The real drama took place between Kollontai and Smidovich. The two women, both former directors of the Zhenotdel, each regarded herself still as a leader of the socialist women's movement. And although Smidovich spoke from a position of power, as a member of the Central Control Commission, and Kollontai spoke ostensibly from weakness, as a former member of the Central Committee and the Council of Commissars who could no longer live and work in Moscow, we will see that each woman had her followers. The Soviet press would be witness to a bitter confrontation, the culmination of several years of hostility between Smidovich and Kollontai. Zhenotdel workers withdrew to the sidelines, leaving the two outspoken opponents to battle the issues.

We recall Smidovich's opposition to Kollontai's plan in 1920 to deal with prostitution; it had seemed to her to endorse rather than to discourage it. Kollontai's advocacy in 1923 of "special societies" of unemployed women appeared to Smidovich as a feminist threat. Now Kollontai's proposal for a General Insurance Fund to replace individual alimony convinced Smidovich that Kollontai not only advocated promiscuity but sought to free men from the responsibility of providing for their children. Smidovich was probably unaware that it was she, not Kollontai, who sounded like a cruel caricature of a feminist as she lashed out at men. "Let them pay!," Smidovich angrily retorted in a speech rejecting Kollontai's argument that working-class men could not afford alimony.[70] Smidovich perceived herself as a member of an older, more staid generation; she wanted to

68. Iaroslavskii, "Moral' i byt," p. 150.
69. For example, Iaroslavskii carefully pointed out that Kollontai's oppositionist views in 1921 were no longer her views in 1926. See Iaroslavskii's introduction to Zorkii, p. 5. Nor does he mention her by name in "Moral' i byt."
70. For Smidovich's remark, see the report of a debate at the Polytechnic Institute in *Brak i sem'ia*, p. 93.

protect young women from the "African" sexual passions and irresponsibility of young men. To a visitor inquiring about sexual mores in the revolutionary society, Smidovich distinguished between generations. "Of course, we older Communists believe that it is best to love one person and stick to him."[71]

The two women, each 54, each a long-time Bolshevik, and each a leader of the socialist women's movement, took different positions on the new marriage code partly because each saw herself representing a different constituency. Kollontai, although an outcast, had become something of a celebrity. She gazed boldly—still quite beautiful—from the cover of the popular magazine *Ekran*. In its pages she argued for the General Insurance Fund on behalf of "new women" who were strong and wanted to move forward to a transformed, freer life. Smidovich, on the other hand, acted on behalf of a Party leadership that was in this instance singularly united. She considered herself an orthodox militant defending the proletarian vanguard against the bourgeois intelligentsia, correcting the inadequate notions of the "great mass of our proletarian youth" on the question of sexual relations. In her widely published criticism of Kollontai's proposals, Smidovich took the line that the Soviet Union was still in the transitional era, moving painfully from capitalism to socialism; consequently Kollontai's ideas were premature and would lead only to promiscuity.[72]

No doubt Smidovich believed she had no choice. Iaroslavskii and Smidovich, like Lenin before them, were hobbled not only by the Marxist paradigm that saw changes in material conditions necessarily preceding changes in social relationships, but by a suspicion of sexuality as prejudicial to revolutionary performance. In his much-quoted conversation with Clara Zetkin in 1920, Lenin indicated his fear of "orgiastic" situations that endangered the Revolution. Youth, he knew, was rebelling with all the impetuosity of its years, and nothing could therefore be "more false than to preach monkish asceticism. . . ." But he warned of a threat to the concentration of revolutionary forces if sex were to become youth's main mental concern.[73] Lenin would not have been interested in knowing that Freud, too, was analyzing the cultural uses of repressed sexual energies.[74] As he

71. Smith, p. 102.
72. See Smidovich, "O liubvi," p. 268, and "Otmenit'."
73. Lenin to Zetkin as cited in Zetkin, p. 48.
74. See Sigmund Freud, *Civilization and Its Discontents* (New York, 1962), pp. 50–51.

told Zetkin, he distrusted Freudianism, scorning "eternal theories and discussions about sexual problems. . . ." Instead of the "present, widespread hypertrophy in sexual matters," Lenin advocated "healthy sport, swimming, racing, walking, bodily exercises of every kind, and many-sided intellectual interests."[75] Lenin's assumption that energy expended in athletic competition and intellectual activity was wholesome, and not harmful to revolutionary concentration, underscored his own rejection of free sexuality as inimical to political control.

The Old Bolsheviks Lenin, Smidovich, and Iaroslavskii thought it unwise for Communists like Kollontai to push the Revolution into areas of innovation beyond a definition of woman's liberty that meant freedom from the constraint of bourgeois marriage and the family laws of the bourgeois state.[76] Presumably these Old Bolsheviks did not share Kollontai's interest in a redefinition of sexual roles.

Smidovich's use of the term "transitional" is curiously suggestive, for in reading Smidovich's views on *byt* ("daily life") one senses that Smidovich herself was transitional. She was one of the earliest Bolshevik leaders in the 1920's to espouse publicly the views on sex that were to become policy in the 1930's, one of the first frankly to break the nineteenth-century bond between socialism and female sexual liberty to which Bebel alluded.[77] Attacking the elegant Kollontai— in her aristocratic appearance and language so obviously outside the new Soviet culture, so clearly a holdover of the *intelligentsiia*—Smidovich appealed to basic prejudices. Here was a preview of the assault on the *intelligentsiia* that took place a few years later. Paradoxically, in the case of sexual questions, it was Kollontai, the *intelligentka*, who spoke for the younger generation of Communists. The attitudes of Kollontai, Smidovich, and their followers by no means exhaust the range of controversies about *byt* that were raging in the Soviet Union in the 1920's, but the published views of these two women leaders define the coordinates by which nearly all the elements of the controversy can be located. For this reason, it will be useful to discuss an exchange of letters that appeared in *Komsomol'skii byt* between

75. Zetkin, pp. 45, 50.
76. *Ibid.*, p. 48. This kind of liberty was defined in the marriage code of 1918 in provisions for legal and political equality for each marriage partner. Such equality was symbolized by the right to divorce, by the termination of the wife's obligation to follow her husband if he changed his residence, and by the right of the married couple to use the wife's surname.
77. Bebel, pp. 82–85.

Smidovich and two young Komsomol women. This exchange brings into focus the image of women suggested by the debates on the new marriage code.

Of the young woman named Lida who wrote to Smidovich, we know only that she was a *komsomolka*, was nineteen years old, and lived far from Moscow. She wrote seeking guidance on sex and love, and wanted to know whether she should succumb to male desires and engage in transient love affairs that meant the possibility of crippling abortions or of raising a child alone. It was not material comforts Lida sought. She just wanted to live openly, not even necessarily in a registered marriage, but in a lasting union with the man she loved.[78] To Lida's fearful questions, which reflected the traditional attitudes in regions far from the center of revolutionary ferment, Smidovich gave answers that were on balance more conservative than avant-garde. She did not object to unregistered unions so long as they were serious and responsible. But advising Lida to trust her cautious, womanly instincts, Smidovich explained that for a woman love was not transient passion but an extended process of birth, nursing, and child-rearing. Smidovich was committed intellectually to the radical concept of children's homes where, as on the Israeli kibbutz, children would spend their days and visit their parents when the adults were free from work; emotionally, though, she was ambivalent.[79] Thus Smidovich told Lida that a woman's relationship to love was determined to a large degree by her role as mother. How much this seemed true Smidovich indicated in her revealing remark that she would not even discuss with Lida marriages without children: they were so rare as not to merit consideration.[80]

To discuss childless marriages would have involved mention of birth control, an awkward subject for Smidovich. Overpopulation did not trouble Russians: with their vast potential resources they could provide sustenance for many more people. And to many Marxists who saw no lack of food and material resources but only their unequal

78. "Pis'mo Komsomolki k tov. Smidovich," in Razin, ed., pp. 172–73.
79. For Smidovich's private conflict, see her remarks to Jessica Smith, who visited her at home with her closely knit, loving family. She loved her children, Smidovich told Smith, but she believed in children's homes. "There is no question that if we had well-equipped, well-run institutions for children, they would be better off than they are in the majority of homes. I love my own children, but after all, how much do I see of them? I am at work all day, and usually in the evenings too. . . . If they were in a Children's Home they would be getting better training and better care than I can give them, and they would be living a more stimulating life." See Smith, pp. 102–3.
80. Smidovich, "Otvet na pis'mo komsomolki," pp. 174–75.

distribution, birth control seemed a gesture of bourgeois defeatism. Smidovich's failure even to mention birth control to Lida, as well as her attitude toward sexual mores in her articles in *Komsomol'skii byt*, suggests a negative attitude that stemmed not only from Marxist unease but from a personal reluctance to condone Kollontai's interpretation of the free woman.[81] For Kollontai's vision of the life of socialism's new woman, though it might not please a feminist today, included a sexuality that offended Smidovich's image of woman as the responsible mother.[82]

Not Kollontai but one of the fledgling "new people" whose attitudes she had so often described replied to Smidovich. The *komsomolka* Lida, inexperienced and anxious, had written to Smidovich asking that the older comrade tell her how to live in the new society; now, however, another *komsomolka*, Nina Vel't, launched not a respectful inquiry but an angry attack. She challenged Smidovich's professed concern with the problems of women and marriage. Did Smidovich really care, or was she interested more in Soviet society's need for children? Nina considered Smidovich's advice to Lida "cheap moralizing" that neither she nor Lida needed. Rejecting Smidovich's admonition, in effect, to be continent or to be willing to assume the care of a family, Nina reminded Smidovich that the socialist does not bow to the laws of nature but seeks instead to alter them. Motherhood should result from choice, not inevitability. Nina ridiculed the Party's ambivalence about birth control as an attitude that led not to ointment being applied to a hurt finger, as she put it, but rather to amputation of the entire hand.[83] Yes, abortions could be crippling; Nina did not like them either. But in favoring larger families did Smidovich think that four sickly children whose parents were unable to support them properly were better for society than two healthy ones? And what of the mother's life? With two children there was still some chance for employment, but four children excluded the possibility. Did Smidovich even know the "new woman"? Surely she was not the married woman cut off from society and dependent for her living on a man because she had abandoned work and studies for motherhood. Nor could she be the pathetic person whom Smidovich

81. See, for example, Smidovich, "O liubvi," p. 268.
82. For Kollontai's own assumption that motherhood was a socialist woman's responsibility, see Kollontai, *Polozhenie zhenshchiny v evoliutsii khoziaistva*, p. 178.
83. Vel't, pp. 181–83. See the report of a 1927 medical conference in Kiev where demands were made for development and production of adequate contraceptives as an alternative to abortion (reprinted in Schlesinger, ed., pp. 183–87).

suggested Lida emulate, a woman who defined herself in terms of her relationship to a man. A fear for the kind of future the Party had in mind caused Nina to press her attack, questioning Smidovich's larger image of Soviet society. Why did Smidovich write approvingly of Lida's assertion that she did not seek a comfortable existence but wanted only to live with a man in an enduring relationship? Intuiting that Smidovich was using asceticism as a defense against sensuality, Nina demanded: Why should a Communist woman not want life's comforts? Did socialism have to be drab? Was a silk blouse a sign that one must be driven from the Party?[84]

Was the bold Nina a typical *komsomolka*, or was the undemanding Lida more usual? The issues of morality and way of life were so widely debated that one might point to either young woman as representative. Certainly the Central Control Commission's concern with the issue of "debauchery" (*raspushchennost'*) and their fear that the institution of the family might be further weakened unless *de facto* marriage carried legal consequences suggest the existence of sizable numbers of "new women" like Nina who expressed "Kollontaish thinking."[85] The Party's concern over "sexual chaos," expressed through those provisions of the new marriage code that would widen the scope of male responsibility for women and children, and its attacks on Kollontai did not mean that Soviet youth was debauched. Sexual chaos and debauchery were subjective terms to which Kollontai refused to subscribe: where others saw chaos, she saw healthy sexuality. Would the Party, she wondered, prefer that its youth resort to old-fashioned bourgeois prostitution?[86]

The more Smidovich wrote, the more apparent it became that she rejected the idea of female sexual freedom and appealed instead to the idea of victimization. One article in particular typified her thinking. In it she analyzed the reasons for the suicide of a young Party member, a woman named Davidson. Smidovich blamed the girl's

84. Vel't, p. 184. For support of her position, see the speech by the Komsomol Secretary at the Seventh All-Union Komsomol Congress in 1932: "For this reason we are not opposed to music, we are not opposed to love, we are not opposed to flowers or beautiful wearing apparel. We are not ascetics and do not preach asceticism. We are for a full, rich, beautiful life" (quoted in Winter, p. 36). For an example of Communist asceticism, see the interchange between Iakov Sverdlov, then Chairman of the Central Executive Committee of the Soviet, and Polina Vinogradskaia in which Sverdlov chided Vinogradskaia for assuming that Communist women must cut their hair short and look austere. Vinogradskaia, *Sobytiia*, p. 167.

85. See Sosnovskii.

86. Kollontai, "Brak i byt," p. 366. For a view of sexual morality among youth in the 1920's, see Mehnert.

death on the cruel insensitivity of her husband, Koren'kov, also a Party member and a man who flaunted his affairs with other women and forced Davidson to submit to three abortions. Although Smidovich must have known that a more self-confident, stable woman would not have remained in such a damaging marriage, she directed her anger at Party comrades who, despite their closeness to the dismal situation, had refrained from interfering, inhibited by a "misguided" belief that marital relations were not the business of the Party. Smidovich countered in anger that if Koren'kov had so much as uttered an "anti-Semitic abuse" his exclusion from the Party would have been certain.[87]

Smidovich, who was committed to the eradication of male chauvinism, insisted on the political need to punish men like Koren'kov. What she ignored was the danger to individual privacy. The questions Smidovich raised about interference in the private lives of Party members were not new. The Party's approach to the issue had never been monolithic. Prior to the Revolution, Lenin had shocked the *Iskra* staff by insisting that the suicide of an abandoned, pregnant Party member was a private not a Party matter.[88] Smidovich had no doubts about the correct Communist approach, but Iaroslavskii would write in *Bolshevik* in 1931, "I must emphatically condemn the Central Control Commission's rummaging into the private lives of Communists."[89] Kollontai's opinion was the exact opposite of Smidovich's: she believed that the proposal to classify women under the new marriage law as registered wives, unregistered wives, or casual lovers was a gross violation of privacy.[90]

Perhaps the Bolshevik leaders of the Zhenotdel came closest to agreement in matters of marriage and the family on the issue of abortion, and it is noteworthy that this was one area the Marriage Code of 1926 left unaltered. The legalization of abortion in 1920

87. Smidovich, "O Koren'kovshchine," pp. 132–33. This article also appeared in 1926 in *Molodaia Gvardiia*.

88. Getzler, p. 67.

89. As quoted in Winter, p. 26. Even friendly observers commented in the late 1920's on the degree of Party interference in private lives. See Mehnert, p. 216. By 1929, in a Party "cleansing," offenses against morality headed the list of causes for expulsion: 22.9 percent of those expelled from the Party were accused of "noncommunist conduct toward women," debauchery, and drunkenness.

90. For indications that others shared her view, see the critical comments of V. Boshko, "The Registration of Marriage and Its Importance Under Soviet Law," *Sovetskaia Iustitsiia*, 1939, no. 17–18, translated in Schlesinger, ed., pp. 348–57.

was by no means intended to launch a permanent social institution; rather, it had been a response to an emergency need arising from the misery of the Civil War. The operation was legalized amid Bolshevik agonizing over a move that went counter to Party belief about the need for socialist mothers to produce children for the future. Aversion to abortion was general, if not always for precisely the same reasons.[91]

Krupskaia, belying the puritanical, sexless, and humorless image of her presented by certain male historians,[92] boldly criticized Party members in 1920 who opposed legalized abortion. In the tones of a radical "new woman," Krupskaia poked fun at "our intellectuals," who, although generally free in their own sexual views, sounded like members of the bourgeoisie when they objected even to contraception on the grounds that it led to debauchery. Then, distinguishing very carefully between abortion and contraception as social remedies, Krupskaia spoke in favor of birth control, pleading the psychological needs of mothers who would be spared the emotional pain of abortion —as well as its physical risks—if the regime were to make contraceptives available as they were in Western Europe.[93] Kollontai agreed with Krupskaia that abortion was a necessary evil, permissible if dictated by harsh economic need and the lack of facilities for child care. The feminist idea that women had a right to control their own bodies seemed to her bourgeois selfishness, a failure on the part of women to understand their responsibility to provide the collective with future workers.[94]

Those who hold to the feminist belief that women have the right to control their own bodies might wonder how Kollontai's criticism of abortion as "bourgeois selfishness" differed substantially from Smidovich's own objections. Women like Kollontai and Krupskaia condoned abortion but disliked it, regarding the taking of a new life as an "offense" to the maternal instinct, and at the very least selfish.[95] Smidovich, however, took a different view, linking abortion, like birth control, not with bourgeois selfishness but with promiscuity. Refusing to separate sex from procreation, Smidovich rejected all reasons for abortions other than to save a mother's life as the irrespon-

91. For Soviet society's agonizing over the question of legalizing abortion, see N. Semashko, "Eshche o bol'nom voprose," *Kommunistka*, 1920, no. 3–4, pp. 19–21. Iaroslavskii referred to abortion figures in Moscow and Leningrad as "horrifying." See Carr, *Socialism in One Country*, vol. 1, p. 43.

92. For a typically negative view of Krupskaia, see Ulam.

93. Krupskaia, "Voina i detorozhdenie," pp. 19–20.

94. Kollontai, *Polozhenie zhenshchiny v evoliutsii khoziaistva*, p. 178.

95. Krupskaia, "Voina i detorozhdenie," p. 20.

sible rationalization of young men eager to be rid of their problems. She drew pathetic pictures of abortion waiting rooms where pale, haggard girls yearned hopelessly for maternity. If abortions were illegal, men would not feel justified in "forcing" them on their wives.[96]

We cannot overlook the feelings of women about a subject so emotionally charged as abortion. Kollontai, Krupskaia, and Smidovich all believed in the maternal instinct.[97] Smidovich, however, seemed to doubt the vigor of female sexual desires, assuming that sexual activity was being unfairly urged on young women by self-seeking men in the name of a new way of life. Smidovich believed in the full equality of women. Women should share political power with men, to be sure. But Smidovich was unable to accept the concept of a sexually free "new woman." She bridged the gulf between the small group of radicals represented by Kollontai and the social conservatives who later became dominant. There was no way to compel women to produce children and to make caring for them their primary role. What could be done was to put women in a situation where maternity and child care were the logical outcome. Smidovich urged stable marriages, ignored birth control, and condemned abortion. Smidovich's position culminated in 1936 when the Stalinists, going far beyond what she herself had advocated, made divorce difficult to obtain and abortion a crime.

It would be ten years before the reaction toward which Smidovich pointed was legitimized and given unambiguous legislative expression. When the new marriage code was promulgated in 1926 it was mistakenly regarded in the West as so radical that it threatened the very institution of marriage. Did it not consider living together with neither legal nor clerical documents a marriage? Could divorce not be obtained by the simple application of one party? To these charges of the "bourgeois" press, Kurskii's aide Brandenburgskii indignantly replied that the law was not radical at all, that it encouraged marital stability and responsibility because it was promulgated out of concern for the potentially abandoned mother and child.[98] The Western bour-

96. Smidovich, "O liubvi," pp. 268–73.
97. Krupskaia, "Voina i detorozhdenie," p. 20.
98. *Izvestiia*, Jan. 14, 1926. In 1944 the law was changed and only registered marriage was given legal recognition.

geois simply misunderstood the Soviet motivation in recognizing non-registered marriage; rather than attacking the marital institution, it was formalizing the *de facto* relationship.[99] The code even defined a *de facto* marriage so that it would not be equated with a casual liaison. The fact of living together, a joint household, and the announcement of such to a third party—the concept of marriage arrived at during debates in the Central Executive Committee—appeared as Article 12 in the published version of the code.[100]

Rather than undermine the family, the obligation of relatives (even relatives by marriage and step-relatives) to support one another was expanded so that the responsibility of parents for children and children for their needy parents now included responsibility for one's grandparents in need.[101] True, one could point to progressive new features. The absolute right to divorce granted in 1918 remained intact and was even simplified in 1926. Where the original 1918 code required "verification that the petition for divorce actually issues from both parties," the 1926 legislation registered a divorce upon the petition of one party. In the original law of 1918 the right to maintenance of a needy former spouse unable to work was to be preserved until a change in the spouse's condition took place; the 1926 legislation, in the interests of a second family, limited alimony to a former spouse to one year. This change was added after the public discussions in 1925. On the other hand, alimony now covered not only the ex-wife who was unable to work, as in the 1918 law, but the wife who was simply unemployed[102] and who upon divorce now became entitled to half the property acquired since marriage. On balance, the code's progressive features did not outweigh its basically conservative stabilizing function, particularly in light of the overwhelming fact that unregistered marriage, which meant the prevailing form, would now carry legal consequences.

Some attempt was made in the final version of the code, in response to the year of discussion, to mollify objections to the original project;

99. Essentially, *de facto* marriages were to be afforded protection only with respect to property rights and alimony. For other privileges arising from marriage, such as the right to join a communal dwelling, it was still necessary to register.

100. In the code's first version in 1925 there was no definition of marriage. See the 1925 code in *Brak i sem'ia*, pp. 25–35. For Article 12, see "Kodeks zakonov o brake, sem'e i opeke," in USSR, [23], p. 126.

101. Similarly, grandparents were responsible for needy grandchildren if the children were unable to obtain support from their parents and were under age or incapacitated (USSR, [23], p. 131).

102. But in the final 1926 version, the stipulation "for six months only" was added (USSR, [23], p. 126).

but the fundamental opposition was simply not resolved. As we have seen, *de facto* marriage was painstakingly clarified so as to alleviate fears of alimony suits that might result from casual liaisons. But peasant objections persisted despite the new threefold definition of marriage and the quite reasonable time periods limiting payment of alimony to a former wife. Other efforts to ease anxiety were no more successful. A new section explained explicitly that the rights of parents and children with regard to the property of a peasant *dvor* were to be "determined by the pertinent sections of the Land Code," which sought to preserve intact the farming establishment. The rather muddled principles of the Land Code of 1922 were now clarified and strengthened. The Marriage Code of 1926 stated explicitly that neither land nor inventory nor livestock was to be distributed. Support payments of peasants were to be in the form of money or products of the household economy.[103] One might conclude that the male peasant proprietor received preferential treatment in the realm of property compared to the urban working man, half of whose family goods acquired since marriage would go to his wife. Still, the peasant persisted in seeing a marriage code that legalized *de facto* marriage as antagonistic.

The Secretary of the Central Executive Committee, Aleksei Kiselev, declared his agreement with Preobrazhenskii that the new code was necessary. But Kiselev, who as a member of the Workers' Opposition had objected to government neglect of the proletariat in 1921, was troubled now that the peasants felt ignored; that a hundred million peasants found their interests neglected by the code, he thought, could not go unchallenged.[104] He did not know that in retrospect 1926 would be considered an idyllic time, that the new law, coming two years before the onset of the First Five-Year Plan, was among the last pieces of Soviet legislation that would take into account any of the peasant's fundamental interests.

Did the peasants prefer Kollontai's plan for a General Insurance Fund? No, and they were unlikely to have accepted it without persuasion. Based on the principle of collective responsibility for mothers and children, it seemed too radical. But had the General Insurance Fund received strong government support, peasant and proletarian worker both could probably have been convinced of its

---

103. *Ibid.*, p. 131.
104. Schlesinger, ed., p. 148. For the view that the government in 1921 was ignoring basic interests of the proletariat, see Kollontai, *Rabochaia oppozitsiia*.

merits. The cost to the individual was small, and it would have removed what in the mind of the peasant was the most oppressive
feature of alimony, and the most divisive issue between the generations: the fact that one member's personal "mistake" could quite
suddenly threaten the economy of the entire *dvor*.

Was there a larger significance to Kollontai's campaign against the
new marriage law? Virtually alone among leading Bolsheviks she
tried in 1926 to revive socialist promises in the area of marriage and
the family. She spoke to women and to youth, both groups that she
perceived as subordinate in the traditional family structure.[105] For
them she tried to keep alive, in the face of Party indifference, the
heroic spirit of October. Nor did she criticize men. Nothing in Kollontai's speeches and articles in 1925–26 could have caused Vinogradskaia to revive her earlier charge that Kollontai's slogan was "down
with men." Instead, with earthy humor she addressed groups of working-class men and explained how her plan would relieve husbands
and fathers of support payments she knew they could ill afford.[106]
Her General Insurance Fund aimed not only at easing the hostilities
between men and women by replacing alimony with a collectivist
responsibility for children, but at reducing the harmful distinctions
between generations in both town and country, and at bringing Soviet
society, rather gently, toward a more humane socialism.

Party negativism toward Kollontai's proposal provides us with another perspective from which to analyze what Communists meant
when they continued, through the 1920's (sounding oddly like Kollontai), to refer to the "withering away of the family" and the advent
of the "new woman." For Kollontai and her small group of followers
these twin concepts were myths in what Robert Tucker calls their
truest meaning, a projection of one's own internal conflicts and needs
on to society.[107] For others, the "withering away of the family" and
the "new woman" were Communist myths in the looser sense of
ritual slogans. The marriage code controversy of 1925–26 not only
underscored peasant commitment to the status quo; it crystallized
the Communist Party's attachment to familiar images of women. It
should come as no surprise that the concepts of the "withering away
of the family" and the "new woman" moved within ten years from

105. Kollontai appealed to youth on this basis in her speech to the Komsomol Congress in 1919. See Kollontai, *Izbrannye stat'i i rechi*, p. 298.
    106. Kollontai, "Brak i byt," pp. 363–78.
    107. Robert Tucker, *Philosophy and Myth in Karl Marx* (Cambridge, Eng., 1971),
pp. 218–32.

myth to heresy, with Kollontai's writings cited as their "undoubtedly harmful" source.[108]

The switch in Communist rhetoric signaling that the family would not wither away, that the institution of marriage and the mother's role in it would remain essentially unchanged, coincided with the consolidation of the Stalin revolution of the 1930's. Should we conclude, as is customary, that Stalin determined the outcome? Not necessarily. His daughter Svetlana has asserted that her father, despite his public remarks about women's contribution to the economy, did not believe in their equality. His concept of home, of family, and of woman's role in each was conservative.[109] But Stalin would need only to welcome the strong forces in the Party throughout the 1920's that—as we have seen—moved in traditional directions, counter to the myths of the Revolution. He neither originated nor compelled them.

108. V. Svetlov, "Socialist Society and the Family," translated and reprinted from *Pod znamenem marksizma*, 1936, no. 6, in Schlesinger, ed., pp. 315–47. Whether Soviet society regarded revolutionary promises concerning the family with any enthusiasm is a matter of controversy. E. H. Carr contends that by the mid-1920's the Party had rejected Kollontai's position on the family, that it was already diverging in "practice and opinion" from Engels' doctrine of the liberation of women from domestic labor. Carr cites Trotsky's symposium for Party workers in 1923 to illustrate a desire for traditional life. More accurately, the symposium revealed the conflict between the conventional family attitudes of men and the desire for greater freedom on the part of women. See Trotsky, *Voprosy byta*, pp. 84–88. For Carr's view, see *Socialism in One Country*, vol. 1, pp. 39–43. Many men no doubt preferred the traditional family, but many women eagerly awaited fulfillment of the promises of Party workers from the Zhenotdel who, recognizing the growing response to their efforts, could do little about the lack of government support for social institutions except express distress and frustration in the pages of *Kommunistka*. Where "officially" but in the clubs, lamented a woman worker, could one even summon the collective spirit? *Kommunistka*, 1926, no. 12, pp. 32–36.
109. Alliluyeva, pp. 381–82.

CHAPTER TWELVE

The Survivor

*... to begin one's life anew every day, as though it were just begin-
ning. . . . My stronger, more courageous will, which nothing could break,
saved me—my unconscious will to self-preservation.*

—*Kollontai, quoting Goethe, 1913*

THE mid-1920's, when Kollontai fought her last open battle
with the Party, was a time of tension and rivalry among the
Bolsheviks. But paradoxically, on the larger Soviet scene it
was almost a peaceful lull, an "idyllic moment before the storm." The
cataclysms of war, revolution, civil strife, and the great famine had
ended by 1922, and recovery had begun under the NEP. A brief seven
years later, in 1928, the NEP would end and another social upheaval
would begin, a violent state-directed transformation of society from
above in which "much of the previous social fabric, Tsarist and Soviet,
was dispersed and destroyed."[1] The period after 1928 was one of forced
collectivization, industrialization, and mass terror. But for the Party,
the worst lay still ahead. Stalin would turn against his Bolshevik comrades in the shattering purges of the late 1930's, and in a series of incredible trials that defy rational explanation he would send Communists, old and new, to the death cellars of Lubianka prison and the
nightmare camps of Siberia. Among the millions who perished were
Kollontai's comrades from her days on the Central Committee and in
the Council of Commissars, along with nearly all the Communists of
her earlier years: Shliapnikov and Dybenko, Bukharin and Rykov,
Iakovleva, Piatakov, Rakovskii, Krylenko, Sol'ts, Riazanov, Osinskii,
Krestinskii, Sosnovskii, Radek, Zinoviev, Kamenev, and finally Trotsky, exiled in 1928 and murdered in 1940. This staggering list is only
partial.[2]

In a series of show trials, Lenin's most trusted colleagues and Kollontai's comrades, those whom she opposed and those whom she sup-

---

1. See Moshe Lewin, "Society, State, and Ideology during the First Five Year Plan,"
in Fitzpatrick, ed., pp. 41–42.
2. For a comprehensive picture, see Conquest.

ported, "confessed" that in collaboration with Trotsky they had conspired to betray to a foreign enemy the Party, the Soviet state, and the cause of socialism. The upheavals of Soviet society that began in 1928 have been called a "prolonged Walpurgis night" in which "nobody was left unharmed," and in which "all the survivors became thoroughly disfigured."[3]

Kollontai was a survivor—one of the few. But the woman who like Cassandra had predicted the future, who had challenged Lenin at the Tenth Party Congress to remedy the Party's "illness," and who had single-handedly opposed conservative social policies was vastly changed. A friend explained that there were "two Kollontais."[4] After certain blows, as F. Scott Fitzgerald put it, one does not recover but "becomes a different person. . . . Eventually, the new person finds new things to care about."[5] Where was Kollontai when the Old Bolsheviks were meeting their violent end? By what route did she reach her position? And who was the Kollontai who survived?

꒭꒭꒭꒭

It was a slow transformation from leader of the Worker's Opposition to Soviet diplomat, and to understand how Kollontai made it we need briefly to turn back to the early years of her exile. Kollontai continued in opposition, but it was an opposition that defied simple categories. Contemporaries described her as a Trotskyist sympathizer,[6] but she never joined the Communists who in late 1923 rallied around the Commissar of War in the Appeal of the Forty-six, although her friends Osinskii, Iakovleva, Piatakov, and Evgeniia Bosh were among those who did. The Appeal was a secret statement submitted to the Politburo in October that bore some similarity to Kollontai's *Workers' Opposition*. The Forty-six did not demand workers' control of industry, but they protested against the unlawful system of appointment from above and asserted that the time had come to put into operation the resolution on "inner-party democracy" that had been adopted at the Tenth Congress. They called attention to Communist fear to speak out at meetings, to the disappearance of discussion, and to the stifling of free opinion. Trotsky headed the Opposition, admit-

3. Lewin, "Society, State, and Ideology," p. 42.
4. Moscow interview, Aug. 1973.
5. F. Scott Fitzgerald, *The Crack-Up* (New York, 1945), p. 76.
6. Serge, p. 205. Boris Souvarine stated that she remained an oppositionist (personal communication, Mar. 26, 1974). Trotsky's widow suggested that Kollontai was privately sympathetic to Trotsky. See Serge and Sedova Trotsky, p. 155.

ting that once he had been skeptical of such arguments but claiming now that it was time for workers' democracy within the Party.[7]

Possibly Kollontai refrained from supporting the Trotskyist Opposition in 1923 because she feared further involvement in factionalism. Yet she continued to take chances, keeping in contact, for example, with the Communist outcasts Shliapnikov and Balabanoff. And in 1924, outraged by Moscow's denunciation of Balabanoff, she protested to the Central Committee.[8] She received no reply. Remembering Trotsky's harshness toward the Workers' Opposition, Kollontai probably underestimated the degree to which in 1923 he shared her fears. She would publicly praise Trotsky in 1926—a risk by that time—for his support of the women's movement, but he seemed to her too rigorous and too little human to be a great leader. She may have shared the suspicion of another Communist that Trotsky did not want to destroy the bureaucracy so much as he wanted to control it.[9]

Even when the broader United Opposition of Trotsky, Zinoviev, and Kamenev formed in 1925 and her comrades Nikolaeva and Krupskaia joined Iakovleva in support of it, Kollontai stood apart. But by 1925 it was not simply lack of faith in Trotsky and Zinoviev that motivated Kollontai; there were more personal factors.[10] For the first time since she had joined the Party, questions of Bolshevik politics were ceasing to absorb her. The Communist Kollontai was yearning for the freedom she had happily forsaken in 1915 in exchange for camaraderie. "It won't be long before I become free," she exulted to F. Ström.[11]

Why did Kollontai contemplate leaving the Bolsheviks? The factor

7. On the Appeal, see Carr, *The Interregnum*, pp. 374–80. For opposition, see Daniels, pp. 216–17.

8. See undated letters to F. Ström, presumably of 1924, referring to correspondence with her old friends and to her futile protest on behalf of Balabanoff. Ström Archive, Univ. of Gothenburg. Also see Body, p. 17, and Balabanoff, *My Life as a Rebel*, pp. 301–2.

9. Body, p. 20, quoting a conversation with V. Serge. For Kollontai's praise of Trotsky, see *Autobiography*, p. 42. Kollontai's correspondence suggests her lack of enthusiasm for Trotsky as a leader. She was noncommittal in 1924 when she recommended to Ström that he read Trotsky's latest work, *The New Course* (undated letter in Ström Archive). Body recalls her enmity toward Trotsky, a result of his harshness both toward the Workers' Opposition and toward Dybenko when he came before a Party tribunal on treason charges in 1918. Body, p. 17. Kollontai sent letters Lenin had written her that were critical of Trotsky to Kamenev, editor of the *Leninskii Sbornik*, in 1924. See Chapter 2 above.

10. Kollontai shared the prevailing view that Zinoviev was a vain man, puffed up with a sense of his own power, which she believed he abused in Leningrad. Body, p. 18. Supposedly, Zinoviev admired Kollontai. See Body, p. 13.

11. See undated letter to Ström, presumably 1924, Ström Archive.

that attracted her to the Party—the wholeness of Communist life—was missing at the embassy in Norway.[12] The life of a diplomat lacked the rigor and intellectual demand, the totality of commitment—what Bukharin called the "tenseness"—of Moscow politics.[13] Nor did Kollontai expect to regain the unity, the sense of being merged with the Party, that had long defined Communism for her. The Party, aware that the remnants of the defeated Workers' Opposition wanted her to represent them abroad, harassed and distrusted her. They suspected her friendships, particularly the one with Marcel Body, the French-speaking Communist who was First Secretary of the Soviet embassy. A critic of Moscow's policies, Body had requested in 1921 that he be assigned a diplomatic post away from the capital. He was already established in Oslo when Kollontai arrived. Efforts were made to separate Kollontai and Body when their mutual affinity became apparent, and Body was recalled in 1925 for reassignment to the Far East. We know Kollontai had tired of diplomatic life. Body believed that his reassignment influenced her to resign.[14]

In a curious episode that began with their departure from Oslo for Berlin in December 1925, Kollontai tried to convince Body to join her in a new life. At one level, Kollontai's relationship with Body was the rapport of two oppositionists. After she continued on to Moscow, she wrote to him nearly daily throughout the winter about the dismal struggle between Stalin and Trotsky.[15] At another level, their relationship was personal. Yet it had not progressed to an intimacy that would enable Kollontai to confide her feelings fully. In Berlin, where she returned in the spring of 1926 for medical treatment, she asked Body by means of a letter left on the table with his name on it (she claimed she did not trust herself with the words) if he would remain with her. Because the letter is so revealing, it is worth quoting in full.[16]

12. Kollontai was elevated to Soviet Minister to Norway in March 1923, when Surits moved on to Turkey.

13. "We are all accustomed to things there and to the tenseness of life," Bukharin explained. Nicolaevsky, p. 6.

14. Body, p. 18. The gist of Body's recollections is usually accurate, though details of time and place are frequently in error. For example, he described a series of articles in *Pravda*, falsely signed AMK that presented crude distortions of Kollontai's ideas on marriage and the family. There are no such articles. Yet Bertram D. Wolfe has testified both to Body's closeness to Kollontai and to his integrity. Body discussed his friendship with Kollontai in a letter to the author of Feb. 28, 1974.

15. When they met again in Berlin, she shared with him her "worst fears" that blood would flow. Body, p. 18.

16. Body, p. 19.

Dear Marcel Iakovlevitch,

It is after deep reflection that I want to propose that we continue to work together. This implies that we must loyally inform the Central Committee of our decision. We will establish ourselves in France or in another country. And there we will write. Once free, we will tell objectively, honestly, what we know of the events and the people of the Revolution and warn people against the excesses to which partisan politics are leading. Tell me what you think of the idea!

A pathetic letter! Kollontai contemplated a break with the Party and a life as a free writer, but she could not do what Angelica Balabanoff had done: become a voluntary exile, renounce the collective, as it were, and live abroad alone.

Body, who had a wife and child in Oslo, was unnerved by Kollontai's invitation. She was asking him to do something "very grave," he told her. Whatever their explanation, the Central Committee would interpret their decision as a political break. The Party did not permit its members to depart freely to write memoirs. Had she forgotten how Balabanoff was persecuted after she left? Was her health strong enough for *Pravda*'s attack? She was one of the last Communists to whom victims could appeal. He reminded her of her intervention earlier to the heads of the GPU (political police), Dzerzhinskii and Menzhinskii, on behalf of those unjustly accused. If she departed, to whom could the innocent turn? Kollontai doubted she would be able to help people much longer, given the worsening political climate in Moscow, but Body countered with other arguments.[17]

In his anxiety to avoid committing himself, Body must have seemed familiar to Kollontai. Russian literature offered abundant examples of the "hero" unable to cope with the plans of a Russian woman. Body was Onegin informing Tat'iana that he was not the man for her, Oblomov telling Ol'ga that she would be happier with someone else, Rudin leaving Nataliia. Appealing to Kollontai's sense of history as well as to her self-image as a court of last resort, he pointed out that her projected memoirs would suffer if she were to cut herself off from her observation post.

Apprehension made Kollontai vulnerable. Only recently she had urged F. Ström to contact their mutual friend, Angelica Balabanoff, who was lonely and saddened as a result of her expulsion from the Party.[18] The life of a free writer had so little reality after a decade as a Bolshevik that Kollontai continued in a sad sort of way to define her

17. *Ibid.*
18. Undated letter to Ström, presumably 1924, Ström Archive.

image of freedom in terms of how Communists in Moscow would react.[19] Abandoning her plan, she returned to the Soviet Union in July.[20]

※※※※

Late in 1926 Kollontai was assigned as a Soviet representative to the embassy in Mexico, a punishment for her boldness that had begun the previous year with her resignation. Not only had she been fighting the new marriage law, she had written a brief autobiography for a German series, *Leading Women in Europe*. Anticipating freedom, Kollontai overstepped Party bounds. She needed now to revise her manuscript, already in galley proof, to bring it within acceptable Party lines. The galleys of her autobiography were recently published in Germany along with her corrections: thus we are afforded a rare glimpse into the mind of a Bolshevik who became her own censor. It would be the first of Kollontai's acts of self-abnegation.

Kollontai's revisions may be summed up as both a critique of individualism and a stifling of her identification with the socialist women's movement. Wherever her ego came into prominence, Kollontai suppressed it. Even the innocent recollection that as a young girl she "wanted to be free" seemed inappropriate.[21] Her recognition that "to go my way, to work, to struggle, to create side by side with men" was her subconscious motive, the force behind her life and activity, sounded on rereading too individualistic.[22] She deleted all references to her popularity as a revolutionary leader and to her bravery.[23] She eliminated discussion of her closeness with Lenin—for example her boast that when Lenin delivered his famous "April Theses" only she supported him.[24]

Kollontai's most severe deletions related to the double standard of sexual morality, to women's relationship to love, and to the Party's lack of support for the woman question. She expunged her frank revelation that she realized for the first time as early as 1905 "how

19. See Body, p. 19.
20. A close friend of Kollontai's in Moscow does not believe that Kollontai seriously intended to leave the Party. Moscow interview, Aug. 1973.
21. Kollontai, *Autobiography*, p. 9. I cite the English translation unless otherwise indicated.
22. *Ibid.*, p. 4.
23. See such deleted phrases as "my followers, factory workers and women-soldiers, numbered thousands" (*ibid*, p. 30) and "I received countless threatening letters, but I never requested military protection. I always went out alone, unarmed and without any kind of a bodyguard. In fact I never gave a thought to any kind of danger" (p. 39).
24. *Ibid.*, p. 31.

little our Party concerned itself with the fate of the women of the working class and how meager was its interest in women's liberation." Similarly she eliminated discussion of the significance to the woman question of her diplomatic appointment: "When I was appointed as Russian envoy to Oslo, I realized that I had thereby achieved a victory not only for myself, but for women in general . . . a victory . . . over conventional morality and conservative concepts of marriage. . . . A woman, like myself, who has settled scores with the double standard and who has never concealed it, was accepted into a caste which . . . staunchly upholds tradition and pseudo-morality."[25]

She erased references to political battles, ignoring her pledge that one day when the pain was less sharp she would give an account of the "dark time" surrounding her resignation in protest against the Treaty of Brest-Litovsk. And, in a final gesture of self-denial, she deleted her promise that the complete liberation of the working woman and the creation of a new sexual morality would always remain "the highest aim of my activity, and of my life."[26] Such massive revisions needed explanation. Kollontai apologized to the editor, offering to bear the cost for changes that were necessary now that she was an "official person"[27]—indeed, a Soviet representative abroad. Then Kollontai departed for Mexico. It was October 1926, the peak of the factional struggle. Trotsky, after condemning Stalin as "the gravedigger of the Revolution," was excluded from the Politburo and Zinoviev was deposed from the Presidency of the Comintern.[28]

Mexico was a misery. The altitude affected Kollontai's heart. That the Party was tearing itself apart increased her anxiety. But, maintaining discipline, she refused to discuss politics with outsiders, even sympathetic ones to whom her unhappiness was apparent.[29] She wrote to Ström alluding to the troubles in Moscow, commenting sadly "how much nicer the first hard years were." Still she had hopes for the "big goals." "If there were just some *other* way!"[30]

Kollontai remained only one year in Mexico. When the opportunity

25. *Ibid.*, pp. 5–6.   26. *Ibid.*, pp. 47–48.

27. See inserted letter of July 1926 to Elga Kern in Kollontai, *Autobiographie einer sexuell emanzipierten Kommunistin* (omitted in the English edition).

28. Bukharin took Zinoviev's place. See Deutscher, *The Prophet Unarmed*, vol. 2, p. 296.

29. Comments of Ella Wolfe to author. Mrs. Wolfe was Kollontai's houseguest at the Soviet embassy in Mexico.

30. Undated letter to Ström, italics in original. Ström Archive.

arose to regain her Norwegian post, she seized it.[31] But there was a price to pay. She would have to join those Communists who, rather than see the Party torn apart, were openly denouncing the United Opposition, which had been routed by Stalin at the Fifteenth Party Conference in October 1926. There Clara Zetkin had denounced Trotsky and Zinoviev.[32] Stalin had earlier announced triumphantly that "Comrade Krupskaia" had forsaken the Opposition. Shliapnikov and Medvedev "confessed" their errors and repented. Varvara Iakovleva broke with the Trotskyists after their street demonstrations in November 1927.[33]

At the end of October 1927, in *Pravda*, Kollontai, too, denounced the Opposition. But her act ought not to be interpreted primarily as capitulation. How then to regard it? Kollontai had not lightly abandoned her dream of living as a free writer, with the individualism it implied. Renouncing opposition and individualism both, Kollontai was elevating her search for personal authenticity, which took the form of a renewed submission to the larger authority of the Party, into a worship of collectivism and discipline. The spirit that inspired the massive revisions of her *Autobiography* was reflected in *Pravda* on a larger scale. Kollontai's ode to collectivism contrasted with her earlier glorification of *samodeiatel'nost'*. During the Civil War creative spontaneity had been useful, but it sometimes degenerated into "anarchistic individualism."[34] *Samodeiatel'nost'* was her motif in 1921. Discipline replaced it in 1927. With a convert's zeal, she wrote that collective work had produced "an utterly new idea of the meaning of discipline," not a conventional submission to orders but a "merging of one's own will with the will of the collective."

Kollontai was harsh: the masses do not trust the Opposition. Based on the near unanimous vote against the Opposition in the selection of delegates to the upcoming Fifteenth Party Congress, Kollontai concluded that in the depths of the Party the mood was anger at the Op-

31. For details, see Hauge, pp. 114–26, and Body, pp. 22–23.

32. See Deutscher, *The Prophet Unarmed*, vol. 2, p. 308.

33. For Krupskaia, Shliapnikov, and Medvedev, see Souvarine, p. 438. See Serge, pp. 225–26 for the street demonstrations.

34. See "Oppozitsiia i partiinaia massa," *Pravda*, Oct. 30, 1927. Kollontai did not renounce the demands of the Workers' Opposition, but she did deplore the excesses of *samodeiatel'nost'*. The Soviet interpretation that Kollontai regretted her leadership of the Workers' Opposition is contradicted by her correspondence with Ström, in which she indicates pride in her earlier leadership. See undated letter to Ström, presumably 1924. For the view that Kollontai recognized and corrected her "errors," see Stasova's "Introduction" to Itkina's biography of Kollontai, p. 4. Itkina suggests the same thing on p. 215.

position for transgressions of Party discipline.[35] Once Kollontai had declared that if the Opposition were driven out of the Party, working-class passivity would increase. That was in 1922 when she believed that the Opposition not only expressed the will of the masses but that the Workers' Opposition *was* the masses. In 1927, on the contrary, the Trotsky-Zinoviev Opposition was being rejected by those same masses. Krupskaia would express a similar sentiment at the Fifteenth Party Congress when she charged that the Opposition had lost "the feeling for what animates the working class."[36] Kollontai spoke sharply: does the Opposition think the masses have forgotten that the Oppositionists themselves helped build the defects they now attacked? Her reference, of course, was to the call for a restoration of inner-party democracy. And she repeated the workers' jeer heard in the factories: who gave the Oppositionists the right to speak for us?

How could Kollontai not sound superior? What the Oppositionists protested in 1927 she had condemned in 1921. But members of the United Opposition were not prepared even in 1927 to acknowledge that the former Workers' Opposition had correctly described the Communist Party's illness. At a meeting somebody recalled that the Workers' Opposition in 1920–21 had analyzed the bureaucratization of the Party and the condition of the working class in terms that, as one Oppositionist put it, "we scarcely dared repeat aloud seven years later." At the suggestion that this "bygone Opposition" had been right in criticizing Lenin, Opposition leader Karl Radek became angry. He argued that it was "a dangerous idea. If you take it up, you will be finished as far as we are concerned. In 1920 there was no Thermidor in sight, Lenin was alive, and the revolution was simmering in Europe."[37]

Kollontai rejected the Opposition, but she did not turn her "eloquent idealism" to "the service of Stalin's organization."[38] She was far from endorsing Stalin in 1927. How far, she indicated in her conclusion, astonishing in the light of the power struggle, that the masses in the unions, in the Soviets, in committees, had accustomed themselves to working as a group, that they no longer relied on "leaders." Leaders, she thought, still in the spirit of *State and Revolution*, were becoming less relevant as workers matured in the collective spirit.[39]

Kollontai remained unbroken; her embrace of collectivism was

35. See "Oppozitsiia i partiinaia massa."
36. Daniels, p. 319.
37. Serge, p. 221.
38. For the view that she did so, see Daniels, p. 309.
39. "Oppozitsiia i partiinaia massa."

enthusiastic, not abject. She still took chances and acted boldly. In November 1927, on the eve of the Fifteenth Party Congress, which would expel the Left Oppositionists from the Party, she wrote an article about the heroines of October. She could never forget Evgeniia Bosh, passionately tensed for struggle: thus Kollontai honored the Trotskyist who shot herself in despair after the failure of the Opposition in 1923. She also recalled how Varvara Iakovleva, another Trotskyist, fought on the barricades in October, bravely restoring courage to the waverers.[40] Ten years later, Kollontai would not dare recall these women by name.

Had she been active in Moscow after 1922 rather than an outcast, Kollontai might have succumbed to the romance of opposition and to the entreaties of old friends like Christian Rakovskii who pleaded with her to join them.[41] The Oppositionists' beleaguered cohesiveness has been made almost palpable in memoirs.[42] But kept at a distance, Kollontai could be detached. In the autumn of 1927, the walls of the embassy in Norway shielded her from the agony of the Opposition after they were expelled from the Party. She did not witness the arrests or hear the loudspeakers on street corners blaring demands for reprisals.[43] Sent to Norway in October, she missed by a month the enforced departure from their Kremlin apartments of the leaders of the Left after their exclusion from the Party. Memoirs offer poignant vignettes: Radek, her friend in Scandinavia in July 1917 who warned her not to return to Russia to certain arrest by the Kerensky government, grimly sorting his papers preparatory to departing his Kremlin rooms, surrounded by a deluge of old books spread out over the carpet. ("Would you like some books? Take what you want," he offered a friend.) It was the night that A. A. Ioffe, one of Trotsky's closest associates, shot himself. Ioffe left a letter. "My death is a gesture of protest against those who have reduced the Party to such a condition that it is totally incapable of reacting against this disgrace" (the expulsion of Trotsky and Zinoviev from the Central Committee). Ioffe's widow sat nearby in "a little room full of children's toys" talking in a low voice to some comrades.[44]

40. See Kollontai, *Izbrannye stat'i i rechi*, p. 373.
41. Rakovskii chided her in the summer of 1926 for refusing still to join the Opposition. He predicted that Stalin's triumph was by no means assured. See Body, p. 21, and Eastman, p. 443, on Rakovskii's friendship with Trotsky. In fact, at no time from 1921 to 1927 did members of the former Workers' Opposition support the Trotskyists.
42. See, for example, Serge, p. 275.
43. *Ibid.*, p. 277.
44. *Ibid.*, pp. 228–29.

Nor did Kollontai witness a few years later the disgrace of her friends on the Right. She was preparing again to move, this time to the embassy in Sweden, when the Stalinists in 1929, having launched the first of the Five-Year Plans, committed themselves to the "highest conceivable speed of economic development," far outstripping anything the Trotskyists had envisioned.[45] The story of the subsequent opposition of the Right—of how Bukharin, Rykov, and Tomskii protested the "military-feudal exploitation" of the peasant, excessive bureaucratization, and the absence of democracy within the Party—has been told elsewhere.[46] Open political opposition in Soviet Russia ended as the 1920's drew to a close. Its demise was symbolized by the confession of error that Bukharin, Rykov, and Tomskii signed and published in *Pravda*.[47]

Oppositionists were puzzled by Kollontai's subsequent conformity. Angelica Balabanoff wrote that "for old revolutionists like Kollontai it was a punishment to be separated from the field of revolutionary activity," but after years in Norway, Mexico, and Sweden as Soviet minister and ambassador, Kollontai "seemed to become reconciled to her position and to fall completely into line."[48] Victor Serge repeats the same bemused conclusion. Kollontai was an Oppositionist who "subsequently conformed."[49] Trotsky, who received no help from Kollontai when he sought to obtain a visa to live in Norway, and who believed that as ambassador to Sweden she objected to his later appeal for a Swedish visa, described her bitterly. Kollontai in the early years took "an ultra-left stand, not only toward me but toward Lenin as well. She waged many a battle against the 'Lenin-Trotsky' regime, only to bow most movingly later on to the Stalin regime."[50] But Trotsky never explained—any more than did Balabanoff or Serge—why Kollontai capitulated.

Fear was a factor. Yet Kollontai did not early succumb to it. As late

45. See Daniels, p. 358.
46. See Daniels, pp. 322–69, and Cohen, *Bukharin*, pp. 270–336.
47. Daniels, pp. 368–69. When Bukharin and Rykov were removed from the Politburo, Kollontai, according to Body, was required to denounce the Old Bolsheviks of the Right just as three years earlier she had denounced former comrades of the Left. See Body, p. 23. According to a friend, Kollontai shared the right wing's criticism of collectivization. Moscow interview, Aug. 1973.
48. Balabanoff, *My Life as a Rebel*, p. 252.
49. Serge, p. 205.
50. For Trotsky's unsuccessful Swedish visa attempts, see Deutscher, *The Prophet Outcast*, vol. 3, p. 188. For his bitterness toward Kollontai, see Trotsky, *My Life*, p. 274.

as the mid-1930's Kollontai was far from anticipating the terror ahead. On a visit to Moscow at the beginning of 1936, a period of relaxation and reconciliation after the first wave of fear, Kollontai wrote to her closest friend in Sweden, Dr. Ada Nilsson (who was also her physician), that Moscow was beautiful. Everyone was full of vitality and good humor.[51] The thought of returning to Stockholm at the end of the month was not pleasant. If not for you, Kollontai told Nilsson, Stockholm would be cold and empty. She was glad that "we have each other."[52] In August 1936 the tranquility broke. The first of the Moscow trials began. Zinoviev and Kamenev were convicted and executed. Tomskii committed suicide. Stalin resumed a war of nerves and terror against Kollontai. Aware of Soviet agents watching her, she anticipated arrest.[53] One never knew what the agents would find and write in their reports, she told Nilsson in 1937.[54] In July of that year Kollontai was recalled to Moscow. The savage purge of the Commissariat of Foreign Affairs was under way.[55] She left a letter in Sweden asking that Nilsson save all her personal letters, notes, and diaries for ten years in case "I become the victim of an unfortunate accident."[56] But Kollontai survived and returned to Stockholm. A year later, after the conviction and execution of the fallen Rightists Bukharin and Rykov, newspapers in Sweden announced "Minister Kollontai is strongly suspected." Before journeying again to Moscow, Kollontai gave Nilsson

51. For the relaxation of tension at this time, see Cohen, *Bukharin*, p. 347.

52. Kollontai to Nilsson, Jan. 1936. Nilsson letters, University of Gothenburg Archive. According to Nilsson, the Swedes occasionally acted coldly toward Kollontai, expressing their anti-Russian feeling. See Nilsson, "Det Stora Uppdraget," no. 35, p. 11. Nilsson was a board member of the Soviet-Swedish Society. For Nilsson's autobiography, see her *Glimtar ur mitt liv som läkare* (Stockholm, 1963).

53. For Kollontai's awareness that she was watched, see Nilsson, "Det Stora Uppdraget," no. 36, p. 16.

54. *Ibid.*, no. 35, p. 38.

55. Medvedev, p. 198. Among those purged in 1937–38 in the Commissariat of Foreign Affairs were L. M. Karakhan, deputy commissar; K. K. Iurenev, ambassador to Japan; Ia. Kh. Davtian, ambassador to Poland; M. A. Karskii, ambassador to Turkey; V. Kh. Tairov, ambassador to Mongolia; Bogomolov, ambassador to China; M. S. Ostrovskii, ambassador to Rumania; I. S. Iakubovich, ambassador to Norway; E. A. Asmus, ambassador to Finland; A. V. Sabinin, Neiman, V. M. Tsukerman, and Fekhner, heads of departments; F. F. Raskol'nikov, ambassador to Bulgaria; A. G. Barmin, ambassador to Greece. Of all those who were ordered to return to face almost certain death in Moscow, only the last two refused. For a fuller list, which includes deputy foreign commissars N. I. Krestinskii and G. Ia. Sokol'nikov among the victims, see Teddy J. Uldricks, "The Impact of the Great Purges on the People's Commissariat of Foreign Affairs," *Slavic Review*, no. 2 (June 1977), pp. 188–89.

56. Kollontai asked Nilsson to turn these materials over to the Institute of Marxism-Leninism in Moscow at the end of that time to be published if it appeared appropriate to do so in the Soviet Union. Kollontai to Nilsson, July 4, 1937, Nilsson Archive. Kollontai included the address of Misha, her son, who was then living with his wife and child in Kew Gardens, New York.

a pile of letters to burn. She also gave her friend a letter with detailed directions to follow in case she heard nothing from Kollontai during the coming year or learned for certain that Kollontai was dead.[57] We do not know whether Kollontai was aware of rumors that a special trial of diplomats was being planned.[58] But she felt death near as she prepared, for a second time, to return to Moscow.[59] As she later recalled, "When I arrived in Moscow . . . I was full of fear. I refused to understand anything at all. My friends and comrades in previous struggles disappeared one by one. Later I got to know that Pavel Dybenko had also lost his life."[60]

Again Kollontai survived. We do not know what happened, what interrogations she was subjected to, what demands were made of her. We know only that in the autumn of 1937 Kollontai began rewriting Bolshevik Party history. Consider her article "Women in 1917" and how it differed from her 1927 tribute to the heroines of October. In 1937 she dealt not with personalities but with broad events: the strike of the laundresses in 1917 and the first Petrograd Conference of Working Women. Not even Krupskaia or Lenin's sisters could safely be mentioned. She dared name in 1937 only Klavdiia Nikolaeva and Vera Slutskaia. Nikolaeva, elected to the Central Committee in 1934 at the Seventeenth Party Congress, survived, despite the purge of 70 percent of that Central Committee, to be reelected in 1939 at the Eighteenth Congress. Vera Slutskaia, killed early in the Revolution, was not associated with controversy.[61] Instead of women, Kollontai em-

57. Kollontai to Nilsson, July 21, 1938. Kollontai had sorted her materials—photographs, notes, and letters—into two suitcases. She asked Nilsson not to publish anything in the one until 1972—100 years after her birth—and in the other until 1950. If Nilsson heard nothing from Kollontai during the coming year or knew for certain that she was dead, she should send both suitcases together with her instructions concerning publication to the International Bureau in Geneva. (Presumably she meant the International Labor Office.) Her printed materials were to be sent to the Institute of Marxism-Leninism.

58. The rumored trial of diplomats never materialized. See Uldricks, "The Impact of the Great Purges," p. 189.

59. In her reflective letter to Nilsson of July 21, 1938, Kollontai assessed her life. The reality of the Soviet Union represented fulfillment of her long struggle as a revolutionary. The emancipation of women was another triumph. Her sorrow stemmed from everything brutal and unjust.

60. As quoted by Hauge, p. 275, from the Soviet film documentary "Vremia, kotoroe vsegda s nami" (Leningrad, 1965). The film is described in Hauge, p. 310. Hauge assumed that Kollontai referred to her arrival in 1937.

61. See Kollontai, "Zhenshchiny v 1917 godu," pp. 12–13. For the purges of the Central Committee and for the survivors in 1939, see Daniels, p. 431. For Khrushchev's secret speech at the Twentieth Party Congress in 1956, which discusses the purge of the Central Committee, see R. V. Daniels, ed., *A Documentary History of Communism* (New York, 1960), vol. 2, p. 227.

phasized Comrade Stalin, "leader of genius" and Lenin's mainstay. An artist's imagined sketch of Lenin, Stalin, and Molotov, smiling, at a table editing *Pravda*, replaced the customary pictures of the heroines of October.[62]

Another article indicated more sharply still in its early and late versions the extent to which Kollontai participated in the all-pervasive lying in Stalinist Russia. Contrast the essay Kollontai published in 1919 recalling the famous meeting in Sukhanov's and Flakserman's apartment when the Bolsheviks voted to move toward a seizure of power with the revision that appeared in *Izvestiia* in 1937: it makes depressing reading. Her original version praised "Comrade Trotsky" for his revolutionary faith. His speeches she compared to the sounding of a bell.[63] No such rhapsodic appreciation appeared in 1937: "Judas-Trotsky" was a traitor and a future Gestapo agent. She eliminated friendly references to Zinoviev and Kamenev, the "two Opposition-ists" at the historic meeting, part of the lively group of Bolsheviks gathered around the samovar in the early hours of the morning eating cheese and sausages. What had been camaraderie in 1919 became con-spiracy in 1937. Kollontai added vicious descriptions of Zinoviev and Kamenev, dead since 1936, to the *Izvestiia* version. Zinoviev and Kam-enev were cowardly enemies who opposed Lenin and the Party, traitors whom Lenin endured with difficulty. Stalin had not figured in the original version of the article, but in 1937 Kollontai ranked him as the "clearest and most determined interpreter of Lenin's and the Party's policy." In 1917, Stalin had unmasked the future gang of counterrevolutionary traitors, Trotsky, Zinoviev and Kamenev.[64]

How should we interpret Kollontai's participation in the Stalinist lie? According to Marcel Body, Kollontai admitted "I have put my principles in a corner of my conscience and I carry out as well as pos-sible the policies dictated to me."[65] It has been suggested that Bolshe-viks had to "join the witchhunt against Trotskyists to prove their Bolshevism."[66] For Kollontai, the reverse was true: she joined the witchhunt not to prove her Bolshevism but to exorcise her Bolshevism,

62. That she was in prison and not present at the Sixth Party Congress did not keep Kollontai in 1937 from describing how at that meeting Stalin emerged as "the heart, the brain, and the will of the Sixth Congress." See "Zhenshchiny v 1917 godu," p. 13.
63. See Kollontai, "Ruka istorii," p. 71.
64. Compare Kollontai, "Ruka istorii," and *Izvestiia*, Oct. 24, 1937, p. 3.
65. Body, p. 23.
66. Robert Tucker, speaking at a panel of the American Association for the Advance-ment of Slavic Studies, Washington, D.C., Oct. 1977.

for she understood that it would be emotionally impossible—indeed, physically impossible—to survive if she remained what she had been. Taking her cue from Stalin, who in 1935 had abolished the Society of Old Bolsheviks (of which Sof'ia Smidovich had been Secretary) because it was the home of "fault-finding old men" unable to grasp the "needs of the times," she did Stalin's work for him.[67] She began in 1937 to destroy her political self.

What was a Bolshevik? After the first of the Moscow trials had begun, with Zinoviev and Kamenev soon to be executed, Bukharin and others explained Stalin's definition. Old Bolsheviks, having grown up under the conditions of revolutionary struggle, were trained in the psychology of opposition. Their minds worked in directions critical of the existing order, seeking everywhere its weaknesses. In short, they were wreckers, not builders. The conclusion to be drawn was clear: the critical mood of the Bolshevik was appropriate to the past but not to the present, when the Soviet Union must occupy itself with building. It was impossible to build anything enduring with skeptics and critics. As one Communist put it: "All of us Old Bolsheviks who have any sort of prominent revolutionary past are now hiding in our lairs, trembling. For has it not been demonstrated theoretically that . . . we are an undesirable element?"[68] Hatred of the Bolsheviks was manifested in the mass arrests and executions of the *Yezhovshchina*, which began in 1937. With what ecstasy Yezhov, the Commissar of Internal Affairs who directed the purge in 1937 and 1938, badgered the old Oppositionists whenever he had a chance. A great store of bitterness had accumulated in his soul against all those who had formerly occupied prominent posts in the Party, against intellectuals who were good speakers.[69] What were the Old Bolsheviks to do? They were *"all obliged to lie*: it is impossible to manage otherwise."[70]

The Menshevik Boris Nicolaevsky described the Old Bolsheviks

67. For Old Bolsheviks, see Nicolaevsky, *Power and the Soviet Elite: "The Letter of an Old Bolshevik" and Other Essays*, p. 57.

68. The "Letter of an Old Bolshevik" is purportedly Bukharin's account of the Party up to 1936. Nicolaevsky claims (pp. 8–9) to have written it from memory after having destroyed the notes of a conversation with Bukharin. For the period after 1936 Nicolaevsky relied on other Communist sources. Kollontai was not technically an Old Bolshevik, unless the definition is extended to include those who joined the Party after 1903 but before 1917.

69. Nicolaevsky, p. 49.

70. *Ibid.*, p. 54. Italics in original.

as people who "found themselves in a new, Stalinist environment and who were dying in it."[71] Kollontai, like other Bolsheviks, was destroying herself as a critic of the existing order so that she might live. She was driven to capitulate also by her fear for the survival of others. Here lies an answer to perplexing questions: why Kollontai returned to Moscow in 1937 and 1938 instead of seeking asylum abroad; why she remained in the diplomatic service continuing to maintain an uncongenial "façade," serving as a "porter" carrying other people's messages.[72] The safety of her son Misha and his family does not seem a major reason, since they were not in Russia. Mikhail Kollontai had not followed his mother's path. He was what Communists call "non-Party."[73] A well-educated, soft-spoken engineer, he spent most of his time away, working for Soviet trade. During the 1920's he lived in Berlin. Later, during the NEP, he worked in Stockholm as a controller, facilitating large Soviet purchases from Swedish factories. When trade credits to the Soviet Union were canceled in 1928, his work ended and he moved to the United States, not to return home until 1939.[74]

Kollontai may have returned to Moscow in 1937 because Stalin held another hostage—not Misha, but Dybenko. I suspect that Kollontai's capitulation in that year can be explained partly by her fear for her former husband, who had risen to be military commander of the Leningrad district but whose life was endangered in 1937 when Stalin and Yezhov began their campaign against the officer corps.[75] Letters to Nilsson, conversations with Body, and Kollontai's memoirs suggest that Dybenko was still on her mind.[76]

Stalin began his sudden assault on the army in June 1937 with the announcement that the "flower of the Red Army Command" had been charged with treason. Dybenko was one of the nine judges on the military tribunal that sentenced to death General Tukhachevskii, Iakir, and others. But the officers who sat on the tribunal understood that

71. *Ibid.*, p. 10.

72. For the "façade" reference, see Kollontai to Zoia Shadurskaia, Feb. 6, 1932, as quoted in G. Petrov, "Posol revoliutsii," in Zhak and Itkina, eds., p. 207. For the "porter" reference, see Nilsson, "Det Stora Uppdraget," no. 36, p. 16.

73. Moscow interview, Aug. 1973.

74. Nilsson, "Det Stora Uppdraget," no. 37, p. 18. A letter from Kollontai to Palencia of Nov. 5, 1939, reports that Misha and his family had returned to Moscow. Palencia, p. 274.

75. Medvedev (p. 307) suggests that Dybenko was already under suspicion in 1937. The Swedish press circulated rumors of Dybenko's arrest in Feb. 1937 but later reported him serving as commander of the Leningrad Military District. See *Nya Dagligt Allehanda*, Feb. 8, 1937, cited in Hauge, p. 196.

76. See Body, p. 24; undated letter to Nilsson; and Hauge, p. 275.

they were all threatened. Il'ia Ehrenburg wrote of how painful it had been for the military leaders to sign the sentences, how one of them told him "And tomorrow I'll be put in their place." [77] No one in command was safe. [78] Kollontai feared for Dybenko. An undisciplined, impetuous man, how could he survive? But if she hoped that her capitulation might protect him, or if she had been given assurances to that effect, it was to no avail. Dybenko was dismissed from his post in Leningrad for "insufficient vigilance." Appointed Deputy Commissar of Forest Industry, he was sent to the Urals. In April 1938 he was arrested. [79] Another source reports that once in the Urals, Dybenko was shot as he got off the train. [80] Kollontai mournfully told Marcel Body of Dybenko's death. Body was baffled: why Dybenko? He hated Trotsky with a passion and had not taken part in opposition. There had been a purge of the army, she explained, and Dybenko did not know how to keep quiet. [81]

Had Dybenko not been a hostage, Kollontai might still have remained at her diplomatic post. At 64 she was an unlikely émigré. The thought of regaining her independence had frightened her when she contemplated it ten years earlier. And strange as it may seem to the non-Communist mind, and although the Party played an ever-diminishing role in her life, she valued its esteem. [82]

The torment of the would-be exile was a problem endemic to the Russian intelligentsia from Aleksandr Herzen in the 1840's to Aleksandr Solzhenitsyn in the 1970's. Anna Akhmatova told the historian Isaiah Berlin that she disapproved of emigration. She felt "it was important to die with one's country. Compared to this, dying *for* one's country was easy." [83] But why, when Kollontai was already abroad, did she not defect *after* 1938 to a Scandinavian country where she felt comfortable? If she did not, it was because of what her Communist commitment still represented. To be sure, the Party's hold over her had diminished. In the past it had provided comradeship and engagement of all her moral energies. In Stockholm, Kollontai experienced

77. As quoted by Medvedev, pp. 405–6.
78. See Conquest, pp. 226–28.
79. Medvedev, p. 307. Dybenko was remarried; after his execution, his wife was sent to a camp. *Ibid.*, p. 342.
80. See Haupt and Marie, p. 125.
81. Body, p. 24. Body has this conversation misdated as taking place in 1936 before the army purge and Dybenko's death.
82. An old friend attests that by this time Kollontai lived virtually as a non-Party person. Moscow interview, Aug. 1973.
83. Haight, p. 142.

the Party only in the most attenuated sense. And in 1938, when Kollontai knew only a handful of people in Moscow, camaraderie existed only as nostalgia.[84] What was left? In place of the former melding of one's self with the collective was the compensating satisfaction of being part of history moving forward, of representing the first socialist state. When Kollontai thought she was facing death in 1938 and assessed her life, she thought not of the Party but of the reality of the Soviet Union. Its existence, the fulfillment of her long struggle as a revolutionary, was a source of joy.[85]

Other Communists expressed similar views. Bukharin, on his trip to Europe in 1936, explained his feelings to friends who were urging him to remain abroad. He used the image of a stream. It was as though they, the Bolsheviks, were part of a stream that was running to the shore. If one leaned out of the stream, one was ejected. The stream went through the most difficult places. But it still went forward.[86]

❀❀❀

Kollontai stayed on, suffering from insomnia, high blood pressure, and heart trouble. For a woman who lived to 80 Kollontai had a remarkable record of ill health.[87] David Joravsky has commented on the evidence that Party activists suffered from an especially high incidence of hypertension and other cardiovascular disorders.[88] The poet Boris Pasternak put it well, summing up the psychological and physical consequences of constant pretense: "The great majority of us are required to live a life of systematic duplicity. Your health is bound to be affected if, day after day, you say the opposite of what you feel, if you grovel before what you dislike."[89]

There were psychological blows of another sort. Kollontai, the old pacifist and internationalist, a Soviet representative to the League of Nations in the mid-1930's, grieved over Spain, China, and Czechoslovakia, and the failure of the Western nations to understand what seemed clear, that the Soviet Union wanted peace.[90] Thoroughly anti-

84. See Body, p. 23.

85. Letter to Nilsson, July 21, 1938.

86. Nicolaevsky, p. 25. And see Kollontai to Nilsson in the same vein, Sept. 7, 1939.

87. For examples, see letters to Nilsson of June 6, 1937, and July 9, 1938.

88. He quoted Dr. L. L. Rokhlin: "To, chem zhivet partaktiv—mozgom i serdtsem—tem on bol'she vsego boleet." (That by which the party *aktiv* lives, the brain and the heart, that is what ails him most of all.) See Joravsky, p. 113.

89. As quoted by Max Hayward, "What Is to Be Done?" *The New York Times Book Review*, May 7, 1978, p. 12.

90. For her "grieving," see her letter to Nilsson from Geneva, Sept. 22, 1938; on Spain, see her letters to Nilsson of Apr. 22, 1936, and Oct. 4, 1936.

fascist, she feared a German attack. According to Nilsson, she was un-
prepared for the Nazi-Soviet pact in August 1939. Marcel Body, on the
other hand, claimed that Kollontai suspected in the mid-1930's (as did
other Bolsheviks, notably Bukharin) that Stalin wanted a pact with
Hitler.[91]

The treaty was so hateful that Kollontai felt almost relieved when
Hitler broke the alliance by attacking the Soviet Union in June 1941.[92]
That knowledge makes it more painful to read Kollontai's letter to
Nilsson written immediately after the German invasion of Poland in
September 1939. It was a desperate attempt to rationalize Soviet com-
plicity, a depressing example of how a good person could be trapped
by her Communist commitment into pathetic self-deception. Kollontai's idealism became the source of her intellectual blindness. In a
rapid handwriting, frequently crossing out words, she scrawled page
after page in agitated German, choosing a curious line of defense.[93]
She might have argued with some plausibility that Stalin, concerned
only for Soviet survival in a hostile world, was forced to conclude a
nonaggression pact with Germany, that Britain and France were encouraging German Fascism against the Soviet Union and had frustrated negotiations for a mutual-assistance pact with Litvinov.[94] But
instead of noting the danger of a Western design to pit Germany
against the Soviet Union, she fell back on a simple faith that revealed
her continuing hunger for absolutes. The Soviet Union was evolving
a new way to move international relations forward. When she was
young, did Nilsson not wish that the world would break away from its
traditions? Well, now the world was in the process of change, what they
both wished for when they were young. The quality of her thought

91. According to Body, p. 24, Kollontai thought Stalin thereby hoped to avoid
German aggression against Russia. For a discussion of the political background under-
lying assumptions that Stalin wanted a pact with Hitler, see Robert Tucker, *The Soviet
Political Mind* (New York, 1972), pp. 73–74. Stalin and Bukharin were presumably
exponents of the two main opposing foreign-policy orientations regarding Germany.
For discussion of these two opposing views, and this theory, see Robert M. Slusser,
"The Role of the Foreign Ministry," in Ivo J. Lederer, ed., *Russian Foreign Policy:
Essays in Historical Perspective* (New Haven, Conn., 1962).

92. Nilsson, "Det Stora Uppdraget," no. 36, p. 16.

93. See letter to Nilsson, Sept. 7, 1939. Kollontai would switch from Swedish or Norwegian to German or French when she became excited. Evidently Nilsson did not know
Russian.

94. For this view see Medvedev, p. 411, and Ehrenburg, p. 305. Litvinov, Surits, and
Maiskii each said the pact was necessary, since by it Stalin succeeded in thwarting plans
for a Western coalition intent on destroying the Soviet Union. For the controversy over
Stalin's foreign policy, see Robert Tucker, "The Emergence of Stalin's Foreign Policy,"
Slavic Review, 4 (Dec. 1977), pp. 563–89, criticisms by T. Uldricks and A. Dallin, in the
same issue, and Tucker's reply (also in the same issue).

remained apocalyptic: mankind simply did not understand that the current turmoil indicated the onward march. There was no single method to solve conflicts among nations, but was it not more humane to solve problems through negotiations rather than with weapons? She insisted with astonishing blindness that a Nazi-Soviet pact was in the spirit of the League of Nations. But people were not willing to understand. A pathetic argument; Kollontai at her weakest. She denied that she was pessimistic. How could she be when the Soviet Union was moving the world forward? One too easily forgot that the Soviet Union was the "first" Soviet nation. But *that is* the *important* thing!"[95]

A postscript revealed that Kollontai was less sanguine than she claimed. She told of a threatening letter she had received from Polish refugees who wanted revenge against her, the Soviet representative, for the Nazi invasion. They warned her to leave Sweden if she valued her life. She could only smile. Was her life so dear to her? Her death, through an act of vengeance, might even arouse sympathy for the Soviet Union and be a crowning end to her service. She thought of Misha and speculated morosely that her "modest, wise, dear Misha" might benefit from her death. It would make his position easier. If Kollontai viewed herself as a hostage, her existence limiting Misha's behavior abroad and even assuring his return, she did not elaborate. She concluded that unfortunately threats were rarely carried out. Forgetting that she had insisted earlier in her letter that she was not pessimistic, she wrote of her depression. Her writing was not going well. She must avoid long discussions, not give in to painful thoughts, think introspectively. Did Ada understand?[96]

The saddest part of this letter was Kollontai's need to compose it. She wrote not to convince Nilsson of the peaceful intent of Soviet foreign policy, even when that policy switched from Litvinov's quest for collective security to Stalin's Nazi-Soviet pact, but to convince herself. She was not able to confront the possibility that the Soviet Union—the first socialist state—might be motivated not by the interests of international peace but by naked self-interest. Indeed, the most curious part of her letter was her notion that Soviet policy was still consistent with the goals of the League of Nations. This is not the place to discuss the historians' controversy over whether Stalin was merely marking time throughout the 1930's until a pact with Hitler could be con-

95. Letter of Sept. 7, 1939, to Nilsson. Underlined in original.
96. *Ibid.*

cluded. We should simply note that Kollontai had no sense of Stalin's long-range purpose as it existed in August 1939: Soviet-guided revolutions in contiguous countries and the annexation of territory to which Russia laid historical claim. Neither could it occur to her that such a policy would be furthered by a pact with Hitler that precipitated a European war.

᛭᛭᛭᛭

After the German attack on the Soviet Union in 1941, the moral ambiguities were fewer. But Kollontai's health continued to deteriorate. A combination of influences were shattering her constitution: 1937–38, and the endless line of dead comrades behind her; anxiety over the war; perhaps even guilt that while Russia was besieged she was secure with her son, who was again safe, this time in neutral Sweden. She had gone to Moscow in 1940 to fetch Misha when he, too, was stricken with heart trouble.[97] She may have known that other women were also in Moscow that year trying, unsuccessfully, to help their sons. Anna Akhmatova was one of them, hoping to obtain her son's release from prison.[98]

Kollontai collapsed finally in 1942 of a stroke. She recovered— though part of her face and her left hand remained paralyzed, and she was obliged thereafter to conduct diplomacy from a wheelchair. A go-between in efforts to end the Russo-Finnish war, she contributed to bringing about peace and was even nominated for a Nobel Peace Prize in 1946. But in Moscow, Kollontai was never fully trusted. When war with Finland loomed in 1939, and Kollontai expressed sadness at the prospect to Molotov (who had replaced Litvinov as Commissar for Foreign Affairs at the time of the Nazi-Soviet pact), he responded with an infuriating reference to "your Finland."[99]

Moscow feared that Kollontai was too sympathetic to the interests of both the Swedes and the Finns. Her years abroad and her many friends in Swedish intellectual, artistic, and diplomatic circles aroused suspicion.[100] Vladimir Petrov, the NKVD agent whom Moscow assigned to the Stockholm embassy in the early 1940's to watch Kollon-

97. Nilsson, "Det Stora Uppdraget," no. 37, p. 18. Misha returned to the Soviet Union in 1939.

98. Haight, p. 108.

99. Nilsson, "Det Stora Uppdraget," no. 36, p. 18. Nilsson gives details of Kollontai's negotiations during the Winter War.

100. See Petrov and Petrov, pp. 193–94, on Moscow's fear of Kollontai's foreign contacts.

tai (and who later defected to the United States), recalled the awe with which he spied on Lenin's comrade, the "legendary" Kollontai. Moscow even sent a second agent to watch the elderly ambassador, a woman named Elena who posed as a secretary and kept the NKVD informed of Kollontai's conversations and visitors. But nothing compromising turned up. The agents were directed to obtain the notes and drafts of Kollontai's memoirs, which Moscow knew she was writing. During one of Kollontai's absences the NKVD agents opened a locked chest in her embassy apartment. For three nights they worked, photographing her voluminous notes. From these the NKVD learned of Kollontai's grief at Dybenko's execution and her incredulity at the notion that he was a traitor.[101]

The Party might be wary of Kollontai's worldliness and her foreign contacts. The Commissar for Foreign Affairs might suspect her special fondness for Sweden, or for Finland, where she had spent childhood summers. But Moscow had nothing to fear from Aleksandra Kollontai. She was thoroughly subservient. Was the change in Kollontai a function primarily of illness and aging? Victor Serge asked himself that question on a Moscow street when he caught a glimpse of Maxim Gorky as he drove by sitting in the rear seat of a large Lincoln. Literature was dying in Soviet Russia, but Gorky, at 60, was silent. "Here was an ascetic, emaciated figure, with nothing alive in it except the will to exist and think." Could it be, Serge wondered, some kind of inner drying, stiffening, and shrinking peculiar to old age? Later he was reassured by the humanity and clear sightedness of André Gide and thought gratefully of John Dewey.[102] Age and illness were only partial explanations for the crumbling of Kollontai's critical posture; she was well into middle age and frequently in poor health at the peak of her boldest opposition. Her rejection of politics occurred several years before her stroke. The decision to lead an apolitical existence was Kollontai's rational choice, her only means for survival, both emotionally and physically. And how can those who did not share her awesome experiences question it?

❧❧❧

The nearly 400 letters Kollontai wrote to her beloved friend Ada Nilsson after retirement in 1945 and her return to Moscow are invaluable to our understanding. More than simply documenting her last

101. *Ibid.*, pp. 190–93.
102. Serge, pp. 268–69. Gorky did break with Stalin shortly before his death.

years, they provide a final perspective from which to interpret her earlier life. We will return to this assumption; it suffices here to comment briefly on one aspect. The letters testify to Kollontai's commitment to intimate and enduring bonds of female friendship, relationships found more commonly among nineteenth-century than twentieth-century women. Kollontai's experiences bear out the conclusion that such intense friendships appeared entirely compatible with heterosexuality.[103] Kollontai's relationship with Zoia Shadurskaia, her girlhood companion, was unaltered, we recall, by her romantic involvement with Vladimir Kollontai. Her marriage did not diminish either her love for Zoia or her desire to be with her. Indeed, in a manner not uncommon in the nineteenth century, Kollontai integrated Zoia into her married household. Accustomed to a loving relationship with a woman, Kollontai again, when life was lonely and her relationships with men disappointing, sought sustenance in an emotional bonding with a member of her own sex.[104] Ada Nilsson, like Zoia, who died shortly before the war, functioned as Kollontai's soul mate, one of the few people she trusted completely, whose conversation and companionship she yearned for and to whom in letter after letter she poured out her heart. Kollontai confided her fears, her disappointments, and her joys, *po dusham*—literally "soul to soul." Having shared some of Kollontai's most perilous moments, Nilsson could understand when Kollontai called one message not a letter but "a cry from my tired nerves." At their most intense, her letters to Nilsson reveal Kollontai's capacity for deep sharing and document her conclusion that ultimately long-term, loving friendships were more satisfying and supportive than romantic liaisons.[105] But for other reasons they make gloomy reading. Their emotional force does not conceal the image of a life reduced to banal activities and private concerns, a depressing contrast to what Kollontai had expected for herself and for revolutionary Russia.

The letters speak for themselves. One of the earliest described the three-room apartment in a ministry building on Bol'shaia Kaluzhskaia Street that the foreign office provided her, along with the title

103. See Carroll Smith-Rosenberg, "The Female World of Love and Ritual: Relations Between Women in Nineteenth-Century America," *Signs*, 1 (1975), pp. 1–29.
104. For Kollontai's conclusion that her romantic relationships were disappointing, see *Autobiography*, p. 7.
105. For her "cry," see letter of Jan. 15–18, 1949. For her evaluation of friendship as compared to romance, see Kollontai's remarks to Nilsson, "Det Stora Uppdraget," no. 35, p. 9.

of Councillor of the Ministry of Foreign Affairs. The apartment was "not big," but it was "light and clean, and very nice." Kollontai's grandson Volodia, a student at an institute in Moscow, visited daily. Emy Lorentsson, her secretary-companion, who accompanied Kollontai to Moscow, ran the household.[106] Kollontai worried about Misha, who remained behind in Stockholm with his wife Irina. Anxious about his heart, she wrote joyfully in 1947: "My dearest, dearest friend Ada, have you heard that Misha and Ira are soon coming home?" Misha's return focused Kollontai's anxieties.[107] "Misha is still in the clinic, his heart is better, but they told me today he shall have to remain three weeks longer, as his ulcer has reappeared." Letter after letter expressed her concern and told of her efforts to arrange work that Misha could do at home. His physical condition, she feared, would not permit him long or late hours at the Ministry of Trade.[108]

Kollontai detailed their life, describing (in English) a day at a rest home. "To keep still on the terrace, Misha is painting and he does it well! Then a walk, dinner at four o'clock and then—imagine! Emy teaches Ira, Misha, and even me to play bridge. I don't understand all the finesses of the play, but we have much fun and laughter just because we all are bad and new players. Emy is called by us Culbertson, as the master. So you see we are all right and enjoy the summer."[109] In the autumn Kollontai felt better because Misha was a pensioner and his health was improved. His pension was not enough to live on, even when combined with his wife's earnings as a teacher of English in the Foreign Ministry. Kollontai helped financially.[110]

Letters thanking Ada for packages—medicines for Misha, cooking

106. See letter to Nilsson, Oct. 12, 1945. For grandson, letter of Mar. 27, 1945. For household arrangements, Jan. 5, 1948, and Oct. 7, 1947.

107. Letters of Jan. 22, 1947, and Mar. 24, 1947. Barbara Clements is incorrect in her assumption (p. 270) that Misha died during the war.

108. For Misha's illness, see letters to Nilsson of May 1948. For Kollontai's fear that Misha could no longer carry out his Ministry of Trade work, see her letter of July 18, 1948. In a letter of July 11, 1948, Kollontai wrote Nilsson in English: "Just now I am fixing some plans for Misha in the future. I think he can't work as before so that it must be arranged." Letter of Aug. 7, 1948: "I have a lot to do trying to arrange for an easier job for Misha, who is still at the sanitarium."

109. Letter of June 20, 1948. (Another survivor, Maxim Litvinov, also played bridge during his isolation. See Uldricks, "The Impact of the Great Purges," p. 193, and Ehrenburg, pp. 276–78.) Other letters described Kollontai at home. On July 11, 1948, she wrote in English: "I am in town now, with Emy and cat, Alexander. It is nice in our apartment, not too hot, the balcony is green with beans, the vine with red flowers, so one does not feel the stones of a town. And I have my writing table, my privacy, and my newspaper every day. . . . Emy is giving me charming summer meals: vegetables and all what I like."

110. Letter of Dec. 12, 1948.

supplies for Emy, and books for Aleksandra—suggested the difficulty of adjustment to life in grim, gray Moscow after fifteen years abroad.[111] But politically Kollontai could have been anywhere. Little in the hundreds of emotional letters to Nilsson suggests that Kollontai was living in the oppression of Stalinist Russia, an era defined by mass terror, worship of the despot, and indulgence in the big lie.[112] It was a bizarre world, in which her fallen comrades were pictured as agents of foreign powers who, before they were purged, had been plotting for twenty years against the Soviet state. Proof was replaced by invective: "Trotskyite-Bukharinite outlaws," "a band of murderers and spies," "fascist lackeys," "the dregs of the human race."[113] Repression continued, but on a lesser scale than in the 1930's. The Soviet intelligentsia was again attacked in the persecution of writers, composers, and drama critics that began in 1946–47. A series of speeches by Zhdanov providing guidelines for socialist realism resulted in the expulsion of Anna Akhmatova from the Union of Writers.

The closest Kollontai came to suggesting an atmosphere of fear was to report a visit from another survivor, her friend Maxim Litvinov. The former Commissar for Foreign Affairs, since the purges of 1937, had been keeping a revolver on his bedside table. If there were to be a ring at the door in the night, he was not going to wait for what came next.[114] After he left, Kollontai noted casually, she and Emy worked on desk drawers and "threw out old papers, etc."[115] Ordinarily she filled her letters with trivia, whimsy about feeding the birds and the moods of her cat Aleksandr. Say hello to my trees, she told Ada: the "big pine tree at the side of the road and the friendly spruces."[116] She was alive and reasonably well. It was all she could safely convey.

How did Kollontai react privately to repression? She was "writing over my old diaries and tearing up old letters."[117] The destruction of a Bolshevik continued. A friend insists that despite the illusion of respect, Kollontai was really an "internal exile." Thus, the few old friends who were still alive tended to stay away; they understood her

111. A list of some of the items Nilsson sent is revealing: quick-cooking oatmeal, slippers, good quality cotton sheets and pillow cases, an aluminum kettle, moth spray, shampoo, combs, a watch for Emy, paper towels, toilet paper, and cleaning cloths.
112. There were occasional lapses in her discretion, which will be discussed later in the chapter.
113. Medvedev, p. 500.
114. Ehrenburg, p. 277. Litvinov was neither arrested nor purged. He died in 1952.
115. Kollontai to Nilsson, Oct. 13, 1946.
116. For Kollontai's greeting to the trees, see her letter of Oct. 24, 1948.
117. Kollontai to Nilsson, Sept. 22, 1947.

ambiguous status and were fearful of visiting the former Opposition-ist.[118] There is no reason to doubt the authenticity of this recollection. On the other hand, Kollontai did have some visitors—acquaintances from the diplomatic corps, and foreign Communists—and she was pleased by such small signs of recognition as inclusion in a Russian diplomatic encyclopedia, occasional invitations to the "writers' club" to talk about Lenin, and official greetings on her birthday.[119] Pleased, but fundamentally unconcerned. Her life was apolitical. Kollontai tried to ignore the terror by retreating in a fascinating way into an interior existence. A large segment of the population in postwar Russia followed the same route—"inwardly emigrating."[120] Ironically, in the last decade of her life Kollontai came full circle back to the role of an anxious mother focusing on her son—the kind of narrow, private, "egotistical" existence she had condemned for over half a century.

The insight into Kollontai's emotions provided by her letters to Ada Nilsson makes it tempting to argue that Kollontai's quest for the collective spirit had all along been a source of conflict, an unconscious effort to combat her individualism. Kollontai yearned to merge with the collective, but during much of her political life she was unable to be a conforming Communist. She was always balancing tensions, fighting the "atavistic" desires that intellectually she rejected. She called for an end to overwhelming, exclusive, maternal love and for communal upbringing of children, yet she yearned at the same time to be with her son. She condemned sexual possessiveness and jealousy, yet she reproached Dybenko for loving another woman. She longed to subordinate herself to the collective, yet she dreamed of fleeing to live as a free writer.

Kollontai reacted to terror by succumbing to barely suppressed aspects of her personality. An "internal exile," a survivor in Stalinist Russia, partially paralyzed, she was free *only* to pursue private inclinations. Thus she spent the last years of her life, when quite literally she had no other choice, in profoundly personal enterprises: writing memoirs, caring for her son, and guarding her privacy.[121]

---

118. Moscow interview, Aug. 1973.

119. See her letters to Nilsson of Jan. 22, 1947, and May 6, 1948. In the latter Kollontai wrote of the "good article" written about her. Only the "most known" Russian diplomats were included. Kollontai was referring to the first edition of *Diplomaticheskii slovar'* (Moscow, 1948). None of the purged diplomats was named.

120. Tucker, *The Soviet Political Mind*, p. 189.

121. The old exponent of communal life complained that her flat was a "gypsy camp" occupied by acquaintances awaiting their apartments. For her concern with privacy, see letters to Nilsson of June 26, 1947, and Aug. 18, 1947.

Kollontai retreated further into her prerevolutionary self by indulging her fondness for the old Russian holidays. Once she had disdained even the celebration of birthdays by Communists.[122] Now she looked warmly on Christmas, a nostalgia that Lenin is said also to have shared. "My dearest Ada," she wrote, "in these Christmas days I think very much of you. . . . I remember how you arranged a surprise Christmas tree in 1942, when I was in the hospital. It was just like a nice dream, the tree, the music and all." Another letter thanked Ada for packages, remarking that when the family opened them, it was "just like Christmas." Elsewhere she wished Ada a happy Easter and commented that in her thoughts she celebrated Easter together with her.[123]

꙰꙰꙰

Kollontai might ignore Stalinism in her private world, but the rest homes where she received special care, the comfortable apartments (one for herself and Emy, another for Misha and Ira, at a time when others in Moscow were scrambling for living space), and the early pension she arranged for Misha were rewards for her support of the regime. If Kollontai felt uneasy, if she contrasted her by no means luxurious but still privileged life with that of the ordinary citizen (as in the old days she would have done), we have no record of it. Instead, we have her message to Ada not to worry: she had permission from the authorities to live quietly, in peace.[124] Surprising, although not difficult to understand, was the way in which even Kollontai adjusted to class privilege. She reflected the traditional social assumptions of her youth: thus on the one hand she reported that the young girl who worked as a domestic in her apartment would be leaving to start in a factory, and that her old Anna Ivanovna was returning to take her place; on the other, she took for granted that her grandson and his student wife would work on advanced degrees. Volodia was preparing to be a professor, she wrote proudly.[125]

From time to time Kollontai, like others, made the required obeisances. She renounced the "withering away of the family" in an article

122. See *Vasilisa Malygina*, p. 284.
123. For Christmas, see letters to Nilsson of Dec. 30, 1945, Feb. 22, 1948. For Easter, see the letter of Apr. 17, 1949. For Lenin and Christmas, see Harrison Salisbury, *Black Night, White Snow* (New York, 1978), pp. 549–50.
124. Kollontai to Nilsson, Aug. 30, 1945.
125. See letters to Nilsson of Dec. 8, 1949, and Feb. 9, 1951.

in which she thanked the Soviet state for giving women access to all areas of creative activity and at the same time providing all necessary conditions to enable them to fulfill their "natural duty" as mothers, bringing up their own children as mistress of their own home.[126] Humiliating words for the author of *The Family and the Communist State*. Or in old age had Kollontai's attitude toward the nuclear family in fact mellowed? Politically isolated, a matriarch surrounded by "my four children," Kollontai needed the family as a refuge from an uncongenial society.

Publicly she praised Stalin. When the first (and only) installment of her memoirs appeared in 1945, they described Stalin as Lenin's "beloved pupil, aide, and friend," whom Lenin loved especially to have close by.[127] Kollontai had become accustomed to political lying. Privately, no doubt, she despised her distortions of the past that safeguarded her family and provided them with comforts. Other Russian mothers made the same sacrifice of pride. Akhmatova, fearing for her imprisoned son's life, wrote a cycle of poems in 1950, "In Praise of Peace," lauding Stalin. Her friends believed that this act probably saved her son.[128] Memoir jottings reflect Kollontai's feeble defiance. She wrote of the long years of friendship in the Party, adding in a parenthesis, "under Lenin's direction."[129]

Regretting Kollontai's capitulation or sadly comparing Kollontai the survivor with Kollontai the Bolshevik is difficult to avoid. Yet such regrets or comparisons are also presumptuous. The years after 1937 may have been her bravest. Her acquiescence was based on resignation, not on calm, as indicated by her constant requests to Dr. Nilsson for tranquilizers for her melancholy, nerves, and insomnia.[130]

※※※※

But capitulation was not enough to ensure survival. Why did Stalin spare Kollontai? Il'ia Ehrenburg remarked, thinking of the

126. See *Izbrannye stat'i i rechi*, p. 378.
127. See Kollontai, "Iz vospominanii," pp. 85–86. The editors indicated that the memoirs would be continued, but no further installments appeared. We know Lenin's real feelings toward Stalin. In his "testament," written in Dec. 1922, Lenin used the word *"grubyi"* [rude, coarse] to describe Stalin, urging his dismissal from the post of General Secretary. Other examples of Kollontai's cautious lip-service to Stalin include a postcard to a friend admonishing her to read and to study Stalin. See Fortunato, p. 187.
128. Haight, p. 159.
129. See *Iz moei zhizni i raboty*, p. 367.
130. For a typical request for tranquilizers, in which Kollontai added "(as usual)," see letter to Nilsson of Mar. 28, 1946.

Old Bolsheviks, that probably only Lunacharskii and Kollontai "were lucky enough to die in their own beds." By 1939 there remained at liberty only a small group of Communists who held any significant position in the 1920's or before. Kollontai was among them.[131] Nadezhda Mandelstam has concluded that survival was "a matter of pure chance."[132] Still one wonders how Kollontai escaped. One theory holds that a curious remnant of Caucasian chivalry caused Stalin to spare Bolshevik women. Krupskaia, Stasova, and Fotieva, Lenin's secretary, survived. So too did Kollontai's protégé Nikolaeva, the former Zinovievite, and Vinogradskaia, the Trotskyist and wife of Preobrazhenskii.[133] (Varvara Iakovleva, on the other hand, was purged.)

It is tempting to seek a pattern, but Caucasian chivalry seems an unlikely one. Probably several motives were involved, and in Kollontai's case sexual sadism could have been one. We know from Trotsky's memoirs that for Stalin, Kollontai's relationship with Dybenko was a subject of sexual titillation in which he took lewd delight. Possibly Stalin enjoyed keeping the aristocratic old exponent of free love alive and at his mercy, subject to his terror. We know of Stalin's contempt for those he called *intelligenty*. Roy Medvedev included Kollontai in his list of Old Bolshevik *intelligenty* who escaped arrest but who were "pushed out of the leadership, terrorized, deprived of any influence," and treated by Stalin with "undisguised contempt." Stalin's daughter Svetlana recalled her father's scorn for the intellectual Bolshevik women active early in the Revolution. He called them "herrings with ideas."[134] A refusal to recognize women as important seems a more convincing explanation than chivalry.

There may be yet another reason. All the prominent Bolsheviks who opposed Stalin were purged. But Kollontai never opposed Stalin per se. She protested against Lenin, Trotsky, Zinoviev, and Bukharin, but not Stalin. Marcel Body thought Stalin spared Kollontai because it was "expedient" to do so.[135] Kollontai was really quite a useful link to Lenin. Stalin needed to have a few Bolsheviks around who could

131. See Ehrenburg, p. 306. Lunacharskii died in 1933. See Daniels, p. 388, for the survivors.
132. Mandelstam, p. 378.
133. To this list we might add R. S. Zemliachka and Artiukhina, a Central Committee member from 1927 to 1930. For the theory about Georgian chivalry, see Conquest, p. 80, and Daniels, p. 389.
134. See Medvedev, p. 200, and Alliluyeva, p. 381.
135. Body, p. 12.

be counted on to attest to the special closeness between himself and Lenin.

Kollontai was, above all, a convenient token. Servile and no threat, but a well-known international figure, she could be pointed to as a visible sign of Soviet progress in achieving equality for women: the first woman ambassador in history. Stalin indicated privately, however, his lack of respect for her: a diplomatic dinner in honor of a foreign dignitary took place once while she was in Moscow, but Ambassador Kollontai was excluded. The dinner was for men only.[136]

Could Kollontai in her old age have come to believe in Stalin? The pervasiveness of the commonplace in her life, the focusing of her interests on family, her pride in Russia's postwar recovery—all this suggests that Kollontai could conceivably have blended with the mass of self-concerned citizenry and become a believer. The majority of Soviet people, according to Roy Medvedev, had faith in Stalin and were sincerely indignant against "enemies of the people." A source in Moscow who was close to Kollontai during the 1930's and again during her last years has testified, however, to Kollontai's contempt for Stalin and his chief prosecutor, Vyshinskii.[137] Russians who never knew the reality of Lenin's relationship to Stalin or Stalin's actual role in Party history might admit that the "cult of personality" swayed their judgment, but Kollontai, who participated in writing the fictitious version of revolutionary history, knew the part official instruction played in developing that cult.[138] We have further evidence of her negative feelings toward Stalin. For what they do *not* say, the mass of Kollontai's letters silently indict Stalinism. Not once in the hundreds of letters to Nilsson written during the peak of the Stalin cult did she mention his name! In her private world, as I have said before, Stalin simply did not exist.

On the other hand, Kollontai had begun in the mid-1930's to fit the Stalinist dictatorship into a Russian framework. The Revolution had come too soon. Russia, lacking culture, was not ready to pass from absolutism to freedom. The cult of the tsar, the ideology of absolutism, was ingrained. The dictatorship of Stalin or someone else—maybe

---

136. Hauge, p. 135.
137. Moscow interview, Aug. 1973. And Kollontai no doubt remembered that in 1922 Stalin tried to have her expelled from the Party. See above, Chapter 8.
138. For acknowledgment of being so swayed, see Ehrenburg, p. 302.

Trotsky—was inevitable. How many decades would have to pass before Russia could achieve a free government she could not predict.[139]

Earlier, Kollontai had refused to accept the inevitability of suffering. Now she echoed this very Russian theme when she acknowledged that, though everything that was brutal and unjust hurt her, suffering would always be present during transformations of sociopolitical and economic systems. It was painful, but historically ordained.[140] Kollontai explained the lack of freedom in Soviet life in terms of Russia's backwardness, but she did not explain Stalinism. Her rigid determinism made Stalin largely irrelevant. Her determinism also exculpated Stalin's evil. Her letters suggest that she never succumbed to the Stalinist cult, but we do not know if she was aware of the degree to which Stalin personally was responsible for the attack on the Bolsheviks or if, like others, she ascribed mass repressions to a Communist death struggle, to the sadism of the miserable Yezhov, or simply to Stalin's "misinformation."

The survivor did not lose all resemblance to the Bolshevik. The Cold War brought Kollontai to political life. In 1949 the North Atlantic Pact was concluded, Germany was divided, and the Chinese People's Republic came into being. When, during the summer of 1950, fighting began in Korea, it seemed that the Third World War was imminent. One Russian writer recalled the apprehension of ordinary Russians, not yet recovered from the grief of the Second World War, as they began laying in stores of soap and salt.[141] Kollontai reacted with her old anger: the atmosphere of Cold War "removed all happiness from life." She followed the left-wing world peace movement. "Our enemies won't dare start a new war," she predicted. The Soviet will for peace made Russia too strong. She despaired of the Western half of the globe but declared it a joy to see Russia and China standing for peace and better living conditions. She thought in terms of simple, democratic truths. If more than half the globe was for peace, then peace would win.[142] With her faith in human goodness and her optimism born of a belief in progress, Kollontai's world view

139. Body, p. 24.
140. Letter to Nilsson, July 21, 1938.
141. Ehrenburg, p. 197.
142. Letters to Nilsson: undated, no. 282, 1950; Jan. 12, 1950; Apr. 26, 1950; Nov. 9, 1950.

was closer to nineteenth-century Marxism than to the twentieth-century world of Stalin.

⁂

Kollontai was sustained at the end of her life not by a belief in the Party—that faith had long since disappeared. She understood that since the purges in the mid-1930's there was no longer in any real sense a ruling Bolshevik Party. The one-party system had given way to a one-person system.[143] She looked not to the remnants of what once was Bolshevism but to two solid achievements: the Soviet state which was moving forward, and the emancipation of women.[144] The Bolshevik Kollontai had been destroyed. The feminist survived. It is to the woman question, which has received special emphasis in this study, that I would like now to turn.

It may seem paradoxical to conclude that Kollontai took comfort in the situation of women, since much of Stalin's family legislation was conservative. One might expect Kollontai, returning from Sweden in 1945, to have been appalled by new Soviet laws: the 1936 ban on all nontherapeutic abortions (which lasted until 1955), and the legislation of 1944, which included increased penalties for default on support payments and placed new difficulties in the way of divorce. The changes in the divorce provisions, of course, were a source of dismay, as was the reactionary law of 1943 that decreed an end to coeducation for boys and girls and the establishment of separate sex-based curricula.[145] But the ban on abortions fell into a different category. Kollontai, believing in motherhood as a social obligation, rejected abortion as a remnant of bourgeois society to be condoned only in a situation of national poverty. The family legislation of 1944 provided state allowances for mothers, married or not, and offered mothers the option of placing a child in a state home, thus making abortion theoretically unnecessary. Whatever Stalin's motives, Kollontai's aim when she introduced the idea of a General Insurance Fund in 1925 was coming closer to fulfillment in at least one sense. The 1944 family legislation, with its state protection for mothers, provided the possi-

143. Tucker, *The Soviet Political Mind*, p. 179.
144. See letter to Nilsson of July 21, 1938. When Kollontai anticipated death, she comforted herself with the existence of the Soviet Union. On women, see Itkina, p. 175, and *Iz moei zhizni i raboty*, p. 364.
145. See "Abolition of Co-Education in Soviet Schools," in Schlesinger, ed., pp. 363–66.

bility for women to be less dependent on individual men. So too did increased female employment.[146]

Kollontai listed change in the status of women as the major achievement of her 60 years of work for the Revolution. She considered herself the founder of the Russian socialist women's movement. "Our generation pierced the wall," she wrote in her journal. "Drops of my energy, my thinking, my struggle, and the example of my life are in this achievement. We, our generation, with our own hands, laid the path. It is difficult for the present generation to imagine the strength it took."[147]

How do we assess the achievements Kollontai hailed, what do we make of the "equality" of women in the Soviet Union? Do we evaluate the status of Soviet women by comparing them with women elsewhere? Or with their relative progress from their own past? Or with Kollontai's dreams? It has been pointed out that the Soviet Union has "failed precisely in those areas where its founders had made particular, utopian claims: the areas of uniquely communist expectations and promises."[148] The Soviet woman's phenomenal entry into the work force and public life has been accompanied by alteration of the original blueprint. Private domesticity and the nuclear family have survived as woman's sphere, thus doubling her work. And yet this outcome did not keep Kollontai, the feminist author of the blueprint, from cheering. Kollontai needed to believe that her life work was not in vain. But that she herself evaluated progress from where Russian women had been should not eliminate more rigorous criteria of judgment.[149]

At the All-Russian Congress of Worker and Peasant Women in 1918 Kollontai proclaimed that there would be nothing Soviet women would not be able to do. But in the Soviet Union (as elsewhere), women have not risen to the highest positions in the professions, in

146. See "The Family Law of July 8, 1944," in Schlesinger, ed., pp. 367–90. For commentary on the 1944 law, see Juviler.

147. Itkina, p. 175. A Soviet writer in 1971 attributed Soviet achievement in the area of aid to women to the groundwork of the Old Bolsheviks, Kollontai in particular. See Emel'ianova, as quoted in Mandel, p. 72. Kollontai saw her ambassadorship as a triumph for women. See Maiskii, p. 109. Few Old Bolshevik women saw the results of their labor. Armand, Samoilova, and Slutskaia died during the revolutionary era. Smidovich, Krupskaia, and Stal' died before the Second World War, Nikolaeva in 1944. Vinogradskaia, Moirova, and Stasova lived on in obscurity. For their biographies, see Zhak and Itkina, eds., pp. 559–70.

148. See Alexander Dallin, "Conclusion," in Atkinson, Dallin, and Lapidus, eds., p. 386.

149. For Kollontai's evaluation, see *Izbrannye stat'i i rechi*, p. 379.

management, or in government. One statistic seems particularly revealing. Girls and young women are often as politically active as their male counterparts—probably more so in school, where 52.4 percent of all Komsomol members are women, as are 57.1 percent of all secretaries of primary Komsomol organizations. But the overall level of female participation declines sharply with marriage and motherhood. "A mere 5 percent of all women between the ages of 31 and 60 are party members, compared with some 22 percent of all men in that age group."[150] Scholars observe no visible counterpart in the Soviet Union to the current feminist movement in the West. If Soviet women have not rebelled against the half-way position in which they find themselves even to the point of questioning why they cannot share power with men,[151] the explanation is connected, at least in part, with the destruction of the Women's Section that Kollontai imposed on the Central Committee in 1917.

Pushing aside models of revolutionary change dictated from above, and looking at the pervasiveness of deeply rooted cultural values, we find that what the remarkable old leaders of the Zhenotdel dismissed as "bourgeois remnants" have proven not to be ephemeral at all.[152] The married woman in Russia still feels that her first responsibility is to her individual family. Accordingly, her career objectives are usually more limited than a man's. Women do not generally aspire to top positions requiring travel or long hours away from home.[153] This reason—the failure of women to alter their priorities—perhaps more than the burdens of domesticity, may explain women's secondary status. Indeed, as one analyst has commented, many women "seem relieved that housework provides an acceptable excuse for avoiding political activity."[154]

If traditional social values are to be changed, there must be a "critical mass" of protesters such as existed during the first decade of Soviet power when women were organized in an interest group.[155] The preservation of a Women's Section in the Communist Party was

150. See Hough, p. 362.
151. *Ibid.*, p. 371.
152. Lapidus, "Sexual Equality in Soviet Policy," p. 117.
153. See Chapman, p. 235.
154. Hough, p. 372.
155. For this idea, see W. H. Chafe, "The Paradox of Progress," in Jean E. Friedman and William G. Shade, eds., *Our American Sisters: Women in American Life and Thought* (Boston, 1976), pp. 390–91. A number of Soviet writers use the Zhenotdel as a model and urge state and Party to intervene—as the Women's Section did—to inculcate egalitarian norms and, in women, a sense of their equality with men. See Lapidus, *Women in Soviet Society*, p. 332.

thus crucial. The women of the Zhenotdel were not monolithic, but even a "conservative" like Smidovich advocated children's homes where children would live apart from their parents.[156] The abolition in 1930 of the coherent center that furnished the radical model made it unlikely that a break with traditional values would occur.[157]

⹌⹌⹌

Kollontai could not openly question women's double burden or regret their failure radically to alter their priorities. She hoped that life would get better. About her own situation she had few illusions. Russians say "Being old is no fun." She hated old age and longed not for youth but for the years between 40 and 50 when she had fought for the Revolution.[158] Nearly every morning she worked methodically on memoirs that she knew would not be published. With a very Russian belief in the potency of the written word, she regretted that her writing was "not for this historical era," that her memoirs would remain untranslated, and *only* in the Institute.[159] If one were to publish all that I have written in the last two years, she speculated in 1949, it would come to ten volumes of 320 pages each.[160] It was difficult to write, to gather up sheets of paper with one hand, or to hold a book without having it close unexpectedly. Her eyes weakened. She wondered nervously if she would finish. She longed for a tranquility she did not possess. She needed two more years, she told Nilsson. Three years later, in March 1952, she died.[161]

Kollontai pondered her life. So sharp were the contrasts of its chapters that she concluded she had lived several lives. She had experienced

156. Smidovich to Smith, in Smith, p. 103.

157. The endurance of familiar priorities helps explain the willingness of Soviet men to accept women in professions hitherto closed to them. Wherever they may be employed, Soviet wives maintain domestic roles and outward deference to male superiority. Vera Dunham, "Surtax on Equality," paper presented to the Conference on Women in Russia, Stanford University, May 29–June 1, 1975. The situations in which women compete with men and in which women exercise authority over men are limited. See Lapidus, *Women in Soviet Society*, p. 280. A wife's wages are usually less, and are a second income. See Chapman, pp. 225–39, and Hough, p. 366.

158. See letter to Nilsson of Feb. 10, 1949.

159. See letters to Nilsson of Dec. 12, 1948, and Jan. 1948 (no. 18). *"Only,"* underlined, appears in the Jan. letter. Maiskii has written that the memoirs are of great interest and should be published. See Maiskii, p. 111.

160. A typist worked on her material each day. See the letter of Apr. 17, 1949. That she reported her memoirs complete for 1922–40, with only the war years remaining, suggests that Kollontai may have omitted 1917–22. Letter of Sept. 20, 1950.

161. See letters of Dec. 12, 1948, and Jan. 15–18, 1949. Her last letter to Nilsson was dated Sept. 22, 1951. Misha died in 1953. See editor's note in Dazhina, ed., "Amerikanskie dnevniki A. M. Kollontai," p. 157.

hard work, success, recognition, but also hatred, prison, failure, mis-
understandings of her convictions, and painful breaks with comrades.[162] One would like to know more about her recollections. We
have only excerpts from her memoirs—which, as she feared, are se-
questered in the Institute of Marxism-Leninism—and only samplings
from her correspondence. Still, by putting together bits and pieces
it is possible to obtain some final insight into the state of mind of
Kollontai the survivor, who, toward the end of her life, recalled that
she still possessed the "talent to live."[163]

Kollontai became immersed in the past, a natural outcome of
memoir-writing. She wrote to Elizaveta Mravinskaia, her sister-in-law.
"Remember our youth? . . . The Balls? Springtime at Kuuza, white
nights, the pungent fragrance of violets at night in my room? Remember how Mama knocked on the wall: 'Girls, girls, enough chattering,
you must go to sleep. . . .' But how could we sleep, in the springtime
of our lives, with the future so enticing, with so much promised, so
much new and yet to be experienced? . . . That's the way it was . . .
youth. Balls and satin shoes in which we danced holes, and the white
nights. . . . But now it seems to me that I only read about it in some
old and forgotten book."[164]

In old age, Kollontai was again sleepless. She took two pills. One
used to be enough. "What would one do to be able to sleep? . . . I
think and think."[165] Now she was kept awake not by a joyous future,
but rather by the sadness of the past and by the "problems of the
world."[166] She tried to make sense of the present and the contrasts with
1917. It was futile to dwell on the deformities of the Stalin era when
much of the core of the Revolution and its achievements survived.
Better to remember that the October Revolution promised power to
the workers and equal rights to women. It opened the road to culture and education for the masses. Leaders might fail. But the "creative" Russian people, although with setbacks, were still going forward on the road taken in October.[167] She remembered. And, as
she said, she thought and thought. Did Kollontai's experiences of
Stalinism alter the quality of her thinking and make her a less rigid

162. Kollontai, *Iz moei zhizni i raboty*, pp. 367–68.
163. *Ibid.*, p. 367.
164. Itkina, p. 15.
165. Letter to Nilsson of Dec. 12, 1948.
166. Letter to Nilsson of Feb. 10, 1949.
167. For this sentiment, see undated letter to Nilsson (no. 282) and letter of Nov.
9, 1950.

Communist? Did it provide her with a greater ability to encompass the shades of intellectual nuance that confront most thoughtful people? Almost certainly. But Kollontai could not bear ambiguity. She needed still to have a defined position. The Soviet Union was, after all, the first socialist state, the only major power, she was convinced, that was working for peace. There are times, another Russian wrote, that compel "the finest people to think in terms of history."[168] So it was with Kollontai. She philosophized: "Everything is going to straighten out with time. And more humane ideas always win. I read historical books and it calms me. Reactionary tendencies don't last long, never. History shows this in all countries and among all people."[169] But occasionally her optimism faltered. The Soviet Union is advancing economically and culturally, she wrote to Nilsson.[170] "I don't know why I am so often very melancholic. . . ."

168. Ehrenburg, p. 156.
169. Letter to Nilsson of Mar. 22, 1949. Political comments were interspersed among domestic details.
170. Letter to Nilsson of May 26, 1947.

Reference Matter

Selected Bibliography

I cite here those materials that have been most helpful in preparing this book. Occasional items referred to only once or twice in the footnotes are cited in full where they occur as a convenience to the reader. In particular, I have omitted some of Kollontai's early writings and some of her publications in *Pravda* and *Izvestiia*. For an annotated bibliography of works by and about Kollontai, consult Henryk Lenczyc, "Alexandra Kollontai. Essai bibliographique," *Cahiers du Monde Russe et Soviétique* (Jan.–Jun. 1973), pp. 205–41. The fullest bibliography appears in Barbara Clements, *Bolshevik Feminist* (Bloomington, Ind., 1979). Another useful bibliography, which includes the Lenin Library list of published Kollontai holdings as of August 1970, is contained in Kaare Hauge, "Alexandra M. Kollontai: The Scandinavian Period, 1922–1945" (unpublished Ph.D. dissertation, University of Minnesota, 1971). Two collections of Kollontai's writings edited by I. M. Dazhina et al.—*Izbrannye stat'i i rechi* (Moscow, 1972) and *Iz moei zhizni i raboty* (Moscow, 1974)—bring together publications hitherto scattered in the periodical press, along with archival material, and provide useful biographical and autobiographical details.

The single most valuable archival source is Kollontai's more than 350 letters to Dr. Ada Nilsson (spanning the 1930's, 1940's, and early 1950's), which are located in the University of Gothenburg Library. Most are in Swedish and Norwegian (some are in German, French, and English). The Fredrik Ström collection, also in the University of Gothenburg (and written mostly in German and in Swedish) contains Kollontai's letters to that Swedish Communist and are an important source for the prerevolutionary years and the 1920's. Frequently, however, these letters are undated.

Among the Soviet scholars who have used Kollontai's unpublished papers in the Institute of Marxism-Leninism in Moscow are I. M. Dazhina, A. M. Itkina, E. Mindlin, V. S. Nevolina, N. V. Orlova, and G. Petrov. The reader should consult their respective introductions to recently published Kollontai archival materials for occasional illumination of still unpublished papers. These sometimes lengthy introductions are meticulously edited and contain useful biographical sketches and explanations of references. Kollontai, however, out of political caution, may have edited the diaries and letters she deposited in the Institute of Marxism-Leninism. She told Ada Nilsson that she was "writing over my old diaries and tearing up old letters" (letter of Sept. 22, 1947).

ALEKSANDRA KOLLONTAI: WRITINGS AND SPEECHES

"Antimilitarizm rabochikh v Amerike," *Nashe Slovo*, Apr. 30, 1916, May 1, 1916, pp. 2–3.
Autobiography of a Sexually Emancipated Communist Woman, trans. Salvator Attanasio, ed. Iring Fetscher. New York, 1971. (First published in Munich in

1926 as *Ziel und Wert Meines Lebens,* in the "Leading Women of Europe" series edited by Elga Kern.) The German edition, *Autobiographie Einer Sexuell Emanzipierten Kommunistin* (Munich, 1970), is more complete than the English translation. Both the American and the German editions contain the galleys that reveal Kollontai's cautious revisions of her original text to eliminate personal material and references to her political opposition. The afterword written by Iring Fetscher is marred, unfortunately, by errors.

"Avtobiograficheskii ocherk," *Proletarskaia Revoliutsiia,* 1921, no. 3, pp. 261–302. (This autobiographical sketch is particularly useful for Kollontai's political activities prior to 1921. She skims lightly over her opposition in 1921 and does not discuss personal affairs.)

" 'Belyi' i 'zheltyi' kapitalizm," *Nashe Slovo,* June 20, 1915, pp. 1–2.

Bol'shaia liubov'. Moscow, 1927. (There is an English translation by Lily Lore, *A Great Love* [New York, 1929].)

"Brak i byt," *Rabochii Sud,* 1926, no. 5, pp. 364–76.

"Brak, zhenshchiny, alimenty," *Ekran,* 1926, no. 5, p. 1.

"Chto delat'? Otvet Sotsialistkam," *Nashe Slovo,* Feb. 19, 1915, p. 1.

"Dorogu krylatomu erosu!," *Molodaia Gvardiia,* 1923, no. 3 (May), pp. 111–24.

"Dva techeniia," *Obrazovanie,* 1907, no. 10, pp. 46–62. (Written on the occasion of the first International Women's Conference in Stuttgart.)

"Dve pobedy norvezhskikh rabochikh," *Nashe Slovo,* May 23, 1915, p. 2.

"Finskie sotsialisty v Amerike," *Nashe Slovo,* May 6, 1916, pp. 1–2; May 7, 1916, p. 2.

"Germanskaia sotsialdemokratiia v pervye dni voiny (lichnaia nabliudeniia)," *Nashe Slovo,* Apr. 4, 1915, pp. 1–2; Apr. 9, 1915, pp. 1–2; Apr. 10, 1915, p. 1.

"Gigant dukha i voli: golos Lenina," *Oktiabr',* 1963, no. 1, pp. 4–5.

"Gotoviatsia k voine," *Nashe Slovo,* Jan. 6, 1916, p. 1.

"Itogi Manngeimskago S"ezda," *Sovremennyi Mir,* no. 11, pt. 2 (Nov. 1906), pp. 1–19.

Izbrannye stat'i i rechi, ed. I. M. Dazhina et al. Moscow, 1972.

Iz moei zhizni i raboty, ed. I. M. Dazhina et al. Moscow, 1974. (Contains excerpts from Kollontai's archival memoirs.)

"Iz vospominanii," *Oktiabr',* 1945, no. 9, pp. 59–89. (This "first installment," dealing primarily with Kollontai's youthful years—although containing some flashes forward to the revolutionary era and lip service to Stalin—was never continued.)

K voprosu o klassovoi bor'be. St. Petersburg, 1905.

"K vozrozhdeniiu," *Nashe Slovo,* Apr. 28, 1915, p. 1.

"Kak my sozvali pervyi vserossiiskii s"ezd rabotnits i krest'ianok," *Kommunistka,* 1923, no. 11, pp. 3–8.

"Klassovaia voina i rabotnitsy," *Kommunistka,* 1920, no. 5, pp. 6–9.

"Kogo poteriali rabotnitsy?," *Kommunar,* Mar. 21, 1919. (In memory of Iakov Sverdlov.) Reprinted in Dazhina, ed., *Izbrannye stat'i i rechi,* pp. 266–67.

Komu nuzhna voina? (Published by the Bolshevik Central Committee, Berne, 1916.)

"Kongress norvezhskoi sots-dem," *Nashe Slovo,* June 13, 1915, pp. 1–2.

"Kopengagenskaia konferentsiia," *Nashe Slovo,* Jan. 29, 1915, p. 2; Feb. 2, 1915, p. 1.

"Krest materinstva," *Kommunistka,* 1921, no. 8–9, pp. 22–29.

"Krest materinstva i Sovetskaia respublika," *Pravda,* no. 210 (Oct. 1918). Reprinted in Dazhina, ed., *Izbrannye stat'i i rechi,* pp. 237–42.

"Krizis v Shvedskoi partii," *Nashe Slovo*, May 13, 1915, p. 1.

"Lenin dumal o bol'shom i ne zabyval o malom" (Jan. 1946), in Dazhina, ed., *Izbrannye stat'i i rechi*, pp. 384–86.

"Lenin v Smol'nom" (1947), in Dazhina, ed., *Izbrannye stat'i i rechi*, pp. 387–90.

Liubov' pchel trudovykh. Moscow, 1923. This collection contains the novel *Vasilisa Malygina* (largely autobiographical) and the short stories "Liubov' trekh pokolenii" and "Sestry." There is an English translation by Cathy Porter, *Love of Worker Bees* (London, 1977). *Vasilisa Malygina* later appeared separately as *Svobodnaia liubov'* (Riga, 1925) and also exists in English translation as *Red Love* (New York, 1927).

"Liubov' trekh pokolenii." This short story appeared in the collection *Liubov' pchel trudovykh* (q.v.) and in another collection, *Sestry* (Moscow, 1927), which includes the short story of that name. Page references in the notes to "Liubov' trekh pokolenii" are to this latter edition.

Ne bud' dezertirom! Kiev, 1919.

"Ne 'printsip', a 'metod'," *Pravda*, Mar. 20, 1923, p. 4.

"Ne uprazdnenie, a ukreplenie," *Kommunistka*, 1921, no. 16–17, pp. 25–27.

"Notes autobiographiques," *Bulletin Communiste* (Paris), nos. 1–9 (1925), pp. 11–141. (This is the same autobiographical sketch that appeared in *Proletarskaia Revoliutsiia*.)

Novaia moral' i rabochii klass. Moscow, 1918, 1919. This collection contains "Novaia zhenshchina" (which first appeared in *Sovremennyi Mir*, 1913, no. 9, pp. 151–85), "Liubov' i novaia moral'" (which first appeared in *Novaia Zhizn'*, 1911, no. 8, pp. 174–96, as "Na staruiu temu"), and "Otnoshenie mezhdu polami i klassovaia bor'ba" (which first appeared in *Novaia Zhizn'*, 1911, no. 9, pp. 155–82, as "Polovaia moral' i sotsial'naia bor'ba").

"Novaia ugroza," *Kommunistka*, 1922, no. 8–9, pp. 5–9.

"Novaia zhenshchina," *Sovremennyi Mir*, 1913, no. 9, pp. 151–85.

Obshchestvo i materinstvo. Petrograd, 1916.

"Obshchii kotel ili individual'nye alimenty?," *Komsol'skaia Pravda*, no. 26 (209) (Feb. 1926), p. 2.

"Oktiabr'skaia revoliutsiia i massy," *Molodaia Gvardiia*, 1922, no. 6–7, pp. 211–18.

"O linii mezhevaniia," *Nashe Slovo*, Sept. 7, 1915, p. 2.

"Oppozitsiia i partiinaia massa," *Pravda*, Oct. 30, 1927.

"O rabote mezhdunarodnogo zhenskogo sekretariata," *Kommunisticheskii Internatsional*, no. 19 (Dec. 17, 1921), cols. 5,097–5,100.

Otchet. See *Vsesoiuznaia kommunisticheskaia partiia (bol'shevikov)*.

Otryvki iz dnevnika. 1914g. Leningrad, 1925. (This autobiographical account of Kollontai's years as an internationalist exile in Germany explains her disillusionment with the German socialists who supported the war in 1914.)

"Pamiati bortsov revoliutsii: tvorcheskoe v rabote tovarishcha K. N. Samoilovoi," *Kommunistka*, 1922, no. 3–5, pp. 8–11.

"Pervaia mezhdunarodnaia konferentsiia kommunistok, 1920g.," *Kommunistka*, 1920, no. 1–2, pp. 3–5.

"Pis'mo k rabotnitsam krasnogo Petrograda" (letter of Nov. 1918). Reprinted in Dazhina, *Izbrannye stat'i i rechi*, pp. 246–47.

"Pis'ma k trudiashcheisia molodezhi. Moral', kak orudie klassovogo gospodstva i klassovoi bor'by," *Molodaia Gvardiia*, 1922, no. 6–7, pp. 128–36.

"Pis'ma k trudiashcheisia molodezhi o 'Drakone' i 'beloi ptitse'," *Molodaia Gvardiia*, 1923, no. 2, pp. 162–74.

"Pis'ma Rozy Liuksemburg," *Kommunistka*, 1921, no. 8–9, pp. 36–38.

"Pochemu molchal" proletariat" Germanii v" iiul'skie dni?," *Kommunist*, 1915, no. 1–2, pp. 159–61.

Polozhenie zhenshchiny v evoliutsii khoziaistva (lectures presented at Sverdlov Communist University). Moscow-Petrograd, 1923.

"Popy eshche rabotaiut," *Pravda*, Dec. 29, 1918. Reprinted in Dazhina, ed., *Izbrannye stat'i i rechi*, pp. 250–53.

Po rabochei Evrope. St. Petersburg, 1912.

"Pora pokonchit' s 'chernymi gnesdami'," *Pravda*, Nov. 10, 1918. Reprinted in Dazhina, ed., *Izbrannye stat'i i rechi*, pp. 248–49.

"Posledniaia rabynia," *Kommunistka*, 1920, no. 7, pp. 24–26.

"Profsoiuzy i rabotnitsa," *Pravda*, May 22, 1921. Reprinted in Dazhina, ed., *Izbrannye stat'i i rechi*, pp. 319–21.

"Proizvodstvo i byt," *Kommunistka*, 1921, no. 10–11, pp. 6–9.

Prostitutsiia i mery bor'by s nei. Moscow, 1921.

Rabochaia oppozitsiia. Moscow, 1921. An English translation of this work, without the first five pages of the original, appeared as *The Workers' Opposition in Russia* (Chicago, 1921).

"Rabochaia zhizn' v Norvegii," *Nashe Slovo*, May 15, 1915, p. 1.

Rabotnitsa i krest'ianka v Sovetskoi Rossii. Petrograd, 1921.

Rabotnitsa mat'. St. Petersburg, 1914.

Rabotnitsa za god' revoliutsii. Moscow-Petrograd, 1918.

"Rabotnitsy i uchreditel'noe sobranie," *Pravda*, Mar. 21, 1917.

"Rabotnitsy, zanimaite svoi revoliutsionnye posty!," *Pravda*, Nov. 10, 1917.

"Ruka istorii: Vospominaniia A. Kollontai," *Krasnoarmeets*, 1919, no. 10–15, pp. 68–71.

Selected Writings of Alexandra Kollontai. Trans. with an introduction and commentaries by Alix Holt. Westport, Conn., 1977.

Sem'ia i kommunisticheskoe gosudarstvo. Moscow, 1918.

"Sem'ia i kommunizm," *Kommunistka*, 1920, no. 7, pp. 16–19.

"Sestry," *Kommunistka*, 1923, no. 3–4, pp. 23–26.

Skoro (cherez 48 let). Omsk, 1922. An English translation is available in Alix Holt's *Selected Writings of Alexandra Kollontai*.

Sotsial'nye osnovy zhenskago voprosa. St. Petersburg, 1909.

"Sovetskaia zhenshchina—polnopravnaia grazhdanka svoei strany," *Sovetskaia Zhenshchina*, 1946, no. 5 (Sept.–Oct.), pp. 3–4. Reprinted in Dazhina, ed., *Izbrannye stat'i i rechi*, pp. 378–83.

"Starost'—ne prokliat'e, a zasluzhennyi otdykh," *Vechernie Izvestiia*, Oct. 30, 1918. Reprinted in Dazhina, ed., *Izbrannye stat'i i rechi*, pp. 243–45.

"Tezisy o kommunisticheskoi morali v oblasti brachnyk otnoshenii," *Kommunistka*, 1921, no. 12–13, pp. 28–34.

"The Attitude of the Russian Socialists," *The New Review*, Mar. 1916, pp. 60–61.

"The Third International," *The American Socialist*, Oct. 23, 1915, p. 2.

"Tretii internatsional i rabotnitsa," *Pravda*, Nov. 13, 1921. Reprinted in Dazhina, ed., *Izbrannye stat'i i rechi*, pp. 349–52.

"Trudovaia povinnost' i okhrana zhenskogo truda," *Kommunistka*, 1920, no. 1–2, pp. 25–27.

"Trudovaia respublika i prostitutsiia, *Kommunistka*, 1920, no. 6, pp. 15–17.

"Tvorcheskoe v rabote tovarishcha K. N. Samoilovoi," *Kommunistka*, 1922, no. 3–5, pp. 8–11.

"Udarnitsa proletarskoi revoliutsii," *Pravda*, Jun. 23, 1933, p. 2. (On the death of Clara Zetkin.)

Udvalgte Skrifter. Copenhagen. 1977, 3 vols.
Vasilisa Malygina. See under *Liubov' pchel trudovykh.*
"V Germanii," *Nashe Slovo,* Apr. 8, 1915, p. 1.
"Vesti iz Finliandii," *Nashe Slovo,* Aug. 5, 1915, pp. 1–2; Aug. 6, 1915, pp. 1–2.
"Vesti iz Rossii," *Nashe Slovo,* June 16, 1915, pp. 1–2.
"Vesti iz Rossii: interv'iu s 'obyvatelem'," *Nashe Slovo,* Apr. 15, 1916, p. 1; Apr. 18, 1916, p. 1.
"Vmesto 'Zhenskogo dnia'—internatsional'naia demonstratsiia sotsialistok," *Nashe Slovo,* Feb. 25, 1915, p. 2.
Vospominaniia ob Il'iche. Moscow, 1959.
"Vseobshchaia zabastovka v Norvegii," *Nashe Slovo,* June 23, 1916, p. 1; June 24, 1916, p. 1.
Vsesoiuznaia kommunisticheskaia partiia (bol'shevikov). Tsentral'nyi Komitet. Otdel po rabote sredi zhenshchin. Otchet. Moscow, 1921?
"V tiur'me Kerenskogo," *Katorga i Ssylka,* 7, no. 36 (1927), pp. 25–53. (Kollontai's recollections of imprisonment in the summer of 1917.)
"Zadachi rabotnits" v" bor'be s" prostitutsiei," *Golos Sotsial'demokrata,* 1910, no. 21 (Apr.), pp. 3–4. (Written under the pseudonym A. Mikhailova.)
"Zhenshchina—rabotnitsa na pervom" feministskom" Kongresse v" Rossii," *Golos Sotsial'demokrata,* 1909, no. 12 (Mar.), pp. 6–7.
Zhenshchina na perelome. Moscow, 1923. (Kollontai published this collection of short stories under her maiden name, Domontovich.)
"Zhenshchiny—bortsy v dni Velikogo Oktiabria," *Zhenskii Zhurnal,* 1927, no. 11 (Nov.), pp. 2–3. Reprinted in Dazhina, ed., *Izbrannye stat'i i rechi,* pp. 370–74.
"Zhenshchiny v 1917 godu," *Rabotnitsa,* 1937, no. 31 (Nov.), pp. 12–13.
"Zhenskii den'," *Nashe Slovo,* Mar. 18, 1915, p. 2.
"Zhenskii sotsialisticheskii internatsional' i voina," *Nashe Slovo,* Mar. 7, 1915, pp. 3–4.

GENERAL WORKS

Alliluyeva, Svetlana. *Only One Year.* New York, 1969.
Armand, Inessa Aleksandrovna. "Pis'ma Inessy Armand," *Novyi Mir,* 1970, no. 6 (June), pp. 196–218.
Armand, Inessa Fedorovna. *Stat'i, rechi, pis'ma.* Moscow, 1975.
Artiukhina, A. V. "Na vysshuiu stupen'," *Kommunistka,* 1930, no. 2–3, pp. 6–7.
Artiukhina, A. V., et al., eds. *Zhenshchiny v revoliutsii.* Moscow, 1959.
Arvatov, B. "Grazhd. Akhmatova i Tov. Kollontai," *Molodaia Gvardiia,* 1923, no. 4–5, pp. 147–51.
Atkinson, Dorothy, Alexander Dallin, and Gail W. Lapidus, eds. *Women in Russia.* Stanford, Calif., 1977.
Avrich, Paul. *Kronstadt 1921.* Princeton, N.J., 1970.
Baevskii, D. "Bor'ba za III Internatsional do Tsimmerval'da," *Proletarskaia Revoliutsiia,* 1934, no. 4, pp. 13–36.
Bailes, Kendall. "Alexandra Kollontai et la nouvelle morale," *Cahiers du Monde Russe et Soviétique,* 1965, no. 4 (Oct.–Dec.) pp. 472–96.
Balabanoff, Angelica. *Impressions of Lenin* (trans. Isotta Cesari). Ann Arbor, Mich., 1968.
———. *My Life as a Rebel.* New York, 1968.
Barmine, Alexander, *One Who Survived.* New York, 1945.

Basanov, V., et al., eds. *V. I. Lenin, A. B. Lunacharskii. Perepiska, doklady, dokumenty.* Moscow, 1971.

Bebel, August. *Woman Under Socialism.* Trans. Daniel De Leon. New York, 1971. (Originally *Die Frau in der Vergangenheit, Gegenwart und Zukunft.* Zurich, 1883.)

Berezovskaia, Sof'ia G. *Trudiashchiesia zhenshchiny v sotsialisticheskoe stroitel'stvo.* Moscow, 1931.

Bessonova, A. F., ed. "K istorii izdaniia zhurnala 'Rabotnitsa,'" *Istoricheskii Arkhiv,* 1955, no. 4 (July–Aug.), pp. 25–53.

Bettelheim, Bruno. *The Children of the Dream.* New York, 1969.

Blonina, Elena (pseud. Inessa Armand). "Formy mezhdunarodnoi organizatsii i kommunisticheskie partii," *Kommunistka,* 1920, no. 1–2, pp. 5–7.

———. "Rabotnitsa i organizatsiia proizvodstva," *Kommunistka,* 1920, no. 1–2, pp. 23–25.

———. "Volostnoe delegatskoe sobranie krest'ianok," *Kommunistka,* 1920, no. 1–2, pp. 34–35.

Bobroff, Anne. "The Bolsheviks and Working Women, 1905–1920," *Soviet Studies,* 1974, no. 4 (Oct.), pp. 540–67.

Bochkarëva, E., and S. Liubimova. *Svetlyi put'.* Moscow, 1967.

Bochkarëva, E., and S. Lyubimova. *Women of a New World.* Moscow, 1969.

Body, Marcel. "Alexandra Kollontai," *Preuves,* 1952, supplement no. 14, pp. 12–24.

Bogdanov, Ivan M. *Gramotnost' i obrazovanie v dorevoliutsionnoi Rossii i v SSSR.* Moscow, 1964.

Bosh, Evgeniia. "Bernskaia konferentsiia 1915 g.," *Proletarskaia Revoliutsiia,* 5, no. 40 (1925), pp. 179–82.

———. *God bor'by.* Moscow-Leningrad, 1925.

Boxer, M., and J. Quataert, eds. *Socialist Women.* New York, 1978.

Brak i sem'ia. Sbornik statei i materialov, Molodaia Gvardiia. Moscow-Leningrad, 1926.

Bryant, Louise. *Mirrors of Moscow.* New York, 1973 (original ed. 1923).

———. *Six Red Months in Russia.* New York, 1918.

Bukharin, N., and E. Preobrazhenskii. *Azbuka Kommunizma.* N.p. 1919.

Bunyan, James. *The Origin of Forced Labor in the Soviet State, 1917–1921: Documents and Materials.* Baltimore, Md., 1967.

Carr, E. H. *A History of Soviet Russia: The Bolshevik Revolution, 1917–1923.* London, 1971 (original ed. New York, 1950–53). 3 vols.

———. *A History of Soviet Russia: The Interregnum, 1923–1924.* Baltimore, Md., 1969 (original ed. New York, 1954).

———. *A History of Soviet Russia: Socialism in One Country, 1924–1926.* Baltimore, Md., 1970 (original ed. New York, 1958–64). 3 vols.

Chapman, Janet G. "Equal Pay for Equal Work?" in Atkinson et al., eds., pp. 225–39.

Clements, Barbara. *Bolshevik Feminist: The Life of Aleksandra Kollontai.* Bloomington, Ind., 1979.

Cohen, Stephen F. "Bolshevism and Stalinism," in R. C. Tucker, ed., pp. 3–29.

———. *Bukharin and the Bolshevik Revolution: A Political Biography, 1888–1938.* New York, 1973.

Conquest, Robert. *The Great Terror.* New York, 1968.

Daniels, Robert V. *The Conscience of the Revolution: Communist Opposition in Soviet Russia.* Cambridge, Mass., 1960.

Dazhina, I. M. "V vodovorote novoi Rossii. Pis'ma A. M. Kollontai V. I. Leninu i N. K. Krupskoi v Shveitsariiu," *Novyi Mir*, 1967, no. 4 (Apr.), pp. 235–42.

Dazhina, I. M., ed. "Amerikanskie dnevniki A. M. Kollontai (1915–1916 gg.)." *Istoricheskii Arkhiv*, 1962, no. 1 (Jan.), pp. 128–59. (Excerpts from Kollontai's American diary, 1915–16.)

Dazhina, I. M., and R. Tsivlina, eds. "Iz arkhiva A. M. Kollontai (Dnevniki, pis'ma, stat'i 1915–1917 gg.)," *Inostrannaia Literatura*, 1970, no. 1 (Jan.), pp. 226–36; 1970, no. 2 (Feb.), pp. 226–45. (Excerpts from Kollontai's diaries in Scandinavia and America and from her correspondence with Lenin and Krupskaia.)

———. "Skoree v Rossiiu! (vospominaniia A. M. Kollontai)," *Sovetskie Arkhivy*, 1967, no. 2, pp. 23–33. (An exile in Norway, Kollontai recalls events from news of the downfall of the tsar to her return to Petrograd in March 1917.)

Deiateli SSSR i Oktiabr'skoi Revoliutsii: Entsiklopedicheskii slovar'. Moscow, 1925–28. 44 vols. Vol. 41, parts 1–3, contains capsule biographies or autobiographies of the leading personalities of the early Soviet years. See especially those of Evgeniia Bosh (cols. 42–43), Pavel Dybenko (cols. 128–33), Nikolai Nikolaevich Iakovlev (cols. 274–75), Varvara Iakovleva (cols. 278–80), Aleksandra M. Kollontai (cols. 194–201), Elena Fedorovna Rozmirovich (cols. 206–12), and Aleksandr Gavrilovich Shliapnikov (cols. 244–51).

Deutscher, Isaac. *The Prophet Armed: Trotsky, 1879–1921.* New York, 1965 (original ed. 1954).

———. *The Prophet Unarmed: Trotsky, 1921–29.* New York, 1965 (original ed. 1959).

———. *The Prophet Outcast: Trotsky, 1929–40.* New York, 1965 (original ed. 1963).

Dewar, Margaret. *Labour Policy in the USSR, 1917–1928.* London, 1956.

Dodge, Norton. *Women in the Soviet Economy.* Baltimore, Md., 1966.

Draper, Theodore. *The Roots of American Communism.* New York, 1957.

Dunham, Vera S. "The Strong-Woman Motif," in Cyril E. Black, ed., *The Transformation of Russian Society* (Cambridge, Mass., 1960), pp. 459–83.

Dunn, Robert W. *Soviet Trade Unions.* New York, 1925.

Eastman, Max. *Love and Revolution: My Journey Through an Epoch.* New York, 1964.

Edmondson, Linda, "Russian Feminists and the First All-Russian Congress of Women," *Russian History*, 1976, no. 2, pp. 123–49.

Egorova, Mariia. "Kak organizovat' rabotu sredi krest'ianok," *Kommunistka*, 1920, no. 1–2, pp. 32–34.

Ehrenburg, Ilya. *The Post-War Years: 1945–54* (trans. Tatiana Shebunina). New York, 1967.

Emel'ianova, E. D. *Revoliutsiia, partiia, zhenshchina (Oktiabr' 1917–1925 gg.).* Smolensk, 1971.

Engel, Barbara, and Clifford Rosenthal, eds. *Five Sisters: Women Against the Tsar.* New York, 1975.

Engels, Friedrich. *The Origin of the Family, Private Property, and the State.* New York, 1972 (original ed. 1884).

Farnsworth, Beatrice, "Bolshevism, the Woman Question, and Aleksandra Kollontai," *The American Historical Review*, 81, no. 2 (Apr. 1976), pp. 292–316.

Figner, Vera. *Zapechatlennyi trud. Vospominaniia v dvukh tomakh.* Moscow, 1964.

Fischer, Ruth. *Stalin and German Communism.* Cambridge, Mass., 1948.

Fitzpatrick, Sheila, ed. *Cultural Revolution in Russia, 1928-1931.* Bloomington, Ind., 1978.

Flakserman, Iu., "Stranitsy proshlogo," *Novyi Mir,* 1968, no. 11, pp. 208-41.

Fortunato, Evgeniia, "Nash drug Aleksandra Kollontai," *Neva,* 1959, no. 3, pp. 182-87.

Fueloep-Miller, René. *The Mind and Face of Bolshevism. An Examination of Cultural Life in the Soviet Union.* New York, 1965.

Futrell, Michael. *Northern Underground.* New York, 1963.

Gankin, Olga H., and H. H. Fisher. *The Bolsheviks and the World War: The Origin of the Third International.* Stanford, Calif., 1940.

Gasiorowska, Xenia. *Women in Soviet Fiction, 1917-1964.* Madison, Wisc., 1968.

Geiger, H. Kent. *The Family in Soviet Russia.* Cambridge, Mass., 1968.

Getzler, Israel. *Martov.* Cambridge, Eng., 1967.

Gitelman, Zvi. *Jewish Nationality and Soviet Politics: The Jewish Sections of the CPSU, 1917-1930.* Princeton, N.J., 1972.

Gladkov, F. *Tsement.* Moscow, 1928. There is an English translation, *Cement* (New York, 1960).

Glavkomtrud i Narkomtrud, krest'ianstvo i trudovaia povinnost'. Moscow, 1920.

Glebov, A. G. *Inga,* in his *P'esy* (Moscow, 1934), pp. 219-94.

Glickman, Rose. "The Russian Factory Woman, 1880-1914," in Atkinson et al., eds., pp. 63-83.

Goldberg, Rochelle. "The Russian Women's Movement: 1859-1917." Unpublished Ph.D. dissertation, Univ. of Rochester, 1976.

Goldman, Emma. *My Disillusionment in Russia.* New York, 1970 (original ed. London, 1925).

Golubeva, V. "K diskussii po voprosam brachnogo i semeinogo prava." *Kommunistka,* 1926, no. 1, pp. 50-53.

———. "Rabota zhenotdelov v novykh usloviiakh," *Pravda,* Feb. 1, 1923, p. 3.

———. ("Rabota zhenotdelov v novykh usloviiakh") "(otvet na vozrazheniia)," *Pravda,* Apr. 13, 1923, p. 4.

———. "S"ezd rabotnits i krest'ianok, kak pervyi etap raboty partii sredi zhenskikh trudiashchikhsia mass," *Kommunistka,* 1923, no. 11 (Nov.), pp. 16-18.

Gorky, Maxim. *Days with Lenin.* New York, 1932.

Grunfeld, Judith. "Women's Work in Russia's Planned Economy," *Social Research,* 9, no. 1 (Feb. 1942), pp. 22-45.

Haight, Amanda. *Anna Akhmatova.* New York, 1976.

Halle, Fannina W. *Woman in Soviet Russia.* New York, 1935.

Halvorsen, Carsten. *Revolutionens ambassadør. Alexandra Kollontays liv och gärning* (aaren 1872-1917). Stockholm, 1945. (This biography is based on material provided by Kollontai.)

Hauge, Kaare. "Alexandra Mikhailovna Kollontai: The Scandinavian Period, 1922-1945." Unpublished Ph.D. dissertation. Univ. of Minnesota, 1971.

Haupt, G., and J. J. Marie. *Makers of the Russian Revolution* (trans. C. I. P. Ferdinand and D. M. Bellos). Ithaca, N.Y., 1974. (Contains translations of many *Deiateli* entries.)

Hayden, Carol E. "The Zhenotdel and the Bolshevik Party," *Russian History,* 1976, no. 2, pp. 150-73.

Holt, Alix, ed. and trans. *Selected Writings of Alexandra Kollontai.* Westport, Conn., 1977.

Honeycutt, Karen. "Clara Zetkin: A Left-wing Socialist and Feminist in Wilhelmian Germany." Unpublished Ph.D. dissertation, Columbia Univ., 1975.

Hough, Jerry F. "Women and Women's Issues in Soviet Policy Debates," in Atkinson et al., eds., pp. 355–73.

Iakovleva, Varvara. "K voprosu a kvalifikatsii zhenskogo truda," *Kommunistka,* 1923, no. 6, p. 16.

———. "Katorga i ssylka," *Proletarskaia Revoliutsiia,* 2, no. 8 (1922), pp. 199–202.

———. "Partiinaia rabota v Moskovskoi oblasti v period Fevral'–Oktiabr' 1917 g.," *Proletarskaia Revoliutsiia,* 3, no. 15 (1923), pp. 196–204.

———. "Podgotovka Oktiabr'skogo vosstaniia v Moskovskoi oblasti," *Proletarskaia Revoliutsiia,* 10, no. 22 (1922), pp. 302–6.

Iaroslavskii, Emelian, ed. *Kakim dolzhen byt'. Kommunist staraia i novaia moral'. Sbornik.* Moscow, 1925.

———. "Moral' i byt proletariata v perekhodnyi period," *Molodaia Gvardiia,* 1926, no. 3 (May), pp. 138–53.

Itkina, Anna. *Revoliutsioner, tribun, diplomat: Stranitsy zhizni Aleksandry Mikhailovny Kollontai.* Moscow, 1970 (original ed., 1964).

Joravsky, David. "The Construction of the Stalinist Psyche," in Fitzpatrick, ed., pp. 105–28.

Juviler, Peter H. "Women and Sex in Soviet Law," in Atkinson et al., eds., pp. 243–65.

Kamenev, L. B., ed. *Pis'ma V. I. Lenina, A. G. Shliapnikov i A. M. Kollontai, 1914–1917 gg.* Leningrad, 1925.

Katkov, George. *The Trial of Bukharin.* New York, 1969.

Keep, John L. H. *The Debate on Soviet Power: Minutes of the All-Russian Central Executive Committee of Soviets: October 1917–January 1918.* Oxford, 1979.

Kingsbury, Susan M., and Mildred Fairchild. *Factory, Family and Women in the Soviet Union.* New York, 1935.

Knight, Amy. "The Fritschi: A Study of Female Radicals in the Russian Populist Movement," *Canadian-American Slavic Studies,* 1975, no. 1 (Spring), pp. 1–17.

Koni, A. F. *Vospominaniia o dele Very Zasulich.* Moscow, 1933.

Kotov, G. N. "Iz vospominanii o T. Inessa i T. Arteme," *Proletarskaia Revoliutsiia,* 1921, no. 2, pp. 115–22.

Kritsman, L. N. "Geroicheskii period velikoi Russkoi Revoliutsii (opyt analiza t. n. 'voennogo kommunizma')," *Vestnik Kommunisticheskoi Akademii,* vol. 9 (Moscow, 1924).

Krupskaia, N. K. "Voina i detorozhdenie," *Kommunistka,* 1920, no. 1–2, pp. 18–20.

———. *Vospominaniia o Lenine.* Moscow, 1957.

Lapidus, Gail W. "Sexual Equality in Soviet Policy," in Atkinson et al., eds., pp. 115–38.

———. *Women in Soviet Society: Equality, Development, and Social Change.* Berkeley, Calif., 1978.

Lasch, Christopher. *Haven in a Heartless World.* New York, 1977.

Lavrov, E. "Polovoi vopros i molodezh'," *Molodaia Gvardiia,* 1926, no. 3 (Mar.), pp. 136–48.

Lelevich, G. "Anna Akhmatova," *Na Postu,* 1923, no. 2–3, pp. 178–202.

Lenczyc, Henryk. "Alexandra Kollontai. Essai bibliographique," *Cahiers du Monde Russe et Soviétique,* 1973, no. 1–2 (Jan.–June), pp. 205–41.

Lenin, V. I. *Polnoe Sobranie Sochinenii,* 5th ed. Moscow, 1958–65. 55 vols.

———. *Selected Works.* Moscow, 1960. 3 vols.

———. *Sochineniia,* 2d ed. Moscow-Leningrad, 1926–32. 32 vols.

———. *Sochineniia.* 3d ed. Moscow, 1927–37. 30 vols.

———. *Sochineniia.* 4th ed. Moscow, 1941–60. 39 vols.

Leningradki: Vospominaniia, Ocherki, Dokumenty. Leningrad, 1968.

Leninskii Sbornik. Moscow, 1924–40. 33 vols.

Levidova, S. M., and E. G. Salita. *Elena Dmitrievna Stasova.* Leningrad, 1969.

Levytsky, Boris. *Stalinist Terror in the Thirties.* Stanford, Calif., 1974.

Lewin, Moshe. *Russian Peasants and Soviet Power: A Study in Collectivization* (trans. Irene Nove). Evanston, Ill., 1968.

———. "The Social Background of Stalinism," in R. C. Tucker, ed., pp. 111–36.

Lilina, Z. "Rol' obshchestvennogo pitaniia v zhizni rabotnitsy," *Kommunistka,* 1920, no. 3–4, pp. 24–26.

Lin, I. "Eros iz rogozhsko-simonovskogo raiona (mysli vslukh o stat'e tov. Kollontai 'dorogu krylatomu erosu')," *Molodaia Gvardiia,* 1923, no. 4–5, pp. 152–55.

Liubimova, S. *V pervye gody.* Moscow, 1958.

Livshits, S. "Partiinaia shkola v Bolon'e (1910–1911 gg.)," *Proletarskaia Revoliutsiia,* 1926, no. 3, pp. 109–43.

Lorimer, Frank. *The Population of the Soviet Union: History and Prospects.* Geneva, 1946. (A League of Nations publication.)

Lunacharskii, A. *O byte.* Moscow, 1927.

———. *Revoliutsionnye siluety.* Kharkov, 1924. (An English translation, *Revolutionary Silhouettes* [trans. and ed. Michael Glenny] was published in New York in 1968.)

Maiskii, I. M. "A. M. Kollontai," *Oktiabr',* 1962, no. 7, pp. 107–12.

———. *Vospominaniia sovetskogo posla.* Moscow, 1964.

Malia, Martin. *Alexander Herzen and the Birth of Russian Socialism.* New York, 1965.

Mandel, William M. *Soviet Women.* New York, 1975.

Mandelstam, Nadezhda. *Hope Against Hope. A Memoir* (trans. Max Hayward). New York, 1970.

Massell, Gregory. *The Surrogate Proletariat. Moslem Women and Revolutionary Strategies in Soviet Central Asia, 1919–1929.* Princeton, N.J., 1974.

McNeal, Robert H. *Bride of the Revolution. Krupskaya and Lenin.* Ann Arbor, Mich., 1972.

———. *Guide to the Decisions of the Communist Party of the Soviet Union, 1917–1967.* Toronto, 1972.

———. "Women in the Russian Radical Movement," *Journal of Social History,* 1971–72, no. 2 (Winter), pp. 143–63.

Medvedev, Roy A. *Let History Judge: The Origins and Consequences of Stalinism* (trans. Colleen Taylor, ed. David Joravsky and Georges Haupt). New York, 1973.

Mehnert, Klaus. *Youth in Soviet Russia* (trans. M. Davidson). New York, 1933.

Meyer, Alfred G. "Marxism and the Women's Movement," in Atkinson et al., eds., pp. 85–112.

Mindlin, E. *Ne dom, no mir: Povest' ob Aleksandre Kollontai.* Moscow, 1969. (This work is partly fiction but is based on Kollontai archives.)

———. *Neobyknovennye sobesedniki.* Moscow, 1968.

Mitchell, Juliet. *Psychoanalysis and Feminism: Freud, Reich, Laing and Women.* New York, 1974.

Moirova, V. "Piat' let raboty sredi zhenshchin," *Kommunistka,* 1923, no. 11, pp. 9–13.

Morozova, Vera. *Rasskazy o zemliachke; Klavdichka; Konkordiia.* Moscow, 1970.

Nettl, J. P. *Rosa Luxemburg.* New York, 1966.

Nevolina, V. S., and N. V. Orlova, eds. "O mezhdunarodnoi zhenskoi sotsialisticheskoi konferentsii v 1915 g: Dokumenty instituta Marksizma-Leninizma pri Tsk KPSS," *Istoricheskii Arkhiv*, 1960, no. 6, pp. 106–25.

Nicolaevsky, B. *Power and the Soviet Elite: "The Letter of an Old Bolshevik" and Other Essays*. New York, 1965.

Nikolaeva, K. "Slovo k molodym rabotnitsam," in Artiukhina et al., eds., pp. 117–21.

———. "O pervom mezhdunarodnom soveshchanii kommunistok," *Kommunistka*, 1920, no. 3–4, p. 5.

Nilsson, Ada. "Det Stora Uppdraget," *Vi*, 1961, no. 35, pp. 9–11, 38; no. 36, pp. 16–18; no. 37, pp. 18–19, 40; no. 38, p. 16.

Niurina, F. "Zhenotdely RKP, ili 'osobye obshchestva'," *Pravda*, Feb. 7, 1923.

Palencia, I. *Alexandra Kollontay*. New York, 1947. (This is a useful biography for its excerpts from Kollontai's letters and recollections of conversations. Kollontai considered it accurate in general, if not in detail.)

Parsons, Talcott, and Robert F. Bales. *Family, Socialization and Interaction Process*. Urbana, Ill., 1955.

Pertsoff, Margaret H. "Lady in Red, a Study of the Early Career of Alexandra M. Kollontai." Unpublished Ph.D. dissertation, Univ. of Virginia, 1968.

Pethybridge, Roger. *The Social Prelude to Stalinism*. New York, 1974.

Petrov, G. D. "Aleksandra Kollontai nakanune i v gody pervoi mirovoi voiny," *Novaia i noveishaia istoriia*, 1969, no. 1, pp. 67–81.

———. "A. M. Kollontai v gody pervoi mirovoi voiny," *Istoriia SSSR*, 1968, no. 3, pp. 83–97.

———. "Aleksandra Kollontai v SShA," *Novaia i noveishaia istoriia*, 1972, no. 3, pp. 128–42.

———. "O broshiure A. M. Kollontai 'Komu nuzhna voina?'," *Sovetskie Arkhivy*, 1968, no. 5, pp. 109–11.

———. "Meridiany druzhby," *Moskva*, 1967, no. 1, pp. 162–69.

Petrov, Vladimir, and Evdokia Petrov. *Empire of Fear*. New York, 1956

Podliashuk, Pavel. *Tovarishch Inessa*. Moscow, 1973.

Preobrazhenskii, Evgenii. "Evgeniia Bogdanovna Bosh," *Proletarskaia Revoliutsiia*, vol. 5 (37), no. 2 (1925), pp. 5–16.

Price, M. Phillips. *My Reminiscences of the Russian Revolution*. London, 1921.

Proletarskaia Revoliutsiia sistematicheskii i alfavitnyi ukazatel' 1921–1929. Moscow, 1930.

Quataert, Jean H. *Reluctant Feminists in German Social Democracy, 1885–1917*. Princeton, N.J., 1979.

Rabinowitch, Alexander. *The Bolsheviks Come to Power: The Revolution of 1917 in Petrograd*. New York, 1976.

Ransel, David L., ed. *The Family in Imperial Russia*. Urbana, Ill., 1978.

Ravich, Ol'ga. "Mezhdunarodnaia zhenskaia sotsialisticheskaia konferentsiia 1915 g.," *Proletarskaia Revoliutsiia*, 10, no. 45 (1925), pp. 165–77.

———. "Bor'ba s prostitutsiei v Petrograde," *Kommunistka*, 1920, no. 1–2, pp. 21–23.

Razin, I. M., ed. *Komsomol'skii byt. Sbornik*. Moscow-Leningrad, 1927.

Reed, John. *Ten Days That Shook the World*. New York, 1960 (original ed. 1919).

Reichenbach, Bernhard. "Moscow, 1921," *Survey*, 1964, no. 50–53 (Oct.), pp. 16–22.

Riazanov, David. "Marks i Engels o brake i sem'e," *Letopisi Marksizma*, 1927, no. 3, pp. 13–35.

Rigby, T. H. *Communist Party Membership in the USSR. 1917–1967.* Princeton, N.J., 1968.

Sadoul, Jacques. *Notes sur la Révolution Bolchevique.* Paris, 1919.

Samoilova, K. N. *Krest'ianka i sovetskaia vlast'.* Moscow, 1921.

———. "O rabote sredi krest'ianok," *Kommunistka,* 1920, no. 7, pp. 31–34.

———. "Organizatsionnye zadachi," *Kommunistka,* 1920, no. 6, pp. 26–28.

———."Trudovoi front i rabotnitsa," *Kommunistka,* 1920, no. 5, pp. 10–12.

———. *V ob"edinenii-zalog pobedy.* Moscow, 1921.

Saumoneau, L. "The Case of Louise Saumoneau," *The Socialist Review,* 1916, no. 76 (Jan.–Mar.), pp. 44–50.

Schapiro, Leonard. *The Origin of the Communist Autocracy: Political Opposition in the Soviet State. First Phase, 1917–1922.* 2d ed. Cambridge, Mass., 1977.

Schlesinger, Rudolf, ed. *The Family in the USSR: Documents and Readings.* London, 1949.

Scott, Hilda. *Does Socialism Liberate Women? Experiences from Eastern Europe.* Boston, 1975.

Selishchev, A. M. *Iazyk revoliutsionnoi epokhi: iz nabliudenii nad Russkim iazykom poslednikh let. 1917–1926.* Moscow, 1928.

Selivanova, N. N. *Russia's Women.* Westport, Conn., 1975 (original ed. New York, 1923).

Serebrennikov, G. N. *Zhenskii trud v SSSR.* Moscow, 1934.

Serge, Victor. *Memoirs of a Revolutionary, 1901–1941* (trans. Peter Sedgwick). London, 1963.

Serge, Victor, and Natalia Sedova Trotsky. *The Life and Death of Leon Trotsky.* Trans. A. J. Pomerans. New York, 1975.

Shliapnikov, A. *Kanun semnadtsatogo goda.* Moscow, 1928.

———. "K Oktiabriu," *Proletarskaia Revoliutsiia,* 1922, no. 10, pp. 3–42.

———. *Semnadtsatyi god.* Moscow-Leningrad, 1927.

Shorter, Edward. "Female Emancipation, Birth Control, and Fertility in European History," *The American Historical Review,* vol. 78, no. 3 (Jun. 1973), pp. 605–40.

Smidovich, S. "Nashi zadachi v oblasti pereustroistva byta," *Kommunistka,* 1926, no. 12, pp. 18–25.

———. "O Koren'kovshchine," in Razin, ed., *Komsomol'skii byt,* pp. 132–40.

———. "O liubvi," in Razin, ed., *Komsomol'skii byt,* pp. 268–73.

———. "O novom kodekse zakonov o brake i sem'e," *Kommunistka,* 1926, no. 1, pp. 45–50.

———. "Otmenit' li registratsiiu braka i sistemu alimentov," *Komsomol'skaia Pravda,* 37, no. 220 (1926), p. 2.

———. "Otvet na pis'mo komsomolki," in Razin, ed., *Komsomol'skii byt,* pp. 174–75.

———. "Rabota partii sredi zhenshchin v Moskve i Moskovskoi gubernii," *Kommunistka,* 1923, no. 11, pp. 19–22.

———. "Soveshchanie zavedyvaiushchikh oblastnymi zhenotdelami," *Kommunistka,* 1923, no. 5, pp. 8–11.

———. "XII S"ezd partii o rabote sredi rabotnits i krest'ianok," *Kommunistka,* 1923, no. 8, pp. 4–5.

Smith, Jessica. *Woman in Soviet Russia.* New York, 1928.

Sosnovskii, L. *Bol'nye voprosy.* Leningrad, 1926.

Souvarine, Boris. *Stalin: A Critical Survey of Bolshevism.* New York, 1939.

Spiro, M. *Children of the Kibbutz.* New York, 1972.

——. *Kibbutz: Venture in Utopia*. New York, 1971.

Stal', L. "Nasha rabota v kustarnoi promyshlennosti," *Kommunistka*, 1920, no. 7, pp. 14–16.

——. "Novye zhenshchiny," *Kommunistka*, 1920, no. 6, pp. 17–20.

——. "Rabota sredi zhenshchin v Terskoi oblasti," *Kommunistka*, 1920, no. 5, pp. 39–41.

——. "Rabotnitsa v Oktiabre," *Proletarskaia Revoliutsiia*, 1922, no. 10, pp. 299–301.

Staryi drug [Old Friend]. "Zlata Ionovna Lilina," *Proletarskaia Revoliutsiia*, vol. 9, no. 6 (1929), pp. 204–11.

Stasova, E. D. *Stranitsy zhizni i bor'by*. Moscow, 1960.

——. *Uchitel' i drug*. Moscow, 1972.

——. *Vospominaniia*. Moscow, 1969.

Stavrakis, Bette. "Women and the Communist Party in the Soviet Union, 1918–45." Unpublished Ph.D. dissertation, Case Western Reserve Univ., 1961.

Stites, Richard, "Kollontai, Inessa, Krupskaia," *Canadian-American Slavic Studies*, 9, no. 1 (Spring 1975), pp. 84–92.

——. *The Women's Liberation Movement in Russia. Feminism, Nihilism, and Bolshevism, 1860–1930*. Princeton, N.J., 1978.

——. "Women and the Russian Intelligentsia: Three Perspectives," in Atkinson et al., eds., pp. 39–62.

——. "Zhenotdel: Bolshevism and Russian Women, 1917–1930," *Russian History*, 1976, no. 2, pp. 174–93.

Stora-Sandor, Judith, ed. *Alexandra Kollontai: Marxisme et révolution sexuelle*. Paris, 1973.

Sukhanov, N. *The Russian Revolution* (trans. and ed. Joel Carmichael). New York, 1962 (original ed. 1955). 2 vols.

——. *Zapiski o revoliutsii*. Berlin, 1922–23.

Sverdlova, K. T. *Iakov Mikhailovich Sverdlov*. Moscow, 1957.

Trotsky, L. *My Life*. New York, 1970. (Originally *Moia Zhizn'*, Berlin, 1930. English edition originally published London, 1930.)

——. *O Lenine, materialy dlia biografa*. Moscow, 1924.

——. *Sochineniia*. Moscow, 1924–27, 21 vols.

——. *Stalin*. New York, 1941.

——. *The History of the Russian Revolution* (trans. Max Eastman). New York, 1932, 3 vols.

——. *Voprosy byta*. Moscow, 1923.

Trudy I-go vserossiiskago zhenskago s"ezda pri russkom' zhenskom' obshchestve v' S. Peterburge. 10–16 Dekabria. 1908 goda. St. Petersburg, 1909.

Tucker, Robert C. *Stalin as Revolutionary, 1879–1929*. New York, 1973.

Tucker, Robert C., ed. *Stalinism: Essays in Historical Interpretation*. New York, 1977.

Tucker, Robert C., and Stephen F. Cohen. *The Great Purge Trial*. New York, 1965.

Ulam, Adam. *The Bolsheviks*. New York, 1968 (original ed. 1965).

USSR, Official and Semiofficial Publications:

1. *Dekrety Sovetskoi Vlasti* (ed. G. D. Obichkin, S. N. Valk, et al.). Moscow, 1957–59. 2 vols.

2. *Desiatyi S"ezd RKP (b). Mart 1921 goda. Stenograficheskii otchet*. Moscow, 1963.

3. *Deviataia konferentsiia RKP (b). Sentiabr' 1920 goda. Protokoly.* Moscow, 1972.
4. *Deviatyi S"ezd RKP (b). Mart-Aprel' 1920 goda. Protokoly.* Moscow, 1960.
5. *Dvenadtsatyi S"ezd Rossiiskoi Kommunisticheskoi Partii (Bol'shevikov). Stenograficheskii Otchet.* Moscow, 1923.
6. *Kommunisticheskaia partiia sovetskogo soiuza v rezoliutsiiakh i resheniiakh s"ezdov, konferentsii i plenumov TsK.* Moscow, 1953–54. 3 vols.
7. *Krest'ianstvo i trudovaia povinnost'.* Moscow, 1920.
8. *Odinnadtsatyi S"ezd (b). Mart–Aprel' 1922 goda. Stenograficheskii Otchet.* Moscow, 1961.
9. *Otchet Otdela TsKRKP (b) po rabote sredi zhenshchin za god raboty.* Moscow, 1921.
10. *Pervyi Vserossiiskii S"ezd Sovetov RiSD.* Moscow-Leningrad, 1931.
11. *Protokoly S"ezdov i Konferentsii Vsesoiuznoi Kommunisticheskoi Partii (b): Sed'moi S"ezd. Mart 1918 goda.* Moscow, 1928.
12. *Protokoly tsentral'nogo komiteta RSDRP (b). Avgust 1917–Fevral' 1918.* Moscow, 1958.
13. *Sbornik instruktsii otdela TsKRKP po rabote sredi zhenshchin.* Moscow, 1920.
14. *Sed'moi Ekstrennyi S"ezd RKP (b). Mart 1918 goda. Stenograficheskii otchet.* Moscow, 1962.
15. *Sobranie Uzakonenii i rasporiazhenii rabochego i krest'ianskogo pravitel'stva. Sbornik dekretov 1917–18 gg.* Moscow, 1920.
15a. *Sobranie Uzakonenii i rasporiazhenii rabochego i krest'ianskogo pravitel'stva. Sbornik dekretov za 1920 god.* Moscow, 1921?
16. *Spravochnik partiinogo rabotnika,* Moscow, 1921–35.
17. *Stenograficheskii Otchet X S"ezda Rossiiskii Kommunisticheskoi Partii (8–16 Marta 1921 g).* Petrograd, 1921.
18. *Tretii Vsemirnyi Kongress Kommunisticheskogo Internatsionala. Stenograficheskii Otchet.* Petrograd, 1922.
19. *Tretii Vserossiiskii S"ezd Professional'nykh Soiuzov. 6–13 Aprelia 1920 goda. Stenograficheskii Otchet.* Moscow, 1921.
20. *Vos'moi S"ezd RKP (b). Mart 1919 goda. Protokoly.* Moscow, 1959.
21. *Vtoroi Vserossiiskii S"ezd Professional'nykh Soiuzov. Stenograficheskii Otchet.* Moscow, 1921.
22. *Vtoroi Vserossiiskii S"ezd RKSM, 5–8 Oktiabria 1919 goda. Stenograficheskii Otchet.* Moscow, 1926.
23. *III Sessiia Vserossiiskogo Tsentral'nogo Ispolnitel'nogo Komiteta XII Sozyva. Postanovleniia.* Moscow, 1926.

Valentinov, N. V. (pseud. for N. Vol'skii). *Vstrechi s Leninym.* New York, 1953.
Vavilina, V., et al., eds. *Vsegda s vami: sbornik, posviashchennyi 50-letiiu zhurnala "Rabotnitsa."* Moscow, 1964.
Vel't, Nina. "Otkrytoe pis'mo tovarishchu Smidovich," in Razin, ed., *Komsomol'-skii byt,* pp. 178–86.
Vinogradskaia, P. "Itogi III-go vserossiiskogo sovesch. [*sic*] zavgubotdelov po rabote sredi zhenshchin. *Kommunistka,* 1920, no. 7, pp. 3–6.
———. "Oktiabr' v Moskve," *Novyi Mir,* 1966, no. 4, pp. 143–86.
———. *Pamiatnye vstrechi* [2d ed. of *Sobytiia i pamiatnye vstrechi*]. Moscow, 1972.
———. "Serdtse, otdannoe narodu," *Novyi Mir,* 1969, no. 2, pp. 186–204.
———. *Sobytiia i pamiatnye vstrechi.* Moscow, 1968.
———. "Voprosy byta (po povodu stat'i tov. Trotskogo)," *Pravda,* July 26, 1923, pp. 4–5.

————. "Voprosy morali, pola, byta i tov. Kollontai," *Krasnaia Nov'*, 6, no. 16 (Oct.–Nov. 1923), pp. 179–214.

Vvedenskii, A. I. *Tserkov' i gosudarstvo*. Moscow, 1923.

Wade, Rex A. *The Russian Search for Peace, February–October 1917*. Stanford, Calif., 1969.

Weiss, Louise. *Memoirs d'une Européenne (1919–1934)*. Paris, 1970.

Williams, Albert Rhys. *Journey into Revolution: Petrograd. 1917–1918*. Chicago, 1969.

Winter, Ella. *Red Virtue: Human Relationships in the New Russia*. New York, 1933.

Wolfe, Bertram D. "Lenin and Inessa Armand," *Slavic Review*, 1963, no. 1, pp. 96–114.

Zaitsev, P. "V Kronshtadte," *Novyi Mir*, 1957, no. 7, pp. 167–72.

Zalkind, A. B. "Polovaia zhizn' i sovremennaia molodezh'," *Molodaia Gvardiia*, 1923, no. 6, pp. 245–49.

Zasulich, V. *Vospominaniia*. Moscow, 1931.

Zetkin, C. *Reminiscences of Lenin*. New York, 1934.

Zhak, L. P., and A. Itkina, eds. *Zhenshchiny Russkoi Revoliutsii*. Moscow, 1968.

Zhenshchiny goroda Lenina. Leningrad, 1963.

Zorkii, M. S. *Rabochaia oppozitsiia. Materialy i dokumenty. 1920–26*. Moscow, 1926.

Index